Parenting Plan Evaluations

Parenting Plan Evaluations

Applied Research for the Family Court

EDITED BY ■

KATHRYN F. KUEHNLE

LESLIE M. DROZD

Oxford University Press, Inc., publishes works that further Oxford University's objective of excellence in research, scholarship, and education.

Oxford New York
Auckland   Cape Town   Dar es Salaam   Hong Kong   Karachi   Kuala Lumpur   Madrid   Melbourne
Mexico City   Nairobi   New Delhi   Shanghai   Taipei   Toronto

With offices in
Argentina   Austria   Brazil   Chile   Czech Republic   France   Greece   Guatemala   Hungary   Italy
Japan   Poland   Portugal   Singapore   South Korea   Switzerland   Thailand   Turkey   Ukraine
Vietnam

Copyright © 2012 by Oxford University Press

Published by Oxford University Press, Inc.
198 Madison Avenue, New York, New York 10016
www.oup.com

ISBN: 9780199754021
A copy of this book's Cataloging-in-Publication Data is on file with the Library of Congress.

9 8 7 6 5 4 3 2

Printed in the United States of America
on acid-free paper

CONTENTS

SECTION IV: Children's Disorders that Require Specialized Parenting

SECTION V: Parent Behaviors Affecting Co-parenting and the Stability
of the Parent–Child Relationships

SECTION VI: Present and Future Cultural and Political Issues

SECTION VII: Science and the Law

SECTION VIII: Conclusion

CONTRIBUTORS

William G. Austin, Ph.D.
Licensed Psychologist, CO &
  NCForensic Psychology
Clinical & Medical Psychology
  Specializing in Child Custody
  Evaluation and Trial Consultation
Lakewood, Colorado

Nicholas Bala, L.S.M.
Faculty of Law
Queen's University Kingston
Ontario, Canada

Alexander S. Berk, J.D., L.P.C., M.Ed.
Dallas, Texas

Rachel Birnbaum, Ph.D., R.S.W., L.L.M.
King's University College
The University of Western Ontario
London,
Ontario, Canada

Sanford L. Braver, Ph.D.
Prevention Research Center
Department of Psychology
Arizona State University
Tempe, Arizona

Brianna Coffino, Ph.D.
Child Trauma Research Program
University of California, San Francisco
San Francisco General Hospital
San Francisco, California

Marilyn Coleman, Ed.D.
Department of Human Development
  and Family Studies
University of Missouri
Columbia, Missouri

Carolyn Pape Cowan, Ph.D.
Professor Emerita
Department of Psychology
University of California, Berkeley
Berkeley, California

Philip A. Cowan, Ph.D.
Professor Emeritus
Department of Psychology
University of California, Berkeley
Berkeley, California

Jillian S. Diamond, B.S.
University of Vermont
Burlington, Vermont

Priscila Diaz, M.A.
Department of Psychology
Arizona State University
Tempe, Arizona

William V. Fabricius, Ph.D.
Department of Psychology
Arizona State University
Tempe, Arizona

Barbara Jo Fidler, Ph.D. C. Psych.,
   Acc.FM
Family Solutions
Toronto, Ontario, Canada

Lawrence Ganong, Ph.D.
Department of Human Development
   and Family Studies
University of Missouri
Columbia, Missouri

Jennifer L. Hardesty, Ph.D.
Department of Human and
   Community Development
University of Illinois, Urbana-Champaign
Urbana, Illinois

Megan L. Haselschwerdt, M. S.
Doctoral Candidate in Department of
   Human and Community Development
University of Illinois, Urbana-Champaign
Urbana, Illinois

Liza Cohen Hita, Ph.D. LISAC
School of Social and Family Dynamics
Arizona State University
Tempe, Arizona

Suzanne M. Johnson, Ph.D.
Department of Psychology
Dowling College
Oakdale, New York

Michael P. Johnson, Ph.D.
Sociology, Women's Studies, and African
   and African American Studies
The Pennsylvania State University
State College, Pennsylvania

Janet R. Johnston, Ph.D.
San José State University
San José, California

Joan B. Kelly, Ph.D.
Psychologist
Corte Madera, California

Suzanne E. U. Kerns, Ph.D.
Department of Psychiatry and
   Behavioral Sciences
University of Washington
Seattle, Washington

Gerald P. Koocher, Ph.D.
School of Health Sciences
Simmons College
Boston, Massachusetts

Nina Koren-Karie, Ph.D.
Center for the Study of Child
   Development
University of Haifa
Israel

Lucyna M. Lach, M.S.W., Ph.D.
School of Social Work
Montreal, Québec, Canada

Michael E. Lamb, Ph.D.
Department of Social and
   Developmental Psychology
University of Cambridge
United Kingdom

Alicia Lieberman, Ph.D.
Child Trauma Research Program
University of California, San Francisco
San Francisco General Hospital
San Francisco, California

Jennifer Ma, M.S.W.
Graduate Student in Social Work
University of Toronto
Toronto, Ontario, Canada

Radha MacCulloch, M.S.W.
School of Social Work
McGill University
Montreal, Québec, Canada

Nicole E. Mahrer, M.A.
Prevention Research Center
Arizona State University
Tempe, Arizona

Graham McCaulley, M.A.
Doctoral Student
University of Missouri
Columbia, Missouri

Jennifer E. McIntosh, Ph.D.
School of Public Health
La Trobe University
Bundoora, Victoria, Australia

Lauren Mednick, Ph.D.
Children's Hospital Boston
Department of Psychiatry
Boston, Massachusetts

John A. Moran, Ph.D.
Forensic Psychologist
Scottsdale, Arizona

Elizabeth O'Connor, Ph.D.
Department of Psychology
Dowling College
Oakdale, New York

David Oppenheim, Ph.D.
Center for the Study of Child Development
University of Haifa
Israel

Ronald J. Prinz, Ph.D.
Parenting and Family Research Center
Psychology Department
University of South Carolina
Columbia, South Carolina

Marsha Kline Pruett, Ph.D., M.S.L.
School for Social Work
Smith College
Northampton, Massachusetts

Michael Saini, Ph.D., M.S.W., R.S.W.
Faculty of Social Work
University of Toronto
Toronto, Ontario, Canada

Irwin Sandler, Ph.D.
Arizona State University
Prevention Research Center
Tempe, Arizona

Donald T. Saposnek, Ph.D.
Department of Psychology
University of California, Santa Cruz
Santa Cruz, California

Daniel W. Shuman, J.D.
Dedman School of Law
Southern Methodist University
Dallas, Texas

Gwynneth Smith, J.D., Ph.D.
Child Trauma Research Program
University of California, San Francisco
San Francisco General Hospital
San Francisco, California

Bruce Smyth, Ph.D.
Australian Demographic and Social
    Research Institute
Australian National University
Australia

Karina R. Sokol, Ph.D.
Department of Psychology
Glendale Community College
Glendale, Arizona

Steven N. Sparta, Ph.D., ABPP
Department of Psychiatry
University of California, San Diego
Thomas Jefferson School of Law
San Diego, California

Patricia Van Horn, Ph.D., J.D.
Child Trauma Research Program
University of California, San Francisco
San Francisco General Hospital
San Francisco, California

David Weinstock, J.D., Ph.D.
Forensic Counseling & Evaluations,
    P.L.L.C.
Scottsdale, Arizona

Emily B. Winslow, Ph.D.
Prevention Research Center
Arizona State University
Tempe, Arizona

Sharlene Wolchik, Ph.D.
Prevention Research Center
Arizona State University
Tempe, Arizona

INTRODUCTION

STEVEN N. SPARTA

The family court must address serious matters of great consequence to children and families. When mental health professionals offer opinions in highly contested cases, conclusions and recommendations should be derived from data of reasonable relevance and quality to substantiate the opinion. Professionals must remind themselves not to overreach the extent of their data and not to substitute values for scientifically supported facts, and must know when to inform fact-finders about the extent of the limits to knowledge. This book provides an essential contribution to the professional literature by focusing attention on the research associated with many of the most important topics within the family court, describing the studies and methods associated with a wide variety of crucial topics. The range and depth of studies reviewed in this book are intended to inform evaluators about scientifically derived knowledge from the empirical literature, complementing other professional literature concerning itself with the best practices procedures for assessment.

This book consists of seven sections, addressing personality development (attachment and parent insightfulness); factors associated with children's adjustment to parents' separation; factors associated with children's adjustments to time-sharing; children's disorders that require specialized parenting; parent behaviors affecting co-parenting and parent–child relationships; present and future cultural and political issues; and science and the law.

The first chapter examines the concept of attachment as applied to child custody determinations. Although there is no consistency among all of the different state statutes defining the best interests of the child, there is universal recognition that the nature and extent of a parent–child relationship are extremely important. The concept of attachment has been increasingly referenced in child custody proceedings in the past decade. G. Smith, B. Coffino, P. Van Horn, and A. Lieberman examine the ways in which attachment theory can increase the scientific rigor of parenting evaluations. Their chapter examines a number of relevant issues: What is the degree to which attachment theory can be extended to the practical questions of particular parenting plans? Is it proper to use attachment measures developed in another context within parenting evaluations? Are some professionals consulting with the family court confusing attachment and comforting or nurturing? These questions and many others are considered from an examination of the current literature, including discussions about specific attachment measures and the professional debate of whether the attachment literature has relevance for parenting plan recommendations involving overnights with young children.

D. Oppenheim and N. Koren-Karie examine the concept of parental insightfulness and the relevance to parenting plan evaluations. Research has shown that parents form internal representations about the emotional meaning they attribute to the child and his or her behavior. Parents may not be aware of their internal representations about their children, but research has shown that parenting is greatly influenced by such beliefs. The Insightfulness Assessment is described as a semi-structured interview in which parents are shown video segments of their child interacting with the parent, simulating moments from everyday life. The empirical support for this procedure is described, along with a more general discussion about how parents' insightfulness helps them understand the motives or feelings of their children. Being able to empathetically understand the child's needs would be relevant in assessing parenting effectiveness.

J. Kelly discusses risk and protective factors associated with adjustment following separation and divorce. Empirical research is reviewed over the past two to three decades, showing the refinement of sample size, methodology, and advanced statistical analysis. The familial and external factors that increase risk or foster resilience are illuminated in the increasingly complex and varied research reviewed by Kelly. Kelly explains how the research could inform child custody evaluators in many different ways, such as developing more risk-focused interviews; assessing protective factors that may ameliorate negative outcomes for children; protecting against relationship loss; risks and protective factors associated with remarriage and cohabitation; family structure transitions; and writing reports that are more easily defended because they are anchored by empirical research.

The quality of parenting following separation and divorce is examined by I. Sandler, S. Wolchik, E.B. Winslow, N.E. Mahrer, J.A. Moran, and D. Weinstock. The authors recognize that various professional practice guidelines recognize the importance of the quality of parenting, but such guidelines do not specify how the quality of parenting is conceptualized or measured. The authors examine the most influential factors for high-quality parenting following separation and divorce; the strengths and weaknesses of available studies; and whether the quality of parenting can be improved. Detailed information is presented on the measures used in the research literature as well as the empirical studies related to the quality of maternal and paternal parenting.

M. Kline Pruett, C. P. Cowan, P. A. Cowan, and J. S. Diamond review the support of fathers after separation and divorce. The authors review a burgeoning literature on how fathers play an important and different role than mothers. They describe an evidence-based intervention program, with suggestions about how to adapt the derived information for separating parents. Information is reviewed from over 700 families participating in a series of research phases.

J.E. McIntosh and B. Smyth examine shared parenting, sometimes called joint physical custody or dual residence. Their review notes the increasing trend toward shared parenting plans, including how some jurisdictions make such arrangements a rebuttable legal presumption. Belgium and Italy are two countries with such laws, while Sweden has moved away from shared care presumptions. The authors interpret the empirical literature on shared parenting and risk and comment on some of the problems of the existing research literature, including the shortcomings of the small body of literature, methodological complexity across studies, and the problems with undifferentiated grouping of research participants. Many important issues are considered within the review of research, including whether shared time is used in high-conflict populations to appease the parties although rather than helping, it may increase damaging conflict.

Parenting conflict poses questions about risk to children, so should parenting time be limited to some parents in such situations? The quality of parenting with and without conflict and the amount of time made possible for fathers are among the different questions reviewed by W.V. Fabricius, K.R. Sokol, P. Diaz, and S.L. Braver. They examine older and newer findings from the available literature, including data from a 2005–2006 survey of 1,030 students whose parents divorced before they were 16 years old. They describe how the evidence suggests that parent conflict alone should not be the basis for limiting parent time, and that the amount of parenting time can exert a causal influence on parent–child relationships. The authors suggest several considerations and cautions, including that courts have better options to deal with children's exposure to conflict than simply considering reducing parenting time, and that reducing the quantity of parenting time might risk damaging father–child relationships.

M.E. Lamb provides a critical analysis of research on parenting plans and children's well-being. The author notes that since the early 1990s, growing numbers of researchers have provided increasingly rich and sophisticated data to inform decision-makers. Following a review of many different research findings, the chapter concludes with a concise list of cautions and considerations: most children have psychologically meaningful relationships with both parents; most children benefit from the opportunity to maintain meaningful contact with both parents after separation; in a minority of cases, children should not be forced to endure schedules with parents who are not interested in supporting the child; and when conflict between parents is endemic and deep, children may not benefit from contact with both parents, and it may be necessary to identify the more competent and committed parent and minimize contact with the other parent.

L. Mednick and G.P. Koocher analyze the literature on the vulnerable population of chronically medically ill children and their co-parenting situations. Assessment considerations include the parents' differential ability to deliver and adhere to medical treatments of varying complexity, understanding of treatment alternatives, an evaluation of family dynamics, and providing for the safety and optimal quality of the child's life. The authors note various cautions in interpreting the research, including the limitations in illness groups studied.

Another vulnerable group involves a heterogeneous set of conditions called neurodevelopmental disorders. Children with these conditions are discussed in terms of the implications for co-parenting situations. Such conditions include autism spectrum disorders, cerebral palsy, epilepsy, and learning or intellectual disabilities. R. Birnbaum, L. Lach, D. Saposnek, and R. MacCulloch note how parents experience significant tension related to the multiple and competing demands and how both parents can coordinate their parenting plans in the interest of the child.

S. Kerns and R. Prinz note that attention-deficit/hyperactivity disorder (ADHD), oppositional defiant disorder (ODD) and conduct disorder (CD) are the most commonly encountered mental health concerns for practitioners and the courts. Parents of children with ADHD are more likely to find fault in their partner's parenting, withdraw from parenting situations, or disagree about parenting tasks compared with parents of children without ADHD. Caregiver strain is exacerbated when children have ADHD plus ODD or CD problems. The authors describe treatment options and how effective treatment can promote consistency between caregivers.

L. Ganong, M. Coleman, and G. McCaulley note that the professional literature richly documents the importance for children to maintain emotional bonds with non-residential parents after separation/divorce, yet parents often struggle mightily with continuing care as co-parents. The authors examine research on the role of "gatekeeping" by one parent, affecting the ability of the other parent to maintain meaningful post-separation relationships with a child. Restrictive or rather protective gatekeeping can have a legitimate function in cases that warrant protection of the child, such as in instances of intimate partner violence. The research reviewed examines the various contexts in which to consider the role of gatekeeping, including times when parents unnecessarily inhibit facilitative relationship functions with the other parent. The authors critique the available research and measures used and discuss the concept as applied to controversial issues such as parental alienation.

The next chapter represents a logical transition from the previous one and involves an empirical examination of alienation by M. Saini, J.R. Johnston, B. J. Fidler, and N. Bala. Any experienced professional working within the family court is aware of the tensions and controversies associated with this concept. Definitions and assumptions linked to the term *alienation* are often varied and are sometimes inaccurately applied in matters that have tremendous importance for the lives of children or parents. The authors correctly note that clinical observations or first-person accounts should not substitute for knowledge of the available empirical evidence. The chapter considers the quality of research designs for the studies reviewed, and the authors provide a cautious review sufficient to permit responsible generalizations from multiple findings. A total of 29 published papers and 10 doctoral dissertations were reviewed after meeting selection criteria about quality. It is sobering to note that of the 39 studies reviewed, no study was judged as scoring high in research quality. One of the many important points made in the conclusion of the chapter is that professionals should recognize the dangers of oversimplification, applying only broad labels of parental alienation without adequate attention to specific descriptions of child–parent behaviors and how they are best understood within the total context of the relevant family.

Domestic violence allegations are not uncommon in conflicted family court cases. Misconceptions about domestic violence and inadequate training among professionals complicate the appropriate handling of such cases. The chapter on domestic violence and child custody by J.L. Hardesty, M.L. Haselschwerdt, and M.P. Johnson reviews the empirical research on several important aspects relevant to parenting plan evaluations, including explanations of the subtypes of domestic violence, a summary of the effects of domestic violence on children, and a discussion of the options available for parenting plans that prioritize safety and long-term adjustment of parents and children. The failure of a professional to adequately differentiate subtypes, including cases of intimate terrorism/coercive control, increases the risk for inadequate interventions tailored to the specific needs of the parents, or mislabeling appropriately protective parents as "alienating." The research illuminates not only that meta-analyses have well documented the detrimental effects of domestic violence on children, but also that there may be different effects depending upon the age and gender of the child. "One-size-fits-all" conclusions or recommendations risk serious errors in divergent directions, including inappropriately over-pathologizing or stigmatizing some parents who will needlessly suffer unwarranted estrangement from their child, or tragically failing to protect the child from a parent with serious and potentially dangerous parenting deficits.

The next section of the book concerns present and future cultural or political issues. Examining the research in these neglected areas is a valuable contribution to professionals who work in the family court. The first chapter in this section, by L. Hita and S.L. Braver, concerns never-married parents in family court. The relevance to professionals is immediately established in the beginning of the chapter, which notes that only 12% of children were born outside a marriage in the United States in 1970, while studies conducted in 2003–2004 note that one third of all children were born to an unwed mother. The never-married parent has a different legal status than divorcing parents, and there are often informal arrangements regarding parenting plans, or such parents do not come to the attention of the court. The chapter reviews the research on psychosocial risk factors, economic strain, lack of social support, relocation, and family restructuring related to this population but notes that the scientific literature has seriously lagged behind the increasing numbers of these families appearing in family court.

S. Johnson and E. O'Connor discuss the relevant research involving gay and lesbian parents in family court. The chapter describes the different pathways to parenthood, including biological parenthood through the use of sperm donors, surrogacy, adoption, or individual families that include children who arrived through a combination of different pathways. There is much more research regarding lesbian mothers, with a greater need to focus on gay fathers, ethnic and racial minorities, multiracial families, lower-class families, adoptive families, and those living in rural areas. The chapter examines each study's methodology and findings, including strengths and weaknesses—for example, whether study samples were random, whether selection criteria were clearly stated, and whether the sample size was adequate. Among the important findings are studies showing that in controlled studies, children and adolescents from gay and lesbian families are not at heightened risk for maladjustment, problem behavior, or delinquency. Factors associated with children's adjustment and behavior were levels of parenting stress, parental interpersonal conflict, and levels of love expressed between the parents. The research results also include that the overwhelming majority of children with gay and lesbian parents identify as heterosexual in adulthood.

The chapter concerning cultural dynamics of divorce and parenting by M. Saini and J. Ma notes that families in North America are quite diverse, transforming conventional notions of multiculturalism, multilinguistic services, and multireligious observances. The increased diversity of families involved in family court requires professionals to know the research in this area and to apply it respectfully. Examining families solely based on traditional definitions limits understanding of family formations, expectations, and experiences. The research is considered from a variety of perspectives, including whether the context of the research adequately mirrors the complexity of the populations served with the court.

W.G. Austin examines the research on relocation in child custody cases. The chapter notes that relocation law follows different standards and procedures adopted by the 50 states and the District of Columbia, and that there has been an evolution reflecting changing family roles and responsibilities, where fathers are now much more involved in childrearing. This complex area of family law litigation is examined from many perspectives, including the sufficiency of relationship harm to the non-residential parent; crafting long-distance plans to mitigate harm; the fact that relocation and economic changes associated with divorce are the two most potent predictors of the child's adjustment; and the concept of parental gatekeeping, when one parent acts in a facilitative or restrictive fashion in reference to the other parent, and why this is relevant to relocation disputes.

The final section and concluding chapter of the book, by D.W. Shuman and A.S. Berk, examines the best interests of the child and the *Daubert* and *Frye* evidentiary frameworks. The chapter begins with an examination of how legal determinations for child custody are based on the best interests of the child, although this standard has been criticized since its inception in part for its ambiguity and lack of consistency among jurisdictions. While mental health professionals were increasingly used by the courts to help address the psychological best-interests question in family court, over a 76-year period the U.S. Supreme Court was reinventing the standard for the admissibility of expert opinion. From 1923, in *Frye v. United States*, to 1993, in *Daubert v. Merrell Dow Pharmaceuticals*, the authors explain the court went from a standard of qualification only, to scrutinizing the methods and procedures by experts, requiring proof of testimonial relevance and reliability. The authors note that child custody adjudications occur in state courts that may not have adopted *Daubert*, and jurisdictions may vary in their evidentiary standards. The authors discuss guidelines for identifying reliable mental health testimony, including whether the witness qualifies as an expert (e.g., is a licensed mental health professional); whether the expert opinion comports with applicable professional standards; whether there is an unreasonable analytical gap between the data and the conclusion; whether the testimony speaks to the legal standard at issue; and judicial self-assessment for objectivity (i.e., whether judges can perform their objective adjudicative duty). The authors express concern that the ambiguity of the best interests of the child standard, combined with a lack of adherence to evidentiary qualification, has led to subjective and inconsistent judicial determinations.

K.F. Kuehnle and L.M. Drozd remind us of the importance of evidence-based practice in all parenting plan evaluations. The authors note that scientists rely on the scientific method and empirical investigation, while the pseudoscientist relies on subjective clinical judgments and intuition. In highly charged parenting plan evaluations, questions are often extremely complex, frequently beyond the limits of what professionals can answer, while the parties demand answers or opinions. Professionals offering opinions to the court would be wise to heed these authors' caution, "the confidence and perhaps arrogance of the testifying expert is not always equal to his or her level of competence."

Empirical research represents a way to increase knowledge, derived from or relating to experiments and observation rather than theory, to better answer questions. The research covered in this book is extensive and complements other professional literature of interest to mental health professionals working in the family court. The above chapters provide a timely and necessary contribution, broad in scope and focused on important and controversial issues, and facilitate a better understanding of a vulnerable and heterogeneous population of adults and children at a most stressful time in life.

Parenting Plan Evaluations

Foundation of Personality Development: Attachment and Parent Insightfulness

Attachment and Child Custody

The Importance of Available Parents

GWYNNETH SMITH, BRIANNA COFFINO,
PATRICIA VAN HORN, AND
ALICIA LIEBERMAN ■

INTRODUCTION

The aim of this chapter is to provide an overview of attachment theory and its foundations in research, to discuss how it can enhance the understanding of parent–child relationships, and to urge caution in the overextension of the tools and findings of attachment research to child custody evaluations. *Attachment* is a word that is liberally used in forensic contexts but often erroneously conflated with notions of parent–child bonding or warmth (Calloway & Erard, 2009). This misuse is partially a function of the gulf that continues to exist between academic attachment researchers and forensic child practitioners (Calloway & Erard, 2009). As a rule, attachment theory and assessment tools were developed for research purposes, and this has rarely included custody litigant samples (Calloway & Erard, 2009). Although this divide currently limits the practical utility of attachment measures in a forensic context, the theory remains an important source of conceptualization for the issues involved in custody decisions.

Children are biologically programmed by human evolution to seek protection from their caregivers in times of danger or threat. This exceedingly simple and yet profoundly functional drive—the desire to "be near Mommy" or "be near Daddy" when scared, sad, or confused—is the subject of attachment theory. There is a biological reason that this bond is so important to children's development. The attachment system promotes survival when children are vulnerable and unable to function independently. Human children, relative to other mammals, are born significantly underdeveloped, unable to feed themselves or to be mobile in the face of danger. This is due in large part to humans' large brain size relative to body size, which requires that children be born with much brain development yet to come in order for the child's head to fit through the birth canal (Friedlander & Jordan, 1995). As a species, the survival of our young is dependent upon the formation of an exceptionally powerful relationship between child and parent to compensate for the physical helplessness of the young. From an evolutionary perspective, children who survived to adulthood and perpetuated the species were those who were members of parent–child partnerships (dyads) where the parent fiercely protected the child, and the child invariably sought out the parent in situations of danger and uncertainty. The child's tendency to turn to the parent for protection and the parent's motivation to keep the child safe from danger make up the attachment system.

John Bowlby (1969/1982, 1988) was the creator of attachment theory and focused primarily on the relationship between mothers and young children, but research in the past decades has expanded to include fathers and other caregivers. Findings from dozens of studies demonstrate that children whose parents are sensitively attuned to their signals of need tend to develop most successfully, showing a healthy balance between exploration of the world in safe situations and seeking protection from their parents when uncertain or endangered (De Wolff & van IJzendoorn, 1997). This careful balance is essential to children's optimal development because the stimulation provided by exploration is necessary to further early brain development, while a protective, nurturing relationship is vital to keep young children safe and to make to make them feel confident in exploring. The attachment relationship between parent and child is the incubator of this process.

ATTACHMENT THEORY AND CHILD CUSTODY

Despite occupying a central place in developmental psychology for decades, attachment theory and its methods of assessment have only recently been adopted for use in child custody evaluations (Calloway & Erard, 2009; Garber, 2009). Because of this, best practices and standards are still developing for the role of attachment theory and its clinical application in a forensic context (Byrne, O'Connor, Marvin, Whelan, 2005; Calloway & Erard, 2009; Garber, 2009; Rivas, Handler, & Sims, 2009). The reasons for the current forensic interest in attachment theory are understandable. Attachment theory, at least in some part, seeks to explain the very question that custody evaluators, family law attorneys, and judges ask in each custody case: What is the nature of the relationship between this child and each of his or her parents? However, the degree to which attachment theory can be then extended to the practical questions of particular custody and visitation schedules is less clear.

Potential Value of Attachment Theory Within a Custody Context

There are several reasons that attachment theory holds the potential to inform custody decision-making. First, it is a well-understood construct within the context of early childhood development and disruptions in relationships. At a time when more than 40% of contemporary first marriages end in divorce, and the number of never-married couples having children has increased drastically (40% of U.S. children are born to unmarried parents), parental separation is a common experience for America's children (Wilcox, 2009; National Center for Health Statistics [NCHS], 2009). Moreover, children whose parents divorce tend to be young. Two thirds of children who experience divorce by age 12 are very young, under the age of 6 (Furstenberg, Nord, Peterson, & Zill, 1983). Second, cases that are referred for custody evaluations tend to be the most complex and fraught within the family court system (Smith & Kerner, 2010). Only 5.2% of cases proceed to evaluation before settling, while 1.5% eventually go before a judge, and it is these cases that are most likely to necessitate a custody evaluation because they tend to present with complex environmental and interpersonal issues (Emery, Otto, O'Donohue, 2005; Maccoby & Mnookin, 1992). As divorce and parental separation continue to disproportionately affect individuals with fewer financial and educational resources in what is termed the *marriage divide*, these families frequently present with profound external stressors, in addition to the stress of dissolution itself (Wilcox, 2009). Finally, when judges apply the "best interests of the child" standard they are required to consider a range of factors, including the "quality of the relationships between children, parents, siblings, and significant others, the child's social needs, and the mental and physical health of all parties involved" (Jaffe & Mandeleeuw, 2008; Uniform Marriage and Divorce Act, 1974). Attachment theory clearly lends itself to better understanding these issues.

Within the strictures of professional guidelines (those that relate both to custody evaluations and to the practice of forensic psychology broadly), the use of attachment theory presents an opportunity to increase scientific rigor applied within an area that has sometimes seemed to be an "intuition-based practice" (Rivas et al., 2009). There are three primary sets of custody evaluation guidelines that have substantial overlap and collectively represent the consensus in the field as to professional competence (American Psychological Association [APA], 2010; Herman, S. P., 1997 [American Academy of Child and Adolescent Psychiatry, AACAP]; Martindale, 2006 [Association of Family and Conciliation Courts, AFCC]). All require that evaluators be able to offer testimony as to the "best interests of the child." Some states also have "rules of court" set forth by the state judicial counsel that also emphasize the importance of assessing those areas that are in the "best interests of the child" (Cal. Rule of Court 5.220, 2007). The requirement to assess the attachment relationship is implicit in some guidelines (APA, AFCC), and explicit in others (AACAP). As experts seek to meet the expert testimony admissibility standard of *Daubert/Frye* and progeny, employing methodologies with a rigorous girding in research is essential (*Daubert v. Merrell Dow Pharmaceuticals, Inc.*, 1993; *Frye v. United States*, 1923; Garber, 2009; Rivas et al., 2009). However, a competent application of attachment theory to a custody context is simultaneously guided by forensic practitioner guidelines, which require mental health professionals to be forthright about the "scientific bases and limitations of methods and procedures that they employ" (Committee on Ethical Guidelines for Forensic Psychologists, 1991, p. 658). Because the use of attachment theory within custody is in its infancy, practitioners are required to be forthright about its limitations and potential methodological issues. Judges often lean heavily upon evaluator testimony and recommendations as some of the most important factors in making rulings in custody cases (Byrne et al., 2005; Herman, S. P., 1997; Waller & Daniel, 2004). Along with the great power afforded to the recommendations of custody evaluators comes great responsibility.

INTRODUCTION TO ATTACHMENT THEORY

This section provides a broad overview of attachment theory. This includes the definition of attachment theory, attachment classification, the positive and negative outcomes related to attachment classification, and the stability of attachment (whether attachment status remains the same over time). The authors conclude with cautionary statements regarding the application of traditional attachment theory to forensic child custody evaluations.

Bowlby's (1969/1982, 1988) attachment theory has spurred considerable research within the area of child development. The body of compelling research linking attachment to outcomes in social, emotional, behavioral, and interpersonal areas has fostered the extension of attachment theory to new contexts, including policy and custody evaluations. To evaluate the appropriateness of applying attachment theory to custody evaluations, it is important to understand the original pillars of attachment theory, research findings in this area, and the tools used to measure attachment. An understanding of attachment theory will also help child custody evaluators use the theory of attachment to inform how they interpret an assessment, if not actually provide tools.

Definition of Attachment

As mentioned earlier, attachment theory is based on the premise that the caregiver–child attachment is an evolutionarily based behavioral system that functions to ensure the infant's survival by promoting proximity to the caregiver in times of danger (Bowlby, 1969/1982). Infants' behavior with their parents during times of stress or danger reflects their cumulative experience with caregivers. A history of caregiving that is sensitive and responsive promotes the child's ability to use that parent as a "secure base" to explore the world. Because infants develop distinct attachment relationships with each caregiver based on the history of interactions with that specific caregiver, a child may have a different attachment classification with each caregiver. In other words, attachment is not a characteristic of the individual child or parent, but rather it describes the quality of the relationship between them. This means that in sibling groups, different children may have different attachment classifications with the same parent.

An infant may have multiple attachment relationships (Howes & Speiker, 2008), a finding that is of particular significance in the context of custody evaluations. While Bowlby (1969/1982) originally proposed that an infant's mother was the primary caregiver, recent theorists have begun to reconsider how to determine who meets the criteria to be an attachment figure (Howes & Spieker, 2008; van IJzendoorn, Sagi, & Lambermon, 1992). This inquiry is partially related to the changing landscape of infants' daily lives. Infants spend considerably more time in non-familial care than when Bowlby originated attachment theory. However, for infants who attend day care, attachment is not related to day care per se, but to parents' psychological adjustment and the quality of parenting when the infants are with their parents (National Institute of Child Health and Human Development [NICHD], 1997). While there is some debate regarding how to determine who is an attachment figure other than the mother, the following set of guidelines provides a starting point. An attachment figure other than the mother is a caregiver who provides emotional and physical caregiving, is consistently involved with the child, and is emotionally invested in the child (Howes, 1999). Fathers are capable of meeting this definition, and in many cases they are a child's primary attachment figure (Lamb & Lewis, 2010). In fact, most children growing up in nuclear families are likely to become attached to both parents and may turn preferentially to one or the other parent depending on the specific situation.

Attachment Classification and Assessment

While Bowlby originated attachment theory, Mary Ainsworth was the first to create a procedure to measure attachment in babies aged 12 to 20 months old (Ainsworth, Blehar, Waters, & Wall, 1978). Ainsworth's laboratory assessment (the Strange Situation) is generally considered the "gold standard" of attachment research measures. The Strange Situation is a semi-structured, mildly stressful laboratory procedure composed of a series of short separations and reunions between a caregiver and an infant, and it yields a categorical dyadic classification. Only infant behaviors are measured in this procedure because according to attachment theory, an infant will behave in a way consistent with its history of interactions with a caregiver. Special attention is paid to how the child uses closeness to the caregiver as a means of balancing the competing developmental demands of protection and exploration. Based on their balance of exploration and attachment-seeking behaviors, as well as on their responses to reunions and separations, infants are classified into one of four categories: Secure (i.e., the child signals appropriately and effectively when distressed, is soothed by the caregiver, and actively explores), Insecure-Resistant (i.e., the child is focused on the caregiver and when distressed does not settle easily), Insecure-Avoidant (i.e., the child is focused on exploration and may appear to ignore its caregiver), and Disorganized (i.e., the infant displays inconsistent or illogical behavior or appears frightened by the caregiver). Secure attachment is associated with a parent's level of sensitivity and attunement to the internal need states of the child, levels of empathy, and the parent's ability to gain insight into the child's experience of the world (Koren-Karie, Oppenheim, Dolev, Sher, & Etzion-Carasso, 2002; Oppenheim, Koren-Karie, & Sagi, 2001).

To reach conclusions from the Strange Situation procedure, it must be conducted in a way that is consistent with the original guidelines. Primarily, the Strange Situation is intended to be a mildly stressful procedure (Ainsworth et al., 1978). In fact, an infant's stress level in this procedure involves various factors. An infant's amount of contact with strangers, and complementarily separation from caregivers, influence both how stressful the procedure is and how the infants show that they are stressed. Initially, it can be hypothesized that an infant's history of separations from caregivers will influence how the infant reacts to the separations in the Strange Situation. While separations are not in and of themselves detrimental, they may become so when they are emotionally charged or unpredictable (Lieberman & Van Horn, 2008). This seems especially relevant in a custody context, which may be a time of acute parenting stress and conflict surrounding exchanges. Infants who have experienced parental separations that are frequent, unpredictable, or accompanied by hostility, despair, or anger from the parent may be expected to feel greater anxiety in the separations in the Strange Situation procedure. For this reason, there is current debate in the field as to whether and how the Strange Situation protocol should be used with families in the midst of parental separation.

For infants who have a history of traumatic experiences, including the potential trauma of highly conflicted parental separation, parental entrances and departures in the Strange Situation procedure may be experienced as a trauma trigger, thereby violating the guideline that the Strange Situation be a *mildly* stressful procedure. Moreover, for infants who have been exposed to trauma, parents themselves can become trauma triggers for the child. Triggers can include tone of voice, facial expressions, sounds, and even certain emotions themselves (Lieberman, 2004). In addition, environmental stimuli (e.g., sights, sounds, and smells present at the time of the trauma) can function as trauma triggers (Pynoos, Steinberg, & Piancentini, 1999). Although beyond the scope of this chapter, it is also crucial to keep the concept of trauma triggers in mind when assessing distressed child behavior during exchanges between parents. This distressed behavior may be a manifestation of trauma in response to unpredictable or emotionally charged separations themselves, rather than indicative of Disorganized or Insecure attachment to one parent or the other. Exchanges in high-conflict post-separation scenarios may rise to the level of trauma, depending upon the presence of violence, chronic unpredictability, or emotional chaos. In theory, this could affect the quality of the attachment relationship because parents may be emotionally unavailable or frightening at precisely the time that the child needs protection (for a comprehensive review of the impact of trauma on attachment, see Lieberman, 2004).

Certain practical precautions must be acknowledged with the assessment of attachment. The procedure should be the first in a battery of tests and is discouraged if the infant is sick or extremely fatigued. This awareness is essential as any infant will display indices of disorganization when unduly stressed. In addition, the procedure must be administered and interpreted consistent with Ainsworth's guidelines. This requires that experts in attachment theory and assessment train the individuals who administer and score the Strange Situation. Without this training, evaluators and therapists should not use this procedure. Any modification to the Strange Situation invalidates the results and prevents extrapolating findings from attachment research. Finally, the Strange Situation yields a categorical classification (one of four primary categories) rather than a dimensional rating. This means that the nuances of an attachment relationship (i.e., showing some indications of security simultaneous to some indications of insecurity) are not reflected in the current categorical attachment classification system. This reduces the natural complexity of human relationships to four categories when in fact there may be notable variability within the same category. For these reasons, untrained evaluators should not employ the Strange Situation procedure, and even when employed by trained professionals it should be interpreted with great caution.

Adult Attachment Theory

A comparable attachment measure is widely used to measure adults' current mental representations of their own attachment experiences. The Adult Attachment Interview (AAI) is a semi-structured interview that probes for childhood and current experiences with caregivers as well as for opinions on the significance of those relationships (Main & Goldwyn, 1984). The coding of the AAI reflects individuals' mental representations (specifically, the degree of reflection and coherence in their description) of childhood experiences rather than the quality of those childhood experiences per se. This means that the focus of the AAI is on the way adults think and speak about their own early attachment experiences, which may hold clinical value for understanding how they view their own current role as a parent.

An AAI assessment yields four categories that parallel the infant coding scheme described above. Secure-Autonomous adults value attachment experiences, describe them coherently, are objective, and are not openly angry. Insecure-Preoccupied adults are preoccupied and involved with memories, openly angry, non-objective, and incoherent. Insecure-Dismissing adults are defensive, provide minimal detail, idealize parents, and deny the developmental importance of attachment relationships. Unresolved adults have not completed mourning the death of an attachment figure. Infant and adult attachment categories parallel each other in the following way: Secure/Autonomous, Resistant/Preoccupied, Avoidant/Dismissing, and Disorganized/Unresolved.

Some propose that adult attachment measures, including the AAI interview, may be useful in custody evaluations and hold potential for understanding parenting capabilities (Rivas et al., 2009). However, to date, the application of these measures to custody evaluations has not been rigorously tested (Rivas et al., 2009). It will be important for developmental researchers and practitioners to collaborate in order to consider the utility of using this measure in forensic settings.

Notably, other tools have been developed to measure attachment at different ages and using different methods (e.g., the Attachment Q Sort, the Macarthur Story Stem Battery, preschool attachment). These tools vary in the amount of training required to administer and score them, psychometric properties, and predictive power. Other measures, related to attachment assessment, have also recently been developed to help further elucidate the quality of the parent–child relationship and its role in child functioning (for a detailed discussion of parental insightfulness, see Oppenheim & Koren-Karie, 2012 [Chapter 2 in this volume]).

Outcomes of Attachment Classification

The predictive power of attachment underlies the trend to integrate attachment into custody evaluations (Garber, 2009). A rich body of longitudinal research has linked attachment to outcomes in later childhood and adulthood (e.g., Sroufe, Egeland, Carlson, & Collins, 2005). For instance, Secure attachment classification has been associated with higher self-esteem, resourcefulness with teachers, peer competence, and romantic relationship competence (Sroufe, 1989; Sroufe et al., 2005). On the other hand, Disorganized attachment in infancy has been related to child behavior problems in childhood and adolescence as well as psychopathology in adolescence (Carlson, 1998). Conceptually, early experiences with caregivers (i.e., attachment histories) influence children's expectations of others, the experiences that they pursue, and the meaning they ascribe to those encounters. Therefore, attachment patterns can be conceived as initiating a pathway that may be altered based on subsequent experience. Attachment "in infancy, even Disorganized attachment, does not make later pathology certain or even highly likely, it merely increments the probability of such an outcome. This is why we describe attachment as an organizational construct rather than as a 'causal trait.'" (Sroufe et al., 2005, p. 241).

Attachment Stability

Attachment is a reflection of interactive experience between a child and caregiver and thus is expected to change as caregiving changes. Parenting capacity is influenced by multiple factors, including parent characteristics, child characteristics, and contextual sources of stress and support (Belsky, 1984). In fact, Insecure attachment classification has been related to a host of negative factors, including violence in the home and conflict between parents, parental separation or death, the birth of a sibling, and poverty (Kelly & Lamb, 2000). Therefore, as contextual factors (parents' levels of stress and support) change, it is expected that this will influence parents' ability to be responsive to their children, which in turn will affect the attachment between parents and children.

In general, change in attachment status has been associated with changes in life stress (e.g., Bar-Haim, Sutton, Fox, & Marvin, 2000). For instance, in one longitudinal study, 38% of infants changed in attachment classification measured in the Strange Situation at 12 and 18 months. A change from Insecure to Secure attachment was related to a decrease in parents' life stress (Vaughn, Egeland, Sroufe, & Waters, 1979).

This is especially relevant to custody evaluators, as divorce and litigation may be a period of particular instability, with acute consequences in caregiving capabilities as well as attachment status. Research suggests that attachment measured at such a chaotic time may not necessarily be consistent with how attachment would have been classified before or after the spike in parents' stress levels. Similarly, while some researchers have found notable consistency between infant and adult attachment classifications (e.g., Waters, Treboux, Crowell, Merrick, & Albersheim, 2003), others have found little stability (Grossman, Grossman, & Zimmerman, 1999; Weinfeld, Sroufe, & Egeland, 2000). Conditions of chronic life stress, instability, or poverty may make long-term attachment continuity less likely and more likely to change from infancy to adulthood (see Solomon & George, 1999b, for discussion).

Van IJzendoorn (1995) completed a meta-analysis[1] on the association between a parent's attachment status on the AAI and the classification of the attachment relationship between that parent and his or her child. Van IJzendoorn (1995) found a 63% to 75% concordance between parents' attachment status and their infants' attachment classification. The range depended on how many classification categories were considered in the analysis. These findings have been cited in a discussion of the use of the AAI in custody evaluations (Rivas et al., 2009) However, there are four considerations before extrapolating from this study (van IJzendoorn, 1995).

1. Inherent in the discussion of the magnitude of effect sizes is the reality of publication bias in social science literature. In other words, people are less likely to publish nonsignificant findings, although this meta-analysis did include some unpublished work to address publication bias.
2. In addition, the ability to predict infant attachment from the father's own attachment representation was weaker than the ability to predict from the mother's attachment representation.
3. There was not a one-to-one correspondence between adult and infant attachment classifications.

4. Finally, the way that adult attachment representations influence children's attachment is only partially understood. Sensitive and responsive parenting only partially accounted for the relationship between adult and infant attachment.

Until the mechanism that underlies the possible transmission of attachment style from parent to child is better understood, extreme caution must be employed before applying these types of findings to custody decisions.

Overall Considerations

While the framework of attachment theory may be useful in conceptualizing parent–child relationships, there are some cautions before using the tools and findings of attachment research in custody evaluations.

- Attachment findings are based on group data and always include some measurement error, requiring caution in applying group findings to individuals.
- Attachment measures were developed for research purposes, and any modification in the administration of attachment tools invalidates their relationship to empirical findings.
- Attachment procedures (e.g., the Strange Situation, Adult Attachment Interview) should be administered and interpreted only by trained and certified coders.
- Attachment is not necessarily a stable construct over the life of the child. Because external stressors influence attachment, a given child can become Insecure in the wake of divorce or family transitions and then become Secure once the environment stabilizes (Kelly & Lamb, 2000). In addition, the parental conflict and stress that may accompany custody evaluations can initiate the development of a Disorganized attachment pattern (see Lee, Kaufmann, & George, 2009). Empirical research supports that certain risk factors have been associated with Disorganized attachment, including marital strife, witnessing domestic violence, and emotional dysregulation in the environment (Lee et al., 2009).
- Moreover, as other experts have highlighted, attachment, though very important, is only one lens through which to understand the development of children in the context of their primary relationships. The central contribution to functioning of other child factors such as temperamental flexibility and tolerance of stress cannot be overlooked (Thomas & Chess, 1984). These findings alert custody evaluators to consider contextual risk factors in the overall conceptualization of the child.

General guidelines for conducting early childhood evaluations are relevant to custody evaluations of young children. The DC: 0–3R manual (Zero to Three: National Center for Infants, Toddlers, and Families, 2005) provides recommendations for completing evaluations of young children. Guidelines include that the evaluation be conducted over multiple sessions, in multiple contexts, and with a range of caregivers in order to gain a comprehensive understanding of the child's functioning and needs. Evaluations may occur in multiple types of settings as long as the clinicians are competent, the tools are appropriately used, and the settings provide an adequate backdrop to evaluate particular domains of child functioning. These guidelines suggest that a comprehensive early childhood evaluation requires significant time and resources as well as a clinician who has expertise in multiple areas of child functioning or a multidisciplinary team of clinicians.

SPECIAL CONSIDERATIONS: CUSTODY SCHEDULES FOR YOUNG CHILDREN

One of the issues for which expert testimony on child attachment is most often introduced is related to parenting plans and schedules for young children. In particular, there is much debate in the field surrounding how attachment theory may inform the question of if and when overnight shared care should be initiated with the "non-primary" parent (Biringen et al., 2002; McIntosh & Smyth, Chapter 6 in this volume; Solomon & Biringen, 2001; Solomon & George, 1999a; Warshak, 2000, 2002). Reflective of the state of research within custody litigant samples as a whole, there is a limited amount of empirical data focusing on the questions of child outcomes broadly, and attachment in particular, in the context of overnight care for young children (Lamb, Chapter 8 in this volume). Because of this, there continues to be substantial disagreement within the field between those who believe the research shows that overnight visitations may harm the infant–primary parent attachment (Biringen et al., 2002; Solomon & Biringen, 2001) and those who urge that, in many cases, overnights for young children are developmentally beneficial (Kelly & Lamb, 2000; Warshak, 2000, 2002). The following discussion reviews points of view on the impact of overnights on attachment on either side of this debate and the studies that are most often cited by experts, and it concludes with author recommendations for how best to understand the current dialogue in the field and apply it within a custody context.

How Does Overnight Shared Care Affect Attachment Security?

The pioneering work of Solomon and George (1999a), which looked at the impact of overnight visitation schedules for young children on attachment classification, initiated this debate. In this work, Solomon and George (1999a) looked at a group of 145 infants and their parents, some from intact families and some from separated families, to see whether there were significant differences in attachment security according to whether the children spent overnights with the "non-primary parent." The results, though illuminating, were complex. There was not a straightforward relationship found between the type of shared care schedule and the child's well-being as measured by attachment classification (Solomon & George, 1999a).

Specifically, Solomon and George (1999a) highlighted three primary findings. First, infants of separated parents who had overnight care provided by their fathers were less likely to be classified as Secure in their relationships with their mothers compared to infants from married families. Second, mothers of infants in the overnight care group who were found to be Disorganized were more likely to report low parent communication and high parent conflict. Finally, infants from separated families (both those who had overnights and those who did not) were more likely to be classified as Disorganized in their relationships with their fathers than infants from married families (Solomon & George, 1999a).

The complexity of these findings was accompanied by a detailed discussion of how to best understand them as well as the limitations inherent to the study design (Solomon & George, 1999a). Both of these factors are crucial to understand when extrapolating from this important research to decision-making in custody cases. Most importantly, the authors emphasized that although they found an associated negative effect of overnights on infant–mother attachment classification, this was moderated by the level of reported conflict between the parents and the mother's perception that she was able to be protective of her child even when he was with the other parent (Solomon & George, 1999a). This finding can be understood to support what custody professionals have long known anecdotally: It is not parental separation itself that necessarily negatively affects children, but it is the way in which parents act out their conflicts and the degree to which they are able to collaborate on behalf of their child that is a deciding factor. This means that the message communicated to the child, both implicitly and explicitly, about the other parent is a crucial factor (see Pruett, Cowan, Cowan, & Diamond, Chapter 5 in this volume). While Solomon and George's (1999a) research yields important cautions regarding shared care within a highly conflicted family system, the authors advised against the wholesale conclusion that overnights are categorically detrimental to the attachment of young children. Limitations to the study design that require consideration in the generalizability of findings include that attachment was assessed at a time of high family stress; that the infants and fathers in the overnight group, in some cases, had very limited contact prior to the onset of overnights; and that samples were not as representative as would be desired.

The Ensuing Debate Regarding How to Apply These Findings

In the wake of the publication and discussion of Solomon and George's (1999a) work, a fervent debate arose between experts in the field as to what was implied for decision-making regarding overnights. On one hand were experts who emphasized the developmental benefit to children of maintaining, wherever possible, Secure attachments to both parents. They proposed that not only could infants tolerate frequent overnight transitions between parents, but also that in many cases this was the preferred arrangement because of the way it fostered these multiple attachments (Kelly & Lamb, 2000; Warshak, 2000, 2002). Conversely, another group of attachment experts cautioned that more data were needed before it could be said that frequent overnight transitions were a desirable arrangement for young children (Biringen et al., 2002; Solomon & Biringen, 2001). This group emphasized the importance of maintaining at least one Secure attachment to a primary attachment figure, usually the mother, and warned that overnights may present a special kind of disruption, particularly in highly conflicted couples, that could harm this primary attachment.

Kelly and Lamb (2000) were among those who support maintaining connections for young children via frequent overnight transitions. They proposed that rather than being the exception, this arrangement was preferable because it minimized the negative impact that extended separations and limited caregiving roles could have on the attachment relationship with either parent. Overnight care, in contrast to daytime visitation, provided the parent–child dyad with a unique opportunity to engage in important caregiving experiences like bathing, bedtime, and other night-time rituals, and caregiving in this varied context was important to maintaining a Secure attachment (Kelly & Lamb, 2000; Lamb, Sternberg, & Thompson, 1997; Warshak, 2002). They emphasized that relational consistency, rather than geographic consistency, was most important for young children and that this meant robustly supporting the connection between the child and both parents (Kelly & Lamb, 2000). Proponents drew on data from a large study of day care arrangements to support the notion that children could thrive in an environment of multiple caregivers and tran-sitions between them when the quality of caregiving was sufficient and caregivers were supportive of each other (Kelly & Lamb, 2000; NICHD, 1997; Warshak, 2002). How the day care findings might translate to a highly conflicted separation situation, however, was less well understood.

The issue of overnight care was connected to the highly fraught area of gender politics within the custody field, and experts observed that overwhelmingly fathers tended to be left with very limited contact with their young children, a factor that had negative implications for the future of these relationships, and even for the level of fathers' financial support of children after separation (Kelly & Lamb, 2000; Warshak, 2002). They objected that the Solomon and George (1999a) data were often cited to discourage overnight visitation when in fact that data had not shown that infants with overnight schedules were more likely to be insecurely attached than their separated counterparts who had daytime visitation schedules. This group also said that those who opposed overnights overlooked the limitations of the Solomon and George (1999a) research design (Warshak, 2002).

In response to this somewhat provocative recommendation that overnights be commonly considered in custody arrangements, others from the attachment field voiced their concerns, including Judith Solomon, the lead author of the initial study. The concerns of this group rested on the feeling that the data in the field were too preliminary to say that frequent transitions are desirable for young chil-dren, and moreover, that overnight separations from primary caregivers—unlike daytime separations—may present a special potential detriment to the attachment relationship (Biringen et al., 2002; Solomon & Biringen, 2001). The authors argued that while "mothering is not synonymous with good parenting," there is a hierarchy of attachment figures, and that at times of instability the child's level of contact with the primary attachment figure should be given priority (Solomon & Biringen, 2001, p. 361). They concluded that for these reasons, when relationships are con-flicted and parental communication is low, overnights away from primary caregivers should be avoided for infants and toddlers (Biringen et al., 2002; Solomon & Biringen, 2001). However, the authors acknowledged that a wider variety of schedules were possible in lower-conflict family systems (Biringen et al., 2002; Solomon & Biringen, 2001).

Essentially, proponents on either side of the divide drew upon the absence of robust replicated research to support their conclusions, one side saying that in the absence of evidence to the contrary, children should not be deprived of Secure attachment relationships to their fathers, and the other side citing the same lack of data to issue a warning against frequent overnight transitions until the phenomenon and its longer-term effect on children are better understood.

Subsequent Research

Since the publication of Solomon and George's (1999a) work, there has been a limited amount of additional research on how shared overnight schedules affect outcomes for young children. It is important to note that the two studies described here look at a broader range of behavioral outcomes, not attachment status, to elucidate the consequences of various overnight schedules. This was done deliberately, both because of the nature of the study designs and because the authors felt that attachment classification alone was too narrow a construct to understand the global affects of overnight separations (McIntosh, Smyth, & Kelaher, 2010; Pruett, Ebling, & Insabella, 2004).

In the study by Pruett, Ebling, and Insabella (2004), the authors wanted to better understand how overnight shared care, schedule consistency, and number of caregivers affected young children's social and emotional functioning after divorce. They studied 132 families both at the initiation of custody proceedings and then 15 to 18 months later and found that children's behavioral health was affected by all three variables on a measure of child symptomatology, the Child Behavior Checklist. The most powerful variables (those that were most strongly associated with problematic child behaviors) were the consistency of schedules and numbers of caregivers. The presence or absence of overnights was not itself the most predictive factor. The authors stated, "Overnights do matter, but what matters more to these children is whether they occur on a regular unchanging schedule" (p. 56). In particular, the authors noted that children's successful adaptation to post-divorce life was highly contingent upon their parents' ability to provide them with stability and predictability in relationships and schedules, factors that buttress Secure attachments and optimal development.

McIntosh, Smyth, and Kelaher (2010) is a recent body of work, commissioned by the Australian government, that represents a significant step forward for the field in the breadth and size of its sample and its longitudinal design. Conducted as part of the Longitudinal Study of Australian Children, which follows 10,000 children and families from around Australia, this sub-analysis looked at 2,050 children aged birth to 5 years old whose parents were separated. These children had a variety of caregiving arrangements, from virtually no overnights to nearly equally shared overnight care. The researchers wanted to understand how different levels of overnight-shared care, in conjunction with children's ages, affected emotional well-being. Controlling for the independent effects of parent's socioeconomic status, parenting warmth, and co-parenting relationship, they found that overnight-shared care was associated with different outcomes depending on the child's age. Children under age 2 with more shared care were found to be more irritable and more vigilant in monitoring the location of and proximity to the primary caregiver, two behaviors related to the functioning of the attachment system. Children aged 2 to 3 with more shared care showed lower levels of persistence in tasks, more problematic behaviors on a caregiver report of child functioning, and more distressed behaviors within the parent–child dyad, including separation anxiety, worry, lack of responsiveness, feeding problems, and aggression towards the primary parent. Significantly, for children older than 4 years, no negative effects of shared overnight care were found. The authors noted that there were limitations to their study design, including the small sample size of parents actually practicing shared care (N = 160 children) and the inability to consistently collect data from "non-primary" parents, which were excluded from the study as a result. Based on their findings, the authors cautioned that shared overnight care for young children under 4 years old may independently affect elements of early emotional development associated with affect regulation.

Conclusion: Attachment and Custody Schedules for Young Children

For forensic practitioners and courts, who do not have the luxury of deferring decision-making in complex cases until a convergence of expert opinion occurs, a debate like this in the field, while merited and important, is difficult to extract actionable knowledge from. The authors of this chapter, in line with statements made by the experts cited above, have sought to draw broad conclusions where consensus exists and to highlight areas where the field still does not yet have enough data to draw bright-line conclusions.

A review of this dialogue reveals that perhaps the most important threshold consideration for decision-makers is not the age of the child but the level and nature of interparental conflict. Where communication is good and levels of conflict are low (or the child is effectively insulated from conflict), overnight schedules, even for very young children, may be preferable to keep the child closely connected to both parents across a range of caregiving contexts (Biringen et al., 2002; Kelly & Lamb, 2000; Solomon & Biringen, 2001; Warshak, 2002). Parents must be able to maintain these schedules in predictable and consistent ways (Pruett et al., 2004).

Where there are high levels of ongoing conflict, conclusions are less clear. In these circumstances, children's ability to form one Secure attachment, let alone a Secure attachment with each caregiver, may be compromised (Solomon & George, 1999a). Their overall functioning, beyond the attachment domain, may suffer as well (McIntosh et al., 2010; Pruett et al., 2004). In these types of cases, which are the most difficult and therefore the most likely to present for custody evaluation, children may need to be protected from environmental stressors by emphasizing a primary attachment relationship in forming the custodial schedule. Where conflict is high, frequent transitions can exacerbate it (Amato & Rezac, 1994). This is not to say that there is no detrimental consequence to potentially losing out on the depth of relationship they may have otherwise had with their other parent. But protecting attachment security, when parents are unwilling or unable to cooperate, will become the primary objective. Ultimately, decisions should continue to be made on a case-by-case basis, assessing the functioning of the entire family system. No blanket mandate either for or against overnights for young children can currently be supported by the research.

SUMMARY

Attachment theory and its application to the child custody context continues to be an area both of great promise and great challenge within forensic psychology.

On one hand, insights from attachment theory directly bear on the central inquiry of custody disputes, the nature of the relationship between young parents and children, and the developmental implications of their disruption. On the other hand, many experts agree that the application of attachment assessment tools to a family system in the midst of crisis is insufficiently understood at the current time (Calloway & Erard, 2009; Garber, 2009). In a practical sense, this dramatically limits the application of attachment theory within forensic evaluations.

This chapter has sought to outline the current dialectic within the attachment field with respect to child custody evaluations. A review of attachment theory was provided, with special focus on those aspects that most closely pertain to questions arising with child custody. Particular attention was devoted to the current state of the research on the implications of shared overnight care on the parent–child attachment relationship.

In closing, the authors join the call of others in the field for a redoubling of research efforts to better understand the implications of attachment theory specifically within a custody litigant context (Calloway & Erard, 2009; Garber, 2009; Ludolph, 2009). In particular, Garber (2009) is prescient in outlining the most important areas on which future research needs to focus, including how to address the practical issues of using existing attachment assessment tools validly in a custody context, how to overcome the practical and ethical challenges of including custody litigant samples in research, how to accurately assess attachment during a time of high familial stress, and ultimately how best to incorporate attachment findings into the practicalities of parenting plans. Until these basic methodological issues are surmounted, attachment theory remains an extremely useful theoretical construct, with limited practical implications to the custody arena.

GUIDELINES: CONSIDERATIONS AND CAUTIONS

- Attachment findings are based on group data and always include some measurement error, suggesting caution in applying group findings to individuals.
- Any modification in the administration of attachment tools invalidates their relationship to empirical findings.
- Attachment classification between a parent and child may change over the life of the child.
- Because it is influenced by external stressors, attachment can become Insecure in the wake of divorce or family transitions and then become Secure once the environment stabilizes.
- Classifying parent–child relationships into one of four categories does not reflect the complexity in parent–child relationships; there may be notable variability within the same attachment classification.
- Attachment research within custody litigant samples remains very much in its infancy. Therefore, until more well-designed research is conducted with this particular sample, professionals must be cautious in extrapolating from attachment theory in general to its particular manifestation within a family in crisis.

NOTES

1 A meta-analysis is a "statistical synthesis of related studies" that allows researchers to combine data from different pieces of research on the same question to come to broad conclusions (Lehrer, 2010).

REFERENCES

Ainsworth, M. D. S., Blehar, M. C., Walters, E., & Wall, S. (1978). *Patterns of attachment: A psychological study of the stranger situation.* Hillsdale, NJ: Erlbaum.

Amato, P. R., & Rezac, S. (1994). Contact with nonresident parents, interparental conflict, and children's behavior. *Journal of Family Issues, 15*(2), 191–207. doi: 10.1177/0192513X94015002003

American Psychological Association. (2009). Guidelines for child custody evaluations in family law proceedings. Retrieved January 10, 2011, from http://www.apa.org/practice/guidelines/child-custody.pdf.

American Psychological Association. (2010). Guidelines for child custody evaluations in family law proceedings. *American Psychologist, 65*(9), 863–867. DOI: 10.1037/a002125.

Association of Family and Conciliation Courts. (2007). Model standards of practice for child custody evaluations. *Family Court Review, 45*, 70–91. doi: 10.1111/j.1744-1617.2007.129_3. x

Bar-Haim, Y., Sutton, D. B., Fox, N. A., & Marvin, R. S. (2000). Stability and change of attachment at 14, 24, and 58 months of age: Behavior, representation, and life events. *Journal of Child Psychology and Psychiatry, 41*(3), 381–388. doi: 10.1111/1469-7610.00622 PMid: 10784085

Belsky, J. (1984). The determination of parenting: A process model. *Child Development, 55*, 83–96. doi: 10.2307/1129836 PMid: 6705636

Biringen, Z., Greve-Spees, J., Howard, W., Leith, D., Tanner, L., Moore, S., Williams, L. (2002). Commentary on Warshak's "Blanket restrictions: Overnight contact between parents and young children." *Family Court Review, 40*(2), 204–207. doi: 10.1111/j. 174-1617.2002. tb00831. x

Bowlby, J. (1969/1982). *Attachment and loss, Vol. 1: Attachment.* New York: Basic Books.

Bowlby, J. (1988). Developmental psychiatry comes of age. *American Journal of Psychiatry, 145*(1), 1–9. PMid: 3276225

Byrne, J. G., O'Connor, T. G., Marvin, R. S., & Whelan, W. F. (2005). Practice review: The contribution of attachment theory to child custody assessments. *Journal of Child Psychology and Psychiatry, 46*(2), 115–127. doi: 10.1111/j. 1469-7610.2004.00396. x PMid: 15679522

California Rule of Court 5.220. Retrieved February 25, 2011, from http://www.courtinfo.ca.gov/rules/index.cfm?title=five&linkid=rule5_220.

Calloway, G., & Erard, R. E. (2009). Introduction to the special issue on attachment and child custody. *Journal of Child Custody, 6*, 1–7. doi: 10.1080/15379410902894825

Carlson, E. A. (1998). A prospective longitudinal study of attachment disorganization/disorientation. *Child Development, 69*(4), 1107–1128. PMid: 9768489

Committee on Ethical Guidelines for Forensic Psychologists. (1991). Specialty guidelines for forensic psychologists. *Law & Human Behavior, 15*, 655–665. doi: 10.1007/BF01065858

Daubert v. Merrell Dow Pharmaceuticals Inc., 509 U.S. 579 (1993).

De Wolff, M. S., & van IJzendoorn, M. H. (1997). Sensitivity and attachment: A meta-analysis on parental antecedents of infant attachment. *Child Development, 68*(4), *571–591.*

Emery, R. E., Otto, R. K., & O'Donohue, W. T. (2005). A critical assessment of child custody evaluations: Limited science and a flawed system. *Psychological Science in the Public Interest, 6*, 10–29. doi: 10.1111/j. 1529–1006.2005.00020. x

Friedlander, N., & Jordan, D. K. (1995). Obstetric implications of Neanderthal robusticity and bone density. *Human Evolution (Florence), 9*, 331–342.

Frye v. United States, 293 F. 1013 (D.C. Cir. 1923)

Furstenberg, F. F., Jr., Nord, C. W., Peterson, J. L., & Zill, N. (1983). The life course of children of divorce: Marital disruption and parental contact. *American Sociological Review, 48*(5), 656–668. doi: 10.2307/2094925

Garber, B. D. (2009). Attachment methodology in custody evaluation: Four hurdles standing between developmental theory and forensic application. *Journal of Child Custody, 6*, 38–61. doi: 10.1080/15379410902894841

Grossman, K. E., Grossman, K., & Zimmerman, P. (1999). A wider view of attachment and exploration: Stability and change during the years of immaturity. In J. Cassidy & P. R. Shaver (Eds.), *Handbook of Attachment* (1st ed., pp. 760–786). New York: Guilford.

Herman, J. (1997). *Trauma and recovery: The aftermath of violence from domestic abuse to political terror.* New York: Basic Books.

Herman, S. P. (1997). Practice parameters for child custody evaluation. *Journal of the American Academy of Child and Adolescent Psychiatry, 36*(10), 57s–68s. PMid: 9334565

Howes, C. (1999). Attachment relationships in the context of multiple caregivers. In J. Cassidy & P. R. Shaver (Eds.), *Handbook of attachment* (1st ed., pp. 671–687). New York: Guilford.

Howes, C., & Spieker, S. J. (2008) Attachment relationships in the context of multiple caregivers. In J. Cassidy & P. R. Shaver (Eds.), *Handbook of attachment* (2nd ed., pp. 317–332). New York: Guilford.

Jaffe, A. M., & Mandeleeuw, D. (2008). Essentials of a forensic child custody evaluation. *Family Advocate, 30*, 16–21. Retrieved on January 10, 2011, from http://www.california-divorce.com/articles_custody/Jaffe_%20MandeleewABASpring08TTArticles.pdf.

Kelly, J. B., & Lamb, M. E. (2000). Using child development research to make appropriate custody and access decisions for young children. *Family and Conciliation Court Review, 38*(3), 297–311. doi: 10.1111/j. 174–1617.2000. tb00577. x

Koren-Karie, N., Oppenheim, D., Dolev, S., Sher, E., & Etzion-Carasso, A. (2002). Mothers' insightfulness regarding their infants' internal experience: Relations with maternal sensitivity and infant attachment. *Developmental Psychology, 38*(4), 534–542).

Lamb, M. (2012). Critical analysis of research on parenting plans and children's well-being. In K. Kuehnle & L. Drozd (Eds.), *Parenting plan evaluations: Applied research for the family court.* New York: Oxford University Press.

Lamb, M., & Lewis C. (2010) The development and significance of father-child relationships in two parent families. In M. Lamb (Ed.), *The role of the father in child development* (5th ed., pp. 94–153). Hoboken, NJ: Wiley.

Lamb, M. E., Sternberg, K., & Thompson, R. A. (1997). The effects of divorce and custody arrangements on children's behaviour, development and adjustment.

Family and Conciliation Courts Review, 35, 393–404. doi: 10.1111/j. 174–1617.1997.
tb00482. x

Lee, S. M., Kaufman, R., & George, C. (2009). Disorganized attachment in young
children: Manifestations, etiology, and implications for child custody. *Journal of
Child Custody*, 6, 62–90. doi: 10.1080/15379410902894858

Lehrer, J. (2010). The truth wears off: Is there something wrong with the scientific
method? *The New Yorker Magazine*, Dec. 13.

Lieberman, A. F. (2004). Traumatic stress and quality of attachment: Reality and
internalization in disorders of infant mental health. *Infant Mental Health Journal*,
25(4), 336–351. doi: 10.1002/imhj. 20009

Lieberman, A. F., & Van Horn, P. (2008). *Psychotherapy with infants and young
children: Repairing the effects of stress and trauma on early attachment*. New York:
Guilford.

Ludolph, P. (2009). Answered and unanswered questions in attachment theory
with implications for children of divorce. *Journal of Child Custody*, 6, 8–24. doi:
10.1080/15379410902894817

Maccoby, E. E., & Mnookin, R. H. (1992). *Dividing the child: Social and legal
dilemmas of custody*. Cambridge, MA: Harvard University Press.

Main, M., & Goldwyn, R. (1984). Predicting rejection of her infant from mother's
representation of her won experience: Implications for the abused-abusing
intergenerational cycle. *Child Abuse and Neglect*, 8(2), 203–217. doi: 10.1016/
0145-2134(84)90009-7

Martindale, D. A., et al. (2006). Model Standards of Practice for Child Custody
Evaluation. *Association of Family and Conciliation Courts*. Retrieved on January
9, 2011, from http://www.afccnet.org/pdfs/Model%20Stds%20Child%20Custody
%20Eval%20Sept%202006.pdf

McIntosh, J., & Smyth, B. S. (2012). Shared-time parenting: An evidence-based
matrix for evaluating risk. In K. Kuehnle & L. Drozd (Eds.), *Parenting plan evaluations: Applied research for the family court*. New York: Oxford University Press.

McIntosh, J., Smyth, B. S., Kelaher, M., Wells, Y., & Long, C. (2010). *Parenting arrangements post-separation: Patterns and developmental outcomes, Part II: Relationships
between overnight care patterns and psycho-emotional development in infants and
young children*. Victoria, Australia: Family Transitions.

National Center for Health Statistics. (2009). *Changing patterns of nonmarital childbearing in the United States*. Vital Health Statistics Series. Retrieved on January 10,
2011, from http://www.cdc.gov/nchs/data/databriefs/db18.pdf.

National Institute of Child Health and Human Development. (1997). The effects of
infant child care on infant-mother attachment security: Results of the NICHD
study of early child care. *Child Development*, 68(5), 860–879. doi: 10.1111/j. 1467–
8624.1997. tb01967. x doi: 10.2307/1132038

Oppenheim, D., & Koren-Karie, N. (2012). Parents' insightfulness: the importance
of keeping the inner world of the child in mind for parenting plan evaluations. In
K. Kuehnle & L. Drozd (Eds.), *Parenting plan evaluations: Applied research for the
family court*. New York: Oxford University Press.

Oppenheim, D., Koren-Karie, N., & Sagi, A. (2001). Mothers' empathic understanding of their preschoolers' internal experience: Relations with early attachment.
International Journal of Behavioral Development, 25(1), 16–26.

Pruett, M. K., Cowan, C. P., Cowan, P. A., & Diamond, J. S. (2012). Supporting
father involvement in the context of separation and divorce. In K. Kuehnle &

L. Drozd (Eds.), *Parenting plan evaluations: Applied research for the family court.* New York: Oxford University Press

Pruett, M. K., Ebling, R., & Insabella, G. (2004). Critical aspects of parenting plans for young children: Interjecting data into the debate about overnights. *Family Court Review, 42*(1), 39–59. doi: 10.1177/1531244504421004 doi: 10.1111/j. 174–1617.2004. tb00632. x

Pynoos, R. S., Steinberg, A. M., & Piancentini, J. C. (1999). A developmental psychopathology model of childhood traumatic stress and intersection with anxiety disorders. *Biological Psychiatry, 46*(11), 1542–1554. doi: 10.1016/S0006-3223(99)00262-0

Rivas, E. M., Handler, L., & Sims, C. R. (2009). Adult attachment measures and their potential utility in custody cases. *Journal of Child Custody, 6,* 25–37. doi: 10.1080/15379410902894833

Smith, G., & Kerner, M. J. (2010). Child custody evaluations: Standards and recommendations. *Psychiatric Malpractice Risk Management, 6,* 39–51.

Solomon, J., & Biringen, Z. (2001). Another look at the development research: Commentary on Kelly and Lamb's "Using child development research to make appropriate custody and access decisions for young children." *Family Court Review, 39*(4), 355–364. doi: 10.1111/j. 174–1617.2001. tb00617. x

Solomon, J., & George, C. (1999a). The development of attachment in separated and divorced families: Effect of overnight visitation, parents and couple variables. *Attachment and Human Development, 1*(1), 2–33. doi: 10.1080/14616739900134011

Solomon, J., & George, C. (1999b). The measurement of attachment security in infancy and childhood. In J. Cassidy & P. R. Shaver (Eds.), *Handbook of attachment* (pp. 287–318). New York: Guilford.

Sroufe, L. A. (1989). Relationship, self, and individual adaptation. In A. J. Sameroff & R. N. Emde (Eds.), *Relationship disturbance in early childhood: A developmental approach* (pp. 70–94). New York: Basic Books.

Sroufe, L. A., Egeland, B., Carlson, E., & Collins, A. (2005). *Development of the person.* New York: Guilford.

Thomas, A., & Chess, S. (1984). The genesis and evolution of behavioral disorders: From infancy to early adult life. *American Journal of Psychiatry, 141*(1), 1–9. PMid: 6691419

Uniform Marriage and Divorce Act, § 402, 9A U.L.A. 561 (1974).

van IJzendoorn, M. H. (1995). Adult attachment representations, parental responsiveness, and infant attachment: A meta-analysis on the predictive validity of the adult attachment interview. *Psychological Bulletin, 117*(3), 387–403. doi: 10.1037/0033-2909.117.3.387 PMid: 7777645

van IJzendoorn, M. H., Sagi, A., & Lambermon, M. W. E. (1992). The multiple caretaker paradox: Data from Holland and Israel. In R. C. Pianta (Ed.), *Beyond the parent: The role of other adults in children's lives* (pp. 5–24). San Francisco: Jossey-Bass.

Vaughn, B. E., Egeland, B. R., Sroufe, L. A., & Waters, E. (1979). Individual differences in infant-mother attachment at twelve and eighteen months: Stability and change in families under stress. *Child Development, 50*(4), 971–975. doi: 10.2307/1129321 PMid: 535447

Waller, E. M., & Daniel, A. E. (2004). The purpose and utility of child custody evaluations: From the perspective of judges. *Journal of Psychiatry and the Law, 32,* 5–27.

Warshak, R. A. (2000). Blanket restrictions: Overnight contact between parents and young children. *Family and Conciliation Courts Review, 38*, 422–445. doi: 10.1111/j. 174–1617.2000. tb00583. x

Warshak, R. A. (2002). Who will be there when I cry in the night? Revisiting overnights—A rejoinder to Biringen et al. *Family Court Review, 40*(2), 208–219. doi: 10.1111/j. 174–1617.2002. tb00832. x

Waters, E., Treboux, D., Crowell, J., Merrick, S., & Albersheim, L. (2003). Attachment security in infancy and early adulthood: A twenty-year longitudinal study. In M. E. Hertzig & E. A. Farber (Eds.), *Annual progress in child psychiatry and child development: 2000–2001* (pp. 63–72). New York: Brunner-Routledge.

Weinfield, N. S., Sroufe, L. A., & Egeland, B. (2000). Attachment from infancy to young adulthood in a high-risk sample: Continuity, discontinuity and their correlates. *Child Development, 71*(3), 695–702. doi: 10.1111/1467–8624.00178 PMid: 10953936

Wilcox, W.B. (2009). The evolution of divorce. *National Affairs, 1*, 81–94.

Zero to Three: National Center for Infants, Toddlers, and Families. (2005). *Diagnostic classification of mental health and developmental disorders of infancy and early childhood* (DC: 0–3R) (rev.). Washington, DC: Author.

Parents' Insightfulness

The Importance of Keeping the Inner World of the Child in Mind for Parenting Plan Evaluations

DAVID OPPENHEIM AND NINA KOREN-KARIE ■

When professionals evaluate families during child custody litigation, they are often asked to examine parental functioning and competence. Based on their findings, they provide recommendations to the family court regarding parenting plans that will meet the "best interest" of the children. Much attention is naturally given to parental behaviors in such assessments. For example, professionals may need to examine how parents independently and cooperatively handle disciplinary issues, disagreements regarding their children, or decisions about their children's schedules. Assessment of these parenting behaviors provides important information regarding a parent's capacity and motivation to meet the needs of his or her children. However, staying at the level of what parents do—how they react, respond, or handle their children—may provide only part of the picture. Studies have revealed that it is equally important to pay attention and assess another level—the level referred to as parental *internal representations* (Main, Kaplan, & Cassidy, 1985). Internal representations reflect the emotional meaning that the parent attributes to the child and his or her behavior, the self, the spouse, and family relationships (Oppenheim, 2006). While parents may or may not be aware of these attributions, research and clinical work have shown that they exert a powerful effect on parental caregiving and on the parent–child relationship (Fraiberg, Adelson, & Shapiro, 1975; Main et al., 1985). The research on internal representations provides professionals working with families new ways to think about how parents' internal processes promote or impede healthy child development in times of stressful family transitions.

This chapter will focus on one component of parental internal representations, which is referred to as *insightfulness*. Insightfulness involves the parents' ability to see things from the child's point of view and to empathically think about and consider the motives underlying their children's behavior. The Insightfulness Assessment (IA; Oppenheim & Koren-Karie, 2009) was developed to examine this capacity and will be presented. The chapter will address the theory and empirical data on which this assessment tool is based, and examples will illustrate how insightfulness (or lack of insightfulness) is expressed in parents' speech about their children.

INSIGHTFULNESS: BACKGROUND

The concept of insightfulness is rooted in the work of clinicians and developmental researchers who have argued that a full understanding of parent–child relationships, and particularly those relationships that are under stress, requires an appreciation of the parent's internal depiction of the child. Perhaps the best-known and most emotionally evocative expression of this point of view was presented over three decades ago by Fraiberg et al. (1975). These authors described how unresolved parental childhood conflicts may distort the representation of the child in the mind of the parent. The mother's representations of her child can be so intensely colored by trauma and unmet needs from her own history that she cannot, in effect, "see" the child. In such situations mothers experience difficulties in developing insight into the motives and emotions underlying the child's behavior and responding empathically to the child's signals and the emotional needs that underlie them.

Assessments of Parents' Representations of Their Children

Based on Fraiberg et al. (1975) as well as on Bowlby's concept of internal working models (Bowlby, 1982), several researchers developed assessments of parents' representations of their children using interviews (see George & Solomon, 2008, for a review). This body of research has shown that mothers of Secure children are flexible, balanced, and integrated in their interviews about their children. Their narratives reflect their commitment, trust, cooperation, knowledge of self and child as individuals, open communication with the child, and joy in the parenting experience. Mothers of Insecure children are not flexible, balanced, or integrated. They receive lower ratings of sensitivity, reflective functioning, and mind-mindedness than mothers of Secure children.

In sum:

- Clinical work has revealed that unresolved conflicts and traumas from parents' past may distort their perceptions of their children's experience and behavior.
- Research using maternal interviews has shown that balanced and flexible maternal representations are associated with Secure attachment.

THE INSIGHTFUL ASSESSMENT

Further investigation of parents' internal representations of their children by Oppenheim and Koren-Karie (2009) resulted in the construction of a semi-structured interview, the Insightfulness Assessment. In this assessment parents are shown several video segments of their child interacting with the parent and are asked about the child's thoughts and feelings during the segments. Thus, this assessment reveals how parents' general representations of their children are applied to a specific and concrete moment in the life of the child. The goal of this procedure is to simulate moments from everyday life in which parents try to make sense of their children's behavior and understand the motives and emotions that may underlie the behavior. Unlike "real-life" moments, however, in which these meaning-making processes are implicit and operate mostly outside of awareness, the IA requires parents to make these processes explicit by responding to questions presented by an interviewer regarding their children's thoughts and feelings. In this way the IA allows the evaluator to understand parents' feelings, perceptions, and thoughts that are believed to underlie parental caregiving behavior. Before describing the IA procedure in more detail, the central components of insightfulness will be described.

To summarize:

- In the Insightfulness Assessment parents are interviewed regarding their children's thoughts and feelings after they view short video segments of their children interacting with them.
- Parents' responses in the IA reveal their ability to understand their children's inner experiences during specific and concrete moments.

INSIGHTFULNESS: CENTRAL COMPONENTS

Insightfulness involves three main features: *insight* regarding the motives for the child's behaviors, an *emotionally complex* view of the child, and *openness* to new and sometimes unexpected information regarding the child.

Insight

This concept refers to the parent's capacity to think about the motives that underlie the child's behavior. Considering such motives is based on accepting the child as a separate person with plans, needs, and wishes of his or her own. The motives insightful parents suggest are framed positively and match the behavior they are intended to explain. Both understanding and acceptance are needed when considering such motives. The parent should be able to *understand* the motives underlying the child's behavior and accompany such understanding with *acceptance* of these motives. This stance provides the basis for appropriate and growth-promoting parental responses, especially toward challenging or unrewarding child behavior.

Emotionally Complex View of Child

This feature involves a full and integrated portrayal of the child as a whole person with both positive and negative features. Positive features, which typically outweigh negative features, are described openly and are supported by convincing examples from everyday life. Frustrating, unflattering, and upsetting aspects of the child are discussed within an accepting framework and in the context of attempts to find reasonable and appropriate explanations for the child's negative behavior.

Openness to New Information

Rather than imposing a preconceived notion of who their child is, insightful parents see not only the familiar and comfortable aspects of their children but are also open to see, without distortion, unexpected behaviors, and they may update their view of the child as they talk. Openness also involves a parent's attitude towards her or his own self: Insightful parents can reflect on these self-observations and child observations without excessive criticism or defensiveness.

While the three positive features discussed above are associated with insightfulness, two negative features constitute barriers to insightfulness.

Shift of Focus from Child due to Anger and Worry

When high levels of anger or worry are expressed in parents' interviews, they often shift the focus of discussion from the child's experience. For example, parents' preoccupations with issues such as their marital relationship can dominate the interview and lead to a shift in the focus of the interview from the child's experience to the parent's self or other issues related to marital discord. Such shifts in focus prevent the parent from flexibly considering a wide range of possible motives or explanations for the child's behavior.

Lack of Acceptance

Lack of acceptance is expressed in derogation of the child, detachment from or indifference to the child's internal experience, or rejection of certain child behaviors or even of the child as a whole. Such a stance violates the basic function of insightfulness, which is to provide the foundation for caregiving that promotes healthy emotional development in the child. Interestingly, such lack of acceptance can sometimes be observed even in conjunction with a moderate degree of insight into the child's motives and some understanding of what may lead the child to behave or feel in a certain way. For example, a mother may compellingly describe her son's shy, embarrassed, and self-conscious behavior but proceed to ridicule him for this behavior. In this example the child does not benefit from his parent's understanding of the motives underlying his behavior. On the contrary, from the child's point of view the combination of knowing that the parent understands his internal experience but, at the same time, rejects it can be particularly painful and confusing.

In sum, factors that promote insightfulness are:

- *Insight* into the motives underlying the child's behavior and acceptance of these motives
- *A complex, multidimensional, and integrated view* of the child that is primarily positive and in which negative aspects are presented in a non-blaming way within the specific context in which they emerge
- *Openness* to see the child in new, unexpected ways; flexibility to change one's view when the "data"—the observation of the child—is not consistent with what the parent expects and "knows" about the child

Factors that inhibit insightfulness in parents are:

- *Shifting the focus* from the child: Strong negative emotions, stress, and certain personality characteristics of the parent may lead the parent to drift

from focusing on the child, his or her behavior, and the possible underlying motives for the behavior to a focus on the self or on other unrelated topics.
- *Lack of acceptance* of the underlying motives for the child's behavior, even when they are understood by the parent

ASSESSMENT OF INSIGHTFULNESS

In the IA, parents and children are first videotaped in three interactional contexts. Parents subsequently watch short segments from the videotaped interactions and are interviewed regarding their children's and their own thoughts and feelings. Three vignettes representing different aspects of the parent–child relationship (e.g., caregiving, play, and teaching) are selected. The vignettes are drawn from interactions that are age-appropriate. In the study of adolescents the vignette may involve a problem-solving task; in school-age children it may involve a competitive mother–child game; in preschoolers it may involve co-constructing a play narrative using dolls and props; and in infants it may involve a free play episode using various toys. The IA is introduced to parents as an opportunity to better understand their children, with a particular emphasis on what they believe their child is thinking or feeling. They are also asked whether the behaviors they saw on the video are typical of their child and about the way they felt when they were watching the video. These questions are presented following each of the three segments, and at the end of the interview mothers are asked two general questions about their children and invited to share their own thoughts and feelings regarding their children and their parental role. Throughout the IA, parents are asked to support their statements with examples from the observations of the videotaped segments and from everyday life events with the child (Table 2.1). The IA has been used with children between the ages of 1 and 18 years.

Interview transcripts are rated on 10 scales and, based on the profile from the 10 scale scores, classified into one of four groups (Table 2.2). The first of the four groups, Positive Insightfulness, indicates the capacity for insightfulness, while the remaining three (One-Sided, Disengaged, and Mixed) indicate a lack of insightfulness (Koren-Karie & Oppenheim, 2001).

Research has primarily focused on the four insightfulness *classifications* because these categories are thought to capture the overall capacity to show insightfulness or the specific difficulty in showing insightfulness. The IA *scales* (i.e., Insight into child's motives, Openness, Complexity in description of child, Maintenance of focus on child, Richness of description of child, Acceptance, Anger, Worry, Separateness from child, Coherence of thought) can also be very useful, particularly for describing the parent's strengths and weaknesses. For example, in a divorce situation a parent may show good acceptance of the child and even a moderate capacity for insight, and these qualities can be captured on the Acceptance and Insight scales. At the same time, the parent can be flooded by anxiety and worry regarding times when the child is separate from him or her, and this may be captured by the Concern scale. Additionally, this emotional response may lead the parent to lose the capacity to focus on the child and see things from the child's point of view. The child may, in fact, be doing well even when he or she is not with the parent, but the parent's anxiety can overwhelm his or her capacity to focus on the child (Focus and Separateness scales). Thus, the profile of the parent on the IA scales can point to areas of strength in the

Table 2.1 INSIGHTFULNESS ASSESSMENT QUESTIONS

Part 1: The first three questions are posed after each of the three video segments parents watch:

1. What do you think went through (child's name) mind? What did s/he feel and think during this segment? Where in the segment did you see that (child's name) felt/ thought _____? Can you give me an example from everyday life of a similar situation?
2. Is this segment characteristic of (child's name) more generally? Does it tell you something about his personality or about his characteristics?
3. How did you feel while watching this segment? Did anything concern you, surprise you, or make you happy?

Part 2 (After completing the interview regarding all three video segments):

1. From what we talked about during this interview until now, and from what you know about (child's name) in general, what characterizes him/her as a person, as a child? What makes (child's name) (child's name) (e.g., "What makes Sally Sally?").
2. Thinking about your child in general, are there things about him/her that surprise you, concern you, or make you happy?
3. What is the thing that, in your opinion, most characterizes the relationship between your child and yourself? (After the parent answers, ask:) What are your expectations for the future regarding your relationship with your child for the next year?

Table 2.2 INSIGHTFULNESS ASSESSMENT SCALES

IA Scale	Low	High
Insight into child's motives	Mother[1] does not talk about possible motives for her child's behavior.	Mother tries to understand the thoughts and feelings that may underlie her child's behavior; she moves freely between the videotaped observations and her knowledge about her child, draws parallels between the two, and tries to gain deeper understanding.
Openness	Mother is not open to the information of the videotaped observations, but rather speaks about her fixed and preset ideas about the child; the observation may be dismissed as not typical of the child.	Mother is open to the information arising from the videotaped observations; she compares what she knows about her child with the video observations and modifies her perceptions if needed.
Complexity in description of child	Mother describes the child in a uni-dimensional, one-sided way, emphasizing either only positive or only negative aspects of the child.	Mother provides a believable description of the child in which the child is described as a "whole" with both positive and negative aspects.
Maintenance of focus on child	The child is not the focus of discussion; rather, the focus is on the mother and her feelings and thoughts or other irrelevant issues.	The child is the focus of discussion; if mother talks about herself, it will be when she is asked to do so or regarding her maternal role.
Richness of description of child	Limited responses that lack substance or full responses with mostly irrelevant details	Mother responds to the interview questions in a full, comprehensive, and vivid way.

Table 2.2 INSIGHTFULNESS ASSESSMENT SCALES (Continued)

IA Scale	Low	High
Acceptance	Mother expresses dissatisfaction or disappointment in the child or talks about the child in a derogatory way.	Mother accepts the full range of her child's behaviors and shows tolerance and understanding towards challenging aspects; she is open about difficulties in her child's behavior and conveys a deep acceptance of the child.
Anger	Mother's speech does not include current anger, even though she can talk about behaviors that caused her to feel angry in the past.	Current anger towards the child is a central feature of mother's talk; the child is described as having many irritating traits, and many of his or her behaviors on the videotaped observation elicit anger in mother.
Worry	Mother expresses belief in herself and her child's capacity to cope with challenges.	Mother's worry regarding the child, her maternal behavior, or their relationship is a central, repetitive theme throughout the interview.
Separateness from child	Mother finds it difficult to talk about the child with a sense of clear boundaries; she may talk about the child's thoughts as if spoken out loud or refers to ideas regarding what the child *might* think or feel as facts.	Mother sees the child as a separate person and accepts that the child may sometimes have needs and wishes that are different from or even contradictory to hers.
Coherence of thought–Overall Scale	Mother's speech does not convey a consistent and clear picture, and it is difficult to understand what she means; responses may contain digressions and contradictions, or mother may ignore the videotaped observations.	Mother is focused on the videotaped segments, and in her answer she develops ideas in a consistent, connected, and relaxed way; her speech forms an integrated and clear picture linked both to the videotaped segments and the child as a whole.

[1] Scales apply to fathers or other caregivers as well.

parent but also to "blind spots" in which the parent has difficulties seeing things from the child's point of view. Such refined understanding can provide the basis for developing parenting plans that are more nuanced and tailored to the parent.

The IA Classifications

As mentioned above, the rating scales serve as a basis for the classification of the transcripts into one insightful and three non-insightful categories. Categories reflect more than a simple summation of scale scores. Rather, the coding manual provides guidelines regarding various constellations and combinations of scale scores that lead to specific categories. The four categories are:

1. *Positively Insightful (PI):* The main characteristic of these parents is their ability to see various experiences through their child's eyes and to try to understand the motives underlying their child's behavior. They are flexible

when viewing their child on the video segments, and they may gain new insights as they talk. Positively Insightful parents convey acceptance of the child, and their speech is coherent. These parents talk openly about both positive and negative aspects of their child's personality and behavior as well as of their own caregiving. While all Positively Insightful parents share the above characteristics, they are also quite varied. Some talk about their child in a very warm and emotional manner while others are more reserved and have a matter-of-fact, focused style of speech. Other parents in this group have a didactic style and focus on their child's cognitive competencies and achievements, and still others are most noted by their self-reflection. Thus when parents are grouped into one classification, it is not surface similarity that is looked at; instead, the underlying features that reflect these parents' capacity to "see the world from the child's point of view" are identified (see Table 2.3 for excerpts from an interview classified as Positively Insightful).

2. *One-sided (Os):* One-sided parents have a preset conception of the child that they impose on the videotaped segments, and this conception does not

Table 2.3 TRANSCRIPTS OF AN IA INTERVIEW CLASSIFIED AS POSITIVELY INSIGHTFUL (18-MONTH-OLD CHILD)

Interviewer:	What went through your child's head? What was he thinking and feeling? (The question refers to a segment in which the mother and the father were filling out questionnaires and the child was playing by himself next to them.)
Father:	What was he thinking? Uhhm, there are several things happening. First, he sees new toys, toys that I think most of them are new for him, so he is curious. He wants to examine the toys, and at the same time he wants to share his discoveries with us. He wants to show us his new things, which I find very sweet. As you can see, we tried to follow your instructions and to be busy with the questionnaires, and that is why we tried to get him back to the toys, and we didn't really interact with him as we usually would. But you know, it is interesting, because he returned to whatever he was doing quite happily, which for me is an expression of him feeling secure. He knows that we are there with him, and that's what he needs: our presence. That's nice. For me it felt as if we were setting here some limits, but he didn't feel that way. He did not seem to be bothered. As I said, I see it as a sign of confidence. We are with him, and even if we are busy, for him that is enough.

Features of the Positively Insightful classification in this interview:

- *Complex view of the child:* The father does not simply describe his child as curious but rather puts his behavior into a context, explaining that the child's curiosity stems from the novelty of the toys.
- *Acceptance:* The father describes his child's attempts to gain his attention while he was trying to concentrate on completing the questionnaires in a positive way. He interprets the child's behavior as indicating his wish to share his discoveries with his parents, thus providing an accepting and insightful explanation for his child's behavior. This behavior could be described by a non-insightful parent as representing less positive features of the child such as dependency, impatience, or lack of appropriate self-control.
- *Openness to new information:* Although the father felt that directing the child back to the toys would be experienced negatively by the child, he was open to see that the child was, in fact, content even though his parents did not respond as they usually would.
- *Coherence:* Father's speech is coherent, as reflected in the freshness, richness, and flow of his narrative.

appear open to change. These parents often find it difficult to maintain the focus of their speech on the child, and switch to discussing their own feelings or to other, irrelevant issues. Some One-sided parents overemphasize the child's positive qualities without being able to support their statements with episodes from everyday life or from the video segments. Others may describe the child as "all negative" and talk only about his or her faults and misbehaviors. Still others may show a good understanding of the child's underlying motives, but that understanding is coupled with a rejection of these motives. In other words, such parents show understanding without empathy (see Table 2.4 for excerpts from an interview classified as One-sided).

Table 2.4 Transcripts of an IA Interview Classified as One-sided
(18-month-old child)

Interviewer:	What went through your child's head? What was she thinking and feeling? (The question refers to a segment in which both mother and father were asked to fill out questionnaires while the child was playing next to them.)
Mother:	Mom, why don't you want to play with me? Okay, that's not so bad, I'll play by myself. Mom, play with me! Why don't you want to play with me? Mom, why don't you give me that pen you are writing with? Okay, so sometimes she doesn't let me use her pen, but why she doesn't give it to me now? That is why I gave her the pen.
Interviewer:	Where in the segment did you see that she was thinking that way?
Mother:	She tried to get her father's attention. Most of the times when we are together with her she won't approach him, so this means she was desperate. She understood that I won't play with her, so she tried to get his attention. She didn't expect him to play with her. You could see it, too: he didn't pay attention to her at all; he continued writing. This is so typical of him, being completely stuck in his own business. The same thing happens at home. Let's say I need to prepare dinner, and I need to cook or to do something in the kitchen that is dangerous for the child, so I tell him, take her, play with her. When I play with her I do a lot of funny and interesting things for her. I dance with her, do all kinds of arts and crafts. I do such things and not ordinary games. It takes a lot from me; I'm really dedicated. That is why she didn't think that I will play with her with that hammer. She knew that I will watch her but won't play with her. I do a lot of activities with her, not such games. That is me (laughing), that's my character.

Features of the One-sided classification in this interview:

- *Boundary dissolution:* The mother speaks for the child, quoting from her thoughts as if the child is transparent. Note that this "knowing" of the child's thoughts is very different from the attempts of insightful parents who try to think of possible meanings for their children's behavior, with clear awareness of the separateness between the parent and child.
- *Shift of focus:* Mother's thoughts and feelings become the main focus of her response. For example, when asked to point out where in the video she saw that the child was thinking in a certain way, she gave a long and emotionally loaded answer that focused on the differences between her husband's way of interacting with the child and her own. In this example one can see how the child's perspective and voice fades into the background, while the mother's perceptions, concerns, and feelings move to the front of the stage. Consequently, the questions regarding the child's motives and intentions were left unanswered.
- *Incoherence:* Mother's speech is overwhelming and dysfluent. She jumps from one idea to another and from one topic to another. As a result, the reader gets a lot of information regarding her thoughts and feelings but an incomplete, fragmented description of the child with only few (if any) insights into the child's inner world.

3. *Disengaged (De):* Disengaged parents are characterized by their lack of emotional involvement during the interview. Their answers are short and limited, and they do not use the observation as an opportunity to reflect upon their child's and their own behavior. Attempts for understanding what is on their child's mind are novel to them and they do not find them pleasurable or valuable. When asked what their child might be feeling in the video segment they viewed, they provide answers like, "I don't know." As a result, the interviewer does not get a sense of who the child is. Disengaged parents talk very little about their children's emotions and focus more on their children's behavior. Many of them emphasize the child's ability to be on his or her own and are pleased with the child's lack of need for others (see Table 2.5 for excerpts from an interview classified as Disengaged).

4. *Mixed (Mx):* This category involves parents who do not show one style of narration as defined in the above categories. Rather, such parents may respond to one video segment in one style, and to another segment with a different style, and the reader cannot judge which of the styles is dominant. For example, a parent may sound overwhelmed, unfocused, or hostile in

Table 2.5 TRANSCRIPTS OF AN IA INTERVIEW CLASSIFIED AS DISENGAGED
(18-MONTH-OLD CHILD)

Interviewer:	What went through your child's head? What was she thinking and feeling? (The question refers to a segment in which the parents were filling out questionnaires and the child was playing by herself next to them.)
Mother:	What was he thinking? (Long pause) I don't know. (Long pause) She looked curious to find out what was the source of the beep. Other than that—nothing in particular.
Interviewer:	Okay, can you tell me where in the segment you saw her curiosity?
Mother:	That she looked around. She was looking for the source of that noise.
Interviewer:	Okay, so that is what she was thinking. What about what she was feeling?
Mother:	Nothing in particular. She was playing. That's it.
Interviewer:	Do you have any example from everyday life in which your child is curious?
Mother:	(long pause) No, I . . . she does many things all the time, I don't have a specific example.
Interviewer:	Do you think that this segment is typical for your child? Do you see any of her characteristics?
Mother:	Well, ye . . . she likes to play . . . she plays a lot . . . other than that—I don't know.

Features of the Disengaged classification in this excerpt:

- *Lack of insight:* This is evident at the beginning with the mother's claim that she has no idea what her child may be thinking. Moreover, the mother does not seem to be bothered by this and does not try to come up with a fuller answer.
- *Lack of complexity:* The mother provides shallow descriptions that do not portray a complex picture of her child. The child appears to be "curious," and she appears to "like to play." When the mother is asked to give an example from everyday life for her child's curiosity, she gives a global answer that does not go deeper into the child's underlying motives and preferences: "she does many things all the time." The mother does not provide a description of a specific event in which child was curious.
- *Low cooperation:* The mother's cooperation with the interviewer's questions is very limited. She does not show interest in speaking about her child's mind and internal experience, and she appears comfortable saying that she does not know what is going on in her head.

the responses to the three video segments, but insightful, complex, and open in the response to the two general questions.

In sum, the assessment of Parental Insightfulness asks:

- Does the parent try to understand the reasons for the child's behavior or misbehavior—the thoughts, feelings, and motives that underlie the behavior?
- Can the parent empathize with the child's feelings and point of view, even when this includes feelings that are difficult for the parent to accept?
- Can the parent keep the focus on the child's experience, or do the parent's emotions, such as anxiety or anger, color the parent's view of the child?
- Can the parent contextualize the child's behavior and think about the specific events and reasons that may have led to the child's behavior?
- Does the parent coherently and logically link specific behaviors to the child's general traits and characteristics?

EMPIRICAL SUPPORT FOR THE INSIGHTFULNESS ASSESSMENT

Insightfulness Assessment and Attachment

The conceptual foundations of the IA are strongly rooted in attachment theory. This theory, developed by John Bowlby (1982) and Mary Ainsworth (1989), is the most widespread and accepted theory regarding parent–child relationships and their importance for children's healthy emotional and psychological growth. Attachment theory has received extensive empirical support during the past 40 years in numerous studies across a wide range of cultures (Cassidy & Shaver, 2008). Attachment refers to the strong and enduring emotional ties that young children develop toward a specific number of caregivers, ties that provide them with a secure base from which they venture to explore the environment and to which they return in times of distress or need (Bowlby, 1982). While all children develop attachments toward their caregivers, the degree to which these attachments are secure depends on the sensitivity and responsiveness of the caregiver to the child's signals and emotional needs. Such sensitivity and responsiveness, which refers to the parent's behavior toward the child, was described by Ainsworth, Blehar, Waters, and Wall (1978) as being based on "seeing things from the child's point of view," a capacity operationalized by Oppenheim and Koren-Karie (2009) as insightfulness.

Based on this theorizing, the goal of the initial studies using the IA was to establish its links with children's attachment to their parents. Importantly, when possible, these studies attempted not only to match the IA with infant attachment patterns at the global level (i.e., insightful/non-insightful with Secure/Insecure), but also to match each of the four IA classifications (Positive Insightfulness, One-sided, Disengaged, Mixed) with each of the four infant attachment classifications respectively (Secure, Ambivalent, Avoidant, Disorganized; Ainsworth et al., 1978; Main & Solomon, 1990; see Table 2.6). These specific concordances were seen as important because attachment theory and research describe the specific adaptations (i.e., types

Table 2.6 INFANT ATTACHMENT CLASSIFICATIONS

Note: These classifications are based on observing 12- to 18-month-old infants in the Strange Situation Procedure (Ainsworth et al., 1978), which involves exposure of the infant to stress due to two brief separations from the mother in an unfamiliar environment.

- *Secure (B):* The baby is happy to see the parent upon reunion; if upset, the baby is able to draw comfort from the parent's presence and to return to playful exploration.
- *Insecure Avoidant (A):* The baby does not show distress upon separation and does not greet the parent upon reunion; the baby actively avoids and ignores the parent on reunion and shows no signs of pleasure upon the parent's return.
- *Insecure Resistant/Ambivalent (C):* The baby shows high distress throughout the procedure with little exploration; the baby is preoccupied with the parent and fails to settle and take comfort in the parent upon reunion.
- *Insecure Disorganized (D):* The baby displays Disorganized behaviors in the parent's presence such as contradictory, incomplete, stereotyped, or fearful behaviors.

of Secure and particularly Insecure attachment) children make to specific types of sensitive and particularly insensitive parental care (Weinfield, Sroufe, Egeland, & Carlson, 1999).

The hypotheses linking the IA classifications to children's attachment were as follows:

1. *Positively Insightful parents will have children with Secure attachment:* This hypothesis was based on the idea that insightfulness facilitates correct interpretations and empathic responses to children's signals, as well as open examination of the appropriateness (or inappropriateness) of the parent's caregiving behavior based on the child's reactions. Such caregiving is likely to be experienced by the child as matched to his or her emotional needs and thus to contribute to a Secure infant–mother attachment (Ainsworth et al., 1978; Weinfield et al., 1999).

2. *One-sided parents will have children with Insecure/Ambivalent attachment:* The uni-dimensional view of the child characteristic of One-sided parents is likely to be associated with inconsistent care: When the child's behavior is congruent with the mother's expectations, she may respond appropriately, whereas when the child's behavior is not congruent with the mother's expectations, she may ignore or respond in a way that is not matched to the child's needs. Mothers classified as One-sided are also often preoccupied with their own emotional issues, and consequently their availability and capacity to focus on the child's inner world may be impaired. The parenting of mothers classified as One-sided may be experienced by the child as frustrating and confusing—the kind of caregiving found to lead to ambivalent attachment (Cassidy & Berlin, 1994).

3. *Disengaged parents will have children with Insecure/Avoidant attachment:* The lack of emotional engagement characteristic of the Disengaged parent may lead to minimizing or even ignoring the child's bids for closeness and protection, which is likely to be experienced by the child as rejection. Disengaged parenting may leave children with the feeling that while their external behavior may be acknowledged, their emotional and psychological

needs are unrecognized by their caregivers (Slade, 1999). These experiences are likely to lead to the child's inhibition of his or her emotional expression, particularly of negative affect and vulnerability, which is the hallmark of children with Avoidant attachment (Zeanah, Benoit, Hirshberg, Barton, & Regan, 1994).

4. *Parents classified as Mixed will have children with Insecure/Disorganized attachment*: The lack of a coherent strategy for understanding the child's motives and feelings may be reflected in competing or contradictory caregiving behaviors when interacting with the child. Such strategies have been described by Lyons-Ruth and colleagues (Lyons-Ruth, Bronfman, & Atwood, 1999) as being expressed in disruptive parental affective communication and leading to Disorganized attachment.

In sum:

- The IA is based on the idea that parents who see things from their children's point of view foster Secure attachments.
- Insightful parents are expected to have Securely attached children; One-sided parents are expected to have Ambivalent/Resistant children; Disengaged parents are expected to have Avoidant children; and Mixed parents are expected to have Disorganized children.

VALIDITY OF THE INSIGHTFULNESS ASSESSMENT: ASSOCIATION BETWEEN PARENTAL INSIGHTFULNESS AND CHILDREN'S SECURITY OF ATTACHMENT

A growing body of research supports the validity of the IA, and it is reviewed next. While the studies provide support for the IA's validity, additional research on this topic is needed and is under way. Two studies of mothers and their typically developing infants investigated the association between the IA and infant–mother attachment (Koren-Karie, Oppenheim, Dolev, Sher, & Etzion-Carasso, 2002; Oppenheim, Koren-Karie, & Sagi, 2001) (Table 2.7).

In the Oppenheim et al. (2001) study, in which children with Insecure attachments were oversampled, 38% of the mothers were classified as *PI*, 43% as *Os*, 11% as *De*, and 8% as *Mixed*. In the Koren-Karie et al. (2002) study, in which attachment was distributed normally, 62% of the mothers were classified as *PI*, 21% as *Os*, 12% as *De*, and 5% as *Mixed*. In both studies mothers classified as *PI* had Secure children, mothers classified as *Os* had Insecure/Ambivalent children, and mothers classified as *Mixed* had children classified as Insecure/Disorganized. Unexpectedly, no associations were found between the *De* classification and children's attachment, perhaps because the samples (like all those based on studies conducted in Israel; van IJzendoorn & Sagi, 1999) included very few children classified as Avoidant.

Two studies of mothers and their atypically developing children also supported the associations between insightfulness and attachment (Oppenheim, Feniger-Shaal, & Koren-Karie, 2010; Oppenheim, Koren-Karie, Dolev, & Yirmiya, 2009). Due to the limited size of the samples in both studies, the associations were only examined dichotomously, linking insightfulness versus non-insightfulness with security versus

Table 2.7 STUDIES USING THE IA

Source	Participants			Procedures
	N	Mean Age of Children	Sample Characteristics	
Low-Risk Samples				
Oppenheim et al., 2001	118	4.5 years	Low risk	IA, Strange Situation
Koren-Karie et al., 2002	129	1 year	Low risk	IA, Strange Situation, Maternal Sensitivity rating
Fridman, 2005	127	1 year	Low risk	IA, Mind-mindedness coding
Oppenheim et al., 2005	107	4 years	Low risk	IA, Theory of Mind task
Children with Atypical Development				
Oppenheim et al., 2010	22	4 years	Children with intellectual disability	IA, Strange Situation, Maternal Sensitivity rating
Oppenheim et al., 2009; Oppenheim et al., 2011	45	4 years	Children with autism spectrum disorder (ASD)	IA, Strange Situation, Maternal Sensitivity rating
Hutman et al., 2009	67	4.5 years	Children with ASD	IA, maternal synchrony during play interactions
Kuhn, 2007	70	2 years	Children with ASD	IA, maternal synchrony during play interactions
High Socio-Emotional Risk Samples				
Koren-Karie & Oppenheim, 2010	60	11 years	Foster care	IA of foster caregiver with two children

Analysis and Results	Weaknesses	Strengths
Insightful mothers were more likely to have Securely attached children than non-insightful mothers.	Insightfulness was assessed 3.5 years *after* the assessment of attachment.	Longitudinal associations across 3.5 years.
Insightful mothers were more likely to have Securely attached children than those classified as non-insightful. Also, insightful mothers were rated in observations as more sensitive to their children's communication than non-insightful mothers.	All assessments were concurrent.	IA was associated both with maternal sensitivity and child attachment.
Insightful mothers used fewer inappropriate "mind-minded" comments when talking to their infants compared to non-insightful mothers.	No differences were found regarding appropriate mind-minded comments.	The study pinpoints one possible mechanism by which insightfulness is expressed during interaction.
Maternal insightfulness but not infant attachment predicted 4-year-olds' Theory of Mind.	The prediction of children's Theory of Mind was carried primarily by only one of the non-insightful groups (Disengaged).	Insightfulness was a better predictor of children's Theory of Mind than attachment.
Insightful mothers were more likely to have Securely attached children than those classified as non-insightful. Also, insightful mothers were rated in observations as more sensitive to their children's communication than non-insightful mothers.	The sample was small.	Extends the use of the IA to an understudied population.
Insightful mothers were more likely to have Securely attached children than those classified as non-insightful and were more sensitive during interactions with their children.	Assessments were concurrent.	The IA is useful even with children with ASD whose communicative skills are severely impaired.
Insightful mothers were more synchronous with their children during observations of mother–child interactions.	Assessments were concurrent.	Maternal behavior was assessed using a detailed microanalytic technique.
No differences in synchrony were found between insightful and non-insightful mothers.		Maternal synchrony predicted gains in children's verbal IQ.
Although children in foster care can be very challenging, foster caregivers showed insightfulness towards the children irrespective of the degree of challenge they presented.	Other contextual variables that may explain the findings were not assessed.	Extends the use of the IA to non-parental caregivers.

(Continued)

Table 2.7 STUDIES USING THE IA (*Continued*)

Source	Participants			Procedures
	N	Mean Age of Children	Sample Characteristics	
Yuval-Adler, 2010.	60	11 years	Foster care.	IA, Emotion Dialogue Procedure.
Oppenheim et al., 2004.	32	4.5	Children with behavior and emotion disorders.	Pre- and post-treatment IA.

insecurity. Oppenheim et al. (2009) reported that in a sample of preschool-age boys with autism spectrum disorder (ASD), maternal insightfulness was associated with child attachment: Mothers who were insightful (42%) had Securely attached children and mothers who were non-insightful (58%) had children with Insecure attachments. Additionally, Oppenheim et al. (2009) did not find an association between insightfulness and either the severity of the child's diagnosis on the autism spectrum or the child's IQ, suggesting that insightfulness (or lack thereof) is more a reflection of the parent's capacity to see the world from the child's point of view and less sensitive to the specific characteristics of the child. Oppenheim et al. (2010) found similar associations in a sample of children with intellectual disability. Mothers who were insightful (43%) had Securely attached children, and mothers who were non-insightful (57%) had children with Insecure attachments.

Taken together, the studies of Oppenheim and Koren-Karie of typically and atypically developing children have shown the theoretically predicted associations between maternal insightfulness and child Secure attachment. Importantly, because the studies involved both typically developing children and those with atypical development, the data suggest that parental insightfulness is possible even when the child's capacity to signal and communicate his or her needs is impaired or atypical, such as in the case of autism or intellectual disability. Furthermore, studies of atypically developing children suggest that not only is insightfulness possible with regard to such children, it is also associated with child security in the same way as with typically developing children. While these studies are encouraging, clearly more research is needed to replicate them and to extend them to other types of disabilities.

In sum:

- In studies of typically developing children, maternal insightfulness was associated with Secure infant–mother attachment.
- In studies of children with disabilities (ASD and intellectual disability), maternal insightfulness was associated with Secure infant–mother attachment.

Analysis and Results	Weaknesses	Strengths
Insightful foster caregivers guided emotional dialogues with their children more sensitively than non-insightful caregivers.	Concurrent assessments preclude causal inferences.	Links between the way caregivers talk *about* their children and *with* their children.
Children whose mothers shifted from a non-insightful to an insightful stance during treatment showed a higher decrease in their behavior problems than children of mothers who did not make the shift.	Small sample and impossible to determine the direction of effects.	Pre–post design that shows coherent changes in mothers and children.

Association Between Insightfulness and Behavior of Parents

Because insightfulness is thought to be expressed in sensitive and emotionally regulating caregiving behavior, studies using the IA have investigated associations between the IA and maternal sensitivity. In the Koren-Karie et al. (2002) study of typically developing infants mentioned above, mothers classified as insightful were more sensitive in their interactions with their infants in both home and laboratory observations than those not classified as insightful. Koren-Karie et al. (2002) concluded that insightfulness has its effects on child attachment, at least in part, through sensitive caregiving behavior. Oppenheim, Koren-Karie, Dolev, and Yirmiya (2011) replicated the insightfulness–sensitivity link in the sample of children with ASD described earlier (Oppenheim et al., 2009). They found that insightful mothers were rated as more sensitive during their interactions with their children compared to non-insightful mothers. Similar results have been reported by Hutman, Siller, and Sigman (2009), who found that mothers of children with ASD classified as Positively Insightful (34%) were more synchronous in their interactions with their children than mothers classified as non-insightful (66%). Kuhn (2007) also studied mothers of children with ASD. She identified 54% of the mothers as Positively Insightful but failed to replicate the insightfulness–synchrony association. Finally, in their study of children with intellectual disability, Oppenheim et al. (2010) found, as expected, that insightful mothers were rated as more sensitive during their interactions with their children compared to non-insightful mothers.

Two additional studies linked insightfulness to other aspects of maternal behavior that are closely related to maternal sensitivity. Fridman (2005) studied the "mind-minded" comments (Meins, Fernyhough, Wainwright, Gupta, & Tuckey, 2002) of the mothers from the Koren-Karie et al. (2002) study. Such comments of mothers toward their infants reflect the mothers' orientation to their children as mental agents and individuals who have thoughts and intentions that guide their behavior. As expected, Fridman (2005) found that insightful mothers used fewer inappropriate mind-minded comments than non-insightful mothers. No differences were found regarding appropriate mind-minded comments. A recent study of foster mothers (Koren-Karie & Oppenheim, 2010; Yuval-Adler, 2010) showed a link between insightfulness and the mothers' sensitive guidance of emotional dialogues with their children. The mothers, each of whom fostered several children, were observed with both the most and the least challenging child in their care while co-constructing a conversation about emotional themes. Insightful mothers (47%) guided the conversation more sensitively than non-insightful mothers (53%), and this was true of their interactions with both the least challenging and most challenging child.

In sum:

- Insightful mothers show more sensitive behavior when interacting with their normally developing children than non-insightful mothers.
- Insightful mothers of children with developmental disabilities show more sensitive and synchronous behavior when interacting with their children than non-insightful mothers.
- Insightful mothers use fewer inappropriate mind-minded comments when interacting with their infants compared to non-insightful mothers.
- Insightful foster caregivers guided emotional dialogues with their children more sensitively than non-insightful foster caregivers.

EFFECTS OF INSIGHTFULNESS ON THE CHILD

As mentioned above, the main source of validity for the IA was its associations with child attachment, and several studies reviewed above documented such associations. Two additional studies examined the effects of insightfulness on other aspects of children's development. The first study (Oppenheim, Koren-Karie, Etzion-Carasso, & Sagi-Schwartz, 2005) involved a low-risk sample in which maternal insightfulness was assessed when children were 1 year of age, and children's Theory of Mind—their capacity to understand that the behavior of others is governed by internal thoughts, feelings, and beliefs—was assessed when children were 4 years old. The authors hypothesized that maternal insightfulness would promote children's Theory of Mind, and the findings supported this hypothesis. Mothers who were insightful when children were 1 year of age had children who showed at the age of 4 years higher Theory of Mind scores than children of mothers who were non-insightful when they were infants (Oppenheim et al., 2005).

The second study showed the contribution of insightfulness to children's therapeutic gains. In this study (Oppenheim, Goldsmith, & Koren-Karie, 2004), preschoolers with emotional and behavioral problems were in a day treatment program, and mothers received parent therapy. Only 9% of the mothers were classified as Positively Insightful prior to treatment, but 50% were so classified following treatment. The findings showed that the gains mothers made in treatment were associated with improvements in children's behavior problems: Children of mothers who shifted from non-insightfulness to insightfulness showed a reduction in their behavior problems, whereas children of mothers who did not make the shift did not show such a reduction. Although it was not possible to determine whether changes in the mothers elicited changes in the children or vice versa, the findings nonetheless point to the potential importance of maternal insightfulness in supporting therapeutic gains in young children.

In sum:

- Early maternal insightfulness was associated with higher Theory of Mind scores in children.
- Improvements in the insightfulness of mothers of children attending a therapeutic preschool were associated with a reduction in children's behavior problems.

SUMMARY

When families are seen in family court, they are typically at a very vulnerable and tumultuous moment. Family life during such times—which often follow an extended period of family conflict, negative interactions, and sense of failure in resolving differences—is often characterized by uncertainty and feelings of threat to the family's ties. Under such circumstances parents are often overwhelmed by negative affects, adopt rigid and uni-dimensional perspectives about family members and relationships, and may experience difficulties in thinking about others and adopting complex and contextual perspectives. These difficulties may even characterize families who under typical situations, prior to the emergence of the conflict, functioned well. The ability to take the perspective of an external observer, the ability to regulate one's affect, and the ability to think in complex ways—all critical for insightfulness—are typically reduced under stress. Overwhelmed by their own turmoil, parents are likely to have difficulties focusing on their children's experiences and understanding and accepting how their children experience the family's crisis. However, it is in these very moments that children need their parents' focused empathic attention and support in order to make emotional sense out of their experience.

The research on parental insightfulness indicates that even when families are faced with challenges, a substantial group of parents are able to maintain a complex, open, and insightful view of their children's inner experiences, and that such support is of great importance for the children's adjustment and coping. While at this point the IA cannot be used as a standardized measure for forensic mental health evaluators due to the lack of studies regarding the IA in the family court context, it is hoped that future studies will provide the empirical basis needed for such use. The absence of such research notwithstanding, it is important for professionals dealing with families in the courts to consider parents' capacity to take into account and accept the motives underlying their children's behavior when making recommendations regarding family plans and children's placements.

GUIDELINES: CONSIDERATIONS AND CAUTIONS

- Insightfulness involves the parents' ability to see things from the child's point of view and to empathically think about and consider the motives underlying their children's behavior. Parental insightfulness provides the basis for sensitive caregiving and for Secure child–parent attachment.

- Insightfulness involves insight regarding the motives for the child's behaviors, an emotionally complex view of the child, and openness to new and sometimes unexpected information regarding the child. Barriers to insightfulness include shifting the focus from the child and lack of acceptance of the motives for the child's behavior.
- In the Insightfulness Assessment (IA) parents are interviewed regarding their children's thoughts and feelings after they view short video segments of their children interacting with them. Parents' interviews are classified into one of four groups. The first, Positive Insightfulness, indicates the capacity for insightfulness, while the remaining three (One-Sided, Disengaged, and Mixed) indicate a lack of insightfulness.
- Support for the validity of the IA comes from studies showing its links with maternal caregiving behavior and with children's attachment. Additional research to support the use of the IA in forensic mental health evaluations is needed. In addition, because most of the studies with the IA were conducted with mothers, more research on fathers' insightfulness is needed.
- Lack of insightfulness in parents going through marital conflict may reflect either current stress or more chronic difficulties. Therefore, more research is needed to discriminate between the two scenarios. In particular, the IA scales, which provide a more refined picture of parental insightfulness, may be helpful for this discrimination. However, until more research is conducted regarding insightfulness in custody cases, it is not possible to use the IA as a standardized instrument for forensic mental health evaluators.
- Appropriate use of the IA requires specialized training provided by the authors for the administration of the procedure and coding of the interviews. Without such training, it is not possible to draw valid conclusions regarding parental insightfulness from the procedure.

REFERENCES

Ainsworth, M. D. S. (1989). Attachment beyond infancy. *American Psychologist, 44,* 709–716. Retrieved from http://www.apa.org/pubs/journals/amp/index.aspx.

Ainsworth, M. D. S., Blehar, M. C., Waters, E., & Wall, S. (1978). *Patterns of attachment: A psychological study of the strange situation.* Hillsdale, NJ: Erlbaum.

Bowlby, J. (1982). *Attachment and loss: Vol. 1. Attachment.* New York: Basic Books.

Cassidy, J., & Berlin, L. (1994). The insecure/ambivalent pattern of attachment: Theory and research. *Child Development, 65,* 971–991. doi:10.2307/1131298

Cassidy, J., & Shaver, P. R. (2008). *Handbook of attachment: Theory, research, and clinical applications* (2nd ed.). New York: Guilford.

Fraiberg, S., Adelson, E., & Shapiro, V. (1975). Ghosts in the nursery: A psychoanalytic approach to the problems of impaired infant–mother relationships. *Journal of the American Academy of Child Psychiatry, 14,* 387–421. doi:10.1016/S0002-7138(09)61442-4

Fridman, A. (2005). *Maternal mind-mindedness: Relations with maternal insightfulness and infant behavior at one year* (Unpublished master's thesis). University of Haifa, Israel.

George, C. & Solomon, J. (2008). The caregiving system: A behavioral system approach to parenting. In J. Cassidy & P. Shaver (Eds.), *Handbook of attachment: Theory, research, and clinical applications* (pp. 833–856). New York: Guilford.

Hutman, T., Siller, M., & Sigman, M. (2009). Mothers' narratives regarding their child with autism predict maternal synchronous behavior during play. *Journal of Child Psychology and Psychiatry, 10,* 1255–1263. doi:10.1111/j.1469-7610.2009.02109.x

Koren-Karie, N., & Oppenheim, D. (2001). *Insightfulness procedure administration and coding manual.* Unpublished manual, University of Haifa, Israel.

Koren-Karie, N., & Oppenheim, D. (2010). *Parenting challenging children: Caregivers' insightfulness, emotional investment, and guidance of dialogues in a sample of foster caregivers and their children.* Unpublished manuscript, University of Haifa, Israel.

Koren-Karie, N., Oppenheim, D., Dolev, S., Sher, E., & Etzion-Carasso, A. (2002). Mothers' empathic understanding of their infants' internal experience: Relations with maternal sensitivity and infant attachment. *Developmental Psychology, 38,* 534–542. doi:10.1037/0012-1649.38.4.534

Kuhn, J. C. (2007). *Maternal synchrony predicts joint attention and language gains in toddlers with autism* (Unpublished doctoral dissertation). University of Massachusetts, Boston, MA.

Lyons-Ruth, K., Bronfman, E., & Atwood, G. (1999). A relational diathesis of hostile-helpless states of mind: Expressions in mother-infant interaction. In J. Solomon & C. George (Eds.), *Attachment disorganization* (pp. 33–70). New York: Guilford.

Main, M., Kaplan, N., & Cassidy, J. (1985). Security in infancy, childhood, and adulthood: A move to the level of representation. In I. Bretherton & E. Waters (Eds.), Growing points in attachment theory and research. *Monographs of the Society for Research in Child Development, 50* (1–2, Serial No. 209), 66–104. Retrieved from http://www.wiley.com/bw/journal.asp?ref=0037-976x.

Main, M., & Solomon, J. (1990). Procedures for identifying infants as disorganized/disoriented during the Ainsworth Strange Situation. In M. T. Greenberg, D. Cicchetti, & E. M. Cummings (Eds.), *Attachment in the preschool years: Theory, research, and intervention* (pp. 121–160). Chicago, IL: University of Chicago Press.

Meins, E., Fernyhough, C., Wainwright, R., Gupta, M. D., & Tuckey, M. (2002). Maternal mind-mindedness and attachment security as predictors of Theory of Mind understanding. *Child Development, 73,* 1715–1726. doi:10.1111/1467-8624.00501

Oppenheim, D. (2006). Child, parent, and parent–child emotion narratives: Implications for developmental psychopathology. *Development and Psychopathology, 18,* 771–790. doi:10.1017/S095457940606038X

Oppenheim, D., Feniger-Shaal, R., & Koren-Karie, N. (2010). *Insightfulness of mothers of young children with intellectual disability.* Unpublished raw data.

Oppenheim, D., Goldsmith, D., & Koren-Karie, N. (2004). Maternal insightfulness and preschoolers' emotion and behavior problems: Reciprocal influences in a day-treatment program. *Infant Mental Health Journal, 25,* 352–367. doi:10.1002/imhj.20010

Oppenheim, D., & Koren-Karie, N. (2009). Parents' insightfulness regarding their children's internal worlds: Assessment, research, and clinical implications. In

C. Zeanah (Ed.), *Handbook of infant mental health* (3rd ed., pp. 266–280). New York: Guilford.

Oppenheim, D., Koren-Karie, N., Dolev, S., & Yirmiya, N. (2009). Maternal insightfulness and resolution of the diagnosis are related to secure attachment in preschoolers with Autism Spectrum Disorder. *Child Development, 80,* 519–527. doi:10.1111/j.1467-8624.2009.01276.x

Oppenheim, D., Koren-Karie, N., Dolev, S., & Yirmiya, N. (2011). *Maternal representations and child attachment in children with Autism Spectrum Disorder: The mediating role of maternal sensitivity.* Unpublished manuscript, University of Haifa, Israel.

Oppenheim, D., Koren-Karie, N., Etzion-Carasso, A., & Sagi-Schwartz, A. (2005, April). *Maternal insightfulness but not infant attachment predicts 4-year-olds' Theory of Mind.* Poster session presented at the biennial meeting of the Society for Research in Child Development, Atlanta, GA.

Oppenheim, D., Koren-Karie, N., & Sagi, A. (2001). Mothers' empathic understanding of their preschoolers' internal experience: Relations with early attachment. *International Journal of Behavioral Development, 25,* 16–26. doi:10.1080/01650250042000096

Slade, A. (1999). Representation, symbolization, and affect regulation in the concomitant treatment of a mother and a child: Attachment theory and child psychotherapy. *Psychoanalytic Inquiry, 19,* 797–830. doi:10.1080/07351699909534277

van IJzendoorn, M. H., & Sagi, A. (1999). Cross-cultural patterns of attachment: Universal and contextual determinants. In J. Cassidy & P. R. Shaver (Eds.), *Handbook of attachment: Theory, research, and clinical applications* (pp. 713–734). New York: Guilford.

Weinfield, N. S., Sroufe, L. A., Egeland, B., & Carlson, E. A. (1999). The nature of individual differences in infant–caregiver attachment. In J. Cassidy & P. Shaver (Eds.), *Handbook of attachment: Theory, research, and clinical applications* (pp. 68–88). New York: Guilford Press.

Yuval-Adler, S. (2010). *Emotion dialogues between challenging and easy foster children and their mothers: Associations with maternal insightfulness.* Unpublished master's thesis, University of Haifa, Israel.

Zeanah, C. H., Benoit, D., Hirshberg, L., Barton, M. L., & Regan, C. (1994). Mothers' representations of their infants are concordant with infant attachment classifications. *Developmental Issues in Psychiatry and Psychology, 1,* 9–18.

Factors Associated with Children's Adjustment to Parents' Separation

## 3

Risk and Protective Factors Associated with Child and Adolescent Adjustment Following Separation and Divorce

Social Science Applications

JOAN B. KELLY ∎

The effects of separation and divorce on children attracted considerable attention as the divorce rate began its rapid increase 50 years ago. Initial conviction that the experience of divorce was responsible for lasting emotional, behavioral, and social damage in children and adolescents has gradually shifted to a more accurate and nuanced view of the varied impacts of the separation and divorce process on children. As empirical studies over the past two to three decades improved in sample size and diversity, methodology, and advanced statistical analyses, it became evident that outcomes for children and adolescents following divorce were complexly determined, varied considerably, and could be best understood within a framework of familial and external factors increasing risk and fostering resilience.

This chapter first describes the extent of risk associated with divorce for children when compared to married-family children. Then, two important risk factors for children *prior* to the separation are discussed: intense marital conflict and problematic parenting. The main focus of the chapter is the major factors associated with increased risk and enhanced resilience in children and adolescents following divorce for which consensus has emerged from thousands of empirical studies. Child custody evaluations will benefit from familiarity with this literature by: (a) developing more risk-focused interviews of parents, children, and collaterals, and selecting relevant objective and standardized measures; (b) assessing the existence of, or potential for, protective factors that may ameliorate negative outcomes for children; (c) preparing empirically based reports that are useful both for families and family courts and more defensible in the increasingly demanding forensic setting; and (d) making recommendations for appropriate interventions that emerge from risk and resilience analyses within each family and that might lead to reduced risk and more positive outcomes for children and adolescents.

Some characteristics of empirical research in the child divorce field are noted: (a) most studies were conducted after divorce, not after separation, and reflect the predominant post-divorce family structure in which children live primarily with their mothers and spend generally small amounts of time with their nonresident fathers; (b) early studies focused primarily on children who had lived in Caucasian, middle-class, married families; many samples now include never-married, cohabitating, and remarried families; (c) second-generation studies typically use large community or nationally representative samples with diverse racial backgrounds and economic circumstances; (d) most studies focused on children from 7 to 17 years of age and young adults, and the impacts of separation and divorce on children from birth to 7 have been little understood until recently; and (e) more longitudinal studies including pre-separation and post-divorce variables have helped to disentangle the effects of the pre-separation family environment and child's adjustment and divorce effects. Research findings reported in this chapter were all statistically significant and typically controlled for demographic and other relevant family differences in addition to the effects of the variables hypothesized to contribute to children's outcomes.

DOES RISK INCREASE WHEN PARENTS SEPARATE AND DIVORCE?

Children in Married, Divorced, and Separated Families

RISK IN MARRIED-FAMILY AND DIVORCED-FAMILY CHILDREN
A large body of empirical research confirms that divorce increases the risk for psychosocial maladjustment and academic problems in children and adolescents when compared to children in continuously married families (Amato, 2000, 2001, 2010; Carlson & Corcoran, 2001; Clarke-Stewart & Brentano, 2006; Emery, 1999; Hetherington, 1999; Hetherington & Kelly, 2002; Kelly, 2000; Kelly & Emery, 2003; Lansford, 2009; McLanahan, 1999; Potter, 2010; Simons et al., 1996; Sun & Li, 2001). The extent of risk varies depending on the time elapsed since the divorce. Recent and more sophisticated studies show smaller effect sizes of divorce because they generally control for pre-divorce variables. However, the risk remains more than twice as large: 25% of children whose parents divorced had adjustment problems, compared to 10% of children and adolescents in still-married families.

Two meta-analyses of 93 and 97 studies conducted by Amato (2001) a decade apart confirmed that the largest effects were seen in externalizing problems, including conduct disorders; impulsivity; antisocial behaviors and delinquency; relationship problems with parents, peers, and authority figures; and academic achievement. Internalizing symptoms, including depression, anxiety, and lower self-esteem, are more common in divorced-family children, although the findings are less consistent than findings for externalizing problems. Children in post-divorce families also have weaker ties and poorer relationships with their parents compared to those in married families, particularly with nonresident parents (Amato, 2001, 2010; Aquilino, 1994; Booth, Scott, & King, 2010; Hetherington & Kelly, 2002; King & Sobolewski, 2006; McLanahan, 1999; Schwartz & Finley, 2009; Sun, 2001).

Children from divorced families have lower academic performance and achievement test scores compared to married-family children. These effects are reduced after controlling for education and income but do not disappear (Manning & Lamb, 2003; McLanahan, 1999; Sun & Li, 2001). The school dropout and pregnancy rate of adolescents in divorced families is two to three times as high compared to adolescents in still-married families.

School dropout and poorer academic performance have long been associated with poverty or low income regardless of family structure (see McLanahan & Sandefur, 1994). Two large nationally representative longitudinal studies (N = 16,000; N = 9,524) of students from eighth to 12th grade found that families that separated during the study were poorer at the beginning of the study compared to still-married families (Pong & Ju, 2000), and the adolescents living in these families had lower scores on tests of math and reading before and after separation, compared to the adolescents in still-married families. The parents who divorced during the study provided fewer parental resources (financial, social, and human capital) to their children at the beginning of the study and were less involved in their children's education (e.g., parental help on homework) compared to still-married families (Sun & Li, 2001). Potter (2010) confirmed that younger children whose parents divorced between kindergarten and fifth grade also had lower reading and math scores prior to separation and lost ground immediately after divorce; being divorced exacerbated the gap over time (N = 10,061).

It is important to note that the size of the group differences between married- and divorced-family children were modest rather than large in magnitude (see Amato, 2001; Clarke-Steward & Brentano, 2006, for examination of effect sizes), and symptoms and problems described were not universal. There is considerable overlap between groups of married- and divorced-family children, as some married-family children have serious adjustment and academic problems and substantial numbers of divorced-family children function well. A relevant 17-year longitudinal study (N = 629) found that those in high-conflict marriages whose parents remained married had *more* adjustment problems than children in divorced families. Children and adolescents in low-conflict marriages had the most positive outcomes (Booth & Amato, 2001). Hetherington and Kelly (2002) reported that by 2 years after divorce, 75% to 80% of divorced-family children functioned within the average range on psychological adjustment, social, and behavioral measures. Among those children and adolescents who fall into the 25% risk category, problems persist in varying degrees into adulthood, particularly in lowered well-being, socioeconomic attainment, and poorer relationships with parents (Amato, 2001; Aquilino, 1996; Booth & Amato, 2001; Chase-Lansdale, Cherlin, & Kierman, 1995).

RISK IN NEVER-MARRIED AND COHABITING-FAMILY CHILDREN

Studies comparing children in never-married and continuously married families indicate that those born out of wedlock are more likely to experience a variety of emotional, cognitive, and behavioral problems and have less education and earnings and more troubled marriages compared to those reared in continuously married families (Aquilino, 1996; Teachman, 2008). The differences between children in never-married and divorced families are not substantial. Children living with cohabiting biological parents have more emotional and behavioral problems and less school involvement and a higher risk of parental separation compared to those in married families. While some of the differences can be explained by the lower education, income, and well-being of cohabiting parents, the increased risk remains (Brown, 2004).

Age and Gender as Risk Factors

Is the Child's Age at Divorce a Risk Factor?
Studies have been mixed with regard to whether the timing of divorce matters in child adjustment. A confounding methodological problem has been that children's ages correspond to the beginning of the study, not the time of separation or divorce, resulting in wide variations in children's experience of divorce. Younger children were found to have more problems than older youngsters in several early studies, leading some to conclude that their more limited cognitive and emotional capabilities, anxieties about abandonment, and inability to take advantage of outside resources made it more difficult for them to cope with the divorce (Hetherington, 1999). Infants and toddlers have extremely limited understanding of the disappearance of important attachment figures and become more insecure, anxious, and fretful as a result (Lamb & Kelly, 2009).

Others have reported that risk escalates as children move into adolescence (Chase-Lansdale et al., 1995; Cherlin et al., 1991). Chase-Lansdale et al. compared the effects of separation for children between ages 7 and 11 and ages 11 and 16 and found that separations in the older age group were more likely to lead to adverse mental health outcomes in adulthood. A longitudinal study of children (N = 1,265) assessed at birth, at 4 months, and annually to age 16 focused on age at parental separation and adolescent attachment to parents. After controlling for family background factors, parent conflict, child behavior at 3 years, and mother–child interaction from birth to 3 years, Woodward, Fergusson, and Belsky (2000) found that the younger the child at the time of parental separation, particularly in the birth-to-5 cohort, the lower the attachments to parents as reported by adolescents, and the lower their perceptions of caring by mothers and fathers. There were no gender differences. Attachments to parents and perceptions of caring were higher among adolescents whose parents did not separate.

It is likely that some adverse outcomes are related to tasks that children must negotiate at each stage of development, such as consolidating attachments to parents and caregivers, learning to control behavior, identity formation, developing social relationships, or developing effective study/work habits. Using child age at the time of parental divorce, and following adjustment from 1 year before divorce to 3 years after divorce, Lansford et al. (2006) found that divorce from kindergarten to Grade 5 had more adverse effects on internalizing and externalizing symptoms; from Grades 6 to 10 there were more adverse effects on grades.

Gender of the Child
While preadolescent boys were at greater risk for externalizing symptoms in some studies (Amato, 2001; Hetherington, 1999), no gender differences linked to divorce were found in others (Sun & Li, 2001; Vandewater & Lansford, 1998). A recent study of 6,647 adults whose parents divorced before age 18 reported that men were two to three times more likely to have seriously considered suicide than women, after

controlling for many other factors (Rabin, 2011), but there were no data about when or how serious the thoughts were. The interaction between gender, age, pre-separation adjustment, conflict, and parent–child relationships is complex and confounds efforts to clarify the role of gender.

To summarize:

- Studies indicate that the risk of emotional, behavioral, social, and academic problems for children of divorced parents is more than double that of children whose parents were continuously married.
- The differences between married- and divorced-family children are modest and not universal, and one should not assume that children in divorcing families either have or will develop adjustment problems. ¹
- Between 75% and 80% of children of divorce fall within the average range or better on objective measures by 2 to 3 years after divorce.
- Children raised in a single-parent or cohabiting family are at higher risk for adjustment difficulties compared to married-family children.
- Age at time of divorce may be a critical determinant of later outcomes, but the impact is likely related to developmental tasks to be mastered before and after separation. There are no consistent gender differences attributable to divorce.

The Pre-separation Experiences of the Child

ARE CHILDREN AT RISK BEFORE DIVORCE?

Children come to the separation process with a family history that may determine their ability to cope with separation and their longer-term risk. An important early longitudinal study using a large British sample that assessed children at 7, 11, 15, and 23 years of age found that as many as half of the behavioral and academic problems of children whose parents later divorced were observed 4 to 12 years before the separation, with symptoms similar to those reported in divorced children (Cherlin et al., 1991). Similarly, 3-year-old boys in 101 families whose parents later divorced were more impulsive, disorderly, and inconsiderate with other children, compared to 3-year-olds whose parents did not divorce (Block, Block, & Gjerde, 1986).

A study of 5,530 adolescents (mean age = 16.4 years) from the National Longitudinal Study of Adolescent Health investigated the effects of separation on adolescent delinquency and depression and found that the quality of the pre-separation father–son relationship was predictive of delinquent behavior after separation 18 months later (Videon, 2002). When separated from fathers and living with mothers by Wave 2, adolescent boys who had higher levels of satisfaction with the father–son relationship before separation had a greater increase in delinquent behaviors at Wave 2. For adolescent girls who were less than satisfied with the mother–child relationship prior to separation, living with fathers by Wave 2 was associated with reductions in delinquent behaviors by Wave 2. Separation did not have a significant effect on adolescent depression regardless of which parent they lived with, but the quality of pre-separation relationships with opposite-sex parents did influence adolescent depression regardless of living arrangements (Videon, 2002). Such research indicates the importance of directly obtaining and giving weight to adolescent views of each pre-separation parent–child relationship and to input about living arrangements after separation.

MARITAL CONFLICT

Many early studies confirmed the link between marital conflict and children's adjustment problems (see Cumming & Davies, 1994; Grych, 2005; Kelly, 2000). Problems of aggression, impulsivity, peer difficulties, delinquency, depression, and impairments in concentration and academic achievement were more often found in children of high-conflict marriages compared to those in low-conflict marriages (Vandewater & Lansford, 1998). And more negative parent–child relationships and lower parent–child affection were found in high-conflict marriages, with effects accelerating more for fathers than mothers after divorce (Amato & Booth, 1996). Stocker and Youngblade (1999) found that marital conflict was associated with more hostile parenting behavior of both fathers and mothers, which in turn was linked to problematic sibling relationships, including less warmth and higher levels of conflict and rivalry between siblings. Regardless of family structure, a high level of marital conflict experienced during childhood has been linked to more depression and other psychological disorders in young adults compared to those reporting lower conflict levels during childhood (Amato, 2001; Zill, Morrison, & Coiro, 1993). In a diverse sample of 649 college students, exposure to nonviolent interparental conflict during childhood significantly increased the odds of having a subsequent episode of major depressive disorder and alcohol abuse or dependency disorder, controlling for demographic factors, divorce, and parent-to-child physical abuse (Turner & Kopiec, 2006).

The presence of verbal conflict is not a reliable predictor of child adjustment, and it should not be assumed that children who experienced marital conflict will have problems. High-frequency conflict is associated with more anger and distress in children compared to moderate to low frequency, but it is not the most powerful predictor of child problems. Conflict is often viewed as a uni-dimensional construct. To understand the impact of conflict on children, a more nuanced differentiation of conflict behaviors and child experiences as well as the presence of protective buffers available to the child is essential (Birnbaum & Bala, 2010; Grych, 2005; Kelly, 2000; Kelly & Emery, 2003).

The intensity of conflict, the conflict style of parents, and the focus of the conflict are critical variables to assess. Intensity or severity of conflict more reliably predicts negative outcomes for children. And intense conflict that occurs frequently is certainly more likely to be associated with adjustment problems. High-intensity fighting is associated with more insecure attachments and anxiety in infants and toddlers and distress and insecurity in young children. In older children and adolescents, intense conflict had the largest and most consistent impact and was associated with more externalizing and internalizing symptoms in both boys and girls, compared with low-intensity conflict (see Cummings & Davies, 1994).

Violence in the marriage has an independent negative effect on child adjustment and is more potent in predicting negative outcomes. Children have more symptoms in violent, high-conflict marriages compared to nonviolent, high-conflict marriages (McNeal & Amato, 1998), and symptoms are more severe when children observe the use of knives and guns (Jouriles et al., 1998). There are higher rates of sibling violence in families with violent parents compared to siblings with nonviolent parents, with the highest rates among brothers. Severe sibling violence cascades down the sibling hierarchy, and parents rarely identify a perpetrator and victim. Children who are victims of sibling violence are more likely to have poor peer relationships, depression, inability to trust, poor self-esteem, and substance abuse (Graham-Berman, Cutler, Litzenberger, & Schwartz, 1994). None of the above research has differentiated among patterns of marital violence in assessing children's adjustment (Kelly & Johnson, 2008). (See Hardesty, Haselschwerdt, & Johnson, Chapter 14 in this volume, for a more extensive consideration of violence and child adjustment.)

In married and divorced families, overtly hostile conflict styles (physical and verbal affect and behaviors such as slapping, screaming, contempt, derision) were more strongly associated with externalizing and internalizing behaviors than either covert conflict styles or frequency of conflict. In contrast, covert conflict styles such as triangulation of the child and parental passive-aggressive behaviors were linked to more internalizing symptoms, including depression, anxiety, and withdrawal (Buehler, Krishnakumar, Stone, Anthony, Pemberton, Gerard, & Barber, 1998). Marital conflict that focused on the child was also more predictive of child adjustment problems, particularly self-blame, shame, and fear of being drawn into the conflict, compared to intense conflict that was not child-centered (Grych, 2005). Parent–child conflict was found to be more destructive for children than marital conflict because of the constant negative focus on the child (Demo & Cox, 2000).

MEDIATING LINKS BETWEEN MARITAL CONFLICT AND CHILD ADJUSTMENT

There are both direct and indirect effects of high levels of marital conflict on child adjustment (for reviews, see Cummings & Davies, 1994; Grych, 2005; Kelly, 2000). *Direct* negative effects include modeling aggressive parental behaviors in response to frustration and rage, failing to learn appropriate social interaction skills, and experiencing strong physiological effects that interfere with affective regulation, particularly when intense marital conflict is accompanied by violence. A study of 6-year-old children's distress responses to interparental conflict found support for elevated cortisol levels, particularly when children showed high levels of involvement in the conflicts (Davies, Sturge-Apple, Cicchetti, & Cummings, 2008).

For two decades, social scientists have sought to understand the mechanisms that link high marital conflict to child adjustment problems. *Indirect* negative effects of marital conflict are mediated through the mother–child and father–child relationship, primarily in the quality of parenting. Quality of parenting is consistently one of the best predictors of children's psychological and social adjustment (Amato, 2001; Amato & Gilbreth, 1999; Hetherington, 2006; Simons et al., 1996). Persistent, intense marital discord and marital dissatisfaction pervasively undermine parenting, and inappropriate and hostile parenting styles lead in turn to more behavioral, social, and emotional problems in children and adolescents. In a meta-analysis of 39 studies, Krishnakumar and Buehler (2000) found that discipline and parental acceptance were the aspects of parenting most affected by high conflict, an association that was stronger for children in middle childhood and adolescence than younger children. In a multiethnic, low-income sample of 97 children ages 9 to 11, Gonzales, Pitts, Hill, and Roosa (2000) reported that children's reports of parental acceptance, inconsistent discipline, and hostile control were associated with child depression and conduct problems.

A number of studies confirmed that compared to mothers in low-conflict marriages, mothers in high-conflict marriages were less warm and empathic toward their children; demonstrated less affection; were more rejecting; and used harsher, erratic, and coercive discipline, with more yelling and physical punishment. Fathers were more likely to withdraw from the parenting role and from their children in high-conflict marriages, compared to fathers in low-conflict marriages, and interactions with their children were more insensitive and intrusive (Amato & Booth, 1996; Belsky, Youngblade, Rovine, & Volling, 1991; Cummings & Davies, 1994; Harrist & Ainslie, 1998; Kline, Johnston, & Tschann, 1991). A more recent prospective study of 225 families with 6-year-old children found that marital hostility and withdrawal were associated with increases in parental emotional unavailability over a 1-year period (Sturge-Apple, Davies, & Cummings, 2006). The quality of maternal and paternal parenting fully mediated the associations between marital conflict and child internalizing and externalizing behaviors in a sample of 226 families with a school-age child (Kaczynski, Lindahl, Malik, & Laurenceau, 2006). High marital conflict was also associated with more problematic and hostile sibling relationships in 7- and 10-year-olds, mediated by the separate hostility of both parents (Stocker & Youngblade, 1999).

Parents in high-conflict marriages are also more depressed than those in low-conflict marriages (Vandewater & Lansford, 1998; Whisman, 2001), which is likely to limit emotional responsiveness to their children and lower tolerance for their misbehavior. In a community sample of 235 families with kindergarten children, Cummings, Keller, and Davies (2005) found that increased maternal and paternal depressive symptoms were associated with increased marital conflict and insecure marital attachment, less parental warmth, more psychological control in parenting, greater internalizing and externalizing symptoms in children, and more peer exclusion. The link between high marital conflict and reduced quality of parenting was found to be stronger in married than divorced families (King & Heard, 1999).

Other investigators have sought to understand pathways between marital conflict and child adjustment that assess the child's reactivity to conflict (e.g., the emotional security model; Davies & Cummings, 1994). Support for this explanatory mechanism was found in two prospective studies with parents and children in two age groups, 9 to 18 and 5 to 9 years (Cummings, Schermerhorn, Davies, Goeke-Morey, & Cummings, 2006). In the older group, Time 1 parental discord predicted Time 2 emotional insecurity, which in turn predicted Time 2 internalizing and externalizing problems. In the younger group, Time 1 parental discord predicted Time 2 emotional insecurity in children 1 year later, which in turn predicted Time 3 externalizing and internalizing problems after controlling for earlier levels of child adjustment.

PROTECTIVE BUFFERS AMELIORATING IMPACT OF CONFLICT

Because not all children in high-conflict families have negative outcomes, researchers sought to identify which factors in the family experience reduced the negative impacts of marital conflict for some children. A good, caring relationship with at least one parent, caregiver, or mentor had a buffering effect, as did parental warmth (Amato & Gilbreth, 1999; Harrist & Ainslie, 1998; Neighbors, Forehand, & McVicar, 1993; Vandewater & Lansford, 1998). Further, if parents demonstrated some ability to resolve significant conflict, using either compromise or negotiation styles rather than verbal attacking styles, children had fewer behavioral problems and were less distressed and fearful (Cummings & Davies, 1994). Positive sibling support (feeling understood, confiding, caring), as reported in retrospective reports of 194 university students, was associated with more positive self-esteem and competent social relationships in both high- and low-conflict families, compared with those students who described low sibling support (Caya & Liem, 1998). Similarly, preadolescents in high-conflict families with close sibling relationships were found to be as well adjusted as youngsters in low-conflict families (Jenkins & Smith, 1990).

To summarize the research on marital conflict and child adjustment:

- The intensity, conflict style, and focus of marital conflict in married and divorced families are better predictors than frequency of conflict or legal conflict.
- There are both direct and indirect effects of high levels of conflict that contribute to children's psychological and social adjustment problems. Children often model their parents' aggressive behavior in their own social interactions and fail to learn appropriate social skills. The indirect effects on child adjustment are mediated through the intervening variables of quality of parenting (emotional availability and discipline) and decreases in children's emotional security.
- Having a good relationships with at least one caregiver or mentor and supportive sibling relationships serve as protective buffers against negative effects of high marital conflict.

RISK AND RESILIENCE FACTORS ASSOCIATED WITH CHILD ADJUSTMENT FOLLOWING SEPARATION AND DIVORCE

Risk factors linked to negative outcomes following divorce for children and adolescents include parental conflict, psychological adjustment of the parents, quality and type of parenting and parent–child relationships, loss of important relationships, cohabitation and remarriage, family structure transitions, and economic resources. These variables have the most robust empirical support and consensus among social scientists in the fields of child development, sociology, and psychology. Protective factors linked to resilience in children following divorce include reduced or encapsulated co-parental conflict, good adjustment of the residential parent, competent parenting of both parents and cooperative or parallel co-parenting styles, higher levels of involvement of the nonresident parent, limited number of family transitions, and economic stability.

Parent Conflict After Divorce

CONFLICT AND RISK
Children in separating and divorcing families have widely varying family histories of exposure to conflict prior to separation. Between 20% and 25% of children experienced high conflict in the marriage, and the risk of child adjustment problems is likely to be high in this group at separation. Nearly one quarter of parents who divorced were in low-conflict marriages and approximately 50% experienced moderate levels of marital conflict, with only slightly elevated risk to children in either

group (Booth & Amato, 2001; Hetherington, 1999; Wallerstein & Kelly, 1980). Pre-divorce conflict is not a good predictor of the amount of post-divorce conflict (Booth & Amato, 2001), however, and it should not be assumed that high-conflict parents will continue the same level of conflict following separation once they are living apart and no longer confronting each other. As a result, some children of high-conflict families may experience significantly less conflict on a daily basis, particularly if parenting plans are well structured and all transitions occur in neutral places such as school or day care (Kelly, 2005, 2007).

In contrast, longitudinal clinical studies found that some parents with low or moderate pre-separation conflict escalated into protracted and heated battles after separation as a result of a number of factors, including a significant imbalance in the desire for separation, angry feelings resulting from feeling abandoned, mental illness and personality disorders, and highly adversarial litigation over the parenting plan and financial support (Johnston, Kuehnle, & Roseby, 2008; Kelly, 2003; Wallerstein & Kelly, 1980).

There is little research focusing on the prevalence of different psychological responses early in the separation, but at least 50% of parents are moderately to extremely angry during the separation period, and some engage in hostile exchanges and accusations and openly criticize and denigrate the other parent (Johnston et al., 2008; Kelly, 1982, 2004). The normative course for most parents is a reduction in anger and hostile behaviors over 2 to 3 years as they disengage emotionally from their former partners and move ahead with their separate lives (Hetherington, 1999; Maccoby & Mnookin, 1992; Wallerstein & Kelly, 1980). However, 8% to 12% of parents remained highly conflicted (Hetherington, 1999; King & Heard, 1999), and parents in this group frequently litigated their disputes, were more likely to have psychiatric illness or personality disorders, and were more likely to expose their children to verbal and physical aggression and hostile attitudes and behaviors (Johnston et al., 2008; Wallerstein & Kelly, 1980).

The label of *high-conflict parents* presumes that *both* parents are angry and actively fueling the conflict and litigation. Practitioners in the divorce field recognize that a substantial percentage of parents (perhaps 35%) have disengaged emotionally from the former partner and have no interest in conflict, litigation, or exposing the children to hostile exchanges (Friedman, 2004; Kelly, 2003; Kelly & Emery, 2003). Like the children, they are also victims of the other parent's vindictive rage or personality disorder and deplete emotional and financial resources to defend themselves or their divorce agreement from repeated allegations or noncompliance of the other parent.

Studies yield mixed results on whether pre-separation or post-divorce conflict is more likely to be associated with child adjustment problems. Some found that marital conflict was a more potent predictor of children's adjustment (Buehler et al., 1998; King & Heard, 1999; Kline et al, 1991), Hetherington (1999) reported that post-divorce conflict had more adverse effects than marital conflict, and Booth and Amato (2001) found no relationship. The different findings may reflect the timing of the study after divorce and different measures of conflict and adjustment.

Many children and adolescents have painful experiences and feelings as a residue of the divorce even if their emotional, social, and behavioral adjustment is average or better (Kelly & Emery, 2003). A decade after divorce, college students whose parents had remained in conflict reported greater feelings of loss and were more likely to view their lives through the lens of divorce compared to students whose parents had low conflict. However, these two groups of students did not differ on measures of depression and anxiety (Laumann-Billings & Emery, 2000). Similarly, college students who experienced high conflict for years after divorce reported high levels of distress, which was independent of how much time they spent with their fathers (Fabricius & Leucken, 2007).

The type of parent conflict most consistently associated with negative outcomes after divorce was the use of children by parents to express their anger and disputes. The parent behaviors included asking children to carry hostile messages to the other parent, asking intrusive questions about the other parent, creating a need in the child to hide information or conceal positive (or negative) feelings about the other parent, and denigrating the other parent. Such behaviors were associated with increased depression and anxiety in children. However, when parents with similarly high conflict did *not* use their children in this way, their children did not differ in adjustment from children with low-conflict parents (Buchanan, Maccoby, & Dornbusch, 1996). Fosco and Grych (2010) assessed the outcomes of triangulation of adolescents (N = 171, ages 14–19) into parental conflict at two points in time. Adolescents who experienced greater threat in response to intense, frequent parent conflict were more likely to triangulate themselves into the parental conflict, and this predicted greater self-blame and poorer parent–adolescent relationships at Time 2 for both boys and girls, in married and divorced families. Adolescents who reported triangulation at Time 1 also reported increased levels of anger and conflict with parents 6 months later (Time 2). Similarly, demeaning or putting down the other parent in the presence of children was associated with increased anger, stress, and less close parent–child relationships in studies of college students and young adults (Amato & Afifi, 2006; Fabricius & Hall, 2000). Feelings of being caught between parents appear to diminish in the decade following divorce (Amato & Afifi, 2006), but not for all children and young adults (Johnston et al., 2008). Of interest is that the amount of legal conflict related to the separation or divorce was *not* associated with child adjustment (Goodman, Bonds, Sandler, & Braver, 2004).

Reducing Risk Through Protective Buffers after Divorce

Some conflict between parents after divorce is normative and even acceptable to parents (King & Heard, 1999). Since low levels of parental conflict after separation or divorce are protective, early interventions that have been demonstrated to minimize or reduce conflict (e.g., mandated research-based divorce education programs, custody mediation) are important for families (Emery, 1994; Haine, Sandler, Wolchik, Tein, & Dawson-McClure, 2003; Kelly, 2002, 2004; Kelly & Emery, 2003). Transitions between parents are conflict-free for children when one parent drops off the children at school or day care and the other picks them up later. There are protective benefits when angry parents refrain from using their children to express parental disputes (Buchanan et al., 1996). Similarly, Hetherington (1999) found that when parents shielded children from conflict (encapsulation of conflict), it was beneficial. Warm, caring, authoritative, and involved parenting from at least one parent or caregiver is an important protective factor in buffering or minimizing effects of intense post-divorce parent conflict (Amato & Gilbreth, 1999; Neighbors et al., 1993; Vandewater & Lansford, 1998). In the presence of high conflict, two warm parents were better than one (Sandler, Miles, Cookston, & Braver, 2008). Positive and close sibling relationships in high-conflict families were also a protective buffer, associated with better adjustment, compared to children with low support or hostile sibling relationships (Caya & Liem, 1998; Jenkins & Smith, 1990).

In summary:

- Parents' post-separation conflict levels cannot be predicted by level of conflict prior to separation, and findings are mixed as to whether pre- or post-divorce conflict is more likely to result in negative child outcomes. High conflict is stressful in both situations.
- Between 8% and 12% of parents remain highly conflicted 2 to 3 years after divorce. In differentiating aspects of the conflict, it is also important to determine each parent's separate contributions to fueling conflict and litigation, including whether a parent has emotionally disengaged and is not invested in keeping the conflict going.
- The most destructive post-divorce conflict is when parents use their children to express their anger and disputes and make demeaning and contemptuous comments to the children about the other parent. Conversely, the amount of legal conflict between parents is not associated with child adjustment.
- Protective buffers against high conflict after separation and divorce include warm, competent parenting; shielding children from conflict by encapsulation of anger and disputes; not using the children to express anger; refraining from demeaning or attacking the other parent; and positive sibling relationships.

Parent Psychological Adjustment

PARENT ADJUSTMENT AND RISK

One of the best predictors of child adjustment after separation or divorce, and in all family structures, is the adjustment of mothers who are the primary caregivers (Cummings & Davies, 1994; Cummings, Keller, & Davies, 2005; Keitner & Miller, 1990). After divorce, living in the custody of mothers with significant psychiatric illness or personality disorders, including depression and anxiety, is associated with longer-term increased emotional, social, and academic problems in children of all ages (Carlson & Corcoran, 2001; Emery, Waldron, Kitzmann, & Aaron, 1999; Hetherington, 1999; Kline et al., 1991; Meadows, McLanahan, & Brooks-Gunn, 2007; Pruett, Williams, Insabella, & Little, 2003).

A longitudinal study of 340 mothers and their children in never-married, separated, and married families assessed children's cognitive and social development during their first 3 years (Clarke-Stewart, Vandell, McCartney, Owen, & Booth, 2000). Maternal depression predicted poorer child development, as did lower capacity to provide stimulation and support to the children. Children of separated parents had poorer cognitive ability, were less securely attached, and had less positive mother–child interactions than children in married families. Children of never-married mothers had the lowest scores on cognitive ability and more negative mother–child interactions by age 3, after controlling for income and maternal education. Levels of maternal depression were similar in both groups, and these indices of diminished parenting were observed in never-married and in separated mothers *before* separation. Using the national longitudinal Fragile Families and Child Well-Being Study sample, Meadows et al. (2007) examined the associations between parental major depressive episodes and generalized anxiety disorders and child behavior problems among 3-year-olds in 2,120 families in four family types (married, cohabiting, involved nonresident father, noninvolved nonresident father). In all family structures, maternal depression and anxiety were associated with increased likelihood of anxious/depressed, attention-deficit, and oppositional/defiant disorders in children. Paternal anxiety and depression alone was not related to these problems, but if both father and mother were anxious/depressed and father was co-resident, there was an increased likelihood of child anxiety and depression (Meadows et al., 2007). Using data from the same longitudinal survey and a sample of 2,427 mostly unmarried mothers of 5-year-old children, Turney (2011) found that maternal depression reported by mothers during the prior 5 years was associated with worse behavioral but not cognitive outcomes at entry into school. Children with chronically depressed mothers were the most vulnerable, but children exposed to maternal depression at any time over the first 5 years, compared to those with no exposure to maternal depression, had more externalizing and internalizing behaviors. Boys were more vulnerable to maternal depression than girls, and socioeconomic advantage did not buffer children from the negative effects of maternal depression. In this sample, 34% of children had a mother who reported at least one episode of depression during the first 5 years, a rate higher than the general population, and 5% reported depression at each of the three data-collection points (Turney, 2011).

While fathers' involvement with infants in married families with depressed mothers moderated the extent of internalizing behaviors as seen later in kindergarten (Mezulis, Hyde, & Blark, 2004), it is unlikely that such buffering of maternal depression will be effective after separation, given the brief and infrequent contacts that most fathers have with their infants. A study of 149 divorcing families with children from birth to age 6 found that a greater number of psychological symptoms in either parent was associated with more negative changes in the parent–child relationship, which mediated the link between parent symptoms and child adjustment (Pruett et al., 2003).

There is increased risk for children when parents abuse illicit drugs and alcohol. Fathers are more likely to use alcohol and illicit drugs than are mothers and to develop substance abuse problems during early to middle adulthood, when many men are fathering children. They are also more likely to appear in family court for a variety of legal actions compared to fathers who do not abuse substances. Children of fathers with alcohol or drug abuse histories are more likely to be overactive, oppositional, defiant, and aggressive; have poorer academic achievement; and develop substance abuse problems as they move through adolescence into adulthood, compared to children whose fathers have no history of alcohol or drug abuse. As is true with maternal substance abuse, paternal substance abuse contributes to compromised family environments in a number of ways. Children of substance-abusing fathers are more likely to be affected by antisocial personality disorders and other psychiatric disorders; more traumatic events, including conflict and violence; poor parenting practices; and negative father–child relationships (for review, see McMahon & Giannini, 2003). In family court, allegations of drug and alcohol abuse are often combined with other allegations, including domestic violence and child and sexual abuse.

PARENT ADJUSTMENT AND PROTECTIVE FACTORS

Living in the post-divorce custody of a psychologically adequate parent(s) is a protective factor strongly associated with longer-term positive outcomes in boys and girls. In most of these studies, children lived primarily with their mothers. There have not been specific studies of the relationship between the mental health of both parents and children's outcomes in more shared custody arrangements. If both parents are within the normal range of adjustment, having two parents significantly involved in their lives is beneficial (Sandler et al., 2008).

To summarize:

- The adjustment of the parent with primary custody, usually the mother, is one of the best predictors of children's psychological adjustment after divorce. Depression, anxiety disorders, mental illness, and personality disorders are associated with longer-term externalizing, internalizing, and academic problems.
- Significant psychological problems of all types interfere with quality of parenting and the parent–child relationship, which in turn is associated with children's adjustment problems.
- Studies of the impact of depression in nonresident fathers on their children show mixed results, and it is unclear whether fathers can buffer the effects of maternal depression if they have a limited amount of time with their children.

Quality of Parenting and Co-parental Relationships

PARENTING AS RISK FACTOR

Quality of parenting has emerged as a central variable and major predictor of children's outcomes after divorce and must be considered as important as conflict in assessing risk—if not more so. Parenting problems contribute to children's emotional, behavioral, and academic problems in all family structures, and many studies have demonstrated that separation is likely to diminish the quality of parenting, at least temporarily. Stressed, preoccupied, emotionally labile, and angry parents have difficulty providing warmth and affection, monitoring and supervising their children, and disciplining effectively, and parent–child conflict increases while family cohesion decreases. They are less involved and emotionally supportive and use more coercive and harsh forms of discipline (Amato, 2001; Buchanan et al., 1996; Cummings & Davies, 1994; Hetherington, 1999; Simons et al., 1996; Wallerstein & Kelly, 1980).

PARENTING AS A PROTECTIVE FACTOR

Effective involved parenting has been demonstrated to ameliorate the negative impacts of both divorce and conflict on children's outcomes (Amato & Gilbreth, 1999; Hetherington & Kelly, 2002; Simons et al., 1996; Videon, 2005). In a meta-analysis of 63 studies, Amato and Gilbreth found that specific aspects of parenting for mothers and fathers were associated with positive child adjustment after divorce. Core aspects of mothers' parenting included warmth, authoritative discipline, academic skill encouragement, and monitoring of child activities. For fathers, behaviors linked to positive adjustment in children were active involvement, authoritative discipline, and monitoring activities. Active involvement included help with homework and projects, emotional support and warmth, talking about problems, and involvement in school (e.g., attendance at events and meetings). Sandler et al. (2008) found that having a warm parent was a protective factor, including in high-conflict situations. To enable such involvement, fathers must have sufficient time to parent, including midweek and weekend overnights. See Sandler, Wolchik, Winslow, Mahrer, Moran, and Weinstock, Chapter 4 in this volume, for an extensive discussion of quality of parenting and parenting skills important in child adjustment after divorce.

Menning (2002) explored the relationship between different types and frequency of activities jointly shared, financial support (court-ordered and informal), and educational attainment in an adolescent sample of 269 father–adolescent pairs. Increased activities and financial support did not independently increase educational attainment, but the combination of shared, different activities and financial support increased both the probability of earning a high school diploma and college attendance. Menning (2006) then looked at school failure and level and type of father involvement among 2,550 adolescents in Grades 7 to 12. The father involvement variable included measures of communication, number of overnight stays, the number of nine different activities participated in during the prior month, and how close the adolescent felt to the father. Higher levels of father involvement at Time 1 were related to less school failure (e.g., less truancy, suspension, expulsion, dropping out) at Time 2. Greater variety of activities at Time 1 and increases in father–child activities between Time 1 and Time 2 were associated with lowered school failure. Ongoing school-related discussions (e.g., grades, homework, other school issues) between fathers and children were most significant in lowering the probability of school failure from Time 1 to Time 2. Ethnic and racial differences were found in the extent of involvement of fathers as well as the type of activities engaged in by fathers and adolescents (King, Harris, & Heard, 2004).

CO-PARENTAL RELATIONSHIPS AND RISK
Understanding the three categories of post-divorce co-parental relationships is valuable in work with parents (Hetherington & Kelly, 2002; Maccoby & Mnookin, 1992). *Cooperative co-parenting*, characterized by joint planning for the children, coordination of children's activities, offering parental support, and some flexibility in schedules, is achieved by 25% to 30% of divorced parents in the years after divorce. This type of parenting promotes resiliency in children not only because they benefit from parental cooperation and low conflict but also because good mental health and maturity are most likely characteristic of these parents.

The majority of parents—more than half—settle into a *parallel co-parenting* style in which emotional disengagement from each other, low conflict, and low communication predominate. They generally follow rules but provide parenting separately in their own domains and often fail to coordinate child-rearing practices or scheduling issues. While less optimal, children do thrive in these arrangements, particularly when the parenting in each home is nurturing and adequate (Hetherington & Kelly, 2002).

Between 20% and 25% of parents have a continuing *conflicted co-parenting* relationship characterized by poor communication, low cooperation, high distrust, control and dependency, and failed decision-making.

To summarize:

- Quality of parenting is a major predictor of emotional and social adjustment and academic performance after separation and divorce, of equal if not greater importance than conflict in determining risk.
- Effective parenting, more paternal involvement, and close father–child relationships are associated with positive adjustment, and when fathers discuss homework, grades, and other school issues, school dropout and failure rates are reduced.
- Children will thrive in cooperative co-parenting relationships and in parallel co-parenting relationships when both parents provide adequate and nurturing parenting in each home.

Parent–Child Relationships

PARENT–CHILD RELATIONSHIPS AND RISK AFTER DIVORCE

Fathers are typically less involved than mothers in their children's care in married and particularly in never-married families, although married fathers have significantly increased their level of care and involvement in the past three decades, a trend that continues (Casper & Bianchi, 2002). Following separation, contacts between fathers and children are sharply reduced, as are opportunities for father involvement. Frequency of visits by itself was not related to children's outcomes in a number of studies, although more frequent visits, when coupled with active father involvement and adequate parenting, are linked to positive outcomes (Amato & Gilbreth, 1999; Fabricius, Sokol, Diaz, & Braver, Chapter 7 in this volume).

In a study of 2,733 10- to 14-year-olds, 43% of those in married families rated their fathers as highly involved on seven dimensions, while only 14% did so in divorced families. Lower father involvement was associated with more delinquency, externalizing and internalizing problems, and negative feelings (Carlson, 2006). The seven measures of father involvement studied were talks over important decisions, listens to the adolescent's side of things, knows who the adolescent is with, spends enough time with the adolescent, adolescent feelings of closeness, shares ideas, and talks about things that matter.

A minority of adolescents maintain close relationships with fathers over time after separation and divorce (Scott, Booth, King, & Johnson, 2007). When fathers and adolescents have a close relationship *and* sufficient time to be with each other after divorce, fathers have more opportunities to be effective parents by monitoring activities, communicating with their children, expressing support, and teaching their children. Higher-quality mother–child relationships and positive adolescent well-being were found to help prevent deterioration in father–child relationships after divorce (Scott et al., 2007). There is no evidence that increasing time between fathers and their children, up to equally shared physical custody, diminishes the closeness or importance of the mother–child relationship (Buchanan et al., 1996; Lee, 2002).

The consequences of weakening ties between fathers and children extend into adulthood. Young adults whose parents divorced when they were younger reported less contact with fathers; less affection, closeness, and trust of their fathers; and fewer offers of intergenerational assistance compared to those whose parents remained married (Booth & Amato, 2001; King, 2002).

PARENT-CHILD RELATIONSHIPS AND PROTECTIVE FACTORS AFTER DIVORCE

Father involvement and close father–child relationships are protective factors ameliorating risk in children and adolescents and are associated with better psychological, social, and academic outcomes compared to youngsters with less close relationships (Amato & Gilbreth, 1999; Booth et al., 2010; King & Sobolewski, 2006). In addition, adolescents who are closer to their nonresident fathers reported less delinquency than adolescents who live with a father with whom they are not close (Booth et al., 2010). Further, higher levels of father involvement were associated with fewer behavioral problems on all outcomes (fewer behavioral and delinquency problems, less depression and anxiety), and boys and girls benefited equally. The more that fathers were involved, the smaller the differences between divorced- and married-family adolescents and four other family structures (Carlson, 2006). Distrust in young adults was diminished by a good teen–parent relationship and more frequent contact with fathers after divorce (King, 2002).

Spending overnights with fathers appears to be important for both young children and adolescents. Those adolescents who had 30 or more overnights a year (2.5 per month or more) versus no overnights reported that their nonresident parent was more close to them, more involved, and more aware of their activities and friends. They described their father–adolescent relationships as of better quality compared to those without overnights. The number of overnights was linked to parental trust and conflict, but 30 or more overnights resulted in better father–son relationships after accounting for parent conflict level and overall frequency of visits (Cashmore, Parkinson, & Taylor, 2008). In young children, there was no detriment associated with overnights with fathers in the birth to age 3 cohort. The children from ages 4 to 6 benefited in terms of more positive adjustment and social relationships compared to those without overnights. Consistency of schedule was important (Pruett, Ebling, & Insabella, 2004). Maternal hostility at the beginning of separation is a factor in influencing father–child contacts initially and was linked to fewer visits and overnights 3 years later (Buchanan et al., 1996). Fathers who never married reported more maternal interference in their involvement with their children and less time and fewer overnights with their children compared to divorced fathers (Insabella, Williams, & Pruett, 2003). Maternal gatekeeping also may serve to limit father–child contacts and has a more potent role in determining the extent of father–child involvement and contacts after separation than during the marriage (Allen & Hawkins, 1999; Ganong, Coleman, & McCaulley, Chapter 12 in this volume; Pruett, Cowan, Cowan, & Diamond, Chapter 5 in this volume; Trinder, 2008).

To summarize:

- Lower father involvement is associated with more delinquency and with externalizing and internalizing problems for boys and girls and male and female adolescents.

- Both boys and girls benefit along many measures of adjustment and academic performance from having an involved father and closer father–child bonds.
- More rather than fewer overnights have been found to be beneficial for both young children and adolescents.

Loss of Important Relationships

LOSS AS A CENTRAL THEME OF DIVORCE

Many children are at risk for losing important attachment figures and relationships from their lives, which can have long-term negative consequences. The separation may result in the reduced support of grandparents, cherished day care providers, teachers, close friends, and in particular their father. For four decades, children have reported the loss of the nonresident parent, usually the father, as the most negative aspect of divorce. Even when fathers and children continued to see each other, the majority of relationships declined in closeness over time (Scott et al., 2007; Wallerstein & Kelly, 1980). This has been primarily a result of the traditional visiting pattern of every other weekend, which has been slow to change even in the face of mounting research evidence, and a reluctance to order overnights for young children. (See Fabricius et al., Chapter 7 in this volume; Fabricius, Braver, Diaz, & Velez, 2010; Kelly, 2005, 2007; Kelly & Emery, 2003; Lamb, Chapter 8 in this volume.)

The majority of children from preschool through high school expressed sadness, pain, and great dissatisfaction with such arrangements because of the prolonged separations between contacts and brevity of visits and the resultant loss of shared activities and emotional support (Emery, 1999; Hetherington & Kelly, 2002; Wallerstein & Kelly, 1980). Longing for the father has been a persistent theme. Among school-age children, more than half wanted more contact with their fathers, and one third wanted the contacts to be longer (Smith & Gollop, 2001). In retrospective studies of adolescents and college students, between 50% and 70% indicated that they would have preferred equal time with both parents, or at least a substantial number of overnights with the nonresident parent. They reported that their mothers were opposed to any increases in time (Fabricius & Hall, 2000; Parkinson, Cashmore, & Single, 2005; Smith & Gollop, 2001).

In an ethnically diverse sample of 1,376 college students, reports of and desires for paternal involvement among students from divorced families differed greatly from those of married-family students, whereas those of maternal involvement did not. The divorced-family student sample desired more father involvement in all 20 domains measured, and results were consistent across gender, ethnicity, and parent work schedules (Schwartz & Finley, 2009).

Overall, research points to reduced father–child contacts and father involvement after divorce as a major source of distress about lost nurturance and caring, as perceived by children and adolescents. Comparing the pain and distress reported among college students whose parents were divorced about ten years earlier with a matched sample of students in still-married families, the divorced sample reported more painful childhood feelings and experiences, more worry about many things such as parents attending major events and financial support, and wanting to spend more time with their fathers. Two thirds of the divorced-family students said they missed not having their fathers around, and one third questioned whether they were loved by their fathers. Further, there was more pain, more feelings of loss, and more self-identification as a child of divorce in sole physical custody arrangements compared to those in shared physical custody (Laumann-Billings & Emery, 2000).

In a study of 1,375 college students, Finley and Schwartz (2010) found that the amount of nurturance and involvement reported to be received from mothers and fathers in married families was closely related, but was not at all correlated in divorced families. The total amount of reported nurturance and involvement from both parents, when integrated into a continuum, was related to all measures of psychosocial functioning and troubled ruminations about parents in both family structures, with lower nurturance/involvement associated with poorer functioning. Differences between parents on nurturance and involvement received also had negative effects on self-esteem, life satisfaction, and psychological distress, as well as friendship quality and academic performance, regardless of gender or ethnic background. Longitudinal studies of adolescents living in low-income neighborhoods demonstrated that higher levels of nonresident paternal involvement were associated with lower delinquency and decreases in delinquency over time (Coley & Medeiros, 2007) and a decreased likelihood of smoking (Menning, 2006).

While clearly the majority of children and adolescents want to maintain a meaningful relationship with their fathers after separation and divorce, a small minority do not want and resist contact with the nonresident parent, often quite appropriately. Experiences of parental child abuse, parent violence, substance abuse, estrangement and child alienation, and rigid and insensitive parenting practices with either parent are likely to result in no contact or supervised visits when appropriate, or very limited contact and distancing from that parent over time (Hardesty, Haselschwerdt, & Johnson, Chapter 14 in this volume; Johnston et al., 2008; Kelly & Johnston, 2001; Saini, Johnston, Fidler, & Bala, Chapter 13 in this volume).

PROTECTING AGAINST RELATIONSHIP LOSS

Children and adolescents in separated and divorced families are better adjusted when they have warm relationships with two actively involved and adequate parents, and yet harmful deterioration of father–child relationships over time has been the norm. Generally, it is not the separation or divorce itself but rather the attitudes and practices set in motion that lead to dramatic restrictions in father and child time together, which in turn diminishes the possibility of nurturance and involvement for children.

There are societal, institutional, paternal, maternal, and economic influences that combine to create barriers (see Fabricius et al., 2010 and Kelly, 2007, for extensive discussion of these issues). Among the most important institutional family court barriers have been the historic reliance on *visitation guidelines* (written, or embedded in traditional attitudes by judges, lawyers, or evaluators), which prescribed a one-size-fits-all parenting plan, most often every other weekend with a brief midweek visit, without regard to the quality of the child's relationships with each parent. Such guidelines, ironically framed as "best interests," persist to this day in many jurisdictions (Kelly, 2005, 2007). They were simplistic to apply, took no careful thinking about children's needs, and did not benefit the majority of children. These were developed at a time when there was a strong maternal preference for custody, bolstered by untested and influential psychoanalytic theory that assumed that children had only one "psychological parent" and would be harmed if they were not in the full-time care of this parent—almost without exception mothers—after separation (Kelly, 1994). These attitudes were reflected as well in early attachment research, which exclusively studied infants' attachments to their mothers, because attachments to fathers were not viewed as significant or psychologically meaningful relationships. Only later did research demonstrate that infants form attachments to their mothers and fathers at the same time (around 7 months) in two-parent families (see Kelly & Lamb, 2000; Lamb, 1976; Lamb & Kelly, 2009; Thompson, 1999). Early but not relevant research on infant–mother separations (lengthy wartime and hospital separations from both parents) led mental health professionals to believe that serious detriment would result from separations of young and older children from their mothers, and the primacy given to this "family unit" came at the expense of father–child relationships. Fathers with whom children had lived during their early months or years were essentially perceived as strangers rather than meaningful attachment figures.

The research that demonstrates the benefits of more involvement of fathers with their children, particularly when the parent is an adequate, caring parent, does not usually specify what "more involvement" means in actual time spent with children. For decades, fathers' time with children, when contact was ordered, has most often been in the range of 10% to 20% (Amato, Meyers, & Emery, 2009; Furstenberg, Morgan, & Allison, 1987; Kelly, 1994; Maccoby & Mnookin, 1992; Parkinson, 2011; Selzer, 1991; Smith & Gollop, 2001; Smyth, 2004; Wallerstein & Kelly, 1980). This pattern of contact 4 days per month, sometimes with a brief midweek visit, has contributed to the demonstrated deterioration in closeness in father–child relationships over time, and sadness, longing, and a sense of deprivation among children (Amato, 1987; Fabricius et al, 2010; Fabricius & Hall, 2000; Fabricius et al., Chapter 7 in this volume; Laumann-Billings & Emery, 2000; Wallerstein & Kelly, 1980). Weekend-only time excludes fathers from participating regularly in homework and other school projects and situates fathers and children in a leisure environment, which skews the father–child relationship. In fact, the most common weekend activities of many fathers—playing sports, going shopping, and going to the movies—were not among the activities that promoted more beneficial adjustment (Menning, 2006).

In the face of a growing, extensive body of empirical research over the past two decades demonstrating the advantages of having two involved parents, and children's longing for much more expansive time with fathers, the opposition of the past several decades to shared physical custody has been puzzling (see Parkinson, 2011, for review). Instead of focusing on maintaining continuity and meaning in children's relationships with both caring parents, critics of shared custody focused on the presumed damage to children of being separated from their mothers (but not their fathers) and on the transitions between households (like "ping-pong balls") that were declared to be "confusing." Research does not support these concerns for average children with average parents (Bauserman, 2002; Buchanan et al., 1996; Fabricius et al., 2010; Laumann-Billings & Emery, 2000; Lee, 2002; Maccoby & Mnookin, 1992; Wallerstein & Kelly, 1980). Based on a meta-analysis of 33 studies, children in joint physical custody were better adjusted on multiple measures, including emotional and behavioral adjustment, and academic achievement, compared to children in more limited sole custody arrangements. These advantages persisted independent of the amount of conflict between parents (Bauserman, 2002). Buchanan, Maccoby and

Dornbusch (1996) reported a "drift" away from dual residence to primarily maternal care over time, but a recent study found that 3 years after divorce, the shared physical living arrangements were as stable as sole mother custody arrangements (Berger, Brown, Joung, Melli, & Wimer, 2008).

In some jurisdictions, when parents have conflict (which most often is not differentiated as to type and detriment to children), joint legal and joint physical custody is prohibited because of the conviction that such arrangements will increase conflict, an assumption for which there is little evidence (see Birnbaum & Bala, 2010, and Fabricius et al., 2010, for review of the research and case law). Generally, the majority of time is given to one parent (usually the mother), a practice and policy also promoted by some authors (e.g., Emery, 2004). A rule that automatically reduces contact with one parent, usually the father, or eliminates that parent from any future child-related decision-making, is problematic. It provides an incentive to act and remain angry as a legal strategy, discourages any cooperation or civil communication, and may eliminate an involved, loving parent (who may be less angry). It also does not take into account the research described above that demonstrates the importance of protective buffers—including involved and nurturing fathers—that shield children from the negative effects of conflict. (See Fabricius et al., Chapter 7 in this volume; Fabricius et al., 2010; Kelly, 1994; Lamb, Chapter 8 in this volume; Lamb and Kelly, 2009; and McIntosh and Smyth, Chapter 6 in this volume, for more extensive discussion of these issues.)

To summarize:

- The loss of important relationships is a source of distress, pain, and sadness for most children and adolescents, and the majority report wanting more expansive time with their fathers, including shared physical custody.
- While the level of father contact has increased over time, traditional guidelines and attitudes in many jurisdictions still result in restrictive parenting plans, even when children and fathers have close relationships.
- Conflict by itself should not be a barrier to more expansive or shared legal and physical custody; it should be considered in the context of the quality of parenting—including nurturance and support provided—and child and adolescent views of both parent–child relationship and living arrangements.

Remarriage and Cohabitation

REMARRIAGE AS RISK

Remarriage by itself does not decrease risk for children and adolescents, as children in stepfamily homes are twice as likely to have emotional, social, and academic problems (similar to those in single-parent homes), compared to those in still-married families. Although most parents view the formation of a stepfamily positively, children, particularly older ones, are typically less enthusiastic. Children often rebuff the stepparent's efforts to provide authoritative parenting, and many withdraw to more disengaged roles of chauffeur, handyman, and provider of financial support. Hetherington and Kelly (2002) found that most mothers had three to five serious relationships before remarriage and one third had more than 10; the majority cohabited before remarriage. This study also reported a 5- to 7-year period of desta-bilization and elevated stress after the stepfamily forms. Children in remarried fami-lies also have the risk of another divorce. In a two-wave study of 1,753 adolescents, King (2009) found that stepfamily formation had little consequence for adolescent–nonresident father closeness and that adolescent–mother closeness did not decline when mothers married the partner, but it declined when mothers cohabited. When adolescents were close to their mothers prior to acquiring a stepfather, they were more likely to develop close ties to their married stepfathers. While most adolescents reported being close to their mothers, over half of the adolescents reported not being close to their nonresident parent, and 45% were not close to their stepfathers.

PROTECTIVE EFFECTS OF REMARRIAGE
When the quality of the stepfather–child relationship was rated by adolescents as good, there was a lower risk of externalizing or internalizing symptoms. Having a nurturing relationship with the nonresident father, as opposed to no relationship, was also associated with positive outcomes, as were good relationships with both stepfathers and biological fathers. The benefits of a good relationship with the non-resident father were more independent of the mother than those in the stepfamily, and the quality of relationships with the stepfather was not associated with the child's contacts with the nonresident father or the quality of that relationship (White & Gilbreth, 2001). When adolescents lived with fathers, they were closest to their fathers, followed by closeness to stepmothers, and then nonresident biological mothers. Close relationships with fathers were associated with fewer externalizing and internalizing problems. As occurs with nonresident fathers, adolescent closeness to nonresident mothers decreased over time and was independent of the quality of the relationship with stepmothers (King, 2007).

COHABITATION AFTER SEPARATION AS RISK
Buchanan et al. (1996) reported that cohabitation was associated with more negative child outcomes than remarriage, a finding mirrored in the Manning and Lamb (2003) study of 13,231 adolescents (N = 13,231) on behavioral, delinquency, and academic outcomes. However, adolescents in single-mother, cohabiting, and remar-ried stepfather families were equally more likely to be suspended or expelled from school compared to married families (Manning & Lamb, 2003). Hetherington and Kelly (2002) found that the majority of cohabitation arrangements entered into by mothers were not stable; half of them lasted less than 1 year and only 10% lasted 5 or more years. The quality of parenting in dating and cohabiting families is poorer, particularly in monitoring children's lives and in positive involvement, compared to married or remarried families.

To summarize:

- Remarriage does not decrease risk for children, but when the quality of the stepfather–child relationship was good, there was lowered risk for externalizing or internalizing symptoms. Simultaneous good relationships with nonresident fathers also decreased risk.
- Living in a cohabiting household is associated with more negative outcomes than remarriage. Many cohabitations are short-lived, and children often experience serial cohabitations after separation and divorce.

Family Structure Transitions

FAMILY STRUCTURE TRANSITIONS AS RISK

Research on the number of family structure transitions (e.g., separation, divorce, cohabitation, remarriage, termination of cohabitation, re-divorce) experienced by children following separation and divorce highlights another significant risk factor. Such transitions often require the adaptation of children to new partners and parenting demands, schools, and neighborhoods. With each additional change in family structure, the risk for behavioral problems and delinquency, drug use, and poorer academic achievement increases (Magnuson & Berger, 2009; Manning & Lamb, 2003; Osborne & McLanahan, 2007; Teachman, 2008). Sun and Li (2009) compared 7,897 adolescents in stable post-divorce families with those who had additional transitions over time and found that late adolescents in more unstable post-divorce families, particularly girls, made little progress on math and social studies. Among 1,364 elementary school children who experienced family structure change, Cavanagh and Huston (2008) found that the cumulative level of family instability negatively affected social development by the end of elementary school, particularly for boys, and that early childhood transitions were primarily responsible.

Extending this research to very young children and including dating transitions as well, the relationship between partnership changes, dating transitions, and parenting behavior of 1,975 mothers from the Fragile Families database during their children's first 5 years found that both co-residential and dating transitions were associated with higher levels of parenting stress and harsh parenting (Beck, Cooper, McLanahan, & Brooks-Gunn, 2010). Each additional partnership or dating transition was associated with a higher level of maternal stress and more frequent harsh parenting. Maternal education moderated these associations, with less-educated mothers reacting more negatively to transitions with increases in maternal stress, and more educated mothers providing fewer literacy activities (e.g., reading, singing).

In summary:

- Family structure transitions are associated with increased problems of all types for children, which increase with each subsequent transition.
- Both cohabiting and dating transitions increase maternal stress and harsh parenting with each cumulative transition.

Economic Resources

REDUCED INCOME AS A RISK FACTOR

Most families experience a substantial decline in the income of both maternal and paternal households following separation and divorce, including the amount of economic resources devoted to children (McLanahan & Sandefur, 1994). Some of the differences in child behavioral problems and academic performance between single-mother, cohabiting, and remarried families can be explained by income differences. Twenty-eight percent of single mothers and 11% of single fathers live in poverty, compared to 8% of two-parent families (Grall, 2007). On average, children raised in cohabiting households experience better economic situations than those in single-parent families, but they experience more stressful economic conditions than married families (Manning & Lamb, 2003). Children living with mothers are more likely to have fewer economic resources than those living with fathers and often move to less desirable housing, schools, and neighborhoods. The pathways of economic hardship predicting poorer adjustment of children are increased partner conflict; poorer partner behavioral and emotional functioning; and harsh, inconsistent, and uninvolved parenting (Conger, Conger, & Martin, 2010).

To summarize:

- Decreased economic resources are a particularly important source of stress for single and cohabiting parents.
- Economic hardship increases partner conflict, which in turn leads to poorer parental functioning and more harsh and uninvolved parenting, which predicts poor adjustment for children.

GUIDELINES: CONSIDERATIONS AND CAUTIONS

- The primary objective of this chapter was to familiarize child custody evaluators with important empirical research on the outcomes of separation and divorce for children and adolescents. In particular, the extent of risk for children when parents separate and the major factors associated with increased risk and enhanced resilience for which consensus has emerged are described. Knowledge of the research will assist evaluators in developing more risk-focused procedures and measures, assessing the existence of protective factors available to the children, and preparing more useful reports and recommendations that benefit parents and children.
- Separation and divorce increase the risk for psychological, behavioral, social, and academic problems in children and adolescence, when compared to children in continuously married families. The magnitude of the differences is small, however, and there is considerable overlap between married- and divorced-family children. The majority of children and adolescents whose parents separate are functioning within the average or better range on objective measures and academic tests by 2 to 3 years after divorce. While approximately 12% of children in married families have psychosocial problems, the risk is doubled for children in separated and divorced families. Children raised in single-parent or cohabiting families also have elevated risk compared to married-family children.
- Studies have indicated that some of the psychosocial and academic problems attributed to divorce are evident before the parental separation. Some children are at risk before the separation as a result of their family environment, and this may affect their ability to cope with separation. Intense marital conflict and problematic parenting are the two most important risk factors before separation. When compared to children in low-conflict marriages, children in high-conflict marriages are more likely to have problems of aggression, impulsivity, delinquency, depression, peer

difficulties, and academic achievement. These negative effects are mediated by the quality of parenting, which is less warm and affectionate, more rejecting and erratic, and harsher in discipline, compared to parenting in low-conflict marriages. Intensity of conflict and conflict that focuses on the child are better predictors of child problems than frequency.

- Protective buffers identified to shield children from negative effects of marital conflict include a good, caring relationship with at least one parent or caregiver, parental warmth, parental attempts to resolve the conflict, and positive sibling support.

- Many empirical studies have identified and confirmed the presence of major risk factors following separation and divorce that negatively affect children's outcomes. These factors include parental conflict, psychological adjustment of the parents, quality and type of parenting and parent–child relationships, loss of important relationships, cohabitation and remarriage, family structure transitions, and economic resources.

- Parental separation most often results in increased parent anger and conflict, to which children are variously exposed. Parent conflict and hostile behaviors typically diminish over 2 to 3 years as parents disengage emotionally from their former partners. However, between 8% and 12% of parents remain very hostile and engage in protracted conflict and litigation, more often parents with personality disorders and psychiatric illness. The type of conflict found to be most detrimental to children's adjustment after separation and divorce is when parents use their children to express their anger and disputes. Children placed in the middle of the parental dispute by one or both parents are more likely to be depressed and anxious compared to youngsters whose high-conflict parents did not use their children in this manner. Protective buffers identified that can ameliorate the negative effects of high levels of parent conflict on children include warm, competent parenting; encapsulating the conflict so that children do not see or hear it; refraining from using the children to express hostility to the other parent; and avoiding demeaning comments and attacks on the other parents.

- The adjustment of mothers who are primary caregivers following separation and divorce is one of the best predictors of child and adolescent adjustment in all family structures. Children of all ages who live primarily with mothers with depression, anxiety, personality disorders, and psychiatric illness are more likely in the long term to have increased psychological, social, and academic problems. More psychological symptoms in either parent were associated with more negative changes in parent–child relationships, which in turn contributed to poorer child adjustment. Protective factors include having two parents within the normal range of adjustment involved in children's lives, and living in the custody of a psychologically adequate parent.

- The quality of parenting provided by both parents following separation and divorce is as important as conflict in determining children's outcomes. Effective and involved parenting has been demonstrated to reduce the negative impacts of conflict and divorce on children's adjustment. Specific aspects of mothers' parenting associated with positive adjustment included warmth, authoritative discipline, academic skill encouragement, and monitoring of children's activities and whereabouts. Specific aspects of fathers' parenting linked to positive adjustment included active involvement in their children's lives and school, including emotional support and warmth, authoritative discipline, and monitoring of activities. The combination of father–child shared activities and financial support increased the probability of school success (behavioral and academic) and college attendance.

- The majority of parents settle into a parallel co-parenting style characterized by emotional disengagement, low conflict, low communication, and parenting separately in their own households. While less optimal than cooperative co-parenting, in which parents jointly plan for and coordinate their children's activities, parallel co-parenting can be successful when the parenting in each home is adequate and nurturing. In conflicted co-parenting relationships, parents have high distrust and conflict, poor communication, and low cooperation, and their children are more likely to have adjustment problems.

- Following separation, contact between fathers and their children is substantially reduced, as are opportunities for father involvement. Father–child relationships erode over time with limited amounts of contact. Lower father involvement was associated with more delinquency, aggressive behaviors, depression, and negative feelings about self-worth, compared to children with higher levels of father involvement. There is no evidence that a larger amount of time spent between fathers and children diminishes the closeness or importance of the mother–child relationship. More father involvement and close father–child relationships are protective factors reducing the risk of negative psychological, behavioral, social, and academic outcomes. Overnights are important to maintain closeness and father involvement. In very young children, there was no detriment associated with overnights, and benefits were demonstrated for older preschool children.

- Loss of important relationships is a major risk factor for children, and considerable research documents that the loss of the nonresident parent after separation was viewed by children as the most negative aspect of divorce. From preschool to college age, sadness, pain, distress, depression, and longing for the father have been persistent themes. The majority of children wanted more time and longer contacts with their fathers. A majority of college students reported they would have liked to have equal time or at least a substantial number of overnights with their fathers. Protective factors include maintaining a close relationship with two involved, caring parents, including sufficient time with both parents to sustain nurturance and closeness in parent–child relationships. Shared physical custody arrangements were associated with better emotional and behavioral adjustment, and higher academic achievement, compared to children in more traditional maternal custody arrangements with limited father contacts, and shared custody was beneficial regardless of parent conflict level.

- Remarriage does not decrease risk for children, and cohabitation is associated with more negative outcomes for children, compared to children in remarried families. Good stepfather–child relationships were associated with lowered risk for externalizing or internalizing symptoms, as were good relationships with nonresident fathers.
- Children may experience a substantial number of family structure transitions, and with each additional change in family structure, the risk for behavioral and social problems, delinquency, drug use, and poorer academic achievement increases. Cohabiting and dating transitions increase maternal stress and harsh parenting with each transition.
- Economic hardship is associated with increased partner conflict, poorer partner behavioral and emotional functioning, and harsh and uninvolved parents, which in turn predicts poorer child adjustment.

REFERENCES

Allen, S. M., & Hawkins, A. J. (1999). Maternal gatekeeping: Mothers' beliefs and behaviors that inhibit greater father involvement in family work. *Journal of Marriage & Family, 61*, 199–212. doi:10.2307/353894

Amato, P. (1987). Family processes in one-parent, stepparent and intact families: The child's point of view. *Journal of Marriage and the Family, 49*, 327–337. doi:10.2307/352303

Amato, P. R. (2000). The consequences of divorce for adults and children. *Journal of Marriage and Family, 62*, 1269–1287. doi:10.1111/j.1741–3737.2000.01269.x

Amato, P. R. (2001). Children of divorce in the 1990's: An update of the Amato and Keith (1991) meta-analysis. *Journal of Family Psychology, 15*, 355–370. doi:10.1037/0893–3200.15.3.355 PMid:11584788

Amato, P. R. (2010). Research on divorce: Continuing trends and new developments. *Journal of Marriage and Family, 72*, 650–666. doi:10.1111/j.1741–3737.2010.00723.x

Amato, P. R., & Afifi, T. D. (2006). Feeling caught between parents: Adult children's relations with parents and subjective well-being. *Journal of Marriage and Family, 68*, 222–235. doi:10.1111/j.1741–3737.2006.00243.x

Amato, P. R., & Booth, A. (1996). A prospective study of divorce and parent-child relationships. *Journal of Marriage and the Family, 58*, 356–365. doi:10.2307/353501

Amato, P. R., & Gilbreth, J. (1999). Nonresident fathers and children's well-being: A meta-analysis. *Journal of Marriage and the Family, 61*, 557–573. doi:10.2307/353560

Amato, P. R., Meyers, C., & Emery, R. (2009). Changes in nonresident father contact between 1976 and 2002. *Family Relations, 58*, 41–53. doi:10.1111/j.1741–3729.2008.00533.x

Aquilino, W. S. (1994). Impact of childhood family disruption on young adults' relationships with parents. *Journal of Marriage and the Family, 56*, 295–414. doi:10.2307/353101

Aquilino, W. S. (1996). The life course of children born to unmarried mothers: Childhood living arrangements and young adult outcomes. *Journal of Marriage and the Family, 58*, 293–310. doi:10.2307/353496

Bauserman, R. (2002). Child adjustment in joint-custody versus sole-custody arrangements: A meta-analytic review. *Journal of Family Psychology, 16*, 91–102. doi:10.1037/0893-3200.16.1.91 PMid:11915414

Beck, A. N., Cooper, C. E., McLanahan, S., & Brooks-Gunn, J. (2010). Partnership transitions and maternal parenting. *Journal of Marriage and Family, 72*, 219–233. doi:10.1111/j.1741-3737.2010.00695.x

Belsky, J., Youngblade, L., Rovine, M., & Volling, B. (1991). Patterns of marital change and parent-child interaction. *Journal of Marriage and the Family, 53*, 487–498. doi:10.2307/352914

Berger, L. M., Brown, P. R., Joung, E., Melli, M. S., & Wimer, L. (2008). The stability of child physical placements following divorce: Descriptive evidence from Wisconsin. *Journal of Marriage and Family, 70*, 272–283. doi:10.1111/j.1741-3737.2008.00480.x

Birnbaum, R., & Bala, N. (2010). Toward the differentiation of high-conflict families: An analysis of social science research and Canadian case law. *Family Court Review, 48*, 403–416. doi:10.1111/j.1744-1617.2010.01319.x

Block, J., Block, J., & Gjerde, P. (1986). The personality of children prior to divorce: A prospective study. *Child Development, 57*, 827–840. doi:10.2307/1130360 PMid:3757603

Booth, A., & Amato, P. R. (2001). Parental predivorce relations and offspring postdivorce well- being. *Journal of Marriage & Family, 63*, 197–212. doi:10.1111/j.1741-3737.2001.00197.x

Booth, A., Scott, M. E., & King, V. (2010). Father residence and adolescent problem behavior: Are youth always better off in two-parent families? *Journal of Family Issues, 3*, 585–605. doi:10.1177/0192513X09351507 PMid:20379350

Brown, S. (2004). Family structure and child well-being: The significance of parental cohabitation. *Journal of Marriage and Family, 66*, 351–367. doi:10.1111/j.1741-3737.2004.00025.x

Buchanan, C., Maccoby, E., & Dornbusch, S. (1996). *Adolescents after divorce.* Cambridge, MA: Harvard University Press.

Buehler, C., Krishnakumar, A., Stone, G., Anthony, C., Pemberton, S., Gerard, J., & Barber, B. K. (1998). Interparental conflict styles and youth problem behaviors: A two-sample replication study. *Journal of Marriage and the Family, 60*, 119–132. doi:10.2307/353446

Carlson, M. J. (2006). Family structure, father involvement, and adolescent behavioral outcomes. *Journal of Marriage and Family, 68*, 137–154. doi:10.1111/j.1741-3737.2006.00239.x

Carlson, M. J., & Corcoran, M. E. (2001). Family structure and children's behavioral and cognitive outcomes. *Journal of Marriage and Family, 63*, 779–792. doi:10.1111/j.1741-3737.2001.00779.x

Cashmore, J., Parkinson, P., & Taylor, A. (2008). Overnight stays and children's relationships with resident and nonresident parents after divorce. *Journal of Family Issues, 29*, 707–733. doi:10.1177/0192513X07308042

Casper, L. M., & Bianchi, S. M. (2002). *Continuity and change in the American family.* Thousand Oaks, CA: Sage.

Cavanagh, S. E., & Huston, A. C. (2008). The timing of family instability and children's social development. *Journal of Marriage and Family, 70*, 1258–1269. doi:10.1111/j.1741-3737.2008.00564.x

Caya, M., & Liem, J. (1998). The role of sibling support in high-conflict families. *American Journal of Orthopsychiatry, 68*, 327–333. doi:10.1037/h0080342 PMid:9589771

Chase-Lansdale, P. L., Cherlin, A. J., & Kierman, K. E. (1995). The long-term effects of parental divorce on the mental health of young adults: A developmental perspective. *Child Development, 66*, 1614–1634. doi:10.2307/1131900 PMid:8556889

Cherlin, A., Furstenberg, F., Jr., Lindsay, P., Chase-Lansdale, P., Kiernan, K., & Robins, P. (1991). Longitudinal studies of the effects of divorce on children in Great Britain and the United States. *Science, 252*, 1386–1389. doi:10.1126/science.2047851 PMid:2047851

Clarke-Stewart, A., & Brentano, C. (2006). *Divorce: Causes and consequences.* New Haven, CT: Yale University Press.

Clarke-Stewart, K. A., Vandell, D. L., McCartney, K., Owen, M. T., & Booth, C. (2000). Effects of parental separation and divorce on very young children. *Journal of Family Psychology, 14*, 304–326. doi:10.1037/0893–3200.14.2.304 PMid:10870296

Coley, R. L., & Medeiros, B. L. (2007). Reciprocal longitudinal relations between nonresident father involvement and adolescent delinquency. *Child Development, 78*, 132–147. *doi:10.1111/j.1467–8624.2007.00989.x* PMid:17328697

Conger, R. D., Conger, K. J., & Martin, M. J. (2010). Socioeconomic status, family processes and individual development. *Journal of Marriage and Family, 72*, 685–704. *doi:10.1111/j.1741–3737.2010.00725.x* PMid:20676350

Cummings, E., & Davies, P. (1994). *Children and marital conflict: The impact of family dispute and resolution.* New York: Guilford Press.

Cummings, E. M., Keller, P. S., & Davies, P. T. (2005). Towards a family process model of maternal and paternal depressive symptoms: Exploring multiple relations with child and family functioning. *Journal of Child Psychology and Psychiatry, 46*, 479–489. doi:10.1111/j.1469–7610.2004.00368.x PMid:15845128

Cummings, E. M., Schermerhorn, A. C., Davies, P. T., Goeke-Morey, M. C., & Cummings, J. S. (2006). Interparental discord and child adjustment: Prospective investigations of emotional security as an explanatory mechanism. *Child Development, 77*, 132–152. doi:10.1111/j.1467–8624.2006.00861.x PMid:16460530

Davies, P. T., & Cummings, E. M. (1994). Marital conflict and child adjustment: An emotional security hypothesis. *Psychological Bulletin, 116*, 387–411. doi:10.1037/0033–2909.116.3.387 PMid:7809306

Davies, P. T., Sturge-Apple, M. L., Cicchetti, D., & Cummings, E. M. (2008). Adrenocortical underpinnings of children's psychological reactivity to interparental conflict. *Child Development, 79*, 1693–1706. doi:10.1111/j.1467–8624.2008.01219.x PMid:19037943 PMCid:2597091

Demo, D. H., & Cox, M. J. (2000). Families with young children: A review of research in the 1990's. *Journal of Marriage and Family, 62*, 876–895. doi:10.1111/j.1741–3737.2000.00876.x

Emery, R. (1994). *Renegotiating family relationships: Divorce, child custody, and mediation.* New York: Guilford Press.

Emery, R. (1999). *Marriage, divorce, and children's adjustment* (2nd ed.). Thousand Oaks, CA: Sage.

Emery, R. (2004). *The truth about children and divorce: Dealing with emotions so you and your children can thrive.* New York: Viking/Penguin.

Emery, R. E., Waldron, M., Kitzmann, K. M., & Aaron, J. (1999). Delinquent behavior, future divorce or nonmarital childrearing, and externalizing behavior among offspring: A 14-year prospective study. *Journal of Family Psychology, 13,* 568–579. doi:10.1037/0893–3200.13.4.568

Fabricius, W. V., Braver, S. L., Diaz, P., & Velez, C. E. (2010). Custody and parenting time: Links to family relationships and well-being after divorce. In M. E. Lamb (Ed.), *The role of the father in child development* (5th ed). (pp. 201–240). New York: Wiley & Sons.

Fabricius, W. V., & Hall, J. (2000). Young adults' perspectives on divorce: Living arrangements. *Family & Conciliation Courts Review, 38,* 446–461. doi:10.1111/j.174–1617.2000.tb00584.x

Fabricius, W. V., & Luecken, L. J. (2007). Post-divorce living arrangements, parent conflict, and long-term physical health correlates for children of divorce. *Journal of Family Psychology, 21,* 195–205. doi:10.1037/0893–3200.21.2.195 PMid:17605542

Fabricius, W. V., Sokol, K. R., Diaz, P., & Braver, S. L. (2012). Parenting time, parent conflict, parent-child relationships, and children's physical health. In K. Kuehnle & L. Drozd (Eds.), *Parenting plan evaluations: Applied research for the family court.* New York: Oxford University Press.

Finley, G. E., & Schwartz, S. J. (2010). The divided world of the child: Divorce and long-term psychosocial adjustment. *Family Court Review, 48,* 516–527. doi:10.1111/j.1744–1617.2010.01326.x

Fosco, G. J., & Grych, J. H. (2010). Adolescent triangulation into parental conflicts: Longitudinal implications for appraisals and adolescent-parent relations. *Journal of Marriage and Family, 72,* 254–267. doi:10.1111/j.1741–3737.2010.00697.x

Friedman, M. (2004). The so-called high-conflict couple: A closer look. *American Journal of Family Therapy, 32,* 101–117.doi:10.1080/01926180490424217

Furstenberg, F., Morgan, S., & Allison, P. (1987). Paternal participation and children's well- being after marital dissolution. *American Sociological Review, 52,* 695–701. doi:10.2307/2095604

Ganong, L., Coleman, M., & McCaulley, G. (2012). Gatekeeping after separation and divorce. In K. Kuehnle & L. Drozd (Eds.), *Parenting plan evaluations: Applied research for the family court.* New York: Oxford University Press.

Gonzales, N. A., Pitts, S. C., Hill, N. E., & Roosa, M. W. (2000). A mediational model of the impact of interparental conflict on child adjustment in a multiethnic, low-income sample. *Journal of Family Psychology, 14,* 365–379. doi:10.1037/0893–3200.14.3.365 PMid:11025930

Goodman, M., Bonds, D., Sandler, I., & Braver, S. (2004). Parent psychoeducational programs and reducing the negative effects of interparental conflict following divorce. *Family Court Review, 42,* 263–279. doi:10.1177/1531244504422007 doi:10.1111/j.174–1617.2004.tb00648.x

Grall, T. S. (2007). *Custodial mothers and fathers and their child support: 2005.* Washington, DC: U.S. Bureau of the Census.

Graham-Bermann, S. A., Cutler, S. E., Litzenberger, B. W. & Schwartz, W. E. (1994). Perceived conflict and violence in childhood and violence in childhood sibling relationships and later emotional adjustment. *Journal of Family Psychology, 8,* 85–97. doi:10.1037/0893–3200.8.1.85

Grych, J. H. (2005). Interparental conflict as a risk factor for child maladjustment: Implications for the development of prevention programs. *Family Court Review, 43,* 97–108. doi:10.1111/j.1744–1617.2005.00010.x

Haine, R. A., Sandler, I. N., Wolchik, S. A., Tein, J.-U., & Dawson-McClure, S. R. (2003). Changing the legacy of divorce: Evidence from prevention programs and future directions. *Family Relations, 52,* 397–405. doi:10.1111/j.1741-3729.2003. 00397.x

Hardesty, J. L., Haselschwerdt, M. L., & Johnson, M. P. (2012). Domestic violence and child custody. In K. Kuehnle & L. Drozd (Eds.), *Parenting plan evaluations: Applied research for the family court.* New York: Oxford University Press.

Harrist, A., & Ainslie, R. (1998). Parental discord and child behavior problems. *Journal of Family Issues, 19,* 140–163. doi:10.1177/019251398019002002

Hetherington, E. M. (1999). Should we stay together for the sake of the children? In E. M. Hetherington (Ed.), *Coping with divorce, single parenting, and remarriage* (pp. 93–116). Mahwah, NJ: Erlbaum.

Hetherington, E. M. (2006). The influence of conflict, marital problem solving and parenting on children's adjustment in nondivorced, divorced, and remarried families. In A. Clarke-Stewart & J. Dunn (Eds.), *Families count: Effect on child and adolescent development* (pp. 203–237). New York: Cambridge University Press.

Hetherington, E. M., & Kelly, J. (2002). *For better or for worse.* New York: Norton.

Insabella, G. M., Williams, T., & Pruett, M. K. (2003). Individual and coparenting differences between divorcing and unmarried fathers: Implications for Family Court Services. *Family Court Review, 41,* 290–306. doi:10.1177/1531244503041003003 doi:10.1111/j.174-1617.2003.tb00892.x

Jenkins, J. M. & Smith, M. A. (1990). Factors protecting children in disharmonious homes. *Journal of the American Academy of Child and Adolescent Psychiatry, 29,* 60–69. doi:10.1097/00004583-199001000-00011

Johnston, J. R., Kuehnle, K., & Roseby, V. (2008). *In the name of the child: a developmental approach to understanding and helping children of conflict and violent divorce* (2nd ed.). New York: Free Press.

Jouriles, E., McDonald, R., Norwood, W., Ware, H., Speller, L., & Swank, P. (1998). Knives, guns, and interparent violence: Relations with child behavior problems. *Journal of Family Psychology, 12,* 178–194. doi:10.1037/0893-3200.12.2.178

Kaczynski, K. J., Lindahl, K. M., Malik, N. M., & Laurenceau, J.-P. (2006). Marital conflict, maternal and paternal parenting, and child adjustment: A test of mediation and moderation. *Journal of Family Psychology, 20,* 199–208. doi:10.1037/0893-3200.20.2.199 PMid:16756395

Keitner, G. I., & Miller, I. W. (1990). Family functioning and major depression: An overview. *American Journal of Psychiatry, 147,* 1128–1137. PMid:2201221

Kelly, J. B. (1982). Divorce: The adult experience. In B. Wolman & G. Stricker (Eds.), *Handbook of developmental psychology* (pp. 734–750). Englewood Cliffs, NJ: Prentice-Hall.

Kelly, J. B. (1994). The determination of child custody. *The Future of Children: Children and Divorce, 4,* 121–142.

Kelly, J. B. (2000). Children's adjustment in conflicted marriage and divorce: A decade review of research. *Journal of Child and Adolescent Psychiatry, 39,* 963–973. doi:10.1097/00004583-200008000-00007

Kelly, J. B. (2002). Psychological and legal interventions for parents and children in custody and access disputes: Current research and practice. *Virginia Journal of Social Policy and Law, 10,* 129–163.

Kelly, J. B. (2003). Parents with enduring child disputes: Multiple pathways to enduring disputes. *Journal of Family Studies, 9,* 37–50. doi:10.5172/jfs.9.1.37

Kelly, J. B. (2004). Family mediation research: Is there support for the field? *Conflict Resolution Quarterly, 22,* 3–35. doi:10.1002/crq.90

Kelly, J. B. (2005). Developing beneficial parenting plan models for children following separation and divorce. *Journal of American Academy of Matrimonial Lawyers, 19,* 237–254.

Kelly, J. B. (2007). Children's living arrangements following separation and divorce: Insights from empirical and clinical research. *Family Process, 46,* 35–52. doi:10.1111/j.1545–5300.2006.00190.x PMid:17375727

Kelly, J. B., & Emery, R. E. (2003). Children's adjustment following divorce: Risk and resilience perspectives. *Family Relations, 52,* 352–362. doi:10.1111/j.1741–3729.2003.00352.x

Kelly, J. B., & Johnson, M. P. (2008). Differentiation among types of intimate partner violence: Research update and implications for interventions. *Family Court Review, 46,* 476–499. doi:10.1111/j.1744–1617.2008.00215.x

Kelly, J. B., & Johnston, J. R. (2001). The alienated child: A reformulation of parental alienation syndrome. *Family Courts Review, 39,* 249–266. doi:10.1111/j.174–1617.2001.tb00609.x

Kelly, J. B., & Lamb, M.E. (2000). Using child development research to make appropriate custody and access decisions. *Family & Conciliation Courts Review, 38,* 297–311. doi:10.1111/j.174–1617.2000.tb00577.x

King, V. (2002). Parental divorce and interpersonal trust in adult offspring. *Journal of Marriage and Family, 64,* 642–656. doi:10.1111/j.1741–3737.2002.00642.x

King, V. (2007). When children have two mothers: Relationships with nonresident mothers, stepmothers, and fathers. *Journal of Marriage and Family, 69,* 1178–1193. doi:10.1111/j.1741–3737.2007.00440.x

King, V. (2009). Stepfamily formation: Implications for adolescent ties to mothers, nonresident fathers, and stepfathers. *Journal of Marriage and Family, 71,* 954–968. doi:10.1111/j.1741–3737.2009.00646.x PMid:20161429 PMCid:2786204

King, V., Harris, K. M., & Heard, H. E. (2004). Racial and ethnic diversity in nonresident father involvement. *Journal of Marriage and Family, 66,* 1–21.

King, V., & Heard, H. E. (1999). Nonresident fathers' visitation, parental conflict, and mother's satisfaction: What's best for child well-being? *Journal of Marriage and Family, 61,* 385–396. doi:10.2307/353756

King, V., & Sobolewski, J. M. (2006). Nonresident fathers' contributions to adolescent well-being. *Journal of Marriage and Family, 68,* 537–557. *doi:10.1111/j.1741–3737.2006.00274.x PMid:18270550 PMCid:2239255*

Kline, M., Johnston, J. R., & Tschann, J. (1991). The long shadow of marital conflict: A model of children's postdivorce adjustment. *Journal of Marriage and the Family, 53,* 297–309. doi:10.2307/352900

Krishnakamur, A., & Buehler, C. (2000). Interparental conflict and parenting behaviors: A meta-analytic review. *Family Relations, 49,* 25–44. doi:10.1111/j.1741–3729.2000.00025.x

Lamb, M. E. (Ed). (1976). *The role of the father in child development.* New York: Wiley.

Lamb, M. E. (2012). Critical analysis of research on parenting plans and children's well-being. In K. Kuehnle & L. Drozd (Eds.), *Parenting plan evaluations: Applied research for the family court.* New York: Oxford University Press.

Lamb, M. E., & Kelly, J. B. (2009). Improving the quality of parent-child contact in separating families with infants and young children: Empirical research foundations.

In R. M. Galazter- Levy, J. Kraus, & J. Galatzer-Levy (Eds.), *The scientific basis of child custody decisions* (pp. 187–214). Hoboken, NJ: Wiley.

Lansford, J. E. (2009). Parental divorce and children's adjustment. *Perspectives on Psychological Science, 4,* 140–152. doi:10.1111/j.1745-6924.2009.01114.x

Lansford, J. E., Malone, P. S., Castellino, D. R., Dodge, K. A., Pettit, G. S., & Bates, J. E. (2006). Trajectories of internalizing, externalizing, and grades for children who have and have not experienced their parents' divorce. *Journal of Family Psychology, 20,* 292–301. doi:10.1037/0893-3200.20.2.292 PMid:16756405 PMCid:2750031

Laumann-Billings, L., & Emery, RE. (2000). Distress among young adults in divorced families. *Journal of Family Psychology, 14,* 671–687. doi:10.1037/0893-3200.14.4.671 PMid:11132488

Lee, M-Y. (2002). A model of children's postdivorce behavioral adjustment in maternal and dual-residence arrangements. *Journal of Family Issues, 23,* 672–697. doi:10.1177/0192513X02023005005

Maccoby, E., & Mnookin, R. (1992). *Dividing the child.* Cambridge, MA: Harvard University Press.

Magnuson, K., & Berger, L. M. (2009). Family structure states and transitions: Associations with children's well-being during middle childhood. *Journal of Marriage and Family, 71,* 575–591. doi:10.1111/j.1741-3737.2009.00620.x PMid:20228952 PMCid:2836533

Manning, W. D., & Lamb, K. A. (2003). Adolescent well-being in cohabiting, married, and single-parent families. *Journal of Marriage and Family, 65,* 876–893. doi:10.1111/j.1741-3737.2003.00876.x

McIntosh, J., & Smyth, B. (2012). Shared-time parenting: An evidenced based matrix for evaluating risk. In K. Kuehnle & L. Drozd (Eds.), *Parenting plan evaluations: Applied research for the family court.* New York: Oxford University Press.

McLanahan, S. S. (1999). Father absence and children's welfare. In E. M. Hetherington (Ed.), *Coping with divorce, single parenting, and remarriage: A risk and resiliency perspective* (pp. 117–146). Mahway, NJ: Erlbaum.

McLanahan, S., & Sandefur, G. (1994). *Growing up with a single parent.* Cambridge, MA: Harvard University Press.

McMahon, T. J. & Giannini, F. D. (2003). Substance-abusing fathers in family court: Moving from popular stereotypes to therapeutic jurisprudence. *Family Court Review, 41,* 337–353. doi:10.1177/1531244503041003006 doi:10.1111/j.174-1617.2003.tb00895.x

McNeal, C., & Amato, P. (1998). Parents' marital violence: Long-term consequences for children. *Journal of Family Issues, 19,* 123–139. doi:10.1177/019251398019002001

Meadows, W. O., McLanahan, S. S., & Brooks-Gunn, J. (2007). Parental depression and anxiety and early childhood behavior problems across family types. *Journal of Marriage and Family, 69,* 1162–1178. doi:10.1111/j.1741-3737.2007.00439.x

Menning, C. L. (2002). Absent parents are more than money: The joint effects of activities and financial support on youths' educational attainment. *Journal of Family Issues, 23,* 648–671. doi:10.1177/0192513X02023005004

Menning, C. L. (2006). Nonresident fathering and school failure. *Journal of Family Issues, 27,* 1356–1382. doi:10.1177/0192513X06290038

Mezulis, A., Hyde, J., & Blark, R. (2004). Father involvement moderates the effect of maternal depression during a child's infancy on child behavior problems in kindergarten. *Journal of Family Psychology, 18,* 575–588. doi:10.1037/0893-3200.18.4.575 PMid:15598163

Neighbors, B., Forehand, R., & McVicar, D. (1993). Resilient adolescents and inter-parental conflict. *American Journal of Orthopsychiatry, 63,* 462–471. doi:10.1037/h0079442 PMid:8372913

Osborne, C., & McLanahan, S. (2007). Partnership instability and child well-being. *Journal of Marriage and Family, 69,* 1065–1083. doi:10.1111/j.1741–3737.2007.00431.x

Parkinson, P. (2011). *Family law and the indissolubility of parenthood.* New York: Cambridge University Press.

Parkinson, P., Cashmore, J., & Single, J. (2005). Adolescents' views on the fairness of parenting and financial arrangements after separation. *Family Court Review, 43,* 429–444. doi:10.1111/j.1744–1617.2005.00044.x

Pong, S.-L., & Ju, D.-B. (2000). The effects of change in family structure and income on dropping out of middle and high school. *Journal of Family Issues, 21,* 147–169. doi:10.1177/019251300021002001

Potter, D. (2010). Psychosocial well-being and the relationship between divorce and children's academic achievement. *Journal of Marriage and Family, 72,* 933–946. doi:10.1111/j.1741–3737.2010.00740.x

Pruett, M., Cowan, P., Cowan, C., & Diamond, J. (2012). Supporting father involve-ment in the context of separation and divorce. In K. Kuehnle & L. Drozd (Eds.), *Parenting plan evaluations: Applied research for the family court.* New York: Oxford University Press.

Pruett, M. K., Ebling, R., & Insabella, G. (2004). Critical aspects of parenting plans for young children. *Family Court Review, 42,* 39–59. doi:10.1177/1531244504421004 doi:10.1111/j.174–1617.2004.tb00632.x

Pruett, M. K., Williams, T. Y., Insabella, G., & Little, T. D. (2003). Family and legal indicators of child adjustment to divorce among families with young children. *Journal of Family Psychology, 17,* 169–180. doi:10.1037/0893–3200.17.2.169 PMid:12828014

Rabin, R. C. (2011, Jan. 25). Sons of divorce fare worse than daughters. *The New York Times.* Retreived from http://well.blogs.nytimes.com/2011/01/25/sons-of-divorce-fare-worse-than-daughters/?pagemode=print

Sandler, I., Miles, J., Cookston, J., & Braver, S. (2008). Effects of father and mother parenting on children's mental health in high- and low-conflict divorces. *Family Court Review, 46,* 282–296. doi:10.1111/j.1744–1617.2008.00201.x

Sandler, I., Wolchik, S., Winslow, E., Mahrer, N., Moran, J., & Weinstock, D. (2012). Quality of maternal and paternal parenting following separation and divorce. In K. Kuehnle & L. Drozd (Eds.), *Parenting plan evaluations: Applied research for the family court.* New York: Oxford University Press.

Schwartz, S. J., & Finley, G. E. (2009). Mothering, fathering, and divorce: The influ-ence of divorce on reports of and desires for maternal and paternal involvement. *Family Court Review, 47,* 506–522. doi:10.1111/j.1744–1617.2009.01270.x

Seltzer, J. (1991). Relationships between fathers and children who live apart: The father's role after separation. *Journal of Marriage and the Family, 53,* 79–101.doi:10.2307/353135

Scott, M. E., Booth, A., King, V., & Johnson, D. R. (2007). Postdivorce father-ado-lescent closeness. *Journal of Marriage and Family, 69,* 1194–1211. doi:10.1111/j.1741–3737.2007.00441.x

Simons, R. L., et al. (1996). *Understanding differences between divorced and intact families: Stress, interaction, and child outcomes.* Thousand Oaks, CA: Sage.

Smith, A. B., & Gollop, M. M. (2001). What children think separating parents should know. *New Zealand Journal of Psychology, 30,* 23–31.

Smyth, B. M. (2004). Parent-child contact schedules after divorce. *Family Matters, 69,* 32–43.

Stocker, C. M., & Youngblade, L. (1999). Marital conflict and parental hostility: Links with children's sibling and peer relationships. *Journal of Family Psychology, 13,* 598–609. doi:10.1037/0893-3200.13.4.598

Sturge-Apple, M. L., Davies, P. T., & Cummings, E. M. (2006). Hostility and withdrawal in marital conflict: Effects on parental emotional unavailability and inconsistent discipline. *Journal of Family Psychology, 20,* 227–238. doi:10.1037/0893-3200.20.2.227 PMid:16756398

Sun, Y. (2001). Family environment and adolescents' well-being before and after parents' marital disruption: A longitudinal analysis. *Journal of Marriage and Family, 63,* 697–713. doi:10.1111/j.1741-3737.2001.00697.x

Sun, Y., & Li, Y. (2001). Marital disruption, parental investment, and children's academic achievement. *Journal of Family Issues, 22,* 27–62. doi:10.1177/019251301022001002

Sun, Y., & Li, Y. (2009). Postdivorce family stability and changes in adolescents' academic performance: A growth-curve model. *Journal of Family Issues, 39,* 1527–1555.

Teachman, J. D. (2008). The living arrangements of children and their educational well-being. *Journal of Family Issues, 29,* 734–761. doi:10.1177/0192513X07309742

Thompson, R. (1999). Early sociopersonality development. In W. Damon (ed.), *Handbook of child development (5th Ed.), Vol. 3. Social, emotional, and personality development* (pp. 25–104). New York: Wiley.

Trinder, L. (2008). Maternal gate closing and gate opening in postdivorce families. *Journal of Family Issues, 29,* 1298–1324.doi:10.1177/0192513X08315362

Turner, H. A., & Kopiec, K. (2006). Exposure to interparental conflict and psychological disorder among young adults. *Journal of Family Issues, 27,* 131–158. doi:10.1177/0192513X05280991

Turney, K. (2011). Chronic and proximate depression among mothers: Implications for child well-being. *Journal of Marriage and Family, 73,* 149–163. doi:10.1111/j.1741-3737.2010.00795.x

Vandewater, E., & Lansford, J. (1998). Influences of family structure and parental conflict on children's well-being. *Family Relations, 47,* 323–330. doi:10.2307/585263

Videon, T. M. (2002). The effects of parent-adolescent relationships and parental separation on adolescent well-being. *Journal of Marriage and Family, 64,* 489–503. doi:10.1111/j.1741-3737.2002.00489.x

Videon, T. M. (2005). Parent-child relations and children's psychological well-being: Do dads matter? *Journal of Family Issues, 26,* 55–78. doi:10.1177/0192513X04270262

Wallerstein, J. S., & Kelly, J. B. (1980). *Surviving the breakup: How children and parents cope with divorce.* New York: Basic Books.

Whisman, M. A. (2001). The association between depression and marital dissatisfaction. In S. R. H. Beach (Ed.), *Marital and family processes in depression: A scientific foundation for clinical practice* (pp. 3–24). Washington, DC: American Psychological Association. doi:10.1037/10350-001

White, L., & Gilbreth, J. G. (2001). When children have two fathers: Effects of relationships with stepfathers and noncustodial fathers on adolescent outcomes. *Journal of Marriage and Family, 63,* 155–167. doi:10.1111/j.1741-3737.2001.00155.x

Woodward, L., Fergusson, D. M., & Belsky, J. (2000). Timing of parental separation and attachment to parents in adolescence: Results of a prospective study from birth to age 16. *Journal of Marriage & Family, 62*, 162–174. doi:10.1111/j.1741–3737.2000.00162.x

Zill, N., Morrison, D., & Coiro, M. (1993). Long-term effects of parental divorce on parent-child relationships, adjustment, and achievement in young adulthood. *Journal of Family Psychology, 7*, 91–103. doi:10.1037/0893–3200.7.1.91

Quality of Maternal and Paternal Parenting Following Separation and Divorce

IRWIN SANDLER, SHARLENE WOLCHIK,
EMILY B. WINSLOW, NICOLE E. MAHRER,
JOHN A. MORAN, AND DAVID WEINSTOCK ■

INTRODUCTION

The importance of quality of parenting following separation and divorce has been recognized by statutes and professional practice guidelines for family evaluators (e.g., American Psychological Association, 2002, 2010; Association of Family and Conciliation Courts, 2007; Uniform Marriage and Divorce Act, 1979). This chapter addresses four questions that are critical to the scientific base for evaluations of the quality of parenting following separation and divorce. First, how is quality of parenting by the mother and father conceptualized and measured? Second, what factors influence quality of parenting by the mother and father? Third, what are the strengths and weaknesses of the studies linking quality of parenting by the mother and father to children's post-divorce adjustment? Fourth, is quality of parenting changeable by intervention programs, and if it is changeable, what impact do improvements in quality of parenting have on children's post-divorce adjustment?

The chapter is organized into three major sections. The first two sections review the research that addresses these four questions separately for the mothers and fathers. The sections on quality of parenting following separation or divorce by mothers and fathers differ somewhat. The research on mother's parenting includes more experimental studies than the research on father's parenting, and less attention is given to reviewing the findings of non-experimental research, and additional focus is given to an exciting group of experimental studies that have demonstrated that quality of maternal post-divorce parenting, and consequently child outcomes, can be changed by preventive interventions. The section on paternal parenting[1] focuses on how quality of parenting is conceptualized and measured for fathers, factors that are associated with quality of paternal parenting, and empirical evidence concerning the relations between quality of paternal parenting and children's adjustment following separation or divorce. The third section presents guidelines, considerations, and cautions for the application of the findings from the review to parenting plan evaluations. Two tables are presented for more detailed explication of the major empirical studies reviewed. Table 4.1 presents detailed descriptions of the empirical studies concerning the relations between quality of maternal and paternal parenting, including a description of the methodological strengths and limitations of these studies. Table 4.2 presents detailed information on the measures used in the research literature.

Methodological Issues in Evaluating Research Evidence

The major methodological issues concern sampling, measurement, and design of the study. Studies are conducted on samples of the population of interest, and different sampling frames allow inferences to different populations. No sampling plan allows

Table 4.1 STUDIES OF THE RELATIONS OF QUALITY OF MATERNAL AND PATERNAL PARENTING WITH CHILD ADJUSTMENT

Source	Participants	Design Procedure
Mother Parenting		
Simons, Whitbeck, Beaman, & Conger, 1994	207 separated mothers and their 14-year-old children	Longitudinal design Participants were recruited from a cohort of eighth- and ninth-grade students whose parents had separated within past 2 years. Data were collected annually over three waves of assessment.
Wolchik et al., 1993	70 divorced mothers and their children age 8–15 All children lived primarily with their mothers	Randomized controlled trial Participants recruited through records of divorces over past 24 months Participants assigned to intervention or wait-list control

inference to all populations of potential interest. For example, random probability samples of the nation's families allow inference to the general population, but may be limited in the inferences to be made to specific subpopulations, such as same-sex–parent families or specific ethnic minority groups. Quantitative studies require the use of reliable and valid measures of all constructs. However, even reliable measures have potential biases. For example, different reporters (mothers, fathers, and children) perceive constructs such as parenting or child adjustment from their own perspective, and no single perspective represents absolute truth. Study designs vary in the times of data collection and the approaches used to account for the effects of variables that might affect outcomes of interest. Each design offers different information regarding the link between parenting and children's outcomes. For example, relative to cross-sectional designs in which the variables of interest are measured at the same time, prospective longitudinal designs, in which the predictor (e.g., quality of parenting) is measured before the outcome (e.g., child mental health), strengthen

Measures of Parenting	Analysis and Results	Strengths/Weaknesses
Multi-method assessments included observations of mother–adolescent interactions and mother and adolescent reports. Four dimensions of effective discipline were measured: monitoring, consistency of discipline, harsh discipline, and standards for behavior ($\alpha > 0.80$). Dimensions were summed to assess overall quality of parenting ($\alpha = .70$).	Correlational and regression analyses were used to assess the relations between mother's parenting and adolescent internalizing and externalizing problems. Quality of parenting was negatively associated with externalizing problems for both genders and internalizing problems for boys. Adolescent externalizing problems at the initial assessment were negatively related to mother's parenting 1 year later. Relations between internalizing and externalizing problems at second assessment and mother's parenting 1 year later were non-significant.	*Strengths:* Multi-method and multiple report measures; multiple assessments over time *Weaknesses:* Narrow age range
Mother–child relationship measured using mother and child report on: Parent–Adolescent Communication Scale Open Family Communication Subscale ($\alpha = .86$), Family Routines Inventory ($\alpha = 0.76$), and Child Report of Parenting Behavior Inventory (CRPBI) Acceptance and Rejection subscales ($\alpha = 0.88$). Discipline measured using mother and child report on CRPBI Inconsistency Subscale ($\alpha = 0.68$).	Intervention effects tested using ANCOVA Youths in intervention had fewer behavior problems. Program led to improvements in acceptance and positive communication, positive family routines, and effective discipline. For some outcomes, program effects were stronger for those with poorest initial functioning. Improvement in mother–child relationship quality accounted for reductions in children's behavior problems.	*Strengths:* Experimental design used; sample drawn from divorce records; tested several potential mediators of intervention effects *Weaknesses:* Measures exclusively self-report; small sample size; no follow-up

(Continued)

Table 4.1 Studies of the Relations of Quality of Maternal and Paternal Parenting with Child Adjustment (*Continued*)

Source	Participants	Design Procedure
Wolchik et al., 2000; Wolchik et al., 2002; Wolchik, Sandler, Weiss, & Winslow, 2007; Tein, Sandler, MacKinnon, & Wolchik, 2004; Dawson-McClure, Sandler, Wolchik, Millsap, 2004	240 divorced mothers and their children ages 9–12 All children lived primarily with their mothers.	Randomized controlled trial Participants recruited through records of divorces over past 24 months Participants were randomly assigned to mother program (MP), mother and child program (MPCP), or literature control (LC). Data were collected over six waves of assessment (pre- and post-test; 3-month, 6-month, 6-year, and 15- year follow-ups).
Forgatch & DeGarmo, 1999; Martinez & Forgatch, 2001; DeGarmo, Patterson, & Forgatch, 2004; Forgatch, Patterson, Degarmo, & Beldavs, 2009	238 separated mothers and their sons ages 6–10	Randomized, experimental design Participants were recruited through media and court records of mothers separated in past 3–24 months. Participants were assigned to experimental or control group. Data were collected at nine assessments (baseline, 6 month, 1-year, 1.5-year, 2.5-year, 6-year, 7-year, 8-year. and 9-year follow-ups).

Measures of Parenting	Analysis and Results	Strengths/Weaknesses
Mother–child relationship quality was measured with a composite of measures of acceptance and communication (mother/child-report [α range 0.71–0.86] and observational measures [Kappa range 0.76–0.95]). Effective discipline was measured using child and mother reports on CRPBI Inconsistency Subscale (α = 0.74 and 0.82).	Intervention effects were tested using ANCOVA for continuous variables and logistic regression for dichotomous variables. Mediation analyses were conducted using structural equation modeling. Program effects occurred for the MP vs. LC mother–child relationship quality, effective discipline, internalizing problems, and externalizing problems. Stronger program effects occurred for those who entered the program with poorer functioning. Program effects to reduce externalizing in the MP group at post-test were mediated through improvements in discipline and mother–child relationship quality. 6-year follow-up data showed significant program effects on mental disorder in the past year, externalizing problems, internalizing problems, symptoms of mental disorder, competence, grade-point average, number of sexual partners, alcohol use, marijuana use, and other drug use. For several outcomes, stronger program effects occurred for those who entered the program with poorer functioning. Mediational analyses indicated that improvements in mother–child relationship quality at post-test accounted for improvements in internalizing problems, externalizing problems, and symptoms of mental disorder for youths who entered the program at high levels of risk. Improvements in effective discipline at post-test accounted for the program effects on grade-point average.	*Strengths*: Design was experimental; sample was drawn from divorce records; multi-method, multi-reporter measurement was used; follow-up data collected over a 15-year period; sophisticated statistical analyses. *Weaknesses*: Sample nearly exclusively NHW; restricted age range
Multi-method assessments included structured interviews with mothers and children; observations of mother–child interactions; and mother, child, and teacher reports. Seven domains of parenting practices were obtained from the structured interaction task (effective parenting, positive involvement, skill encouragement, problem-solving, monitoring, negative reinforcement, and inept discipline; α range 0.55–0.93).	Structural equation modeling was used to test effects of the intervention on mother and child outcomes. Improvements in positive parenting and coercive discipline were seen in the intervention group but not the control group. Intervention effects on noncompliance, internalizing problems. and externalizing problems at the 2.5-year follow-up were mediated by change in positive parenting and coercive discipline. Improvement in parenting accounted for reductions in delinquent behaviors at the 9-year follow-up.	*Strengths*: Experimental design; multi-method and multiple reporter measures; follow-up data collected over a 9-year period; sophisticated statistical analyses *Weaknesses*: Sample nearly exclusively NHW; age- and gender-restricted sample

(Continued)

Source	Participants	Design Procedure
Father Parenting		
Amato & Gilbreth, 1999	63 studies about nonresident fathers and children's well-being	Meta-analysis
Simons, Whitbeck, Beaman, & Conger, 1994	207 separated mothers and their 14-year-old children	Longitudinal design Participants were recruited from cohort of eighth- and ninth-grade students whose parents had separated within past 2 years. Data were collected annually over three waves of assessment.
King & Sobolewski, 2006	453 adolescents living with mothers and had fathers living elsewhere	Cross-sectional design Participants from the National Survey of Families and Households

Measures of Parenting	Analysis and Results	Strengths/Weaknesses
Studies assessed child support, frequency of contact, feeling close, and authoritative parenting (e.g.,supportiveness, control).	Meta-analytic methods were used (to assess the relations between children's academic success, internalizing and externalizing problems, and four aspects of father involvement). Payment of child support was related to higher academic success and lower externalizing problems. Frequency of contact was generally not significantly related to child well-being. In more recent studies versus older studies, there was a stronger relation between contact and child well-being. Feelings of closeness and authoritative parenting were significantly related to better academic success, lower externalizing and internalizing problems.	*Strengths*: Meta-analysis; considered methodological limitations of individual studies; examined secular trends over time
Quality of parenting was assessed via mother and adolescent report ($\alpha = 0.90$ for adolescents, $\alpha = 0.86$ for mothers). Contact with father was measured using adolescent report.	Correlational and regression analyses were used to assess the relations between father's parenting and adolescent internalizing and externalizing problems. Quality of father's parenting was negatively associated with externalizing problems. Adolescent externalizing problems at initial assessment were negatively related to parenting 1 year later. Externalizing problems were negatively related to father's parenting for boys. Relations between internalizing and externalizing at second assessment and parenting 1 year later were not significant.	*Strengths*: Multi-method and multiple report measures; multiple assessments *Weaknesses*: Non-experimental design; restricted age range
Adolescents reported frequency of contact ($\alpha = 0.85$), father–child relationship quality ($\alpha = 0.86$), and father responsiveness ($\alpha = 0.77$).	Structural equation modeling was used to test the relations between adolescent child well-being and paternal parenting. Positive father–child relationship and father responsiveness were related to lower adolescent internalizing and externalizing problems, but these relations were reduced in magnitude when mother–child relationship was added as a predictor. Contact with father had an indirect relation with adolescent behavior problems through its relation with father responsiveness. Adolescents who did not have a positive relationship with either parent had the most behavior problems.	*Strengths*: Nationally representative sample; sophisticated statistical methods *Weaknesses*: Cross-sectional design; single-reporter measures

(Continued)

Source	Participants	Design Procedure

Menning, 2006	2,983 youths in grades 7–12	Longitudinal design
		    Participants from the National Longitudinal Study of Adolescent Health
		        Data collected from two waves of assessment across 2 years

Stewart, 2003	1,469 adolescents living with biological mothers, but not biological fathers, and currently enrolled in school	Cross-sectional design Participants from National Longitudinal Study of Adolescent Health
Sandler et al., 2008	182 divorcing families with a child between 4 and 12 years	Cross-sectional design Participants from Dads for Life intervention

Measures of Parenting	Analysis and Results	Strengths/Weaknesses
	Adolescents with a positive relationship with only the father had fewer behavior problems than those who had a poor relationship with both parents (marginal effect).	
Mothers reported on child support. Father involvement was assessed by a composite measure of communication, overnight stays, activities, and closeness measured via child report (Wave 1: $\alpha = 0.86$, Wave 2: $\alpha = 0.82$).	Logistic regression was used to examine the relation between father involvement and child school failure. Father involvement and increases in father involvement over time were associated with lower probability of school failure. Involvement related to school contributed to this effect. No involvement was related to lower overall risk of school failure compared to low or moderate involvement.	*Strengths*: Longitudinal design; nationally representative sample; examined specific types of involvement *Weaknesses*: Single-reporter measures of father involvement
Relationship quality with father was measured using adolescent report of father involvement and closeness.	Multiple regression was used to examine the relation between father involvement and adolescent well-being. Adolescent closeness to the father predicted lower emotional distress. Talking about things at school was related to lower emotional distress, higher grade-point average, and lower emotional distress.	*Strengths*: Nationally representative sample of youth; examined specific types of involvement *Weaknesses*: Cross-sectional design; single-reporter measures
Mother, father, and child report of interparental conflict was measured with the Children's Perception of Interparental Conflict Scale (mother: $\alpha = 0.90$, father: $\alpha = 0.89$, child: $\alpha = 0.88$) and mother and father report on the Braver Conflict Breadth Scale (mother: $\alpha = 0.79$, father: $\alpha = 0.82$). Father and mother warmth (acceptance and rejection subscales) were assessed using child report on the CRBPI (mother acceptance, rejection: $\alpha = 0.82, 0.80$, father acceptance, rejection: $\alpha = 0.92, 0.86$).	Hierarchical regression analyses were conducted to assess the effects of mother warmth, father warmth, and interparental conflict on children's internalizing and externalizing problems. Father and mother warmth were significantly related to lower child externalizing problems. A significant three-way maternal warmth × paternal warmth × interparental conflict interaction showed that the effects of maternal warmth and paternal warmth on internalizing problems differed as a function of the level of interparental conflict. When interparental conflict was high, warmth from either the father or mother compensated for the lack of warmth from the other parent. Children had highest levels of internalizing problems when warmth from both parents was low. When there was higher level of father warmth, internalizing problems decreased, despite the low levels of mother warmth and the high level of interparental conflict. The compensation effect was not found when interparental conflict was low.	*Strengths*: Multi-reporter measures *Weaknesses*: Cross-sectional design; intervention sample may differ from general population

(Continued)

Table 4.1 STUDIES OF THE RELATIONS OF QUALITY OF MATERNAL AND PATERNAL PARENTING
WITH CHILD ADJUSTMENT   (*Continued*)

Source	Participants	Design Procedure
DeGarmo, 2010	230 divorced fathers of children aged 4–11 32% maternal custody, 53% shared custody, 14% paternal custody	Participants were recruited from records of divorces over past 24 months. Data were collected over three waves of assessment (baseline, and 9- and 18 month follow-ups).
Menning, 2002	269 "absent" parents with children under 18 years old	Longitudinal design Participants from the National Survey of Families and Households Data collected at two waves across 6 years
Fabricius & Luecken, 2007	266 college students whose parents had divorced before age 16	Retrospective design

Measures of Parenting	Analysis and Results	Strengths/Weaknesses
Four scales were used to rate harsh discipline ($\alpha = 0.86$), total aversives (Kappa range 0.76–0.81), self-reported harsh discipline ($\alpha = 0.85$), and pro-social parenting ($\alpha = 0.94$); skill encouragement ($\alpha = 0.92$) was measured via behavioral observation of father–child interaction and father self-report. Father–child monthly contact was assessed via father report.	Structural equation modeling was used to test the relation between father parenting, father antisocial personality, and child adjustment. Relation of father contact with child noncompliance differed across levels of antisocial personality of father. Contact was related to higher noncompliance at high levels of antisocial personality and contact was related to lower noncompliance at low levels of antisocial personality. Coercive parenting was related to higher child noncompliance. Father antisocial personality was related to higher child noncompliance. Coercive parenting mediated relation between father antisocial personality and noncompliance.	*Strengths*: Longitudinal design; sophisticated statistical analyses *Weaknesses*: Noncompliance assessed in interaction with father rather than measured in multiple contexts; sample majority NHW
Fathers reported on financial support and father–child activity.	Logistic regression was used to assess the relation between father involvement, economic support, and child educational attainment. Activities and financial support alone were not significantly related to educational attainment. Receiving financial support with higher father–child activity increased the probability that youth would complete high school and go on to college.	*Strengths*: Longitudinal design *Weaknesses*: Single-reporter measures
Living arrangements, parent conflict, and global feelings about divorce were assessed using young adult report. Young adults completed the Parental Bonding Instrument and the Painful Feelings about Divorce scale.	Structural equation modeling was used to evaluate the proposed model. Time living with fathers post-divorce was positively related to current relationships, independent of parent conflict. Higher conflict was related to worse relationships and greater distress about the divorce, independent of time spent living with father. Poor father–child relationships and distress predicted poorer health outcomes.	*Strengths*: Authors articulated and tested a theoretical model *Weaknesses*: Data were gathered retrospectively; single-reporter measures

Table 4.2 Measures Used in the Studies on the Quality of Maternal and Paternal Parenting with Child Adjustment

Measures	Referenced Study	Reporter/Method Items
Multiple Reporters		
Child Report of Parenting Behavior (Schaefer, 1965)	Wolchik et al., 2000; Wolchik et al., 2002; Sandler et al., 2008	Child, Mother, Father report 40 items
Living Arrangements scale (Fabricius & Hall, 2000)	Fabricius & Luecken, 2007	Adolescent, Parent report 1 item
Nonresidential father's parenting (Simons, Whitbeck, Beaman, & Conger, 1994)	Wolchik et al., 2000; Wolchik et al., 2002; Simons, Whitbeck, Beaman, & Conger, 1994	Adolescent and Mother report 14 items adolescent, 8 items mother
Child/Adolescent Report		
Closeness to parents (Buchanan, Maccoby, & Dornbusch, 1996)	Amato & Gilbreth, 1999	Adolescent report 9 items
Father involvement (Menning, 2002)	Menning, 2002; Menning, 2006	Adolescent report 12-items
Father–child relationship quality (King & Sobolweski, 2006)	King & Sobolweski, 2006	Adolescent report 5 items
Parental Acceptance– Rejection Questionnaire (Rohner, 1990)	Amato & Gilbreth, 1999	Child report 60 items
Parent–Adolescent Communication Scale (Barnes & Olson, 1982)	Wolchik et al., 2000; Wolchik et al., 2002	Adolescent report 20 items
Parental support (Young, Miller, Norton, & Hill, 1995)	Amato & ilbreth, 1999	Adolescent report 14 items
Relationship quality (Stewart, 2003)	Stewart, 2003	Child report 4 items
Responsiveness fathering (King & Sobolweski, 2006)	King & Sobolweski, 2006	Adolescent report 3 items

Construct/Scales	Reliability/Validity	Notes and Considerations

Measures parenting behavior
  Three scales: Acceptance, Rejection, Consistency of Discipline
	Test–retest reliability = 0.81; internal consistency reliability ranges from 0.68 to 0.84
	  Evidence of discriminant validity between scales
		Can be used as report of mother or father

Assesses living arrangements of the child	Test–retest reliability = 0.86, inter-rater reliability = 0.92	Qualitative category scales are more interpretable than quantitative scales.
Measures paternal authoritative parenting	Internal consistency reliability = 0.90 for adolescents, 0.86 for mothers	Low correlation between adolescent report and mother report
Measures closeness to parents	Internal consistency reliability = 0.90	Can be used as report of mother or father
Measures father involvement Questions about frequency of communication, overnight stays, activities, and closeness	Internal consistency reliability = 0.86 (wave 1) and 0.82 (wave 2)	Menning measured change in involvement by measuring involvement over time.
Measures quality of father–child relationship	Internal consistency = 0.86	

Measures parenting behaviors
  Four scales: Warmth/affection, Hostility/aggression, Indifference/neglect, Undifferentiated rejection
	Internal consistency reliability ranges from 0.83 to 0.95 for scales, and 0.77 overall.
	  Evidence of construct validity
	  Scales correlate ranging from 0.51 to 0.86.
		Can be used as report of mother or father
		  Highly related scales suggest using the overall scale score.

Measures quality of parent–child communication
  Two scales:
  Open Family Communication, Problems in Family Communication
	Internal consistency reliability range 0.87–0.92; test–retest reliability = 0.78
	  Evidence of construct validity for two subscales
	  Discriminant validity between clinical and non-clinical families
		Can be used as report of mother or father

Measures authoritative parenting and closeness Three scales: Intrinsic support, Extrinsic support, Closeness	Internal consistency reliability = 0.82 (intrinsic), 0.67 (extrinsic, 0.75 (closeness)	Can be used as report of mother or father.
Measures relationship quality with non-residential father Questions assess type of involvement and closeness.		Relationship quality (Stewart, 2003)
Measures responsive paternal parenting.	Internal consistency = 0.77	Responsiveness fathering (King & Sobolweski, 2006)

(Continued)

Table 4.2 Measures Used in the Studies on the Quality of Maternal and Paternal
Parenting with Child Adjustment   (*Continued*)

Measures	Referenced Study	Reporter/Method Items
Parent Report		
Family Routines Inventory (Jensen, Boyce, & Harnett, 1983)	Wolchik et al., 2000	Parent self-report (Note: Some items applicable only to 2-parent families) 23 items
Paternal Involvement in Child-care Index (Radin, 1981)	Amato & Gilbreth, 1999	Father report 16 items
Behavior Observation		
Custodial Mother's Parenting (McGruder, Lorenz, Hoyt, Ge, & Montague, 1992)	Simons, Whitebeck, Beaman, & Conger, 1994	Behavioral observation, Mother report, Adolescent report 1 item per dimension per reporter
Family and Peer Process Code (Stubbs, Crosby, Forgatch, & Capaldi, 1998)	DeGarmo, 2010	Behavioral observation
Interpersonal Process Code (Rusby, Estes, & Dishion, 1991)	Martinez & Forgatch, 2001	Behavioral observation
New Beginnings Coding System (Griffin & Decker, 1992)	Wolchik et al., 2000; Wolchik et al., 2002	Behavioral observation

Note: The measures cited in this table are not intended to be a comprehensive set of measures for
parenting plan evaluations. They can be used as a foundation for selection of measures on quality of
parenting that link with the empirical research.

(but do not prove) the inference that parenting affects a child's mental health. Because
parenting occurs in the context of a dynamic family system in which multiple factors
could affect the child's outcomes and fathers, mothers, and children affect each other,
researchers need to account for the effects of other variables that may also influence
children's adjustment problems. Often, the effects of a variable (e.g., quality of

Construct/Scales	Reliability/Validity	Notes and Considerations
Measures behavioral consistency in the family unit Summary frequency score of number and frequency of family routines	Test–retest reliability ranges from 0.74 to 0.79. Evidence of construct validity	Can be used as report of mother and/or father Developed for use with racially diverse families
Measures father involvement Five scales: Socialization, Responsibility, Availability, Power in decision making, Global estimate of involvement	Internal consistency reliability ranges from 0.67 to 0.75.	Used with white and black American fathers
Measures discipline as indicators of ineffective parenting Four dimensions: Monitoring, Consistency of Discipline, Harsh disciplinary practices, Setting standards	Internal consistency reliability >0.80 for mother and adolescent reports Inter-coder reliability = 0.60 Correlation between mother and adolescent report ranges from 0.25 to 0.35. Intercorrelation among aggregated scales = 0.70	Aggregates mother self-report, adolescent report with videotaped family interaction task
Assesses parenting practices Five codes: Harsh discipline, Total aversives, Pro-social parenting, Positive involvement, Skill encouragement	Inter-rater reliability for total aversives ranges from 0.87 to 0.96. Internal consistency reliability = 0.86 (harsh discipline), 0.94 (pro-social parenting), 0.92 (skill encouragement)	DeGarmo (2010) also used self-report of harsh discipline to supplement behavioral observation.
Measures effective parenting Seven domains: Positive involvement, Skill encouragement, Problem solving, Monitoring, Negative reinforcement, Negative reciprocity, Aversive discipline	Internal consistency ranges from 0.63 to 0.73.	Procedure involves structured interaction tasks: problem-solving discussion, teaching task, unstructured activity, forbidden toy situation.
Measures parent–child interaction Two codes: Pro-social behavior and global negativity	Inter-rater reliability ranges from 0.75 to 1.0.	Procedure involves 3-minute warm-up discussion and 12-minute problem-solving discussion.

paternal parenting on child mental health) differ as a function of another variable (e.g., level of interparental conflict), so researchers conduct moderation analyses to test for such differential effects. Finally, in drawing conclusions from a body of studies, it is important to recognize that each individual study has different strengths and weaknesses. Meta-analysis is a statistical approach to assess the aggregate effects across studies and to identify how different sources of potential bias affect the find-ings. Meta-analyses that have addressed the questions of interest are cited wherever they are available.

QUALITY OF PARENTING BY THE MOTHER FOLLOWING SEPARATION AND DIVORCE

Although the number of families in which the father is the primary parent has increased over the past decade, currently over 80% of children in divorced families live primarily with their mothers (U.S. Census Bureau, 2010). Because most children spend more time with their mothers than fathers after divorce, it is to be expected that the mother–child relationship would be a salient influence on the child's adjust-ment problems following separation or divorce. Reflecting the difference in time that most children spend with their mother and father after divorce, there is a longer his-tory of research on mothers' versus fathers' parenting. Additionally, it is important to note that most of the research on mothers' parenting after divorce was conducted in the 1980s and 1990s, earlier than the research on paternal parenting.

How is Quality of Maternal Post-Divorce Parenting Conceptualized and Measured?

A critical issue faced by parenting plan evaluators as well as researchers is how to conceptualize and assess quality of parenting by the mother. Consistent with the research on quality of maternal parenting in two-parent families, researchers who have studied maternal parenting after separation and divorce and children's adjust-ment problems have focused on two dimensions of parenting: relationship quality (e.g., the degree of warmth, support, encouragement, positive communication, con-flict, and negativity that characterizes the relationship) and effective discipline (e.g., the degree to which the mother enforces age-appropriate rules and expectations, consistently enforces rule compliance, and avoids harsh punishment). As shown in Table 4.2, research has employed multiple methods and multiple measures to assess these two dimensions of maternal post-divorce parenting.

What Factors Influence the Quality of Maternal Parenting Following Separation and Divorce?

Parenting in all types of families is best understood from an ecological perspective in which quality of parenting is affected by characteristics of the mother (e.g., depres-sion), aspects of the environment (e.g., financial strain), interpersonal factors (e.g., social support), and characteristics of the child (e.g., temperament) (Belsky, 1984; Belsky & Jaffe, 2006). A comprehensive review of the literature on the social-contex-tual factors that shape maternal parenting after divorce is beyond the scope of this chapter. In this section, the most well-studied correlates of maternal parenting after divorce are described as a way to highlight the importance of viewing parenting as a dynamic process that is shaped by multiple factors within and outside of the family.

Several researchers have documented changes in the quality of parenting during the process of separation and divorce. Early in this process, mothers often experience multiple changes, including reductions in financial resources, increases in conflict with their ex-spouse, and increases in household responsibilities. The psychological distress associated with these stressors can lead to less effective parenting in the immediate aftermath of separation (e.g., Camara & Resnick, 1989; Hetherington, Cox, & Cox, 1982). For example, in their pioneering research, Hetherington and her colleagues (1982) assessed the parenting skills of divorced mothers of preschool-aged children over a 2-year period. Using a multi-method approach that included diary data and behavioral observations, Hetherington and her colleagues found that 1 year after divorce, mothers made fewer maturity demands of their children, communicated less effectively, were less affectionate, and showed more inconsistency in discipline compared to non-divorced mothers. However, Hetherington and colleagues (1982), as well as other researchers (e.g., DeGarmo & Forgatch, 1999), observed that the quality of maternal parenting improves after this early adjustment period. Hetherington and her colleagues' use of information from several sources reduces concerns about reporter biases, such as mothers' desire to see improvements over time. However, all the mothers in this sample were non-Hispanic whites (NHWs), so caution needs to be used in generalizing the findings to other ethnic groups.

Numerous studies have found significant negative associations between interparental conflict and the quality of maternal parenting following separation or divorce (e.g., Hetherington, 1999; Tschann, Johnston, Kline, & Wallerstein, 1989). Two research groups have conducted meta-analyses on the relation between these two variables. In their meta-analysis, Krishnakumar and Buehler (2000) defined quality of parenting in terms of acceptance, harsh punishment, lax control, and inconsistency, whereas Whiteside and Becker (2000) defined quality of parenting as maternal warmth. Both research groups found that higher levels of interparental conflict were associated with lower quality of maternal parenting. It is important to note that most of the studies in these meta-analyses were cross-sectional, and consequently it is not possible to conclude that interparental conflict led to poorer quality of parenting. For example, poor-quality parenting may have affected interparental conflict. Alternatively, the relation between parenting and interparental conflict may have been due to an unknown third variable, such as poor interpersonal skills, that may be causally related to both these variables. Further, Whiteside and Becker's (2000) meta-analysis included only studies of divorced families with children age 6 or younger, limiting the generalizability of their findings.

Two intrapersonal characteristics of mothers, depression (e.g., Forgatch, Patterson, & Ray, 1999; Hetherington, Bridges, & Insabella, 1998; Simons & Johnson, 1996; Simons, Lin, Gordon, Conger, & Lorenz, 1999) and antisocial personality (e.g., Bank, Forgatch, Patterson, & Fetrow, 1993; Forgatch & DeGarmo, 1999; Simons, Beaman, Conger, & Chao, 1993; Simons & Chao, 1996; Simons & Johnson, 1996), have been found to be related to the quality of maternal parenting after separation and divorce. Illustratively, Forgatch and colleagues (1996) assessed divorced mothers and their elementary-school–aged sons three times over a 4-year period. Two components of discipline, harsh discipline and ineffective monitoring, were measured using maternal self-report and ratings made by interviews after assessments with mothers. Results showed that as depressed mood increased, discipline became harsher and less effective monitoring strategies were used. The use of a longitudinal design in this study strengthens inferences about the causal relation between maternal depression and quality of parenting.

Several researchers have examined the influence of children's characteristics on mothers' quality of parenting. In these studies, maternal behavior is viewed as a *reaction* to behavioral and emotional characteristics of the child rather than an *action* that affects the child's adjustment outcomes (e.g., Hetherington, 1991, 2006; Hetherington et al., 1982; Simons, Whitbeck, Beaman, & Conger, 1994). For example, in a sample of divorced mothers with adolescent offspring, Hetherington (2006) found that externalizing behavior problems at the first assessment were positively related to mothers' monitoring and control at the second assessment.

Several researchers have focused on relations between social support and quality of maternal parenting after divorce (Belsky & Vondra, 1989; DeGarmo & Forgatch, 1999; Simons et al., 1993; Simons, Johnson, Conger, & Lorenz, 1997). Illustratively, DeGarmo and Forgatch (1999) examined the relation between support received from an adult confidant and quality of parenting. Quality of parenting was assessed using a measure of aversive discipline during a mother–child problem-solving task and was assessed using observers' ratings. Less support was associated with more aversive discipline. This relation remained significant even after controlling for maternal distress and confidant negativity. The use of observational data is a significant strength of this study. However, generalizability of the findings is limited given that the sample was nearly exclusively NHW, and only mothers with elementary-school-aged sons were included.

In summary:

- Several contextual factors have been shown to be associated with the quality of maternal parenting after separation and divorce. More specifically, interparental conflict, maternal depression, and maternal antisocial tendencies are associated with lower quality of parenting. Also, social support is positively related to quality of parenting. In addition, children's behavior problems are associated with quality of parenting.
- Although the use of cross-sectional and longitudinal research designs precludes drawing causal inferences between these contextual factors and quality of maternal parenting, the findings on correlates of maternal parenting highlight the importance of conducting an assessment of the social-contextual factors that may affect maternal parenting.
- It is important to note that nearly all the research on factors that are associated with maternal parenting following separation or divorce has been conducted with samples that exclusively or almost exclusively included NHW parents. Therefore, caution must be used in generalizing the findings of these studies to other ethnic groups.

What is the Relation Between Quality of Maternal Parenting Following Separation or Divorce and the Well-Being of Children?

In this section, the literature on the association between mothers' quality of parenting after separation and divorce and children's adjustment problems is reviewed. There is a large body of research that has documented inverse relations between mother–child relationship quality and children's adjustment problems and between effective discipline and children's adjustment problems following separation and divorce (e.g., Buchanan, Maccoby, & Dornbusch, 1996; DeGarmo & Forgatch, 1999; Forgatch et al., 1996; Forgatch, Patterson, & Skinner, 1988; Hess & Camara, 1979; Hetherington et al., 1982, 1992;Krishnakumar & Buehler, 2000; Maccoby, Buchanan, Mnookin, & Dornbusch, 1993; Maccoby & Mnookin, 1992; Neighbors, Forehand, & McVicar, 1993; Simons et al., 1994; Simons & Chao, 1996; Simons & Johnson, 1996; Tschann et al., 1989; Whitbeck, Simons, & Goldberg, 1996). Many of these are cross-sectional studies, in which parenting and children's adjustment problems are measured simultaneously. As noted earlier, cross-sectional studies cannot establish the direction of causal effect between variables and thus can *only* demonstrate that a relation between mothers' parenting and children's adjustment problems exists. It is possible that deficits in parenting cause children's adjustment problems, that children's adjustment problems cause deficits in parenting, or that there is a reciprocal relation between parenting and children's adjustment problems. Longitudinal studies, in which parenting and children's adjustment problems are measured at more than one time point, offer an advantage over cross-sectional studies because tests can be conducted in which there is temporal precedence between variables, allowing a stronger test of the causal direction between parenting and children's adjustment problems (Cowan & Cowan, 2002; Rutter, 2005). Further, longitudinal studies can test whether children's adjustment problems influence, and/or are influenced by, parenting.

In one of the more rigorous longitudinal studies, Simons and his colleagues (1994) followed 207 recently separated mothers and their 14-year-old offspring over a 3-year period. Scores on four dimensions of effective discipline (monitoring, consistency of discipline, harsh discipline, standards for behavior) were aggregated into a single score (after harsh discipline was reverse-scored). Lower scores on this measure were significantly related to subsequent externalizing problems for girls and boys and were also significantly related to internalizing problems for boys. Adolescents' externalizing problems, but not internalizing problems, at the initial assessment were significantly negatively related to quality of parenting assessed a year later. However, neither externalizing nor internalizing problems measured at the second assessment were significantly related to parenting measured a year after the second assessment. These findings suggest that the negative influence of externalizing problems on parenting may be strongest in the initial period of adjustment to the separation. Although inferences about casual relations between parenting and youth adjustment problems are stronger when based on longitudinal studies versus cross-sectional studies, it is important to note that third variables that are shared by mothers and their offspring, such as genetic factors (e.g., antisocial personality traits) or environmental stressors (e.g., decreased economic resources), could explain significant relations observed in longitudinal studies.

Can Intervention Programs Strengthen the Quality of Maternal Parenting Following Separation or Divorce?

Findings from randomized trials of programs designed to improve the quality of maternal parenting allow stronger inferences about the causal effects of maternal parenting on children's adjustment than do findings from correlational studies (Cole & Maxwell, 2003; MacKinnon, 2008). In these trials, families are randomly assigned to a control condition or to an intervention that targets improvements in parenting. If differential changes between the control and intervention groups emerge following the intervention on parenting and children's adjustment problems, it can be concluded that these changes were caused by the intervention. Experimental designs also offer the possibility of examining whether changes in parenting account for changes in children's adjustment problems. For example, when the intervention leads to improvements in both parenting and children's adjustment problems, mediation analyses can be conducted to examine whether the changes in children's adjustment problems are due to changes that occurred in parenting as a result of participation in the program. To date, two research groups have used experimental trials to evaluate whether changes in maternal parenting accounted for improvements in children's post-divorce adjustment problems.

Wolchik and her colleagues have conducted two randomized experimental trials of a 10-session parenting-focused intervention for mothers titled the New Beginnings program (Wolchik et al., 1993, 2000). Over half of the 10 sessions in this program teach skills for enhancing mother–child relationship quality (e.g., increasing positive exchanges, routine use of quality time, active and responsive listening) and improving discipline (e.g., establishing clear and appropriate rules, use of consistent and contingent consequences). The first evaluation was a small-scale, randomized trial comparing an experimental group and a delayed intervention control group (N = 70; youths between ages 8 and 15). Relative to youths in the control condition, youths whose mothers participated in the program had fewer behavior problems at post-test. Also, the program led to improvements in mother–child relationship quality (i.e., acceptance, positive communication, and positive family routines), as well as effective discipline (i.e., consistency of discipline). Participants with poorer functioning at program entry showed the most improvement on consistency of discipline and child behavior problems. Mediation analyses indicated that improvements in mother–child relationship quality accounted for the program effects on children's adjustment problems.

A second, larger-scale randomized trial of the New Beginnings program was designed to examine (a) whether adding a coping-focused program for children to the program for mothers would lead to greater benefits than the program for mothers alone and (b) whether the effects of the program would be maintained over time. In this trial, 240 mothers and their children who were between the ages of 9 and 12 were randomly assigned to one of three conditions: mother program (MP),[2] mother plus child coping program (MPCP), or a literature control condition (LC). Families completed assessments at pre-test, post-test, short-term follow-up (3 months, 6 months), and long-term follow-up (6 years, 15 years). Results from the data collected through the 6-year follow-up are presented below; data from the 15-year follow-up are being analyzed.

Based on findings from the first trial that showed that program effects were strongest for children who entered the program with poorest functioning, analyses incorporated a measure of youths' risk for developing future adjustment problems (Dawson-McClure, Sandler, Millsap, & Wolchik, 2004) as a covariate. At post-test, children in the MP group had fewer internalizing problems and externalizing problems than those in the LC group, with greater benefit occurring for the children who entered the program with higher risk. Also, greater improvement in mother–child relationship quality (assessed by child report and observers' ratings of a mother–child interaction task) and effective discipline (assessed by mother/child report) occurred for mothers in the MP versus those in the LC group. Mediation analyses of the post-test data demonstrated that changes in mother–child relationship quality accounted for improvements in youths' internalizing and externalizing problems and that changes in effective discipline accounted for the improvements in youths' externalizing problems (Tein, Sandler, McKinnon, & Wolchik, 2004). Contrary to expectation, the MP and the MPCP did not have different effects on mother–child relationship quality, children's coping, or children's adjustment problems at post-test or 3-month or 6-month follow-up. Thus, the data from the MP and MPCP groups were combined into one group (referred to below as NBP) and compared to the LC group in the analyses of data from the 6-year follow-up. The analyses at the 6-year follow-up showed program effects to improve a wide array of adolescent outcomes. For example, 23.5% of youths in the LC condition had a mental disorder in the past year versus 14.8% of youths whose mothers participated in the NBP (odds ratio = 2.7). The NBP also had a positive impact to reduce number of sexual partners, externalizing problems, internalizing problems, symptoms of mental disorder, alcohol use, marijuana use, other drug use, and polydrug use, and to increase grade-point average and adolescent self-esteem. Similar to the findings in the earlier assessments, program effects for several outcomes (i.e., externalizing problems, internalizing problems, symptoms of mental disorder, polydrug use, alcohol use, marijuana use, other drug use, and competence) were stronger for youths who, at program entry, were at higher risk. At the 6-year follow-up, improvements in mother–child relationship quality (i.e., mother/child report at post-test) accounted for the effects of the program on internalizing problems, externalizing problems, and symptoms of mental disorder for those youths who entered the program at high levels of risk. Improvements in effective discipline (mother/child report at post-test) accounted for the program effects on grade-point average (Zhou, Sandler, Millsap, Wolchik, & Dawson-McClure, 2008). Further, improvement in monitoring, as assessed at 6-year follow-up, accounted for the program effects on substance use for youths who entered the program at high risk for developing problems (Soper, Wolchik, Tein, & Sandler, 2010).

Forgatch and her colleagues have evaluated their 14-session parenting-focused program, Parenting Through Change, in a sample of 238 recently separated mothers and their sons ages 6 to 10 (Forgatch & DeGarmo, 1999). Mothers were randomly assigned to the intervention or no-intervention control group. The intervention provided training in parenting practices (e.g., discipline, skills encouragement, monitoring, problem solving) and other issues relevant to divorced mothers (e.g., regulation of negative emotions, management of conflict). This program led to increases in positive parenting (i.e., skill encouragement, problem solving, and monitoring) and decreases in coercive discipline (i.e., negative reinforcement, negative reciprocity, and inept discipline) as assessed by mother self-report and observers' ratings of mother–child interactions (Martinez & Forgatch, 2001). Three years after participation, boys whose mothers had participated in the program showed lower levels of noncompliance, delinquent behaviors (lying, cheating, stealing), internalizing problems, and externalizing problems compared to those in the control group. These short-term follow-up effects were accounted for by improvements in positive parenting and coercive discipline (DeGarmo & Forgatch, 2005; DeGarmo, Patterson, & Forgatch, 2004). More recently, Forgatch, Patterson, DeGarmo, and Beldavs (2009) reported that at the 9-year follow-up, boys in the intervention group showed lower levels of delinquent behaviors according to teacher report, fewer arrests according to police records, and a delay in the age at first arrest. Improvements in parenting accounted for the reductions in these measures of adolescent delinquency.

In summary:

- There is a very large body of research that has shown that high-quality parenting by mothers is related to lower levels of children's adjustment problems. Although most of this work has used cross-sectional or longitudinal research designs, three experimental trials of brief interventions designed to improve parenting have shown that improving maternal parenting led to decreases in children's adjustment problems. The results of these experimental trials provide strong support for the inference that high-quality maternal parenting has a causal effect to reduce youths' post-divorce adjustment problems.
- It is important to note that nearly all the research on the relation between maternal quality of parenting and youths' adjustment problems has been conducted with NHW samples. Further, none of the experimental studies has assessed program effects for children younger than 6. Thus, caution must be used in generalizing the results of these studies to mothers with young children and other ethnic groups.

QUALITY OF PARENTING BY THE FATHER FOLLOWING SEPARATION AND DIVORCE

How is Quality of Paternal Post-Divorce Parenting Conceptualized and Measured?

A critical issue faced by custody evaluators involves how to conceptualize and assess quality of parenting by the father following separation or divorce. Some studies assess parenting by the father using the same dimensions commonly used to assess parenting by the mother (i.e., father–child relationship quality and effective discipline). However, because the child typically does not reside primarily with the father following separation and divorce, studies of paternal parenting have also assessed the amount of time the father spends with the child and the degree to which the father is actively involved and has an emotionally close relationship with the child. Table 4.2 presents a summary of the measures used in the empirical research on the relations between quality of paternal parenting and children's well-being following separation or divorce; it includes descriptions of the constructs, assessment methods, reliability and validity of the measures, and issues pertaining to use of these measures in parenting plan evaluations. The table does not include measures of parenting time because this chapter is focused on quality of parenting. Approaches to the measurement of parenting time are reviewed extensively by Fabricius, Sokol, Diaz, and Braver (2012) in Chapter 7 of this volume.

What Factors Influence the Quality of Paternal Parenting Following Separation and Divorce?

Quality of paternal parenting must be understood from an ecological perspective in which both father and child are part of a larger dynamic system involving mutual influences between mothers, fathers, children, and others in the family's social network. Parenting plan evaluators interested in assessing the quality of the father–child relationship need to account for four factors that influence this relationship: (a) the amount and pattern of time the father spends with the child, (b) characteristics of the social context in which parenting occurs, (c) characteristics of the child, and (d) characteristics of the father.

FATHER–CHILD CONTACT

Several authors have proposed that the quality of the father–child relationship following separation or divorce is limited by the amount and timing of contact between father and child (Fabricius, Braver, Diaz, & Velez, 2010; Kelly, 2007). Consistent with this thesis, in a meta-analysis of 12 empirical studies on parental factors and children's adjustment following separation or divorce, Whiteside and Becker (2000) found that more frequent visitation by the father was associated with a higher-quality father–child relationship. Fabicius, Sokol, Diaz, and Braver (2012; Chapter 7 in this volume) propose a theoretical model in which more time a father spends with his child leads to more interactions with the child, which in turn leads to a higher-quality father–child relationship. They present evidence from a survey of college students whose parents had divorced, which showed that increased amounts of time spent with the father following divorce (up to approximately 50% time) was related to a better father–child relationship, with no adverse effects on the quality of the mother–child relationship. Cashmore, Parkinson, and Taylor (2008), in their study of divorced families with adolescents, found that more frequent overnight stays were positively related to the quality of the father–child relationship, but the frequency of contacts without overnight stays was not associated with relationship quality. A major limitation of the aforementioned studies on paternal parenting time is that these studies did not use a prospective design in which parenting time was measured at an earlier point than quality of the father–child relationship. Two studies that used a prospective design did not find significant associations between the amount of father–child contact and later father–child relationship quality (DeGarmo, Patras, & Eap, 2008; Dunn, Cheng, O'Conner, & Bridges, 2004). Thus, although more parenting time appears to be related to a higher-quality father–child relationship, the direction of causality between these variables has not been established, and the exact pattern of living arrangements that leads to a better father–child relationship is not clear.

SOCIAL CONTEXT OF PATERNAL PARENTING

Contextual factors that have been found to be related to the quality of father–child relationships include the relationship between the parents (DeGarmo et al., 2004; Dunn et al., 2004; Fabricius & Luecken, 2007; Whiteside & Becker, 2000), the level of support fathers receive for parenting from their social network (Castillo & Fenzl-Crossman, 2010; DeGarmo et al., 2008), and the level of stress fathers experience

(DeGarmo et al., 2008). Researchers have found positive associations between quality of father–child and mother–child relationships and no significant relations between father–child and stepfather–child relationships (Dunn et al., 2004, White & Gilbreth, 2001). Thus, available evidence indicates that having a positive relationship with the father does not come at the cost of the child's relationships with other parental figures.

CHILD'S CHARACTERISTICS

Characteristics of the child have also been found to predict quality of father–child relationships. Hawkins, Amato, and King (2007) used a nationally representative sample of 3,394 adolescents in Grades 7 through 12 not living with their fathers to study whether adolescents' characteristics predicted fathers' involvement over time. Their results showed that adolescent externalizing and internalizing problems and academic success predicted one or more of the following aspects of father–child relationships 1 year later: contact with fathers, shared activities, and emotional closeness. A similar effect was found in another prospective longitudinal study (Simons et al., 1994), which found that youth externalizing problems predicted the quality of parenting of both the father and the mother 1 year later. The results of these studies indicate that adolescents play an active role in shaping the father–child relationship (as well as the mother–child relationship), and that adolescents who are experiencing maladjustment problems may make it difficult for fathers to be actively involved.

FATHER'S CHARACTERISTICS

The following characteristics of the father have also been found to be related to the quality of the father–child relationship: fathers' antisocial personality (DeGarmo, Reid, Leve, Chamberlain, & Knutson, 2010), level of fathers' pre-separation involvement with the children (Whiteside & Becker, 2000), identification with the fathering role (DeGarmo, 2010) and fathers' educational level (King, Harris, & Heard, 2004). Race and ethnicity were found to be related to differences in specific areas of paternal involvement with their adolescent children (e.g., as compared to the fathers of other ethnicities, Hispanic fathers have a higher rate of working on a school project, African American fathers have a higher rate of attending religious services, and NHW fathers have a higher rate of playing sports). However, no overall difference in level of father involvement was found across race and ethnicity (King et al., 2004).

In an exemplary study, DeGarmo and colleagues (2008) studied the effects of social support, stress, custody arrangement, and fathers' antisocial personality as predictors of the quality of fathers' parenting in a sample of 218 divorced families. A particular strength of the study was the use of a multi-method approach for assessing paternal parenting, including behavioral observation ratings of parent–child interactions and fathers' self-ratings. Quality of parenting was assessed as pro-social parenting (i.e., composite of positive involvement and skill encouragement observed in a structured father–child interaction task) and coercive parenting (i.e., composite of harsh and punitive discipline and verbal and physical aggression directed towards the child). The use of a cross-sectional as well as longitudinal design allowed them to study predictors of parenting quality at a single point in time and predictors of changes in parenting over 9 months. In the cross-sectional analysis, they found that antisocial personality, interparental conflict, and father full custody predicted higher levels of coercive parenting by the father. In the longitudinal analysis, they found that a higher level of stress from an overload of time commitments predicted increases in coercive parenting over the 9 months. They also found that social support for fathers' parenting reduced the negative effects of interparental conflict on pro-social parenting concurrently and on coercive parenting longitudinally. Social support also reduced the negative effects of daily stress on pro-social parenting longitudinally.

In summary:

- A positive relationship between parenting time and quality of paternal parenting is found in most studies, although the direction of causality between time and quality of parenting has not been well established. In addition, some kinds of contact, such as overnight visits, have been more strongly related to quality of paternal parenting than others. Amount and type of contact should be considered as factors that enable the father to establish a better quality of relationship.
- Quality of paternal parenting following separation or divorce is the result of a dynamic process in which multiple factors influence paternal parenting, including the social context in which parenting occurs (i.e., social support for parenting, stressors in father's life, interparental conflict), characteristics of the child (i.e., child mental health problems and academic success), and characteristics of the father (i.e., antisocial personality, involvement with the child prior to the divorce or separation, and father's education level).
- Each of the factors that have been found to influence the quality of parenting should be assessed in parenting plan evaluations. However, the empirical studies have some limitations, so evaluators need to consider the patterns of factors in recommending a parenting plan for specific family situations.

What is the Relation Between Quality of Paternal Parenting Following Separation or Divorce and the Well-Being of Children?

This section will first describe the findings from a major meta-analytic review to summarize empirical evidence concerning the direct relations between different aspects of fathering and children's well-being following separation or divorce. It will then review recent studies that address two critical questions: (a) Are the effects of paternal parenting found after accounting for the effects of the multitude of other factors that might affect children's well-being? (b) Are the effects of paternal parenting found in the difficult family situations that evaluators typically encounter, such as when there is high interparental conflict or when the father has an antisocial personality?

In an influential meta-analysis of 63 empirical studies, Amato and Gilbreth (1999) investigated relations between children's academic success, externalizing problems, and internalizing problems and four aspects of fathers' involvement with children after separation or divorce: (a) payment of child support, (b) amount of contact, (c) feeling close, and (d) authoritative parenting. They found that payment of child support was related to higher academic success and lower externalizing problems. Level of contact between father and child was only very weakly related to children's academic success and internalizing problems. Measures of feeling close were assessed as the children's positive emotional relationship to the father and were significantly but weakly related to better academic success and lower externalizing and lower internalizing problems. Measures of authoritative parenting included supportiveness (e.g., responsiveness, positive encouragement) and control (e.g., consistent discipline). Authoritative parenting had small relations to measures of academic success and externalizing and internalizing problems. Amato and Gilbreth (1999) noted that although these relations are statistically small, they are meaningful at the population level. For example, in a hypothetical population of separated or divorced families in which 30% of the children without an authoritative father had a behavior problem, only 20% of the children with an authoritative father would have that behavior problem (i.e., a 34% decline in the probability of experiencing that behavior problem associated with having an authoritative father).

Does Quality of Paternal Parenting Predict Child Well-Being After Controlling for Other Factors?

This question can be addressed using analyses in which the effects of paternal parenting are assessed while statistically controlling for the effects of other critical factors. Several methodologically strong studies that used multi-method assessments and/or separate reporters of fathering and child outcomes have found evidence that the quality of paternal parenting predicts child and adolescent adjustment, controlling for other factors. Specifically, a three-wave longitudinal study of parenting previously described in the section on maternal parenting (Simons et al., 1994) also studied the effects of paternal parenting quality on the child's well-being, controlling for the effects of mothers' parenting, interparental conflict, family income, and amount of child support payments. The study tested the prospective relations between paternal parenting and adolescent externalizing and internalizing problems. Fathers' parenting was assessed using reports of fathers' involvement in a wide range of activities (e.g., talking about what is going on in the child's life, discipline). The results showed a longitudinal effect of lower paternal parenting quality, as reported by the adolescent, to predict externalizing problems for boys and girls 1 year later. Maternal report of lower-quality parenting by the father also predicted externalizing problems for boys.

King and Sobolewski (2006) provided a more in-depth study of how quality of paternal parenting predicted the child's well-being, controlling for quality of mother–child relationship and frequency of father–child contact. They studied the relations between child well-being and two measures of quality of paternal parenting: quality of father–child relationship as measured by adolescent ratings of positive father–child relationship (e.g., how positive is the relationship, how much they admire their father) and fathers' responsiveness (e.g., discusses decisions with child). They found that the child's report of having a positive relationship with his or her father and the father's responsiveness were both related to lower maternal reports of internalizing and externalizing problems. Although these relations were reduced in magnitude when the mother–child relationship was added as a predictor, they remained significant or marginally significant. They also investigated the joint effect of having a positive relationship with both the mother and the father. As expected, children who did not have a positive relationship with either parent had the most behavior problems.

There was a marginally significant effect for those who had a positive relationship with only the father to have fewer internalizing and externalizing problems than those who had poor relationships with both parents.

Several studies investigated whether specific kinds of father involvement had effects on specific outcomes controlling for other factors. A longitudinal study with a nationally representative sample of youths in Grades 7 through 12 investigated whether specific kinds of father involvement were related to child failure in school (Menning, 2006). They found that higher levels of involvement with fathers after separation or divorce predicted lower school failure over a 1-year period; controlling for a wide range of other predictors, including maternal household income, mothers' closeness to the child, and youths' prior school performance (Menning, 2006). Specific kinds of paternal involvement (i.e., the variety of activities the father engaged in with the youth and discussion of schoolwork and other school issues) accounted for the effects of paternal involvement on school failure. In a study of adolescents, Stewart (2003) provided further evidence of the effects of specific aspects of paternal involvement predicting the child's well-being, controlling for a wide range of other factors, including family income and the children's closeness to the mother. Specifically, closeness to the father predicted lower emotional distress, and talking about things happening at school was related to lower emotional distress and higher grade-point average.

Is High-Quality Paternal Parenting Beneficial for Children in the Presence of Other Conditions that Threaten Children's Well-Being?

Evaluators frequently confront family situations where there is a high level of interparental conflict or where one or both parents have personality or mental health problems. The evaluators need to consider whether the benefits of high-quality paternal parenting will still be seen under these conditions. An early longitudinal study with a sample of divorcing families entrenched in disputes over custody and parenting time found that greater father–child contact was related to higher levels of child behavior problems (Johnston, Kline, & Tschann, 1989). Although this study assessed only paternal contact rather than quality of parenting, it raised a serious concern over whether paternal involvement is helpful or harmful when there is a high level of conflict. Several other studies have reported inconsistent findings regarding the relation between amount of father–child contact and children's well-being in the context of high interparental conflict (Amato & Rezac, 1994; Fabricius & Luecken, 2007; Healy, Malley, & Stewart, 1990; Kurdek, 1986; Trinder, Kellet, & Swift, 2008). Although there have been inconsistent findings regarding the benefits of frequent father–child contact under conditions of interparental conflict, the two studies that have examined fathers' parenting quality have found that high-quality paternal parenting was related to lower child externalizing problems, and that this relation was not affected by the level of interparental conflict (Sandler, Miles, Cookston, & Braver, 2008; Simons et al., 1994). In the study by Sandler and colleagues (2008), a more complex pattern of relations was found for internalizing problems. This study investigated the joint effects of interparental conflict and quality of parenting by both the mother and father. Quality of parenting was measured using children's reports of parental warmth. When interparental conflict was high, warmth from either the father or mother compensated for the lack of warmth from the other parent. Specifically, children had the highest levels of internalizing problems when warmth from both parents was low. However, when there was a high level of warmth from the father, children's internalizing problems were lower, despite low warmth from the mother and high interparental conflict. The compensation effect was not found when interparental conflict was low.

Characteristics of the father, particularly mental health or substance abuse problems, may also affect how paternal parenting influences children's adjustment. DeGarmo (2010) found two pathways by which paternal antisocial personality was related to children's adjustment in a sample of 230 children (ages 4–11) from divorced families. They measured coercive parenting as a composite of harsh discipline, aversive interactions, and pro-social interactions. A notable strength of this study was the use of multiple methods, including behavioral observation and paternal report, in their measurement of coercive parenting. Children's noncompliant behavior was used as an outcome variable because it had previously been found to predict child problem behaviors. Assessments were done at three time points over an 18-month period. In a prospective longitudinal analysis, the researchers found that more frequent father–child contact was related to higher child noncompliance if fathers scored high on antisocial personality, whereas for fathers who were low on antisocial personality, more contact was related to lower noncompliance. In addition, paternal antisocial personality was directly related to higher coercive parenting, which in turn was related to higher child noncompliance.

Low child support is another factor that appears to reduce the benefits of high-quality paternal parenting for children's well-being. Menning (2002) found that the relation of paternal involvement to youth academic success differed as a function of the amount of economic support fathers had provided 5 years earlier. They assessed paternal involvement as the sum of activities fathers engaged in with their children and the father's provision of economic support as the total amount of money the father provided to support the child in the prior year. At low levels of child support, there was little or no effect of paternal involvement on youths' educational achievement, but at high levels of economic support, paternal involvement was strongly predictive of educational success.

In summary:

- The quality of paternal parenting following separation or divorce, defined as involvement in multiple aspects of children's lives and emotional closeness, predicts children's behavioral and academic adjustment, controlling for a wide range of other factors, including the quality of maternal parenting, interparental conflict, and mothers' income.
- There is no evidence that the beneficial effects of high-quality paternal parenting are reduced under conditions of high interparental conflict. In fact, there is some evidence that high paternal warmth can compensate for the negative effects of interparental conflict and low maternal warmth on children's adjustment. The evidence is mixed concerning how the impact of father–child contact on children's well-being is affected by interparental conflict.
- There is evidence that fathers' antisocial personality and low economic support for the child reduce the beneficial effects of fathers' involvement on children.

Can Intervention Programs Strengthen the Quality of Paternal Parenting Following Separation or Divorce?

There are no experimental trials of parenting programs for separated or divorced fathers that have demonstrated findings comparable to the impressive studies of programs for separated or divorced mothers described earlier (Forgatch et al., 2009; Wolchik et al. 2002). One experimental trial of a program for divorced fathers, the Dads for Life program, reduced interparental conflict, improved co-parenting, and reduced mental health problems for children who had higher problems when their fathers initiated the program. However, the program did not improve the quality of paternal parenting, perhaps because only 3 of the 8 sessions focused on parenting, considerably fewer than the 9 to 14 sessions on parenting in the effective programs for separated and divorced mothers. Nevertheless, evidence from parenting programs with fathers in other contexts supports the expectation that separated and divorced fathers can learn effective parenting skills. A meta-analysis of 11 parenting programs involving fathers and mothers of children experiencing disruptive behavior problems found a significant overall effect of the programs to improve paternal parenting at post-test and at least 2 months following program completion (Lundahl, Tollefson, Risser, & Lovejoy, 2008). Positive effects to promote effective paternal parenting have also been reported for programs in other contexts, including stepfathers (DeGarmo & Forgatch, 2007) and African American fathers not residing with their children (Caldwell, Rafferty, Reischl, DeLoney, & Brooks, 2010). Programs to promote high-quality paternal parenting following separation or divorce will also need to help fathers deal with the disruptors of parenting described in this chapter and in other chapters (e.g., see Pruett, Cowan, Cowan, & Diamond, 2012; Chapter 5 in this volume), but it is reasonable to expect that such programs can be effective. In view of the strong evidence that high-quality paternal parenting is related to better child adjustment, there is good reason to expect that strengthening the quality of paternal parenting will improve the well-being of children following separation and divorce.

GUIDELINES: CONSIDERATIONS AND CAUTIONS

- Many factors that are the focus of evaluations (e.g., interparental conflict, parents' psychopathology, co-parenting, and amount of parenting time) are seen as important because of their impact on quality of parenting. Although these factors are important, this chapter encourages evaluators to focus directly on the assessment of quality of parenting. The research reviewed in this chapter provides scientific evidence to support and guide the evaluation of quality of parenting. Because studies on quality of parenting following separation and divorce were not conducted in the context of parenting plan evaluations, evaluators need to consider both the implications and limitations of the research findings for their practice.
- How is quality of parenting conceptualized and measured for mothers and fathers?
- There is consistency across research studies on the dimensions of parenting quality that are important to measure. For mothers, quality of parenting has

been assessed on the dimensions of relationship quality (e.g., high levels of warmth and support and low levels of negative interactions) and effective discipline (e.g., setting and enforcing appropriate rules consistently). Although these measures also have been applied to paternal parenting, other constructs (e.g., degree of involvement in specific activities, closeness of the relationship) have also been used to assess father–child relationships. Reliable measures of each of these constructs have been developed and shown to predict child outcomes. It is critical to note that no single measure is the gold standard; rather, multi-method assessments (including behavioral observation of parent–child interactions) and multiple reporters should be used to assess parenting. Although researchers either report findings separately for different measures or statistically form composites that represent the shared attribute across measures, evaluators have a more difficult task. The evaluator must base conclusions on the configuration of data from multiple sources in light of the biases inherent in each source of data. An impediment to using these scales is that there are no national norms for them and no algorithm for defining a diagnosis of "deficient parenting." Rather, the evaluator needs to use professional judgment to assess the relative strengths and problems in parenting.

- What factors influence quality of parenting by the mother and father?
- Factors identified by research as influencing quality of parenting are often the focus of evaluations. For both mothers and fathers, they include characteristics of the parent (e.g., depression, antisocial personality), the social and family context (e.g., social support for parenting, interparental conflict), and the characteristics of the child (e.g., child externalizing problems). For fathers, an additional factor that relates to quality of parenting is the amount and type (i.e., overnights or day visits) of time they have with their children. These findings strongly suggest that the quality of parenting be viewed within an ecological context in which multiple factors may influence each other over time. It is important to note the limitations of this research for evaluators. First, while each of these factors potentially influences quality of parenting, they do not "cause" it in a direct linear way. High-quality parenting can occur despite the presence of factors that make it more difficult, and the presence of these factors should not be used as a substitute for the direct assessment of parenting. For example, parents can provide high-quality parenting despite there being a high level of interparental conflict, though it may be more difficult to do so. Second, the factors presented in this chapter are not exhaustive of the factors that may influence parenting. Other factors that have not been addressed in the scientific literature (e.g., father's depression, mother's new partners) may also be important in specific cases.
- What are the strengths and limitations of the evidence linking quality of parenting by the mother and father to children's adjustment following separation or divorce?
- Making causal inferences based on correlational studies is inherently problematic. There are always other unmeasured variables that might account for the significant effects found and other potential sources of bias

that might influence the findings. That being said, a rather substantial literature has emerged over the past 15 years that supports the relations between quality of maternal and paternal parenting and measures of children's well-being following separation or divorce. Multiple studies conducted in the 1980s and 1990s using strong research designs found that quality of maternal parenting was related to children's mental health following divorce. However, the strongest evidence for the causal effect of maternal parenting on children's well-being comes from experimental studies.

- There is now consistent evidence that quality of paternal parenting is related to children's well-being following separation or divorce, controlling for a wide range of other factors that might be alternative explanations for this relationship, including the quality of maternal parenting, interparental conflict, and economic factors. Furthermore, research now provides guidance on a question of critical importance to evaluators: How is the effect of paternal parenting on children affected by the presence of a high level of interparental conflict? In addressing this issue a distinction needs to be made between quality of paternal parenting and paternal parenting time. There is no evidence that the positive effects of high-quality paternal parenting on a child's well-being are diminished when interparental conflict is high. Thus, if there is high-quality paternal parenting, the research evidence does not support reducing paternal parenting time in the presence of interparental conflict. However, the evidence is mixed concerning whether more paternal parenting time is related to more or fewer child behavior problems in high-conflict families. Thus, in the absence of information concerning quality of paternal parenting, there is no clear scientific foundation for recommendations concerning how paternal parenting time should be modified when the level of interparental conflict is high.

- Is the quality of parenting changeable by currently available intervention programs?

- There is now strong scientific evidence from two independent studies that quality of parenting by divorced or separated mothers is changeable through skill-building parenting programs. Furthermore, these studies find that changing parenting has positive effects on children's well-being many years following the intervention, including reduced rates of diagnosed mental disorder, reduced internalizing and externalizing problems, improved academic success, reduced use of drugs and alcohol, and reduced arrests. Furthermore, one study finds that the long-term effects are strongest for families in which children are experiencing high levels of problems and the families have higher levels of stress and interparental conflict. The major limitations of these findings are that they need to be replicated across ethnic groups and with preschool-age children. Comparable evidence is not currently available for skill-building parenting programs with fathers following divorce and separation, although positive effects of parent training programs with fathers in other contexts provide reason for optimism. These programs have important implications for recommendations for parenting plan evaluators. Successful parenting programs have been demonstrated to have their effects through working with one parent in the family; they did not focus on the co-parenting relationship or work with both parents. In cases where cooperative co-parenting cannot be accomplished, there is reason to believe that strengthening the quality of individual parenting can have long-term positive effects on children.

ACKNOWLEDGMENTS

Work on this chapter was supported by grants from the NIMH (R01 MH071707and P30 MH06868–01), which are gratefully acknowledged.

NOTES

1 The term *paternal parenting* or *fathers' parenting* will be used throughout the text to refer to the parenting of the father who is not the primary residential parent following separation and divorce. The research literature on fathers following divorce has used a number of terms to refer to fathers (e.g., noncustodial, nonresidential) that gloss over distinctions between parenting plans. For the sake of simplicity of presentation and to avoid inaccuracies of depiction (i.e., many fathers either have joint custody or reside with the child for a certain proportion of time), the simple term *paternal parenting* or *fathers' parenting* is used.

2 The MP focused on improving effective discipline and mother–child relationship quality. In the MPCP, the mothers participated in the MP and the children participated in the child program, a concurrent but separate group for children that focused on promoting adaptive appraisals and coping. In the LC, mothers and children received three books about divorce adjustment (Wolchik et al., 2000). Both the mother and child programs included didactic presentations and skills practice. Participants were expected to try the program skills at home and, in each session, leaders and participants discussed each participant's use of the skills.

REFERENCES

Amato, P. R., & Gilbreth, J. G. (1999). Nonresident fathers and children's well-being: A meta-analysis. *Journal of Marriage & Family, 61*, 557–573. doi: 10.2307/353560

Amato, P. R., & Rezac, S. J. (1994). Contact with nonresidential parents, interparental conflict, and children's behavior. *Journal of Family Issues, 15*(2), 191–207. doi: 10.1177/0192513X94015002003

American Psychological Association. (2002). Ethical principles of psychologists and code of conduct. *American Psychologist, 57*, 1060–1073. doi: 10.1037/0003–066X.57.12.1060

American Psychological Association. (2010). Guidelines for child custody evaluations in family law proceedings. *American Psychologist, 65*(9), 863–867. doi: 10.1037/a0021250

Association of Family & Conciliation Courts. (2007). Model standards of practice for child custody evaluation. *Family Court Review, 45*, 70–91. doi: 10.1111/j.1744–1617.2007.129_3.x

Bank, L., Forgatch, M. S., Patterson, G. R., & Fetrow, R. A. (1993). Parenting practices of single mothers: Mediators of negative contextual factors. *Journal of Marriage and Family, 55*(2), 371–384. doi: 10.2307/352808

Barnes, H., & Olson, D. H. (1982). Parent-adolescent communication scale. In D. H. Olson, H. I. McCubbin, H. Barnes, A. Larsen, M. Muxen, & M. Wilson (Eds.), *Family inventories: Inventories used in a National Survey of Family Life Cycle* (pp. 438–447). St. Paul, MN: University of Minnesota.

Belsky, J. (1984). The determinants of parenting: A process model. *Child Development, 55*, 83–96. doi: 10.2307/1129836

Belsky, J., & Jaffee, S. R. (2006). The multiple determinants of parenting. In D. Cicchetti & D. J. Cohen (Eds.), *Developmental psychopathology* (Vol. 3: *Risk, disorder and adaptation*, pp. 739–795). New York: Wiley.

Belsky, J., & Vondra, J. (1989). Lessons from child abuse: The determinants of parenting. In D. Cicchetti & V. Carlson (Eds.), *Child maltreatment: Theory and research on the causes and consequences of child abuse and neglect* (pp. 153–202). Cambridge, England: Cambridge University Press.

Buchanan, C. M., Maccoby, E. E., & Dornbusch, S. M. (1996). *Adolescents after divorce.* Cambridge, MA: Harvard University Press.

Caldwell, C., Rafferty, J., Reischl, T., De Loney, E., & Brooks, C. (2010). Enhancing parenting skills among nonresident African American fathers as a strategy for preventing youth risky behaviors. *American Journal of Community Psychology, 45*, 17–35. doi: 10.1007/s10464–009-9290–4

Camara, K. A., & Resnick, G. (1989). Styles of conflict resolution and cooperation between divorced parents: Effects on child behavior and adjustment. *Journal of Orthopsychiatry, 59*, 560–575. doi: 10.1111/j.1939–0025.1989.tb02747.x

Cashmore, J., Parkinson, P., & Taylor, A. (2008). Overnight stays and children's relationships with resident and nonresident parents after divorce. *Journal of Family Issues, 29*, 707–733. doi: 10.117/0192513X07308042

Castillo, J. T., & Fenzl-Crossman, A. (2010). The relationship between non-marital fathers' social networks and social capital and father involvement. *Child & Family Social Work, 15*(1), 66–76. doi: 10.1111/j.1365–2206.2009.00644.x

Cole, D. A., & Maxwell, S. E. (2003). Testing mediational models with longitudinal data: Questions and tips in the use of structural equation modeling. *Journal of Abnormal Psychology, 112*, 558–577. doi: 10.1037/0021–843X.112.4.558

Cowan, P. A., & Cowan, C. P. (2002). Want an intervention design reveals about how parents affect their children's academic achievement and behavior problems. In J. G. Borkowski, S. L. Ramey, & M. Bristol-Power (Eds.), *Parenting and the child's world: Influences on academic, intellectual, and social-emotional development* (pp. 75–97). Mahwah, NJ: Erlbaum.

Dawson-McClure, S. R., Sandler, I. N., Wolchik, S. A., & Millsap, R. E. (2004). Risk as a moderator of the effects of prevention programs for children from divorced families: A six-year longitudinal study. *Journal of Abnormal Child Psychology, 32*, 175–190. doi: 0091–0627/04/0400–0175/0

DeGarmo, D. (2010). A time varying evaluation of identity theory and father involvement for full custody, shared custody, and no custody divorced fathers. *Fathering, 8*, 181–202. doi: 10.3149/fth.1802.181

DeGarmo, D. S., & Forgatch, M. S. (1999). Contexts as predictors of changing maternal parenting practices in diverse family structures: A social interactional perspective of risk and resilience. In E. M. Hetherington (Ed.), *Coping with divorce, single parenting, and remarriage: A risk and resilience perspective* (pp. 227–252). Mahwah, NJ: Lawrence Erlbaum Associates Publishers.

DeGarmo, D. S., & Forgatch, M. S. (2005). Early development of delinquency within divorced families: Evaluating a randomized preventive intervention trial. *Developmental Science, 8*, 229–239. doi: 10.1111/j.1467-7687.2005.00412.x

DeGarmo, D. S., & Forgatch, M. S. (2007). Efficacy of parent training for stepfathers: From playful spectator and polite stranger to effective stepfathering. *Parenting, 7*, 331–355. doi: 10.1080/15295190701665631

DeGarmo, D. S., Patras, J., & Eap, S. (2008). Social support for divorced fathers' parenting: Testing a stress-buffering model. *Family Relations, 57*(1), 35–48. doi: 10.1111/j.1741-3729.2007.00481.x

DeGarmo, D. S., Patterson, G. R., & Forgatch, M. S. (2004). How do outcomes in a specified parent training intervention maintain or wane over time? *Prevention Science, 5*(2), 73–89. doi: 10.1023/B:PREV.0000023078.30191.e0

DeGarmo, D. S., Reid, J. B., Leve, L. D., Chamberlain, P., & Knutson, J. F. (2010). Patterns and predictors of growth in divorced fathers' health status and substance use. *American Journal of Men's Health, 4*(1), 60–70. doi: 10.1177/1557988308329454

Dunn, J., Cheng, H., O'Conner, T. G., & Bridges, L. (2004). Children's perspectives on their relationships with their nonresident fathers: Influences, outcomes and implications. *Journal of Child & Psychiatry, 45*, 553–566. doi: 10.1111/j.1469-7610.2004.00245.x

Fabricius, W. V., Braver, S. L., Diaz, P., & Velez, C. E. (2010). Custody and parenting time: Links to family relationships and well-being after divorce. In M. E. Lamb (Ed.), *The role of the father in child development* (5th ed., pp. 201–240). Hoboken, NJ: John Wiley & Sons.

Fabricius, W. V., Diaz, P., & Braver, S. L. (2012). Parenting time, parent–child relationships and children's health. In K. Kuehnle & L. Drozd (Eds.), *Plan evaluations: Applied research for the family court*. New York: Oxford University Press.

Fabricius, W. V., & Hall, J. A. (2000). Young adults' perspectives on divorce living arrangements. *Family Court Review, 38*, 446–461. doi: 10.1111/j.174-1617.2000.tb00584.x

Fabricius, W. V., & Luecken, L. J. (2007). Postdivorce living arrangements, parent conflict, and long-term physical health correlates for children of divorce. *Journal of Family Psychology, 21*(2), 195–205. doi: 10.1037/0893-3200.21.2.195

Forgatch, M. S., & DeGarmo, D. S. (1999). Parenting through change: An effective prevention program for single mothers. *Journal of Consulting & Clinical Psychology, 67*, 711–724. doi: 10.1037/0022-006X.67.5.711

Forgatch, M. S., Patterson, G. R., Degarmo, D. S., & Beldavs, Z. G. (2009). Testing the Oregon delinquency model with 9-year follow-up of the Oregon Divorce Study. *Development and Psychopathology, 21*, 637–660. doi: 10.1017/S0954579409000340

Forgatch, M. S., Patterson, G. R., & Ray, J. A. (1996). Divorce and boys' adjustment problems: Two paths with a single model. In E. M. Hetherington & E. A. Blechman (Eds.), *Stress, coping, and resiliency in children and families* (pp. 67–105). Mahwah, NJ: Lawrence Erlbaum Associates, Inc.

Forgatch, M. S., Patterson, G. R., & Skinner, M. L. (1988). A mediational model for the effect of divorce on antisocial behavior in boys. In E. M. Hetherington & J. D. Arasteh (Eds.), *Impact of divorce, single parenting and stepparenting on children* (pp. 135–154). Hillsdale, NJ: Lawrence Erlbaum.

Griffin, W. A., & Decker, A. (1992). *New Beginnings coding system* (Tech Rep. No. 92–01). Tempe, AZ: Arizona State University, Prevention Intervention Research Center.

Hawkins, D. N., Amato, P. R., & King, V. (2007). Nonresident father involvement and adolescent well-being: Father effects or child effects? *American Sociological Review, 72*, 990–1010. doi: 10.1177/000312240707200607

Healy, J. M., Malley, J. E., & Stewart, A. J. (1990). Children and their fathers after parental separation. *American Journal of Orthopsychiatry, 60*, 531–543. doi: 10.1037/h0079201

Hess, R. D., & Camara, K. A. (1979). Post-divorce family relationships as mediating factors in the consequences of divorce for children. *Journal of Social Issues, 35*(4), 79–96. doi: 10.1111/j.1540–4560.1979.tb00814.x

Hetherington, E. M. (1991). Presidential address: Families, lies, and videotapes. *Journal of Research on Adolescence, 1*, 323–348. doi: 10.1111/1532–7795.ep11298087

Hetherington, E. M. (1999). Should we stay together for the sake of the children? In E. M. Hetherington (Ed.), *Coping with divorce, single parenting and remarriage: A risk and resiliency perspective* (pp. 93–116). Mahwah, NJ: Erlbaum.

Hetherington, E. M. (2006). The influence of conflict, marital problem solving and parenting on children's adjustment in nondivorced, divorced and remarried families. In A. Clarke-Steward & J. Dunn (Eds.), *Families count: Effect on child and adolescent development* (pp. 203–237). New York: Cambridge University Press.

Hetherington, E. M., Bridges, M., & Insabella, G. M. (1998). What matters? What does not?: Five perspectives on the association between marital transitions and children's adjustment. *American Psychologist, 53*(2), 167–184. doi: 10.1037/0003-066X.53.2

Hetherington, E. M., Clingempeel, W. G., Anderson, E. R., Deal, J. E., Stanley-Hagan, M., Hollier, E. A., & Lindner, M. S. (1992). Coping with marital transitions: A family systems perspective. *Monographs of the Society for Child Development, 227*(57), Nos. 2–3.

Hetherington, E. M., Cox, M., & Cox, R. (1982). Effects of divorce on parents and children. In M. Lamb (Ed.), *Nontraditional families* (pp. 233–288). Hillsdale, NJ: Erlbaum.

Jensen, E. S., Boyce, W. T., & Harnett, S. A. (1983). The Family Routines Inventory: Development and validation. *Social Science Medicine, 17*, 201–211. doi: 10.1016/0277-9536(83)90117-X

Johnston, J. R., Kline, M., & Tschann, J. M. (1989). Ongoing postdivorce conflict: Effects on children of joint custody and frequent access. *American Journal of Orthopsychiatry, 59*, 576–592. doi: 10.1111/j.1939–0025.1989.tb02748.x

Kelly, J. B. (2007). Children's living arrangements following separation and divorce: Insights from empirical and clinical research. *Family Process, 46*, 35–52. doi: 10.1111/j.1545–5300.2006.00190.x

King, V., Harris, K. M., & Heard, H. E. (2004). Racial and ethnic diversity in nonresident father involvement. *Journal of Marriage and Family, 66*(1), 1–21. doi: 10.1111/j.1741–3737.2004.00001.x

King, V., & Sobolewski, J. M. (2006). Nonresident fathers' contributions to adolescent well-being. *Journal of Marriage and Family, 68,* 537–557. doi: 10.1111/j.1741–3737.2006.00274.x

Krishnakumar, A., & Buehler, C. (2000). Interparental conflict and parenting behaviors: A meta-analytic review. *Family Relations, 49,* 25–44. doi: 10.1111/j.1741–3729.2000.00025.x

Kurdek, L. A. (1986). Custodial mothers' perceptions of visitation and payment of child support by noncustodial fathers in families with low and high levels of pre-separation interparent conflict. *Journal of Applied Developmental Psychology, 7,* 307–323. doi: 10.1016/0193–3973(86)90002-x

Lundahl, B. W., Tollefson, D., Risser, H., & Lovejoy, M. C. (2008). A meta-analysis of father involvement in parent training. *Research on Social Work Practice, 18*(2), 97–106. doi: 10.1177/1049731507309828

Maccoby, E. E., Buchanan, C. M., Mnookin, R. H., & Dornbusch, S. M. (1993). Postdivorce roles of mothers and fathers in the lives of their children. *Journal of Family Psychology, 7*(1), 24–38. doi: 10.1037/0893–3200.7.1.24

Maccoby, E., & Mnookin, R. (1992). *Dividing the child.* Cambridge, MA: Harvard University Press.

MacKinnon, D. P. (2008). *Introduction to statistical mediation analysis.* New York: Erlbaum.

Martinez, C. R. J., & Forgatch, M. S. (2001). Preventing problems with boys' non-compliance: Effects of a parent training intervention for divorcing mothers. *Journal of Consulting and Clinical Psychology, 69,* 416–428. doi: 10.1037/0022–006X.69.3.416

McGruder, B., Lorenz, F. O., Hoyt, D., Ge, X. J., & Montague, R. (1992). *Dimensions of parenting: A technical report.* Ames, IA: Iowa State University, Center for Family Research in Rural Mental Health.

Menning, C. L. (2002). Absent parents are more than money. *Journal of Family Issues, 23,* 648–671. doi: 10.1177/0192513x02023005004

Menning, C. L. (2006). Nonresident fathering and school failure. *Journal of Family Issues, 27,* 1356–1382. doi: 10.1177/0192513x06290038

Neighbors, B., Forehand, R., & McVicar, D. (1993). Resilient adolescents and inter-parental conflict. *American Journal of Orthopsychiatry, 63,* 462–471. doi: 10.1037/h0079442

Pruett, M., Cowan, P. A., Cowan, C. P., & Diamond, J. (2012). Supporting father involvement in the context of separation and divorce. In K. Kuehnle & L. Drozd (Eds.), *Parenting plan evaluations: Applied research for the family court.* New York: Oxford University Press.

Radin, N. (1981). The role of the father in cognitive, academic, and intellectual devel-opment. In M. E. Lamb (Ed.), *The role of the father in child development* (2nd ed., pp. 379–427). New York: Wiley.

Rohner, R. P. (1990). *Handbook for the study of parental acceptance-rejection.* Storrs, CT: Rohner Research Publications.

Rusby, J., Estes, A., & Dishion, T. (1991). *The interpersonal process code.* Unpublished coding manual. (Available from Oregon Social Learning Center, 207 East 5th Avenue, Ste. 202, Eugene, OR.)

Rutter, M. (2005). Environmentally mediated risks for psychopathology: Research strategies and findings. *Journal of the American Academy of Child and Adolescent Psychiatry, 44*(1), 3–18. doi: 10.1097/01.chi.0000145374.45992.c9

Sandler, I. N., Miles, J. C., Cookston, J. T., & Braver, S. L. (2008). Effects of father and mother parenting on children's mental health in high and low conflict divorces. *Family Court Review, 46*, 282–296. doi: 10.1111/j.1744–1617.2008. 00201.x

Schaefer, E. S. (1965). Children's reports of parental behavior: An inventory. *Child Development, 36*, 413–424. doi: 10.2307/1126465

Simons, R. L., Beaman, J., Conger, R. D., & Chao, W. (1993). Stress, support, and antisocial behavior trait as determinants of emotional well-being and parenting practices among single mothers. *Journal of Marriage and Family, 55*, 385–398. doi: 10.2307/352809

Simons, R. L., & Chao, W. (1996). Conduct problems. In R. L. Simons et al. (Eds.), *Understanding differences between divorced and intact families: Stress, interaction, and child outcome* (pp. 125–143). Thousand Oaks, CA: Sage.

Simons, R. L., & Johnson, C. (1996). Mother's parenting. In R. L. Simons et al. (Eds.), *Understanding differences between divorced and intact families: Stress, interaction and child outcome* (pp. 81–93). Thousand Oaks, CA: Sage.

Simons, R. L., Johnson, C., Conger, R. D., & Lorenz, F. O. (1997). Linking community context to quality of parenting; A study of rural families. *Rural Sociology, 62*, 207–230. doi: 10.1111/j.1549–0831.1997.tb00651.x

Simons, R. L., Lin, K.-H., Gordon, L. C., Conger, R. D., & Lorenz, F. O. (1999). Explaining the higher incidence of adjustment problems among children of divorce compared with those in two-parent families. *Journal of Marriage & Family, 61*, 1020–1033. doi: 10.2307/354021

Simons, R. L., Whitbeck, L. B., Beaman, J., & Conger, R. D. (1994). The impact of mothers' parenting, involvement by nonresidential fathers, and parental conflict on the adjustment of adolescent children. *Journal of Marriage and Family, 56*, 356–374. doi: 10.2307/353105

Soper, A. C., Wolchik, S. A., Tein, J. Y., & Sandler, I. N. (2010). Mediation of a preventive intervention's six-year effects program effects on health risk behaviors. *Psychology of Addictive Behaviors, 24*, 300–310. doi: 10.1037/a0019014

Stewart, S. D. (2003). Nonresident parenting and adolescent adjustment. *Journal of Family Issues, 24*, 217–244. doi: 10.1177/0192513x02250096

Stubbs, J., Crosby, L., Forgatch, M. S., & Capaldi, D. M. (1998). *Family and Peer Process Code: Training manual: A synthesis of three OSLC behavior codes.* Eugene, OR: Oregon Social Learning Center.

Tein, J.-Y., Sandler, I. N., MacKinnon, D. P., & Wolchik, S. A. (2004). How did it work? Who did it work for? Mediation and mediated moderation of a preventive intervention for children of divorce. *Journal of Consulting and Clinical Psychology, 72*, 617–624. doi: 10.1037/0022–006X.72.4.617

Trinder, L., Kellet, J., & Swift, L. (2008). The relationship between contact and child adjustment in high conflict cases after divorce or separation. *Child and Adolescent Mental Health, 13*(4), 181–187. doi: 10.1111/j.1475–3588.2008.00484.x

Tschann, J. M., Johnston, J. R., Kline, M., & Wallerstein, J. S. (1989). Family process and children's functioning during divorce. *Journal of Marriage and Family, 51*, 431–444. doi: 10.2307/352505

U. S. Census Bureau. (2010). *American's families and living arrangements: 2010.* Retrieved December 5, 2010, from http://www.census.gov/population/www/soc-demo/hh-fam/cps2010.html.

Uniform Marriage and Divorce Act. (1979). 9A Uniform Laws Annotated, Sec. 316.

Whitbeck, L. B., Simons, R. L., & Goldberg, E. (1996). Adolescent sexual intercourse. In R. L. Simons et al. (Eds.), *Understanding differences between divorced and intact families* (pp. 144–156). Thousand Oaks, CA: Sage.

White, L., & Gilbreth, J. G. (2001). When children have two fathers: Effects of relationships with stepfathers and noncustodial fathers on adolescent outcomes. *Journal of Marriage and Family, 63*(1), 155–167. doi: 10.1111/j.1741–3737.2001.00155.x

Whiteside, M. F., & Becker, B. J. (2000). Parental factors and the young child's postdivorce adjustment: A meta-analysis with implications for parenting arrangements. *Journal of Family Psychology, 14*(1), 5–26. doi: 10.1037/0893–3200.14.1.5

Wolchik, S. A., Sandler, I. N., Millsap, R. E., Plummer, B. A., Greene, S. M., Anderson, E. R., ... Haine, R. A. (2002). Six-year follow-up of a randomized, controlled trial of preventive interventions for children of divorce. *Journal of the American Medical Association, 288*, 1874–1881. doi: 10.1001/jama.288.15.1874

Wolchik, S. A., Sandler, I., Weiss, L., & Winslow, E. B. (2007). New Beginnings: An empirically-based program to help divorced mothers promote resilience in their children. In J. M. Briesmeister & C. E. Schaefer (Eds.), *Handbook of parent training: Helping parents prevent and solve problem behaviors* (pp. 25–62). New York: John Wiley & Sons.

Wolchik, S. A., West, S. G., Sandler, I. N., Tein, J.-Y., Coatsworth, D., Lengua, L., ... Griffin, W. A. (2000). An experimental evaluation of theory-based mother and mother–child programs for children of divorce. *Journal of Consulting and Clinical Psychology, 68*, 843–856. doi: 10.1037/0022–006X.68.5.843

Wolchik, S. A., West, S. G., Westover, S., Sandler, I. N., Martin, A., Lustig, J., ... Fisher, J. (1993). The children of divorce parenting intervention: Outcome evaluation of an empirically based program. *American Journal of Community Psychology, 21*, 293–331. doi: 10.1007/BF00941505

Young, M. H., Miller, B. C., Norton, M. C., & Hill, E. J. (1995). The effect of parental supportive behaviors on life satisfaction of adolescent offspring. *Journal of Marriage and Family, 57*, 813–822. doi: 10.2307/353934

Zhou, Q., Sandler, I. N., Millsap, R. E., Wolchik, S. A., & Dawson-McClure, S. R. (2008). Mother–child relationship quality and effective discipline as mediators of the 6-year effects of the New Beginnings Program for children from divorced families. *Journal of Consulting and Clinical Psychology, 76*, 579–594. doi: 10.1037/0022–006X.76.4.579

## 5

Supporting Father Involvement in the Context of Separation and Divorce

MARSHA KLINE PRUETT, CAROLYN PAPE COWAN,
PHILIP A. COWAN, AND JILLIAN S. DIAMOND ■

Ellen: "He doesn't pay child support, so he doesn't get to see the kids when he wants."
John: "I don't get to see my kids, so the hell if I'm going to pay her child support."
Ronnie: "He never paid that much attention to the kids when we were married. Now he wants to see them. He's just doing that to pay less support, or to get me back for leaving. I'm not sure which."
Ryan: "I wasn't a very involved father. I loved my kids, but Ronnie had a death grip on their schedules, and on what I was or was not allowed to do, and how I was supposed to do it. It was easier just to back away. Now that we're divorcing, I can be the kind of father I always wanted to be."

In these and countless other examples, a standoff ensues, a cycle in which neither parent wants to capitulate to the other because the stakes are so high. The stakes ultimately concern each parent's place in the child's heart, but they are fought out in terms of sharing time with the children and precious financial assets. One result of these types of ongoing parental conflicts may be reduced father involvement, as anger and bitterness become entrenched between parents, leaving the child at risk (Krishnakumar & Buehler, 2000; Sturge-Apple, Davies, & Cummings, 2006). Solutions to these dilemmas lie in how father involvement and co-parenting get conceptualized and implemented in the context of parenting time and decision-making. The ambiguity inherent in such decisions when the court is left to make them was first poignantly depicted for popular audiences in the movie *Kramer vs. Kramer* (1979), and it continues to get played out in family court cases that involve the structure of children's living arrangements, overnights, and relocations, among other issues.

To provide a context for discussion of father engagement when parents separate or divorce, this chapter begins with three brief sections summarizing research on married and cohabiting couples. A burgeoning literature indicates that fathers play an important role in their children's development, a role that is often quite different than that of mothers. Further, a plethora of recent studies show that when parents have high levels of unresolved conflict, or cold and withdrawn relationships, their children are at risk for behavioral, social, and emotional symptoms, as well as difficulties meeting academic challenges in school. After developing and summarizing these studies as relevant background, some central issues of father involvement when couple relationships dissolve but co-parenting obligations continue will be considered:

- Dilemmas about continuing a collaborative co-parenting relationship even though the partners are in conflict with each other
- Special problems of father involvement associated with maternal gatekeeping and establishing overnights with children

Finally, an evidence-based intervention designed to support and enhance father involvement prior to separation and divorce is described, with suggestions about how it could be adapted for separating and divorcing couples.

THE IMPACT OF FATHER ENGAGEMENT ON CHILDREN'S DEVELOPMENT

In this chapter, father involvement connotes feeling responsible for and behaving responsibly toward the child; being emotionally engaged; being physically accessible; providing material support to sustain the child's needs; being involved in caring for the child; and/or exerting influence in childrearing decisions. In a recent conceptualization, Pleck (2010) defines these components as positive activity engagement, warmth-responsiveness, control, indirect care, and process responsibility (responsibility for indirect care such as scheduling appointments). The components are interrelated, especially the first three, while the latter two are more independent from each other and the others, indicating that there are various pathways to father involvement that matter for child development in novel, as well as compounding, ways.

Paralleling societal shifts in gender roles and partly in response to them, there has been an impressive increase in research concerning the critical role fathers play in their children's healthy development (see Lamb, 2010, for a comprehensive review). This research has advanced our understanding of the importance of fathers' involvement in their children's lives, regardless of whether the men live with their children. A majority of the studies found that across family structures, cultures, and living circumstances, when fathers are positively engaged with their children, the children derive cognitive, emotional, and social benefits in terms of adjustment and resilience in the face of familial troubles and environmental risks and vulnerabilities. For example, one review of longitudinal studies indicated that children with involved fathers tend to have higher performance and verbal literacy skills, lower levels of emotional distress, and lower incidences of substance use, teen pregnancy, and delinquency (Sarkadi, Kristiansson, Oberklaid, & Bremberg, 2007). A summary of over 160 studies (Pruett, 2000), shown in Table 5.1, resulted in an extensive list of benefits accruing to children when fathers are positively engaged in their lives.

Table 5.1 CHILD OUTCOMES OF INVOLVED FATHERING

Behavioral

Reduced contact with juvenile justice

Delay in initial sexual activity, reduced teen pregnancy

Reduced rate of divorce

Less reliance on aggressive conflict resolution

Educational

Higher grade completion, graduation rates, and income

Math competence in girls

Verbal strength in boys and girls (literacy)

Enjoy school more

Emotional/Social

Greater problem-solving competence and stress tolerance

Greater empathy and moral sensitivity; reduced gender stereotyping

Initiative and self-direction

Positive peer relationships

UNIQUE CONTRIBUTIONS OF PATERNAL PARENTING

When partners become parents, their gender as well as their role differences are often accentuated, leading to slightly or somewhat different parenting responses and behaviors. Children will embrace these differences, but they also learn to "play up" the differences, creating a wedge between parents if such differences evoke anger and blame when they result in miscommunication, unmet expectations, and ultimately resentment (Pruett & Pruett, 2009). Understanding modal differences between parents in gendered behaviors and inclinations (*word of caution*: there are always individual differences as well, and they often take precedence) helps parents and legal professionals identify typical gender differences that often get attributed to personal failings of the ex-spouse.

By 6 weeks of age, babies respond differently to their father than their mother. In one study, when mothers approached and held their babies, the babies would partially close their eyes and relax their shoulders, and their heart rate slowed. By contrast, when approached by their fathers, the babies hunched their shoulders and opened their eyes wide, and their heart rates accelerated (Yogman, Kindlon, & Earls, 1995). Fathers were associated with novelty and excitement, mothers with calming nurturance. Further, mothers are likely to lift their babies consistently in the same manner—to their chests—while fathers' approaches are unpredictable; they might roll the baby over or lift him or her into the crook of their arm. When a child is distressed, mothers tend to soothe, fathers to distract. Mothers often teach in their play; fathers tend to engage in more tactile and open-ended exploration. She prepares the child for relationships, focusing on social interactions as important for future success. He tends to explain his risk-taking, problem-solving, and frustration-tolerating behaviors as preparation for the "real world" children must enter. Fathers spend more time playing with their young children, even when they are the primary caretakers of those children. Although mothers spend more absolute time playing with their children, play is more prominent in father–child interactions, and the stimulation and novelty fathers introduce may render their play especially salient to their children (Lamb, Frodi, Hwang, & Frodi, 1982). Fathers tend to demand exploration, and children respond, for example, by using more advanced speech patterns with their fathers than with their mothers. Fathers also discipline differently than mothers: they spend less time reasoning, use fewer words, and expect greater compliance more quickly; they use more imperatives and fewer reciprocal bargaining techniques; and they are more willing to confront their children and enforce discipline. These tendencies in gender differences translate into concrete behavioral differences: Fathers tend to activate and stimulate, emphasizing independence, competence, and frustration tolerance. Mothers, on the other hand, tend to regulate and soothe, helping their young children to navigate life's challenges feeling cared for and secure. These gender differences extend throughout the early years of a child's life (see Pruett, 2000, for a fuller explication of studies).

WHEN MATERNAL AND PATERNAL DIFFERENCES EVOLVE INTO CONFLICT

Children benefit from parenting styles that typify typical paternal and maternal proclivities, especially if both styles are conducted within an overall frame of sensitivity to the child's needs and limits and an overall acceptance of the other parent's different style and parenting qualities (Pruett & Pruett, 2009). Married and cohabiting couples with different ideas and behavioral strategies concerning how to parent their children find themselves increasingly working out a co-parenting relationship, yet it is usually far more difficult to establish a collaborative co-parenting relationship when parents are living separately and in a state of conflict about financial and/or emotional aspects of their lives. For example, children respond to the novel and stimulating approach of fathers in ways that may cause difficulties in a divorcing family where differences are accentuated and mistrusted. Consider this common theme heard in clinical consultations: Separated, co-parenting mothers attribute their children's return from the father's house "all jazzed" as a sign that he is not attending to his children's needs faithfully. He may be crossing a line in judgment, or he is often doing things differently than she would choose or desire. Sorting this out can be critical in deciding if a parenting plan is ill advised for the child versus uncomfortable for the parent to whom the child returns, but not necessarily a serious problem for the child.

Whether living together or apart, parents who fail to establish a satisfactory cooperative relationship place their children at risk. Parents with high levels of conflict and/or high levels of relationship unhappiness have children who are likely to be more aggressive, depressed, or both (Cowan, Cowan, Ablow, Johnson, & Measelle, 2005; Cummings & Keller, 2006; Harold, Aitken, & Shelton, 2007; Johnston, 2006; Sandler, Miles, Cookston, & Braver, 2008). The mechanisms linking couple conflict with negative child outcomes include emotional distress at witnessing or becoming triangulated in parental fighting, but they also include a spillover from couple to parent–child relationships. It is difficult for both fathers and mothers to be warm and firm with their children when their relationship with their partners is not a source of support for them (Kaczynski, Lindahl, Malik, & Laurenceau, 2006; Sturge-Apple et al., 2006).

CO-PARENTING IN DIVORCING FAMILIES

When parents dissolve their couple relationship, the co-parenting relationship becomes the focus of the distinct part of their relationship that must evolve into a new form but remain strong. It is generally accepted that it is beneficial for children if parents maintain a positive co-parenting relationship, except in situations in which involvement of one or both parents is not healthy or desirable for the family. When there is a history of severe drug or alcohol abuse, intimate partner (domestic) violence, or child abuse, parental access may be limited, supervised, or suspended in accord with children's best interests (Dalton, Carbon, & Olesen, 2003; Jaffe, Johnston, Crooks, & Bala, 2008).

Ongoing parental conflict is an indicator that a co-parenting alliance may be difficult or impossible to achieve. In divorcing families, it is more often father involvement that is limited when parents cannot cooperate. Although the focus of this chapter is on the benefits to children of active and positive father involvement in their life, that stance in no way implies that children require a male parent to develop social, emotional, and cognitive competence, as there is ample research to suggest otherwise (Silverstein, 2002). To the contrary, the argument presented turns on the empirically supported assumption that a second positively involved parent can provide added significant support for children's development. When the second parent is a male, it may offer unique protective factors to the child and family.

Successful co-parenting after separation or divorce requires that parents maintain a shared focus on their child's well-being even when they are not in a romantic or contractual relationship with each other. This requirement is typically translated in family court into encouraging or mandating that major decisions be made together (e.g., health care, education) and/or sharing parental responsibilities and division of time spent with the children. Additional components of co-parenting that broaden the opportunities to work with families and establish mutuality through parenting plans include (a) striving to agree on who their child is and what his or her needs are; (b) expressly and implicitly valuing the importance of the other parent's contributions to childrearing; (c) recognizing gender differences that lead partners to think, feel, and behave in distinct ways with respect to childrearing; (d) allowing children's needs to dictate how conflicts get resolved; and (e) creating a "team" that extends beyond parallel parenting and commits to backing each other up when children need two firm but loving parents to hold them on course when they are veering off in some unknown or ill-informed direction (Pruett & Pruett, 2009). Parents may display a high level of sensitive responsiveness to a child individually, but they also may criticize, blame, or neglect the other parent in front of the child. This undermines the capacity of the co-parenting alliance to function as the child's safety net. Co-parenting can counteract compromised parenting styles and enhance the quality of parent–child relationships (Feinberg & Kan, 2008), thereby supporting the child's disrupted sense of security from the transition to separate households and family units (Nair & Murray, 2005).

Among the thorniest issues facing family courts are (a) how to encourage parents to cooperate in the face of hurt or conflict; (b) how to support both parents' role in the child's life without splitting the child's time and life arbitrarily in half; and (c) how to overcome barriers to ongoing father involvement created by social roles that establish mothers as primary caretakers, often right up to the point of a legal dispute.

Faced with these dilemmas, family practitioners from legal and mental health professions have put their faith in the promise of co-parenting, without ample evidence regarding how it can best be implemented.

Research findings on co-parenting and father involvement in intact families may be useful in helping divorcing parents to design appropriate parenting plans. First, fathers may find it difficult to negotiate the kind of parenting plan they desire when their children are very young and their ex-partners want to remain the primary parent. Yet fathers who stay collaboratively involved during the first 3 months of a newborn's life also tend to be in relationships in which couple distress is less likely to spill over into co-parenting over the first year of the baby's life (McHale, 2007). In other words, fathers who stay the course despite rocky relationships with their partners—"resilient dads"—strengthen the bedrock of the co-parenting relationship. There is some evidence that men who are active from early on in their children's life experience hormonal (Storey, Walsh, Quinton, & Wynne-Edwards, 2000) and brain (Feldman, Swain & Mayes, 2005; Swain et al., 2008) changes that support their capacity to respond to and empathize with their child. Activating the nurturing potential in men early seems to support their ongoing parenting and co-parenting competence.

A father's involvement with his children is often contingent upon the mother's attitude towards, and expectations of, support from him (Carlson, McLanahan, & Brooks-Gunn, 2008; Cohen & Finzi-Dottan, 2005; Pruett, Arthur, & Ebling, 2007). Mothers are a force in co-parenting negotiations and compromises, and parenting plans should be constructed within this social reality.

INVOLVEMENT AS A FUNCTION OF QUALITY OVER QUANTITY TIME

One reality of maternal primacy in the family domain is that divorced fathers often are in court wanting more time with their child than they have spent historically or currently. In research concerning father involvement, there has been a shift from discussing the frequency or amount of time fathers spend with their children to assessing the quality of their involvement (Cowan, Cowan, Cohen, Pruett, & Pruett, 2008; Lamb, 2010; Shonkoff & Phillips, 2000). It has been shown that non-residential fathers' involvement may have less impact on their children than resident fathers' involvement due to differences in level of involvement or in characteristics of the men who remain living with their children (see Carlson & McLanahan, 2010; Jaffee, Caspi, Moffitt, Taylor, & Dickson, 2001). Although children benefit most from having fathers who are engaged in their care on a number of levels, research also has clearly indicated that it is the quality—not the quantity—of time that matters most to children's outcomes. Studies have not established the bare minimum quantity of time that supports ongoing parent–child relationships, nor will they ever likely do so, since what constitutes an acceptable minimum is a product of a number of factors that cannot all be accounted for simultaneously and in the same family: child age, gender, temperament, quality of attachment to each parent, proximity in living situation, and so on. In the absence of a bright-line decision marker, quantity as much or more than quality time continues to lie at the heart of legal disputes. These disputes are fueled by the fact that spending less time together causes distress to parent and/

or child and raises fears about whether they will be able to maintain closeness over time in the face of ongoing family transitions. On the other end of the spectrum, in terms of supporting time sharing, joint legal and physical custody research generally finds positive outcomes for parents and children compared to sole custody (see Pruett & Barker, 2009), though recent research suggests that shared parenting splits may work best only under cooperative conditions for school-age children (McIntosh, Wells, Smyth, & Long, 2008). Although the generalizations that can be justified from empirical data are relatively few, research offers more instructive guidelines than a generation ago, when exploration of how to turn the value of father involvement into a viable shared parenting arrangement began in earnest.

Summary points of the co-parental relationship:

- Research shows that father involvement is good for the child's and father's adjustment and for the strength of the co-parental relationship.
- However, father's involvement is strongly influenced by the mother's attitudes towards his competence and about his desirability as a parent for their child.
- There are multiple indicators of father involvement and co-parenting. Maintaining a broad definition opens doors for more types of shared arrangements to be adopted and reinforced.
- It is the quality of time and parenting—not the quantity—that is more highly related to closeness between parent and child. While some quantity is needed to establish sufficient opportunity to establish and maintain closeness, the minimum point has not been established. Similarly, no amount of time nearing equality has been established as helpful or harmful to children in general; individual considerations take precedence.

TWO FACTORS THAT PLACE FATHERS' INVOLVEMENT WITH YOUNG CHILDREN AT SPECIAL RISK

It has been well established that children's adjustment with both parents influences their adjustment throughout life. Young children and fathers face particular risks to their relationship that place the child's adjustment in jeopardy early in the developmental trajectory. With the average marriage lasting 8 years in the United States, and unmarried relationships averaging a shorter duration, a majority of families who are separating and divorcing have children under age 6 (Maccoby & Mnookin, 1992; Pruett & Jackson, 2002). Recently, researchers have focused on exploring two types of dynamics in families with young children that are focal points for contention and controversy in legal disputes: maternal gatekeeping and overnights in parenting plans for young children.

Maternal Gatekeeping

A reality in both married and divorced families is that the mother often functions as a gatekeeper in ways that can either facilitate or inhibit father–child relationships (Allen & Hawkins, 1999; Fagan & Barnett, 2003) through her influence on his access and decision-making latitude. Gatekeeping is usually justified in terms of its protective function, keeping children appropriately safe from external dangers, but it also may serve as a vehicle for expression of maternal anger, fear, or distrust of fathers' parenting competence. While either or both parents may engage in gatekeeping behaviors, maternal gatekeeping is more commonly discussed due to women's traditional role as the primary caretaker and tendency toward more restrictive gatekeeping in comparison with fathers. In contrast, research has shown that positive, unrestrictive maternal gatekeeping is associated with higher levels of cooperation between parents, lower parental conflict and hostility, and increased father involvement (Pruett et al., 2007).

CHARACTERISTICS OF GATEKEEPING

Although gatekeeping occurs between married as well as divorced parents, it is especially important to address it in separated and divorced parents, in which the father–child relationship is particularly vulnerable. Several recent studies have extended the knowledge of what characterizes maternal gatekeeping, its antecedents, and the effect it has on paternal involvement.

Using data from the Collaborative Divorce Project (Pruett, Insabella, & Gustafson, 2005), a subsequent study of maternal gatekeeping behaviors sought to better understand patterns of gatekeeping, as well as to determine whether an intervention could reduce restrictive behaviors (Pruett et al., 2007). Among significant findings from the study, mothers' retrospective perceptions of their past marriage and supportiveness of the ex-spouse were directly associated with their gatekeeping behaviors following the divorce, as well as their perceptions of father involvement. Negative gatekeeping may be, in part, her payback for his treatment of her (not only the children) during the marriage. Positive gatekeeping (that which supports collaborative childrearing) was linked to the mother's belief that the father's involvement with the child is important and that it is her parental duty to facilitate it. The father's positive gatekeeping response was linked to his acknowledgment that the mother's role in his relationship to his child is a central one.

In addition, mothers were twice as likely to report ways in which they supported father involvement than ways they hindered access, while fathers viewed mothers as equally helping and hindering of contact with their children. Although men and women agreed that mothers were often helpful, mothers saw themselves as being more helpful than fathers did, suggesting that one mechanism for her frustration may be that she is not being appreciated and for his frustration that he does not view her as helpful as she claims.

A co-parenting intervention was implemented in the study that combined a brief psychoeducation program (6 hours) and court-assisted mediation to coach mothers and fathers to identify gatekeeping behaviors and work at greater cooperation. Mothers who participated in the intervention became four times more likely to acknowledge and describe ways in which they hindered paternal access. Their greater awareness led to more clarity about behaviors that hindered fathers' access to the children that they had not realized and often had not intended. The intervention also encouraged fathers to "step up to the plate" and take responsibility for knowing their children's needs and responding to them with personal initiative rather than leaving it to their ex-wives to orchestrate.

While gatekeeping is often prompted by mothers' feelings about fathers' competence, it also may be affected by mothers' own internal factors. Gaunt (2008) found that mothers who identified highly with their parental role and had low self-esteem were more likely to be restrictive gatekeepers. Similarly, father involvement may have more to do with fathers' own characteristics and beliefs about parenting than maternal beliefs and actions (Schoppe-Sullivan, Cannon, Brown, Mangelsdorf, & Sokolowski, 2008). Assessing the extent to which gatekeeping is operating within a family, and for what reasons, may help evaluators and legal professionals promote parenting plans that are less likely to destabilize without the watchful eye of the court.

From the current research, the following conclusions can be reached about maternal gatekeeping:

- Mothers' retrospective opinions of their marriage may play a role in their gatekeeping behaviors.
- Restrictive maternal gatekeeping is sometimes conducted with little awareness and can be associated with mothers' low self-esteem.
- An intervention program that teaches about the effects of gatekeeping can help make mothers aware of their gatekeeping tendencies and promote positive gatekeeping among mothers (support for father's role) and fathers (support for mother's role).
- Assessing what is happening in a family in regard to gatekeeping and the validity of restrictive or protective parenting supports the development of parenting plans that support father involvement appropriate to an individual family situation.

Overnights for Young Children

Historically, parenting plans for young children (under age 6) have specified that one parent, typically the mother, maintains primary residential status, with the other parent spending less time with the children. Early psychological literature that emanated from assessment and evaluation data of custody disputes between biological and foster or adoptive parents supported the notion that stability in residence and consistency in caretaking are critical elements for young children's healthy adjustment (Goldstein, Solnit, & Freud, 1973; Goldstein, Solnit, Goldstein, & Freud, 1996). The authors described children's foreshortened sense of time and their resulting need for regular contact and few or short separations from adults with whom they were developing secure attachments. Goldstein et al.'s analysis relied on the knowledge of attachment that was available at the time of their research. Much of the theory Goldstein et al. relied on about the role of secure attachment in children has been borne out over time and research, but recent studies also have expanded what is known about multiple attachments in general, and the role of the father in particular (Lamb & Lewis, 2010; Paquette, 2004).

In brief, separation responses of infants become stronger as attachments to caregivers solidify between 6 and 24 months. There is often a primary caregiver whom the child prefers and seeks comfort from when distressed, although this preference fluctuates at different developmental stages in the first few years of life (see Lamb & Lewis, 2010). Yet the non-preferred caregivers remain important figures, and the preference diminishes and often disappears by the time the child is 18 months of age (Lamb, 2002). Although infants and toddlers may resist transitions between parents in their second year, just as they sometimes protest "even more strongly" (Lamb & Kelly, 2009, p. 190) when transitioning to out-of-home care providers, they generally comfort quickly once the transition has been made. The final phase of attachment formation begins when children are approximately 2 years old (Greenberg, Cicchetti, & Cummings, 1990), when the cognitive and linguistic abilities of 2- to 3-year-olds enable them to tolerate longer separations with less distress. This is especially likely when both parents have been providing regular care to the baby, including feeding, soothing, putting to bed, and so on, so that attachments to both caregivers are being consolidated and strengthened on an ongoing basis (Lamb & Kelly, 2009). It is now understood that the basis for secure attachments begins and solidifies early in life, but that attachment also changes across childhood, varies across caregivers, and is subject to change in conjunction with early life events, especially adverse ones (see Cassidy & Shaver, 2008).

After separation, the problem lies in balancing children's needs for stability with their needs for regular interaction with both caregivers around important aspects of care, such as sleep routines. When there have been overnights with the less seen or non-residential parent built into the parenting plan, conventional wisdom suggested that fewer overnights, ideally once the child was 3 years old, maximized children's potential to develop secure attachment to the primary caregiver and maintain their sense of safety and comfort. A current area of disagreement among professionals surrounding parenting plans for young children is whether overnight visits with a secondary caretaker (typically the father) is developmentally facilitative for children under 5 years of age. With increased knowledge of child development as well as the benefits of father involvement, some child development experts question the validity of the historically held belief that overnights with secondary caretakers are disruptive to development. They assert that children are not only capable of adjusting to overnights with both parents but can also benefit from this experience (Kelly & Lamb, 2005). Other experts assert that overnight visits are inadvisable for infants and young toddlers (Solomon & Biringen, 2005).

These scholars agree on some critical points and disagree on others (Pruett, 2005). They agree that:

1. Attachment theory offers an empirically founded lens through which to consider and examine children's separation responses and relationships to their parents, with different features associated with secure attachment in infancy, toddlerhood, and childhood.
2. Children develop multiple attachments; fathers as well as mothers constitute important attachment figures in children's lives, and father–child attachments are independent from and distinct in quality from mother– child attachments.
3. Separations are not inherently harmful for children, and the work of early attachment theorists may not be directly germane to divorce situations.

The scholars have different views on three equally important assumptions:

1. The relative import for child attachment and bonding to the non-primary caregiver(s), and the degree to which attachment to a second parent or parent figure compensates for separations from the primary attachment figure;

2. The weight to assign to the child's preference for the mother at different ages, especially at approximately 18 months old, when children's preference for the primary attachment figure begins to fluctuate between caretakers;

3. In divorce situations, how to balance the importance of consistency in residence and overall stability of care with support for high levels and quality of father–child relationships. Empirical research does not offer clarity about the relative import of these factors vis-à-vis each other.

These three issues are examined with respect to a body of child development and attachment literature that focused on different research questions. Experts disagree about how to interpret the available literature, which findings are most relevant, and how meaning attributed to the findings gets made. Individual value systems and theoretical preferences are implicated in the debate; developmental theorists, family systems theorists, and psychoanalytically oriented theorists tend to see the same world through different lenses. Compared to the volumes of studies that indirectly address considerations of how children feel and stay connected to important adults in their life, and how children maintain equilibrium when they separate, make transitions, and adapt to stress (e.g., Cassidy & Shaver, 2008), there are only a few studies that directly address the question of how overnights for young children directly impinge on optimal development. Four relevant studies are described, with strengths and limitations of each summarized in Table 5.2. In the absence of more specific data, mental health and legal professionals are left to make individual decisions based on the best clinical evidence that can be gleaned in each family's situation.

The first study examined how the occurrence and structure of overnight visits relates to psychological and behavioral problems in 132 young children (Pruett, Ebling, & Insabella, 2004). Significant findings included the importance of consistent schedules each week, and a gender difference in which girls benefited from parenting plans that involved overnights and multiple caregivers, while boys did not reap the same benefit. Inconsistent schedules were more difficult for boys than for girls. Outcome indicators included children's depression/anxiety, sleep problems, aggression, and social withdrawal. In this study, the youngest children (0–2-year-olds) were not assessed, though this fact is not always recognized by professionals citing this study. The 2- to 3-year-olds neither benefited nor developed behavioral symptoms as a result of overnights or multiple caretakers; overnights with 4- to 6-year-olds had benefits.

In path analyses using the same sample of parents (Pruett & Barker, 2009), the maternal model showed that overnights and consistent schedules week to week were related indirectly to child outcomes through their reciprocal relationship to mothers' support of fathers 15 to 18 months after the divorce. The same variables were significant in the paternal model, except that there was a direct correlation to child outcomes. Less couple conflict and more cooperation were associated with overnights and a consistent schedule, which was in turn associated with both parents' views of the child as having fewer behavioral problems. These analyses indicate that the overnights and parenting plan variables operate in the larger family context of parental relations that locate them as one of many dynamics influencing how overnights affect child adjustment and development.

A second recent study assessed children in three age groups—0 to 2 years (n = 248 overnighters), 2 to 3 years (n = 487 overnighters), and 4 to 5 years (n = 1,215

Table 5.2 Four Seminal Overnights Studies

	Participants	Procedures
Pruett, Ebling, & Insabella, 2004	132 families, including 101 divorcing and 31 unmarried parents with children ages 0–6 Families predominantly Caucasian, predominantly low to moderate income levels; range of parental conflict levels	After both parents agreed to participate, parents completed a self-report questionnaire at the time of filing for divorce and again 15–18 months later. Widely used self-report measures provided data on parent–child relationships (Negative Changes in Parent–Child Relationship), conflict (Content of Conflict Checklist [CCC]), and demographics. Child problems were measured by CBCL (Achenbach) filled out by both parents separately. Zero- to 1-year-olds were not assessed in this study because the CBCL is not normed for that age group. Parenting plan information was coded by research staff based on court-provided information (for control group) or clinician-provided information (for intervention group). Parenting plan variables included the number of overnights; the number of caretakers, which assessed the number of significant people (parents and others) the child spent significant waking time with; consistent schedules (yes, no) was measured as the same schedule on weekdays (M–F) across weeks.
McIntosh, Smyth, Kelaher, Wells, & Long, 2010	From a very large sample that included intact families, 835 separated/divorcing families with children ages 3 months to 5 years were studied. Families were representative of the general Australian population. The children were assessed in three groups: <2 years, 2–3 years, and 4–5 years. They were also divided into groups based on overnight status:	Data were collected for the Longitudinal Study of Australian Children (LSAC); collection techniques included face-to-face interviews, brief observations, and mail-in self-report questionnaires. Primary caregivers filled out surveys for demographic, parenting, parental relationship, and outcome data. Outcomes pertained to emotional dysregulation and psychosomatic symptoms. Parents rated psychosomatics as wheezing, health status (PEDS), and

Findings and Analysis	Strengths	Weaknesses
Data analytic strategies: bivariate correlations followed by hierarchical regression analysis Poorer parent–child relationships were related to various negative child outcomes. Parent conflict also explained child behavior problems. Overall: Fathers reported that children with overnights, more caretakers, and consistent schedules had fewer social problems. Mothers reported that children with overnights and more caretakers had fewer social problems and attention problems. Both parents reported fewer internalizing problems when consistent schedules were maintained. Mothers also reported that having more caretakers was associated with sleep disturbances and anxiety/depression. Gender differences: Girls benefited from overnights and more caretakers, boys did not. Age differences: Overnights did not benefit or cause distress to the toddlers (2–3) and benefited 4- to 6-yr-olds. After accounting for parent–child relationship changes and parental conflict, the parenting plan variables were still significantly related to cognitive and social outcomes for children, but the differences were not large in absolute terms.	Both mothers and fathers were assessed. Study relied on measures that are widely used in the field. Overnight data were reported by a third (objective) source. Number of caregivers and schedule consistency are variables not previously assessed; they account for important aspects of parenting plans for young children beyond the presence of overnights.	The sample size was too small to make conclusions about interactions with age and gender together in the sample. Outcomes for 0- to 1-year-olds were not assessed in this report (though they were part of the larger study). The parenting plan variables were measured simply and with limited information since intervention, not parenting plans, was the focus of the larger study.
Data analytic strategies: Hierarchical regression analysis using linear or logistic regression depending on the type of outcome variable There were no significant findings relating overnights to psychosomatic outcomes. Children <2 years in shared arrangements had higher irritability than children in primary care. The degree of monitoring	Obtaining data from LSAC allowed researchers to use an array of developmentally appropriate variables and to employ a large sample size. Use of multiple age groupings allowed for comparison. Data were collected from multiple sources. Overnights were explicated with age appropriate	Data were not collected from the secondary caretaker. Despite the overall large sample size, the number of infants and young children in shared overnight arrangements was comparatively small, which affects the capacity to obtain significant findings. Findings were based upon emotional regulation, not attachment *per se*. This is not

(Continued)

Table 5.2 Four Seminal Overnights Studies   (*Continued*)

	Participants	Procedures
	Infants (0–1) *Rare*: less than 1 ovn/yr *Primary care*: between 1 ovn/mo and 1 ovn/wk *Shared*: 1+ ovn/wk **2- to 6-yr-olds** *Rare*: <1 ovn/yr *Primary care*: between 1 ovn/mo and 5 ovn/2 wks *Shared*: 5+ ovn/2 wks	a Global Health Measure. Emotional dysregulation included parent ratings of proximity monitoring behaviors with the primary caregiver (three items taken from Communication and Symbolic Behavior Scales), irritability (Short Temperament Scale for Infants), problems (Brief Infant-Toddler Social-Emotional Assessment [BITSEA]), and emotional development. Caregivers rated conflict with caregiver, and observers rated negative response to parent (yes/no). Some different measures were used for each of the three age groups.
Altenhofen, Sutherland, & Biringen, 2010	24 divorcing mothers and their children, ages 1–6 Families predominantly Caucasian Averaged 8 months since separation	Mother and child engaged in free play while parent completed self-report questionnaires. This was designed to simulate parents' normal home environment (multitasking). This process was taped and scored for maternal emotional availability (EA). Lastly, the mother participated in a semi-structured interview related to the parenting plan. Widely used qualities such as age at onset of overnight stays, interparental conflict and communication, and EA were examined for their importance in child attachment security and dependency. Attachment security and dependency were assessed using Waters' Attachment Q-Set. EA includes four caregiver scales (Sensitivity, Structuring, Nonintrusiveness, and Nonhostility) and two child scales (Responsiveness to the Caregiver and Involvement of the Caregiver). Shared parenting = avg. 8 overnights/ month. No range given and S.D. large (which means great variability within small sample).

Findings and Analysis	Strengths	Weaknesses
proximity to the primary caretaker did not differ across these groups. Children age 2–3 in shared arrangements exhibited lower levels of persistence with tasks, as well as more problematic behaviors. There were no significant group differences for sleep difficulties, relations with peers, social adjustment, and emotional symptoms. Conflict with caregiver and observed negative interactions also were not significantly different across groups. The 4- to 5-year-olds in shared arrangements showed no negative effects in comparison with children in primary care. Variation in behavior and emotional regulation in this group was explained by parental conflict and emotional variability rather than residential arrangements.	definitions and more detail than in previous studies. Findings were based upon specific and age appropriate outcomes of emotional dysregulation.	a weakness of the study, but a caution to others interpreting the results in variance with and beyond the data.
Data Analytic Strategies: bivariate correlations followed by hierarchical regression analysis 54% of children showed insecure attachment (no comparison group). Age of onset of overnights was not significantly related to attachment or dependency. Mothers who rated themselves as using higher-conflict tactics had low emotional availability. No regression equations were significant. That is, when considered in unison, the variables were unrelated to outcome variables	Data were obtained using measures common to this area of research. Child attachment is an important variable to assess in the study of overnights.	Only mother report is included. No control group is included to put results in an appropriate context. The children experienced recent parent separation, so insecure attachment is not surprising and may only be transient. The statistical procedures violate statistical assumptions (insufficient sample size). This limitation and others are not noted in the study.

(Continued)

Table 5.2 FOUR SEMINAL OVERNIGHTS STUDIES   *(Continued)*

	Participants	Procedures

Solomon & George, 1999	126 mother–toddler pairs
	   Avg. child age 29 months
	   Married mothers had higher income and higher education, and were less likely to work full-time.
	   3 overnight groups:
	   overnights (n = 55),
	   no overnights (n = 29),
	   married families (n = 42).
	   Many of the families had changed overnight status within the past year from
	   no overnights to overnights.
		Children's attachment status was classified as organized, disorganized, or unclassifiable, based on prior studies.
		   In a Strange Situation procedure paradigm, pairs attended a single session in a laboratory playroom.
		   They were videotaped doing two interactive tasks: a problem-solving task and a cleanup task. Brief separations and reunions (3 and 5 minutes) were arranged between tasks.
		   Measures:
		   Problem-solving task: mother's supportive presence and child's task orientation.
		   Cleanup task: mother's authoritativeness and child's self-control.

overnighters)—with children living primarily with one parent used as comparable control groups (McIntosh, Smyth, Kelaher, Wells, & Long, 2010). According to data from primary caretakers, usually the mothers, children under age 2 with frequent overnights (averaging four or more nights every two weeks) were more irritable than those in primary care. Also, they more vigilantly monitored visual proximity with the primary parent than did infants with rare overnights (less than once per month or holidays only), but there were no differences from those in primary care, so it is a bit unclear what this distinction signifies. Among 2- to 3-year-olds, children in a shared care arrangement exhibited lower levels of persistence (the ability to play continuously, stay with routine tasks, etc.) and more distressed parent–child interactions than those with rare overnights or living in primary care. The authors note that children at this age still exhibit distress when separated from their primary caregiver, despite their growing cognitive ability to be aware of and comprehend the separations. No group differences were found for emotional symptoms, conflict with the caregiver, response to strangers, or psychosomatic symptoms. Similar to Pruett et al.'s (2004) results, the 4- to 5-year-olds exhibited no negative effects from having frequent overnight visits with a secondary caregiver. By this age children are generally

Findings and Analysis	Strengths	Weaknesses

Analytic strategies:
  ANOVAs and ANCOVAs with attachment status and family group.
  Married and non-overnight groups were combined.
  Problem-solving task: Unclassifiable mothers provided more support in overnight than in comparison families.
  Within the overnight families, organized and unclassifiable mothers provided more support than disorganized mothers.
  Cleanup task: No significant effects across family groups. Authors questioned if lack of results is due to the task being less developmentally appropriate for toddlers than other task.
  Tasks were then combined:
  Post-separation child "breakdowns" (low self-control score but adequate problem-solving score) were significantly more common among the overnight group (54% to 27%). Larger differences were found across attachment groups as well.
	Used a well-known paradigm for attachment assessment and adapted widely used measures
	  First study to focus specifically on overnights and toddlers using attachment measures
		The authors acknowledge that no construct-validated classification system for attachment existed for children 20–36 months old, so the measures' validity for the children in the study is unknown (p.147).
		  Information was obtained only from mothers.
		  The procedures used a 5-minute separation between laboratory tasks as an analogy to overnight separations and how children might respond, although the correspondence between real-life situations and the laboratory is not known and its applicability has been widely questioned.
		  The significant movement into the overnights group from non-overnight families within the past year (n = 30 to 55) suggests many of the children were in transition, with most change evident in the overnights group, which may partially account for group differences.

able to separate from their primary caregiver with minimal distress as long as they are given a clear plan about reunion before the separation (Marvin & Britner, 2008). In both McIntosh's and Pruett's studies, assessments of child behaviors relative to separations and reunions were not collected.

A third study about the effects of overnight visits with secondary caretakers examined the maternal-reported attachment security of 24 children ages 12 to 73 months who were currently experiencing overnights (averaging eight nights per month) compared to that of children in non-divorced families (Altenhofen, Sutherland, & Biringen, 2010). Children whose parents divorced showed a higher incidence of insecure attachment to their primary caregiver (54%) versus 30% to 33% found in other studies of non-divorced families; the families had only recently separated (average = 8 months), and the transition was still underway for those families. Age of onset of overnights was not a significant predictor of security; emotionally available mothers had more securely attached children, introducing an external factor that may eclipse the effects of overnights per se.

The final study (Solomon & George, 1999) compared 126 mother–toddler pairs: 40 had overnights in a baseline study conducted 1 year prior, 42 had no overnights but did have paternal involvement 1 year prior, and 44 were married when assessed 1 year prior. The status of many of the families had recently changed: at this time of assessment 55 were families with overnights, 29 had no overnights, and 42 were married (note that many of the no-overnight families had begun overnights within the last year or less). Using procedures in which families were not assessed in their homes but in a laboratory environment, problem-solving skills (supportive presence of mother and task orientation of toddler) and behavior during a clean-up session (authoritativeness of mother and self-control of toddler) were measured. There were no differences between groups; when the no-overnights and marrieds were combined, children in the overnight group were more likely than the comparison children to have meltdowns in the clean-up session.

It is noteworthy that another Solomon study (cited in Solomon, 2005) using a similar methodology is often quoted in custody and access disputes. Since we could not obtain the full-text article of the study despite extensive efforts, a summary of the study is mentioned below but is not included on Table 5.2. In this study, 145 mothers and infants 12 to 18 months were assessed. Also, 42 intact and 43 separated fathers were assessed. The groups were divided by overnight status into roughly three equal groups: regular overnights (one or two overnights/week or biweekly), no overnights, or dual-parent (intact). Findings indicated that significantly more infants with overnights were classified as disorganized or unclassifiable in attachment compared to infants in intact families. *Neither the pattern of overnights nor the total amount of time away from the mother predicted disorganized attachment.* Instead, insecure attachment in the overnight group was associated with parental conflict and low communication. Maternal insensitivity to the child was also related to disorganized attachment. Overnight time and patterning was not related to father–child attachment security. Low parent communication again was significantly related to the father–child attachment, similar to results for mother–child pairs. Thus, the relationship between parents, not the overnights, explained differences in child attachment.

Table 5.2 indicates similarities and differences among the studies. It is noteworthy that the Pruett et al. study (2004) did not examine attachment, but rather emotional and behavioral problems that emerged once parent–child relationship quality and parental conflict were accounted for in analyses. Only the Pruett et al. (2004) study reported data from both parents. The latter three studies assessed attachment behaviors or proxies of such; McIntosh et al. (2010) and Solomon (2005) reported finding some difficulties experienced by the children studied, while Altenhofen et al. (2010) did not, perhaps due to a number of methodological weaknesses of that study. All four studies showed that the *context in which overnight arrangements occur is critical.* In particular, high conflict between parents and less effective parenting exacerbate the vulnerabilities that children making more frequent transitions face and appear to override any potential benefits children may derive from spending overnights. Parents with high-conflict relationships must actively communicate, respond sensitively to their child's feelings about transitioning, and strive to shield their children from their conflicts if they are to protect their child's sense of security. This can be tricky, if not downright impossible, for some parents to accomplish, and the benefits of overnight access get mitigated through additional opportunities for parents to have conflict with each other. In these cases, parents can try communicating through e-mail or a log passed back and forth (Deutsch, 2010), but this may not be a sufficient degree or type of communication to reassure the children.

In sum, the current research on parenting plans for young children indicates:

- Factors such as low conflict between parents and their emotional availability play a crucial role in the success of overnights.
- While overnights seem clearly beneficial for older preschoolers, the benefits and drawbacks for younger children are less clearly delineated and await further clarification from larger, longitudinal research samples. Studies to date suggest that caution is warranted and that when young children are spending regular overnights in two homes, follow-ups that assess children's ongoing adaptation or distress should be built into parental agreements.

In aggregate, these studies show that overnights either have no connection or a negative one to child outcomes. Infants and toddlers are most vulnerable to the potentially negative effects. However, these effects were modest and do not simultaneously account for benefits that are derived over time from keeping fathers involved. In the absence of such data, one may speculate that beginning overnights early benefits father–child relationships (Kelly & Lamb, 2005), but that the benefits that accrue directly to children are more likely to manifest later. Cashmore, Parkinson, and Taylor (2008) found that older children and adolescents with frequent overnight visits reported a closer relationship with their father than those with infrequent or no overnight visits. But at what age the overnights must begin to initiate and maintain such relationships is an unsettled question. Therefore, practitioners and families are encouraged to address questions of parenting plans early, accounting for child temperament, parental, familial, and structural (how close do parents live?) factors, making case-by-case decisions with follow-up monitoring and evaluation built in. When infants or toddlers are at issue, follow-ups scheduled with consultants, mediators, or court designates every few months provide responsible oversight. It is also important to bear in mind that the mother's (or primary caretaker's) attitude toward the overnights and the father's sensitive attunement to the child—especially at transition points—are critical components of how well the child will adjust.

Supporting Father Involvement: An Evidence-Based Intervention for Fathers and Co-parents

A review of the research indicates that it is often difficult for divorced or separated parents to establish a collaborative co-parenting relationship. If they can do so, fathers are more likely to stay actively and positively involved with their children. In addition, there are specific aspects of the couple relationship that affect whether fathers stay involved—whether the couple can overcome a tendency toward restrictive gatekeeping by mothers, and whether the couple can work out overnights in a way that keeps the child's needs in focus. But it is not enough just to hope that divorcing parents will find a way to work together for their children. Many couples need help to accomplish this Herculean task. While there are mediators available to help resolve property and custody disputes, there are few resources available for divorcing couples to work on improving their co-parenting relationship. The Supporting Father Involvement (SFI) intervention, developed and evaluated by the senior authors of this chapter, draws on a couple-oriented approach to enhance father involvement, primarily but not exclusively in low-income families. This intervention is discussed, along with considerations of how this approach could be readily adapted for separated or divorcing couples (Table 5.3).

SFI is the first research-based program in the United States designed to encourage fathers from diverse backgrounds to be positively involved with their children, and to systematically evaluate the effectiveness of the program with a randomized clinical trial research design (Cowan, Cowan, Pruett, Pruett, & Wong, 2009). The SFI intervention study was designed to help mothers and fathers develop skills and resources to have healthier family relationships, decrease stress, and reduce abusive and/or neglectful behavior. The program aims to improve functioning in multiple aspects of family life (helping the parents increase their satisfaction and well-being as individuals and as a couple, develop healthy relationships with their children, become aware of and improve three-generational patterns of childrearing, and learn to access support from persons and institutions) based on previous literature suggesting that father engagement is associated with all of these areas (Cowan, Cowan, Pruett, & Pruett, 2006).

Since the inception of this study, over 700 families have participated in a series of research phases. Participants have been recruited at family resource centers in five California counties. Criteria for involvement included (a) both parents agreed to participate, (b) the couple had a child 0 to 7 years of age, later increased to 11 years, (c) parents reported no mental health or substance abuse issues that impaired their daily functioning to a degree that they could not participate, and (d) domestic violence was not reported in the family in the past 12 months, and neither partner was afraid to be in the intervention with the other. The intervention phase that is currently under way was recently expanded to include families who are involved in the child welfare system for abuse or violence issues, but again, partners are carefully assessed and deemed not to be at present risk for hurting each other or their child.

For the first wave of published data (Cowan et al., 2009), 289 families completed pre- and post-tests. Of these, 67% were Mexican American and 33% were Caucasian (an African American sample joined in a subsequent phase). Most of the parents were married (75%), and most of the rest were cohabiting (20%).

Couples who agreed to participate were randomly assigned to one of three interventions: a 16-week (32-hour) group for fathers, a 16-week (32-hour) group for couples, or a low-dose comparison condition with the couple attending a single 3-hour group information session where they learn about the importance of fathers' family involvement to the children and the parents. The group interventions are psychoeducational and therapeutically oriented and were co-led by trained clinicians, although they are not therapy groups. All families were also assigned a case manager to help them access other needed services. The case managers stayed in close contact with the families and helped them maximize attendance in the intervention groups and access other services as needed. Findings to date indicate that for partners who are willing and able to attempt co-parenting together, the curriculum is leading to benefits for the parents as individuals, as couples, and as parents, and shows positive effects on the children's acting out and withdrawn, depressed behaviors. Parents report that the program is enjoyable, helpful, and highly relevant to their everyday situations.

The group curricula for fathers and couples groups cover identical topic areas and have similar activities and exercises but are either geared primarily towards self-discovery and skill development or focused on dyadic application, depending upon which group the parents are offered in a random process. Couples were recruited from their communities broadly, and many of them were in conflict. Few of them had been involved in legal conflicts at the time of group enrollment, although the staff members at several of the sites are considering offering the intervention to couples with higher conflict or who are divorcing.

A number of significant and encouraging outcomes have emerged from the SFI study thus far. To name a few, at an 18-month follow-up, parents from both the fathers and couples groups reported decreased levels of depression/anxiety, parenting stress, and violent problem-solving. This stands in contrast to parents in the control condition, in which all of these indicators worsened over the same period. In addition, children of parents in the intervention groups were found to have stable levels of behavior problems, in contrast with consistent increases in problem behaviors in children of parents from the control condition. Participants in the couples groups also maintained their relationship satisfaction while the control groups' satisfaction declined, in line with normative trends found in longitudinal studies of the transition to parenthood (Twenge, Campbell, & Foster, 2003). The couples group participants also showed reduced parenting stress, while fathers group and comparison participants showed no change. Finally, interviews with staff of the SFI project, family resource centers that hosted the study, and counties in which they were located, along with more widely collected agency self-assessment questionnaires, indicated that the family centers were becoming more father-friendly following the study. They reached out to fathers and adapted their policies, procedures, programs, and practices to be more welcoming and inclusive of fathers. This finding has far-reaching systemic effects so that clinical intervention is not the only place and method for increasing fathers' family involvement. When agencies—especially female-dominated ones—also nurture and sustain such efforts, the likelihood of change toward positive father involvement is increased, and resources for ongoing support are built into the agency offering the program.

Perhaps the greatest achievement of the SFI project is its ongoing adaptability to diverse populations. So far SFI is effective with both English and Spanish speakers, immigrants and non-immigrants, parents with high and low socioeconomic status, parents with initially high and low conflict levels and satisfaction as couples, and parents entering with high and low levels of depression. Caucasian, Hispanic, and African American families have participated. The intervention program is currently being replicated and adapted through not-for-profit agencies in four locations in Alberta, Canada as well as in Great Britain, New Zealand, and with teen parents in Hartford, CT.

What has been demonstrated through SFI so far:

- Low-income families facing a myriad of problems in their personal and social environments can be recruited and retained in ongoing group interventions with clinically trained leaders. They not only attend on average 75% of the sessions but have consistently asked for more group time. This attendance factor is likely a large contributor to the intervention's success, as attendance is high relative to federally funded fatherhood and co-parenting interventions that have met with less success (Wood, McConnell, Moore, Clarkwest, & Hsueh, 2010).

- SFI success rests on targeting multiple aspects of family life (individual, parenting, co-parenting, three-generation transmission of behaviors, and how to balance life stress with social support). Addressing the full family environment helps ensure that family changes, such as increased father involvement, endure subsequent to the intervention.
- Positive change was sustained in individuals' levels of well-being (anxiety and depression), their satisfaction with their couple or co-parenting relationships, parenting stress, and violent means of problem-solving. Their children's behavioral adjustment remained steady, whereas problem behaviors of control group children worsened over the same period.
- This intervention can be effective for many types of families and also supports positive change toward father inclusion in the agencies that serve families and the communities in which they live.

The existence of both fathers-only and co-parenting/couples groups within one model that strengthens co-parenting makes this intervention particularly relevant and applicable for separating or divorcing families. In divorce interventions, it is generally assumed that parents must be separated in order to be effective. Support groups exist, but intervention groups are typically reserved for children. Groups offer natural supports that can help parents garner their internal and familial resources to better sustain their children through the transition. And co-parenting is best developed *in vivo* rather than through separate intervention groups. Though being together in a group will not be effective or desirable for all couples, when it is safe and practical to do so, the relief that both married and unmarried or divorced parents experience from acting together on their children's behalf can be immediate. Such collaboration reduces the likelihood of polarizing through the legal process. Moreover, SFI addresses the critical issues of cooperation, conflict reduction, and maternal (or paternal) gatekeeping, which have been identified through research as salient issues among divorcing families. The SFI curriculum could readily be adapted to include content on parenting plans generally, and overnights specifically. It would serve as a preventive intervention that could not only shore up the family to assume healthier relationships in the future but also minimize some of the most deleterious aspects of divorce.

SUMMARY

The current research on father involvement is an important area of study that is expanding the knowledge base of family functioning after divorce. The preponderance of scientifically informed evidence has shown that fathers play an important role in their children's development in married and unmarried families, and recent research has shed light upon the nuances regarding *which* fathers, for *which* children, and under *what circumstances*. As developmental and family researchers continue to explore co-parenting models and their limitations, paternal involvement with young children, and the family processes such as maternal gatekeeping and overnight stays with fathers that promote or inhibit father involvement, new issues will emerge for study. As the science expands, it will be essential for professionals working with

Table 5.3 SUPPORTING FATHER INVOLVEMENT (SFI) PROJECT

Supporting Father Involvement Intervention Program

	Philip A. Cowan, Ph.D. Carolyn Pape Cowan, Ph.D. University of California, Berkeley	Marsha Kline Pruett, Ph.D., M.S.L. Smith College School for Social Work Rachel Ebling, Ph.D. Smith College Postdoctoral Student	Kyle D. Pruett, M.D. Yale Child Study Study Center
Designed and Adapted:			
Curricula:			
Target:	Fathers	Couples/Co-parents	Educational/Control group for research
Size:	8–12 fathers	5–6 couples	Any
Length:	16 weeks/32 hours	16 weeks/32 hours	3 hours
Structure:	Open-ended check-in Didactic/ Instructional	Open-ended check-in Didactic/ Instructional	Information on importance of father involvement
	Activities/Experiential applications	Activities/Experiential applications	Video: *Show Your Love*
	Homework to reinforce learning	Homework to reinforce learning	Question and answer
Focus/ Domains:	Individual	Individual well-being	
	Couple/partners	Couple/co-partners	
	Parenting	Parenting	
	Three-generational/ families of origin	Three-generational/ families of origin	
	Life stress/social support balance	Life stress/social support balance	
Evidence base:	>800 couples assessed to date; 6-, 18-, and 42-month follow-ups. Substantive and lasting effects: Individual depression/anxiety, couple satisfaction and communication, parenting stress, violent methods of problem-solving, couple conflict, child hyperactivity and aggression; agency father-friendliness. Successful across income levels, ethnicity, mental health levels, conflict levels		

For more information: www.supportingfatherinvolvement.org

families within and just outside of the legal system to stay informed about how best to support these families.

GUIDELINES: CONSIDERATIONS AND CAUTIONS

- **Moving the Paternal Role Towards Center.** The role of the father in family life has shifted from one of more peripheral parent to a position closer to the center of family life. Coupled with this shift, researchers have sought and identified numerous contributions that fathers make to the development of healthy children. Those contributions include parenting in ways that are, on average, different from maternal parenting styles such that father involvement plays an active role in promoting children's self-sufficiency, problem-solving, frustration tolerance, and cognitive competence and achievement. Moreover, involved fathers play an important role in fostering control behaviors in children, thereby serving a protective function for children's positive adaptation in environmentally vulnerable or socially risky situations. In family law situations, this research adds up to a vote of confidence for including fathers and other significant male figures whenever it is feasible and safe to do so for all family members. It forms an imperative to help families identify and construct parenting plans that secure paternal involvement in children's lives.
- **Involving Fathers as Non-residential Parents.** Involving fathers as non-residential parents may pose significant obstacles. Although co-parenting is now a norm in intact families (though not approaching equal time by both parents), it often leads to complications in post-divorce parenting plans. Helping parents to stay focused on their ongoing team functions may be easier to accomplish if they understand the variety of co-parenting aspects in which they might involve themselves. Theories of co-parenting have progressed to a point where legal professionals can make themselves and families aware of the many aspects of and opportunities for successful co-parenting.
- **The Paternal Role with Young Children is Vulnerable.** Father involvement is especially vulnerable in divorcing families with young children, where fathers may leave the child's residence before they can establish a firm footing in their relationship with their children. Maternal gatekeeping varies from openly supportive to appropriately protective to restrictive behaviors that constrain fathers' involvement with their children. Interventions indicate that raising awareness of mothers' power in this regard helps them identify situations in which they could facilitate rather than hinder fathers' time with their children. Facilitating positive gatekeeping includes each parent's acknowledgement of the other's importance in the family triangle, and fostering behaviors that result in greater cooperation, reduced conflict, and greater father involvement.
- **Overnights for Young Children.** Recent research suggests that frequent overnights for very young children may be associated with attachment difficulties and emotional regulatory problems, though the research is far

from conclusive. Studies to date concur that schedule consistency and parents' emotional availability and sensitivity around transition times can facilitate children's adjustment. In the face of parental conflict, infant/child distress, and poor parental communication, overnights with infants and toddlers should be considered cautiously. The kinds of distress focused on in current studies have not produced robust results, nor are they sufficiently longitudinal to assert whether these effects are temporary and balanced by the support overnights lend to father involvement, or whether the effects will translate into longer-term difficulties for the child. Parental and parent–child relationships continue to emerge as unassailable factors within and across studies, and so far the particulars of parenting plans provide less useful information than the child's response to each parent and across contexts. In other words, whether the child is coping well in various contexts (home, child care) matters a great deal for the determination of whether current parenting plans should be sustained.

- **Father-Supportive Interventions.** In the absence of more specific data, interventions that strengthen family relationships with respect to and beyond the divorce—parent–child and co-parent relationships—offer promising solutions to the conundrums faced by families trying to plan for parenting schedules. The Supporting Father Involvement program is offered as an example of a program that could provide a cost-effective alternative to family evaluations and a more comprehensive support than family mediation does at present. It is conceivable that with minor adaptations to the curriculum, parenting plans could be developed by partners in the co-parenting intervention and jointly considered by the leaders and other members of the group.

- **How Professionals Can Support Fathers.** Educating ourselves about the role of fathers, how to engage fathers and enhance their relationships within the divorcing family, and understanding and managing our own biases and expectations about gender roles will go a long way to increasing public perception that there is a level playing field for fathers and mothers who are separating and involved in the family court system.

REFERENCES

Allen, S. M., & Hawkins, A. J. (1999). Maternal gatekeeping: Mothers' beliefs and behaviors that inhibit greater father involvement in family work. *Journal of Marriage and the Family, 61*, 199–212. doi:10.2307/353894

Altenhofen, S., Sutherland, K., & Biringen, Z. (2010). Families experiencing divorce: Age at onset of overnight stays, conflict, and emotional availability as predictors of child attachment. *Journal of Divorce and Remarriage, 51*, 141–156. doi:10.1080/10502551003597782

Carlson, M. J., & McLanahan, S. S. (2010). Fathers in fragile families. In M. E. Lamb (Ed.), *The role of the father in child development* (5th ed., pp. 241–269). Hoboken, NJ: John Wiley & Sons.

Carlson, M. J., McLanahan, S. S., & Brooks-Gunn, J. (2008). Coparenting and nonresident fathers' involvement with young children after a nonmarital birth. *Demography, 45*(2), 461–488. doi:10.1353/dem.0.0007 PMid:18613490

Cashmore, J., Parkinson, P., & Taylor, A. (2008). Overnight stays and children's relationships with resident and nonresident parents after divorce. *Journal of Family Issues, 29*, 707–733. doi:10.1177/0192513X07308042

Cassidy, J., & Shaver, P. R. (2008). *Handbook of attachment: Theory, research, and clinical applications*(2nd ed.). New York: Guilford Press.

Cohen, O., & Finzi-Dottan, R. (2005). Parent–child relationships during the divorce process: From attachment theory and intergenerational perspective. *Contemporary Family Therapy, 27*, 81–99. doi:10.1007/s10591–004–1972–3

Cowan, P. A., Cowan, C. P., Ablow, J. C., Johnson, V. K., & Measelle, J. R. (2005). *The family context of parenting in children's adaptation to elementary school.* Monographs in Parenting series, xvii (p. 414). Mahwah, NJ: Lawrence Erlbaum.

Cowan, C. P., Cowan, P. A., Cohen, N., Pruett, M. K., & Pruett, K. (2008). Supporting fathers' engagement with their kids. In J. D. Berrick & N. Gilbert (Eds.), *Raising children: Emerging needs, modern risks, and social responses* (pp. 44–80). New York: Oxford University Press.

Cowan, C. P., Cowan, P. A., Pruett, M. K., & Pruett, K. (2006). An approach to preventing coparenting conflict and divorce in low-income families: Strengthening couple relationships and fostering fathers' involvement. *Family Process, 46* (1), 109–120.doi:10.1111/j.1545–5300.2006.00195.x PMid:17375732

Cowan, P. A., Cowan, C. P., Pruett, M. K., Pruett, K., & Wong, J. J. (2009). Promoting fathers' engagement with children: Preventive interventions for low-income families. *Journal of Marriage and Family, 71*, 663–679. doi:10.1111/j.1741–3737.2009.00625.x

Cummings, E. M., & Keller, P. S. (2006). Marital discord and children's emotional self-regulation. In D. K. Snyder, J. Simpson, & J. N. Hughes (Eds.). *Emotion regulation in couples and families: Pathways to dysfunction and health* (pp. 163–182). Washington, DC: American Psychological Association. doi:10.1037/11468–008

Dalton, C., Carbon, S., & Olesen, N, (2003). High conflict divorce, violence, and abuse: Implications for custody and visitation decisions. *Juvenile& Family Court Journal, 54*(4), 11–33. doi:10.1111/j.1755–6988.2003.tb00084.x

Deutsch, R. M. (2010). When the conflict continues: The right parenting plan can help defuse tensions. *Family Law, 33*(1), 40–45.

Fagan, J., & Barnett, M. (2003). The relationship between maternal gatekeeping, paternal competence, mothers' attitudes about the father role, and father involvement. *Journal of Family Issues, 24*(8), 1020–1043. doi:10.1177/0192513X03256397

Feinberg, M. E., & Kan, M. L. (2008). Establishing family foundations: Intervention effects on coparenting, parent/infant well-being, and parent–child relations. *Journal of Family Psychology, 22*, 253–263. doi:10.1037/0893–3200.22.2.253 PMid:18410212ı

Feldman, R., Swain, J., & Mayes, J. (2005). Interaction synchrony and neural circuits contribute to shared intentionality. *Behavior and Brain Sciences, 28*(5), 697–698. doi:10.1017/S0140525X0529012X

Gaunt, R. (2008). Maternal gatekeeping: Antecedents and consequences. *Journal of Family Issues, 29*(3), 373–395. doi:10.1177/0192513X07307851

Goldstein, J., Solnit, A.J., & Freud, A. (1973). *Beyond the best interests of the child.* New York: Free Press.

Goldstein, J., Solnit, A.J., Goldstein, S., & Freud, A. (1996). *The best interests of the child: The least detrimental alternative.* New York: Free Press.

Greenberg, M. T., Cicchetti, D., & Cummings, E. M. (Eds.). (1990). *Attachment in the preschool years: Theory, research, and intervention.* Chicago: University of Chicago Press.

Harold, G. T., Aitken, J. J., & Shelton, K. H. (2007). Inter-parental conflict and children's academic attainment: A longitudinal analysis. *Journal of Child Psychology and Psychiatry,* 48(12), 1223–1232. doi:10.1111/j.1469-7610.2007.01793.x PMid:18093028

Jaffe, P. G., Johnston, J. R., Crooks, C. V., & Bala, N. (2008). Custody disputes involving allegations of domestic violence: The need for differentiated approaches to parenting plans. *Family Court Review, 46*(3), 500–522. doi:10.1111/j.1744-1617.2008.00216.x

Jaffee, S. R., Caspi, A., Moffitt, T. E., Taylor, A., & Dickson, N. (2001). Predicting early fatherhood and whether young fathers live with their children: Prospective findings and policy recommendations. *Journal of Child Psychology and Psychiatry,* 42(6), 803–815. doi:10.1111/1469-7610.00777 PMid:11583253

Johnston, J. R. (2006). A child-centered approach to high-conflict and domestic-violence families: Differential assessment and interventions. *Journal of Family Studies, 12*(1), 15–35. doi:10.5172/jfs.327.12.1.15

Kaczynski, K. J., Lindahl, K. M., Malik, N. M., & Laurenceau, J. P. (2006). Marital conflict, maternal and paternal parenting, and child adjustment: A test of mediation and moderation. *Journal of Family Psychology, 20*, 199–208. doi:10.1037/0893-3200.20.2.199 PMid:16756395

Kelly, J. B., & Lamb, M. E. (2005). Using child development research to make appropriate custody and access decisions for young children. In *Overnights and young children: Essays from the Family Court Review* (pp. 13–27). Madison, WI: Association of Family and Conciliation Courts.

Krishnakumar, A., & Buehler, C. (2000). Interpersonal conflict and parenting behaviors: A meta-analytic study. *Family Relations, 49*, 25–44. doi:10.1111/j.1741-3729.2000.00025.x

Lamb, M. E. (2002). Infant-father attachments and their impact on child development. In C. S. Tamis-LeMonda & N. Canrera (Eds.), *Handbook of father involvement: Multidisciplinary perspectives* (pp. 93–117). Mahwah, NJ: Erlbaum.

Lamb, M. E. (2010). How do fathers influence child development? Let me count the ways. In M.E. Lamb (Ed.), *The role of the father in child development,* 2nd ed.(pp.1–26). Hoboken, NJ: John Wiley & Sons.

Lamb, M. E., Frodi, A. M., Hwang, C. P., & Frodi, M. (1982). Varying degrees of paternal involvement in infant care: Attitudinal and behavioral correlates. In M. E. Lamb (Ed.), *Nontraditional families: Parenting and child development* (pp.117–138). Hillsdale, NJ: Erlbaum.

Lamb, M. E., & Kelly, J. B. (2009). Improving the quality of parent–child contact in separating families with infants and young children: Empirical research foundations. In R. M. Galatzer-Levy, L. Kraus, & J. Galatzer-Levy (Eds.), *The scientific basis of child custody decisions* (2nd ed., pp. 187–214). Hoboken, NJ: John Wiley & Sons.

Lamb, M. E., & Lewis, C. (2010). The development and significance of father–child relationships in two-parent families. In M. E. Lamb (Ed.), *The role of the father in child development* (2nd ed., pp. 94–153). Hoboken, NJ: John Wiley & Sons, Inc.

Maccoby, E. E., & Mnookin, R.H. (1992). *Dividing the child: Social and legal dilemmas of custody*. Cambridge, MA: Harvard University Press.

Marvin, R. S., & Britner, P. A. (2008). Normative development. The ontogeny of attachment. In J. Cassidy & P. Shaver (Eds.), *Handbook of attachment: Theory, research and applications* (2nd ed., pp. 269–294). New York: Guilford Press.

McHale, J. P. (2007). *Charting the bumpy road of coparenthood: Understanding the challenges of family life*. Washington, DC: Zero to Three Press.

McIntosh, J. E., Wells, Y. D., Smyth, B. M., & Long, C. M. (2008). Child-focused and child-inclusive divorce mediation: Comparative outcomes from a prospective study of post-separation adjustment. *Family Court Review, 46*(1), 105–124. doi:10.1111/j.1744–1617.2007.00186.x

McIntosh, J. E., Smyth, B. M., Kelaher, M., Wells, Y. D., & Long, C. (2010). *Post-separation parenting arrangements: Patterns and developmental outcomes for infants and children* (Report to the Attorney-General's Department). Victoria, Australia: Family Transitions.

Nair, H., & Murray, A. D. (2005). Predictors of attachment security in preschool children from intact and divorced families. *Journal of Genetic Psychology, 166*, 245–263. doi:10.3200/GNTP.166.3.245–263 PMid:16173670

Paquette, D. (2004). Theorizing the father–child relationship: Mechanisms and developmental outcomes. *Human Development, 47*, 193–219. doi:10.1159/000078723

Pleck, J. H. (2010). Paternal involvement: Revised conceptualization and theoretical linkages with child outcomes. In M. E. Lamb (Ed.), *The role of the father in child development*, 2nd ed. (pp. 58–93). Hoboken, NJ: John Wiley & Sons.

Pruett, K. D. (2000). *Fatherneed*. New York: Free Press.

Pruett, K. D., & Pruett, M. K. (2009). *Partnership parenting*. New York: De Capo.

Pruett, M. K. (2005). Applications of attachment theory and child development research to young children's overnights in separated and divorced families. In *Overnights and young children: Essays from the Family Court Review* (pp. 5–12). Madison, WI: Association of Family and Conciliation Courts.

Pruett, M. K., Arthur, L. A., & Ebling, R. (2007). The hand that rocks the cradle: Maternal gatekeeping after divorce. *Pace Law Review, 27*(4), 709–739.

Pruett, M. K., & Barker, R. (2009). Children of divorce: New trends and ongoing dilemmas. In J. H. Bray & Stanton, M. (Eds.), *The handbook of family psychology* (pp. 463–471). New York: Blackwell. doi:10.1002/9781444310238.ch31

Pruett, M. K., Ebling, R., & Insabella, G. (2004). Critical aspects of parenting plans for young children: Interjecting data into the debate about overnights. *Family Court Review, 42*(1), 39–59. doi:10.1111/j.174–1617.2004.tb00632.x

Pruett, M. K., Insabella, G., & Gustafson, K. (2005). The Collaborative Divorce Project: A court based intervention for separating parents with young children [Special issue]. *Family Court Review, 43*(1), 38–51. doi:10.1177/1531244504421004

Pruett, M. K., & Jackson, T. (2002). Perspectives on the divorce process: Parental perceptions of the legal system and its impact on family relations. *Journal of the American Academy of Psychiatry and the Law, 29*, 18–28.

Sandler, I., Miles, J., Cookston, J., & Braver, S. (2008). Effects of father and mother parenting on children's mental health in high and low conflict divorces. *Family Court Review, 46*(2), 282–296. doi:10.1111/j.1744–1617.2008.00201.x

Sarkadi, A., Kristiansson, R., Oberklaid, F., & Bremberg, S. (2007). Fathers' involvement and children's developmental outcomes: A systematic review of longitudinal studies. *Acta Paediatrica, 97*, 153–158. doi:10.1111/j.1651–2227.2007.00572.x PMid:18052995

Schoppe-Sullivan, S. J., Cannon, E. A., Brown, G. L., Mangelsdorf, S. C., & Sokolowski, M.S. (2008). Maternal gatekeeping, co-parenting quality, and fathering behavior in families with infants. *Journal of Family Psychology, 22*(3), 389–398. doi:10.1037/0893–3200.22.3.389 PMid:18540767

Shonkoff, J. P., & Philips, D.A., (2000). *From neurons to neighborhoods: The science of early childhood development.* Washington, DC: National Academy Press.

Silverstein, L. B. (2002). Fathers and families. In J. P. McHale & W. S. Grolnick (Eds.), *Retrospect and prospect in the psychological study of families* (pp. 35–64). Mahwah, NJ: Lawrence Erlbaum Associates, Inc., Publishers.

Solomon, J. (2005). An attachment theory framework for planning infant and toddler visitation arrangements in never-married, separated, and divorced families. In L. Gunsberg & P. Hymowitz (Eds.), *A handbook of divorce and custody: Forensic, developmental, and clinical perspectives* (pp.259-280). New York: Analytic Press.

Solomon, J., & Biringen, Z. (2005). Another look at the developmental research: Commentary on Kelly and Lamb's "Using child development research to make appropriate custody and access decisions for young children." In *Overnights and young children: Essays from the Family Court Review* (pp. 28–37). Madison, WI: Association of Family and Conciliation Courts.

Solomon, J., & George, L. (1999). The effects on attachment of overnight visitation on divorced and separated families: A longitudinal follow-up. In J. Solomon & C. George (Eds.), *Attachment disorganization* (pp. 243–264). New York: Guilford.

Storey, A. E., Walsh, C. J., Quinton, R. L., & Wynne-Edwards, R.E., (2000). Hormonal correlates of paternal responsiveness in new and expectant fathers. *Evolution and Human Behavior, 21,* 79–95. doi:10.1016/S1090–5138(99)00042–2

Sturge-Apple, M. L., Davies, P. T., & Cummings, E. M. (2006). Hostility and withdrawal in marital conflict: Effects on parental emotional unavailability and inconsistent discipline. *Journal of Family Psychology, 23,* 215–225. doi:10.1037/a0014198 PMid:19364215 PMCid:2909036

Swain, J., Taskgin, E., Mayes, L., Feldman, R., Constable, R., & Leckman, J. (2008). Maternal brain response to own baby cry. *Journal of Child Psychology and Psychiatry, 49,* 1042–1052. doi:10.1111/j.1469–7610.2008.01963.x PMid:18771508

Twenge, J. M., Campbell, W. K., & Foster, C. A. (2003). Parenthood and marital satisfaction: A meta-analytic review. *Journal of Marriage and Family, 65,* 574–583. doi:10.1111/j.1741–3737.2003.00574.x

Wood, R. G., McConnell, S., Moore, Q., Clarkwest, A., & Hsueh, J. (2010). *Strengthening unmarried parents' relationships: The early impacts of Building Strong Families.* Washington, DC: Mathematica Policy Research, Inc.

Yogman, M. W., Kindlon, D., & Earls, F. (1995). Father involvement and cognitive/behavioral outcomes of preterm infants. *Journal of the American Academy of Child and Adolescent Psychiatry, 34,* 58–66. doi:10.1097/00004583–199501000–00015

Factors Associated with Children's Adjustment to Time-Sharing

## 6

Shared-Time Parenting

An Evidence-Based Matrix for Evaluating Risk

JENNIFER E. McINTOSH AND BRUCE SMYTH ■

THE EMERGENCE OF SHARED-TIME PARENTING

In many countries, shared-time parenting (also referred to as *joint physical custody, dual residence, shared physical placement,* and *shared care*) is emerging as an important modern family form following divorce or separation. Whereas traditional primary care arrangements often involve up to 20% of the child's time being spent in the overnight care of the non-resident parent (often the father), shared-time arrangements are those whereby the child is cared for in equal or nearly equal amounts of time by both parents (with time split ratios typically ranging from 30/70 to 50/50 of overnights).

Sociolegal Impetus for Shared-Time Parenting after Separation

Internationally, family law reform is moving to encourage and support shared-time parenting, from passive preference for shared parenting, to rebuttable presumptions in favor of children's co-residence.[1] The legislative push toward shared-time parenting can be traced to a variety of socioeconomic shifts in normative family caregiving. After parental separation, a shared-time arrangement may (a) mirror the increasingly shared nature of involvement in their children's lives that some parents share before separation, or (b) create new opportunities for the greater involvement of a previously less-involved parent. In the latter cases, separation may represent a rupture that brings with it the realization that time with children is important for an emotionally close relationship to develop and be sustained (Smyth, 2005b).

Empowerment and parental equality paradigms also underpin the movement toward equally shared homes after separation. At least two central assumptions run through these paradigms: (a) through equitable division of the caregiving role after separation, both parents can have "equally" meaningful involvement in their children's lives, and (b) through the shared day-to-day and night-to-night care of each parent, children will be enabled to retain "equally" loving and important relationships with both parents.

As an ideal, shared parenting promises an array of outcomes that most families would wish for in the event of parental separation—for example, children being enabled to retain strong, practical relationships with both parents, and parents retaining maximum shared involvement and influence in the day-to-day care of their children. But all post-separation parenting time schedules are somewhat of an experiment, and all experiments involve an element of risk—sometimes known and calculable and sometimes not.

The task of this chapter is to define what is meant by risk in the context of shared-time parenting after separation, and to detail the current body of literature—particularly new Australian data—that addresses the issue of risk in shared-time parenting. The chapter is in five parts. Part I considers the problem of defining *risk* in the context of shared-time parenting. Part II considers the particular difficulties that pertain to interpreting the current literature pool around shared-time parenting. Part III gives an overview of recent empirical findings about risk factors associated with shared-time parenting, and Part IV considers the details of this literature along three interdependent axes: pragmatic risks, parenting and relationship risks, and developmental risks. In Part V, an empirically based matrix approach to the understanding of risk is summarized, encouraging the interweaving of pragmatic, parenting, and developmental considerations in weighing the risks—and the challenges and chances—of a shared-time lifestyle for a child at various points in infancy, childhood, and adolescence.

PART I. DEFINING RISK IN THE CONTEXT OF SHARED-TIME PARENTING

For Emery (2010), shared parenting can be the best and worst possible parenting arrangement after divorce. How does social science define what "best" and "worst" mean in this context? As shared parenting is brought to life in countless ways by diverse family constellations, social scientists in the 21st century seek to answer the question: What outcomes, positive and negative, are likely to be independently shaped by the amount of time children spend living with each parent, and what outcomes are determined or mediated by the way time and living arrangements are enacted? Recent post-separation parenting research provides a way of understanding probable links between each family's unique characteristics and the risks that exist or are likely to accrue in association with any particular pattern of care and/or its form of enactment.

PART II. INTERPRETING THE EMPIRICAL LITERATURE ON SHARED PARENTING AND RISK

The benefits of a shared care environment for children's well-being have been variously hypothesized, with common assertions being that properties inherent to a shared arrangement may alleviate certain risks to child development that other arrangements would not. For example, advantages to children may include positive, active relationships with both parents, the maintenance of two active social and family support networks, increased attention and stimulation by two involved parents, equitable gender role modeling, less risk of depleted emotional availability associated with single parenting, happier mothers who can maintain work and family balance, and fathers who establish a more gratifying level of involvement than that often achieved in marriage (Bauserman, 2002; Fabricius, Braver, Diaz, & Velez, 2010; Hetherington, Cox, & Cox, 1985; Luepnitz, 1991; McKinnon & Wallerstein, 1986).

Yet, as many have written (Bauserman, 2002; Johnston, 1995; Kline Pruett, Ebling & Insabella, 2004; Pearson & Thoennes, 1990), the idea that any given parenting time arrangement can create these effects in its own right, independent of parenting and relationship qualities and psychosocial resources, is simplistic. Herein lies just some of the complexity of interpreting research about parenting arrangements.

Problems of Interpreting Shared Parenting Research

In considering the empirical findings about the benefits and risks of shared parenting arrangements, there are some important caveats to include in the task of interpreting findings and applying them to individual cases.

SMALL LITERATURE POOL

The first and most obvious point is the small body of literature specific to the empirical study of families who have exercised shared-time parenting (time splits ranging from 30/70 to 50/50 of overnights). Shared-time parenting remains a minority arrangement, although the numbers are rising. Small population numbers impose significant limits on research samples.

Reported rates of shared-time parenting vary in the United States, according both to legislative definitions and researcher definitions (as explained later, some studies include *any* overnight care in their definition of shared parenting, and many studies conflate joint parental responsibility and care). Defining shared time as arrangements where children spend at least 30% of overnights with each parent, recent international general population estimates range from 9% to 30%: 10% in Norway (Skjørten, & Barlindhaug, 2007); 9% to 17% in the United Kingdom (Peacey & Hunt, 2008); 16% to 17% of recently separated families in Australia (Kaspiew et al., 2009; Smyth, 2009); and about 20% of post-separation arrangements in the United States— although this estimate is higher in some states (e.g., 30% in Wisconsin; Melli & Brown, 2008).

Despite a marked increase in shared-time parenting in the general population in Australia since the introduction of legislation in 2006, new Australian research suggests that only 4% of parents elect to share the care of children under 3 years (Kaspiew et al., 2009). Children living in equal or near-equal time arrangements are most likely to be of primary/elementary school age or early teenagers.

METHODOLOGICAL COMPLEXITY

Methodologically, the phenomenon of shared-time parenting has presented many challenges both to researchers and to practitioners trying to interpret the findings of various studies. The term *shared-time parenting* is used to refer to a variety of different time-sharing arrangements. A uniform operational definition of shared-time parenting has not been established, and thus one needs to be particularly cautious about findings that do not carefully distinguish the types of families and shared residence arrangements they pertain to. There is little research as yet that distinguishes outcomes from 50/50 arrangements with other ratios in which there is a lesser-time co-parent. Patterns of shared-time parenting vary vastly (see Smyth, 2005a), from symmetric time splits (e.g., alternating weeks or months with each parent, or various ways of alternating nights) to asymmetric splits (e.g., four nights mother, three nights father; five nights mother, nine nights father). Research is as yet a poor guide for understanding outcomes associated with various symmetric or asymmetric patterns of shared care.

VARIATION OF SAMPLES USED IN TIME-SHARING RESEARCH
Within the small populations available for study, shared parenting families have been grouped together in some rather undifferentiated ways (i.e., *lumping*), with the attendant risks of masking both underlying family dynamics and legal pathways that may account for important variations in outcomes. There are obvious problems with studies that conflate joint parental responsibility with joint physical custody and that combine cooperative self-selecting families with court-mandated arrangements among high-conflict families. Litigating and high-conflict families who exercise substantially shared care arrangements differ in important ways from cooperative parents who self-select into shared parenting (discussed more fully below). High-conflict families typically enter shared parenting on a different track and stay on that track by different means, with different outcomes. At a finer level of differentiation, recent research shows distinctions in outcomes between groups when disaggregated according to the flexibility or rigidity of the care arrangement (McIntosh, Smyth, Wells, & Long, 2010).

THE PROBLEM OF DATA SOURCES
Most outcome studies in this area rely on parents' reports of their children's well-being, and parent reports about their children typically correlate with reports of the parents' own well-being (i.e., shared method bias; see, for example, Rodgers, Smyth, Son, Esler, & Shephard, 2010). Independent accounts (e.g., by teachers or independent observers) are typically lacking, and although some work exists about children's own views (Haugen, 2010; McIntosh, Wells, & Long, 2009; Smart, 2004), there exists a limited understanding of children's experiences of shared-time parenting.

CONCLUSIONS REACHED
Fehlberg, Smyth, Maclean, and Roberts (2011) draw attention to the danger of forming conclusions that reach beyond those supportable by individual study designs or data. For example, in support of shared parenting, Fabricius et al. (2010) report that many adult children would have liked to see more of an absent father. But such research cannot, for example, be used to conclude that shared parenting would prevent father absence or that shared parenting alleviates longing in children for the parent the child is not with. Indeed, in a prospective longitudinal study, McIntosh, Smyth, Wells, et al. (2010) found 43% of school aged children living in a shared-time arrangement, and thus who spent regular overnights with each parent, privately longed for more time with their mothers. The cautionary note here is this: The methods used to study a phenomenon, such as the child's experience of parent absence, should reflect the complexity of causation and association inherent within the phenomenon itself.

Section Summary

The key points in this section are that:

- Research on shared parenting can offer deceptively simple or indeed profoundly confusing guidance.
- Studies use different definitions of shared care and employ markedly different designs, research questions, and samples.
- It is important to understand the limits of the various research designs, and the extent to which group data can be applied to an individual case.

The next section sets out the literature to date on the nature of risk associated with shared parenting in specific contexts and identifies key findings as groundwork for considering probable intersections of risk.

PART III. OVERVIEW: RECENT RESEARCH CONSIDERING RISK IN SHARED-TIME PARENTING

Empirical approaches to considering risk in the context of shared-time parenting include risk that the arrangement may not be durable, that it might have an adverse impact on family members' relationships and contentment, and/or it might affect developmental outcomes. Few studies have considered the interaction of these factors. Table 6.1 outlines the literature that has considered risks in shared parenting arrangements.

Table 6.1 sets out the key attributes, strengths, and weaknesses of 10 relatively recent empirical studies and two meta-reviews addressing the risks for children and parents of shared-time parenting arrangements. It is important to describe each study's key attributes because the findings from each will necessarily reflect and be limited by such things as the measures used, the respondents, the way in which respondents were recruited, the method of their response, and the way in which these data were analyzed.

A Note on Recent Australian Research

Table 6.1 features several recent studies conducted in Australia, a country currently at the vanguard of family law reform. Since 2006, there has been sweeping change across the entire family law system (e.g., new services, wide-ranging legislative and procedural changes, and a new child support scheme)—most notably with new legislation mandating that disputing parents, lawyers, mediators, and judges must consider equal or near-equal shared-time arrangements. Given the depth and breadth of these changes, significant money and resources have been invested by government to monitor the operation and impacts of the reforms.

The central plank of the Australian research program is a large evaluation study conducted by the Australian Institute of Family Studies (AIFS). While the AIFS evaluation (Kaspiew et al., 2009) comprises many disparate components, one aspect is

Table 6.1 REVIEW OF 12 RECENT (POST-2000) INTERNATIONAL STUDIES/REVIEWS ADDRESSING RISKS
FOR CHILDREN AND PARENTS IN SHARED-TIME PARENTING ARRANGEMENTS

Source	Areas of risk addressed	Participants	Procedure
Bagshaw, Brown, Wendt, Campbell, McInness, Tinning, Batagol, Sifris, Tyson, Baker, & Fernandez Arias, 2010. [Australia]	The effect of family violence on post-separation parenting arrangements	Non-probability, convenience samples– recruited via e-mail to networks of separated parents, and children　Web survey: 931 adults (677 women, 236 men);　Web survey: 105 children started survey (aged 5–25 years); 68 children completed survey　Phone interview: 105 parents　(47 women, 41 men); follow-up: 33 (13 men, 20 women) in Queensland (Qld) and South Australia (SA)　Phone interviews: 12 children: 4 boys, 8 girls (aged 9–17 years) in Qld and SA	Mixed methods: web surveys (adults & children); phone interview
Bauserman, 2002 [USA]	Children's overall adjustment; behavioral adjustment; emotional adjustment;　self-esteem; family relations/parental behavior; academic and scholastic achievements/ performance (including IQ); and child adjustment/ experience of divorce	Combined sample size of 1,846 children in sole custody arrangements and 814 in joint custody　Analysis of 33 studies with five different sample types: court and divorce records (11), convenience samples (12), school-based samples (6), national sample (1), clinical/service-based samples (2), and sampling unknown (1)	Meta-analysis of quantitative studies that compared outcomes for children in joint custody (legal or physical) and children in sole custody.　Secondary meta-analyses of intact families, paternal sole custody, and joint custody.

Statistical analyses	Findings	Study strengths	Study weaknesses
Descriptive statistics: frequencies/ crosstabs Content analysis of qualitative data	Women and children are more likely than men to be victims of severe abuse and threats. Men and women construct their experiences of violence differently. Two thirds of the 59 children surveyed felt "frightened or scared" when their parents fought; around half felt "helpless" because they could not stop their parents from fighting. Some children wanted no involvement with an abusive non-resident parent.	Focus on family violence Insights from children	Non-probability, convenience sampling No multivariate analyses No quantitative child outcome data reported Strong claims on the basis of biased samples; some samples small Government-commissioned research, not necessarily peer-reviewed
Meta-analysis of 33 studies— 10 published, 23 unpublished	Children in joint custody (legal or physical) are behaviorally and psychologically better adjusted than children in sole custody (where sole custody was almost exclusively maternal custody). Children in joint custody arrangements fare no differently across the measures of child adjustment to children in intact families. Joint custody arrangements are identified as potentially beneficial to children regardless of their family, emotional, behavioral, and academic attributes.	Systematic meta-analytic review Comparative data analysis of joint and sole custody cases	Implicitly conflates joint legal and joint physical custody No consistent definition of joint custody across the studies Study coverage (few probability samples; 22 studies are student theses) Data collected between 1982 and 1999 Only 8 studies used in the analysis of paternal and intact families comparisons Sole custody cases were almost exclusively maternal custody arrangements. Measures used to identify behavioral and psychological adjustment varied between the studies & ranged from standardized scales to author-constructed scales or variables.

(Continued)

Source	Areas of risk addressed	Participants	Procedure
Cashmore, Parkinson, Weston, Patulny, Redmond, Qu, Baxter, Rajkovic, Sitek, & Katz, 2010 [Australia]	Parenting and relationship resources– particularly interparental conflict and concerns about children's safety Children's socio-emotional progress and language development	*Primary data:* 169 separated parents recruited via solicitors, etc.; 859 separated parents recruited from the Child Support Agency; 136 children surveyed online. Plus 40 follow-up interviews with parents by telephone. *Secondary data:* HILDA Wave 7: 606 separated mothers, 381 separated fathers (60 and 67 with shared care, respectively) *LSAC-Wave 1:* 733 separated mothers (84 with shared or near shared care) *Caring for Children sample:* 486 separated mothers, 314 separated fathers (60 and 63 with shared care, respectively) *Family Characteristics Survey:* weighted to population	*Primary data:* Mail survey– Non-probability (recruited via professionals); probability (recruited via Child Support Agency "opt-in" sample) *Secondary data:* HILDA, LSAC-Wave 2, ABS FCS/FCTS = national random samples involving in-person interview Caring for children: CATI
Haugen, 2010 [Norway]	Parental conflict, loss of social and economic capital, and life stress	In-depth interviews with 15 children (aged 9–18 years) in shared care arrangements drawn from Families after Divorce study (96 children) Children's parents divorced in Norway in 1992 or 1995 Shared care arrangements varied from alternating weeks, split weeks, and weekend care, and between time-sharing arrangements (flexible, ambiguous, and rigid)	Face-to-face in-depth interviews coded using within-case and cross-case analysis
Kaspiew, Gray, Weston, Moloney, Hand, Qu, & the Family Law Evaluation Team, 2009 [Australia]	Parenting and relationship resources, particularly interparental conflict and concerns about children's safety	Longitudinal Study of Separated Families (LSSF)[*] 10,002 parents registered with the CSA who separated in 2007 (around half the parents in the study had a child aged 0–2 years)	Computer-assisted telephone interviews

Statistical analyses	Findings	Study strengths	Study weaknesses
Primary data: descriptive statistics (frequencies and crosstabs) *Secondary data:* descriptive statistics (frequencies and crosstabs); multivariate analysis of LSAC-Wave 2 (K-cohort) 2006 data—children aged 6–7 years	Shared care in Australia is unusual but on the rise. A small select group of parents exercise shared care, typically the cooperative group. Shared care can work well for some families; parents often like this arrangement. Relationship quality matters more than the care pattern to children's outcomes. Mothers with shared-care arrangements who report high levels of interparental conflict or have serious concerns about the safety of children are more likely to report negative outcomes for children than when children are in maternal sole care.	*Primary data:* Interviews with children Data triangulation *Secondary data:* National random samples Focus on children aged 6–7 years in LSAC sample	*Primary data:* Low response rate No multivariate analyses Non-random samples of lawyers, mediators, etc. Combined samples from very different populations into a single sample Small non-random samples of children Government-commissioned research, not necessarily peer-reviewed
Not applicable (thematic analysis of qualitative data)	For children, shared residence can be experienced as "both a pleasure and a burden." Shared residence can work well when children have an opportunity to speak and be heard, provided feelings of responsibilities are not placed on them to ensure their parents' well-being. Children caught in high levels of interparental conflict do not benefit from shared residency.	Interviews and insights from children provide rich qualitative data.	Small sample size Data collected in 2000 No comparative data
Combination of descriptive and multivariate statistics	Shared care in Australia is unusual but on the rise. Small select group of parents exercise shared care, typically cooperative parents. But violence and safety concerns were present in some of these families.	Large national random sample including large random sample of shared-care parents Subsample of ex-couple dyads Rigorous design and analysis Recent snapshot	Very recent separations only; not representative of general population of separated parents Sample bias (e.g., CSA population; those with phone numbers on CSA records) Parents' reports only** Cross-sectional data*** Brief CATI telephone interview

(Continued)

163

Table 6.1 Review of 12 recent (post-2000) international studies/reviews addressing risks for children and parents in shared-time parenting arrangements *(Continued)*

Source	Areas of risk addressed	Participants	Procedure
Kline Pruett & Barker, 2009 [USA]	Impact of joint (legal and/or physical) custody on child adjustment	Analysis of 17 joint *legal* custody (only 1 post-2000); 20 studies of joint *physical* custody (only 1 post-2000); 2 studies of joint *legal* and *physical* custody (1 post-2000)	Examined literature on child adjustment post-divorce that focuses on custody as a variable of interest
Kline Pruett, Ebling, & Insabella, 2004 [USA]	Child problem behavior (using the Child Behavior Checklist)	161 families with children aged 0–6 years recruited upon filing for divorce or child custody. 132 families participated in a follow-up 15–18 months after initial contact. Sample drawn from the *Collaborative Divorce Project*.	Inclusion criteria: biological child had to be 6 years or younger; no "significant" history of parental substance use or family violence in family Data collected from mothers and fathers, teachers/child care providers, and attorneys

Statistical analyses	Findings	Study strengths	Study weaknesses
	Most significant increase in incidence of shared care has been in litigated cases since new laws. Shared care generally works well, and parents often like arrangement. Children in 50/50 time-splits were typically aged between 5 and 14 years. Link is evident between mothers' safety concerns and poor child outcomes, especially in shared care.		Crude safety and well-being measures Government-commissioned research, not necessarily peer-reviewed
Not applicable (narrative review of existing studies)	Compared with sole custody, joint custody gives children "an edge." That said, joint custody parents appear to be different from sole custody parents (e.g., they tend to be more cooperative, child-focused, and better educated and have higher SES than other divorcing families). Fathers with joint custody report more satisfaction than non-resident fathers. "Joint custody can be successful under conditions of low to moderate levels of conflict" (p. 437).	Covers key early North American studies Identifies key moderating variables, and key themes in the literature	Joint legal and physical custody often conflated in the narrative review Studies examined are anachronistic. No assessment of the quality of studies in the review Treats joint physical custody as a single homogenous group
Bivariate correlations, regression and hierarchical regression—relationship between the predictors and outcome variable of child behavior	Poor parent–child relationships were associated with child attention problems, social problems, and externalizing behaviors. Family relationships (child–parent and parent–parent) predict a range of adverse child behaviors.	Comparison between randomly assigned intervention group and the remaining families Mother and father reports (dyadic data) Data from "collateral informants" also sought	Small, non-probability sample; lack of statistical power Cross-sectional data: correlation does not mean causation Sample bias: youngest child is focus child; consent from both parents needed for participation→ cooperative relationships— all families made parenting plans together, with the help of Family Services and/ or their lawyers

(Continued)

Table 6.1 Review of 12 recent (post-2000) international studies/reviews addressing risks for children and parents in shared-time parenting arrangements *(Continued)*

Source	Areas of risk addressed	Participants	Procedure
McIntosh, Smyth, Wells, & Long, 2010a [Australia]	Children's adjustment over 4 years (post-mediation)	Longitudinal follow-up (4 years post-mediation) of 133 families (106 mothers, 93 fathers, 196 children); 67 ex-couples (50% of sample) Average age of children = 13 yrs (SD = 3.64, range 6–19 years). 54 families had continuous sole care arrangement; 36 had continuous shared care; 23 started with shared care but changed to sole care; 18 started with sole care but moved to shared care. Sample drawn from Children in Focus (CIF) study	Survey: T1 = paper-pencil; T2, T3, T4 face-to-face/phone (before med; on agreement; 1 yr post-agreement; 4 years post-agreement) Children: 1:1 play-style interviews at each interval
McIntosh, Smyth, & Kelaher, 2010b [Australia]	Young children's adjustment in different patterns of parenting after separation	2,059 families with children ages 3 months to 5 years, where parents separated Three groups of children: 258 children 0–2 yrs; 509 children 2–3 years; 1,292 children 4–5 years (weighted)	Face-to-face interviews, brief observations, and mail-out self-report. Surveys given to "primary" parent and child's day care provider (if applicable). Independent observer data available. (Data from second parent not available.)

Statistical analyses	Findings	Study strengths	Study weaknesses
	Overnight stays and consistent care arrangements were associated with fewer social problems for young children. Girls who have overnight stays were less likely to display withdrawn behaviors. The determinants of child behavioral outcomes differed according to mothers' and fathers' reports.	Subjective reports of the number of nights, access, and parental responsibilities were derived from parenting plans.	
Descriptive statistics; ANOVAs, regression analyses including mother, father, and child responses	Shared care was a less stable pattern than sole care. Cooperative shared-care arrangements were more likely to be sustained than arrangements involving high interparental conflict and acrimony. Four years after mediation, children in shared care (especially those in rigid arrangements) were less satisfied with the arrangements than other groups. After adjusting for initial levels of conflict, children in the shared-care groups reported higher levels of interparental conflict 4 years after mediation than children in the sole care or changing care groups.	Prospective, repeated-measures design High conflict focus Comparison groups Comprehensive child outcome data Mother, father, child reports (i.e., multiple perspectives)	Small, non-probability sample Government-commissioned research, but with (non-blind) peer review
Descriptive statistics, regression analyses	Pattern of care appears to have an independent effect on emotional regulation outcomes for children <4. Infants <2 years with overnights one or more nights per week had higher irritability than	Strong theoretical framework Comprehensive infant/child outcome measures Random sample representative of general population Statistical controls	Small sub-samples, especially in shared care groups: lack of statistical power Second parent report not available Government-commissioned research, but with (non-blind) peer review

(Continued)

Table 6.1 Review of 12 recent (post-2000) international studies/reviews addressing risks for children and parents in shared-time parenting arrangements *(Continued)*

Source	Areas of risk addressed	Participants	Procedure
		Sample drawn from Longitudinal Study of Australian Children. (LSAC) Families representative of the general Australian population	Variables included demographic, psychosomatic variables, and emotional/behavioral regulation variables. Different measures used for each of the three age groups.
Smart, 2004; see also Smart et al., 2001 [UK]	Children's well-being over time in shared parenting arrangements	21 children, aged 8–20 years (majority aged 11–15) still in 50/50 shared care arrangements since 1st interview	Face-to-face interviews with 60 children (out of 117 followed up 3–4 years after 1st interview: 30 were in shared care at 1st interview)
Smyth, Caruana, & Ferro, 2004; Smyth, Qu, & Weston, 2004 [Australia]	Parenting and relationship resources	10 focus groups: 54 parents (including 2 ex-couples). Groups drawn from *Caring for Children after Parental Separation Study.* National random sample of separated parents with at least one child <18 years: 632 separated mothers (32 with shared care); 407 separated fathers (31 with shared care). Sample drawn from Household and Income and Labour Dynamics in Australia (HILDA) Survey.	Focus groups Interviewer-administered survey

Statistical analyses	Findings	Study strengths	Study weaknesses
	infants in primary care, as well as more vigilant monitoring of and maintenance of proximity with primary parent. Children aged 2–3 with frequent overnights exhibited lower persistence with tasks than same-age children with rare or no overnights, as well as more problematic behaviors, and more distressed behaviors in interaction with the primary parent. 4- to 5-year-olds with frequent overnights showed no negative effects in emotional dysregulation compared with children who had rare or no overnights. Variation in behavior and emotional regulation was explained by parental conflict and emotional variability rather than frequency of overnights.	Comparison groups Use of multiple data sources (primary parent, independent observers and teachers/child caregivers). Able to differentiate effects for infants and toddlers from preschool children	
Not applicable (thematic analysis of qualitative data).	Three factors influenced children's satisfaction with shared care: (1) whether arrangement was child-focused or adult-focused; (2) whether arrangements was flexible; (3) whether children felt "at home" in both parents' houses.	Children's perspectives Longitudinal Rich insights about children's experience of shared care over time	Small, non-probability sample
Descriptive statistics	Small select group of families exercise shared care in Australia. Shared care can work well for some families; parents often like this arrangement.	Mixed-methods— depth and generalizability Focus on different patterns of parenting after separation	Small samples Parents' reports only Cross-sectional data No multivariate analyses

Table 6.1 Review of 12 recent (post-2000) international studies/reviews addressing risks
for children and parents in shared-time parenting arrangements   *(Continued)*

Source	Areas of risk addressed	Participants	Procedure
Whiteside & Becker, 2000 [USA]	Child development skills (cognitive skills and social skills); child adjustment (externalizing and internalizing symptoms); and a general adjustment score (total behavioral problems)	Analysis of 12 studies with different sample types and design: nationally representative survey (3); homogenous sample—white middle-class families (6); clinic sample (1); court records (1); and childcare center-based sample (1). The year of divorce across the studies ranged from the late 1970s to 1990.	Meta-analysis of research analyzing the effects of divorce on children aged 6 years or younger at interview who had experienced their parents' divorce before age 5 years

Notes:
*The AIFS evaluation involved numerous forms of data collection. For brevity, we focus on the LSSF because it is the most relevant data in the context of risk.
** Adolescent data released mid-2011 at the time this chapter was finalized (see Lodge & Alexander, 2010).
*** Longitudinal data released mid-2011 at the time this chapter was finalized (see Qu & Weston, 2010). CATI = computer-assisted telephone interviews.
Shared parenting time refers to parenting arrangements where children spend at least 30% of the time with each parent or where neither is described as the "primary parent."

especially well placed to shed light on the shared-time parenting debate in relation to young children: the Longitudinal Study of Separated Families (LSSF). The LSSF currently represents the largest random sample of recently separated parents in Australia, with 10,000 recently separated parents being tracked at two points in time. Just over half (58%) of the focus children in the first wave of the study were under 3 years old. No other Australian study of separated parents involves this number of young children, and this number of young children in substantially shared parenting arrangements.

In addition to the AIFS evaluation, two other studies were commissioned to improve understanding of shared-time parenting: Cashmore et al. (2010) focused on

Statistical analyses	Findings	Study strengths	Study weaknesses

Meta-analysis using regression modeling	Child behavioral outcomes are directly related to the quality of interparental relationships, father–child relationships, and maternal adjustment. Cooperative co-parenting is associated with better child outcomes.
	
	Relationship quality matters more than the care pattern: child behavioral outcomes are indirectly related to amount of time children spend with father.
	
	Pre-separation factors are important in determining and understanding post-separation child outcomes and interparental and parent–child relationships.
		Systematic statistical analysis
		   Tight conceptual focus
		   Pre-separation family history variables included in analysis
			Small sample sizes across the studies used with which correlations were calculated.
			   Causation cannot be determined on basis of correlation data.
			   Majority of sole-custody cases were maternal custody, and mother-only reports most often used for predictor and outcome variables.
			   No comparative analysis between joint and sole custody
			   Time since separation and family economic status not controlled for in analyses
			   Quality of study measures not included
			   Unable to disentangle effects for infants and toddlers from preschool children

the workability for families of shared-time parenting, and Bagshaw et al. (2010) focused on the impact of family violence on post-separation parenting arrangements and decision-making. Several other reports focusing on family violence were also commissioned by the government (e.g., Australian Law Reform Commission, 2010; Chisholm, 2009; Family Law Council, 2010). Studies led by authors of this chapter (McIntosh, Smyth, et al., 2010; McIntosh, Smyth, & Kelaher, 2010) addressed two potential risk groups: children in high-conflict divorce and children under 5 years. Key parameters of these studies are set out in Table 6.1. One of the core challenges for research, policy, and practice in Australia is how to make sense of the voluminous reports and, in some cases, disparate findings that have recently emerged.

Section Summary

The following conclusions can be drawn from Table 6.1:

- It is unusual for studies to collect and analyze data from mothers, fathers, and children (i.e., from multiple perspectives)—this produces an incomplete picture.
- Large representative samples of post-separation parenting are uncommon in this context (small convenience samples are common).
- Even with large representative samples, the number of families with shared care is typically small, given the uncommon nature of this parenting arrangement and the special population from which it is drawn (i.e., separated parents).
- Longitudinal data are uncommon—this means that causality and change over time cannot be assessed.
- Most studies do not have a comparison or control group.
- Most studies treat shared-care families as one homogenous group, yet court-ordered shared care among litigating parents is typically very different from self-selected arrangements made by cooperating parents.
- Key explanatory information is often lacking in many studies (e.g., pre-separation circumstances, time since separation, level of interparental conflict).
- There is a general lack of comparability among studies, particularly in relation to definitions, sampling, measurement, analytic approaches, and so forth. Different methods will produce different findings, and making sense of this body of research is fraught with difficulty. Some areas of convergence nonetheless emerge.
- Australian studies into shared care have burgeoned due to legislative changes mandating that judges, mediators, and parents consider adopting a shared-time parenting arrangement.

PART IV. ANALYSIS OF THE RISK LITERATURE

Area 1: Pragmatic Resources for Durable, Workable Shared Parenting

Recent Australian research indicates that many shared-time parenting arrangements do not endure long term. In a general population sample, Kaspiew et al. (2009) found 49% of shared-time arrangements were still in place after 4 to 5 years, compared to 87% of primary mother care arrangements (see also Smyth, Weston, Moloney, Richardson, & Temple, 2008). McIntosh, Smyth, Wells, et al. (2010) found similar ratios with a high-conflict sample of 131 families over 4 years: 41% had sustained continuous mother primary care, 27% had sustained shared-time care, and 32% had changed their arrangement during this time.

The independent impacts on family members of changing arrangements are not likely to be uniform. Change is likely to be a productive, responsive outcome in many instances, while in other contexts, change may be sudden and dramatic, or late in coming. Aspects of family law practice emphasize the need for parents to "adhere" to court orders, often for many years, and to take care not to breach them. Sustaining arrangements over time may or may not be helpful, depending on the context. For example, McIntosh, Smyth, Wells, et al. (2010) found children's self-reported outcomes and maternal satisfaction with living arrangements significantly improved with the flexibility and adaptability of the arrangement. Research is yet to define the merits and contexts of change, particularly the circumstances under which changed arrangements are for the better.

There is a strong, well-replicated body of evidence concerning the structural and relational elements of family life that predict the ability to sustain a responsive shared parenting arrangement (see Table 6.1). Several early Australian research studies specifically focused on shared parenting arrangements. Smyth et al. (Smyth, Caruana, & Ferro, 2004; Smyth, Qu, & Weston, 2004) originally identified a group of "classic co-operators" who had key structural and relationship resources that contributed to the workability of their shared parenting arrangements. Confirmed by further studies using large, nationally representative data sets (Cashmore et al., 2010 Kaspiew et al., 2009; McIntosh, Smyth, & Kelaher, 2010), recent findings indicate that risk of a shared-time parenting arrangement ending is increased significantly by the following family profile:

1. Younger parents
2. Lower levels of education and lower incomes
3. Parents did not self-select into the arrangement
4. Parents live far apart (more than a 30-minute drive)
5. Parents do not maintain a business-like parenting relationship
6. Arrangements are not child-focused
7. Lack of support from extended family members and new partners
8. A parent's lack of confidence about the other's parenting competence

Drawing on two data sets, one from a family court sample (111 children, 77 parents) and the other a high-conflict mediation sample (364 children, 169 families), McIntosh and Chisholm (2008) suggested additional, interdependent psychological risk factors within one or both parents, including:

1. Poor capacity to operate from the child's best interests
2. Fixation on achieving parity or equity of time
3. Poor emotional availability to the child
4. Poorly managed interparental conflict and acrimony
5. A perception that the child is unsafe with the other parent
6. The child's insecurity in, or discontentment with, a shared arrangement

The main points in this subsection include:

- The importance of strong pragmatic, parenting, and relationship resources in maintaining shared arrangements
- Well-resourced, responsive, child-focused arrangements growing upon a previously existing base of adequate cooperation between parents, with numerous social and economic structural supports, are key to supporting workability and durability in shared care arrangements.

Area 2: Co-Parenting Relationship and Parenting Attitudes

Several of the new Australian studies demonstrate the greater likelihood that, under conditions of interparental conflict, violence, and/or court-enforced orders, mothers with shared-time arrangements are at much higher risk than fathers for concern and anxiety about their children and for general discontent with the arrangement (e.g., Kaspiew et al., 2009). Cashmore et al. (2010) and McIntosh, Smyth, Wells, et al. (2010) found that mothers who had been involved in litigation or were in rigidly fixed, inflexible living arrangements were equally pessimistic about the arrangements, whether they were in shared-time parenting or primary mother care. Both studies found that in a high-conflict scenario, mothers' satisfaction with shared-time parenting was substantially lower than fathers' satisfaction. McIntosh, Smyth, Wells, et al. (2010) found that children's reports of satisfaction with shared-time parenting were lower than either parent's reports and were lowest of all when arrangements were rigid and inflexible. Children in shared-time arrangements reported feeling significantly more caught in the middle of their parents' conflict than children in other parenting arrangements.

This newer research confirms previous findings from over two decades of research in the U.S. context (Johnston, 1995; Johnston, Kline, & Tschann, 1989) demonstrating a poor fit between the many demands of shared-time parenting arrangements and ongoing high levels of conflict between parents. Many studies suggest that while such difficulties can occur for children in any time-share ratios, they may be more frequently experienced in shared-time situations, especially those marked by co-parenting acrimony (Johnston, 1995; McIntosh, Smyth, Wells et al., 2010; Smart, 2004).

Further along the risk spectrum, a risk of continuing abuse of power by controlling or violent ex-spouses in shared parenting has been documented, together with elevated stress and anxiety for parents concerned about their child's well-being when in the care of the other parent (Chisholm, 2009; Kaspiew et al., 2009). Yet, despite a majority of family court matters involving reports of recent or current domestic violence (Chisholm, 2009), Kaspiew et al. (2009) found a marked increase in shared time among families who attended the Family Court of Australia, with 34% of judicially determined matters in the year of study resulting in equal or near-equal shared parenting. Those authors found:

> . . . a substantial minority [of children] may experience frequent episodes of high inter-parental conflict or an atmosphere generating fear in one parent. In fact, mothers with a shared care-time arrangement were less likely to report friendly or cooperative relationships than mothers who cared for their child most nights and those whose child saw the father during the daytime only (especially the latter group) (Kaspiew et al., 2009, pp. 162–163).

Several have questioned whether shared time is used in the high-conflict population "to appease warring parties" (McIntosh & Chisholm, 2008, p. 39), as a compromise solution to a difficult problem (Eekelaar, Clive, Clarke, & Raikes, 1977), and as a modern version of halving the child under King Solomon's dilemma (Moloney, 2008; Smyth, 2009). Trinder (2010) concludes from her review of the shared-time parenting literature that, contrary to the hopes of some, shared care arrangements in high-conflict cases are not transformative and instead may increase and perpetuate damaging conflict. Hunter (2010) argues that shared-time parenting is particularly fraught with problems for parents entangled in complex grief responses to the divorce; effectively it can be an arrangement that locks parents into frequent contact with each other, making emotional separation more complex. Despite the strong and sometimes urgent desire of a parent to share equally the care of his or her children, some parents may need time and support to evolve toward this care arrangement.

The main points in this subsection include:

- Parents' subjective reports of satisfaction with shared care arrangements are associated with their gender, their level of concern about safety, histories of violence, current conflict levels, and litigation pathways.
- Shared-time parenting in the context of family violence and ongoing interparental conflict is often associated with problematic outcomes for children.

Area 3: Children's Outcomes and Developmental Considerations

The burgeoning divorce literature is replete with evidence of the impacts of interparental conflict on children's psycho-emotional capacities. Even within a supportive caregiving environment, the independent impacts that separation brings to bear on children's development remain notable (Amato, 2000). Cherlin, Chase-Lansdale, and McRae (1998) and others found that, through adolescence and young adulthood, the gap in psychological well-being between children from divorced versus intact families grows.

In research terms, the potential role of parenting arrangements in shaping the effects remains poorly understood. Putting aside the special case of infancy for a moment, the existing evidence shows that simple links between parenting time and the emergence of overt pathological outcomes for children are unlikely—with the exception perhaps of rare or no contact with one parent (see Table 6.1). In this light, questions for future research include: How might a shared-time parenting plan contribute to or detract from the caregiving climate, and with it, the underpinnings of children's psycho-emotional security? Where does shared-time parenting intersect with other known risks? The existing literature available to address these questions is outlined in Table 6.1 and in other studies detailed in the following section.

QUALITY VERSUS QUANTITY: THE FACTS TO DATE

Through their meta-analytic studies, Amato (2000) and Amato and Gilbreth (1999) were among the first to show that while *frequency* of contact is not correlated in a predictive way to children's psychological adjustment, *quality* of parenting and the nature of parent–child relationships are significantly related to child well-being. More recently, in the context of longitudinal data from a high-conflict mediation sample over 4 years, McIntosh, Smyth, Wells, et al. (2010) found that more contact in itself did not lead to a better father–child relationship over time; instead, a better relationship at the outset led to more contact (i.e., the past is predictive of the future).

From his overview of the literature, Smyth (2009, p. 44) concluded that "the idea that a clear linear relationship exists between parenting time and children's outcomes (such that ever-increasing amounts of time necessarily leads to better outcomes for children) appears to lack an empirical basis." Whiteside and Becker (2000, p. 23) summarize the time-risk equation in this way:

> Neither the shape of the care giving network nor the time-sharing schedule has the most potent effects on children's development. Rather, the quality of the parental alliance and the parents' warmth, sensitivity, good adjustment, and discipline style make the difference between a well-adjusted child and one who is angry, scared, or limited in cognitive and social skills.

The recent Australian studies into shared-time parenting suggest that there is no clear relationship between parenting time and child well-being and point to similar intervening relationship factors. In two of the recent Australian studies using national child support samples (Cashmore et al., 2010; Kaspiew et al., 2009), any initial differences in child well-being indices found between parenting arrangements became non-significant after controlling for socioeconomic status, maternal characteristics, and family process variables such as conflict.

SUBSTANTIALLY SHARED TIME AND THE HIGH-CONFLICT FAMILY

In four studies of high-conflict parents in the United Kingdom, the United States, and the Australian contexts, more frequent contact was not associated with global child mental health outcomes, as measured by parents' reports on the Strengths and Difficulties Questionnaire (McIntosh, Smyth, Wells, et al. 2010; Trinder, Kellett, & Swift, 2007) and by independent clinical evaluation (Johnston, 1995; Johnston et al., 1989).

Some studies have probed beyond global outcomes, and beyond cross-sectional data (Johnston, 1995; McIntosh, Smyth, Wells, et al., 2010), finding a cluster of elevated risks posed by shared-time parenting arrangements over time for children in high-conflict climates. McIntosh, Smyth, Wells, et al. (2010; see Table 6.1 for methodological details) explored outcomes over a period of 4 years for children from high-conflict families (high conflict defined by parents' voluntary or mandated attendance at mediation and by self-report scores on acrimony and conflict scales at intake). Parent report and children's self-reports were contrasted for the following four groups: (a) ongoing shared care, (b) ongoing primary care, (c) ongoing rare or no overnights with the parents, and (d) changed arrangements over 3 to 4 years following mediation. Children in ongoing shared-time arrangements (35%+ shared overnights) were reported by both mother and father to have significantly higher hyperactivity/inattention scores than children in all other time-sharing arrangements. This was particularly so for boys and for children living in rigid arrangements (defined as *almost never* having flexibility in their care arrangements, on parent report). This study of high-conflict parents also found significantly higher rates of emotional symptoms in children in rigid, unresponsive care arrangements regardless of whether parents had primary or shared parenting arrangements.

Johnston (1995) suggested that, in a context of severe conflict or violence, a small but important group of children may benefit from loss of contact with a parent. In their longitudinal follow-up of a high-conflict group, McIntosh, Smyth, Wells, et al.

(2010) found that 14% of children (N = 37/259) had little or no overnight contact with the second parent at the 4-year follow-up. On self-report, 68% (N =19 of the 28 children having rare or no contact, who provided satisfaction data) were content with having no overnight contact with one parent, and repeated measures showed significant overall reduction in feelings of being caught in the middle of and distressed by their parents' conflict. Emotional well-being scores (primary parent rated) improved significantly in this group. Reported reasons for loss of contact varied, with the majority being self-selection, followed by court-ordered cessation of contact, and two associated with relocation. Children in this group were older than children in the other care-pattern groups (average age 15 years, SD = 4 years).

What Do Children Themselves Say About Shared Care and Risk?

Trinder (2010) reviewed existing qualitative studies on children's views of shared care and found that despite the diversity of cultures in which they had been conducted (in the United Kingdom context, see Smart, 2004, and Smart, Neale & Wade, 2001; in Norway, see Haugen, 2010; in Australia, see Cashmore et al., 2010), findings were highly consistent. Trinder reported that children's views, like mothers' views, were contingent upon the relationship context in which their care was shared, wherein shared residence could work variously as *a pleasure* and/or *a burden*. Dissatisfaction and accruing risk surrounded the continual movement of children's lives and possessions, the organizational burden this created, further complexity as parents re-partnered and cohabited, not feeling equally at home with both parents, and missing an absent parent, despite the equity of the arrangement. Evidence suggests that children's discontentment with shared-time arrangements increases when they feel uninvolved in decision-making (Cashmore et al., 2010). Trinder (2010) noted that relatively few children appeared able to influence their own care arrangements. The most recent data from a Norwegian study indicated that equal-time arrangements were determined solely by adults in 55% of 527 cases and that the children concerned had had no influence on these decisions (Skjørten & Barlindhaug, 2007).

Regarding the issue of age and differing suitability of shared care, the research evidence converges in many respects. Kaspiew et al. (2009) and McIntosh, Smyth, Wells, et al. (2010) report a peak entry into shared arrangements when children are between 6 and 10 years, becoming less common as children move into adolescence. Smart (2004) reports multiple factors that make it more likely that an adolescent will express a wish for a primary home. Teenagers' independent capacities for maintaining relationships with each parent increase with each year that goes by, their movement between homes becomes self-governed, and their ability to make their views known grows. Among the organizational complexities of living a shared-time lifestyle, a focus on peer relationships and the increasing demands of school may combine to influence an adolescent's ability and desire to cope with a shifting home base.

Summary

The main points in this subsection include:

- Shared-time arrangements are most common with children in primary school years.

- Simple links between parenting time and mental health outcomes for children are unlikely.
- Lack of consultation with the child is a risk factor for children's reported dissatisfaction with shared-time arrangements.
- Elevated risk is more likely when shared-time parenting arrangements co-occur with ongoing parental conflict that triangulates the child and/or heightens exposure to conflict.
- Rigid arrangements (either primary care or shared time) that are not responsive to changing needs are associated with problematic outcomes.

Infancy: A Special Case

Of note, the preceding studies have concerned school-aged children. Does developmental stage alter the risk equation in shared parenting arrangements? Infancy in particular (here defined as the first 4 years) is a time of developmental vulnerability by virtue of the rapid physical, cognitive, language, social, and emotional development going on during this time. The human brain, about 30% formed at birth, expands threefold during the first 3 years (Schore & McIntosh, 2011), with ever-evolving quantity and complexity of synaptic connections. Importantly, much of the growth of the human brain during this time is termed *experience dependent* (Melmed, 2004); that is, the complexity of the brain's development depends on the nature and quality of care the infant receives.

What role do time-share arrangements play in the developmental outcomes of infants? To explore this question, McIntosh, Smyth, and Kelaher (2010; see Table 6.1 for details) employed a large nationally representative Longitudinal Study of Australian Children (LSAC) data set to examine overnight care patterns and psycho-emotional development in infants and young children under 5 years old. The study investigated emotional and behavioral regulation outcomes (on primary parent and carer/teacher/observer reports) for children in shared residence, primary residence, and rare/no overnight contact groups. For 4- to 5-year-olds (N = 1,292), results indicated that interparental conflict and parental warmth were independently linked to developmental outcomes, but time arrangements were not. However, for infants (0–2 years, N = 258) and young children (3–4 years, N = 509) the findings were different. Controlling for socioeconomic variables, parenting warmth, and parents' relationship, shared-care arrangements were independently associated with a cluster of developmental problems indicative of significant stress for babies under 2 years who lived one or more overnights a week with both parents. Specifically, on primary parent and independent observers' reports, in their general day-to-day behavior these babies displayed significantly higher rates of irritability and vigilant efforts to monitor the presence and to maintain proximity with the primary parent than babies who had less or no overnight time away from their primary caregiver. A similar profile was noted for older infants, aged 2 to 3 years, living in shared-time arrangements (35% to 50% overnights with each parent). On primary parent and/or independent observers' reports, the study found significantly higher rates of problem behaviors (e.g., crying or hanging onto the primary parent when leaving, refusing to eat, and hitting, biting, or kicking the parent) and poor persistence in activities and exploration compared with young children with fewer or no shared overnights.

This study is one of the first-generation studies around these questions and needs replication before firm conclusions can be made regarding time-sharing arrangements for very young children. However, its findings are consistent with the only other study of infants in overnight care, conducted by Solomon and George (1999), who also documented a picture of developmental strain for the infant when involved in repeated overnight separations from the primary caregiver at the rate of one night per week or more. This strain took the form of greater propensity for anxious, unsettled behavior in infants when reunited with the primary caregiver, and greater propensity for development of insecure and disorganized attachment with the primary caregiver.

These two infant studies have considerable methodological differences. The Solomon and George study provides data that are both longitudinal and in depth in nature, using formal attachment measures and structured clinical observations. This has been cited by various reviewers as both a strength and a weakness—for example, Kline Pruett et al. (2004, p. 41) name the main difficulty with the Solomon and George study as its failure to explore "the possibility that overnights may not account for children's adjustment beyond what is accounted for by the quality of the parents' relationship to each other or to the child." The McIntosh, Smyth, and Kelaher (2010) study did control for the independent impact of shared overnights, but it did not have rich data from attachment measures, nor was it longitudinal.

From these differing methodological perspectives, both sets of findings nonetheless converge in many of their conclusions, suggesting a need to apply particular attention to likely risks inherent in a shared parenting arrangement for children under 4 years. The findings of these two studies also converge with a significant body of developmental studies of attachment conducted outside of the divorce arena, across cultures, and over several decades. These wider studies also suggest that during the first years of life, repeated and prolonged absence from the primary caregiver is uniquely stressful, and related distress is typically expressed on reunion with the primary caregiver, through the infant's irritable, unsettled, angry, or ambivalent behaviors, and over time, through psychosomatic symptoms (Bakermans-Kranenburg, van IJzendoorn, & Juffer, 2003; Belsky & Fearon, 2008; Schore & McIntosh, 2011; van IJzendoorn & Sagi-Schwartz, 2008). (See also other relevant papers in the *Family Court Review*, July 2011, a special edition on attachment and family court matters.)

Extrapolating from his 30-year study of child development in risk contexts, Sroufe (Sroufe & McIntosh, 2011) suggests that shared-time parenting with infants and preschool children is likely to create a set of additional risks that, if not necessary, should be avoided, with parents supported to wait for the child's attachment, cognitive, and language development to be ready for the task of repeat separation from a primary caretaker. Sroufe (Sroufe & McIntosh, 2011, p.466) explains it this way:

Can the child get used to it, can they survive? Yes, *but you're making their job harder.* What I want people to do is think about it from the infant's situation. What is the infant's task? Their task is to try to organize their behavior, to make the world be a predictable and understandable place where they can get their needs met and they will not be too stressed. Their job is to try and keep their arousal modulated. They are unable to do that by themselves. They can only do that with adult help. Their job is the easiest when things are regular, predictable, and responsive to them. Their job is harder the more transitions they have to deal with, the more uncertainty there is.

The main points in this subsection include:

- Only two focused studies of infants in the context of divorce and shared overnight care have been conducted, each with different methodologies.
- The empirical base is embryonic, and further research is needed.
- Early findings, however, converge around probable independent risks of shared-time arrangements for children under 4 years.

PART V. TOWARD A MATRIX FOR UNDERSTANDING RISK IN SHARED PARENTING

Despite its various shortcomings, the small body of shared parenting literature does spotlight several factors likely to give rise to a context of risk for children in shared-time parenting arrangements after parental separation. These factors fall roughly onto three interdependent dimensions: pragmatic resources, parenting/relationship resources, and the child's developmental resources, as summarized in Figure 6.1.

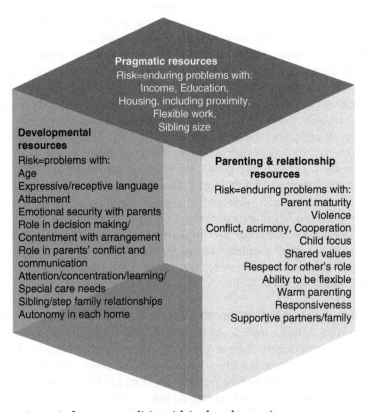

Figure 6.1 A matrix for conceptualizing risk in shared parenting

Future research needs to further investigate the risks listed in the matrix and the intersection of these factors. The literature to date, as reviewed in this chapter, suggests the following summary of risk levels across this matrix:

1. **Low current risk:** Across all axes, there is an existing, developmentally supportive context for shared-time parenting. The parents (and their new partners, extended family) are able and willing to mutually self-select into shared care to effectively support all members of the family within a shared-time arrangement, at a time in which the child's development and well-being are fully supported by this particular parenting arrangement. Parents are able to monitor the welfare of all concerned and adapt arrangements fluidly and responsively as family needs require. Parents are child-focused and able to manage their conflict and communication without unduly burdening the child.
2. **Moderate current risk:** Risks are evident on one or two axes. There is potential to establish a developmentally supportive context for shared-time parenting, but movement toward shared care will involve an evolution of skills, resources, and capacities in parents and/or developmental readiness in the child, or willingness in the child.
3. **High current/future risk:** Risks are substantial, if not numerous (e.g., parents do not live proximally) or are evident across all three axes. Shared-time parenting at this time and/or for the foreseeable future is incompatible with the developmental welfare of the child. These are families for whom shared time is not currently a logical, integrated outcome, where parent capacities or pragmatics are such that resources for shared parenting do not currently exist.

Future Research: The Need for Developmental Frameworks

One further conclusion from this review of the risk literature is that researchers do not share a common lens when operationalizing their developmental terms. This is likely to complicate any attempt to translate the implications of key findings for practice. Frameworks such as that offered in the *Psychodynamic Diagnostic Manual* (PDM; 2006) specifically consider trajectories of childhood psycho-emotional development known to be vulnerable to parenting and family functioning, and to be implicated in lifespan outcomes. The nine trajectories are (PDM, 2006, pp. 183–190):

1. Capacity for regulation, attention and learning
2. Capacity for interpersonal relationships
3. Quality of internal experience
4. Affective experience, expression, and communication
5. Defensive patterns and capacities
6. Capacity to form internal representations
7. Capacity for integration and differentiation
8. Self-observing capacity
9. Capacity to construct and use internal standards and ideals

The PDM gives a useful rubric for considering existing research findings and promotes nuanced developmental hypotheses about children's well-being in various family constellations. Following the PDM or like frameworks, researchers of the future might better distinguish the nature of psycho-developmental risk as it pertains to any particular time-share pattern, employing questions such as these: In what contexts do specific parenting-time schedules:

- Enable parents to provide a predictable, supportive, low-stress, warm environment for their child?
- Promote the child's experience of personal and relationship safety?
- Protect a child from unhelpful aspects of their parents' conflict?
- Enable the child to know and express his or her own feelings?
- Help the child internalize moral, cultural, religious, or other guidelines for coping with and responding to life?
- Employ a healthy range of defenses to manage life stressors?
- Support stage-appropriate independence, autonomy, and important relationships beyond the immediate family?

GUIDELINES: CONSIDERATIONS AND CAUTIONS

- Consensus around the nature and magnitude of risk and benefit for infants and children in shared-time parenting arrangements is some way off.
- Future longitudinal research needs to consider the complex matrix of interaction between time-share agreements, parenting histories, qualities of relationships, and the developmental stages and needs of children.
- The literature to date does however confirm several points, below.
- Shared-time parenting is an arrangement less likely to endure over time than primary home arrangements.
- Parents who maintain two appropriately resourced, proximal homes; cooperate and self-manage the unique communication involved in coordinating care; provide available, responsive parenting; and manage emotions to sufficiently safeguard their children's well-being have a greater chance of success with shared-time parenting than parents enveloped in more complex family dynamics and circumstances.
- Shared-time parenting may maintain or increase the frequency of a child's exposure to conflict or communication difficulties between parents.
- Shared-time arrangements for children growing up in a climate of ongoing conflict between their parents are associated with higher levels of risk for poor socio-emotional outcomes.
- The empirical evidence suggests that children do not like or thrive in parenting arrangements that are rigid and unresponsive to changing needs and that typically result from court orders.
- Even when well supported by cooperative co-parenting, shared care is likely to be a challenging lifestyle for children of any age, requiring skilful support by the parents concerned. Timely, child-focused, flexible, and

responsive arrangements, and the corresponding capacities they entail within parents, appear key to children doing well.

- Equal or near-equal overnight care plans are especially developmentally challenging for infants and preschool children. The developmental stages of infancy and the preschool years are emerging risk factors.
- Unlike the preschool years, by kindergarten or school entry, most children have a more consolidated ability to self-soothe, to organize their own feelings and behavior, to remember and anticipate, and to use and understand language to communicate about past and future events and their emotional states. These elements of development appear crucial to alleviating the risk of strain that accompanies repeated movement between two homes and repeated separation from a primary caregiver.
- Risks in shared-time parenting after separation lie at the intersection of parenting-time arrangements and the method of their enactment and their developmental context.
- Some parents need time and support to evolve toward a shared-care arrangement.
- For a small but significant group, shared parenting may never be appropriate.
- Consideration of a matrix of factors is necessary to understand probable risk in shared-time parenting arrangements after separation.

NOTE

1 Belgium and Italy are two countries with rebuttable presumptions of shared parenting. Australian family law requires decision-makers to consider the merits of shared parenting in matters where shared responsibility is not rebutted. At the time of writing, Canada and the United Kingdom are reviewing the relevant laws. Countries such as Sweden have moved away from shared-care presumptions. A minority of U.S. states (e.g., Wisconsin, Iowa) have amended their family law legislation to endorse shared parenting. Others have considered and declined to legislate for shared-time outcomes (e.g., New Zealand). Others further down the track have retracted earlier provisions that once encouraged shared-time outcomes (Sweden and California) (see Fehlberg et al., 2001 for an international perspective, and http://ec.europa.eu/civiljustice/parental_resp/parental_resp_gen_en.htm for a review of European rulings).

REFERENCES

Amato, P. R. (2000). The consequences of divorce for adults and children. *Journal of Marriage and the Family, 62,* 1269–1287. doi: 10.1111/j. 1741–3737.2000. 01269

Amato, P. R., & Gilbreth, J. G. (1999). Non-resident fathers and children's well-being: A meta-analysis. *Journal of Marriage and the Family, 61,* 557–573. doi: 10.2307/353560

Australian Law Reform Commission. (2010). *Family violence–A national legal response*. ALRC, Sydney. Retrieved from http://www.alrc.gov.au/publications/family-violence-national-legal-response-alrc-report-114

Bagshaw, D., Brown, T., Wendt, S., Campbell, A., McInnes, E., Tinning, B., & Fernandez Arias, P. (2010). *Family violence and family law in Australia: The experiences and views of children and adults from families who separated post-1995 and post-2006*. Canberra: Attorney General's Department.

Bakermans-Kranenburg, M. J., van IJzendoorn, M. H., & Juffer, F. (2003). Less is more: Meta-analyses of sensitivity and attachment interventions in early childhood. *Psychological Bulletin, 129*, 195–215. doi: 10.1037/0033–2909.129.2.195

Bauserman, R. (2002). Child adjustment in joint-custody versus sole-custody arrangements: A meta-analytic review. *Journal of Family Psychology, 16*(1), 91–102. doi: 10.1037/0893–3200.16.1.91

Belsky, J., & Fearon, R. M. P. (2008). Precursors of attachment security. In J. Cassidy & P. R. Shaver (Eds.), *Handbook of attachment: Theory, research, and clinical applications* (pp. 295–316). New York: Guilford Press.

Cashmore, J., Parkinson, P., Weston, R., Patulny, R., Redmond, G., Qu, L., . . . Katz, I. (2010). *Shared care parenting arrangements since the 2006 Family Law Reforms: Report to the Australian government Attorney General's Department*. Sydney, Australia: Social Policy Research Centre, University of New South Wales. Retrieved from http://www.ag.gov.au/

Cherlin, A. J., Chase-Lansdale, P. L., & McRae, C. (1998). Effects of parental divorce on mental health throughout the life course. *American Sociological Review, 63*, 239–249. doi: 10.2307/2657325

Chisholm, R. (2009). *Family courts violence review: A report by Professor Richard Chisholm*. Canberra: Attorney General's Department. Retrieved from http://www.ag.gov.au/www/agd/agd.nsf/Page/Families_FamilyCourtsViolenceReview

Eekelaar, J., Clive, E., Clarke, K., & Raikes, S. (1977). *Custody after divorce: The disposition of custody in divorce cases in Great Britain*. Oxford, England: Wolfson College, Oxford, Centre for Socio-Legal Studies.

Emery, R. E. (2010, October). *Making parenting arrangements after separation. How can we improve?* Conference presentation at the 14th Annual National Family Law Conference, Canberra, Australia.

Fabricius, W. V., Braver, S. L., Diaz, P., & Velez, C. E. (2010). Custody and parenting time: Links to family relationships and well-being after divorce. In M. Lamb (Ed.), *The role of the father in child development* (5th ed., pp. 201–240). Hoboken, NJ: John Wiley and Sons.

Family Law Council. (2010). *Improving responses to family violence in the family law system: An advice on the intersection of family violence and family law issues*. Retrieved from http://www.ag.gov.au/www/agd/agd.nsf/Page/FamilyLawCouncil_Publications_ReportstotheAttorney-General_FamilyViolenceReport

Fehlberg, B., Smyth, B., Maclean, M., & Roberts, C. (2011). Legislating for shared time parenting after separation: A research review. *International Journal of Law, Policy and the Family, 25*(3).

Haugen, G. (2010). Children's perspectives on everyday experiences of shared residence. *Children and Society, 24*(2), 112–122. doi: 10.1111/j. 1099–0860.2008.00198. x

Hetherington, E. M., Cox, M., & Cox, R. (1985). Long-term effects of divorce and remarriage on the adjustment of children. *Journal of the American Academy of Child Psychiatry, 24*, 518–530.

Hunter, R. (2010). Decades of panic. *Griffith Review*, 10(Family Politics). Retrieved from http://www.griffithreview.com/edition10/97/302.html

Johnston, J. R. (1995). Research update: Children's adjustment in sole custody compared to joint custody families and principles for custody decision making. *Family and Conciliation Courts Review, 33*, 415–425. doi: 10.1111/j. 174–1617.1995. tb00386. x

Johnston, J. R., Kline, M., & Tschann, J. M. (1989). Ongoing postdivorce conflict: Effects on children of joint custody and frequent access. *American Journal of Orthopsychiatry, 59*, 576–592. doi: 10.1111/j. 1939–0025.1989. tb02748. x

Kaspiew, R., Gray, M., Weston, R., Moloney, L., Hand, K., Qu, L., & the Family Law Evaluation Team. (2009). *Evaluation of the 2006 family law reforms*. Melbourne: Australian Institute of Family Studies.

Kline Pruett, M., & Barker, C. (2009). Joint custody: A judicious choice for families– But how, when, and why? In R. M. Galatzer-Levy, L. Kraus, & J. Galatzer-Levy (Eds.), *The scientific basis of child custody decisions* (2nd ed., pp. 417–462). New Jersey: John Wiley & Sons.

Kline Pruett, M., Ebling, R., & Insabella, G. (2004). Critical aspects of parenting plans for young children. *Family Court Review, 42*, 39–59. doi: 10.1111/j. 174– 1617.2004. tb00632. x

Lodge, J., & Alexander, M. (2010). *Views of adolescents in separated families: A study of adolescents' experiences after the 2006 reforms to the family law system*. Melbourne: Australian Institute of Family Studies.

Luepnitz, D. A. (1991). A comparison of maternal, paternal and joint custody: Understanding the varieties of post-divorce family life. In J. Folberg (Ed.), *Joint custody and shared parenting* (2nd ed., pp. 105–114). New York: Guildford Press.

McIntosh, J. E., & Chisholm, R. (2008). Cautionary notes on the shared care of children in conflicted parental separations. *Journal of Family Studies, 14*(1), 37–52. doi: 10.5172/jfs. 327.14.1.37

McIntosh, J. E., Smyth, B., & Kelaher, M. (2010). Overnight care patterns and psycho-emotional development in infants and young children. In J. McIntosh, B. Smyth, M. Kelaher, Y. Wells, & C. Long (Eds.), *Post-separation parenting arrangements and developmental outcomes for children: Collected Reports; Report to the Australian Government Attorney-General's Department: Canberra* (pp. 85–168). Retrieved from http://www.ag.gov.au/www/agd/ agd.nsf/Page/Families_FamilyRelationshipServicesOverviewofPrograms_ ResearchProjectsonSharedCareParentingandFamilyViolence

McIntosh, J. E., Smyth, B., Wells, Y. D., & Long, C. M. (2010). Parenting arrangements post-separation: Patterns and outcomes. A longitudinal study of school-aged children in high conflict divorce. In J. McIntosh, B. Smyth, M. Kelaher, Y. Wells, & C. Long (Eds.), *Post-separation parenting arrangements and developmental outcomes for children: Collected Reports; Report to the Australian Government Attorney-General's Department: Canberra* (pp. 23–84). Retrieved from http://www.ag.gov.au/www/ agd/agd.nsf/Page/Families_FamilyRelationshipServicesOverviewofPrograms_ ResearchProjectsonSharedCareParentingandFamilyViolence

McIntosh, J., Wells, Y. & Long, C. (2009). *Children beyond dispute. A four-year follow-up study of outcomes from child-focused and child-inclusive post-separation family dispute resolution*. Canberra, Australia: Australian Government Attorney General's Department. Retrieved from http://www.ag.gov.au/www/agd/agd.nsf/ Page/Publications_ChildrenBeyondDispute-April2009

McKinnon, R., & Wallerstein, J. S. (1986). Joint custody and the preschool child. *Behavioral Sciences and the Law, 4*(2), 169–183.

Melli, M. S., & Brown, P. R. (2008). Exploring a new family form—The shared time family. *International Journal of Law, Policy and the Family, 22*(2), 231–269.

Melmed, M. E. (2004, June). *Statement of Matthew E. Melmed, Executive Director, Zero to Three: National Center for Infants, Toddlers and Families.* Before the House Committee on Ways and Means Subcommittee on Human Resources.

Moloney, L. (2008). The elusive pursuit of Solomon: Faltering steps toward the rights of the child. *Family Court Review, 46*(1), 39–53. doi: 10.1111/j. 1744–1617.2007.00182. x

Peacey, V., & Hunt, J. (2008). *Problematic contact after separation and divorce? A National Survey of Parents.* London, England: One Parent Families/Gingerbread.

Pearson, J., & Thoennes, N. (1990). Custody after divorce: Demographic and attitudinal patterns. *American Journal of Orthopsychiatry, 60*(2), 233–249. doi: 10.1037/h0079166

Psychodynamic Diagnostic Manual. (2006). A collaborative effort of the American Psychoanalytic Association, International Psychoanalytical Association, Division of Psychoanalysis (39) of the American Psychological Association, American Academy of Psychoanalysis and Dynamic Psychiatry, National Membership Committee on Psychoanalysis in Clinical Social Work. Retrieved from http://www.pdm1.org

Qu, L., & Weston, R. (2010). *Parenting dynamics after separation: A follow-up study of parents who separated after the 2006 family law reforms.* Melbourne: Australian Institute of Family Studies.

Rodgers, B., Smyth, B., Son, V. Esler, M., & Shephard, A. (2010, November). *The child support reform study: Some early pre- and post-reform comparisons relating to shared care.* Paper presented at the 3rd National Family Relationships Services Australia Conference, Melbourne, Australia.

Schore, A. N., & McIntosh, J. (2011). Family law and the neuroscience of attachment. *Family Court Review, 49*(3), 501–512.

Skjørten, K., & Barlindhaug, R. (2007). The involvement of children in decisions about shared residence. *International Journal of Law, Policy and the Family, 21*(3), 373–385. doi: 10.1093/lawfam/ebm011

Smart, C. (2004). Equal shares: Rights for fathers or recognition for children? *Critical Social Policy, 24*(4), 484–503. doi: 10.1177/0261018304046673

Smart, C., Neale B., & Wade, A. (2001). *The changing experience of childhood: Families and divorce.* Cambridge, England: Polity Press.

Smyth, B. (2005a). Parent–child contact schedules after divorce. *Family Matters, 69*, 32–43. Retrieved from http://www.aifs.gov.au/institute/pubs/fm2004/fm69/bs.pdf

Smyth, B. (2005b). Time to rethink time? The experience of time with children after divorce, *Family Matters, 71*, 4–10.

Smyth, B. (2009). A five-year retrospective of post-separation shared care research in Australia. *Journal of Family Studies, 15*(1), 36–59.

Smyth, B., Caruana, C., & Ferro, A. (2004). Fifty-fifty care? In B. Smyth (Ed.), *Parent–child contact and post-separation parenting arrangements* (Research Report No 9, pp. 19–29). Melbourne, Australia: Australian Institute of Family Studies.

Smyth, B., Qu, L., & Weston, R. (2004). The demography of parent–child contact? In B. Smyth (Ed.), *Parent–child contact and post-separation parenting arrangements*

(Research Report No 9, pp 113–122). Melbourne, Australia: Australian Institute of Family Studies.

Smyth, B., Weston, R., Moloney, L., Richardson, N., & Temple, J. (2008). Changes in patterns of parenting over time: Recent Australian data. *Journal of Family Studies*, *14*(1), 23–26.

Solomon, J., & George, C. (1999). The development of attachment in separated and divorced families: Effects of overnight visitation, parent and couple variables. *Attachment and Human Development*, *1*, 2–33. doi: 10.1080/14616739900134011

Sroufe, A., & McIntosh, J. (2011). Divorce and attachment relationships: The longitudinal journey. *Family Court Review*, *49*(3), 464–473.

Trinder, L. (2010). Shared residence: A review of recent research evidence. *Child and Family Law Quarterly*, *22*, 475–498.

Trinder, L., Kellett, J., & Swift, L. (2007). The relationship between contact and child adjustment in high conflict cases after divorce. *Child and Adolescent Mental Health*, *13*(4), 181–187. doi: 10.1111/j. 1475–3588.2008.00484. x

Van IJzendoorn, M. H. V., & Sagi-Schwartz, A. (2008). Cross-cultural patterns of attachment: Universal and contextual dimensions. In J. Cassidy & P.R. Shaver (Eds.), *Handbook of attachment: Theory, research, and clinical applications* (pp. 880–905). New York: Guilford Press.

Whiteside, M. F., & Becker, B. J. (2000). Parental factors and the young child's post-divorce adjustment: A meta-analysis with implications for parenting arrangements. *Journal of Family Psychology*, *14*(1), 2–26. doi: 10.1037/0893–3200.14.1.5

Parenting Time, Parent Conflict, Parent–Child Relationships, and Children's Physical Health

WILLIAM V. FABRICIUS, KARINA R. SOKOL, PRISCILA DIAZ, AND SANFORD L. BRAVER ■

INTRODUCTION

Questions the Chapter Will Address

Two questions often confront family law courts and policymakers: "Is the quantity or the quality of parenting time more important for children's outcomes?" and "Should parenting time be limited in high-conflict families?" Most discussions in the research literature give the following answers: The *quality* of parenting time is more important for children's well-being than the *quantity* of parenting time, and when there is frequent and severe parent conflict, parenting time should be limited because it can seriously harm children. In the present chapter, the authors argue that these long-standing conclusions should be re-examined in the light of new evidence. New data on the correlation between quantity of parenting time and quality of parent–child relationships in families with and without severe parent conflict are presented, and new findings in the health literature on family relationships and children's long-term, stress-related physical health are discussed. The authors conclude that these new findings indicate that the lingering situation of minimal parenting time with fathers for great numbers of children is a serious public health issue.

Model of How Parenting Time and Parent Conflict Affect Children's Health

Figure 7.1 shows the authors' conceptual model, or hypotheses, of how the effects of parenting time ultimately play out to influence children's health outcomes. Fabricius and colleagues (e.g., Fabricius, Braver, Diaz, & Velez, 2010; Fabricius & Luecken, 2007) have tested this type of model, and it is used here to organize the various sections of this chapter. The model indicates that parenting time should have an impact

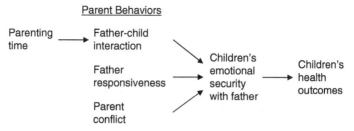

Figure 7.1 Conceptual model relating parenting time to parent behaviors, children's emotional security with father, and children's health outcomes.

on one class of parent behaviors, namely father–child interaction. Interaction is spending time doing things together. *Impact* means that for each father, given his own personal tendency to interact with his child, more parenting time will allow more interaction and less parenting time will allow less. When impact is indicated by an arrow, it usually means both that more of the things on the left end of the arrow causes more of the thing on the right end, and that less of the thing on the left causes less of the thing on the right.

Parenting time should not normally have an impact on father responsiveness, which is the reliability of the father's tendency to respond when the child expresses wants or needs. It reflects not how frequently the child asks, but how reliably the father responds. Responsiveness can occur with or without face-to-face interaction and can be manifested in deeds or words. Examples include conversations, either in person or on the phone, in which the father really *listens* to the child, buying or making things that the child *wants*, helping with homework when the child *asks*, etc.

The model indicates that both father–child interaction and father responsiveness independently affect the child's felt emotional security in the father–child relationship. Parent conflict also has an impact on the emotional security of the father–child relationship (in this case, more parent conflict causes less emotional security, and less parent conflict causes more emotional security). For simplicity, the analogous factors for mothers have not been included in Figure 7.1, but suffice to say that mother–child interactions, mother responsiveness, and parent conflict have an impact on the mother–child relationship, and both the mother–child and the father–child relationships have an impact on the child's health outcomes. Later in this chapter, more will be said about how parenting time differentially affects the mother–child and the father-child relationships.

IS THE QUANTITY OR THE QUALITY OF PARENTING TIME MORE IMPORTANT FOR CHILDREN'S OUTCOMES?

Old and New Measures of Parenting Time

An influential review of the research on father–child contact after divorce published just over 10 years ago (Amato & Gilbreth, 1999) led to the consensus that quality was more important than quantity. Specifically, Amato and Gilbreth found that *frequency of contact* was less important for children's outcomes than two other dimensions of the father–child relationship that seemed to reflect the quality of the time they spent together: father–child emotional closeness, and father authoritative parenting. The authors coded the following specific behaviors in the studies they reviewed as indicators of authoritative parenting: engaging in projects together, listening to the child's problems, monitoring and helping with schoolwork, giving advice, explaining rules, and using non-coercive discipline. Amato and Gilbreth's finding continues to influence many researchers to be skeptical that increasing *quantity of parenting time* with non-resident fathers benefits children (e.g., Hawkins, Amato, & King, 2007; Stewart, 2003). However, the rest of this section explains why courts and policymakers should be cautious about drawing implications about effects of quantity of parenting time from studies that instead measured frequency of contact.

Amato and Gilbreth (1999) noted that most of the studies prior to 1999 measured frequency of contact and only some measured duration or regularity of visits. When respondents are asked how frequently father–child contact has occurred, they are given a limited number of categories to choose from, such as "once a year," "one to three times a month," "once a week," etc. Frequency poorly represents amount of parenting time. For example, two divorced families that have the same parenting time schedule of every other weekend at the father's home could choose different categories. One family could count it as two *visits* per month, in which case they would report it as "one to three times a month." The other family could count it as four *days* per month, in which case they would report "once a week." Even if both families reported it as "one to three times a month," it might be a two-day weekend visit for one family and a three-day weekend visit for the other. Argys et al. (2007) recently compared several large surveys, four of which measured frequency, and concluded, "What is most striking about the reports of father–child contact . . . and perhaps most alarming to researchers, is the magnitude of the differences in the reported prevalence of father–child contact across the different surveys" (p. 383). This inherent unreliability makes it difficult to find consistent relations between frequency measures and child outcomes. Many of the pre-1999 studies, and many studies today, are based on several national surveys[1] that measured frequency; other national and state surveys[2] as well as individual researchers (e.g., Coley & Medeiros, 2007; Laumann-Billings & Emery, 2000) continue to use measures of frequency.

Despite all the research on divorce since the 1980s, there is no standard measure of amount of parenting time. Argys et al. (2007) noted that in the surveys they examined, "variation in the phrasing of the questions [about father–child contact] is significant" (p. 382). The authors hope that the Argys et al. review will initiate the dialogue necessary for the field to arrive at valid, reliable measures of amount of parenting time, because courts and policymakers are in great need of that information. Some progress is being made. Smyth (2004) describes the telephone survey designed by the Australian Institute of Family Studies.[3] Smyth et al. used these questions to sort families into discrete groups to reveal the variety of parenting plans in use. These questions could also be used to calculate the amount of parenting time. One shortcoming of these questions, however, is that they do not apply to parents who do not have a set parenting plan, or to those who live far apart and have yearly plans. A second shortcoming is that they capture only the parenting plan that is in place at the time the questions are asked. If the plan changes later, as a result of relocation for example, then the data for that family may not represent the parenting plan the child experienced for most of his or her life.

A different approach was taken by Fabricius and Luecken (2007), who asked young adults four retrospective questions about the typical number of days and nights they spent with their fathers during the school year and vacations.[4] The amount of parenting time can be calculated from these questions, and this is the approach used below in the new data. An advantage of this retrospective approach is that respondents can focus on the time period after the divorce that was most typical or representative.

Having valid measures of parenting time is one prerequisite for addressing the issue of the relative importance of quantity versus quality of parenting time, but so is having valid measures of the quality of the time. That issue is discussed next.

To summarize:

- Skepticism about benefits of parenting time stems from data collected with old measures.
- Old measures reflected frequency of visits rather than quantity of parenting time.
- New measures reflect quantity of parenting time.

Distinctions Between Quantity of Time and Quality of Time

Argys et al. (2007) also concluded, "There is no consensus on which measures of the quality of [non-resident] parent–child interaction matter most" (p. 396). This lack of consensus is illustrated in Table 7.1, which shows two recent studies of high-quality father involvement. Both of these studies use the National Longitudinal Study of Adolescent Health 1995-1996 (ADD HEALTH 95; Harris, Florey, Tabor, Bearman, Jones, & Udry, 2003), but the researchers defined different constructs from the same survey questions. This large national survey, like many others, includes items that tap into the central constructs in the model (Figure. 7.1); namely, the quantity of interaction (IN) parents and children have, the degree to which parents are responsive (RE) to children's needs and requests, and children's emotional security (ES) in the parent–child relationship. Table 7.1 shows how each set of researchers idiosyncratically mixed IN, RE, and ES items to form their constructs.

The field needs more principled, theoretical analyses of the quality of non-resident parent involvement and how it relates to parenting time. The authors believe that the scheme represented in Figure 7.1 has good theoretical grounds and also that it makes good intuitive sense. First, according to the classic analysis of Lamb, Pleck, and Levine (1987), the time that parents and children spend together can be divided into the time during which the parent is *available* to the child, and the time during which they actually *interact*. For non-resident parents, parenting time (PT) provides availability. However, the scheme represented in Figure 7.1 further distinguishes interaction into quantity (IN) and quality (RE). The authors do not mean to suggest that other parent behaviors are not also important, such as consistent discipline, monitoring, etc. The point here is to distinguish between parent behaviors (IN) that are more likely to be related to parenting time and parent behaviors (RE) that are less likely to be related to parenting time. When researchers mix IN and RE measures, they blur the distinction. For example, Amato and Gilbreth (1999) mixed

Table 7.1 CONSTRUCTS, ITEMS, AND SOURCE OF DATA IN TWO STUDIES OF
HIGH-QUALITY FATHER INVOLVEMENT AND HOW THE ITEMS
MAP ONTO THE CONSTRUCTS IN OUR MODEL IN FIGURE 7.1

Study, Construct, and Items	Data set	PT	IN	RE	ES
Hawkins, Amato, & King, 2007	ADD HEALTH 95				
Active fathering					
Frequency of contact		x			
Leisure, recreational, religious activities			x		
Talked about important personal or school issues				x	
How close do you feel to father					x
Stewart (2003)	ADD HEALTH 95				
Leisure and recreational activities					
Went shopping together			x		
Played a sport together			x		
Went to movie, play, museum, concert, sports event			x		
Authoritative parenting					
Worked together on school project			x		
Talked about important personal or school issues				x	
Closeness to father					
How close do you feel to father					x

PT = Parenting Time; IN = Interaction; RE = Responsiveness; ES = Emotional security with father

IN measures (engaging in projects together) and RE measures (listening and helping) into their construct of authoritative parenting. When researchers create a mixed measure and label it a measure of quality, they inadvertently stack the deck toward finding that quality of time is more important than quantity of parenting time.

Second, these three dimensions (IN, RE, and ES) are grounded in the central constructs of attachment theory (Bowlby, 1969), in which parent availability for interaction and responsiveness to the child both contribute to the security of the young child's emotional connection to the parent, and ultimately to the development of healthy independence. Parent availability and responsiveness are parent behaviors that convey meaning to the child about the reliability of the parent's continued support and caring. As Robert Karen (1998) summarized attachment theory after reviewing its historical development and current research, "All your child needs in order to thrive both emotionally and intellectually is your availability and responsiveness" (p. 416).

Third, these three dimensions are also foremost in adolescents' minds when they think about their relationships with their parents. The authors recruited 393 families for a longitudinal study of the role of fathers in adolescent development. Children were asked to describe their relationships with each of their parents in open-ended interviews when they were in seventh grade and again when they were in 10th grade. The families were equally divided between Anglo-American and Mexican American families, and between intact and stepfather families (see Baham, Weimer, Braver, & Fabricius, 2008, and Schenck, Braver, Wolchik, Saenz, Cookston, & Fabricius, 2009, for sample details). Regardless of which parent they described (resident mother, resident biological father, resident stepfather, and non-resident biological father), virtually all adolescents at both ages and in both ethnic groups spontaneously evaluated their relationships with their parents in terms of IN (e.g., "She does a lot with us." "Sometimes he'll take me out to basketball." "Most of the time we really don't spend time with each other."), RE (e.g., "He's always there for me." "He tries not to ignore me." "When I ask for help, she's always too busy"), and ES (e.g., "He can make me feel better." "She's nice but she can be mean." "He yells at me a lot."). It is remarkable that adolescents still monitor and distinguish the same general types of parent behaviors (IN and RE) that, according to attachment theory, initiated their attachment and emotional security with each of their parents when they were infants. This is consistent with Aquilino's (2006) finding that frequent contact during adolescence was the most important predictor, among other measures of father involvement, of close relationships with fathers in young adulthood. The fact that these parent behaviors (IN and RE) continue to be important in adolescents' representations of their relationships with their parents provides further justification for maintaining this fundamental distinction in the scheme represented in Figure 7.1. As Bowlby (1969) always emphasized, attachment processes continue to operate throughout one's life.

Figure 7.1 illustrates why the authors believe questions such as, "Is quantity of time or quality of time more important for child outcomes?" or "Is parenting time or the parent–child relationship more important?" are straw man comparisons that need to be retired from the debate. As shown in Figure 7.1, parenting time helps build emotionally secure relationships via interaction, but so do other things, including the parent's responsiveness. Emotionally secure parent–child relationships help ensure positive child outcomes. Thus, parenting time is farthest to the left in the causal chain, and things like parent responsiveness and the emotional security of the parent–child relationship (which are different constructs usually subsumed under the rubric "quality") are farther to the right and closer to child outcomes. Things closer to child outcomes in the causal chain will have stronger correlations to child outcomes than things farther away. Asking whether parenting time or various indices of quality are more important presupposes a theoretical model in which they occupy positions in the causal chain the same number of links away from child outcomes, but no such models are on offer. In the absence of such a model, it is an unfair question. In the model represented in Figure 7.1 it is fair to ask, for example, whether IN or RE is more important for ES. The question focused on below, however, is the more important one for courts and policymakers, and the one for which there are new data: What is the strength of the relationship between PT and ES with the father?

To summarize:

- Researchers usually measure but often confuse three things: the amount of direct interaction parents and children have, the degree to which parents are responsive to children's needs and requests, and the child's emotional security in the parent–child relationship.

- These distinctions are grounded in attachment theory and also in adolescents' representations of their relationships with their parents.
- The model represented in Figure 7.1 specifies connections among two aspects of quality and two aspects of quantity: the *quantity* of parenting time should have an impact on the *quantity* of father–child interaction, which in turn should have an impact on the *quality* (i.e., security) of father–child relationship; parenting time should not affect the *quality* of father–child interaction (i.e., the fathers' responsiveness).
- The question of whether quantity or quality of time is more important is a straw man.

New Findings on the Quantity of Parenting Time and the Quality of Parent–Child Relationships

During the 2005–2006 academic year, two of the authors of this chapter, Fabricius and Sokol, surveyed 1,030 students who reported their parents had divorced before they were 16 years old. On average their parents had divorced about 10 years earlier. They completed an online survey administered by the Psychology Department for Introductory Psychology credit, and for which Institutional Review Board human subjects approval was received. The survey included the parenting time questions in Footnote 4, as well as a large number of questions about their past and current family relationships and situations that allowed the researchers to capture several aspects of the emotional security of their relationships with their parents with a single score for each relationship. Because these scores represent how the students viewed their relationships at the time of the survey, when they were generally 18 to 20 years of age, they allowed the researchers to assess long-term associations between PT and ES.

Figure 7.2 shows the relation between PT and ES with the fathers. The vertical line divides the PT scale at 13 to 15 days per "month" (i.e., 28 days). This represents 50% PT with each parent. The father–child relationship improved with each increment of PT from 0% time with father to 50% ($r = .51$, $N = 871$, $p < 0.001$). From 50% to 100% PT with father, the father–child relationship did not show statistically significant change ($r = .15$, $N = 152$); the smaller sample sizes in these categories in which children lived primarily with their fathers mean that the zigzags are not reliable and probably represent random variation.

For simplicity in Figure 7.2, the mother–child relationship scores are not shown. As Fabricius and colleagues have found in other studies (Fabricius, 2003; Luecken & Fabricius, 2003), the long-term mother–child relationship mirrored the father–child relationship; that is, it remained constant with each increment of PT from 0% to 50% time with father, and declined thereafter. These findings indicate that when either parent has the child living with him or her for a majority of the time, increasing PT with the second parent is not associated with any risk of harm to the relationship with the first parent. Instead, increasing PT with the second parent is associated with improvements in that relationship, and benefits continue to accrue up to and including equal PT. At 50% PT, it appears that each relationship achieves its highest level of emotional security.

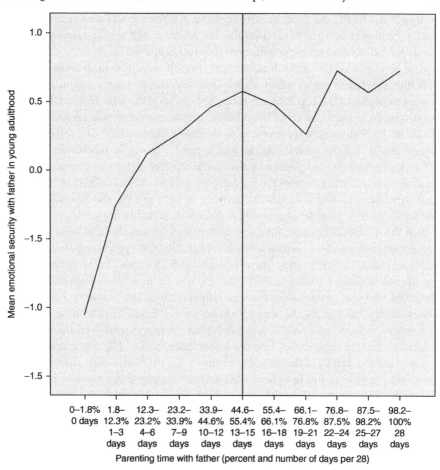

Figure 7.2. Relation between the amounts of parenting time per month (4 weeks) students had with their fathers and the emotional security of their relationships with their fathers in young adulthood.

The strength of the association between PT and ES with father is substantial. A correlation of .51 means that about 25% of the variability in relationship security across students can be explained by PT. In the model represented in Figure 7.1, PT is just one of the things that affects ES, and it does so only indirectly, through the amount of father–child IN that it makes possible. (Fabricius et al. [2010] reported other evidence that PT correlated significantly with IN, and that it did not correlate with RE.) The fact that PT accounted for about one fourth of relationship security so many years later is important. The authors' hypothesis is that PT causes these changes. The alternate hypothesis that the increase in ES across PT categories from 0% to 50% was due to different fathers self-selecting into different categories of PT. This might happen in two ways. Most of the disinterested fathers—those who would ultimately end up with the worst relationships with their college-aged children—might choose, or be given, 0% PT, and progressively fewer such fathers might choose or be given each PT category up to 50%. Or a similar, but reversed, self-selection process might occur for fathers who are especially committed and capable.

The authors examined the feasibility of the self-selection explanation by first splitting the father relationship scores into five equal groups (quintiles) from lowest to highest. The top 20% are those fathers with the best relationships and, according to the self-selection hypothesis, are the most committed and capable. Those in the bottom 20% are presumably the most disinterested. The self-selection hypothesis is that the increase in the security of father–child relationships across PT from 0% to 50% is explained by the distribution of especially committed and/ or disinterested fathers across the PT categories. It would be unlikely according to that hypothesis to find a significant correlation between PT and ES *within either the top or bottom quintile.* That would require a remarkable degree of precision by which those especially committed or disinterested fathers chose or were given PT categories that matched their abilities to eventually achieve corresponding levels of relationship security with their college-aged children. In fact, there were significant positive correlations between PT and ES in *both* the top and bottom quintiles, and also in two of the three middle quintiles. This suggests that the self-selection explanation for the association between PT and ES, in which the most committed fathers were sorted into the higher categories of PT and/or the least interested fathers were sorted into the lower categories of PT, is not sufficient to account for the details of the data. Fabricius et al. (2010) also considered the self-selection hypothesis, but in light of the common finding that fathers and children generally want more PT with father. They concluded that "the self-selection hypothesis should be viewed with a new sense of skepticism" (p. 214). The new data shown in Figure 7.2 provide additional cause for skepticism. The available evidence is not sufficient to reject the hypothesis that PT causes changes in father–child relationship security.

Studies in the past (i.e., those reviewed by Amato & Gilbreth, 1999) focused more on associations between father–child contact and child outcomes such as depression, aggression, and school success than on associations between contact and father–child relationships. This is changing, however. Fabricius et al. (2010) reviewed the studies that focus on associations between contact and parent–child relationships. In contrast to the weak findings in studies of contact and outcomes, these studies find consistent associations between contact and relationships. These studies are summarized in Table 7.2.

To summarize:

- Consistent with the model represented in Figure 7.1, the long-term father–child relationship improves at each level of PT; benefits continue to accrue up to and including equal PT; the long-term mother–child relationship remains constant at each level of PT, up to and including equal PT.
- The evidence to date is consistent with the hypothesis that amount of PT exerts a causal effect on father–child relationship security.
- Many other studies also find consistent associations between father–child contact and father–child relationships.

Table 7.2 STUDIES OF ASSOCIATIONS BETWEEN FATHER–CHILD CONTACT
AND FATHER–CHILD RELATIONSHIPS

Study	Measures	Findings
Buchanan et al., 1996	Amount of parenting time, including number of overnights	Adolescents with 2 or more overnights per week had better relationships with both parents than those in sole residence; those in sole mother residence had better relationships with father if they had some parenting with him.
Dunn et al., 2004; King, 2006; Sobolewski & King, 2005; King & Sobolewski, 2006; Aquilino, 2006	Frequency of father–child contact	Strong associations between frequency of contact and higher father–child relationship quality
Peters & Ehrenberg, 2008	Amount of parenting time	Young adults who had more parenting time experienced higher levels of affective, nurturing fathering, which was likely an indication of father–adolescent closeness.
Fabricius, 2003; Fabricius & Luecken, 2007; Luecken & Fabricius, 2003	Amount of parenting time	College students who had more parenting time had better relationships with fathers.
Struss, Pfeiffer, Preuss, & Felder, 2001	Quantity of father–child interaction during parenting time	More father–child interaction predicted adolescents' positive feelings about visiting.
Clarke-Stewart & Hayward, 1996	Quantity of father–child interaction during parenting time; frequency and length of visits	Quantity of interaction and frequency and length of visits were related to the father–child relationship.
Whiteside & Becker, 2000	Meta-analysis of studies of frequency of father–child contact	More frequent contact related to better father–child relationships.

Trends in Parenting Time

Courts and policymakers need to be aware of changes in cultural values and norms regarding parenting because custody policy and practice derive their legitimacy in part from accurate reflection of parenting values and norms (Fabricius et al., 2010). There is now a strong consensus among the general public that equal parenting time is best for the child. Large majorities favor it in all the locales and among all the demographic groups in the United States and Canada in which this question has been asked, and across several variations in question format, including variations that ask respondents to consider differences in how much pre-divorce child care each parent provided, and differences in parent conflict. It should be noted that none of the polls asked about cases in which there is domestic violence, and the public consensus for equal parenting time should not be taken to apply to such cases. Table 7.3 summarizes these polls. This public consensus about equal parenting time

Table 7.3 Public Opinion Polls about Equal Parenting Time

Reference	Participants	Questions	Responses
Fabricius & Hall, 2000	AZ college students	What is the best living arrangement for children?	70% to 80% said "equal time with both parents;" no difference due to gender or whether their parents were divorced.
Braver, Fabricius, & Ellman, 2008	Tucson, AZ, jury pools; Phoenix, AZ, & Riverside, CA, parents	What is the best living arrangement for children?	Most frequent response was "equal time with both parents" for men (67%) and women (46%).
Massachusetts ballot 2004 http://www.boston.com/news/special/politics/2004_results/general_election/questions_all_by_town.htm	Voting citizens	Should there be a presumption for joint physical custody?	85% said yes.
Fabricius, et al. (2010)	Tucson, AZ, jury pools	Repeated wording of the MA ballot question	90% said yes; no differences due to any demographic variables.
Canadian National Poll 2009 http://www.familylawwebguide.com.au/forum/pg/topicview/misc/4171/index.php&keep_session=204584127	Random telephone survey of 1,002 Canadians from March 13 to March 18, 2009	Do you support legislation to create a presumption of equal parenting in child custody cases?	78% said yes.
Braver, Ellman, Votruba, & Fabricius (2011)	Tucson, AZ, jury pools	Hypothetical cases in which participants were asked to award parenting time.	Participants most commonly awarded equal parenting time even when one parent had provided most child care and when there was high mutual parent conflict; when one parent instigated the conflict, they awarded more time to the other.

is probably best characterized as a cultural value rather than mere opinion, given both its connection to the long-term historical trend toward gender equality, and the evidence for its universality and robustness. This cultural value is consistent with the findings in Figure 7.2.

Regarding norms of practice, there appears to be a slow trend toward greater amounts of PT with fathers, especially equal PT. In the data collected in 2005–2006 in which the students' parents had divorced on average 10 years earlier, about 9% of students reported equal PT (50%). In Wisconsin the percentage of divorced parents with equal PT increased from 15% in 1996–1999 to 24% in 2003–2004 (Brown & Cancian, 2007). In Washington, the percentage of divorced parents with equal PT was approximately 20% in 2008–2009 (George, 2009). In Arizona the percentage of case files specifying equal PT tripled from 5% in 2002 (Venohr & Griffith, 2003) to 15% in 2007 (Venohr & Kaunelis, 2008). The Arizona case files included both divorced and never-married parents, whereas the other rates reflected only divorced parents.

The above makes clear that the practice of equal PT lags the consensus about its value. Braver, Ellman, Votruba, and Fabricius (2011) and Fabricius et al. (2010) discuss the possible complex reasons for the lag. One possibility is a self-fulfilling prophecy stemming from belief that family courts are biased toward mothers. Such a belief appears to exist among divorce attorneys in Maryland, Missouri, Texas, and Washington (Dotterweich & McKinney, 2000) and in Arizona (Braver, Cookston, & Cohen, 2002), and also among the public in Arizona (Braver et al., 2011; Fabricius et al., 2010). Belief that the courts have a maternal bias could dissuade fathers from pressing for shared parenting or entice mothers to resist. If so, it is important for the public to know whether the bias is real.

Some evidence exists (Stamps, 2002) that judges in four Southern states may have a maternal bias. Fabricius (in preparation) received Institutional Review Board human subjects approval to present to approximately 30 Arizona family court judges and commissioners two of the hypothetical cases involving child custody previously used with the public by Braver et al. (2011; Study 2). In each case the two parents ask for as much PT for themselves as possible, and in each case there are no issues with parental fitness, or ability to care for the children, or domestic violence. The difference is that in one there is little conflict between the parents, while in the other there is a great deal of current conflict between the parents, equally often initiated by the father and the mother. Whereas about two thirds of the public said that if they were the judge they would grant equal PT in each case (Braver et al., 2011), about 90% of the judges and commissioners said they would grant equal PT in each case. This question format using hypothetical cases representing judges' daily professional experience produced more responses from judges that reflected the cultural value placed on equal PT than from members of the lay public. This suggests that skepticism about the court's willingness to award shared parenting in Arizona at least might be unwarranted.[5]

Family courts also derive legitimacy from scientific findings. The findings about families that have joint residential parenting are clear. In 2002, Robert Bauserman published a comprehensive review of the research comparing joint versus sole custody. This review included 11 published and 22 unpublished (almost all doctoral dissertations) studies, comprising 1,846 sole-custody and 814 joint-custody children. The category of "joint custody" included *joint physical* custody as well as *joint legal* custody with sole maternal physical custody. Children in joint custody were significantly better off than those in sole custody (and about as well off as those in which the parents remained married) in terms of general adjustment, family relationships, self-esteem, emotional and behavioral adjustment, and divorce-specific adjustment. The joint legal custody families and the joint physical custody families showed similar benefits, and both involved a "substantial proportion of time actually spent living with each parent" (p. 93).

At issue, though, is the possibility that the "better" parents may have been the ones to want joint residential custody. In the classic Stanford Child Custody Study (Maccoby & Mnookin, 1992), the researchers statistically controlled for characteristics that might predispose parents both to want joint residential custody and also to have more parenting skills and resources, including education, income, and initial levels of interparental hostility. Even after controlling for these characteristics, though, children in joint residential custody were still the ones who showed the greatest satisfaction with their parenting arrangements and had the best long-term adjustment (Maccoby, Buchanan, Mnookin, & Dornbusch, 1993).

Moreover, the great majority of joint residential parents did *not* initially want and agree to joint residential custody. Maccoby and Mnookin (1992) gathered data at the pre-decree interview about parents' initial preferences ("what he or she would personally like in terms of residential custody, regardless of what in fact had been or would be requested in the legal proceedings," p. 99). Using the now publically available early waves of the Stanford Child Custody Study (www.socio.com/srch/summary/afda/fam25-27.htm), the current authors determined that there were 92 families with joint residential custody in which the parents had expressed wishes for either sole or joint residential custody. Both parents had initially wanted joint custody in only 19 of those 92 families. The largest subgroup of the joint residential custody families (N = 37) were those where the mother had wanted sole residential custody for herself and the father had wanted joint custody. In 19 other families each parent had wanted sole custody for himself or herself. Thus, very few parents initially agreed on joint residential custody, and the great majority had to accept it over their initial objections. About half accepted it after using some level of court services (mediation, custody evaluation, trial, or judicial imposition). Nevertheless, those with joint residential custody had the most well-adjusted children years later. This finding validates the responses of the Arizona judges and commissioners discussed above that they would impose equal PT when each parent wanted the majority of time for himself or herself.

Having considered the evidence and the underlying theory for the impact of quantity of PT on emotional security of parent–child relationships, and the consistency between the science and contemporary cultural parenting values, the next section considers whether any of that changes in high-conflict families.

To summarize:

- All public opinion findings to date indicate widespread public endorsement of equal PT.
- There is a slow trend toward equal PT in practice.
- Family law attorneys and the public appear to believe that family courts have a maternal bias, but initial data suggest courts may be more willing to order equal PT than generally believed.

- Children who have joint residential custody fare better than children in sole residential custody, and these findings do not seem to be due simply to "better" parents choosing joint residential custody.

SHOULD PARENTING TIME BE LIMITED IN HIGH-CONFLICT FAMILIES?

Previous Research is Mixed but Can Be Sorted Out

One of the vexing questions confronting courts and policymakers concerns PT when there is high conflict between parents.[6] The argument is often made that more PT exposes children to more of the conflict, but that argument is a bit muddled. It is not clear that more PT per se necessarily exposes children to more parent conflict; PT schedules that give more *frequent* discrete periods of PT and thus more *transitions* between parents are more likely to do so. In addition, it is not often acknowledged, but the previous research on this question is in fact quite mixed. On the one hand, Amato and Rezac (1994) and Hetherington, Cox, and Cox (1978) found that more frequent contact in high-conflict families was related to poorer child outcomes. Johnston, Kline, and Tschann (1989) found that among the very high-conflict families referred to court services for custody disputes that composed their sample, greater amounts of visitation in sole custody arrangements were generally harmful. These findings have led some commentators (e.g., Amato, 1993; Emery, 1999) to advocate limiting PT when high conflict prevails.

On the other hand, there is at least as much contrary evidence. Buchanan, Maccoby, and Dornbush (1996) did not find that greater amounts of visitation were harmful in high-conflict families, and Crosbie-Burnett (1991) did not find that more frequent contact was harmful in high-conflict families. Johnston et al.'s (1989) finding was restricted to sole custody families; the children with equal PT (in which children spent 12 to 13 days a month with their fathers) did not have worse adjustment than those in sole custody. Amato and Rezac's (1994) finding was restricted to boys; girls who had more frequent contact in high-conflict families did not have poorer outcomes. Healy, Malley, and Stewart (1990) and Kurdek (1986) found the opposite pattern: that more frequent visitation was actually associated with fewer adjustment problems when parent conflict was high. Similarly, Fabricius and Luecken (2007) found that more PT was associated with improvements in father–child relationships in families with both high and low frequency of conflict, and served to counteract the negative effects of parent conflict on father–child relationship security.

The divergence of findings among these studies can be partly explained by whether researchers measured frequency of contact or amount of PT. Most researchers measured frequency of contact (Amato & Rezak, 1994; Crosbie-Burnett, 1991; Healy et al., 1990; Hetherington et al., 1978; Kurdek, 1986), and among those studies the results are mixed. However, results were consistent among studies that measured amount of PT. Buchanan et al. (1996) and Fabricius and Luecken (2007) found that more PT was not harmful in high-conflict families, and Johnston et al. (1989) found that equal PT was not harmful in families referred to court services for custody disputes. Johnston et al. (1989) did find that greater amounts of PT in sole custody arrangements were harmful, but in their study amount of PT and frequency of transitions happened to be substantially correlated. Thus, sometimes studies indicate that more frequent contact and *transitions* between conflicted parents' homes can be harmful, presumably because they expose children to more instances of conflict. However, there are two ways to limit transitions: one is to eliminate some visits, and the other is to combine some visits into longer, uninterrupted time periods. In the first case amount of PT would decrease, and in the second it could stay the same or increase. The second approach remains viable—and is no doubt preferable—for high-conflict families because there is no evidence that greater *amounts* of PT are harmful for most children of conflicted parents, or that equal PT is harmful for children whose parents are involved in lengthy custody disputes. On the contrary, evidence suggests that father–child relationships can be strengthened through increased PT in high-conflict families as well as in low-conflict families (Buchanan et al., 1996; Fabricius and Luecken, 2007; Johnston et al., 1989), and that strengthened parent–child relationships can shield children from some of the effects of parent conflict (Fainsilber-Katz & Gottman, 1997; Sandler, Miles, Cookston, & Braver, 2008; Vandewater & Lansford, 1998).

To summarize:

- When researchers used the old measures of frequency of contact, the findings sometimes showed that more frequent contact was harmful in families with high parent conflict, and sometimes did not show it was more harmful; the harm might have been due to more transitions in some families with higher frequency of contact.
- When researchers measured amount of PT the findings were more consistent that more PT was not harmful and was beneficial even in high-conflict families.

New Findings When Conflict is Severe

The measure of parent conflict in Fabricius and Luecken (2007) asked about frequency of parent conflict. The new 2005–2006 data set described above included a different measure that asked about the severity of parent conflict before, during, and up to 5 years after their parents' final separation was examined. Results showed that more PT was related to better father–child relationships not only for those students reporting low severity of parent conflict but also for those reporting high severity of parent conflict. These findings on severity of parent conflict replicate and extend the Fabricius and Luecken (2007) findings on frequency of conflict. It is important to state that these findings should not be taken to apply to families in which there is violence or abuse, however.

To summarize:

- The long-term father–child relationship improved with increases in PT in families in which parent conflict was less severe as well as in those in which it was more severe.
- These findings should not be taken to apply to families in which there is violence or abuse, however.

LINKS TO CHILDREN'S LONG-TERM PHYSICAL HEALTH

Risky Families

The divorce literature has long documented the heightened risk for children of mental health problems traceable to the disrupted parent–child relationships and parent conflict that so often accompany divorce. The recent physical health literature that focuses on *risky families* is relevant to divorce research because it indicates profound effects on children's long-term, stress-related physical health attributable to these same family factors. It also gives insight into the underlying physiological mechanisms that are triggered by these factors. The physical health findings have yet to make their way prominently into the divorce literature and appear to be less well known to courts and policymakers.

Rena Repetti, Shelley E. Taylor, and Teresa E. Seeman of the University of California, Los Angeles, published the first review of the physical health literature as it relates to family relationships in 2002 in the prestigious journal *Psychological Bulletin*. They concluded that dysfunctional family relationships "lead to consequent accumulating risk for *mental health disorders, major chronic diseases*, and *early mortality*" (p. 330, emphasis added). They reviewed 15 physical health studies, including several longitudinal studies that began decades ago and fortunately included questions about family relationships in addition to questions about diet, alcohol, exercise, smoking, etc. Findings consistently point to adverse health consequences to children of families characterized not only by high parent conflict, but also by cold, unsupportive parent–child relationships, the so-called risky families. The findings suggested that conflict between the parents and poor parent–child relationships exert similar effects. Family conflict and aggression were related to poorer health in childhood and adulthood, including higher rates of infectious diseases, and to slowed growth, including reduced weight gain in infancy and reduced height at age 7 and in adulthood. Poor parent–child relationships were also related to poorer physical health, including obesity in early adulthood and serious medical conditions in midlife, and to delayed growth during infancy.

For instance, Russek and Schwartz (1997) examined data from Harvard undergraduate men in the early 1950s who were asked to describe their relationship with each parent. Their descriptions were coded as positive ("very close," "warm and friendly") or negative ("tolerant," "strained and cold"). Twelve percent of relationships with mothers and 20% with fathers were coded negative. Thirty-five years later the researchers obtained health status based on in-person interviews and review of available medical records. Of the men who described a negative relationship with either their mother or their father, 85% to 91% had developed cardiovascular disease, duodenal ulcer, and/ or alcoholism, compared to only 45% to 50% of those who had described positive relationships. When assessments of parent–child relationships and parent conflict were made in the same study, researchers found similar effects associated with each. For example, Shaffer, Duszynski, and Thomas (1982) examined data from White male physicians who graduated from medical school between 1948 and 1964 and described their family members' attitudes toward each other as either positive (warm, close, understanding, confiding) or negative (detached, dislike, hurt, high tension). Men who described more negative and less positive family relationships were at increased risk of developing cancer, even after controlling for health risk factors such as age, alcohol use, cigarette smoking, being overweight, and serum cholesterol levels.

It is noteworthy that several of these studies began in the 1950s and 1960s, when mothers were almost exclusive caregivers. The fact that they show that a poor relationship with either the mother or the father had similar effects indicates that the health risks associated with disrupted parent–child relationships are not limited to the primary caregiver.

To summarize:

- Families characterized by either parent conflict or poor parent–child relationships pose serious long-term health risks to children, including early mortality.
- Some of these studies began in the 1950s and 1960s, when mothers were almost exclusive caregivers, and they show that a poor relationship with either the mother or the father had similar effects. Thus, the findings are not limited to just the primary caregiver.

The Stress Response System as the Mechanism by Which Risky Families Can Damage Health

Repetti et al. (2002) found evidence that risky families affect children's physical health via cumulative disturbances established during infancy and early childhood in physiologic and neuroendocrine system regulation (i.e., disruptions in sympathetic-adrenomedullary [SAM] reactivity, hypothalamic–pituitary–adrenocortical [HPA] reactivity, and serotonergic functioning). Such disruptions can have effects on organs, including the brain, and on systems, including the immune system. The emerging consensus (Repetti et al., 2002; Troxel & Matthews, 2004) is that the social processes of parent conflict and poor parent–child relationships cause constant stress in the home, which chronically activates and thereby dysregulates children's biological stress responses, leading to deterioration of cardiovascular system functioning and hypertension (e.g., Ewart, 1991) and coronary heart disease (e.g., Woodall & Matthews, 1989), and possibly hindering children's acquisition of emotional competence and self-regulatory skills (e.g., Camras et al., 1988; Dunn & Brown, 1994; Dunn, Brown, Slomkowski, Tesla, & Youngblade, 1991).

Psychological processes add the cognitive and emotional dimensions to this dysregulation. In modern attachment theory (Bowlby, 1969), poor parent–child relationships lead to feelings of insecurity, anger, distrust in continued parental support, and low self-worth, which can by themselves chronically activate and dysregulate children's biological stress responses. In Davies and Cummings' (1994) attachment-based theory, parent conflict similarly leads to emotional insecurity because the child fears abandonment by one or both fighting parents. This is represented in Figure 7.1, where parent conflict is a parent behavior like parent–child interaction and responsiveness. Parent conflict can also lead parents to withdraw from the children and reduce their interaction and responsiveness (e.g., Fauber, Forehand, Thomas, & Weirson, 1990; Goldberg & Easterbrooks, 1984; Parke & Tinsley, 1983) and thus can also indirectly affect the child's felt security in the parent–child relationship, but for simplicity that more complex path has not been included in the model.

This emotional security mechanism is not an abstract concoction. It incorporates the "fight-or-flight" response system that we experience in acute form when our security is threatened, for example by someone pulling a gun or by hearing footsteps behind us in an empty parking structure. One of the greatest advances in modern psychology has been to see how this system functions during the child's normal development in the family. The primary threats to safety and protection that the helpless human infant and young child's system is attuned to detect are parent absence, parent unresponsiveness, and parent conflict. In acute form, they elicit in children the same shortness of breath, increased blood pressure and heart rate, fear, etc., that we all experience when threatened because they are caused by the instantaneous release of the same powerful hormones. Children in families characterized by dysfunctional parent conflict and unsupportive parent–child relationships experience these threats repeatedly and learn to anticipate them when they are absent. This exposes these children to chronic, low-level doses of these hormones, which is what causes the long-term health problems.

Considering that almost 40% of the college students represented in Figure 7.2 fell into the two lowest categories of PT with their fathers, and now on average as young adults have destroyed relationships with their fathers, and linking that with the lifetime health outcomes of young adults who had reported similarly distant relationships with their parents, should cause alarm among researchers and policy makers at the extent of the personal suffering—and at the scope of the public health problem— that they represent. Further considering that those who also experienced severe parent conflict generally have still worse relationships with their fathers (though, as noted above, even for them more PT is related to improved relationships), should raise even more concern.

To summarize:

- Consistent with attachment theory, when parents are unavailable, unresponsive, or in conflict with each other, children perceive this as a threat to their continued support, which leads to chronic activation of the stress response system.
- Chronic activation can damage organs and systems, and lead to serious long-term health problems.

Mechanisms Available to Courts and Policymakers to Reduce Health Risks to Children of Divorce

These findings indicate that high parent conflict and unsupportive relationships are formidable risks associated with a number of mental health problems and major illnesses later in life. The implication is that family courts and policymakers should give equal consideration to minimizing parent conflict and strengthening parent–child relationships because of their similar long-term health consequences. Many jurisdictions do have policies and interventions regarding reducing parent conflict and strengthening parent–child relationships by promoting positive parenting.

When dealing with the question of whether PT should be limited in high-conflict families, courts should consider the potential risk of damaging parent–child relationships by reducing PT. The evidence indicates that in divorced families with frequent and severe parent conflict, more PT with the father is associated with an improvement in the father–child relationship. Limiting PT when there is parent conflict limits the amount of interaction children can have with that parent, which risks undermining the parent–child relationship and risks making those children doubly vulnerable to long-term damage to their physical health. Courts have better options to deal with children's exposure to parent conflict than reducing PT, such as schedules with fewer transitions, or transitions that do not require face-to-face parent interactions. The evidence suggests that parent conflict alone should not be the basis for limiting PT; rather, the data indicate that courts should weigh the option of increasing PT in high-conflict families. This flies in the face of the accepted wisdom and practice of limiting PT in high-conflict families. But as discussed, the arguments for the accepted wisdom and practice are not based on strong empirical evidence that increased PT is harmful to children in high-conflict families. This recommendation to consider increasing PT in high-conflict families is consistent with Repetti et al.'s (2002) conclusion that parent conflict and parent–child relationships can have independent effects on children's health. That means that parents in conflictual relationships are not necessarily also the ones who are cold and unsupportive with their children. That implies that parent–child relationships can be improved in high-conflict families. Direct evidence that improved parent–child relationships can counteract some harmful effects of parent conflict is available (Fainsilber-Katz &Gottman, 1997; Sandler et al., 2008; Vandewater & Lansford, 1998).

The allocation of PT is an important tool that courts and policymakers have to strengthen parent–child relationships in all families. Evidence and theory both suggest that the quantity of PT affects the long-term quality of the father–child relationship via the increased parent–child interaction it allows. The evidence in Figure 7.2 makes a relatively strong argument that PT exerts a causal influence on parent–child relationships. That argument is also supported by the theoretical explanation of the causal influence provided by attachment theory. It is especially impressive by how important parent–child interaction is to adolescents, as indicated by the central role it plays in their representations of their relationships with their parents. They closely monitor the amount of interaction they have with each of their parents, and evaluate whether it is personally sufficient. Attachment theory identifies parent availability as one of the potential threats that the child's emotional security system is designed to monitor. Time spent interacting is one way that emotionally close and supportive relationships develop, and time lost risks exposing children to chronic stress and disrupted parent relationships, even in adolescence (e.g., Aquilino, 2006).

Courts and policymakers may be reluctant to consider the allocation of PT as a tool to strengthen parent–child relationships because they often receive the following expert advice or testimony: (a) Quality is more important than quantity of PT, and (b) Policies that might encourage any particular level of PT should be avoided because it is not known what level of PT is best for any individual family. The reasons why (a) is an unfair comparison have already been discussed. Here is an analogy regarding (b): Level of education affects the types of jobs people get, which in turn affects their lifetime earnings, but economists do not frame the question as, "Which is more important for determining lifetime earnings, level of education or type of job?" Education has an indirect effect, so this either/or question is not useful. The correlation between job type and earnings will be stronger than the correlation between education level and earnings, but that would not prompt economists to advocate for less attention being given to education.

To carry the analogy further, society takes it for granted that it is not known what level of education is best for any individual, and that policy makers cannot prescribe the same level of education for everyone. But society nevertheless endorses policies that inform people of the importance of education for lifetime earning potential, that make education available to all who want it, and that encourage education even to the extent of prescribing a minimum level for all children. Similarly, courts and policymakers cannot know what level of parent conflict or what level of security of parent–child relationships is acceptable for any family, but they nevertheless institute policies that encourage parents to reduce conflict and strengthen relationships. Likewise, courts and policymakers should institute policies that encourage parents to maximize PT for both parents within the constraints of individual family situations.

The strong connection between PT and father–child relationships in divorced families with both low and high levels of parent conflict, along with the evidence and theoretical understanding that have built over decades about how unsupportive parent–child relationships impair long-term health, means that the lingering situation of minimal PT for great numbers of children is a public health issue that demands the attention of researchers, policymakers, and individual courts. Much research (reviewed in Fabricius et al., 2010) shows that children and divorced fathers generally want more PT. The authors do not see a compelling reason to doubt that absent any unusual circumstances, granting and encouraging more PT, especially in high-conflict families, will be a good thing for children, and for society.

GUIDELINES: CONSIDERATIONS AND CAUTIONS

- Courts and policymakers should give equal consideration to minimizing parent conflict and strengthening parent–child relationships because of their similar long-term health consequences for children.
- Courts have better options to deal with children's exposure to parent conflict than reducing parenting time because that might risk damaging the parent–child relationship; better options include schedules with fewer transitions, or transitions that do not require face-to-face parent interactions.
- Evidence and theory both suggest that quantity of parenting time affects the child's long-term security in the father–child relationship, which makes it another important tool courts have to strengthen parent–child relationships.
- Courts and policymakers should institute policies that encourage parents to maximize parenting time for both parents within the constraints of the individual family situation.

NOTES

1 National Longitudinal Survey of Youth 1979 (NLSY79; http://www.bls.gov/nls/nlsy79.htm); National Survey of America's Families (NSAF; http://www.icpsr.umich.edu/icpsrweb/ICPSR/series/216); National Survey of Families and Households 1987 (NSFH87) and 1992 (NSFH92; Sweet, Bumpass, & Call, 1988).

2 National Longitudinal Study of Adolescent Health 1995–1996 (ADD HEALTH 95; Harris, Florey, Tabor, Bearman, Jones, & Udry,2003); National Longitudinal Survey of Youth 1997 (NLSY97; http://www.bls.gov/nls/nlsy97.htm); Britain's Avon Longitudinal Study of Parents and Children 1991 (ALSPAC91; Golding, 1996), Canada's National Longitudinal Survey of Children and Youth 1994–1995 (NLSCY94; Juby, Billette, Laplante, & Le Bourdais, 2007); Wisconsin Child Support Demonstration Evaluation–Mother Survey, late 1990s (WCSDE; http://www.irp.wisc.edu/research/childsup/csde.htm).

3 "Six questions were asked of parents who reported that a set pattern of face-to-face contact was occurring: Is your contact arrangement based on a weekly, fortnightly, or monthly schedule? Each [week/fortnight/month], how many blocks of contact usually occur? Thinking about [each] block of contact: What day of the week does contact usually start? What time on [day of the week] does the contact visit usually begin? What day of the week does contact usually end? What time on [day of the week] does the contact visit usually end?" (Smyth, 2004, p. 36).

4 "Considering the most typical living arrangement you had after the divorce, what was (a) the number of days you spent any time at all with your father in an average 2-week period during the school year [0 to 14]? (b) the number of overnights (i.e., sleepovers) you spent with your father in an average 2-week period during the school year [0 to 14]? (c) the number of school vacation weeks out of 15 (Christmas = 2 weeks, spring = 1 week, summer = 12 weeks) during which your time with your father was different from what it was during the school year [0 to 15]? And (d) the percentage of time you spent with your father during those vacation weeks above that were different from the regular schedule [0% to 100% in 10% increments]?"

5 It might be important to note that Arizona family court judges had received periodic training during the past decade on research related to parenting time.

6 Because of the complexity of the issue and because of space limitations, we are not including here conflict that reaches the level of physical violence. Lamb and Kelly (2009) have a good discussion of this and reference the quickly changing consensus view observed by Jaffe, Johnston, Crooks, and Bala (2008) and Kelly and Johnson (2008) that types and duration of the physical violence must be distinguished.

REFERENCES

Amato, P. R. (1993). Children's adjustment to divorce: Theories, hypotheses, and empirical support. *Journal of Marriage and Family, 55*(1), 23–38. doi: 10.2307/352954

Amato, P. R., & Gilbreth, J. G. (1999). Nonresident fathers and children's well-being: A meta-analysis. *Journal of Marriage and Family, 61*, 557–573. doi: 10.2307/353560

Amato, P. R., & Rezac, S. J. (1994). Contact with nonresidential parents, interparental conflict, and children's behavior. *Journal of Family Issues, 15*(2), 191–207. doi:10.1177/0192513X94015002003

Aquilino, W. S. (2006). The noncustodial father–child relationship from adolescence into young adulthood. *Journal of Marriage and Family, 68*, 929–946. doi:10.1111/j.1741-3737.2006.00305.x

Argys, L. H., Peters, E., Cook, S. Garasky, S., Nepomnyaschy, L., & Sorensen, E. (2007). Measuring contact between children and nonresident fathers. In S. Hofferth & L. Casper (Eds.), *Handbook of measurement issues in family research* (pp. 375–398). Mahwah, NJ: Erlbaum.

Baham, M. E., Weimer, A. A., Braver, S. L., & Fabricius, W. V. (2008). Sibling relationships in blended families. In J. Pryor (Ed.), *The international handbook of stepfamilies: Policy and practice in legal, research, and clinical spheres* (pp. 175–207). Hoboken, NJ: Wiley.

Bauserman, R. (2002). Child adjustment in joint-custody versus sole-custody arrangements: A meta-analytic review. *Journal of Family Psychology, 16*(1), 91–102. doi: 10.1037//0893-3200.16.1.91

Bowlby, J. (1969). *Attachment and loss: Vol. 1. Attachment*. New York: Basic Books.

Braver, S. L., Cookston, J. T., & Cohen, B. R. (2002). Experiences of family law attorneys with current issues in divorce practice. *Family Relations, 51*(6), 325–334.

Braver, S. L., Ellman, I. M., Votruba, A. M., & Fabricius, W. V. (2011). Lay judgments about child custody after divorce. *Psychology, Public Policy, and Law, 17*, 212–240.

Braver, S. L., Fabricius, W. V., & Ellman, I. M. (2008, May). *The court of public opinion*. Symposium presented to the Annual Conference of the Association of Family and Conciliation Courts, Vancouver, British Columbia.

Brown, P., & Cancian, M. (2007). *Wisconsin's 2004 shared-physical-placement guidelines: Their use and implications in divorce cases*. Madison, WI: University of Wisconsin-Madison Institute for Research on Poverty.

Buchanan, C. M., Maccoby, E. E., & Dornbusch, S. M. (1996). *Adolescents after divorce*. Cambridge, MA: Harvard University Press.

Camras, L. A., Ribordy, S., Hill, J., Martino, S., Spaccarelli, S., & Stefani, R. (1988). Recognition and posing of emotional expressions by abused children and their mothers. *Developmental Psychology, 24*, 776–781. doi:10.1037/0012-1649.24.6.776

Clarke-Stewart, K. A., & Hayward, C. (1996). Advantages of father custody and contact for the psychological well-being of school-age children. *Journal of Applied Developmental Psychology, 17*, 239–270. doi:10.1016/S0193-3973(96)90027-1

Coley, R. L., & Medeiros, B. L. (2007). Reciprocal longitudinal relations between nonresident father involvement and adolescent delinquency. *Child Development, 78*, 132–147. doi:10.1111/j.1467-8624.2007.00989.x

Crosbie-Burnett, M. (1991). Impact of joint versus sole custody and quality of the coparental relationship on adjustment of adolescents in remarried families. *Behavioral Sciences and the Law, 9*, 439–449. doi:10.1002/bsl.2370090407

Davies, P. T., & Cummings, E. M. (1994). Marital conflict and child adjustment: An emotional security hypothesis. *Psychological Bulletin, 116*, 387–411. doi:10.1037/0033-2909.116.3.387

Dotterweich, D., & McKinney, M. (2000). National attitudes regarding gender bias in child custody cases. *Family Court Review, 38*(2), 208–223.

Dunn, J., & Brown, J. (1994). Affect expression in the family, children's understanding of emotions, and their interactions with others. *Merrill-Palmer Quarterly, 40,* 120–137.

Dunn, J., Brown, J., Slomkowski, C., Tesla, C., & Youngblade, L. (1991). Young children's understanding of other people's feelings and beliefs: Individual differences and their antecedents. *Child Development, 62,* 1352–1366. doi:10.2307/1130811

Dunn, J., Cheng, H., O'Connor, T. G., & Bridges, L. (2004). Children's perspectives on their relationships with their nonresident fathers: Influences, outcomes and implications. *Journal of Child Psychology and Psychiatry, 45,* 553–566.

Emery, R. E. (1999). *Marriage, divorce, and children's adjustment* (2nd ed.). Newbury Park, CA: Sage.

Ewart, C. K. (1991). Familial transmission of essential hypertension, genes, environments, and chronic anger. *Annals of Behavioral Medicine, 13,* 40–47.

Fabricius, W. V. (2003). Listening to children of divorce: New findings that diverge from Wallerstein, Lewis and Blakeslee. *Family Relations, 52,* 385–396.

Fabricius W. V., Braver, S. L., Diaz, P., & Velez, C.E. (2010). Custody and parenting time: Links to family relationships and well-being after divorce. In M.E. Lamb (Ed.), *The role of the father in child development* (5th ed., pp. 201–240). New York: Wiley.

Fabricius, W. V., & Hall, J. A. (2000). Young adults' perspectives on divorce: Living arrangements. *Family and Conciliation Courts Review, 38,* 446–461.

Fabricius, W. V., & Luecken, L. J. (2007). Postdivorce living arrangements, parent conflict, and long-term physical health correlates for children of divorce. *Journal of Family Psychology, 21*(2), 195–205. doi: 10.1037/0893-3200.21.2.195

Fainsilber-Katz, L., & Gottman, J. M. (1997). Buffering children from marital conflict and dissolution. *Journal of Clinical Child Psychology, 26*(2), 157–171. doi: 10.1207/s15374424jccp2602_4

Fauber, R., Forehand, R., Thomas, A. M., & Wierson, M. (1990). A mediational model of the impact of marital conflict on adolescent adjustment in intact and divorced families: The role of disrupted parenting. *Child Development, 61,* 1112–1123. doi: 10.2307/1130879

George, T. (2009), *Residential time summary reports filed in Washington from July 2008– June 2009.* Olympia: Washington State Center for Court Research. Retrieved from http://www.courts.wa.gov/wsccr/docs/ResidentialTimeSummaryReport2009.pdf

Goldberg, W. A., & Easterbrooks, M. A. (1984). Role of marital quality in toddler development. *Developmental Psychology, 20,* 504–514.

Golding, J. (1996). Children of the nineties: A resource for assessing the magnitude of long-term effects of prenatal and perinatal events. *Contemporary Reviews in Obstetrics and Gynocology, 9,* 89–92.

Harris, K. M., Florey, F., Tabor, J., Bearman, P. S., Jones, J., & Udry, J. R. (2003). *The National Longitudinal Study of Adolescent Health: Research Design.* Retrieved from http://www.cpc.unc.edu/projects/addhealth/design.

Hawkins, D. N., Amato, P. R., & King, V. (2007). Nonresident father involvement and adolescent well-being: Father effects or child effects? *American Sociological Review, 72*(6), 990–1010. doi: 10.1177/000312240707200607

Healy, J. M., Malley, J. E., & Stewart, A. J. (1990). Children and their fathers after parental separation. *American Journal of Orthopsychiatry, 60,* 531–543. doi:10.1037/h0079201

Hetherington, E. M., Cox, M., & Cox, R. (1978). The aftermath of divorce. In J. H. Stevens, Jr., & M. Matthews (Eds.), *Mother–child, father–child relations.* Washington, DC: National Association for Education of Young Children. doi: 34:851-858

Jaffe, P. G., Johnston, J. R., Crooks, C. V., & Bala, N. (2008). Custody disputes involving allegations of domestic violence: Toward a differentiated approach to parenting plans. *Family Court Review, 46*(3), 500–522. doi:10.1111/j.1744-1617.2008.00216.x

Johnston, J. R., Kline, M., & Tschann, J. M. (1989). Ongoing postdivorce conflict: Effects on children of joint custody and frequent access. *American Journal of Orthopsychiatry, 59,* 576–592. doi:10.1111/j.1939-0025.1989.tb02748.x

Juby, H., Billette, J.-M., Laplante, B., & Le Bourdais, C. (2007). Nonresident fathers and children: Parents' new unions and frequency of contact. *Journal of Family Issues, 28,* 1220–1245. doi: 10.1177/0192513X07302103

Karen, R. (1998) *Becoming attached: First relationships and how they shape our capacity to love.* New York: Oxford.

Kelly, J. B., & Johnson, M. P. (2008). Differentiation among types of intimate partner violence: Research update and implications for interventions. *Family Court Review, 46*(3), 476–499. doi:10.1111/j.1744-1617.2008.00215.x

King, V. (2006). The antecedents and consequences of adolescents' relationships with stepfathers and nonresident fathers. *Journal of Marriage and Family, 68,* 910–928. doi:10.1111/j.1741-3737.2006.00304.x

King, V., & Sobolewski, J. M. (2006). Nonresident fathers' contributions to adolescent well-being. *Journal of Marriage and Family, 68,* 537–557.

Kurdek, L. A. (1986). Custodial mothers' perceptions of visitation and payment of child support by noncustodial fathers in families with low and high levels of pre-separation interparent conflict. *Journal of Applied Developmental Psychology, 7*(4), 307–323. DOI:10.1016/0193-3973(86)90002-X

Lamb, M. E., & Kelly, J. B. (2009). Improving the quality of parent–child contact in separating families with infants and young children: Empirical research foundations. In R. M. Galatzer- Levy, L. Kraus, & J. Galatzer-Levy (Eds.), *The scientific basis of child custody decisions* (2nd ed., pp. 187–214). Hoboken, NJ: Wiley.

Lamb, M. E., Pleck, J. H., & Levine, J. A. (1987). Effects of increased paternal involvement on fathers and mothers. In C. Lewis & M. O'Brien (Eds.), *Reassessing fatherhood* (pp.109–125). London: Sage.

Laumann-Billings, L., & Emery, R. E. (2000).Distress among young adults from divorced families. *Journal of Family Psychology, 14,* 671–687. doi: 10.1037/0893-3200.14.4.671

Luecken, L. J., & Fabricius, W. V. (2003). Physical health vulnerability in adult children from divorced and intact families. *Journal of Psychosomatic Research, 55,* 221–228.

Maccoby, E. E., Buchanan, C. M., Mnookin, R. H., & Dornbusch, S. M. (1993). Postdivorce roles of mothers and fathers in the lives of their children: Families in transition. *Journal of Family Psychology, 7*(1), 24–38. 10.1037/0893-3200.7.1.24

Maccoby, E. E., & Mnookin, R. H. (1992). *Dividing the child: Social and legal dilemmas of custody.* Cambridge, MA: Harvard University Press.

Parke, R. D., & Tinsley, B. R. (1983). The father's role in infancy: Determinants of involvement in caregiving and play. In M. E. Lamb (Ed.), *The role of the father in child development* (2nd ed., pp. 429–458). New York: Wiley.

Peters, B., & Ehrenberg, M. F. (2008). The influence of parental separation and divorce on father–child relationships. *Journal of Divorce and Remarriage, 49,* 78–109. doi: 10.1080/10502550801973005

Repetti, R. L., Taylor, S. E., & Seeman, T. E. (2002). Risky families: Family social environments and the mental and physical health of offspring. *Psychological Bulletin, 128,* 330–366. doi:10.1037/0033-2909.128.2.33

Russek, L. G., & Schwartz, G. E. (1997). Feelings of parental caring can predict health status in mid-life: A 35-year follow-up of the Harvard Mastery of Stress study. *Journal of Behavioral Medicine, 20,* 1–13. doi: 10.1023/A:1025525428213

Sandler, I., Miles, J., Cookston, J., & Braver, S. (2008) Effects of father and mother parenting on children's mental health in high- and low-conflict divorces. *Family Court Review, 46*(2), 282–296. doi: 10.1111/j.1744-1617.2008.00201.x

Schenck, C. E., Braver, S. L., Wolchik, S. A., Saenz, D., Cookston, J. T., & Fabricius, W.V. (2009). Do I matter to my (step- and non-residential) dad?: The relation between perceived mattering and adolescent mental health problems. *Fathering, 7,* 70–90. doi: 10.3149/fth.0701.70

Shaffer, J. W., Duszynski, K. R., & Thomas, C. B. (1982). Family attitudes in youth as a possible precursor of cancer among physicians: A search for explanatory mechanisms. *Journal of Behavioral Medicine, 5,* 143–163.doi: 10.1007/BF00844805

Smyth, B. M. (2004). Parent–child contact schedules after divorce. *Family Matters, 69,* 32–43.

Sobolewski, J. M., & King, V. (2005).The importance of the coparental relationship for nonresident fathers' ties to children. *Journal of Marriage and Family, 67,* 1196–1212. doi: 10.1111/j.1741-3737.2005.00210.x

Stamps, L. E. (2002). Maternal preference in child custody decisions. *Journal of Divorce and Remarriage, 37,* 1–12.

Stewart, S. D. (2003). Nonresident parenting and adolescent adjustment: The quality of nonresident father–child interaction. *Journal of Family Issues, 24*(2), 217–244. doi: 10.1177/0192513X02250096

Struss, M., Pfeiffer, C., Preuss, U., & Felder, W. (2001). Adolescents from divorced families and their perceptions of visitation arrangements and factors influencing parent–child contact. *Journal of Divorce and Remarriage, 35,* 75–89. DOI: 10.1300/J087v35n01_04

Sweet, J., Bumpass, L., & Call, V. (1988). *The design and content of the National Survey of Families and Households.* NSFH Working Paper No. 1.

Troxel, W. M., & Matthews, K. A. (2004). What are the costs of marital conflict and dissolution to children's physical health? *Clinical Child and Family Psychology Review, 7,* 29–57. doi: 10.1023/B:CCFP.0000020191.73542.b0

Vandewater, E., & Lansford, J. (1998). Influences of family structure and parental conflict on children's well-being. *Family Relations, 47,* 323–330. doi: 10.2307/585263

Venohr, J. C., & Griffith, T. E. (2003). *Arizona child support guidelines: Findings from a case file review.* Denver: Policy Studies. Retrieved from http://www.azcourts.gov/Portals/74/CSGRC/repository/2003-CaseFileRev.pdf

Venohr, J. C., & Kaunelis, R. (2008). *Arizona child support guidelines review: Analysis of case file data.* Denver, CO: Policy Studies. Retrieved from http://www.azcourts.gov/Portals/74/CSGRC/repository/2009-CaseFileRev.pdf

Whiteside, M. F., & Becker, B. J. (2000). Parental factors and the younger child's post divorce adjustment: A meta-analysis with implications for parenting arrangements. *Journal of Family Psychology, 14,* 5–26. doi: 10.1037//0893-3200.14.1.5

Woodall, K. L., & Matthews, K. A. (1989). Familial environment associated with Type A behaviors and psychophysiological responses to stress in children. *Health Psychology, 8,* 403–426. doi: 10.1037/0278-6133.8.4.403

Critical Analysis of Research on Parenting Plans and Children's Well-Being

MICHAEL E. LAMB ■

More than a third of a century ago, the "best interests" standard replaced other statutory or judicial rules to determine where children would live after their parents' separation. In theory, this change should have permitted judges, other professionals, and separating parents themselves to evaluate individual circumstances and decide accordingly, but for many years they were guided only by clinical judgment, anecdotes, and personal opinions because the empirical literature was not adequate to provide guidance. Sometimes, the void was filled by simplistic rules of thumb, often advocated or supported by interest groups with appeals to "naturalness," "fairness," or "common sense." Fortunately, the situation has improved markedly since the early 1990s as growing numbers of researchers have provided increasingly rich and sophisticated data to inform those making decisions, even if some of the results have themselves been distorted in the service of diverse social and political agendas. Some of the relevant research has elucidated normative developmental processes documenting both the typical experiences of young children and the factors associated with variations in their outcomes. Other researchers have explored the effects of parental separation under varying circumstances on children's developmental trajectories. Both bodies of research are summarized in this chapter. To begin, research is summarized on normative patterns of social and emotional development, with emphasis on the development and significance of the child–parent attachments that are widely believed to play central roles in shaping children's development. With this as a backdrop, research is then discussed on the effect of parental separation on children's adjustment, focusing primarily on large-scale survey research. The next two sections focus in more detail on parenting plans for younger children, with emphasis on disputes about the amount and types of time children should spend with the two parents and on the effects of conflict on their adjustment. In the final section, focus shifts to four recent studies conducted in Australia to explore the effects of legal reforms in 2006 designed to improve outcomes for children in separating families.

DEVELOPMENT OF PARENT–CHILD RELATIONSHIPS

As described by Bowlby (1969), and largely confirmed by subsequent research (for detailed review, see Thompson, 2006, and Smith, Coffino, Van Horn, & Lieberman, 2012; Chapter 1 in this volume), attachment theory suggests that infants begin to form attachments right after birth as they learn to discriminate among adult caregivers, develop preferences, and gradually develop emotional attachments to those who care for them.

In the first 2 months after birth (phase 1, according to Bowlby), infants indiscriminately accept care from any caregiver and use a repertoire of innate signals, including crying and smiling, to bring and keep potential caregivers close to them. The relief of distress from hunger or pain and the growing interest in and response to social signals from adults are the building blocks for more discriminating attachment processes, but regular interaction is needed to continue the process of attachment formation because very young infants have primitive memories and cognitive abilities. Research has shown that, from the very beginning, fathers are as competent to care for their infants as mothers are (Lamb, 1997, 2002a; Parke, 1996); if gender differences in parental sensitivity develop, this appears to be attributable to differences in the amount of experience mothers and fathers have interacting with their children.

In the period extending from 2 to 7 months of age (phase 2), infants increasingly begin to recognize their parents (and other caregivers) and to prefer interaction with them. They also begin to anticipate caregivers' responses to their signals, although they do not yet understand that people (including caregivers) continue to exist when they are not present. Infants of this age initiate and enjoy social interactions and start to show signs of "attachment in the making." They do not yet typically protest separations from their parents but require frequent contact with their parents for attachment formation to continue.

In the third phase of attachment development (between 7 and 24 months), attachments become increasingly apparent, as infants preferentially seek to be near and to interact with specific caregivers, by whom they are more easily soothed than by strangers. Contrary to Bowlby's initial speculation and widespread common sense, it has been known since the 1970s (e.g., Lamb, 1975) that most infants in two-parent families do not become attached to their mothers first but rather form attachments to both parents at about the same age, around 6 to 7 months (see Lamb, 2002a, for a review), even though fathers typically spend less time with their infants than mothers do (Pleck & Masciadrelli, 2004). This indicates that, although a threshold level of interaction is crucial for attachments to form, time spent interacting is not the only critical dimension. Unfortunately, continued unsubstantiated beliefs on the part of many professionals that babies initially develop attachments to a single primary caretaker have kept alive some of the simplistic rules of thumb that the era of scientifically guided custody determinations was supposed to supplant.

Infants begin to protest when separated from their primary attachment figures around 6 to 7 months of age as they start recognizing that parents continue to exist even when they are not present. Over the ensuing months, infants and toddlers become able to tolerate longer separations from their parents or attachment figures, although such separations may remain stressful. Most infants come to prefer the parents (typically mothers) who take primary responsibility for their care (see Lamb, 2002a, for a review), but this does not mean that relationships with their less-involved parents are unimportant. In fact, many toddlers and preschoolers prefer being with their *traditional* (less involved) fathers in many circumstances, especially when they are not stressed or tired (Lamb, 2002a). However, the relationship with the more involved parent tends to have a greater impact on subsequent behavior and development than the relationship with the less involved parent, albeit not clearly in direct proportion to the relative levels of involvement (Lamb & Lewis, 2010). Nonetheless, both relationships remain psychologically important even when there are disparities in the two parents' levels of participation in child care.

According to attachment theorists, infants form attachments to those who have been available regularly and have responded to the infants' signals and needs (Lamb, Thompson, Gardner, & Charnov, 1985; Thompson, 2006). All caregivers are not equivalently sensitive, of course, and individual differences in responsiveness (but not differences in levels of involvement) affect the quality or security of the attachment relationships that form. The quality of both maternal and paternal behavior is reliably associated with the security of infant–parent attachment (DeWolff & van IJzendoorn, 1997; van IJzendoorn & DeWolff, 1997). Interestingly, the association between the quality of paternal behavior and the quality of infant–father attachment appears to be weaker than the parallel association between maternal behavior and the security of infant–mother attachment. However, the quality of both mother- and father–child interaction remains the most reliable predictor of individual differences in psychological, social, and cognitive adjustment in infancy, as well as in later childhood (Lamb & Lewis, 2010; Thompson, 2006).

As Yarrow (1963; Yarrow & Goodwin, 1973) showed a half century ago, separation responses of infants become increasingly intense as attachments to parents and other important caregivers strengthen between 6 and 24 months. As mentioned earlier, most infants initially come to prefer the parent who provides most of their care and are more likely to seek out their preferred parents for comfort when distressed (see Lamb, 2002a, for a review). Non-preferred parents remain emotionally important, however, and are sought out for other social and emotional needs (e.g., play and companionship) and, when primary caregivers are not available, for comfort. Preference for primary caregivers diminishes with age and often disappears by 18 months of age (Lamb, 2002a). Although infants and toddlers may resist transitions between parents in the second year, just as they sometimes protest (even more strongly) daily transitions to out-of-home care providers, they generally comfort quite quickly once the transition is accomplished. This is particularly likely when both parents have the opportunity to engage in normal parenting activities (feeding, playing, soothing, putting to bed, etc.) while attachments are being established and consolidated.

Infants and toddlers need regular interaction with their "attachment figures" in order to foster, maintain, and strengthen their relationships (Lamb, Bornstein, & Teti, 2002; Thompson, 2006). This means that young children need to interact with both parents in a variety of contexts (feeding, playing, diapering, soothing, reading, putting to bed, etc.) to ensure that the relationships are consolidated and strengthened. In the absence of such opportunities for regular interaction across a broad range of contexts, infant–parent relationships may weaken rather than grow stronger. When toddlers are separated for as little as a few days from all of their attachment figures (for example, both parents) simultaneously, intense distress and disturbances that persist for 6 months after reunion have been reported (Bowlby, 1973; Heinicke, 1956; Heinicke & Westheimer, 1966; Robertson & Robertson, 1971). Reactions are muted, but not always eliminated, when children are cared for by other attachment figures or sensitive substitute caregivers during the separation (Robertson & Robertson, 1971). Extended separations from parents with whom children have formed meaningful attachments are thus undesirable because they unduly stress developing attachment relationships (Bowlby, 1973). The loss or attenuation of important attachment relationships may cause depression and anxiety, particularly in the first 2 years, when children lack the cognitive and communication skills that would enable them to cope with loss. The absence of regular contact slowly erodes relationships, such that, over time, parents who do not interact regularly with their infants effectively become strangers.

In the final phase of attachment formation, which begins around age 2, toddlers better understand why parents come and go, and can enter with their parents into some joint planning of daily activities (Greenberg, Cicchetti, & Cummings, 1990; Thompson, 2006). The increased cognitive and language abilities of 2- to 3-year-olds enable them to tolerate somewhat longer separations from their parents without undue stress. However, their very primitive sense of time prevents them from conceptualizing much beyond today and tomorrow, inhibiting their ability to understand and cope with lengthy separations of several weeks or months.

Relationships with parents continue to play a crucial role in shaping children's social, emotional, personal, and cognitive development into middle childhood and adolescence (Lamb & Lewis, 2010). Indeed, the quality of both mother- and father–child relationships remains the most reliable correlate of individual differences in psychological, social, and cognitive adjustment in infancy, as well as in later childhood (Lamb & Lewis, 2010; Thompson, 2006). Not surprisingly, therefore, children in both two- and single-parent families appear better adjusted when they enjoy warm positive relationships with two actively involved parents (Amato & Gilbreth, 1999; Hetherington, 1999; Lamb, 1999, 2002b; Thompson & Laible, 1999). Children are better off with insecure attachments than without attachment relationships, however, because these enduring ties play essential formative roles in later social and emotional functioning. There is also a substantial literature documenting the adverse effects of disrupted parent–child relationships on children's development and adjustment, with a linear relationship between age of separation and later attachment quality in adolescents. The weakest attachments to parents are reported by those whose parents separated in the first 5 years of their lives (Woodward, Ferguson, & Belsky, 2000). Similarly, in a retrospective study of adolescents whose parents had divorced, Schwartz and Finley (2005) found that age at time of divorce was associated with ratings of both paternal involvement and nurturance, indicating that the earlier the separation, the greater the impact on the quality of the children's relationships with their fathers.

In summary:

- Most infants form attachments to both of their parents.
- The relationships with mothers and fathers are the most important influences on the development of most children.

EFFECTS OF PARENTAL SEPARATION OR DIVORCE

There is clear evidence that, on average, children benefit from being raised in two biological or adoptive-parent families rather than separated, divorced, or never-married single-parent households (Amato, 2000; Amato & Dorius, 2010; Aquilino, 1996; Carlson, 2006; Carlson & McLanahan, 2010; Clarke-Stewart & Brentano, 2006; Clarke-Stewart, Vandell, McCartney, Owen, & Booth, 2000; Hetherington, 1999; Hetherington & Kelly, 2002; McLanahan, 1999; McLanahan & Sandefur, 1994; McLanahan & Teitler, 1999; Simons et al., 1996; Simons, Lin, Gordon, Conger, & Lorenz, 1999), although there is considerable variability within groups, and the differences between groups are relatively small. Indeed, although children growing up in fatherless families are, on average, disadvantaged relative to peers growing up in two-parent families with respect to psychosocial adjustment, behavior and achievement at school, educational attainment, employment trajectories, income generation, involvement in antisocial, delinquent, and even criminal behavior, and the ability to establish and maintain intimate relationships, the majority of children with divorced parents enjoy average or better-than-average social and emotional adjustment as young adults (Booth & Amato, 2001; Clarke-Stewart & Brentano, 2006; Hetherington & Kelly, 2002; Kelly & Emery, 2003). Approximately 20% to 25% of children in post-separation and divorced families give evidence of adjustment problems, compared to 12% in married families. Thus, the majority of children from separated families evince no psychopathology or behavioral symptoms, although they are likely to experience psychic pain for at least some period of time (Emery, 1998; Hetherington & Kelly, 2002; Laumann-Billings & Emery, 2000; Schwartz & Finley, 2005).

Such individual differences in outcomes force us to identify more precisely both the ways in which divorce/single parenthood may affect children's lives and the factors that might account for individual differences in children's adjustment following their parents' separation. As explained in several previous publications (e.g., Lamb 2002a, 2002b; Lamb & Kelly, 2009), five interrelated factors appear to be especially significant.

Economic Stresses

Typically, single parenthood is associated with a variety of social and financial stresses with which custodial parents must cope, largely on their own. Single-parent families are more economically stressed than two-parent families, and economic stresses or poverty appear to account (statistically speaking) for many effects of single parenthood (Hetherington & Kelly, 2002; McLanahan, 1999).

Reductions in Time with Children

Because single mothers need to work more extensively outside the home than married or partnered mothers do, parents spend less time with children in single-parent families and the levels of supervision and guidance are lower and less reliable than in two-parent families (Hetherington & Kelly, 2002; McLanahan, 1999).

Reductions in the level and quality of parental stimulation and attention may affect achievement, compliance, and social skills, while diminished supervision makes antisocial behavior and misbehavior more likely (Hetherington & Kelly, 2002).

Conflict Between Parents

Conflict between the parents commonly precedes, emerges, or increases during the separation and divorce processes, and often continues for some time beyond them. Interparental conflict is an important correlate of children's psychosocial maladjustment, just as marital harmony, its conceptual inverse, appears to be a reliable correlate of positive adjustment (Cummings, Goeke-Morey, & Raymond, 2004; Cummings, Merrilees, & George, 2010; Johnston, 1994; Kelly, 2000). The negative impacts of high levels of marital conflict on the quality of parenting of both mothers and fathers have been well documented. In general, parental conflict is associated with more rejecting, less warm and nurturing parenting by mothers, and with fathers' withdrawal from parenting and engagement in more intrusive interactions with their children (Cummings & Davies, 1994; Grych, 2005). Anger-based marital conflict is associated with filial aggression and externalizing behavior problems, perhaps because such parents and children have similar difficulty regulating negative affect (Katz & Gottman, 1993). These and other data support the observation that some of the effects of divorce are better viewed as the effects of pre-separation marital conflict and violence (Kelly, 2000).

The adversarial legal system tends to promote conflict between already vulnerable parents because of its win–lose orientation and the way it fosters hostile behaviors and demands. Although the adversarial process purports to focus on children's "best interests," parents' psychologically driven legal strategies more often represent their own needs and perceived entitlements, and the effect is to diminish the possibility of future civility, productive communication, and cooperation (Kelly, 2003).

Quality and Type of Parenting

The quality and type of parenting have emerged as important influences on the post-separation/divorce adjustment of school-aged children and adolescents. Deterioration in the quality of parenting after separation has long been recognized (Belsky, Youngblade, Rovine, & Volling, 1991; Clarke-Stewart & Brentano, 2006; Hetherington, 1999; Sturge-Apple, Davies, & Cummings, 2006; Wallerstein & Kelly, 1980). Many parents are preoccupied, stressed, emotionally labile, angry, and depressed around and after separation, and their "diminished parenting" includes less positive involvement and affection expressed with their children, and more coercive and harsh forms of discipline. Additional internal factors affecting quality of parenting include parents' psychological adjustment, violence, and high conflict. External factors such as absorption in dating, new partners, cohabitation, remarriage, and poverty and financial instability are also associated with reductions in the quality of parenting (Amato, 2000; Hetherington, 1999; Kelly, 2000; Pruett, Williams, Insabella, & Little, 2003; Simons et al., 1999; Wallerstein & Kelly, 1980).

Researchers have identified specific aspects of parenting that can moderate the impact of separation/divorce on children's social, emotional, and academic adjustment, and can potentially protect children against the harmful impacts of high conflict. Effective parenting by separated mothers is characterized by warmth, authoritative discipline (setting limits, non-coercive discipline and control, enforcement of rules, appropriate expectations), academic skill encouragement, and monitoring of the children's activities (Amato & Fowler, 2002; Buchanan, Maccoby, & Dornbusch, 1996; Hetherington, 1999; Martinez & Forgatch, 2002; Simons et al., 1999). As described in more detail below, the effective parenting of fathers that is linked to more positive adjustment following parental separation is also associated with effective paternal behaviors, including active involvement (help with homework and projects, emotional support and warmth, talking about problems and involvement in school; Amato & Fowler, 2002; Amato & Gilbreth, 1999; Hetherington, 1999; Finley & Schwartz, 2007).

Disruptions in Relationships with Fathers

Parental separation commonly disrupts one of the child's most important and enduring relationships, that with his or her father. As Amato (1993; Amato & Gilbreth, 1999) has shown with particular clarity, however, the bivariate associations between father absence and children's adjustment are much weaker than one might expect. Indeed, Amato and Gilbreth's (1999) meta-analysis revealed no significant association between the frequency of father–child contact and child outcomes, largely because of the great diversity in the types of "father-present" relationships. We might predict that contacts with abusive, incompetent, or disinterested fathers are likely to have much different effects than relationships with devoted, committed, and sensitive fathers. As expected, Amato and Gilbreth (1999) found that children's well-being was significantly enhanced when their relationships with non-resident fathers were positive, when the non-resident fathers engaged in "active parenting," and when contact was frequent. Dunn, Cheng, O'Connor, and Bridges (2004), Simons et al. (1996), Hetherington, Bridges, and Insabella (1998), and Clarke-Stewart and Hayward (1996) likewise reported that children benefited when their non-resident fathers were actively involved in routine everyday activities, and the conclusion was clearly supported in recent analyses by Carlson (2006) of data from the National Longitudinal Study of Youth. Carlson showed that father involvement was associated with better adolescent adjustment and that paternal involvement partially mediated the effects of family structure (notably divorce or single parenthood) on adolescents' behavioral outcomes. Similarly, higher levels of paternal involvement in their children's schools was associated with better grades, better adjustment, fewer suspensions, and lower dropout rates than were lower levels of involvement (Nord, Brimhall, & West, 1997). Active engagement in a variety of specific activities and ongoing school-related discussions between fathers and their adolescents significantly lowered the probably of school failure when compared to adolescents with less actively engaged fathers.

Another meta-analysis indicated that, on multiple measures of emotional and behavioral adjustment and academic achievement completed by mothers, fathers, teachers, and clinicians, children in joint physical custody were better adjusted than children in sole custody arrangements. In fact, children in shared custody were as well adjusted as children whose parents remained married (Bauserman, 2002). Although joint physical custody parents reported less past and current conflict than did sole physical custody parents, conflict did not explain the superiority of the children in joint custody arrangements. Again, the clear implication is that active paternal involvement, not simply the number or length of meetings between fathers and children, predicts child adjustment. This suggests that post-divorce arrangements should specifically seek to maximize positive and meaningful paternal involvement rather than simply allow minimal levels of visitation. As in non-divorced families, in other words, the quality of continued relationships with the parents—both parents—is crucial (Kelly & Lamb, 2000). Stated differently and succinctly, the better (richer, deeper, and more secure) the parent–child relationships, the better the children's adjustment, whether or not the parents live together (Lamb, 2002a, 2002b).

A recent longitudinal study of representative samples of adolescents living in low-income neighborhoods in Boston, San Antonio, and Chicago nicely illustrated the associations over time between non-resident paternal involvement and adolescent delinquency after statistically controlling for the effects of influences such as demographic factors and the quality of mother–child relationships (Coley & Medeiros, 2007). As expected, non-resident paternal involvement was associated with less delinquency overall; importantly, higher paternal involvement was associated with declines in delinquency over time, particularly among adolescents who were more involved with delinquent activities. In addition, as delinquency increased, paternal involvement increased too, suggesting that fathers were responding to changes in their children's problem behavior. Similarly, in another longitudinal study of adolescents, Menning (2006) showed that adolescents whose non-resident fathers were more involved were less likely to start smoking.

Because fathers' active participation and effective parenting is beneficial, the influence of maternal attitudes on the extent of paternal involvement in the marriage and following separation and divorce is important (Cowdery & Knudson-Martin, 2005; Pleck, 1997). Mothers can be influential gatekeepers of paternal involvement through attitudes and behaviors that limit or facilitate fathers' opportunities to parent and develop close relationships with their children. Mothers' traditional attitudes toward women's roles, identities linked primarily to caregiving, and perceptions that mothers are more competent at child care than fathers are associated with more active inhibitory gatekeeping, particularly following separation, and this is linked with lower levels of father involvement (Allen & Hawkins, 1999; Fagan & Barnett, 2003).

Overall, then, a number of factors help account for individual differences in the effects of divorce, and because they are inter-correlated, it is difficult to assess their relative importance. The ability to maintain meaningful relationships with both parents does appear to be of central importance, however, both in its own right and as a correlate of some of the other factors. As shown later, thoughtful interventions can take advantage of these inter-correlations, initiating processes that minimize the adverse effects on children's adjustment by striving to promote healthy relationships between children and both of their parents, whether or not they live together.

In summary:

- Parents continue to affect children's adjustment whether or not they live together.

- Children are adversely affected by parental conflict, poor relationships with or separations from their parents, and economic circumstances rather than by family structure *per se*.

MINIMIZING THE ADVERSE EFFECTS OF DIVORCE

Even though children's best interests are usually served by keeping both parents actively involved in their children's lives, many custody and access arrangements may not foster the maintenance of relationships between children and their non-resident parents. The use of traditional "visiting guidelines" in many jurisdictions that allocate every other weekend to the non-resident parent (with perhaps a brief midweek visit), or the reliance of mental health professionals on unsubstantiated beliefs that every other weekend is the best parenting plan for children, has caused great dissatisfaction and a sense of loss among the majority of children in post-divorce arrangements. Research on children's and young adults' views of their post-divorce living arrangements indicates that the majority express strong wishes and longing for more time with their fathers, a desire for more closeness, and favorable views of shared physical custody as their preferred schedule (Fabricius & Hall, 2000; Laumann-Billings & Emery, 2000; Smith & Gollop, 2001). Arbitrary and one-size-fits-all restrictions on the amounts of time children spend with their fathers have been the norm regardless of the quality of the father–child relationship. It is no less important to maintain both child–parent attachments when the divorced parents had "traditional" roles before divorce than when they shared parenting responsibilities more equitably. The focus should remain on the children's best interests, not "fairness" to the parents.

Writing on behalf of 18 experts on the effects of divorce and contrasting parenting plans, Lamb, Sternberg, and Thompson (1997, p. 400) observed more than a decade and a half ago that:

> To maintain high-quality relationships with their children, parents need to have sufficiently extensive and regular interactions with them, but the amount of time involved is usually less important than the quality of the interaction that it fosters. Time distribution arrangements that ensure the involvement of both parents in important aspects of their children's everyday lives and routines . . . are likely to keep nonresidential parents playing psychologically important and central roles in the lives of their children.

Consistent with this view, Fabricius and Luecken (2007) subsequently found that the more time a group of university students had lived as children with their fathers, the better were their relationships with their fathers, independent of amount of parent conflict. More time with fathers appeared to be beneficial in both high- and low-conflict families, and more exposure to parent conflict appeared to be detrimental (poorer health status and more distress) at both high and low levels of amount of time with fathers. Interparental conflict should thus be avoided wherever possible, but its presence should not be used to justify restrictions on children's access to either of their parents.

For parents to have a positive impact on their children's development, it is important that parents be integral parts of their children's lives. This remains especially important as children get older and greater portions of their time are occupied outside the family by virtue of friendships, extracurricular activities, sports, and the like. At all ages, it is important for parents to know teachers and friends, what is happening at school or preschool, how relationships with peers are going, what other activities are important or meaningful to the children, etc., and to be aware of daily ups-and-downs in their children's lives. It is hard to do this without regular and extensive first-hand involvement with their children in a variety of contexts.

As Kelly and Lamb (2000; Lamb, 2002b; Lamb & Kelly, 2001, 2009) reiterated, the ideal situation is one in which children with separated parents have opportunities to interact with both parents frequently in a variety of functional contexts (feeding, play, discipline, basic care, limit-setting, putting to bed, etc.). The evening and over-night periods (like extended days with naptimes) with non-residential parents are especially important psychologically for infants, toddlers, and young children. They provide opportunities for crucial social interactions and nurturing activities, including bathing, soothing hurts and anxieties, bedtime rituals, comforting in the middle of the night, and the reassurance and security of snuggling in the morning that 1- to 3-hour-long visits cannot provide. According to attachment theory, as noted earlier, these everyday activities promote and maintain trust and confidence in the parents, while deepening and strengthening child–parent attachments, and thus need to be encouraged when decisions about access and contact are made.

One implication is that even young children should spend overnight periods with both parents when both have been involved in their care prior to separation, even though neo-analysts have long counseled against this (Kelly & Lamb, 2000; Lamb & Kelly, 2001, 2009). As Warshak (2000) has pointed out, the prohibition of overnight visitation has been justified by prejudices and beliefs rather than by any empirical evidence. When both parents have established significant attachments and both have been actively involved in the child's care, overnight visits will consolidate attachments and child adjustment, not work against them.

Solomon and Biringen (2001) challenged Kelly and Lamb's (2000) conclusions regarding the beneficial effects of overnight visits for many young children, citing the results of a study by Solomon and George (1999a, 1999b). Contrary to their assertions, however, the study did *not* show that overnight visits with non-custodial fathers adversely affected the security of infant–mother attachment or that overnights were more problematic for preschoolers than for infants and preschoolers. In addition, many of the infants and toddlers they studied had never lived with their two parents and thus may not have formed attachments to their fathers before the overnight visits commenced; their situation is much different from that of infants and toddlers who have established attachments to two involved parents prior to separation/divorce, which was the context explicitly addressed by Kelly and Lamb (2000). Different steps are needed when promoting the formation rather than the maintenance of attachments, as Kelly and Lamb (2003) pointed out in another paper concerned with young children whose parents live too far apart for children to have regular contact with both of them. Solomon and George (1999a, p. 27) also noted that some of the infants in their study had experienced extended and repeated separations from their fathers, which, as noted above, would have stressed these relationships further.

Pruett, Ebling, and Insabella (2004; see also Pruett, Insabella, & Gustafson, 2005; Pruett, Williams, Insabella, & Little, 2003) studied the adjustment of children aged 6 and under in 132 American families during the 15 to 18 months after separation, a period during which most of the parents agreed on parenting plans with the assistance of family relations professionals. Whereas many of the infants studied by Solomon and George (1999a) had never lived with both parents and/or had suffered extended separations from them, only three of the children studied by Pruett et al. (2004) had not lived with both parents. Most children lived primarily with their mothers following separation, but the majority of the children had one (31%) or more (44%) overnight visits per week with the non-resident parent on a consistent basis, and both sharing overnights and schedule consistency were associated with superior adjustment in the eyes of both mothers and fathers, especially for children over 3 years of age. Only poor parental relationships and parental conflict adversely affected their children's reported behavioral adjustment. Hierarchical regression analyses suggested that having overnights only affected (positively) the fathers' reports of the children's social problems; in all other analyses, the variance was explained by other factors, including demographic variables and measures of the family relationships. As explained by Pruett et al. (2004, 2005), overnights need to be viewed in the context of the broader circumstances.

To minimize the deleterious impact of extended separations from either parent, furthermore, attachment theory tells us there should be more frequent transitions than would perhaps be desirable with older children (Kelly & Lamb, 2000). To be responsive to young children's psychological needs, in other words, the parenting schedules adopted for children under age 2 or 3 should actually involve more transitions, rather than fewer, to ensure the continuity of both relationships and to promote the children's security and comfort. Although no empirical research exists testing specific parenting plans following separation, it is likely, for example, that infants and toddlers would remain most comfortable and secure with a schedule that allowed the child to see his or her father at least three times a week, including at least one overnight extended stay (assuming the father–child relationship is adequate), so that there is no separation of greater than 2 to 3 days. From the third year of life, the ability to tolerate longer separations begins to increase, so that most toddlers can manage two consecutive overnights with each parent without stress.

Interestingly, psychologists have long recognized the need to minimize the length of separations from attachment figures when devising parenting plans, but they have typically focused only on separations from mothers, thereby revealing their presumption that young children are not meaningfully attached to their fathers, or that paternal involvement is a peripheral influence. The lingering resistance to overnights among professionals working with divorcing families appears to view fathers as strangers rather than as important attachment figures. To the extent that children are attached to both of their parents, however, separations from both parents are stressful and at minimum generate psychic pain. As a result, parenting plans that allow children—especially very young children—to see their fathers every other Saturday for a few hours, or every other shortened weekend (with perhaps a brief midweek visit) clearly fail to recognize the adverse consequences of weeklong separations from non-resident parents. It is little wonder that such arrangements lead to attenuation of the relationships between non-resident parents and their children. Instead, it is desirable to promote continued involvement by both parents, striving when necessary to increase the participation of those parents (typically fathers) whose limited prior involvement may initially make overnight contact inappropriate (Kelly & Lamb, 2003).

The quality of the relationships between non-residential parents and their children is also crucial when determining whether to sever or promote relationships between divorced parents and their children. Regardless of the levels of violence, there are many families in which non-resident fathers and children have sufficiently poor relationships—perhaps because of the fathers' psychopathology, substance, or alcohol abuse—that "maintenance" of interaction or involvement may not be of net benefit to the children, but the number of relationships like this remains unknown. Unrepresentative data sets, such as those collected by Greif (1997) in the course of research designed to study fathers and mothers who lose contact with their children after divorce, suggest that perhaps 10% to 15% of parents do not have either the commitment or individual capacities to establish and maintain supportive and enriching relationships with their children following divorce. Taken together, Johnston's (Johnston & Roseby, 1997) and Greif's (1997) estimates suggest that, at most, 15% to 20% (depending on how greatly the two groups of parents overlap) of the children whose parents divorce might not benefit from regular and extended contact with their non-resident parents, and this proportion is consistent with the results reported by Cashmore et al. (2010), below. Stated differently, of course, this suggests that more than three quarters of the children experiencing their parents' divorce could benefit from having and maintaining relationships with their non-resident parents. Instead of "standard" parenting plans, therefore, individual circumstances should be examined to ensure that the arrangements made are sensitive to the parents' and children's strengths, schedules, and needs (Kelly, 2005, 2007; Smyth & Chisholm, 2006).

In summary:

- Most children benefit from the opportunity to maintain meaningful relationships with both of their parents after separation.
- Many parenting plans do not allow meaningful involvement by both parents.
- Continued parental conflict can be harmful to children's post-separation adjustment.

RESTRICTING CONTACT IN RESPONSE TO MARITAL CONFLICT

Of course, there are some cases in which the possible benefits of keeping both parents involved are outweighed by the costs of doing so. Conflict-filled or violent relationships between the parents are most likely to trigger such cost–benefit analyses because, as noted earlier, continuing high conflict is reliably associated with poorer child outcomes following divorce (Johnston, 1994; Kelly, 2000; Maccoby & Mnookin, 1992). Children in high-conflict families who have frequent contact with their fathers sometimes appear more poorly adjusted than those in low-conflict families (Amato & Rezac, 1994; Hetherington, 1999; Johnston, 1994; Johnston, Kline, & Tschann, 1989; Maccoby & Mnookin, 1992), although this may not be true when the relationships with both parents are good. Interparental conflict should thus be avoided wherever possible, but litigation-related conflict and conflict triggered by the high levels of stress around the time of divorce do not appear to have enduring consequences for children. As a result, their occurrence should not be used to justify restrictions on children's access to either of their parents.

Maccoby and Mnookin (1992) cautioned that minor or isolated instances of domestic violence should not affect decisions regarding custody and visitation. The high conflict found harmful by researchers such as Johnston (1994; Johnston & Roseby, 1997) typically involved repeated incidents of spousal violence and verbal aggression between parents with substantial psychiatric problems and personality disorders that continued after divorce at intense levels for extended periods, often in front of the children. As a result, Johnston has emphasized the importance of continued relationships with both parents except in those relatively uncommon circumstances in which intense, protracted conflict or violence occurs and persists. According to Maccoby and Mnookin (1992), somewhere around a quarter of divorcing families experience high levels of conflict around the time of divorce, and perhaps 10% of them may have conflict that is sufficiently severe and intractable that it may not be beneficial for the children concerned to have contact with their nonresident parents (see also Johnston, 1994). Not all entrenched post-divorce conflict involves both parents' participation, however, because in a significant number of cases, one parent has essentially disengaged emotionally from the other parent and is not promoting or instigating the conflict but is a victim of the other parent's rage and vindictiveness, intransigence, and/or failure to comply with parenting and financial orders, and therefore may need to return to court for assistance (Friedman, 2004; Kelly, 2003, 2005).

Significant numbers of children have warm and supportive relationships with parents who have highly conflicted and/or violent relationships with one another, so professionals must be careful regarding reports of parental conflict influencing decisions about parent–child contact (Holden, Geffner, & Jouriles, 1998; Maccoby & Mnookin, 1992; Sternberg & Lamb, 1999). According to Appel and Holden (1998), 60% of the children whose parents were violent with one another were not themselves victims of physical child abuse, suggesting that decision-makers need to assess the children's relationships with parents directly and not simply assume that children must have been abused because their parents were violent with one another. Unfortunately, however, mere allegations of conflict or even marital violence can be powerful tools in an adversarial system, frequently resulting in reduced levels of court-approved contacts between fathers and children (Sternberg, 1997). Disagreements about the occurrence, nature, and perpetrators of violence are quite common, furthermore, and do not always reveal self-serving biases (Braver & O'Connell, 1998; Sternberg, Lamb, & Dawud-Noursi, 1998).

Newer research that differentiates among types of intimate partner violence is directly relevant to these issues of custody and access. Types of partner violence identified include situational couple violence, instigated by both men and women in fairly equal numbers and characterized most often by more minor forms of violence (pushing, shoving, grabbing). Injuries are not as common, and fear of the partner is not typical. Situational couple violence typically arises from arguments that spiral upward and poor conflict-management skills rather than power, coercion, and control as central dynamics (Babcock, Costa, Green, & Eckhardt, 2004; Johnson,

2005; Johnson & Leone, 2005; Johnston & Campbell, 1993; Kelly & Johnson, 2005; Stets & Straus, 1992). In contrast, battering (also called intimate terrorism), seen primarily in shelter and hospital samples, is primarily male-perpetrated, accounts for most of the injuries seen in women, and has coercion, control, and emotional abuse as the primary dynamics. Separation-instigated violence has also been identified in couples whose prior history together did not include any violence or coercion and control (Johnston & Campbell, 1993; Kelly, 1982). Although the experience of parental violence is always distressing, if not traumatic, for children, these differences among types of partner violence have implications for various post-separation interventions, screening, and the development of appropriate parenting plans for children (Jaffe, Johnston, Crooks, & Bala, 2008; Kelly & Johnson, 2005).

Research on the impact of post- as opposed to pre-divorce conflict on children's adjustment has yielded mixed results. Some investigators have found that marital conflict is a more potent predictor of post-divorce adjustment than post-divorce conflict (Booth & Amato, 2001; Buehler, Krishnakumar, Stone, Anthony, Pemberton, Gerard, & Barber, 1998; King & Heard, 1999; Kline, Johnston, & Tschann, 1990), whereas Hetherington (1999) found that post-divorce conflict had more adverse effects than did conflict in married families. McIntosh, Smyth, Wells, and Long (2010), in the research reported more fully below, found that continued conflict between parents was associated with poorer child adjustment, whereas Booth and Amato (2001) reported no association between the amount of post-divorce conflict and later adjustment in young adults. The varied findings may reflect the use of different measures, a failure to differentiate between types of conflict after divorce, differing parental styles of resolution, and/or variations in the extent to which children are directly exposed to anger and conflict. High conflict is more likely to be destructive after divorce when parents use their children to express their anger and are verbally and physically aggressive on the phone or in person (e.g., McIntosh, Smyth, Wells et al., 2010). By contrast, when parents continue to have conflict, but encapsulate it and do not put their children in the middle, children appear unaffected (Buchanan, Maccoby, & Dornbusch, 1991; Hetherington, 1999). Buffers have also been identified that may protect children from the harmful effects of high parent conflict, including a good relationship with at least one parent or caregiver, parental warmth, and emotional support from a sibling (Hetherington & Kelly, 2002; Vandewater & Lansford, 1998).

In addition, most experts agree that conflict localized around the time of separation and divorce is less problematic than conflict that was and remains an intrinsic and unresolved part of the parents' relationship and continues after their divorce (Cummings et al., 2004, 2010; Cummings & O'Reilly, 1997; Johnston & Roseby, 1997). Similarly, conflict from which children are shielded also does not appear to affect adjustment (Hetherington, 1999), whereas conflict that includes physical violence is more pathogenic than high conflict without violence (Jouriles, McDonald, Norwood, Vincent, & Mahoney, 1996; McNeal & Amato, 1998).

In summary:

- Extended contact with both parents after separation may not be beneficial when conflict is high, especially when the children do not have good relationships with both parents.

RECENT AUSTRALIAN LEGAL REFORMS AND THEIR IMPACT

Whereas most North American research on the effects of varying parenting plans was conducted more than a decade ago, there has been considerable recent research conducted in Australia, a country where legal traditions are in some ways similar to those in North America and Great Britain. This research was prompted by major legislative changes and has received a great deal of attention around the world. Because it is easy to misinterpret or over-generalize the results of social research for reasons made clear earlier, the various studies are discussed here in some detail.

In 2006, the Australian government introduced wide-ranging reforms to the policies and practices associated with the dissolution of parents' relationships. One declared goal of the reforms was to minimize the adverse impact of parental separation on the parties involved (especially the children) as well as on society; the reforms were thus motivated in part by reference to the literature reviewed earlier in this chapter. Specifically, the reforms responded to concerns that many children were being exposed to harmful parental conflict and that the common post-divorce parenting arrangements failed to keep many parents meaningfully involved in their children's lives, psychologically and financially, thereby increasing the needed levels of direct (welfare, legal services, court time) and indirect (counseling, educational services, criminal justice services) support from the public purse. As described more fully by Parkinson (2010), the Family Law Amendment (Shared Parental Responsibility) Act 2006 sought to provide support and information (through a network of 65 newly established Family Relationship Centres [FRCs]) to parents who had separated or were contemplating separation, explaining the possible effects on the children and outlining ways in which the parents might minimize these effects. Parents who were unable to resolve their disputes were encouraged to mediate their disagreements. Proponents of the reforms thus expected to reduce the amount of litigation and re-litigation, reduce the amount of conflict to which children were exposed by the separating parents, reduce the numbers who lost contact with one of their parents, increase the proportion spending meaningful amounts of time with both of their parents, and reduce the number of children whose adjustment and well-being was adversely affected by the parents' separation.

By 2010, some early attempts to evaluate the success or failure of this broad reform of Australian family law started to emerge, and four important studies are reviewed here: (a) two large-scale survey-based studies examining the reach and impact of the reforms; (b) a focused examination of young children in the Longitudinal Study of Australian Children (LSAC) whose parents were separated; and (c) a study of 133 divorcing families selected for study because the parents were locked in high levels of conflict. All four studies provide valuable insight into the extent to which interventions of this sort can indeed be effective and into the effects of varying separation arrangements on children's adjustment.

Initial Evaluations of the New System

Kaspiew et al. (2009) conducted an evaluation of the 2006 reforms that involved collecting data from 28,000 parents, grandparents, FRC staff, and legal professionals as well as by analyzing administrative data. Nearly two thirds of the separated mothers and fathers independently reported friendly or cooperative relationships with each other 15 months after separation, with a fifth reporting distant and another fifth highly conflicted relationships. Three quarters of the separating parents sorted out parenting issues within a year of separating, many making little or no use of the available services.

As the FRCs began opening around the country, they came to serve increasing numbers of separating parents, especially those with multiple problems, who might formerly have resorted to the courts. Dispute resolution services were accessed by just under a third of the separating parents, and around 40% of them reached agreements that were still in place around a year later. However, a significant portion of the couples who sought dispute-resolution services involved such levels of family violence that the available services were deemed inappropriate, and FRC staff were surprised and unprepared for the high number of parents with substance abuse, mental health, and violence issues.

More than 80% of the separating parents surveyed by Kaspiew et al. (2009) thought that it was beneficial for children to maintain relationships with both of their parents after separation, but few (16%) of the separating parents chose *shared care* plans (legally defined as arrangements whereby the children spent at least 35% of the overnights with each parent); such plans were most likely to be employed with children in the early school years (26%) and tended to be imposed by judges rather than negotiated. (A third of the cases that were decided by a judge resulted in shared care arrangements.) Traditional arrangements, which were called *primary care* (living with mother but having regular but infrequent overnights with father), were the most durable over time, although *equally shared* arrangements (50/50) and primary father care arrangements were also quite stable, although less common; unequally shared (e.g., 35/65) arrangements tended to become more traditional (primary maternal care) over time, with levels of pre-separation and post-separation involvement significantly correlated. Fathers who shared care equally were more likely to report shared decision-making. Those fathers who had little or no contact with their children after separation tended to be younger, to have lived separately, to live further away from the children after separation, and to have had highly conflicted (often violent) relationships with their former partners.

Most parents reported that their care arrangements were working well for all concerned, and this included three quarters of those who had shared care (65/35) arrangements, even though proportionally more of the parents who shared care reported problematic family dynamics after separation than was true of parents who had traditional arrangements (i.e., living with mother but having regular but infrequent overnights with father). This suggests that some shared care plans were not ideal for the children concerned, insofar as these children may have been more exposed to their parents' conflict. Kaspiew et al. (2009) found no association between physical care arrangement and financial support compliance, but parents who reported joint decision-making (regardless of care arrangements) were more likely to report full child support compliance and to perceive the current levels as fair.

Because the Act extolled the virtues of "equal shared parental responsibility" (*shared legal custody* in American parlance) and of "substantial and significant time with each parent," many parents (especially fathers) expected that they were entitled to 50/50 shared care arrangements, opening the door to more complicated and frequent negotiations (and litigation) when shared care appeared neither practicable nor in the children's best interests. Indeed, many of the legal sector professionals reported a rise in litigation, and negotiation focused on parents' rights rather than the children's needs. On the other hand, lawyers reported a decline in perceptions of the default 80/20 time distribution after reform, with more creative options being considered. They did, however, report an increase in the number of families adopting shared care arrangements for which the levels of conflict made them ill suited, and many professionals felt that the new legal framework made it more difficult to consider children's developmental needs. Many lawyers, and a minority of family relationship professionals, felt that clients were seeking to manipulate the levels of contact to influence their child support responsibilities.

Of course, one key goal of the reform was to improve the outcomes for children. To address this issue, Kaspiew et al. (2009) drew on two data sets: one a targeted survey of children in separated families and one drawing on a representative study of Australian children (LSAC). In both, children who rarely or never saw their fathers had poorer outcomes than those in shared care or primary (maternal) care. Children fared worse (in their mothers' eyes) when the mothers reported concerns about their children's safety, especially when there were shared care arrangements.

Like Kaspiew et al. (2009), Cashmore et al. (2010) drew upon a variety of sources, including the LSAC and other survey data, a targeted survey of parents, an online survey of some children, as well as interviews with parents, to assess the prevalence, characteristics, and impact of shared care arrangements following the 2006 reforms. Survey data showed shared care arrangements (i.e., more than 35% with both parents) in only 8% of the families in which parents did not live together, with care shared equally (50/50) in about half of the families in which care was shared. Many parents attempted to share care after separation but switched to more traditional (i.e., mostly with mother) arrangements over time, often in the face of increased distance between the homes, re-partnering, and other factors. Those who persisted with shared care arrangements (at least 35% of time with fathers) were disproportionately likely to have school-age (rather than younger or teenage) children, and tended to be better educated and more affluent. Families sharing care reported greater flexibility, cooperation, and joint decision-making; these may be consequences of the experience but are perhaps more likely to reflect relationship/ personal characteristics that prompted the shared care arrangements in the first place. Overall, mothers' reports revealed little association between children's adjustment and care patterns, although they thought that children who seldom saw their fathers were the worst off. By contrast, fathers thought that the children who shared care did better. When mothers had serious concerns about the safety of their children or reported high conflict with their former partners, they were more likely to report negative effects on children. Children emphasized the benefits of being able to maintain relationships with both parents, although some (especially older) children found the moves back and forth burdensome. About 10% of the mothers and fathers who shared care arrangements reported that these were unsatisfactory.

Summarizing these findings, Cashmore et al. (2010) concluded that "it is not the care arrangements themselves that make the difference to children's reported well-being. Rather, factors such as the parents' relationship, whether the arrangement was imposed by the court, equitable sharing of family resources . . . and parents' sharing decisions . . . seem to be more significantly associated with children's well-being than the amount of time the children spent with each parent . . . what matters most to children is the quality of the relationship with their parents, not the amount of time in itself" (pp. 143–144).

Survey Research on Overnight Patterns

McIntosh, Smyth, and Keleher (2010) also undertook research on the overnight care patterns experienced by younger children using data from the large nationally representative LSAC. The birth cohort included 5,000 children first studied at 1 year of age, and the kindergarten cohort included 5,000 children first studied as 4-year-olds. From the first wave of the younger cohort, the authors identified 258 babies in separated families, nearly two thirds of whom spent less than one night a year with the non-resident parents; from the second wave they identified 509 2- to 3-year-olds in separated families, 59% of whom never stayed overnight with the non-resident parents; and from the third wave of the first cohort as well as from the first wave of the older cohort, they selected 1,292 4- to 5-year-olds in separated families (40% never stayed overnight). Some of the children in the older age group were also studied at earlier ages, but the analysis was not longitudinal. Shared care and primary care were defined differently for infants and older children because so few of the infants were in shared care arrangements, as defined by the legislation (35% or more of overnights with both parents). Importantly, nothing was known of the children's or parents' behavior prior to the separation.

Infants who spent one or more nights per week with their non-resident parents appeared similar to those in intact families with respect to visual monitoring (mother report) and irritability (observer rated), but differed from those who did not have weekly overnight contact; infants in the latter group had unusually low scores on these measures so that they appeared less irritable or vigilant than those who had one or more overnights. The few toddlers who spent 35% or more of their overnights with the non-resident parents appeared to be less persistent (parent report) and to have more care-provider–reported behavior problems, even when various socioeconomic and parental quality dimensions (which were also associated with poorer adjustment) were taken into account. With similar controls, there were no significant differences between kindergarten children in the shared and primary care groups. Overall, these analyses revealed possible behavioral problems on the part of some 2- to 3-year-olds in shared care arrangements, and some ambiguous differences among the infants who had overnight visits. Children older than 3 years appeared to be unaffected by their living arrangements.

Longitudinal Study of High-Conflict Families

McIntosh, Smyth, Wells, and Long (2010) conducted an extensive longitudinal study of 133 divorcing families with a total of 260 children; 196 of them, ranging in age from 6 to 19, were included in the study. Families were assessed four times over a 4-year period. Baseline information about the families, child care arrangements, and children's adjustment was obtained around the time of mediation conducted to address disputes about post-divorce parenting arrangements that the parents had not been able to resolve satisfactorily on their own—indeed, a majority resorted to judicial determination when mediation was unsuccessful (McIntosh & Chisholm, 2008), underscoring the high levels of conflict characterizing this sample. As the authors emphasized in their report, "these data are solely from families in which the parents experienced significant discord. . . the findings should not. . . be generalised to the population of cooperative separating families characterised by autonomous decision-making and conflict resolution post-separation" (p. 34). The majority of parents reported very high to extreme levels of acrimony and conflict as well as very impoverished co-parenting alliances, indicating that McIntosh, Smyth, Wells, et al.'s (2010) sample was drawn exclusively from among the fifth of divorcing families who had highly conflicted relationships and not at all from the two thirds who had cooperative relationships (Kaspiew et al., 2009). The previous literature implies that many of the children studied by McIntosh, Smyth, Wells, et al. (2010) should be affected adversely by their parents' conflict, especially when care arrangements ensured continued exposure.

Most of the analyses reported by McIntosh, Smyth, Wells, et al. (2010) compared the outcomes for children who (a) lived with one parent (typically the mother) and spent less than 35% of their overnights with the other parent throughout the study (n = 54)—the *primary care* group; (b) spent at least 35% of their overnights with both parents throughout the study (n = 36)—the *shared care* group; (c) changed from one or other of the above groups at least once (n = 41); or (d) had little or no overnight contact with one of their parents (n = 7).

Consistent with trends reported by Kaspiew et al. (2009), mediation was associated with an increase in the number of families who adopted shared care arrangements, but over time many of these families reverted to more traditional (primary care) arrangements. Changes of this sort were more likely to take place when the families included older children (e.g., adolescents) or sibling groups. Families with younger children, especially only one per family, were more likely to maintain or move into shared arrangements over time. These families also tended to involve younger and better educated parents, confident fathers who were more involved in child care before separation, parents who arranged to continue living geographically close to one another after separation, and parents who had higher regard for, felt less hostile to, and had less conflict with partners and parents than those in the other groups. By contrast, older children preferred primary care arrangements at all phases of the study, although, regardless of group, adolescents always reported more contentment with their current living arrangements than younger children did.

Levels of conflict and acrimony tended to decline over time according to both mothers and fathers, regardless of care arrangements. However, after controlling for initial levels of conflict (which were lowest in the shared care families), children in the shared care group reported higher levels of conflict 4 years later, but not when the researchers did not control for initial levels of conflict. At that stage, furthermore, children in the four groups did not report being differentially distressed by their parents' conflict, although children in the shared care group were more likely to feel "caught in the middle" of their parents' disputes. Twenty-three families returned to primary care arrangements from mediation-arranged shared care; as indicated earlier, these families tended to involve older children, larger sibling groups, less educated parents, parents who moved further apart geographically, and parents who experienced more conflict. Interestingly, "children who went on to sustain shared care had significantly better mental health as rated by mothers and fathers than did children who attempted but did not sustain shared care" (McIntosh, Smyth, Wells et al., 2010, p. 50).

Bare majorities of the mothers and fathers who had shared care arrangements (both changing and stable) "reported that their parenting arrangements had at least some flexibility four years [later]" (McIntosh, Smyth, Wells, et al., 2010, p. 51), but it is not clear how many families the 42 children with rigid shared care arrangements belonged to. Not surprisingly, however, this group was characterized by more conflict and litigation, less cooperation, and higher levels of child and maternal distress than the other shared care families.

As one might expect in a high-risk sample like that studied by McIntosh, Smyth, Wells, et al., (2010), the children all appeared significantly more maladjusted overall than children in the general population even at the beginning of the study. There were no group differences in the levels of overall behavior problems, however, although there were some differences with respect to two of the four subscales (emotional symptoms and hyperactivity/inattention).

Analyses of mother- and father-reported scores on the emotional symptoms subscale revealed no differences between children in the four care groups, but significantly greater problems after 4 years on the part of children whose care arrangements were rigid (defined as "contact arrangements . . . [that] were rarely or never responsive to changing needs in family circumstances"; McIntosh, Smyth, Wells, et al., 2010, pp. 60–61). Analyses of scores on the hyperactivity/inattention scale revealed elevated scores on the part of boys in the shared care group, especially those 10 boys whose shared care arrangements had been rigid. (It is a little difficult to evaluate the extent to which rigidity was crucial, however, because differences in the cell sizes reported on pages 63 [Table 7] and 66 [Figure 26] of McIntosh, Smyth, Wells, et al.'s (2010) report are not reconciled.)

As previously reported by McIntosh, Long, and Wells (2009), mediation that specifically included the children rather than mediation that focused on their needs without including them as participants tended to yield parenting plans that involved primary parent arrangements (rather than shared care) and that were less likely to change over time. Mediation-initiated shared care was much less likely to be stable over time than shared care arrangements that evolved prior to mediation.

Probably because they had more extensive contact with both of their parents than children in primary care families, children in shared care arrangements were more likely to report parental conflict and being caught in the middle, but they did not report more distress about the conflict. A subset appeared to be adversely affected by rigid care arrangements; this was a particular problem for the boys in shared care contexts. Hyperactive symptoms were very stable over time, however, suggesting that these boys had initial difficulties that might have been exacerbated by their living arrangements. As McIntosh, Smyth, Wells, et al. (2010) observed: "children already vulnerable to hyperactivity/inattention tended to remain that way over time, regardless of the overnight care arrangement" (p. 75).

Professionals striving to extract lessons or principles from McIntosh, Smyth, Wells, et al.'s (2010) study need to heed the authors' candid caveats concerning both the unrepresentative nature of their sample (see above) and an analytic strategy that was likely to identify as significant group differences that would not be significant if conventional statistical practices were adopted (p. 54).

Overall, McIntosh, Smyth, Wells, et al.'s (2010) findings showed that children's outcomes over time were not simply a function of the care patterns initiated after divorce. The outcomes varied depending upon a number of factors, crucially including the children's temperaments and symptoms as well as pre-divorce arrangements and experiences. In this high-risk sample, shared care arrangements, especially those inspired by mediation in families in which there was not a history of dual parenting and respect, were often difficult to sustain and placed psychological burdens on both the parents and children involved. Even in this sample, however, children benefited from shared care arrangements when their parents had previously shared care more effectively, the children were younger and the families smaller, and the parents recognized the value of continued shared involvement after separation even before mediation. Perhaps the most important lesson to emerge from the study is that families and children have individualized needs and that it is important to choose post-separation arrangements that maximize continuity in children's lives, promote the maintenance of positive parent–child relationships, allow change over time in relation to changing needs and circumstances, and, by recognizing the weaknesses of some parent–child relationships, allow children to escape the damage they might suffer when those parents are not psychologically equipped to promote their children's well-being.

In summary:

- Children tend to benefit when their parents are able to establish parenting plans without litigation.
- Children whose parents were both highly involved before separation benefit from continued involvement by both parents.
- When parents have longstanding conflict without a pattern of joint parenting, children do not benefit from enhanced paternal involvement.
- Children with difficult temperaments may have more difficulty coping with their parents' divorce.
- Because McIntosh, Smyth, Wells, et al. (2010) focused only on high-conflict separating families, it is important not to over-generalize their findings to the majority of separating families.
- The Australian studies, like those conducted elsewhere, show that the majority of children are well adjusted despite their parents' separation/divorce.

SUMMARY

In all, basic research on early social development and descriptive research on the multifaceted correlates of divorce have together yielded a clearer understanding of the ways in which parental separation and subsequent parenting patterns can affect children's well-being. Most importantly, children benefit from supportive relationships with both of their parents, whether or not those parents live together, but it is important to recognize that some children do not have supportive relationships with their parents and that restrictions on the amount of contact with this minority of parents are advisable. Relationships are dynamic and are thus dependent on continued opportunities for interaction. To ensure that committed and psychologically healthy adults can retain meaningful parent–child relationships, post-divorce parenting plans need to encourage participation by both parents in as broad as possible an array of social contexts on a regular basis. Brief dinners and occasional weekend visits do not provide a broad enough or extensive enough basis for such relationships to be fostered, whereas weekday and weekend daytime and nighttime activities are important for children of all ages. In the absence of sufficiently broad and extensive interactions, many fathers drift out of their children's lives, and children see their fathers as increasingly peripheral, placing these children at risk psychologically and materially. Some parents are too bound up in conflict with their former partners to focus sufficiently on children's psychological needs, and in this small minority of cases, it may be in children's longer-term interests to permit only rare (if any) contact with one of the parents. Unfortunately, reasoned discussion about the potential benefits of greater involvement by the vast majority of parents in the lives of their children has been drowned out by poisonous rhetoric from groups and individuals mired in gendered concerns about fairness for parents and from other interest groups who exaggerate the numbers of separating couples whose levels of conflict are sufficiently severe to warrant restrictions on the amounts of time children spend time with both of their parents.

GUIDELINES: CONSIDERATIONS AND CAUTIONS

- Most children have psychologically meaningful relationships with both of their parents.
- Most children benefit from the opportunity to maintain meaningful contact with both parents after separation.
- In a minority of cases, children do not have supportive relationships with both parents, and post-divorce plans should not focus on maintaining them.
- When conflict between the parents is endemic and deep, children may not benefit from continued contact with both parents. In such cases, it may be necessary to identify the more competent and committed parent and minimize contact with the other parent.

ACKNOWLEDGMENTS

I am grateful to Leslie Drozd, Joan Kelly, Kathy Kuehnle, and Patrick Parkinson for helpful comments on a draft of this chapter.

REFERENCES

Allen, S. M., & Hawkins, A. J. (1999). Maternal gatekeeping: Mothers' beliefs and behaviors that inhibit greater father involvement in family work. *Journal of Marriage and the Family, 61*, 199–212. doi: 10.2307/353894

Amato, P. R. (1993). Children's adjustment to divorce: Theories, hypotheses, and empirical support. *Journal of Marriage and the Family, 55*, 23–38. doi: 10.2307/352954

Amato, P. R. (2000). The consequences of divorce for adults and children. *Journal of Marriage and the Family, 62,* 1269–1287. doi: 10.1111/j. 1741–3737.2000. 01269. x

Amato, P. R., & Dorius, C. (2010). Fathers, children, and divorce. In M. E. Lamb (Ed.), *The role of the father in child development* (5th ed., pp. 177–200). Hoboken, NJ: John Wiley & Sons.

Amato, P. R., & Fowler, F. (2002). Parenting practices, child adjustment, and family diversity. *Journal of Marriage and the Family, 64,* 703–716. doi: 10.1111/j. 1741–3737.2002.00703. x

Amato, P. R., & Gilbreth, J. G. (1999). Non-resident fathers and children's well-being: A meta-analysis. *Journal of Marriage and the Family, 61,* 557–573. doi: 10.2307/353560

Amato, P. R., & Rezac, S. (1994). Contact with residential parents, inter-parental conflict, and children's behavior. *Journal of Family Issues, 15,* 191–207. doi: 10.1177/0192513X94015002003

Appel, A. E., & Holden, G. W. (1998). The co-occurrence of spouse and physical child abuse: A review and appraisal. *Journal of Family Psychology, 12,* 578–599. doi: 10.1037/0893–3200.12.4.578

Aquilino, W. S. (1996). The life course of children born to unmarried mothers: Childhood living arrangements and young adult outcomes. *Journal of Marriage and the Family, 58,* 293–310. doi: 10.2307/353496

Babcock, J. C., Costa, D. M., Green, C.E., & Eckhardt, C. I. (2004). What situations induce intimate partner violence? A reliability and validity study of the Proximal Antecedents to Violent Episodes (PAVE) Scale. *Journal of Family Psychology, 18,* 433–442. doi: 10.1037/0893–3200.18.3.433

Bauserman, R. (2002). Child adjustment in joint-custody versus sole-custody arrangements: A meta-analytic review. *Journal of Family Psychology, 16,* 91–102. doi: 10.1037/0893–3200.16.1.91 PMid: 11915414

Belsky, J., Youngblade, L., Rovine, M., & Volling, B. (1991). Patterns of marital change and parent–child interaction. *Journal of Marriage and the Family, 53,* 487–498. doi: 10.2307/352914

Booth, A., & Amato, P. R. (2001). Parental predivorce relations and offspring postdivorce well-being. *Journal of Marriage and the Family, 63,* 197–212. doi: 10.1111/j. 1741–3737.2001.00197. x

Bowlby, J. (1969). *Attachment and loss: Vol. 1. Attachment.* New York: Basic Books.

Bowlby, J. (1973). *Attachment and loss: Vol. 2. Separation: Anxiety and anger.* New York: Basic Books.

Braver, S. L., & O'Connell, E. (1998). *Divorced dads: Shattering the myths.* New York: Tarcher, Putnam.

Buchanan, C. M., Maccoby, E. E., & Dornbusch, S. M. (1991). Caught between parents: Adolescents' experience in divorced homes. *Child Development, 62,* 1008–1029. Doi: 10.2307/1121149 PMid: 1756653

Buehler, C., Krishnakumar, A., Stone, G., Anthony, C., Pemberton, S., Gerard, J. & Barber, B. (1998). Interparental conflict styles and youth problem behaviors: A two-sample replication study. *Journal of Marriage and the Family, 60,* 119–134. doi: 10.2307/353446

Carlson, M. J. (2006). Family structure, father involvement, and adolescent behavioral outcomes. *Journal of Marriage and the Family, 68,* 137–154. doi: 10.1111/j. 1741–3737.2006.00239. x

Carlson, M. J., & McLanahan, S. S. (2010). Fathers in fragile families. In M. E. Lamb (Ed.), *The role of the father in child development* (5th ed., pp. 241–269). Hoboken, NJ: John Wiley & Sons.

Cashmore, J., Parkinson, P., Weston, R., Patulny, R., Redmond, G., Qu, L., Baxter, J., Rajkovic, M., Sitek, T., & Katz, I. (2010). *Shared care parenting arrangements since the 2006 Family Law Reforms: Report to the Australian Government Attorney-General's Department.* Sydney, Australia: University of New South Wales Social Policy Research Centre.

Clarke-Stewart, A., & Brentano, C. (2006). *Divorce: Causes and consequences.* New Haven, CT: Yale University Press.

Clarke-Stewart, K. A., & Hayward, C. (1996). Advantages of father custody and contact for the psychological well-being of school-age children. *Journal of Applied Developmental Psychology, 17,* 239–270. doi: 10.1016/S0193-3973(96)90027-1

Clarke-Stewart, K. A., Vandell, D. L., McCartney, K., Owen, M. T., & Booth, C. (2000).Effects of parental separation and divorce on very young children. *Journal of Family Psychology, 13,* 304–326. doi: 10.1037/0893-3200.14.2.304 PMid: 10870296

Coley, R. L., & Medeiros, B. L. (2007). Reciprocal longitudinal relations between nonresident father involvement and adolescent delinquency. *Child Development, 78,* 132–147. doi: 10.1111/j. 1467–8624.2007.00989. x PMid: 17328697

Cowdery, R. S., & Knudson-Martin, C. (2005). The construction of motherhood: Tasks, relational connection, and gender equality. *Family Relations, 54,* 335–345. doi: 10.1111/j. 1741–3729.2005.00321. x

Cummings, E. M., & Davies, P. (1994). *Children and marital conflict: The impact of family dispute and resolution.* New York: Guilford Press.

Cummings, E. M., Goeke-Morey, M. C., & Raymond, J. (2004). Fathers in family context: Effects of marital quality and marital conflict. In M. E. Lamb (Ed.), *The role of the father in child development* (4th ed., pp. 196–221). Hoboken, NJ: Wiley.

Cummings, E. M., Merrilees, C. E., & George, M. W. (2010). Fathers, marriages, and families: Revisiting and updating the framework for fathering in family context. In M. E. Lamb (Ed.), *The role of the father in child development* (5th ed., pp. 154–176). Hoboken, NJ: Wiley.

Cummings, E. M., & O'Reilly, A. W. (1997). Fathers in family context: Effects of marital quality on child adjustment. In M. E. Lamb (Ed.), *The role of the father in child development* (3rd ed., pp. 49–65). New York: Wiley.

DeWolff, M. S., & van IJzendoorn, M. H. (1997). Sensitivity and attachment: A meta-analysis on parental antecedents of infant attachment. *Child Development, 68,* 571–591. doi: 10.2307/1132107 PMid: 9306636

Dunn, J., Cheng, H., O'Connor, T. G., & Bridges, L. (2004). Children's perspectives on their relationships with their nonresident fathers: Influences, outcomes and implications. *Journal of Child Psychology and Psychiatry, 45,* 553–566. doi: 10.1111/j. 1469–7610.2004.00245. x PMid: 15055374

Ebling, R., Pruett, K. D., & Pruett, M. K. (2009). "Get over it": Perspectives on divorce from young children. *Family Court Review, 47,* 665–681. doi: 10.1111/j. 1744–1617.2009. 012280. x

Emery, R. E. (1998). *Marriage, divorce, and children's adjustment* (2nd ed.). Thousand Oaks, CA: Sage.

Fabricius, W. V., & Hall, J. (2000). Young adults' perspectives on divorce: Living arrangements. *Family and Conciliation Courts Review, 38,* 446–461. doi: 10.1111/j. 174–1617.2000. tb00584. x

Fabricius, W. V., & Luecken, L. J. (2007). Postdivorce living arrangements, parent conflict, and long-term physical health correlates for children of divorce. *Journal of Family Psychology, 21,* 195–205.

Fagan, J., & Barnett, M. (2003). The relationship between maternal gatekeeping, paternal competence, mothers' attitudes about the father role, and father involvement. *Journal of Family Issues, 24,* 1020–1043. doi: 10.1177/0192513X03256397

Finley, G. E., & Schwartz, S. J. (2007). Father involvement and young adult outcomes: The differential contributions of divorce and gender. *Family Court Review, 45,* 573–587.

Friedman, M. (2004). The so-called high-conflict couple: A closer look. *American Journal of Family Therapy, 32,* 101–117. doi: 10.1080/01926180490424217

Greenberg, M. T., Cicchetti, D., & Cummings, E. M. (Eds.) (1990). *Attachment in the preschool years: Theory, research, and intervention.* Chicago, IL: University of Chicago Press.

Greif, G. (1997). *Out of touch: When parents and children lose contact after divorce.* New York: Oxford University Press.

Grych, J. H. (2005). Interparental conflict as a risk factor for child maladjustment: Implications for the development of prevention programs. *Family Court Review, 43,* 97–108. doi: 10.1111/j. 1744–1617.2005.00010. x

Heinicke, C. (1956). Some effects of separating two-year-old children from their parents: A comparative study. *Human Relations, 9,* 105–176. doi: 10.1177/ 001872675600900201

Heinicke, C., & Westheimer, I. (1966). *Brief separations.* New York: International Universities Press.

Hetherington, E. M. (Ed.) (1999). Should we stay together for the sake of the children? In E.M. Hetherington (Ed.), *Coping with divorce, single parenting, and remarriage* (pp. 93–116). Mahwah, NJ: Erlbaum.

Hetherington, E. M., Bridges, M., & Insabella, G. M. (1998). What matters? What does not? Five perspectives on the association between marital transitions and children's adjustment. *American Psychologist, 53,* 167–184. doi: 10.1037/0003–066X. 53.2.167 PMid: 9491746

Hetherington, E. M., & Kelly, J. (2002). *For better or for worse: Divorce reconsidered.* New York: Norton.

Holden, G. W., Geffner, R., & Jouriles E. W. (Eds.) (1998). *Children exposed to family violence.* Washington, DC: American Psychological Association.

Jaffe, P. G., Johnston, J. R., Crooks, C. V., & Bala, N. (2008). Custody disputes involving allegations of domestic violence: Toward a differentiated approach to parenting plans. *Family Court Review, 46,* 500–522.

Johnson, M. P. (2005). Apples and oranges in child custody disputes: Intimate terrorism vs. situational couple violence. *Journal of Child Custody, 2,* 43–52. doi: 10.1300/J190v02n04_03

Johnson, M. P., & Leone, J. M. (2005). The differential effects of intimate terrorism and situational couple violence: Findings from the National Violence Against Women survey. *Journal of Family Issues, 26,* 322–349. doi: 10.1177/0192513X04270345

Johnston, J. R. (1994). High-conflict divorce. *The Future of Children, 4,* 165–182. doi: 10.2307/1602483 PMid: 7922278

Johnston, J. R., & Campbell, L. (1993). A clinical typology of interparental violence in disputed-custody divorces. *American Journal of Orthopsychiatry, 63*, 190–199. doi: 10.1037/h0079425 PMid: 8484424

Johnston, J. R., Kline, M., & Tschann, J. (1989). Ongoing post-divorce conflict in families contesting custody: Effects on children of joint custody and frequent access. *American Journal of Orthopsychiatry, 59*, 576–592. doi: 10.1111/j. 1939-0025.1989. tb02748. x

Johnston, J. R., & Roseby, V. (1997). *In the name of the child: A developmental approach to understanding and helping children of conflict and violent divorce.* New York: Free Press.

Jouriles, E. N., McDonald, R., Norwood, W., Vincent, J. P., & Mahoney, A. (1996). Physical violence and other forms of interpersonal aggression: Links with children's behavior problems. *Journal of Family Psychology, 10*, 223–234. doi: 10.1037/0893-3200.10.2.223

Kaspiew, R., Gray, M., Weston, R., Moloney, L., Hand, K., & Qu, L. (2009). *Evaluation of the 2006 Family Law reforms.* Melbourne: Australian Institute of Family Studies.

Katz, L. F., & Gottman, J. M. (1993). Patterns of marital conflict predict children's internalizing and externalizing behaviors. *Developmental Psychology, 29*, 940–950. doi: 10.1037/0012-1649.29.6.940.

Kelly, J. B. (1982). Divorce: The adult experience. In B. Wolman & G. Stricker (Eds.), *Handbook of developmental psychology* (pp. 734–750). New Jersey: Prentice-Hall.

Kelly, J. B. (2000). Children's adjustment in conflicted marriage and divorce: A decade review of research. *Journal of the American Academy of Child Psychiatry, 39*, 963–973. doi: 10.1097/00004583-200008000-00007

Kelly, J. (2003). Parents with enduring child disputes: Multiple pathways to enduring disputes. *Journal of Family Studies (Australia), 9*, 37–50. doi: 10.5172/jfs. 9.1.37

Kelly, J. B. (2005). Developing beneficial parenting plan models for children following separation and divorce. *Journal of American Academy of Matrimonial Lawyers, 19*, 237–254.

Kelly, J. B. (2007). Children's living arrangements following separation and divorce: Insights from empirical and clinical research. *Family Process, 46*, 35–52. doi: 10.1111/j. 1545-5300.2006.00190. xPMid: 17375727

Kelly, J. B., & Emery, R. E. (2003). Children's adjustment following divorce: Risk and resilience perspectives. *Family Relations, 52*, 352–362. doi: 10.1111/j. 1741-3729.2003.00352. x

Kelly, J. B., & Johnson, M. P. (2008). Differentiation among types of domestic violence: Research updates and implications for interventions. *Family Court Review, 46*(3), 476–499. doi: 10.1111/j. 1744-1617.2008.00215. x

Kelly, J. B., & Lamb, M. E. (2000). Using child development research to make appropriate custody and access decisions for young children. *Family and Conciliation Courts Review, 38*, 297 311. doi: 10.1111/j. 174-1617.2000. tb00577. x

Kelly, J. B., & Lamb, M. E. (2003). Developmental issues in relocation cases involving young children: When, whether, and how? *Journal of Family Research, 17*, 193–205.

King, V., & Heard, H. E. (1999). Nonresident father visitation, parental conflict, and mother's satisfaction: What's best for child well-being? *Journal of Marriage and the Family, 61*, 385–396. doi: 10.2307/353756

Kline, M., Johnston, J., & Tschann, J. (1990). The long shadow of marital conflict: A model of children's postdivorce adjustment. *Journal of Marriage and the Family, 53,* 297–309. doi: 10.2307/352900

Lamb, M. E. (1975). Fathers: Forgotten contributors to child development. *Human Development, 18,* 245–266.

Lamb, M. E. (1997). The development of father infant relationships. In M. E. Lamb (Ed.), *The role of the father in child development* (3rd ed., pp. 104–120, 332–342). New York: Wiley.

Lamb, M. E. (1999). Non-custodial fathers and their impact on the children of divorce. In R. Thompson & P . R. Amato (Eds.), *The post divorce family: Research and policy issues* (pp. 105–125). Thousand Oaks, CA: Sage.

Lamb, M. E. (2002a). Infant-father attachments and their impact on child development. In C. S. Tamis-LeMonda & N. Cabrera (Eds.), *Handbook of father involvement: Multidisciplinary perspectives* (pp. 93–117). Mahwah, NJ: Erlbaum.

Lamb, M. E. (2002b). Placing children's interests first: Developmentally appropriate parenting plans. *Virginia Journal of Social Policy and the Law, 10,* 98–119.

Lamb, M. E., Bornstein, M. H., & Teti, D. M. (2002). *Development in infancy* (4th ed.). Mahwah, NJ: Erlbaum.

Lamb, M. E., & Kelly, J. B. (2001). Using the empirical literature to guide the development of parenting plans for young children: A rejoinder to Solomon and Biringen. *Family Courts Review, 39,* 365–371. doi: 10.1111/j. 174–1617.2001. tb00618. x

Lamb, M. E., & Kelly, J. B. (2009). Improving the quality of parent–child contact in separating families with infants and young children: Empirical research foundations. In R. M. Galatzer-Levy, L. Kraus, & J. Galatzer-Levy (Eds.), *The scientific basis of child custody decisions* (2nd ed., pp. 187–214). Hoboken, NJ: Wiley.

Lamb, M. E., & Lewis, C. (2010). The development and significance of father–child relationships in two-parent families. In M. E. Lamb (Ed.), *The role of the father in child development* (5th ed., pp. 94–153). Hoboken, NJ: John Wiley & Sons.

Lamb, M. E., Sternberg, K. J., & Thompson, R. A. (1997). The effects of divorce and custody arrangements on children's behavior, development, and adjustment. *Family and Conciliation Courts Review, 35,* 393–404. doi: 10.1111/j. 174–1617.1997. tb00482. x

Lamb, M. E., Thompson, R. A., Gardner, W. P., & Charnov, E. L. (1985). *Infant-mother attachment.* Hillsdale, NJ: Erlbaum.

Laumann-Billings, L., & Emery, R. E. (2000). Distress among young adults in divorced families. *Journal of Family Psychology, 14,* 671–687. doi: 10.1037/0893–3200. 14.4.671 PMDid: 11132488

Maccoby, E. E., & Mnookin, R. H. (1992). *Dividing the child: Social and legal dilemmas of custody.* Cambridge, MA: Harvard University Press.

Martinez, C. R. Jr., & Forgatch, M. S. (2002). Adjusting to change: Linking family structure transitions with parenting and boys' adjustment. *Journal of Family Psychology, 16,* 107–111.

McIntosh, J. (2009). Legislating for shared parenting: Exploring some underlying assumptions. *Family Court Review, 47,* 389–400. doi: 10.1111/j. 1744–1617.2009. 01263. x

McIntosh, J., & Chisholm, R. (2008). Cautionary notes on the shared care of children in conflicted parental separations. *Journal of Family Studies, 14,* 37–52. doi: 10.5172/jfs. 327.14.1.37

McIntosh, J. E., Long, C. M., & Wells, Y. (April, 2009). *Children beyond dispute. A four-year follow-up of outcomes from child focused and child inclusive post-separation dispute resolution*. Report to the Australian Government Attorney General's Department, Canberra.

McIntosh, J. E., Smyth, B., Wells, Y., & Long, C. (2010). *Parenting arrangements post-separation: Patterns and outcomes Part I: A longitudinal study of school-aged children in high conflict divorce*. North Carlton, Victoria: Family Transitions.

McIntosh, J. E., Smyth, B., & Keleher, M. (2010). *Parenting arrangements post-separation: Patterns and outcomes Part II: Relationships between overnight care patterns and psycho-emotional development in infants and young children*. North Carlton, Victoria: Family Transitions.

McLanahan, S. S. (1999). Father absence and the welfare of children. In E. M. Hetherington (Ed.), *Coping with divorce, single parenting, and remarriage* (pp. 117–146). Mahwah, NJ: Erlbaum.

McLanahan, S. S., & Sandefur, G. (1994). *Growing up with a single parent: What hurts, what helps*. Cambridge, MA: Harvard University Press.

McLanahan, S. S., & Teitler, J. (1999). The consequences of father absence. In M. E. Lamb (Ed.), *Parenting and child development in "nontraditional" families* (pp. 83–102). Mahwah, NJ: Erlbaum.

McNeal, C., & Amato, P. R. (1998). Parents' marital violence: Long-term consequences for children. *Journal of Family Issues, 19*, 123–139. doi: 10.1177/019251398019002001

Menning, C. L. (2006). Nonresident fathers' involvement and adolescents' smoking. *Journal of Health and Social Behavior, 47*, 32–46. doi: 10.1177/002214650604700103 PMid: 16583774

Nord, C., Brimhall, D., & West, J. (1997). *Fathers' involvement in their children's schools*. National Center for Education Statistics, U.S. Department of Education, Washington, D.C. 20208–25574.

Parke, R. (1996). *Fatherhood*. Cambridge, MA: Harvard University Press.

Parkinson, P. (2010). Changing policies regarding separated families in Australia. In M. E. Lamb (Ed.), *The role of the father in child development* (5th ed., pp. 578–614). Hoboken, NJ: Wiley.

Pleck, J. H. (1997). Paternal involvement: Levels, sources and consequences. In M. E. Lamb (Ed.), *The role of the father in child development* (3rd ed., pp. 66–103). New York: Wiley.

Pleck, J. H., & Masciadrelli, B. (2004). Paternal involvement: Levels, sources, and consequences. In M. E. Lamb (Ed.), *The role of the father in child development* (4th ed., pp. 222–271). New York: Wiley.

Pruett, M. K., Ebling, R., & Insabella, G. (2004). Critical aspects of parenting plans for young children. *Family Court Review, 42*, 39–59. doi: 10.1177/1531244504421004

Pruett, M. K., Insabella, G. M., & Gustafson, K. (2005). The Collaborative Divorce Project: A court-based intervention for separating parents with young children. *Family Courts Review, 43*, 38–51. doi: 10.1111/j. 1744–1617.2005.00006. x

Pruett, M. K., Williams, T. Y., Insabella, G., & Little, T. D. (2003). Family and legal indicators of child adjustment to divorce among families with young children. *Journal of Family Psychology, 17*, 169–180. doi: 10.1037/0893-3200.17.2.169 PMid: 12828014

Robertson, J., & Robertson, J. (1971). Young children in brief separation: A fresh look. *Psychoanalytic Study of the Child, 26*, 264–315. PMid: 5163230

Schwartz, S. J., & Finley, G. E. (2005). Divorce-related variables as predictors of young adults' retrospective fathering reports. *Journal of Divorce and Remarriage, 44*, 145–163. doi: 10.1300/J087v44n01_08

Simons, R. L., et al. (1996). *Understanding differences between divorced and intact families.* Thousand Oaks, CA: Sage Publications.

Simons, R. L., Lin, K. H., Gordon, L. C., Conger, R. D., & Lorenz, F. O. (1999). Explaining the higher incidence of adjustment problems among children of divorce compared with those in two-parent families. *Journal of Marriage and the Family, 61,* 1020–1033. doi: 10.2307/354021

Smith, A. B., & Gollop, M. M. (2001). What children think separating parents should know. *New Zealand Journal of Psychology, 30,* 23–31.

Smith, G., Coffino, B., Van Horn, P., & Lieberman, A. (2012). Attachment and child custody: The importance of available parents in K. Kuehnle & L. Drozd (Eds.), *Parenting plan evaluations: Applied research for the family court.* New York: Oxford University Press.

Smyth, B. M., & Chisholm, R. (2006). Exploring options for parental care of children following separation: A primer for family law specialists. *Australian Journal of Family Law, 20,* 193–218.

Solomon, J., & Biringen, Z. (2001). Another look at the developmental research: Commentary on Kelly and Lamb's "Using child development research to make appropriate custody and access decisions for young children." *Family Courts Review, 39,* 355–364. doi: 10.1111/j. 174–1617.2001. tb00617. x

Solomon, J., & George, C. (1999a). The development of attachment in separated and divorced families: Effects of overnight visitation, parent, and couple variables. *Attachment and Human Development, 1,* 2–33. doi: 10.1080/14616739900134011

Solomon, J., & George, C. (1999b). The effects of overnight visitation in divorced and separated families: A longitudinal follow-up. In J. Solomon & C. George (Eds.), *Attachment disorganization* (pp. 243–264). New York: Guilford.

Sternberg, K. J. (1997). Fathers, the missing parents in research on family violence. In M. E. Lamb (Ed.), *The role of the father in child development* (3rd ed., pp. 284–308, 392–397). New York: Wiley.

Sternberg, K. J., & Lamb, M. E. (1999). Violent families. In M. E. Lamb (Ed.), *Parenting and child development in "nontraditional" families* (pp. 305–325). Mahwah, NJ: Erlbaum.

Sternberg, K. J., Lamb, M. E., & Dawud-Noursi, S. (1998). Understanding domestic violence and its effects: Making sense of divergent reports and perspectives. In G. W. Holden, R. Geffner, & E. W. Jouriles (Eds.), *Children exposed to family violence* (pp. 121–156). Washington, DC: American Psychological Association.

Stets, J., & Straus, M. (1992). *The marriage license as a hitting license. Physical violence in American families.* New Brunswick, NJ: Transaction Publishers.

Sturge-Apple, M. L., Davies, P. T., & Cummings, E. M. (2006). Hostility and withdrawal in marital conflict: Effects on parental emotional unavailability and inconsistent discipline. *Journal of Family Psychology, 20,* 227–238. doi: 10.1037/0893–3200.20.2.227 PMid: 16756398

Thompson, R. A. (2006). Early sociopersonality development. In W. Damon, R. A. Lerner, & N. Eisenberg (Eds.), *Handbook of child development, Volume 3. Social, emotional, and personality development* (6th ed., pp. 24–98). Hoboken, NJ: Wiley.

Thompson, R. A., & Laible, D. J. (1999). Noncustodial parents. In M. E. Lamb (Ed.), *Parenting and child development in "nontraditional" families* (pp. 103–123). Mahwah, NJ: Erlbaum.

van IJzendoorn, M. H., & DeWolff, M. S. (1997). In search of the absent father—Meta- analyses of infant-father attachment: A rejoinder to our discussants. *Child Development, 68*, 604–609.

Vandewater, E., & Lansford, J. (1998). Influences of family structure and parental conflict on children's well-being. *Family Relations, 47*, 323–330. doi: 10.2307/585263

Wallerstein, J., & Kelly, J. (1980). *Surviving the breakup: How children and parents cope with divorce.* New York: Basic Books.

Warshak, R. A. (2000). Blanket restrictions: Overnight contact between parents and young children. *Family and Conciliation Courts Review, 38*, 422–445. doi: 10.1111/j. 174–1617.2000. tb00583. x

Woodward, L., Ferguson, D. M., & Belsky, J. (2000). Timing of parental separation and attachment to parents in adolescence: Results of a prospective study from birth to age 16. *Journal of Marriage and the Family, 62*, 162–174. doi: 10.1111/j. 1741–3737.2000.00162. x

Yarrow, L. J. (1963). Research in dimensions of early maternal care. *Merrill-Palmer Quarterly, 9*, 101–114.

Yarrow, L. J., & Goodwin, M. (1973). The immediate impact of separation: Reactions of infants to a change in mother figures. In L. J. Stone, H. T. Smith, & L. B. Murphy (Eds.), *The competent infant* (pp. 1032–1040). New York: Basic Books.

Children's Disorders that Require Specialized Parenting

## 9

Co-parenting Children with Chronic Medical Conditions

LAUREN MEDNICK AND GERALD P. KOOCHER ■

Understanding the best interests of children with chronic medical conditions in the context of custody decisions requires, in the first instance, a grasp of the nature of the illness and the relevant specialized parenting skills needed to optimize the child's well-being. This may include assessing parents' differential ability to deliver and adhere to medical treatments of varying complexity, an understanding of treatment alternatives, an evaluation of family dynamics (e.g., the impact of the medical condition on siblings), and formulating recommendations for safety and optimal quality of life for the child. The custody evaluator will almost certainly need to become familiar with the nature of the medical condition and the treatment regimen and engage in parental observation and home visits. In addition, the evaluator should become familiar with important case law decisions related to parental behaviors and decision-making in the context of their children's medical conditions.

In the context of this chapter, a chronic medical condition refers to an enduring state of medical illness that requires ongoing management and has the potential to interfere with normal development and long-term functioning. Due to differences in measurement, reporting, and ways of defining chronic medical conditions, estimating the number of children living with chronic medical conditions presents a significant challenge. A recent study conducted by Van Cleave and colleagues (Van Cleave, Gortmaker, & Perrin, 2010), however, suggests that the prevalence has increased over time, with the proportion of children diagnosed with a chronic health condition in 2006 ranging from 3% to 27%, depending on the type of condition. The increased prevalence likely results in part due to the improved medical care that children with several previously life-threatening medical conditions now receive and societal trends such as the growing epidemic of childhood obesity and type 2 diabetes (Han, Lawlor, & Kimm, 2010).

ASSOCIATED BURDEN AND DEMANDS ON THE PARENT

All parents confront the challenge of promoting normal, healthy development in their children. This challenge includes promoting physical growth, and also social, emotional, and intellectual development. Although all children depend on their parents, for children with chronic medical conditions the central role of their parents becomes even more important, and the challenges associated with parenting intensify. In addition to helping their child achieve typical developmental milestones, parents of children with chronic medical conditions often must take on responsibility for carrying out the majority of the child's daily treatment regimen, make important medical decisions, and solve medical challenges. Parents must assume the roles of care coordinator, expert in their child's medical condition, and systems advocate. In addition, childhood illness can interrupt or delay normal developmental trajectories, which may in turn further affect parenting behavior.

The additional needs of a child with a chronic medical condition can often seem overwhelming (e.g., Sullivan-Bolyai, Deatrick, Gruppuso, Tamborlane, & Grey, 2003); parents usually must rearrange their established lifestyle to accommodate the requirements imposed by the medical regimen and treatment demands. Parents interviewed as part of a qualitative examination of the demands of parenting a child with a chronic medical illness reported that their daily tasks for taking care of their child became quite time-consuming (Case-Smith, 2004). In fact, many parents reported needing to change their career plans. Another qualitative study (George, Vickers, Wilkes, & Barton, 2008) examined the impact on the employment of parents with children diagnosed with chronic medical conditions. Findings showed parents often needed to rearrange work schedules, use up their leave time, work difficult hours, change jobs, and ultimately sacrifice their careers to properly care for their chronically ill child.

NECESSARY SPECIALIZED PARENTING SKILLS

Parents of children with chronic medical conditions need to acquire the knowledge necessary to effectively manage their child's chronic medical condition, as they may have to make difficult decisions for their children on a regular basis. In addition, they need to have an accurate understanding of the tasks involved in managing their child's medical condition, acquire technical skills necessary to effectively execute these tasks, and maintain the ability to make adjustments to the tasks when problems arise. The ability to accurately follow a child's medical regimen is essential, as lack of a basic understanding of how to care for a chronically ill child can lead to preventable medical exacerbations. For example, research conducted with parents of children with asthma indicates that children with frequent asthma exacerbations often have parents with inadequate knowledge concerning appropriate use of asthma medications (Deis, Spiro, Jenkins, Buckles, & Arnold, 2010). Other serious adverse consequences for children due to poor management of chronic medical conditions include repeated hospitalizations, poor school attendance, disease-related complications, and death (e.g., Diabetes Control and Complication Trial [DCCT] Research Group, 1994; Dimatteo, 2004).

The specific demands on parents of caring for a child with a chronic medical condition vary tremendously depending on several factors, including intensity of the daily medical regimen, the stage of the illness, and the child's developmental abilities. However, regardless of these factors, the days of parents of chronically ill children often involve many caregiving tasks that demand high levels of planning and structure. Most parents need to maintain a consistent daily treatment regimen that can prove quite time-consuming and may include administering medications, performing medical interventions, following a special diet/administering feedings, and going to therapy and doctor appointments (Table 9.1 lists common medical conditions and the tasks frequently associated with their management).

Fiese and colleagues (Fiese, Wamboldt, & Anbar, 2005) examined the importance of developing consistent routines for medication taking. Their research indicates that compared to parents who reported poorer asthma medication routines, parents who reported better asthma medication routines had children with better medication adherence. The authors suggest that developing predictable routines for a child's medical regimen makes these tasks part of the typical daily schedule, thereby fostering good adherence by minimizing several of the problems often associated with adherence difficulties (e.g., forgetting, conflicts about when to take the medication).

In addition to remembering and enforcing adherence to prescribed daily medical regimen tasks, parents also often need to monitor their child for signs of symptom exacerbations, refill medication prescriptions, order medical equipment, make and attend frequent medical appointments, and create a home environment that decreases health risk (e.g., removing harmful allergens such as smoking and animals for children with asthma, keeping a clean home for children with compromised immune systems). Further, activities that take place outside of the home often require extensive planning and preparation so that the child can safely participate.

Finally, as the child's primary caretakers, parents of children with chronic medical conditions become critical members of their child's health care team and must effectively collaborate with potentially multiple doctors across multiple primary and specialty care settings. This role requires patience, organization, and effective communication skills.

Taken together, although the specific demands of caring for a child with a chronic medical condition vary depending on many factors unique to each child, all parents of chronically ill children must:

- Acquire necessary knowledge about their child's medical condition and treatment regimen
- Attain technical skills necessary for monitoring the child's health and executing the medical regimen
- Remember and enforce adherence to daily medical tasks
- Complete other less frequent tasks associated with the child's medical care (e.g., ordering medications, attending doctor appointments)
- Collaborate with the child's medical providers

PARENTAL INVOLVEMENT AND MONITORING

The importance of parental involvement has been illustrated in numerous studies that suggest that children and adolescents are more likely to adhere to their medical regimen when parents maintain some degree of involvement and oversight in their child's care (e.g., Anderson, Ho, Brackett, Finkelstein, & Laffel, 1997; Eckshtain, Ellis, Kolmodin, & Naar-King, 2010; Ellis et al., 2007). For example, in their study examining parental monitoring of adolescents with type 1 diabetes, Ellis and colleagues

Table 9.1 Common Medical Regimen Tasks by Illness

	Daily Oral Medications	Daily Inhaled Medications	Daily Injections/ Frequent IV Infusions	Dietary Concerns/ Restrictions	Physical Therapy	Frequent Doctor Visits	Other Common Tasks or Issues
Asthma		x				x	
Type 1 diabetes*			x	x		x	Multiple daily blood glucose checks
Cystic fibrosis	x	x		x	x	x	Some patients develop type 1 diabetes
Sickle cell disease	x					x	
HIV	x					x	
Inflammatory bowel disease (Crohn's and colitis)	x			x		x	
Hemophilia			x			x	
Spina bifida	x			x	x	x	Intermittent urinary catheterization
Kidney disease	x			x		x	Dialysis, salt and fluid restrictions
Juvenile arthritis	x		x		x	x	
Epilepsy	x					x	
Cardiovascular disease	x			x		x	Frequent invasive medical tests

Note. This table includes the tasks that the majority of children diagnosed with each illness must do; however, each child's specific medical regimen is unique and may include additional tasks not indicated in the table.

*Type 2 diabetes will require attention to diet and exercise and in serious pediatric cases may require oral medication and/or insulin injections with frequent blood tests.

(2007) found that high levels of parental supervision were directly related to higher regimen adherence and indirectly related to better metabolic control. Berg and colleagues (2008) also found that both parental acceptance of the illness and monitoring were associated with better adherence and metabolic control for adolescents with type 1 diabetes. Such research studies have even led to the American Diabetes Association including a statement about the importance of parental supervision and monitoring in their clinical practice guidelines for families with children with type 1 diabetes.

In summary, research has consistently found that:

- Parental involvement in the child's medical care is associated with better adherence, and in turn better health in the child.

PSYCHOLOGICAL IMPACT ON THE PARENT

The discovery that one's child has a chronic medical condition, and the additional responsibilities and concerns associated with caring for a child with a chronic illness, can become a significant source of distress. Research examining functioning of parents of children with chronic medical conditions consistently finds that these parents experience higher levels of parenting stress and depression compared to parents of healthy children (e.g., Bartlett et al., 2001; Driscoll et al., 2010; Pedersen, Parsons, & Dewey, 2004; Shalowitz et al., 2006).

In their examination of stress experienced by parents of children with various chronic medical conditions who receive nutrition via a feeding tube, Pedersen et al. (2004) reported that compared to parents of healthy children, these parents reported significantly higher levels of stress. Specifically, 42% of the 64 parents in the study scored above the 85th percentile on the Parenting Stress Index. In a more recent study, Lindstrom and colleagues (Lindstrom, Aman, & Norberg, 2010) examined the prevalence of burnout symptoms (physical and psychological fatigue) in the context of parenting a child with a chronic medical condition (i.e., type 1 diabetes and inflammatory bowel disease). Compared to parents of healthy children, significantly more parents of children with chronic medical conditions reported experiencing significant symptoms of burnout (36% compared 20% of parents of healthy children).

Parents who report symptoms of stress and burnout often also describe difficulty with sleep. In a review article examining research conducted on sleep disruptions in parents of children and adolescents with chronic illnesses, Meltzer and Moore (2008) found the prevalence of sleep disruptions to be from 15% to 86% in parents of children diagnosed with numerous medical conditions (see their article for a full review). The review indicated that potential causes of disrupted sleep in these parents included needing to provide medical care for the child during the night, monitoring the child's illness during the night, and stress related to the child's illness. Consequences included poor sleep quality, depression, and anxiety.

Single parent families may be at increased risk for experiencing distress due to having to carry the burden of caring for their child alone. In fact, in their comparison of married and single mothers of children with various chronic medical conditions, Mullins and colleagues (2010) found that single mothers reported experiencing more parenting stress than married mothers.

In addition to increased prevalence of stress, Bartlett and colleagues (2001) found that symptoms of depression were common among inner-city mothers of children with asthma. In a large community-based study, Shalowitz et al. (2006) found that compared to mothers of children without asthma, mothers of children with diagnosed or possible asthma reported more symptoms of depression and life stressors. Driscoll et al. (2010) evaluated the frequency of depressive symptoms in caregivers of children with type 1 diabetes or cystic diabetes. Results indicated that approximately 33% of caregivers reported clinically elevated rates of depressive symptoms. In addition, symptoms of depression in caregivers of both sets of children increased as a function of family stress.

Several articles have reviewed the stressors experienced by parents caring for a chronically ill child that may account for the increased rates of reported stress and depression in this population. Anderson and colleagues (Anderson, Loughlin, Goldberg, & Laffel, 2001) described the following six stressors that families with chronically ill children commonly face: (a) the constant burden of care on parents; (b) physical symptoms that require monitoring; (c) treatments that interfere with the developmental tasks in the parent–child relationship; (d) the child not being able to understand his or her symptoms or the intrusive treatments; (e) strong parental emotions developing from the chronic vigilance around the health of the child (e.g., grief, anxiety, stress, depression); and (f) difficulty in trusting other caregivers, leading to parental isolation.

Patterson and Garwick (1994) listed several additional stressors that affect parents of children with chronic medical conditions: (a) financial strain related to the parents' inability to work, expenses of home modification, nonreimbursable medical expenses, and fears of losing insurance coverage; (b) losses of family privacy and spontaneity; (c) personal stresses of caregiving, worries about the future, and experiences of constant pressure; and (d) problems with service providers and insurers.

In the context of divorce these problems become potentiated by the stresses of the divorce process itself. Marital breakups have emotional and economic costs even when no custody disputes take place. Divorces can force relocations, reduce housing quality, disrupt insurance coverage, and require changes in health care practitioners, and may cause burdens once shared by a couple to fall more heavily on a single parent. The resulting changes hardly ever benefit the ill child's quality of life over the short term.

In sum, research across many disease populations has indicated that compared to parents of healthy children, parents of children with chronic medical conditions:

- Experience multiple additional stressors
- Report experiencing an increased number of depressive symptoms

IMPACT OF PARENTAL STRESS AND EMOTIONAL DIFFICULTIES ON THE CHILD

In addition to potentially affecting the parents' own emotional well-being, the child's emotional and physical health status may also be affected by the impact of the illness on the parent. Importantly, if parents feel too overwhelmed and stressed with caring for their child, management of the illness may become compromised (Bartlett et al., 2001, 2004; Otsuki et al., 2010). For example, distressed caretakers may forget to follow aspects of a prescribed medical regimen, miss cues from their child about his or her health status, underestimate their ability to handle their child's medical needs, or demonstrate impaired problem-solving skills. Such behaviors can directly and indirectly contribute to poor adherence and disease management, which can lead to poor health outcomes in their children.

Several studies have demonstrated a strong relationship between caregiver life stressors/depression and asthma morbidity in children (Bartlett et al., 2001, 2004; Otsuki et al., 2010; Shalowitz, Berry, Quinn, & Wolf, 2001). In a large prospective study that examined the relationship between asthma morbidity in inner-city African American children and maternal depressive symptoms, Otsuki and colleagues (2010) found that maternal depressive symptoms predicted child asthma symptoms. Further, their results indicated that the relationship was not bidirectional, such that asthma symptoms did not predict maternal depressive symptoms. In another study conducted with mothers of inner-city children with asthma, Bartlett et al. (2004) found that mothers indicating high depressive symptoms reported significantly more problems with their child using inhalers properly and forgetting to take their asthma medication. These mothers also made significantly more use of the emergency department for their children's medical care (Bartlett et al., 2001).

Similar findings occur among other illness groups. For example, in their examination of several parenting variables and child self-care behaviors with children diagnosed with type 1 diabetes, asthma, and cystic fibrosis, Bourdeau and colleagues (Bourdeau, Mullins, Carpentier, Colletti, & Wolfe-Christensen, 2007) found that higher levels of parenting stress linked with lower parent ratings of their child's self-care behaviors. Further, studies have indicated that parental stress and depression are associated with worse glycemic control in children with type 1 diabetes (Auslander, Bubb, Rogge, & Santiago, 1993; Driscoll et al., 2010). In their study of families of children taking immunosuppressant medication after kidney transplant, Gerson and colleagues (Gerson, Furth, Neu, & Fivush, 2004) found that increased parental stress was significantly associated with poorer medication adherence.

Other variables such as high parental warmth link to better medical adherence in young children with type 1 diabetes (Davis et al., 2001). This same study found that high parental restrictiveness was associated with poorer metabolic control.

Poor parental functioning also links to psychological adjustment problems in children with chronic medical conditions, which can in turn lead to difficulties with disease management. For example, in their study examining parenting variables associated with poor health outcomes in children and adolescents with type 1 diabetes, Eckshtain and colleagues (2010) found that parental depressive symptoms were significantly related to lower parental warmth towards their children and adolescents. In turn, lower warmth was related to increased report of child and adolescent depressive symptoms, which were significantly associated with poorer metabolic control. In another study examining the associations between parent functioning (i.e., stress, psychosocial adjustment, marital satisfaction) and child adjustment in families of children with spina bifida, Friedman and colleagues (Friedman, Holmbeck, Jandasek, Zuckerman, & Abad, 2004) found that all three of the parental functioning variables predicted child adjustment both concurrently and prospectively. Importantly, analyses examining the bidirectional associations between parent functioning and child adjustment indicated that the direction of effect flowed from parent to child and not child to parent.

Taken together, the findings from these studies suggest that if parents of children and adolescents with chronic medical conditions experience increased stress and depressive symptoms:

- Effective management of the illness may be compromised.
- The child's emotional health may be affected, which in turn can affect physical health.

FAMILY ENVIRONMENT MOST CONDUCIVE TO HEALTHY FUNCTIONING OF CHILDREN

The child's environment has an immense influence on the child's adaptation to his or her disease (e.g., Amer, 1999). In fact, in their study examining the psychological correlates of child adjustment to a chronic illness, Lavigne and Faier-Routman (1993) found family variables to be more strongly correlated than disease factors or socioeconomic status. In a review of research examining the relationship between parent and family functioning and psychological adjustment of children with chronic medical conditions, Drotar (1997) concluded that positive psychological adjustment in children consistently links with more adaptive family relationships (e.g., supportive family relationships, less conflict, family cohesion) and parental psychological adjustment (e.g., less maternal psychological distress), whereas less adaptive family relationships consistently predicted problematic adjustment. Further, research has indicated that poor family functioning can contribute to adverse medical outcomes. For example, Barakat and colleagues (2007) found that families of children with sickle cell disease with poor reports of family functioning had the highest disease severity and health care utilization.

Many studies have examined how specific family variables affect the emotional and physical health in children with chronic medical conditions. For example, research has consistently found a relationship between family conflict and difficulties adhering to a medical regimen (e.g., Hauser et al., 1990; Hentinen & Kyngas, 1998; Lewandowski & Drotar, 2007; Stepansky, Roache, Holmbeck, & Schultz, 2010). In a study with families of adolescents with type 1 diabetes, increased levels of mother–adolescent conflict seemed related to poorer treatment adherence (Lewandowski & Drotar, 2007). In another study examining parental adaptation and coping with caring for their child with a chronic medical condition, results indicate that compared to families reporting fewer conflicts, families experiencing more conflicts had more difficulty with treatment and care of their child (Hentinen & Kyngas, 1998).

In addition to the negative impact of family conflict, research indicates that family cohesion improves the child's health status and treatment adherence (e.g., Cohen, Lumley, Naar-King, Partridge, & Cakan, 2004; Soliday, Kool, & Lande, 2001), likely by offering support and supervision to the child and/or establishing family routines that incorporate disease management tasks. For example, as part of a prospective study conducted with 116 children diagnosed with type 1 diabetes and their parents, Cohen et al. (2004) examined how family functioning predicts medical adherence and glycemic control. Multivariate analyses indicated that family cohesion predicted both better adherence and better glycemic control. In another study using a longitudinal design, Stepansky and colleagues (2010) examined the relationship between medical adherence and family functioning in young adolescents diagnosed with spina bifida. Results indicated that family cohesion correlated positively and family conflict correlated negatively with medical adherence. In addition, family conflict over medical issues was linked to a decrease in medical adherence over time. Soliday and colleagues (2001) examined the effects of the family environment on children with kidney disease and found that whereas higher family conflict predicted more behavioral difficulties and a higher number of prescribed medications, higher family cohesion predicted fewer hospitalizations.

Research has examined other family environment variables and their impact on the child with a chronic medical condition (e.g., Kell, Kliewer, Erickson, & Ohene-Frempong, 1998; LaGreca et al., 1995; Wood et al., 2007). LaGreca et al. (1995) found that adolescent-reported family support was associated with better treatment adherence. In a large study examining the contribution of emotional triggers to asthma severity, Wood and colleagues (2007) found that negative family emotional climate was associated with depressive symptoms in the child, which in turn were associated both directly and indirectly (through emotional triggering) with disease severity. In several studies conducted with adolescents with sickle cell disease, higher family competence (i.e., the ability of the family to manage stressors) was associated with fewer behavioral and emotional problems in the adolescents (Kell et al., 1998) and family problem-solving ability was related to greater adherence (Barakat, Smith-Whitley, & Ohene-Frempong, 2002).

In sum, the literature examining the impact of specific family variables on emotional and physical health in children with chronic medical conditions suggests:

- Children with more positive, structured, cohesive, and supportive family environments better adhere to their medical regimens and have better medical outcomes.
- Lack of family cohesion and increased family conflict may result in a family environment that is more likely to lead to poorer health outcomes.

IMPACT OF A CHRONIC MEDICAL CONDITION ON MARRIAGE AND SIBLINGS

A chronic medical condition has the potential to profoundly disrupt many aspects of family functioning. Quittner and colleagues (1998) examined the impact of illness demands on marital satisfaction, intimacy, and daily mood in 33 couples with a child with cystic fibrosis. The study also included a comparison group of 33 parents of age-matched healthy children. Results indicate that compared to parents of healthy children, parents of children with cystic fibrosis reported greater marital role strain, higher levels of conflict over childrearing issues, more personal time spent in caring for the child, and fewer positive spousal interactions. Couples caring for a child with cystic fibrosis also had less time for social and recreational activities than parents of healthy children.

Healthy siblings also feel the effects of having a brother or sister with a chronic medical condition. In a meta-analysis examining siblings of children with chronic illness, Sharpe and Rossiter (2002) found a significant negative effect for having a sibling with a chronic medical illness. In particular, they reported that chronic medical conditions that involve daily treatment regimens had a more negative impact on the sibling than conditions in which the child needed less day-to-day management.

Similar to the impact on the child with a chronic medical condition, parental functioning can also affect the healthy sibling. In their study examining sibling adjustment to type 1 diabetes, Jackson, Richer, and Edge (2008) found that higher levels of parent stress were linked with poorer sibling adjustment. Additional research examining other variables affecting siblings of children with chronic medical conditions has indicated that family cohesion and feelings of social support are associated with healthy siblings' behavioral functioning (Williams et al., 2002).

PROTECTIVE ROLE OF SOCIAL SUPPORT

Social support has been found to play an important role in the psychological functioning of children and their families (e.g., Hamlett, Pellegrini, & Katz, 1992; Lewandowski & Drotar, 2007; Shalowitz et al., 2006). Hamlett and colleagues (1992) interviewed mothers of children diagnosed with asthma or diabetes and healthy controls and found that maternal social support was one of the variables significantly related to the psychological adjustment of the child. In fact, in their community-based study of mothers of children with asthma, the perception of social support explained a larger proportion of the variation of depressive symptoms than demographic or medical variables (Shalowitz et al., 2006).

Social support in the form of support between spouses also has been examined (Lewandowski & Drotar, 2007). Higher levels of mother-reported spousal support were associated with less mother–adolescent conflict and better adherence to treatment in adolescents with type 1 diabetes (Lewandowski & Drotar, 2007). This suggests that in addition to improving the well-being of the parent, spousal support can affect the quality of the parent–adolescent relationship and adherence.

As suggested by Canam (1993), it appears that when parents form a strong support system, they adapt better to the demands of a child's illness. It is probable that with increased social support, caregivers feel less distress, as they are able to "share the burden" and also may receive increased tangible support (e.g., practical help with taking care of the child, taking the healthy sibling to activities, cooking meals).

SPECIAL CONSIDERATION IN THE EVALUATION

Child custody evaluators will typically interview the parties, the children, and relevant collateral sources as well as review substantial documentation. Many will also conduct home visits and observe parent–child interactions as the situation warrants. When a child has a chronic illness the evaluator will need to consider a number of additional factors relevant to parenting skill, safety, and the best

Table 9.2 Parenting Ability Checklist

- Interview with the Parent
  - Does the parent have a basic understanding of the child's medical condition and the consequences of poor adherence?
  - Can the parent describe the child's daily medical regimen?
  - Does the parent report following a consistent medical management routine?
  - Does the parent receive any help/assistance in caring for the child?
  - If the child takes responsibility for following parts of his or her medical regimen, does the parent regularly check in with and monitor the child's adherence?
  - Does the parent report seeking practical and emotional help for himself or herself when necessary?
  - Does the parent have access to necessary medical care where he or she lives?

- Home Visit
  - Does the parent have a method for organizing the child's medical equipment/medication?
  - Is the home environment free from anything harmful to the child (e.g., secondhand smoke if the child has asthma)?

- Physician Interview(s)
  - Does the parent make and keep necessary medical appointments?
  - Does the parent seek advice and follow recommendations?
  - Does the parent make contact with medical personnel when necessary?
  - Does it seem as though the child is following his or her medical regimen?

---

interests of the child. Table 9.2 summarizes the key points of concern in checklist fashion.

The evaluator will want to assess the parents' understanding of the disease and knowledge of the recommended medical regimen. One can function as a competent and loving parent but still lack the capacity to grasp and implement aspects of care necessary to ensure the well-being of a medically complex child. As part of the process, the evaluator should also consider the stress level of the caregivers and what access they may have to social support, backup, or respite care services, if needed. The evaluator should take note of the living situation and family environment with attention to family and household organization at a level necessary to provide good care to the child.

Contact with the child's treating physician and other care providers (e.g., physical therapist, psychotherapist, or visiting nurse) can also provide important information regarding the parent's ability to deliver appropriate care and monitor the child's condition. With some conditions, parent training to manage the child's condition might take place on an inpatient unit, in a clinic setting, or at home with the assistance of a visiting nurse. Evaluators unfamiliar with particular medical conditions will need to rely on treating clinicians to guide them in making such assessments.

Table 9.3 gives examples of relevant studies relating outcomes to caregiver variables.

WHAT DO ADJUDICATED CASES TEACH US?

Case law decisions can offer some guidance as to how courts will respond to parental actions in withholding treatment or deviating from recommended treatment based

Table 9.3 EXAMPLES OF RELEVANT STUDIES RELATING OUTCOMES TO CAREGIVER VARIABLES

Source	Data Source/Participants	Procedure
Deis et al., 2010	229 parents of children (ages 2–18 years old) diagnosed with asthma	Parents were given an asthma knowledge questionnaire during an emergency room visit for their child.
Eckshtain et al., 2010	61 parents and children (ages 10–17 years old) diagnosed with type 1 diabetes	Parents and children completed self-report questionnaires measuring parenting variables and depressive symptoms. Metabolic control was assessed using HbA1c assays.
Ellis et al., 2007	99 adolescents (ages 12–18 years old) diagnosed with type 1 diabetes and their primary caregivers	Adolescents and their primary caregivers completed several questionnaires concerning diabetes care and family functioning.
Fiese et al., 2005	133 families with children (ages 5–18 years old) diagnosed with asthma	Parents and children independently completed several questionnaires concerning the child's medical regimen. Electronic monitoring and self-report were used to measure adherence.
Friedman et al., 2004	68 families of children diagnosed with spina bifida and 68 healthy control families (ages 8–9 years old at baseline)	As part of a larger longitudinal study, this manuscript reports on baseline and 2-year follow-up data. At each time point the parents and children completed a packet of several self-report questionnaires. An observational measure examined adaptive behavior of the child. Teacher report of behavior was also collected.

Analysis and Results	Weaknesses	Strengths
Descriptive statistics found that parents who bring their child to the emergency department for asthma exacerbations often have an inadequate understanding of daily medication use. Multivariable logistic regression indicated that proper use of these medications was significantly associated with parent education level beyond high school.	This study was limited to parents of children diagnosed with asthma.	This study indicates that proper understanding of how to follow a child's daily medical regimen is an essential part of preventing medical exacerbations. It is likely that similar results would be found with other chronic medical populations.
Results from path analyses suggest that parental depressive symptoms had a significant direct effect on child depressive symptoms through parental involvement. In addition, child depressive symptoms were related to metabolic control.	This study was limited to parents and children diagnosed with type 1 diabetes.	This study illustrates that the presence of parental depressive symptoms influences both child depression and metabolic control through problematic parenting practices. Research conducted with other chronic medical populations has found similar results.
Path analysis revealed that diabetes-specific monitoring was associated with regimen adherence based on both parent and adolescent report. Parental support was also associated with regimen adherence in the bivariate model. However, when parental monitoring was considered simultaneously in the multivariate model, support was no longer significant. Moderate support was found for parental support moderating the relationship between monitoring and adherence.	This study was limited to primary caretakers and adolescents diagnosed with type 1 diabetes.	Parental monitoring and parental support can affect medical regimen adherence, which is linked to medical outcome. Comparable results have been found in studies examining similar constructs with other chronic medical populations.
Correlational analyses found that parents who reported better medication routines had children with better medication adherence.	This study is limited to families with children diagnosed with asthma.	The results from this study illustrate the importance of developing consistent routines for the child's medical regimen, as this can affect adherence. Research conducted with other chronic medical populations is likely to find similar associations.
A series of hierarchical regression analyses were conducted to determine if parent functioning variables were associated both concurrently and prospectively with change in the child's adjustment over time. Results indicate that parenting stress, psychosocial adjustment, and marital satisfaction all predicted child adjustment outcomes. In addition, the direction of the association was from parent to child. These findings were true for both groups.	This study was limited to families with children diagnosed with spina bifida.	The data give strong support for the impact that parental functioning can have on child adjustment both in children with chronic medical conditions and healthy children. Studies with other chronic medical populations have found similar relationships and have further indicated that poor child adjustment is associated with poor medical outcomes.

(Continued)

Table 9.3 EXAMPLES OF RELEVANT STUDIES RELATING OUTCOMES TO CAREGIVER
VARIABLES   (*Continued*)

Source	Data Source/Participants	Procedure
Lewandowski & Drotar, 2007	51 mothers and adolescents (13–18 years old) diagnosed with type 1 diabetes	Mothers and adolescents completed self-report measures of social support, diabetes-related conflict, and diabetes care.
Osterberg & Blaschke, 2005	Review article	Authors analyzed 127 peer-reviewed manuscripts and summarized factors related to adherence to medication in drug therapy.
Otsuki et al., 2010	262 African American mothers of inner-city children (ages 2–12 years old) diagnosed with asthma	Two phone interviews assessing asthma morbidity and maternal depressive symptoms were conducted 6 months apart.
Stepansky et al., 2010	70 families of children (ages 8–9 years old at the start of the study) diagnosed with spina bifida	As part of a 4-year longitudinal study, parents and children diagnosed with spina bifida participated in three interviews, which included completing multiple questionnaires concerning family functioning and medical adherence. Family functioning was also examined through observational measures. Teachers and health professionals completed measures of the child's adherence.

Analysis and Results	Weaknesses	Strengths
Results from regression analyses indicate that increased conflict was associated with poorer treatment adherence, which predicted glycemic control. In addition, higher levels of mother-reported spousal support were associated with less conflict and greater adherence to the medical regimen.	The study was limited to mothers and adolescents diagnosed with type 1 diabetes.	Results from this study provide further evidence for the detrimental effect of family conflict. They also suggest that in addition to enhancing the well-being of the mothers, spousal support can affect the maternal–adolescent relationship and adherence. It is probable that these results could be duplicated with other chronic medical populations.
The ability of physicians to recognize nonadherence is poor, and interventions to improve adherence have had mixed results. Factors that reduce adherence include presence of psychopathology, particularly depression and substance abuse; cognitive impairment; lack of belief in treatment benefit; lack of insight into the illness; poor provider–parent relationships; missed appointments; and barriers to care or medication. Factors that enhance adherence include ample social support, empowering self-management; removing financial barriers; increasing support; and perceived ability to effect disease change/control. No statistical analysis; this was a review article.	The paper focused chiefly on adult adherence behaviors with attention to medication regimens.	The data should generalize to some degree in predicting parental ability to consistently follow medical regimens prescribed for the children. Factors listed may provide a basis for predicting optimal adherence by parents or provide bases for inquiring in detail regarding adherence of those parents displaying risk factors.
Cross-lagged structural path analysis found that maternal depressive symptoms prospectively predicted child asthma symptoms, whereas child asthma symptoms did not predict maternal depressive symptoms.	The study was limited to mothers of African American inner-city children diagnosed with asthma.	The data from this study indicate that maternal depressive symptoms are more likely to influence asthma symptoms than the child's asthma is to influence the parent's mental health over time. Comparable findings have resulted from research examining similar constructs with other chronic medical populations.
Using cross-sectional correlational analyses, family cohesion was correlated positively with medical adherence, whereas family conflict was negatively correlated with medical adherence. Longitudinal regression analyses suggested that over time, family conflict regarding medical issues was related to a decrease in medical adherence, with conflict at time 2 being associated with a decrease in adherence at time 2 and 3.	The study was limited to families with children diagnosed with spina bifida.	The data from this longitudinal study strongly indicate that family functioning variables are significantly associated with medical adherence. Studies conducted with other chronic medical populations have found similar associations.

on personal preferences, religious beliefs, or other practices that may bear on a child's medical condition.

Prince v. Massachusetts

With respect to parental decision-making authority in the context of children's well-being, *Prince v. Massachusetts* (1944) remains an oft-cited classic. In that case the Supreme Court of the United States held that the government has broad authority to regulate the treatment of children. In particular, the court held that parents do have absolute authority and that the courts may restrict some parental preferences in the interest of a child's welfare. Writing for the majority in a 5–4 opinion, Justice Rutledge wrote, "Parents may be free to become martyrs themselves. But it does not follow they are free, in identical circumstances, to make martyrs of their children before they have reached the age of full and legal discretion when they can make that choice for themselves" (Rutledge, 1943).

Although not arising out of a divorce context, this widely cited precedent guides courts to favor decisions that promote the child's survival and well-being over parental religious beliefs that vary from medical advice. Key variables will include the medical certainty of various outcomes, as well as the child's age and ability to participate in the decision.

Phillip Becker

The case of Phillip Becker focused directly on personal parental preferences related to a child's medical care. Born with Down syndrome, significant developmental delay, and ventricular septal defect (VSD), or a hole in the wall between the ventricles of the heart, Phillip spent most of his life in residential care apart from his parents and siblings. Although he did not live with his parents, they reported considering themselves responsible for him and viewing him as part their family. As he approached adolescence, Phillip's need for corrective surgery intensified, but his parents refused permission for the procedure, indicating that they did not want Phillip to outlive them. They expressed the belief that as an older developmentally delayed person with Down syndrome he would not receive good geriatric care after they died. They also reportedly did not want him to become a burden on their other children. When asked who would be better off if Phillip were dead, Mr. Becker replied: "I think it would be best for everyone, including Phillip and the survivors" (Annas, 2002)

On March 31, 1980, the U.S. Supreme Court refused to hear an appeal on behalf of Phillip, noting that his parents, "whose rights had not been terminated," had refused permission. In so doing, the justices appeared to signal a potential next step to Philip's advocates, who successfully sought to have the rights of his biological parents terminated following a 12-day trial. Successful heart surgery followed a 6-year legal battle on Sept. 28, 1983 (In re Guardianship of Phillip B., 1983; In re Phillip B., 1980; Lindsey, 1983).

In this instance the courts placed the survival and quality-of-life rights of the child above the parental rights of an otherwise competent set of biological parents. This precedent could clearly come into play in custody disputes wherein one parent's preference to withhold treatment might contribute to the death or incapacity of the child.

In re E.G.

In re E.G. (1989), the Supreme Court of Illinois addressed the case of a 17-year-old girl who refused blood transfusions for the treatment of acute nonlymphatic leukemia, honoring the tenets of her Jehovah's Witness faith. Her mother, also adhering to the Jehovah's Witness faith, refused to consent to the blood transfusions on behalf of her daughter, though she did consent to all other treatment (Salyer, 1991). The state of Illinois brought charges of neglect against E.G.'s mother, and a trial court appointed temporary guardianship of E.G. to Jane McAtte, the associate general counsel for the University of Chicago Hospital, to authorize the blood transfusions.

The Supreme Court of Illinois reversed the trial court's ruling, noting that a "mature minor may exercise a common law right to consent to or refuse medical treatment, where a trial judge determines that there is clear and convincing evidence that the minor is 'mature' and that such right overrides the four qualified state interests" (Salyer, 1991, p. 421). The four qualified interests of the state are (a) the preservation of life; (b) protecting the interests of third parties; (c) prevention of suicide; and (d) maintaining the ethical integrity of the medical professions.

This case provides examples of how courts might respond in cases where older children with medical conditions have the ability to express preferences in medical care decisions. In custody cases most jurisdictions would require that the judge hear the "voice of the child" with respect to custody decisions in general.

In re Nikolas (1998)

The Supreme Judicial Court of Maine upheld a lower court decision allowing a mother who had been charged with parental neglect to retain custody of her HIV-positive 4-year-old son. She had delayed a recommended but highly aggressive and experimental antiviral drug treatment. Both of the child's divorced parents were HIV-positive, and his older sister had died at age 4 from AIDS complications after receiving the drug therapy. The court found insufficient proof of likely benefit and lack of significant harm from the drug regimen. Furthermore, the court was unable to determine the likely effects of treatment on the child. Consequently, the court decided that the mother's decision to delay new and experimental treatment was not serious parental neglect.

This circumstance is an example of the court considering the parent's decision in the context of likely medical outcome. Since that decision in 1998 significant advances in medical care for people with HIV infections might cause both the court and parents to think differently about treatment decisions. Still, the message that likely outcomes will weigh heavily in judicial decisions remains clear.

Bad Health Habits: The Case of Secondhand Smoke

Courts often consider parental smoking as a factor in custody determinations, particularly when a child has a pulmonary or other condition that may become exacerbated by so-called secondhand smoke (e.g., *Daniel v. Daniel*, 1998; *Gilbert v. Gilbert*, 1996; *Lizzio v. Lizzio*, 1994; *Unger v. Unger*, 1994). Some of these cases involve initial custody determinations, but others have addressed a "change of circum-stances" when a parent failed to curtail smoking or cohabited with a new partner who smoked. We know of such cases only because they reached appellate courts and thus became citable. It seems reasonable to assume that judges often take such situa-tions into account in cases that never progress to the appellate level. We can envision other habit-related problems that courts might consider in determining custody and visitation, such as a parent who could not help a child with type 2 diabetes improve his or her diet and exercise regimens, but to date a case has not been found on record.

SUMMARY

Children with chronic medical conditions are a heterogeneous group with many dif-ferent needs and concerns. The majority of research examining which environments are most conducive to promoting healthy physical and emotional functioning in these children is limited by including only one or two illness groups. Therefore, it is essential to use caution when drawing conclusions about best practices across the entire population of children with chronic medical conditions. However, it is critical to consider many of the factors described within this chapter as potentially having a positive or negative impact on the health of the chronically ill child. Further, when considering the best environment for the child with a chronic medical condition, the medical providers who have a history of working with the family will offer invaluable information about the child's needs, the parents' history of meeting these needs, and their ability to meet the needs in the future.

GUIDELINES: CONSIDERATIONS AND CAUTIONS

- Ascertain that the parents have acquired the knowledge necessary to effectively manage their child's chronic medical condition.
- Confirm parental supervision and monitoring of the child's daily medical regimen.
- Determine whether parents have consistently participated in their child's medical office visits.
- Evaluate parents' ability to cope with the stresses of managing their child's illness.
- Assess the degree to which parental behaviors or the home environment may exacerbate the child's condition.
- When the child is a minor, parents' religious beliefs or personal preferences may not constitute a legal basis for withholding treatment that has proved effective in prolonging or preserving the child's life.

REFERENCES

Amer, K. S. (1999). Children's adaptation to insulin dependent diabetes mellitus: A critical review of the literature. *Pediatric Nursing, 25*, 627–641. Retrieved from http://www.pediatricnursing.net/

Annas, G. J. (2002). Denying the rights of the retarded: the Phillip Becker case. In P. A. Pecorino (Ed.), *Perspectives on death and dying* (5th ed.). Online textbook, downloaded Feb. 25, 2011, at http://www2.sunysuffolk.edu/pecorip/scccweb/ etexts/deathanddying_text/Annas_BeckerI.htm

Anderson, B., Ho, J., Brackett, J., Finkelstein, D., & Laffel, L. (1997). Parental involvement in diabetes management tasks: Relationships to blood glucose monitoring adherence and metabolic control in young adolescents with insulin-dependent diabetes mellitus. *Journal of Pediatrics, 130,* 257–265. doi:10.1016/S0022-3476(97)70352-4

Anderson, B., Loughlin, C., Goldberg, E., & Laffel, L. (2001). Comprehensive, family-focused outpatient care for very young children living with chronic disease: Lessons from a program in pediatric diabetes. *Children's Services: Social Policy, Research, and Practice, 4,* 235–250. doi:10.1207/S15326918CS0404_06

Auslander, W. F., Bubb, J., Rogge, M., & Santiago, J. V. (1993). Family stress and resources: Potential areas of intervention in children recently diagnosed with diabetes. *Health & Social Work, 18,* 101–113. Retrieved from http://www.naswpress.org/publications/journals/hsw.html

Barakat, L. P., Patterson, C. A., Weinberger, B. S., Simon, K., Gonzalez, E. R., & Dampier, C. (2007). A prospective study of the role of coping and family functioning in health outcomes for adolescents with sickle cell disease. *Journal of Pediatric Hematology and Oncology, 29,* 752–760. doi:10.1097/MPH.0b013e318157fdac

Barakat, L.P., Smith-Whitley, K., & Ohene-Frempong, K. (2002). Treatment adherence in children with sickle cell disease: Disease-related risk and psychosocial resistance factors. *Journal of Clinical Psychology in Medical Settings, 9,* 201–209. doi:10.1023/A:1016047210623

Bartlett, S. J., Kolodner, K., Butz, A. M., Eggleston, P., Malveaux, F. J., & Rand, C. S. (2001). Maternal depressive symptoms and emergency department use among inner-city children with asthma. *Archives of Pediatric and Adolescent Medicine, 155,* 347–353. Retrieved from http://archpedi.ama-assn.org/

Bartlett, S. J., Krishnan, J. A., Riekert, K. A., Butz, A. M., Malveaux, F. J., & Rand, C. S. (2004). Maternal depressive symptoms and adherence to therapy in inner-city children with asthma. *Pediatrics, 113,* 229–237. doi:10.1542/peds.113.2.229

Berg, C. A., Butler, J. M., Osborn, P., King, G., Palmer, D. L., Butner, J., & Wiebe, D. J. (2008). Role of parental monitoring in understanding the benefits of parental acceptance on adolescent adherence and metabolic control of type 1 diabetes. *Diabetes Care, 31,* 678–683. doi:10.2337/dc07-1678

Bourdeau, T. L., Mullins, L. L., Carpentier, M. Y., Colletti, C. J. M., & Wolfe-Christensen, C. (2007). An examination of parenting variables and child self-care behavior across disease group. *Journal of Developmental Disabilities, 19,* 125–134. doi:10.1007/s10882-007-9037-9

Canam, C. (1993). Common adaptive tasks facing parents of children with chronic conditions. *Journal of Advanced Nursing, 18,* 46–53. doi:10.1046/j.1365-2648.1993.18010046.x

Case-Smith, J. (2004). Parents of children with medical conditions and developmental disabilities. *American Journal of Occupational Therapy, 58,* 551–560. doi:10.5014/ajot.58.5.551

Cohen, D. M., Lumley, M. A., Naar-King, S., Partridge, T., & Cakan, N. (2004). Child behavior problems and family functioning as predictors of adherence and glycemic control in economically disadvantaged children with type 1 diabetes: A prospective study. *Journal of Pediatric Psychology, 29,* 171–184. doi:10.1093/jpepsy/jsh019

Daniel v. Daniel, 509 S.E.2d 117 (Ga. Ct. App. 1998).

Davis, C. L., Delameter, A. M., Shaw, K. H., LaGreca, A., Edison, M. S., Perez-Rodrigues, J., & Nemery, R. (2001). Brief report: parenting styles, regimen adherence and glycemic control in 4–10 year old children with diabetes. *Journal of Pediatric Psychology, 26,* 123–129. doi:10.1093/jpepsy/26.2.123

Deis, J. N., Spiro, D. M., Jenkins, C. A., Buckles, T. L., & Arnold, D. H. (2010). Parental knowledge and use of preventive asthma care measures in two pediatric emergency departments. *Journal of Asthma, 47*(5), 551–556. doi:10.3109/02770900903560225

Diabetes Control and Complications Trial Research Group. (1994). Effect of intensive diabetes treatment on the development and progression of long-term complications in adolescents with insulin-dependent diabetes mellitus: Diabetes control and complications trial. *Journal of Pediatrics, 125,* 177–188. doi:10.1016/S0022-3476(94)70190-3

Dimatteo, M. R. (2004). Variations in patients' adherence to medical recommendations: A quantitative review of 50 years of research. *Medical Care, 42,* 200–209. doi:10.1097/01.mlr.0000114908.90348.f9

Driscoll, K. A., Johnson, S. B., Barker, D., Quittner, A. L., Deeb, L. C., Geller, D .E., & Silverstein, J. H. (2010). Risk factors associated with depressive symptoms in caregivers of children with type 1 diabetes or cystic fibrosis. *Journal of Pediatric Psychology, 35,* 814–822. doi:10.1093/jpepsy/jsp138

Drotar, D. (1997). Relating parent and family functioning to the psychological adjustment of children with chronic health conditions: What have we learned? What do we need to know? *Journal of Pediatric Psychology, 22,* 148–165. Retrieved from http://jpepsy.oxfordjournals.org/

Eckshtain, D., Ellis, D. A., Kolmodin, K., & Naar-King, S. (2010). The effects of parental depression and parenting practices on depressive symptoms and metabolic control in urban youth with insulin dependent diabetes. *Journal of Pediatric Psychology, 35,* 426–435. doi:10.1093/jpepsy/jsp068

Ellis, D. A., Podolski, C. L., Frey, M., Naar-King, S., Wang, B., & Moltz, K. (2007). The role of parental monitoring in adolescent health outcomes: Impact on regimen adherence in youth with type 1 diabetes. *Journal of Pediatric Psychology, 32,* 907–917. doi:10.1093/jpepsy/jsm009

Fiese, B. H., Wamboldt, F. S., & Anbar, R. D. (2005). Family asthma management routines: Connections to medical adherence and quality of life. *Journal of Pediatrics, 146,* 171–176. doi:10.1016/j.jpeds.2004.08.083

Friedman, D., Holmbeck, G. N., Jandasek, B., Zuckerman, J., & Abad, M. (2004). Parent functioning in families of preadolescents with spina bifida: Longitudinal implications for child adjustment. *Journal of Family Functioning, 18,* 609–619.

George, A., Vickers, M. H., Wilkes, L., & Barton, B. (2008). Working and caring for a child with chronic illness: Challenges in maintaining employment. *Employees Responsibilities and Rights Journal, 20,* 165–176. doi:10.1007/s10672-008-9065-3

Gerson, A. C., Furth, S. L., Neu, A. M., & Fivush, B. A. (2004). Assessing associations between medication adherence and potentially modifiable psychosocial variables in pediatric kidney transplant recipients and their parents. *Pediatric Transplantation, 8,* 543–550. doi:10.1111/j.1399-3046.2004.00215.x

Gilbert v. Gilbert, 1996 Conn. Super LEXIS 2153 (1996).

Hamlett, K. W., Pellegrini, D. S., & Katz, K. S. (1992). Childhood chronic illness as a family stressor. *Journal of Pediatric Psychology, 17*, 33–47. doi:10.1093/jpepsy/17.1.33

Han, J. C., Lawlor, D. A. & Kimm, S. Y. (2010). Childhood obesity. *Lancet, 375*, 1737–1748. doi:10.1016/S0140-6736(10)60171-7

Hauser, S. T., Jacobson, A. M., Lavori, P., Wolfsdorf, J. I., Herkowitz, R. D., Milley, J. E., & Bliss, R. (1990). Adherence among children and adolescents with insulin-dependant diabetes mellitus over a 4-year longitudinal follow-up: II. Intermediate and long-term linkages with the family milieu. *Journal of Pediatric Psychology, 15*, 527–542. doi:10.1093/jpepsy/15.4.527

Hentinen, M., & Kyngas, H. (1998). Factors associated with the adaptation of parents with a chronically ill child. *Journal of Clinical Nursing, 7*, 316–324. doi:10.1046/j.1365-2702.1998.00154.x

In re E. G., 549 N.E. 2d 322 (Ill. App. Ct. 1989). Retrieved March 28, 2010, from http://www.jehovah.to/gen/legal/blood/eg.htm

In re Guardianship of Phillip B., 188 Cal Rptr 781, Cal 1983.

In re Nikolas E. Atl Report. 1998 Nov 19; 720:562–8.

In re Phillip B., 92 Cal App 3d 796, cert denied 445 US 949, 1980.

Jackson, C., Richer, J., & Edge, J. A. (2008). Sibling psychological adjustment to type 1 diabetes mellitus. *Pediatric Diabetes, 9*, 308–311. doi:10.1111/j.1399-5448.2008.00385.x

Kell, R. S., Kliewer, W., Erickson, M. T., & Ohene-Frempong, K. (1998). Psychological adjustment of adolescents with sickle cell disease: Relations with demographic, medical, and family competence variables. *Journal of Pediatric Psychology, 23*, 301–312. doi:10.1093/jpepsy/23.5.301

LaGreca, A. M., Auslander, W. F., Greco, P., Spetter, D., Fisher, E. B., & Santiago, J. V. (1995). I get by with a little help from my family and friends: Adolescents' support for diabetes care. *Journal of Pediatric Psychology, 20*, 449–476. doi:10.1093/jpepsy/20.4.449

Lavigne, J. V., & Faier-Routman, J. (1993). Correlates of psychological adjustment to pediatric physical disorders: A meta-analytic review and comparison with existing models. *Journal of Developmental and Behavioral Pediatrics, 14*, 117–123. Retrieved from http://journals.lww.com/jrnldbp/pages/default.aspx

Lewandowski, A., & Drotar, D. (2007). The relationship between parent-reported social support and adherence to medical treatment in families of adolescents with type 1 diabetes. *Journal of Pediatric Psychology, 32*, 427–436. doi:10.1093/jpepsy/jsl037

Lindsey, R. (1983, October 10). Surgery follows pact on custody. *New York Times*, p. A12.

Lindstrom, C., Aman, J., & Norberg, A. L. (2010). Increased prevalence of burnout symptoms in parents of chronically ill children. *Acta Paediatrica, 99*, 427–432. doi:10.1111/j.1651-2227.2009.01586.x

Lizzio v. Lizzio, 618 N.Y.S.2d 934 (Fam. Ct. Fulton Cty. 1994).

Meltzer, L. J., & Moore, M. (2008). Sleep disruptions in parents of children and adolescents with chronic illness: Prevalence, causes, and consequences. *Journal of Pediatric Psychology, 33*, 279–291. doi:10.1093/jpepsy/jsm118

Mullins, L. L. Wolfe-Christensen, C., Chaney, J. M., Elkin, T. D., Wiener, L., Hullmann, S. E., & Junghans, A. (2010). The relationship between single-parent status and parenting capacities in mothers of youth with chronic health conditions: The mediating role of income. *Journal of Pediatric Psychology.* Advance online publication, Sept. 3, 2010. doi:10.1093/jpepsy/jsq080.

Osterberg, L., & Blaschke, T. (2005). Adherence to medication. *New England Journal of Medicine, 353*, 487–497. doi:10.1056/NEJMra050100

Otsuki, M., Eakin, M. N., Arceneaux, L. L., Rand, C. S., Butz, A. M., & Riekert, K. A. (2010). Prospective relationship between maternal depressive symptoms and asthma morbidity among inner-city African American children. *Journal of Pediatric Psychology, 35*, 758–767. doi:10.1093/jpepsy/jsp091

Patterson, J., & Garwick, A. (1994). The impact of chronic illness on families: A family systems perspective. *Annals of Behavioral Medicine, 16*, 131–142. Retrieved from http://www.springer.com/medicine/journal/12160

Pedersen, S. D., Parsons, H. G., & Dewey, D. (2004). Stress levels experienced by parents of enterally fed children. *Child: Care, Health, & Development, 30*, 507–513. doi:10.1111/j.1365–2214.2004.00437.x

Prince v. Massachusetts, 321 U.S. 158 (1944).

Rutledge, J. (1943). *Opinion of the Court in Prince V. Massachusetts.* Downloaded Feb. 24, 2011, from: http://www.law.cornell.edu/supct/html/historics/USSC_CR_0321_0158_ZO.html

Quittner, A. L., Espelage, D. L., Opipari, L. C., Carter, B., Eid, N., & Eigen, H. (1998). Role strain in couples with and without a child with a chronic illness: Associations with marital satisfaction, intimacy, and daily mood. *Health Psychology, 17*, 112–124. doi:10.1037/0278–6133.17.2.112

Salyer, D. R. (1991). In re E.G., a minor. *Issues in Law and Medicine, 6*(4), 421–424.

Shalowitz, M. U., Berry, C. A., Quinn, K. A., & Wolf, R. L. (2001). The relationship of life stressors and maternal depression to pediatric asthma morbidity in a sub-specialty practice. *Ambulatory Pediatrics, 1*, 185–193. doi:10.1367/1539–4409(2001)001<0185:TROLSA>2.0.CO;2

Shalowitz, M. U., Mijanovich, T., Berry, C. A., Clark-Kaufman, E., Quinn, K. A., & Perez, E. L. (2006). Context matters: A community-based study of maternal mental health, life stressors, social support, and children's asthma. *Pediatrics, 117*, e940–e948. doi:10.1542/peds.2005–2446

Sharpe, D., & Rossiter, L. (2002). Siblings of children with chronic illness: A meta-analysis. *Journal of Pediatric Psychology, 27*, 699–710. doi:10.1093/jpepsy/27.8.699

Soliday, E., Kool, E. M., & Lande, M. B. (2001). Family environment, child behavior, and medical indicators in children with kidney disease. *Child Psychiatry and Human Development, 31*, 279–295. doi:10.1023/A:1010282305881

Stepansky, M. A., Roache, C. R., Holmbeck, G. N., & Schultz, K. (2010). Medical adherence in young adolescents with spina bifida: Longitudinal associations with family functioning. *Journal of Pediatric Psychology, 35*, 167–176. doi:10.1093/jpepsy/jsp054

Sullivan-Bolyai, S., Deatrick, J., Gruppuso, P., Tamborlane, W., & Grey, M. (2003). Constant vigilance: Mothers' work parenting young children with type 1 diabetes. *Journal of Pediatric Nursing, 18*, 21–29. doi:10.1053/jpdn.2003.4

Unger v. Unger, 274 N.J. Super. 532 (1994).

Van Cleave, J., Gortmaker, S. L., & Perrin, J. M. (2010). Dynamics of obesity and chronic health conditions among children and youth. *Journal of the American Medical Association, 303*, 623–630. Retrieved from http://jama.ama-assn.org/

Williams, P. D., Williams, A. R., Graff, J. C., Hanson, S., Stanton, A., Hafeman, C., & Sanders, S. (2002). Interrelationships among variables affecting well siblings and mothers in families of children with chronic illness or disability. *Journal of Behavioral Medicine, 25*, 411–424. doi:10.1023/A:1020401122858

Wood, B. L., Lim. J., Miller, B. D., Cheah, P. A., Simmens, S., Stern, T., & Ballow, M. (2007). Family emotional climate, depression, emotional triggering of asthma, and disease severity in pediatric asthma: Examination of pathways of effect. *Journal of Pediatric Psychology, 32*, 542–551. doi:10.1093/jpepsy/jsl044

## 10

Co-parenting Children with Neurodevelopmental Disorders

RACHEL BIRNBAUM, LUCYNA M. LACH,
DONALD T. SAPOSNEK, AND RADHA MacCULLOCH ■

INTRODUCTION

Neurodevelopmental disorders (NDDs) is an umbrella term used to refer to conditions affecting children's neurologic development. Yeargin-Allsop and Boyle (2002) and Bishop (2010) describe NDDs as a heterogeneous group of conditions that share common long-term effects of developmental delay and differences, resulting from the damage of the neurologic processes that are responsible for developmental functioning. In many cases, the etiology of NDDs may not be known, and the timing of the impairment can be in utero, in the perinatal period, or in the early years of life (Cascio, 2010).

Within the World Health Organization's (WHO) International Classification of Diseases (ICD-10; WHO, 2007), a classification system used to standardize diagnoses worldwide, the category of NDD would include diagnoses associated with the nervous system (Chapter VI; G00–G99), with congenital malformations of the nervous system (Chapter XVII; Q00–Q07), and with symptoms and signs involving the nervous and musculoskeletal systems (Chapter XVIII; R25–29). For the purpose of this chapter, NDD also refers to mental retardation (Chapter V, F70–F79) and disorders of psychological development (F80–F89). Acknowledging that some children and adolescents with NDD also experience challenges with emotional/behavioral dysregulation, the latter is treated here as a comorbidity and not a primary diagnosis.

Examples of neurodevelopmental impairments are epilepsy, cerebral palsy, autism spectrum disorder (ASD), nonverbal learning disabilities, sensory processing disorder, learning or intellectual disabilities, and global developmental delay. Children with NDDs may experience impairments in virtually any aspect of function and development, such as mobility, self-regulation and communication, social reciprocity, interests, and behaviors (Cascio, 2010; Farmer & Deidrick, 2006). These children have significant medical, physical, social, and emotional needs that must be met by their parents, caregivers, and primary care physicians (Miller, 2005). As a result, there needs to be a high degree of communication and cooperation among parents, child care providers, and medical professionals.

Whereas epilepsy, learning disabilities, and global developmental delay are also significant NDDs that affect children, this chapter will focus on ASD and cerebral palsy. These two NDDs prototypically illustrate the variability in function and diverse needs that parents of these children and the courts must understand.

This chapter will review the etiology, the prevalence rates, and the impact on the child's social, emotional, and behavioral development and quality of life with regard to these disorders. It will also examine the impact on families and what treatment, management, and preventive interventions are required for them. Included in this discussion is an examination of the parenting challenges faced by both intact and separated families. The chapter concludes with specific recommendations for forensic evaluators, mediators, and the court to consider in developing parenting plans for these children.

PERSPECTIVES FOR CLASSIFYING NEURODEVELOPMENTAL DISORDERS

Practitioners may draw upon research to inform their understanding of cases that involve children and adolescents with any type of NDD, such as ASD. However, autism or ASD includes children with varying levels of function; that is, the verbal abilities of one child or adolescent with autism may be poor or absent, while those of another may be superior, so the implications for parents of raising a child with "autism" depend upon what actual skills the child brings into the relationship (Sameroff & Mackenzie, 2003). Therefore, the extent to which research that is based on samples of children and/or adolescents with a specific diagnosis must be critically evaluated in light of the fact that their functional abilities might vary considerably. Furthermore, practitioners may also draw on studies of children with other types of NDDs, as their functional impairments may be similar despite their different diagnoses. The following section explores the relevance of a "diagnostic" versus a "functional" approach to research and its implications for using "evidence" to inform decision-making.

"Diagnostic" Versus "Functional" Approach

"DIAGNOSTIC" APPROACH

Much of the research on children with NDDs is categorical in nature; that is, studies focus on children with specific diagnoses, such as epilepsy, cerebral palsy, or autism (Fayed & Kerr, 2009). Given that pediatrics is divided into subspecialties, corresponding expertise and specialized clinics have emerged to deal with children who have specific diagnoses. For example, within neurology, there is a subspecialty of pediatrics, and within pediatrics, neurologists may develop expertise in epilepsy, autism, or multiple sclerosis, as well as other disorders. Along with the proliferation of these subspecialties has been a parallel emergence of clinical studies that seek to better understand these groups of patients and treatments to improve their quality of life. Studies such as these are informative for those who are engaged in providing clinical services to these populations.

Although there are benefits to these kinds of studies, there are drawbacks as well. For example, studies of children with "cerebral palsy" will specify that inclusion criteria include children with that diagnosis, but these studies do not differentiate subject samples based on severity of impairment in mobility, communication, or cognition within this diagnosis. The fact is that children with cerebral palsy have mobility skills that vary in level of impairment, and the extent to which they can communicate verbally, be understood by others, or process information also varies. Therefore, one child with cerebral palsy is not like the next. The significance of this heterogeneity on parenting is that statements regarding the likelihood of separation and/or divorce among parents of children with any particular kind of diagnosis, the impact of a diagnosis on the child/couple/family, or the efficacy of any particular treatment are statements made about *groups* of children, not any individual child. This same issue was recently described by Kazdin (2008) and in an editorial by Rosenbaum (2010), who describes how the heterogeneity of any sample makes the relevance and applicability of findings from randomized control trials challenging, if not questionable. One of the suggestions Rosenbaum (2010) makes is to pay particular attention to both age and function, so that findings within a study are generalized to children of specific age groups and levels of function rather than to all children with that diagnosis.

Another noteworthy drawback of categorical studies is that rare disorders that have a low incidence cannot generate the critical mass required for an adequate sample size. What options do practitioners have when searching for evidence related to rare NDDs such as Prader-Willi or Angelman syndrome? In these cases, reviewing studies of children with other types of NDDs may shed light on the issues faced by these children and their families; however, caution must be used when indiscriminately applying findings to children with a different diagnosis, since comparability of function of a similar sample from one study to the next must be taken into account.

"Functional" Approach

A functional or noncategorical approach to classifying children with NDDs has been advocated over several decades (Pless & Pinkerton, 1972; Stein, Bauman, Westbrook, Coupey, & Ireys, 1993):

> The essence of a noncategorical approach is that children face common life experiences and problems based on generic dimensions of their conditions rather than on idiosyncratic characteristics of any specific disease entity. The lives of children and their families are affected by whether the condition is visible or invisible; whether it is life threatening, stable, or characterized by unpredictable crises; and whether it involves mental retardation, has a cosmetic aspect, affects sensory or motor systems, or requires intrusive and demanding routines of care. (Stein & Jessop, 1982, p. 354)

This suggests that if a diagnostic, or categorical, approach is used for understanding the impact of a particular disorder on parenting needs, practitioners must appreciate the implications of the heterogeneity in these different dimensions of impairment. As stated above, simply knowing the diagnosis is not enough; knowledge is required of these children's ability to understand what others say, to communicate their needs, to remember what they see and hear, to get around in their physical world, and to carry out activities of daily living, and knowledge of their sensitivity to external stimuli is required. An appreciation of the extraordinary challenges involved in parenting a child with an NDD demands that practitioners move beyond quoting the diagnosis in their reports; the complexities associated with parenting have to do with the child's level of function and his or her needs associated with that level of function.

In spite of Stein et al.'s (1993) call for noncategorical research, the dominant paradigm in research and practice remains "diagnostic." If court decisions are to be informed by the "best available evidence," a critical understanding of that evidence is needed to determine how it applies to decision-making about parenting arrangements and parenting plans for a particular child.

In summary:

- Most studies use a diagnostic-specific approach to sampling.
- Children in these samples vary considerably in age and level of function.
- Most consider how the child's age and level of function (e.g., child's ability to process information, communicate, ambulate) inform parenting.

AUTISM SPECTRUM DISORDER

The nomenclature of *autism* and *autism spectrum disorder* can be confusing. Is autism the same as ASD? The following section defines these terms, provides information on how the diagnoses are made, and discusses prevalence and key treatment approaches.

Definition

The *Diagnostic and Statistical Manual of Mental Disorders* (DSM-IV-TR; American Psychiatric Association, 2000) and ICD-10 classify Autistic Disorder (DSM Section 299.00) or Childhood Autism (ICD-10 Section F84.0) as one of several Pervasive Developmental Disorders (PDDs). Diagnoses included in these two classification systems under PDD all involve impairment in reciprocal social interaction skills, communication skills, and/or the presence of stereotyped behavior, interests, and activities. The category of PDD also includes Rett's Disorder/Syndrome (DSM Section 299.80; ICD-10 Section F84.2), Childhood Disintegrative Disorder (DSM Section 299.10; ICD-10 Section F84.3), Asperger's Disorder/Syndrome (DSM Section 299.80; ICD-10 Section F84.5), and Pervasive Developmental Disorder–Not Otherwise Specified (PDD-NOS; DSM-IV-TR Section 299.80; ICD-10 Section 84.9). ASD is an umbrella term used by clinicians and researchers to refer to three of the diagnoses listed above: Autistic Disorder/Childhood Autism, Asperger's Disorder/ Syndrome, and PDD-NOS (Levy, Mandell, & Schultz, 2009).

Establishing a diagnosis of ASD in young children often is a process that occurs over time. The diagnosis is made by licensed practitioners such as pediatricians, pediatric neurologists, geneticists, psychiatrists, psychologists, and speech and language pathologists. Other allied health professionals (e.g., social workers, occupational therapists, and physical therapists) may be involved in the assessment process or in delivering early intervention programs, but their role typically is not to establish a diagnosis. The American Academy of Pediatrics has established an algorithm for the screening, identification, and evaluation of children presenting with developmental symptoms (Myers & Plauche-Johnson, 2007). Given that children typically present with developmental concerns at the primary care level, the protocol provides practitioners with tools for screening and evaluation. The Centers for Disease Control and Prevention (CDC) recommends that professionals rely on parent report as well as on their own clinical observation to make the diagnosis. Standardized tools such as the ADOS-G (Autism Diagnostic Observation Schedule–Generic; Lord et al., 2000), used for evaluating clinical observations, and the ADI-R (Autism Diagnostic Interview–Revised; Lord, Rutter & LeCouteur, 1994), used to obtain a developmental history, are increasingly recommended to confirm the diagnosis. For an overview of screening and diagnostic tools, please refer to the CDC website: http://cdc.gov/ncbddd/autism/hcp-screening.html.

Although the exact causes of ASDs are still unknown, the general consensus is that they are genetic in origin and that environmental factors influence the expression of certain genes (Levy et al., 2009). One of the most controversial research findings that had a powerful influence on the field of autism was the hypothesized link made between the measles-mumps-rubella (MMR) vaccination and the diagnosis of autism (Wakefield et al., 1998). This research was later refuted (Fombonne, Zakarian, Bennett, Meng, & McLean-Heywood, 2006), and the study was retracted by *The Lancet*, the journal that originally published these findings. It is now a well-established scientific conclusion that there is no confirmed link between the MMR vaccine and autism or ASD.

In summary:

- Autism and ASD are not one and the same.
- The procedure recommended by the American Academy of Pediatrics and the CDC for making a diagnosis includes the use of standardized measures and multiple informants.

Prevalence

Prevalence rates of autism vary considerably and depend on a number of factors: (a) when the study was conducted; (b) whether the prevalence rate is being presented for one of the diagnoses included in ASD, or for ASDs or PDDs overall; (c) the sampling procedures and jurisdiction within which the sampling took place; (d) the age range of subjects included in the sample; and (e) the method used to ascertain the presence or absence of the diagnosis (Fombonne, 2003). Most recent figures situate the prevalence rate for ASD between 34 and 64 of 10,000 children (Bertrand et al., 2001; Fombonne et al., 2006; Yeargin-Allsopp et al., 2003). Based on these numbers, up to one out of every 150 to 160 children has the diagnosis of ASD. However, rates have been documented to be as high as one in 110 (CDC, 2009).

In summary:

- Prevalence rates for autism and ASD vary based on where and how the study was conducted.
- Prevalence rates range from one out of every 110 to 160 children.

Level of Functioning

As identified above, the level of functioning among those diagnosed with ASD varies considerably. The extent of the functional impairment of a child diagnosed with an ASD is informed by the specific diagnosis within the spectrum being considered. For example, according to DSM-IV-TR diagnostic criteria, children with Asperger's syndrome have no significant delay in language, cognitive development, self-help skills, adaptive behavior (except social interaction), or curiosity about the social environment, while children with autistic disorder do. Currently, there is no universal classification system to rate the severity of function-related symptoms. Children diagnosed with ASD vary in levels of attention, motor skills, and perception; in how they manage change, fear, and anxiety; in their coordination; in their patterns of eating and sleeping; and in their sensitivity to visual and auditory stimuli. They also vary in the extent to which they are able to process auditory and visual information and communicate both verbally and nonverbally (Charman & Baird, 2002). Any assessment of the needs of children with ASD requires a comprehensive understanding of their level of function in each of a number of domains, since parents must adjust their parenting behaviors accordingly.

In summary:

- Children with ASD vary in their level of attention, motor skills, perception of and sensitivity to visual and auditory stimuli, flexibility in managing change, ability to regulate fear and anxiety, communication of thoughts, and understanding what others are asking of them.
- Parents must adjust their parenting approach to accommodate the child's level of function.

Impact of ASD

Most of the research on the impact of ASD focuses on parents and families. However, studies document that children with this diagnosis are faced with extraordinary cognitive, emotional, behavioral, and social challenges. In a clinical sample of 8- to 16-year-old higher-functioning children with ASD, the younger cohort demonstrated deficits relative to what was expected of them in tests of executive function that evaluated flexibility, in selecting and monitoring their responses to stimuli, and in planning and in working memory that were not as evident in the older cohort (Happe, Booth, Charlton, & Hughes, 2006). This suggests that the gap in executive function lessens as the child grows older. Also, comorbid psychiatric problems are more prevalent in children with ASD than in typically developing children. For example, 17% of the sample scored two standard deviations above the population mean of 50 on a measure of attention-deficit/hyperactivity disorder (ADHD) and depressive symptoms, and 13.6% scored at this level on a measure of anxiety (Kim, Szatmari, Bryson, Streiner, & Wilson, 2000). These children are more likely to have peer issues, to have fewer friends, and to miss school, and parents are more likely to have concerns about their children being bullied and about their learning and achievement (Lee, Harrington, Louie, & Newschaffer, 2008; Orsmond, Krauss, & Seltzer, 2004). The presence of peer relationships was contingent upon the characteristics of the individual child, while participation in social and recreational activities was influenced by aspects of the child's environment, such as greater maternal participation in social and recreational activities, greater number of services received, and inclusion in integrated settings while in school (Orsmond et al., 2004).

The impact of ASD on parents and families is quite significant. Mothers of these children have significantly poorer physical and psychological health than do mothers of age-matched peers (Allik, Larsson, & Smedje, 2006; Montes & Halterman, 2007). These results mirror findings from studies of children with cerebral palsy (Brehaut et al., 2004) and NDDs in general (Lach et al., 2009). Understandably, parental stress is significantly elevated (Montes & Halterman, 2007; Mori, Ujiie, Smith, & Howlin, 2009; Rao & Beidel, 2009), and there are significant implications related to employment and family income. Children with ASD were more likely to live in families that report financial problems, need additional income for the child's medical care, or reduce or stop work because of the child's condition (Brown, MacAdam-Crisp, Want, & Iarocci, 2006; Kogan et al., 2008; Lee et al., 2008; Montes & Halterman, 2008). These studies demonstrate that the annual incomes of these families can be significantly lower than families of children who do not have these same needs. Research findings suggest that these outcomes are influenced by the extent to which the child exhibits behavioral issues (Allik et al., 2006; Bishop, Richler, Cain, & Lord, 2007; Brown et al., 2006; Mori et al., 2009; Rao & Beidel, 2009).

Given the challenges that parents of children with ASD face, many have speculated on the impact that this has on the couple's relationship and more specifically on rates of separation and/or divorce. Received wisdom and common folklore is that these rates are inordinately high (Sobsey, 2004). Recent studies have examined these speculations of increased separation and divorce. Hartley et al. (2010) found that parents of children with ASD had a higher rate of divorce than the comparison group, which consisted of a representative sample of parents whose children did not have the diagnosis. The rate of divorce in the ASD group was 23.5% over time, while the rate in the comparison group was 13.8%—a divorce rate that was twice as high. In contrast, a study by Freedman, Kalb, Zablotsky, and Stuart (2010) noted that children with ASD are no less likely to grow up in an intact two-parent biological or adoptive family than are children without ASD. Using data from the National Survey of Children's Health in the United States, 64% of children diagnosed with ASD live in intact families, compared to 65.2% of children without ASD. Methodological differences between the studies may explain the difference in findings; however, the hypothesis regarding the inevitability of increased rates of separation and/or divorce is challenged by these findings.

In summary:

- Compared to children without ASD, children with ASD have higher rates of symptoms of ADHD, depression, and anxiety and are more likely to have peer problems, to have fewer friends, and to miss school; parents are more likely to have concerns about their children being bullied and about their learning and achievement.
- Mothers of children with ASD have higher levels of compromised physical and psychological health; families of children with ASD are more likely to experience financial and work-related problems.

- Received wisdom regarding elevated rates of separation and/or divorce among families of children with ASD is not clearly substantiated by research.

Intervention: Treatment, Management, and Prevention

Given that ASD is a chronic condition, the primary goals of intervention are to minimize problematic symptoms, maximize functional independence and quality of life, and minimize family distress (Myers & Plauche-Johnson, 2007). A comprehensive review of intervention approaches for children with ASD is beyond the scope of this chapter, as there is a myriad of approaches to treating, managing, and preventing secondary sequelae of ASDs. Preparation for a recent synthesis of intervention studies related to ASD yielded 3,973 articles that were grouped under the following headings: behavioral, pharmacological, social-relational, communication/language, sensory-motor, dietary, developmental, educational, physiological, and non-conventional. The evidence behind these approaches varied from small, qualitative studies to randomized controlled trials (RCTs), suggesting that there is a tremendous range in the type and quality of evidence used to substantiate the use of various approaches. The RCT remains the gold standard for evaluating the efficacy of an intervention, and systematic reviews are increasingly being used to group the studies that evaluate the efficacy of a specific intervention (see http://www.cochrane.org and http://www.campbellcollaboration.org).

A number of common intervention approaches are used to treat children diagnosed with ASD: intensive behavioral intervention (IBI; Smith, Groen, & Wynn, 2000), which is a type of applied behavior analysis (ABA); treatment and education of autistic and related communication-handicapped children (TEACCH; Mesibov, Shea, & Schopler, 2005); and medications such as risperidone. The following sections begin to shed some light on the state of the evidence base for these interventions.

ABA is not a single, specific intervention for individuals with ASD; rather, it is a broad approach to shaping behavior that involves objective measurement of behavior and precise control of the environment and uses procedures that are based on scientifically established principles of behavior (Hagopian & Boelter, 2005). It is used to reduce or eliminate problem behaviors such as self-injury or aggression, as well as to increase the use of adaptive behaviors. IBI is a specific type of intervention that draws on ABA principles and in which the child participates for at least 25 hours of therapy per week. IBI that is implemented early in a child's life (soon after diagnosis is made) is regarded by many families and practitioners as a best practice for children with ASD, as it is more likely to lead to better outcomes than intervention initiated later (Myers & Plauche-Johnson, 2007).

A systematic review of studies evaluating IBI was conducted to ascertain whether any conclusions could be reached about the use of this approach with children with ASD (Mauger- Rothenberg et al., 2009). The search and screening procedure yielded only two RCTs and 14 other types of studies that used less rigorous methods. One of the RCTs showed no statistically significant difference in the rate of improvement between those in the treatment group and those in the control group (Sallows & Graupner, 2005), while results from the second RCT indicated that, at follow-up, the cognitive and communication skills of those in the treatment group were significantly better than those in the control group (Smith et al., 2000). Another systematic review (Ospina et al., 2008) revealed a third RCT that demonstrated no difference between treatment and control groups (Hilton, 2005).

TEACCH is also a "structured teaching" method that relies on predictable sequences of activities, routines with flexibility, and environmental adaptations, such as visual schedules and visually structured work/activity systems (Mesibov et al., 2005). In existence since the 1970s, TEACCH has been broadly adopted in many North American homes and educational settings. Although a number of reports have documented improvements in children (Panerai, Ferrante, & Zingale, 2002), most published studies have not used the gold standard of RCT. A controlled trial conducted by Ozonoff and Cathcart (1998) found that children in the experimental group, treated with a TEACCH-based approach for 4 months, improved significantly more than children in the control group on measures of imitation, fine motor function, gross motor function, cognitive performance, perception, and cognitive verbal performance. Although there was a control group, children were not randomly assigned and evaluators were not blind to group assignment. Welterlin's (2009) study did use random assignment to treatment or waitlist control conditions and found that after a 12-session intervention that taught TEACCH methods to parents of 10 children who were 2 or 3 years old and had autism, children in the treatment group had significant increases in fine motor skills, independence, and visual receptive skills, and decreases in maladaptive behavior and parental distress.

Cochrane reviews regarding the use of gluten-free and casein-free diets (Millward, Ferriter, Calver, & Connell-Jones, 2008) and risperidone (Jesner, Aref-Adib, & Coren, 2007) suggest that the former is not effective while the latter may be, particularly when the child is exhibiting signs of problematic irritability, repetitive behavior, and social withdrawal. Other approaches, such as the use of weighted vests (Stephenson & Carter, 2009) and the use of facilitated communication (American Academy of Pediatrics, Committee on Children with Disabilities, 1998), are not recommended due to a poor evidence base.

In summary:

- There are numerous intervention approaches to ASD.
- Approaches such as IBI and TEACCH are commonly used. However, the science is not advanced enough to predict which child will benefit from which approach and how much exposure to that approach is optimal.
- A number of interventions have not yet been rigorously tested using RCTs.

CEREBRAL PALSY

Definition

Cerebral palsy (CP) is another of the most common NDDs presenting in early childhood and persisting over the lifespan. Like ASD, CP is defined by clinical descriptions only, as there is no definitive test or biomedical marker for it (Blair & Stanley, 1997; Rosenbaum, Paneth, Levitan, Goldstein & Bax, 2007). Both ASD and CP are conditions that are phenomenologically defined and not biomedically defined, for example, the way Down syndrome is defined.

Prevalence

The prevalence of CP is 2 to 2.5 of every 1,000 children born in the Western world (Stanley, Blair, & Alberman, 2000), with a higher incidence in premature infants and in twin births (Nelson & Ellenberg, 1986; Yeargin-Allsop & Boyle, 2002). Parkes and Hill (2010) report that it is unusual to refer to the number of new cases of CP per year because some children die before a diagnosis can be made, and therefore the actual incidence is not known. Nelson (2002) has reported that despite continuing drops in perinatal deaths and intrapartum injuries, over recent decades there has been no net decrease in the occurrence of CP among infants born at or after 37 weeks of gestation. However, Hanna and Law (2006) report that caution must be taken when reporting prevalence rates, as there is no present standard definition that includes both functionality and categorical data on CP rates. Differences are due to how data are collected in different countries and how children with disabilities are defined.

In summary:

- There is no definitive test or biomedical marker for identifying children with CP.
- Prevalence rates vary, as there is no standard definition that includes both functionality and categorical data on CP rates.

Level of Functioning

Similar to ASD, CP presents with many different dimensions. CP is best described as "a group of permanent disorders of the development of movement and posture, causing activity limitation, that are attributed to non-progressive disturbances that occurred in the developing fetal or infant brain" (Rosenbaum et al., 2007, p. 9). Impairments of motor functioning are often accompanied by disturbances of sensation, perception, cognition, and communication, and by secondary musculoskeletal difficulties that may further limit the individual's daily functioning (Rosenbaum et al., 2007). Some authors have noted that because of the heterogeneous nature of CP with respect to etiology, clinical features, severity, and outcome, CP may be best conceptualized as a "symptom complex" rather than as a specific "disease" that individuals share regarding impairments, medical requirements, therapeutic needs, and subsequent challenges in daily living (Kuban & Leviton, 1994; Shevell, Majnemer, & Morin, 2003).

It is important for practitioners to understand the medical and functional abilities of the individual child with CP in order to assist the court when developing parenting plans for these children after separation. In other words, the cluster of signs, symptoms, and diagnosis of CP, similar to the situation with ASD, is only one piece of the puzzle. It is equally important to understand how each child responds with different abilities and different levels of functioning in speech development, sucking or eating, and different degrees of impairment in vision and hearing, cognition, motor functioning, sensation, and urinary incontinence, and with the presence of seizures (Petersen & Palmer, 2001). As a result of the child's maturation and adaptive processes, the child with CP is regularly changing (Ketelaar, Gorter, Vermeer, Hart, & Helders, 2006). Miller (2005) notes that, given the variability of the level of functioning of each individual child, parents must first come to accept and support their child at the child's present level of functioning. Rosenbaum (2009) emphasizes that parents need to accommodate to the child's functional differences, limitations, and capacities in order to allow the child to achieve as much as possible. Therefore, the relationship between parents and professionals must be a partnership in which the families define the priorities for therapeutic intervention (Ketelaar et al., 2006).

In summary:

- CP presents with many different dimensions and levels of functioning.
- Forensic professionals must understand the medical as well as the functional abilities of the individual child with CP.

Impact of Cerebral Palsy

Similar to the impact of ASD on children and parents, much of the research on CP documents significant challenges for the parents of children with CP who have emotional, behavioral, physical, and cognitive impairments. Cheshire, Barlow, and Powell (2010) conducted a comparative study of 70 parents with CP children and 70 parents of children without a long-term health condition in the United Kingdom. They found that parents of children with CP have significantly poorer psychosocial well-being than parents of children without a long-term health condition. The researchers also found that parents of children with CP had lower satisfaction with life and higher levels of anxiety and depressed mood. These results are similar to controlled studies from other countries (Brehaut et al., 2004; Ones, Yilmaz, & Cetinkaya, 2005; Su, 2002; Wang & Jong, 2004) and suggest that interventions to improve well-being for parents of children with CP may be useful in supporting successful parenting.

Arnaud et al. (2008) and Majnemer, Shevell, Rosenbaum, Law, and Poulin (2007) suggest that parental stress is associated with reported negative quality of life for the child with CP that is relatively independent of the child's severity of dysfunction, and they emphasize the detrimental effects of high parental stress and poor family coping on the quality of life of the child. Thus, the quality of parenting a child with CP has significant implications on the medical, physical, and functional well-being of that child and the family. Children with chronic functional limitations can have considerably more difficulties in social and behavioral aspects of their lives than do children without such limitations (Cadman, Boyle, Szatmari, & Offord, 1987). As a result, these children are at a higher risk of being ostracized by their peer groups and of being victimized (Yude & Goodman, 1999). Breslau and Marshall (1985) and Heller, Alberto, and Meagher (1996) report that children with NDDs may have higher risk for psychological problems, such as generalized feelings of helplessness, low self-esteem, anxiety, low academic achievement, and social problems. McDermott et al. (1996) note that, while a substantial proportion of children with CP may experience significant behavioral and social problems, most do not develop these problems and instead demonstrate resilience.

Kee (2005) and Nesseleroade, Musher-Eizenman, and Schmitz (2002) have identified "loss of control" as a factor associated with poorer school adaptation, involvement, and achievements, as well as an increased vulnerability to depression and anxiety. Loss of control has also been examined in regards to disease severity, anxiety, and parenting styles (Cohen, Biran, Aran, & Gross-Tsur, 2008). These researchers collected information from 30 children with CP and 30 healthy siblings on self-report measures such as loss of control, anxiety, and perceived parenting style of the mother. They found that children with CP, regardless of severity, did not differ from their siblings with respect to loss of control, anxiety, or perceived parenting style. The researchers hypothesized that for children with CP, experiencing parental acceptance may enhance the development of resilience-related qualities such as internal loss of control. A supportive family environment is extremely important to facilitate the well-being of the children with CP (Palisano, Snider, & Orlin, 2004).

In summary:

- While some studies demonstrate that parents of children with CP have significantly more psychosocial difficulties, caution must be exercised when examining an individual child and parent–child relationship.
- Parental and family support is important to facilitate well-being of children with CP.

Intervention: Treatment, Management, and Prevention of Cerebral Palsy

The WHO provides a framework to guide clinicians with respect to the treatment and management of CP (Rosenbaum, 2006). "Function" refers to the varied aspects of the child's overall health and well-being, and these aspects must be examined from a variety of perspectives: (a) the functioning of the body; (b) the level of individual activities; and (c) the level of involvement in life situations (Ketelaar et al., 2006).

Considerable progress has been made in identifying outcome measures to evaluate treatment for children with CP. It is important for parents, as well as for the court, to understand how the level of functioning of a child with CP affects treatment and, ultimately, the management of the child's condition. With respect to the child's motor abilities, the Manual Ability Classification System (MACS; Eliasson et al., 2006) provides a classification of the ability of a child with CP to handle objects, and the Functional Mobility Scale (FMS) provides clinicians with a tool to measure changes in the child's ability to walk (Graham, Harvey, Rodda, Nattrass, & Pirpiris, 2004). This latter classification system allows professionals to classify the child's need for assistive devices such as a wheelchair or walking aid. A third scale, the Gross Motor Function Classification System (GMFCS), is based primarily on self-initiated movement of the child with an emphasis on sitting, transfers, and mobility (Palisano et al., 1997). The GMFCS measures the child's or youth's present abilities and limitations in gross motor functioning. Within the GMFCS there are five levels of general functioning that fall under the following distinctions: (a) Level 1: walks without limitations; (b) Level 2: walks with limitations; (c) Level 3: walks using a hand-held mobility device; (d) Level 4: self-mobility with limitations; may use powered mobility; and (e) Level 5: transported in a manual wheelchair (Palisano et al., 1997). It is important to note that the distinctions in Levels 1 and 2 are not as pronounced as they are in the other levels, particularly for infants less than 2 years of age. Palisano et al. (1997) and Palisano, Rosenbaum, Bartlett, and Livingston (2007) emphasize that motor functioning of each individual child with CP is dependent on age and developmental changes over time. While these three scales together provide a detailed description of the levels of the gross and fine motor skills for children with CP, an emerging classification system is being developed for communication (Hidecker et al., 2011). Geytenbeek (2011) reports that clinical studies regarding the level of communication skills or speech and language skills for children with CP remain sparse and dated.

A systematic review of the various intervention approaches for children with CP is beyond the scope of this chapter, as the nature of impairments and functioning abilities of each individual child are so variable. Moreover, each study described in the Cochrane Library Database focuses on a particular drug and its impact on a child, on a particular surgical intervention regarding mobility, or on a variety of forms of assisted communication devices for children of varying disabilities. As noted by Rosenbaum (2009), many of these studies do not address the impact of the intervention on the child, the parent, or the child–parent relationship. Moreover, none of these studies addresses the complexities of implementing interventions in separated and/or divorced families when, for example, parents may have to share medications, mechanical devices and other equipment.

In the final analysis, the goals for managing a child with CP should focus on increasing a child's developmental capabilities and should include, but not be limited to, a combination of interventions that involve developmental, physical, medical, surgical, chemical, and technical modalities to promote function and prevent secondary impairments. For example, providing motorically challenged children with powered mobility as young as 36 months of age has been found to improve social, language, and play skills, in addition to increasing efforts at independent movement (Butler, 1991). A treatment modality that has been found to be helpful for children experiencing communication problems is the early introduction of augmentative communication systems. For example, the use of sign language and picture boards can often promote the development of oral language in children with CP and can enhance communication (Butler, 1991). Geytenbeek (2011) also suggests that a distinction between normal, impaired but understandable, and severely impaired, or no speech (see Andersen et al., 2008) would enhance clarity and provide insights into the prevalence of speech and communication disorders in children with CP.

Rosenbaum (2006) has reviewed the literature of the ever-increasing sophistication of biomedical and surgical innovations in the treatment of CP and concludes that much research still needs to be done for increasing the understanding of primary prevention and how to apply specific interventions to a particular child, based on criteria being used for any particular individual study. He notes, for example, that in a study by Edgar (2001), Botulinum toxin in the appropriate cases can assist in the temporary relief of spasticity; that selective dorsal rhizotomy can be administered for more permanent relief (McLaughlin et al., 2002); and that intrathecal baclofen can be used as a titratable antispasticity agent (Butler & Campbell, 2000). However, Rosenbaum (2006) concludes that very little research has been undertaken on different treatment modalities that might result in developing specific interventions to assist parents with children who have CP. Although complementary treatments have also emerged over the years, very few treatment approaches—whether conventional or alternative—are evidence based. Rosenbaum (2006) refers to many of them as "common-sense approaches," such as the conductive education approach, which is based on educational principles but has been shown to be as effective as, but not better than, conventional approaches (Reddihough, King, Coleman, & Catanese, 1998). On the other end of the spectrum lie many treatment approaches that have little to no demonstrated efficacy for children with CP (Rosenbaum, 2006). For example, Butler and Darrah (2001) and Siebes, Wijnroks, and Vermeer (2002) found no strong evidence for the effectiveness of neurophysiologic approaches to improve daily activities of children with CP. For example, biofeedback has been used to reduce spasticity in children with CP, and while some individuals were able to almost eliminate spasticity, overall improvements in muscle activity did not result in functional improvement (Nielson & McCaughey, 1982). Sensory integration treatment was believed to improve a child's ability to process and integrate sensory information (visual, perceptual, etc.), and while some studies found it to be useful (Schaff & Miller, 2005), others did not (Vargas & Camilli, 1999). Other treatment interventions that have little to no effectiveness range from the use of hyperbaric oxygen (Collet et al., 2001) to electrical stimulation of muscles, to the use of the astronaut suit to promote independent mobility in children with CP (Rosenbaum, 2003).

Palmer (1997) has reviewed the status of the research on the effects of developmental interventions in infants and children with CP. These include physical therapy, occupational therapy, and speech and language therapy, as well as a variety of other early intervention programs (McCarton et al., 1997; McCormick, McCarton, Tonascia, & Brooks-Gunn, 1993). Palmer (1997) found little evidence to support one approach over the other. Finally, Butler and Darrah (2001) concluded from their review of 21 studies on neurodevelopmental treatment interventions that there are too few data to determine whether one intervention approach is more or less effective. Much of the difficulties with the research for children of different ages and what is helpful or not has to do with the methodological limitations of small sample sizes, heterogeneous samples, and limited generalizability of findings.

Preventive medical and well-being care for pregnant women have increased in efforts to reduce the incidence of CP in their children. For example, pregnant women are being tested for the Rh factor and, if negative, they can be immunized within 72 hours of giving birth. There has also been an emphasis on reducing the number of x-rays and medications taken, as well as an emphasis on the importance of self-care prior to conception and throughout pregnancy. Additionally, giving iodine to pregnant women in goiterogenic parts of the world will prevent "cretinism"—possibly the single most common cause of the CP/MR/deafness triad (Rosenbaum, personal communication, Feb. 17, 2011).

Table 10.1 summarizes studies examining ASD and CP.

In summary:

- There is a need for early and continuous parental education and child care so that parents are able to understand and support their child's functional abilities.
- The focus needs to be on the *management* of CP rather than on a *cure.*
- There needs to be an interdisciplinary approach to the treatment and management of CP, with parents playing an active and involved role in their child's life.
- Parent involvement in therapy is an important component for facilitating positive motor and non-motor outcomes for the child.

Table 10.1 STUDIES EXAMINING AUTISM SPECTRUM DISORDER

Source of Research and Purpose of Study	Study Design: Recruitment of Participants, and Research Methodology

Allik, Larsson, & Smedje, 2006
    To evaluate the health-related quality of life (HRQOL) of parents of children with Asperger's syndrome (AS) or high-functioning autism (HFA) between 8–12 years of age and how child behavior characteristics are correlated with HRQOL
	N = 61 parents of 32 children with HFA/AS
	Comparison group:
	N = 59 parents of 32 children with typical development
	Recruitment:
	- Convenience sample
	- Recruited from a pool of 122 potential participants
	Exclusion Criteria:
	- Suspected mental retardation
	- Language delay
	- Physical disability
	- Seizure disorder
	- Medication
	Demographics:
	Age:
	    Mothers of children with AS/HFA: M = 42.4; SD: 6.7; Range = 28–54
	    Fathers of children with AS/HFA: M = 45.6; SD: 6.9; Range: 35–64
	       Children with AS/HFA: M = 10.8; Range: 8–12
	       Comparison group:
	       Mothers: M = 40.3; SD = 5.1; Range: 31–51
	       Fathers: M = 42.7; SD: 4.9; Range: 35–53
	       Children: M = 10.9; Range: 8–13
	Gender:
	    31 mothers and 30 fathers of 32 children with HFA/AS
	    Comparison group:
	    30 mothers and 29 fathers
	SES:
	    Reported as employment of parents
	    Mothers who were gainfully employed: 23/31 (74.1%)
	    Fathers who were gainfully employed: 28/30 (93.3%)
	    Comparison group:
	    Mothers who were gainfully employed: 28/30 (93.3%)
	    Fathers who were gainfully employed: 28/29 (96.5%)
	Ethnicity:
	    Not reported
	Research Methodology:
	• Case-control study
	• Part of a larger, longitudinal study
	Measures:
	- Short-Form Health Survey (SF-12)
	- High-Functioning Autism Spectrum Screening Questionnaire (ASSQ)
	- The Strengths and Difficulties Questionnaire (SDQ)

Bishop, Richler, Cain, & Lord, 2007
    To explore the association between family demographics and perceived negative impact in parents of children with ASD
    To examine the association between perceived negative impact in parents of children with ASD and child behavior characteristics
	N = 110 mothers of children with ASD
	Recruitment:
	- Subsample of a longitudinal study on early diagnosis
	- Those who had completed Child and Adolescent Impact Assessment (CAIA) at age 9 follow-up assessment (N = 116)
	Inclusion criteria:
	- Those who had completed the CAIA at age 9 follow-up assessment
	- Mothers only
	- Participants who identified as Caucasian or African American

Analysis & Results	Study Strengths & Limitations

Statistical Procedures:

Analyses between groups

- Linear regression to compare SF-12 scores between parents in the AS/HFA group and parents in the comparison group
- Linear regression to compare HRQOL scores between mothers and fathers in the AS/HFA group and mothers and fathers in the comparison group
- T-test for paired samples was used to compare ASSQ and SDQ scores between children with AS/HFA and children in the comparison group

Analyses within AS/HFA group

- Linear regression to determine association between HRQOL and child behavior characteristics, ASSQ and SDQ scores

Results:

- Maternal physical health was poorer among mothers of children with AS/HFA than mothers in the comparison group
- Maternal mental health did not differ between groups
- Paternal HRQOL (both physical and mental health) did not differ between groups
- Maternal physical health among mothers of children with AS/HFA was significantly poorer than paternal physical health of fathers of children with AS/HFA
- Parental HRQOL was not significantly correlated with ASSQ scores
- Maternal HRQOL scores were significantly correlated with SDQ scores (higher maternal physical and mental health scores were associated with higher scores of pro-social child behavior and lower scores of child hyperactivity and conduct problems)
- Paternal HRQOL was not significantly associated with SDQ scores

Strengths:

- Use of both parent and teacher reports of child behavior characteristics
- Validated measure of HRQOL (SF-12)
- Children in AS/HFA group had a formal diagnosis of AS or HFA that was further confirmed by lead researcher prior to study participation
- Findings support previous research on the physical health of parents of children with intellectual disabilities, cerebral palsy, and mental disorders

Limitations:

- Small sample
- Parental health was obtained only through self-report

Statistical Procedures:

- Linear regression to identify the predictors of perceived negative impact

Results:

- Only parent ethnicity, number of children in the family, scores on the VABS and restricted and repetitive behavior subscale of the ADI-R, and social support significantly predicted perceived negative impact

Strengths:

- Findings support previous research, which suggests that social support is associated with perceived negative impact

Limitations:

- Parent coping styles, attitudes, and personalities were not measured
- The CAIA has limited reliability and validity testing

(Continued)

Table 10.1 STUDIES EXAMINING AUTISM SPECTRUM DISORDER   *(Continued)*

Source of Research and Purpose of Study	Study Design: Recruitment of Participants, and Research Methodology
	Demographics (of mothers): *Age:* Not reported *Gender:* Female: N = 110 *SES:* Not reported *Ethnicity:* Caucasian: N = 80 African American: N = 30 **Research Methodology:** - Cross-sectional (part of a longitudinal study, but reports on one point in time) **Measures:** - Child and Adolescent Impact Assessment (CAIA) - Autism Diagnostic Interview-Revised (ADI-R) - The Vineland Adaptive Behavior Scale (VABS) - Various child assessment measures (WISC-III, DAS, MSEL and IQ measures included the Peabody Vocabulary Test-3rd edition and the Ravens Progressive Matrices)
Brown, MacAdam-Crisp, Wang, & Iarocci, 2006 To examine the family quality of life across families of children with Down syndrome and autism and those with a child without a disability.	N = 33 families of children with Down syndrome N = 18 families of children with autism N = 18 families of children without a disability **Recruitment:** - Convenience sample - Recruited from Down syndrome and autism organizations in British Columbia, Canada **Inclusion criteria:** - Formal diagnosis of Down syndrome or autism **Demographics of parents across all groups:** *Age:* Mothers: Mean = 38–40 years of age Fathers: Mean = 41–45 years of age *Gender:* Not reported *SES:* Not reported *Ethnicity:* Not reported **Research Methodology:** - Survey with follow-up interview held with a subsample of participants **Measures:** - Family Quality of Life Survey (FQLS) (9 subscales) a. Health b. Financial Well-being c. Family Relations d. Support from other people e. Support from disability-related services f. Spiritual and cultural beliefs g. Careers and preparation for careers h. Leisure and enjoyment of life i. Community and civic involvement

Analysis & Results	Study Strengths & Limitations

- Ethnicity: Caucasian mothers reported significantly lower perceived negative impact than African American mothers
- Number of children in the family: Mothers with fewer children reported significantly higher perceived negative impact
- Scores on the VABS and restricted and repetitive behavior subscale of the ADI-R: Lower scores on both predicted higher perceived negative impact scores
- Social support: Lower social support scores (less social support) predicted higher perceived negative impact scores
- Perceived negative impact and repetitive and restricted behavior scores were not significantly related to child diagnosis or severity of symptoms
- The number of children in the family with a disability was not significantly associated with perceived negative impact

Statistical Procedures:
- Correlations between all of the 9 subscales and the FQLS total score were run

Results:
- Health, financial well-being, family relationships, careers and preparing for careers, and leisure and enjoyment of life domains contributed most to total family quality of life
- Post-hoc F-tests revealed that significant differences across group means generally favored the control group (families with a child without a disability)
- For health, financial well-being, and careers and preparing for careers, the control group differed significantly compared to the Down syndrome and autism groups
- For leisure and enjoyment, a significant difference was found between the autism and control group but not between the Down syndrome and control group
- Families without a child with a disability had statistically significantly higher levels of satisfaction with perceived family quality of life than those families with a child with Down syndrome or autism

Strengths:
- Findings are consistent with previous research

Limitations:
- Small sample
- Self-selected sample (i.e., those who completed and returned the survey by mail)

(Continued)

Table 10.1 Studies Examining Autism Spectrum Disorder   *(Continued)*

Source of Research and Purpose of Study	Study Design: Recruitment of Participants, and Research Methodology

Kogan, Strickland, Blumberg, Singh, Perrin, & van Dyck, 2008
  To examine the health care experiences (care, service, supports) of children with autism and the impact of having a child with autism on the family

N = 2,088 children (3–17 years of age) with special health care needs and autism

N = 9,534 children with special health care needs with emotional, developmental, and behavioral problems excluding autism

N = 26,751 children with other special health care needs

Recruitment:
- Analysis of data from 2005–2006 National Survey of Children with Special Health Care Needs (CSHCN)

Inclusion criteria:
- Screened using the CSHCN screener
- Classified children according to medical, behavioral, or other health condition, expected duration >12 months, resulted in functional impairments, increased need for medication, services, care or therapy

Demographics of children with ASD: (Prevalence of CSHCN with ASD per 10,000)

Age:
3–5 years: 78
6–8 years: 94
9–11 years: 95
12–14 years: 99
15–17 years: 65

Gender:
Male: 133
Female: 37

SES: Reported as Poverty Status % (in 2005, 100% of poverty level was defined as $19,350 for family of 4)
<100: 93
100 to <200: 97
200 to <400: 82
>400: 77

Ethnicity:
Hispanic, any race: 55
Non-Hispanic, White: 100
Non-Hispanic, Black: 81
Non-Hispanic, Other: 68

Research Methodology:
- Cross-sectional study
- Survey–parent/caregiver report
- Details about methodology reported elsewhere

Kuhn & Carter, 2006
  To explore the association between maternal self-efficacy/competency and parenting cognitions including maternal agency, guilt, and knowledge of autism among mothers of children with autism

N = 170 mothers of children with autism

N = 141 mothers participated in completing questionnaires

N = 29 mothers took part in a focus group

Recruitment:
- Recruited from autism service providers, support groups for parents of children with autism, online postings on autism-specific websites

Inclusion criteria:
- Not reported

Demographics of mothers:
Age: Mean = 37 years
Gender: All female

Analysis & Results	Study Strengths & Limitations
Statistical Procedures: - Weighted logistic regression **Results:** - ~535 000 children (3–17 years of age) with SHCN and autism - 5.6% of children with SHCN had ASD - Boys were ~3.5 times more likely to have SHCN and ASD when compared to girls - Children with SHCN and ASD were more likely than children with other SHCN to have unmet needs for particular health care services and family support services, delayed care, difficulty accessing referrals and family-centered care - Families of children with SHCN and ASD were more likely than children with other SHCN to have financial problems, be in need of additional income, spend more than 10 hours per week coordinating care and spend more than $1,000 in the previous year on their child's care related to SHCN or ASD - Children with SHCN and ASD were less likely to have a medical home compared with children with other SHCN - Children without a medical home reported significantly higher financial burden	**Strengths:** - Nationally representative sample **Limitations:** - Parent-report only - Focus on experience with health care system only and not other systems (e.g., education, social, community) - Did not control for comorbid conditions within the SHCN and ASD group (virtually all of the CSHCN and ASD had other conditions [90%]) - Difficult to establish causality between the presence of the medical home and financial burden due to cross-sectional nature of study
Statistical Analyses: - Bivariate correlations between study variables were run - Hierarchical linear regression analysis of variables predicting maternal self-efficacy **Results:** - Parenting stress, depression, and guilt were negatively correlated with maternal self-efficacy - Agency was positively correlated with maternal self-efficacy - Agency was statistically significantly correlated with guilt and autism knowledge	**Strengths:** - Development of two new measures assessing maternal agency and maternal guilt **Limitations:** - Diagnosis was reported by mothers only; sample was biased towards families with high SES

(Continued)

Table 10.1 Studies Examining Autism Spectrum Disorder   (*Continued*)

Source of Research and Purpose of Study	Study Design: Recruitment of Participants, and Research Methodology

	SES: Average annual household income = $60,000
	    Ethnicity: 12% of the sample identified as an "ethnic minority"
	Demographics of child:
	Age: Mean = 6.5 years;
	    Range = 2.4–10.8 years
	Gender: 87% male
	Research Methodology:
	- Cross-sectional
	Measures:
	- Maternal self-efficacy scale
	- Maternal agency questionnaire
	- Maternal guilt questionnaire
	- Maternal autism knowledge questionnaire
	- Center for Epidemiologic Studies Depression Scale (CES-D)
	- Parenting Stress Inventory-Short Form (PSI-SF)

Lee, Harrington, Louie, & Newschaffer, 2008 To examine and compare quality of life across families of children with autism, families of children with ADD/ADHD, and families with children without a disability or medical condition across early childhood, childhood, and adolescence	N = 483 children with autism N = 6,319 children with ADD/ADHD N = 58,953 children without a parent-reported disability or medical condition **Recruitment:** - Analysis of data from the 2003 National Survey of Children's Health - Random-digit dialing of households with children 0–17 across the United States **Inclusion criteria:** - Parent-reported diagnosis of autism or ADD/ADHD - Child between 3 and 17 years of age **Demographics:** *Age of parent:* Not reported *Age of child:* - 3–17 years of age - See full article for a detailed breakdown across groups (autism, ADD/ADHD, and controls) *Gender:* 78.5% mothers 17.3% fathers 4.2% other caregivers *SES:* - See full article for a detailed breakdown across age groups *Ethnicity:* - Most children across all age groups were identified as White - See full article for a detailed breakdown across age groups **Research Methodology:** - Cross-sectional - Data from the National Survey of Children's Health (NSCH) **Measures:** Questions from the NSCH covered the following areas of QOL: - Caring burden - Family outings

- Mothers with high levels of autism knowledge also indicated a high level of agency
- Mothers with low guilt scores had higher agency scores
- Using hierarchical linear regression, having another child with a disability, parenting stress, agency, and guilt all described the unique variance in predicting maternal self-efficacy

Statistical Procedures:
- Bivariate and multivariate regression analyses used to compare outcome measures across all three groups

Results:
- Caring burden, as reported by parents, was significantly higher in the autism group compared to the ADD/ADHD and control group
- Children between 6 and 11 years of age with autism were more likely to repeat a grade in school and to miss more than one week of school and less likely to participate in activities or be involved in the community than the ADD/ADHD and control groups
- Parental concerns about child (child's achievement, self-esteem, stress-coping, learning difficulty, and bullying) were significantly higher for the autism group than the control group without a disability or medical condition

Strengths:
- Nationally representative sample
- Identifies key areas of parental concern for their children

Limitations:
- Diagnosis was obtained through parent-report only
- Child cognitive functioning was not assessed
- Measure of QOL was limited due to nature of questions used in the National Survey of Children's Health

Table 10.1 Studies Examining Autism Spectrum Disorder *(Continued)*

Source of Research and Purpose of Study	Study Design: Recruitment of Participants, and Research Methodology
	- Family meals - Religious service attendance - Impact on employment - Missed school - Participation in activities - Repeating a grade - Independence - Community service

Montes & Halterman, 2007
  To describe and compare the psychological functioning, physical and mental health, family communication, and parenting supports of mothers of children with autism with mothers of children without autism
	N = 61,772 mothers of children between 4 and 17 years of age were surveyed by the NSCH in 2003
	  N = 364 children with autism
	Recruitment:
	- Analysis of data from the 2003 National Survey of Children's Health
	- Random-digit dialing of households with children 0–17 across the United States
	Inclusion criteria:
	- Parent reported diagnosis of autism
	Demographics for families of children with autism:
	Age of child:
	4–17 years of age
	Gender:
	Female: N = 79
	Male: N = 285
	SES:
	Number below the poverty level: N = 108
	Ethnicity:
	White: N = 294
	Black: N = 31
	Multiracial: N = 14
	Other: N = 10
	Research Methodology:
	- Cross-sectional
	- Data from the National Survey of Children's Health (NSCH)
	Measures:
	Likert-scale questions
	- Physical and mental health
	- Parenting stress and parent–child relationship
	- Coping with parenting
	- Parents' support
	- Family communication and domestic violence
	- Child pro-social skills
	- Demographic variables

Montes & Halterman, 2008 To determine the estimated financial impact associated with raising a child with autism	N = 11,684 parents of children in kindergarten to 8th grade N = 131 children with autism N = 2,775 children with other disabilities **Recruitment:** - Analysis of data from 2005 National Household Education Survey-After School Programs - Random-digit dialing of households with children in kindergarten-8th grade

Statistical Analysis:
- Bivariate comparison of maternal functioning between groups
- Multivariate logistic regressions of maternal functioning

Results:
- Overall maternal health between groups was not significantly different
- Maternal mental and emotional health was significantly poorer among mothers of children with autism than other mothers
- Mothers of children with autism were statistically significantly more likely to report that it was harder to care for their child than most other children their age and that they have given up more of their life than expected in the last month
- There was no statistically significant difference in perceived closeness of relationship with child or frequency of anger at child between both groups of mothers
- No difference in coping with parenting, parenting support or resolving household disagreements was found between groups
- In fact, mothers of children with autism were more likely to report that they were coping well with parenting challenges than mothers of children matched according to demographics and social skills

Strengths:
- Nationally representative sample
- Identifies the strengths of mothers of children with autism in coping and caring for their child

Limitations:
- Diagnosis was obtained through parent-report only

Statistical Analysis:
- Ordinal logistic regression analyses to estimate expected income of families of children with autism

Results:
- After controlling for parent education, type of family (two-parent vs. other), parent age, location of household (rural vs. urban), and minority ethnicity, families with a child with ASD significantly decreased the odds of living in a higher income household compared to the other groups

Strengths:
- Nationally representative sample
- First American study to estimate financial impact of raising a child with ASD

Limitations:
- Other causal factors may be associated with loss of household income
- Diagnosis was obtained through parent-report only
- Small sample of children with ASD

(Continued)

Table 10.1 Studies Examining Autism Spectrum Disorder   *(Continued)*

Source of Research and Purpose of Study	Study Design: Recruitment of Participants, and Research Methodology
	Inclusion criteria: Not reported in this article **Demographics:** *Age of children:* Not reported *Age of parents:* Not reported *Gender of parent and/or child:* Not reported *SES:* - Median income for entire sample: $47,500 (US) *Ethnicity of child with ASD:* - White, Non-Hispanic: N = 71 - Minority ethnicity: N = 60 **Research Methodology:** - Cross-sectional - Survey
Mori, Ujiie, Smith, & Howlin, 2009 To assess and compare stress among caregivers of children with Asperger's syndrome with caregivers of children with autism in Japan	N = 193 families N = 30 children with Asperger's N = 163 children with autism **Recruitment:** - Potential participants were identified through a clinic database and invited to participate by mail **Inclusion criteria:** - Diagnosis of autism or Asperger's syndrome - PDD-NOS was excluded - 12 years of age or younger **Child Demographics** (across autism and Asperger's groups): *Age:* Mean = 7.39 years; SD = 2.77 *Gender:* 84.5% male *SES:* Not reported Ethnicity: Not reported **Parent Demographics** (across autism and Asperger's groups): *Age of mothers:* Mean = 38.24 years; SD = 5.25 *Age of fathers:* Mean = 41.05 years; SD = 6.20 *Gender:* Mothers N = 193; Fathers N = 181 *SES:* Not reported *Ethnicity:* Not reported **Research Methodology:** - Cross-sectional **Measures:** - Parenting Stress Index-Short Form - Child and family demographic variables were collected - Information about social support was collected
Orsmond, Kraus, & Seltzer, 2004 To examine the relationship between individual and environmental factors of adolescents and adults with autism who live at home and their peer relationships and involvement in social and recreational activities	N = 235 adolescents and adults with autism who are living at home N = 185 adolescents N = 50 adults **Recruitment:** - Subsample of 407 participants from a four wave longitudinal study **Inclusion criteria:** - Formal diagnosis of autism (based on ADI-R)–Excluded those with Asperger's or PDD-NOS - Adolescent or adult living at home - The mother was the primary respondent

- This finding suggests that families with a child with ASD have a lower-than-expected income (based on factors such as education and other demographic variables)
- Estimated income for the average person was $53,420.45
- Based on the educational and demographic characteristics of families of children with ASD, their expected average income was $51,693.25 if their child did not have a disability
- However, these families reported an average income of $45,486.55, suggesting a 14% loss of income associated with raising a child with ASD

Statistical Analyses:
- Parenting stress between the two groups was assessed using ANCOVA

Results:
- High parental stress scores were found in both autism and Asperger's groups
- Mean parental stress scores were significantly higher among the Asperger's group than the autism group
- Higher parental stress scores were significantly associated with less father involvement, a family history of psychiatric disorders, and an expectation that the child would be dependent on parents later in life
- Correlations between parental stress and child's cognitive functioning (IQ) were not found

Strengths:
- Comparison within the autism spectrum (i.e., comparing autism to AS)

Limitations:
- Sample of parents of children with Asperger's syndrome was small

Statistical Analysis:
- Descriptive analysis of frequencies
- Multiple regression analyses (including logistic regression analysis and OLS regression analysis)

Results:
- 46.4% of the sample reported no peer relationships that met the ADI-R definition of friendship (i.e., peer of the same age who they interact with outside of a pre-arranged setting)
- Going for a walk and engaging in a hobby were the most frequent social or recreational activities reported (independent activities)

Strengths:
- Findings are consistent with previous research
- Examined peer and social relationships across adolescence and adulthood

Limitations:
- Parent-report only
- Involved participants who lived at home; findings may be different for those living in the community or independently

(Continued)

Table 10.1 STUDIES EXAMINING AUTISM SPECTRUM DISORDER (*Continued*)

Source of Research and Purpose of Study	Study Design: Recruitment of Participants, and Research Methodology
	Demographics: *Age of adolescent:* Mean: 15.48 SD: 2.82 *Age of adult:* Mean: 30.74 SD: 7.56 *Mother's age:* Mean: 44.43 SD: 5.75 Range: 32–66 *Gender of adolescent:* Male: 75.7% *Gender of adult:* Male: 62% *SES:* Not reported *Ethnicity:* Not reported **Research Methodology:** - Cross-sectional - Part of a longitudinal study **Measures:** - Friendship and peer relationships were assessed using the parent-report ADI-R - Social and recreational activities were assessed using an adapted version of the National Survey of Families and Households - Revised Activities of Daily Living Index - Inventory for Client and Agency Planning (ICAP) to measure behavior problems - ADI-R to measure language and reciprocal social interaction impairments
Ozonoff & Cathcart, 1998 To evaluate the effectiveness of a home-based, parent-led TEACCH program for children with autism	N = 22 children with autism N = 11 children in the treatment group N = 11 children in the control group **Recruitment:** - Recruited using a study announcement **Inclusion criteria:** Not reported **Demographics of children across groups:** *Age:* Range = 2–6 years of age *Gender:* 18 male; 4 female *SES:* Not reported *Ethnicity:* Caucasian American N = 21 Hispanic American N = 1 **Research Methodology:** - Quasi-experimental **Measures:** - Psychoeducational Profile-Revised (PEP-R) - Childhood Autism Rating Scale (CARS)

- Participating in a group recreational activity and attending a religious service were the second most frequent activities reported
- Age and severity of social impairment predicted peer relationships
- Adolescents (rather than adults) and those participants with less social impairment were more likely to have peer relationships
- Greater involvement in social and recreational activities was predicted by greater independence in activities of daily living, greater internalizing behavior problems, fewer social impairments, more services received, greater maternal involvement in social and recreational activities, and school inclusion

Procedures:
- Treatment group received 4 months of in-home parent training with a focus on developing their child's cognitive, academic and pre-vocational skills
- Pre- and post-test administration of measures
- Treatment sessions ranged from 8–12 (over the course of 10 weeks)
- Control group did not receive home programming and children attending regular day programming

Statistical Analyses:
- Repeated measures multivariate analysis of variance

Results:
- Matched groups, no significant differences
- At 4-month follow-up, children in the treatment group demonstrated significant improvements in imitation skills, fine and gross motor skills, cognitive performance, and overall PEP-R scores compared to the control group
- Pre-treatment PEP-R scores were demonstrated to be significantly correlated with total change scores

Strengths:
- Control group

Limitations:
- Participants were not randomly assigned
- Raters were not blind to group assignment
- Home programs were not manualized

(Continued)

Table 10.1 Studies Examining Autism Spectrum Disorder   (*Continued*)

Source of Research and Purpose of Study	Study Design: Recruitment of Participants, and Research Methodology
Panerai, Ferrante, & Zingale, 2002 To evaluate the effectiveness of a TEACCH program for children with autism	**Intervention Group:** N = 8 children with autism **Control Group:** N = 8 children with autism **Recruitment:** Not explicitly reported **Inclusion criteria:** Not reported **Demographics of children in the intervention group:** *Age:* Mean = 9 years *Gender:* All male *SES:* Low: N = 2 Middle: N = 4 High: N = 2 *Ethnicity:* Not reported **Demographics of children in the control group:** *Age:* Mean = 9 years *Gender:* All male *SES:* Low: N = 2 Middle: N = 5 High: N = 1 *Ethnicity:* Not reported **Research Methodology:** - Quasi-experimental **Measures:** - Psycho-Educational Profile-Revised (PEP-R) - Vineland Adaptive Behavior Scale (VABS)
Rao & Beidel, 2009 To examine the impact of raising a child with high-functioning autism (HFA) on parent stress, family functioning, and sibling adjustment	N = 15 families of children with HFA N = 14 families of matched control children **Recruitment:** - Convenience sample - Parents of children with HFA were recruited from autism clinic - Control group participants were recruited with flyers at a medical center **Inclusion criteria:** - Legal guardian of the child - Child had to be between 8 and 16 years and living in the same home as their parent/legal guardian - Children had to meet autism criteria according to the ADI-R - Children in the control group were interviewed using the Anxiety Disorders Interview Schedule to determine that they did not have a disorder **Demographics:** *Age of children in both groups:* 8–14 years of age

Analysis & Results	Study Strengths & Limitations

Procedures:
- Children in the TEACCH program received individualized educational programming, environmental modifications where appropriate, and alternative communication training
- Children in the control group attended an integrated classroom with support from teachers and outpatient treatment such as speech therapy
- Both groups received the same number of hours
- Measures were administered twice with a one-year interval between administration

Statistical Analysis:
- Wilcoxon test

Results:

PEP-R
- The intervention group had statistically significant improvements in imitation, perception, gross motor skills, hand–eye coordination, cognitive performance, and total score
- In fact, the intervention group had statistically significant improvements across all domains except fine motor skills
- The control had statistically significant improvements in hand–eye coordination only

VABS:
- The intervention group demonstrated statistically significant improvements in personal domains, total daily living skills, play and leisure, and total score
- The control group demonstrated statistically significant improvements in daily living skills only
- Overall, results suggest that the TEACCH program was more effective than the integrated classroom with respect to the domains listed above for children with autism

Strengths:
- Blinded administration of measures

Limitations:
- Used the VABS scale, which only assesses verbal behavior, even though all participants were nonverbal
- Participants were not randomly assigned

Statistical Analysis:
- Independent samples t-tests

Results:
- Significant group difference for total parenting stress
- Parents of children with HFA scored higher on parent stress than the control
- Source of parenting stress was associated with child behavioral factors
- Differences between groups for family functioning did not reach statistical significance; however, analysis of items revealed that parents of controls rated their families as higher in independence (p = 0.05)
- Differences between groups for parent psychological problems and general physical and mental health and sibling adjustment were not statistically significant
- Parent ratings of total behavior problems and internalizing behavior problems was significantly higher for the HFA versus the control group

Strengths:
- Considered child's cognitive functioning (IQ) in measuring impact on parents and family

Limitations:
- Small sample size
- Did not include a comparison group with another condition; therefore it is difficult to determine if these differences are unique to HFA

(Continued)

Table 10.1 STUDIES EXAMINING AUTISM SPECTRUM DISORDER   *(Continued)*

Source of Research and Purpose of Study	Study Design: Recruitment of Participants, and Research Methodology
	Age of HFA caregivers: Mean = 42.5 years *Age of control group caregivers:* 41.6 years *Gender:* HFA group: 12 mothers and 3 fathers Control group: 12 mothers and 2 fathers *SES:* HFA group: Annual family income ranged from $31,000 to $175,000 Control group: Annual family income ranged from $27,000 to $170,000 *Ethnicity:* The majority of children in both groups were Caucasian **Research Methodology:** - Cross-sectional **Measures:** - Parenting Stress Index (PSI) - Family Environment Scale - Symptom Checklist-90-Revised - SF-36 Health Survey - Piers-Harris Children's Self-Concept Scale - Child Behavior Checklist (CBCL)
Sallows & Graupner, 2005 To examine the outcomes of receiving intensive behavioral intervention for children with autism and identify potential predictors or child characteristics associated with positive outcomes	N = 23 children with autism N = 13 children in clinic-led treatment group N = 10 children in parent-led treatment group **Recruitment:** - Recruited through local special education programs for children 0–3 years **Inclusion criteria:** - Between 24 and 42 months at intake - Score of 35 or higher on the Mental Development Index - No severe neurologic impairments - Formal diagnosis of autism **Demographics of children in clinic-led treatment group:** *Age (at intake):* Mean = 33.23 months; SD = 3.89 months *Gender:* 11 male; 2 female *SES:* Median = $62,000; Range = $35–100,000+ **Demographics of children in parent-led treatment group:** *Age (at intake):* Mean = 34.20 months; SD = 5.06 months *Gender:* 8 male; 2 female *SES:* Median = $59,000; Range = $30–100,000+ **Research Methodology:** - Randomized controlled trial **Measures:** - Bayley Scales of Infant Development - Merrill-Palmer Scale of Mental Tests - Reynell Developmental Language Scales

Procedures:
- Children were randomly assigned to one of two groups: (1) early intensive behavioral treatment led by clinic or (2) parent-led behavioral therapy with fewer hours and less supervision
- Treatment in both groups was based on the Lovaas UCLA model

Statistical Analyses:
- ANOVA used to examine treatment effects (2 x 2 ANOVAS)
- Linear and logistic regressions used to predict outcomes

Results:
- Clinic-led group was found to have higher mean IQs than the parent-led group
- Average IQ for all children across both groups increased
- Children with higher IQs at pre-intervention were more likely to have average IQs at 4 years of age
- A group of children demonstrated major improvements over time (N = 11; 5 children from the clinic-led group and 6 children from the parent-led group)
- The remaining 12 children did not demonstrate significant improvements in IQ
- Post-treatment IQ scores were best predicted by receptive language, non-verbal and verbal imitation, pretreatment IQ, and ADI-R scores on social interaction and communication
- The number of hours per week of intervention was not significantly correlated with post-treatment IQ

Strengths:
- Random assignment
- Long-term follow-up

Limitations:
- Lack of no-treatment control group
- Small sample

(*Continued*)

Table 10.1 Studies Examining Autism Spectrum Disorder   (*Continued*)

Source of Research and Purpose of Study	Study Design: Recruitment of Participants, and Research Methodology
	- Vineland Adaptive Behavior Scales - Wechsler Intelligence Scale for Children - Autism Diagnostic Interview-Revised - Personality Inventory for Children - Child Behavior Checklist
Smith, Groen, & Wynn 2000 To examine the effectiveness of intensive behavioral intervention versus parent training for youth with pervasive developmental disorders (autism or PDD-NOS)	N = 28 children with autism or PDD-NOS N = 14 children with autism N = 14 children with PDD-NOS N = 15 children assigned to intensive behavioral intervention group N = 13 children assigned to parent-training group **Recruitment:** - Convenience sample - Children who were referred to the UCLA Young Autism Project between 1989 and 1992 **Inclusion criteria:** - Between 18 and 42 months at intake - Geographically close to treatment center - IQ ratio between 35 and 75 - Formal diagnosis of autism or PDD-NOS - No major comorbid conditions **Demographics for children in intensive behavioral intervention group:** *Age at intake:* Mean = 36.07 months; SD = 6 months *Gender:* 12 male; 3 female *SES:* Median = \$40–50,000; Range = <\$10,000 to \$75–\$100,000 *Ethnicity:* White N = 7 Hispanic N = 4 Black N = 1 Asian N = 3 **Demographics for children in parent-training group:** *Age at intake:* Mean = 35.77 months; SD = 5.37 months *Gender:* 11 male; 2 female *SES:* Median = \$40–50,000; Range = <\$10,000 to \$75–\$100,000 *Ethnicity:* White N = 7 Hispanic N = 2 Black N = 3 Asian N = 1 **Research Methodology:** - Randomized controlled trial **Outcomes measured:** - Intellectual functioning - Language functioning - Adaptive functioning - Socio-emotional functioning - Academic achievement - Class placement - Progress in treatment - Parent evaluation

- At follow-up (2–4 years of treatment), 11 of 23 children had IQs within the normal range (48%)
- Differences between groups were not significant, suggesting that both groups benefited from treatment and pre-treatment variables played a larger role in determining outcomes

Procedures:
- Treatment based on Lovaas UCLA model of early behavioral intervention
- Intensive behavioral intervention involved 30 hours per week over 2–3 years from a team of therapists
- Parent training involved 5 hours per week for 3–9 months to teach parents the Lovaas treatment approach

Statistical Analyses:
- Two-tailed t-tests

Results:
- No statistically significant between-group differences at intake
- At follow-up, the intensive behavioral intervention group scored significantly higher on measures of IQ, visual-spatial skills, and language development but not adaptive behavior
- The intensive behavioral intervention group was also more likely to be placed in less restrictive schools/classrooms
- No statistically significant between group differences on parent and teacher rated child behavior
- There was a trend to suggest that children with PDD-NOS improved more than children with a diagnosis of autism (however, findings were not statistically significant)
- Pre-treatment IQ was not significantly correlated with outcome variables
- Parents in both groups were satisfied with the services they received

Strengths:
- Randomized controlled trial
- Long-term follow-up

Limitations:
- Lack of no-treatment control group
- Small sample
- Many of the measures used were developed for children without disabilities

Table 10.1 Studies Examining Autism Spectrum Disorder   *(Continued)*

Source of Research and Purpose of Study	Study Design: Recruitment of Participants, and Research Methodology
Welterlin, 2009 To evaluate the effectiveness of a home-based TEACCH program for young children with autism	N = 10 children with autism and their parents **Recruitment:** - Convenience sample - Referred to TEACCH program after being placed on a diagnostic assessment wait list **Inclusion criteria:** - Formal or suspected diagnosis of autism - Under 42 months of age - Not receiving other comprehensive early intervention services **Demographics across groups:** *Age:* Mean = 32.2 months; Range = 24.9 months to 39.1 months *Gender:* 9 male; 1 female *Ethnicity:* Caucasian American: N = 8 African American: N = 1 Hispanic: N = 1 *SES:* Household income at or above $50,000: 50% of sample **Research Methodology:** - Randomized, controlled trial **Measures:** - Mullen Early Learning Scales - Parenting Stress Index (PSI) - Scales of Independent Behavior-Revised (SIB-R) - TEACCH Training Quiz (TTQ)
Studies Examining Cerebral Palsy	
Arnaud, White-Koning, Michelson, Parkes, Parkinson, Thyen, Beckung, Dickinson, Fauconnier, Marcelli, McManus, & Colver, 2008 To examine the relationship between type and severity of impairment among children with CP, family psychosocial, social, and economic characteristics and parent-reported child quality of life	N = 818 children with CP (8–12 years of age) **Recruitment:** - Population-based survey from 7 European countries - Recruited from population-based CP register **Inclusion criteria:** - Diagnosis of CP - Between 8 and 12 years of age **Demographics of children:** *Age:* Mean = 10.4 years; Range = 8–12 years *Gender:* 59% male *SES:* Not reported *Ethnicity:* Not reported **Demographics of parents:** *Age:* Not reported *Gender:* Not reported *SES:* Not reported *Ethnicity:* Not reported

Analysis & Results	Study Strengths & Limitations

Procedures:
- Children were randomly assigned to either the treatment or wait-list control group
- Five children were assigned to each group
- Treatment involved 1.5-hour sessions once per week over the course of 12 weeks

Statistical Analyses:
- Independent samples t-test
- One-tailed independent t-test

Results:
- The intervention group demonstrated statistically significantly more improvement on the fine motor skills subscale, the parent stress subscale of the PSI, and externalizing and generalized maladaptive behavior subscales on the SIB-R than the control group

Strengths:
- Random assignment
- Wait-list control group

Limitations:
- Small sample
- Wait-list control group makes long-term follow-up impossible

---

Statistical Analyses:
- Multivariate, multi-level logistic regression analysis

Results:
- Children with poor motor function and lower IQ were more likely to have poorer quality of life
- However, greater severity of QOL was not always associated with poorer QOL
- Pain was significantly associated with poor QOL in physical and psychological well-being and self-perception
- Higher parental stress was associated with poorer child QOL
- In sum, motor and intellectual impairment are associated with parent-reported poor QOL in children with CP

Strengths:
- Examined the impact of impairment severity across all domains of QOL

Limitations:
- Parent-report only
- Cross-sectional methodology hinders drawing causal explanations (i.e., between parental stress and child QOL)

(Continued)

Table 10.1 STUDIES EXAMINING AUTISM SPECTRUM DISORDER   (*Continued*)

Source of Research and Purpose of Study	Study Design: Recruitment of Participants, and Research Methodology
	Research Methodology: - Cross-sectional survey - Population-based **Measures:** - QOL was assessed using the Kidscreen questionnaire (parent-report) - Gross Motor Function Classification System - Child Health Questionnaire - Formal IQ assessment - Parenting Stress Index-Short Form

Brehaut, Kohen, Raina, Walter, Russell, Swinton, O'Donnell, & Rosenbaum, 2004
  To examine and compare the physical and psychosocial health of caregivers of children with CP to a nationally representative sample of parents
	N = 468 caregivers of children with CP
	N = 2,414 parents (from the NLSCY database)
	N = 5,548 parents (from NPHS database)
	Recruitment:
	- Recruited from a previous study
	- Caregivers of children with CP were recruited from 18 public rehabilitation centers in Ontario, Canada
	- Data on parents of children without CP were collected from two national surveys (National Population Health Survey and the National Longitudinal Study of Children and Youth)
	Inclusion criteria:
	- Diagnosis of CP
	Demographics of caregivers of children with CP:
	Age: Mean = 40.3; SD = 6.7; Range = 23–63
	Gender: 94.4% female
	SES: According to household income
	$0–29,999: 25%
	$30–59,999: 34.1%
	$60,000 or more: 40.9%
	Ethnicity: Not reported
	Demographics of NLSCY sample of parents:
	Age:
	Mean = 39.9; SD = 5.4; Range = 18–64
	Gender: 93% female
	SES: According to household income
	$0–29,999: 16.1%
	$30–59,999: 32.5%
	$60,000 or more: 51.4%
	Ethnicity: Not reported
	Demographics of NPHS sample of parents:
	Age: Mean = 40.2; SD = 6.3;
	   Range = 18–75
	Gender: 53.5% female
	SES: According to household income
	$0–29,999: Not reported
	$30–59,999: Not reported
	$60,000 or more: Not reported
	Ethnicity: Not reported
	Research Methodology:
	- Cross-sectional
	Outcomes measured:
	- Psychological health
	- Social Support
	- Physical health

Statistical Analyses:
- Chi-square tests of association and t-tests for comparison of means between groups

Results:
- Caregivers of children with CP and the NLSCY sample were similar but the CP group and NPHS samples differed (more men were sampled in the NPHS study)
- Caregivers of children with CP reported greater financial strain than the NLSCY sample (fewer worked for pay, lower overall reported incomes)
- Caregivers of children with CP had higher scores for distress and chronicity of distress than the NPHS sample
- Caregivers of children with CP and the NPHS sample did not significantly in levels of social support or family functioning however caregivers of children with CP reported a higher frequency of contacts with those in their social support system
- Caregivers of children with CP reported significantly greater physical health problems than the NLSCY sample

Strengths:
- Comparison with nationally representative samples

Limitations:
- As a cross-sectional study, difficult to determine causal explanations

(*Continued*)

Table 10.1 STUDIES EXAMINING AUTISM SPECTRUM DISORDER   (*Continued*)

Source of Research and Purpose of Study	Study Design: Recruitment of Participants, and Research Methodology
Cheshire, Barlow, & Powell, 2010 To examine and compare the positive and negative aspects of psychosocial well-being among parents of children with CP and parents of children with a long-term health condition (LTHC)	N = 70 parents of children with CP N = 70 parents of children without a LTHC **Recruitment of parents of children with CP:** - Convenience sample - Parents of children with CP who were waiting to begin an intervention on massage therapy for their child were invited to take part in the study - Of the 114 parents who were interested, 81 completed the questionnaire and consent form - 11 parents withdrew leaving a final sample of 70 **Recruitment of parents of children without LTHC:** - Convenience sample - Recruited through a university **Inclusion criteria:** - Parents of children with CP **Demographics of CP group:** *Age of parent:* Mean: 39 years SD: 8.7 *Age of child:* Mean: 6.4 years SD: 4.1 *Gender of parent:* Mothers (89%) *Gender of child with CP:* Male: 64% *SES:* Not reported *Ethnicity of parent:* White European (80%) **Demographics of control group:** *Age of parents:* Mean: 39.6 years SD: 6.5 *Age of child:* Mean: 7.3 years SD: 5.0 *Gender of parent:* Mothers (90%) *Gender of child with CP:* Male: 44% *SES:* Not reported *Ethnicity of parent:* White European (97%) **Research Methodology:** - Cross-sectional **Measures:** - Demographic information was collected - Hospital Anxiety and Depression Scale (HADS) was used to assess psychological well-being - Satisfaction with Life Scale was used to assess positive well-being

Analysis & Results	Study Strengths & Limitations
Statistical Analysis: - T-tests and chi-square tests were used **Results:** - Statistically significant differences between groups were found for current work situation and health problems - Parents in the control group were more likely to be employed and had fewer health problems than parents of children with CP - Parents of children with CP had significantly higher rates of anxiety and depression and significantly lower satisfaction with life compared to parents in the control group	**Strengths:** - Assessed both positive and negative aspects of psychosocial well-being **Limitations:** - Potential for sampling bias as parent participants of children with CP were those with an interest in attending an intervention to help their child - Small representation of fathers

(Continued)

Table 10.1 Studies Examining Autism Spectrum Disorder   (*Continued*)

Source of Research and Purpose of Study	Study Design: Recruitment of Participants, and Research Methodology
Cohen, Biran, Aran, & Gross-Tsur, 2008 To investigate the associations between psychosocial factors, specifically locus of control, disease severity, anxiety, and parenting style in children with CP	N = 30 children with CP N = 30 of their siblings (13 male; 17 female) **Recruitment:** - Convenience sample - All families participating in an after-school program for children with CP in regular schools were invited to participate **Inclusion criteria for children with CP:** - Formal diagnosis of CP - Between 6 and 18 years of age - Average intelligence - Attending a regular school - No major comorbid conditions **Inclusion criteria for siblings:** - Healthy - Sibling closest in age to child with CP - Attending a regular classroom within a regular school **Demographics of children with CP:** *Age:* Mean = 11.66 years; SD = 3.17 years; Range = 6–18 years *Gender:* 15 male; 15 female **Demographics of siblings:** *Age:* Mean = 12.16; SD = 3.67; Range = 6–18 years *SES:* Assessed using Abramson's 1982 criteria High SES: 36.7% Middle SES: 30% Low SES: 30% *Ethnicity:* Not reported **Research Methodology:** - Cross-sectional **Measures:** - Locus of control scale for children (child self-report) - Children Reports of Parent Behavior Inventory (mother self-report) - Revised Children's Manifest Anxiety Scale (child self-report) - Gross Motor Function Classification System
Collet, Vanasse, Marois, Amar, Goldberg, Lambert, & Majnemer, 2001 To investigate the effectiveness of hyperbaric oxygen for children with CP	N = 111 children with CP (3–12 years of age) Treatment group (hyperbaric oxygen): N = 57 Control group (slightly pressurized room air): N = 54 **Recruitment:** - Convenience sample drawn from 17 rehabilitation centers in Quebec **Inclusion criteria:** - Formal diagnosis of CP - History of hypoxia in perinatal period - 3–12 years of age - Motor developmental age between 6 months and 4 years - Psychological development of 2 years or more

Analysis & Results	Study Strengths & Limitations
Statistical Analyses: - Pearson correlations - T-tests for matched samples for between-group comparisons - Multiple regression model **Results:** - Age of children with CP and their siblings was significantly correlated with the autonomy-control aspect of the measure of parenting style, suggesting that children's perceptions of autonomy granted by their mothers increased with age - Differences between groups on locus of control, anxiety parenting style were not significant, regardless of disease severity - Within-group analysis revealed that locus of control and anxiety were highly correlated; specifically, higher locus of control was associated with a more external locus of control - External locus of control was significantly correlated with a rejecting and a controlling parenting style - Higher anxiety was significantly correlated with a more rejecting parenting style - A multiple regression revealed that the acceptance/ rejection aspect of parenting style significantly predicted locus of control for children with CP - For siblings, only age and anxiety significantly predicted locus of control (and not parenting style)	**Strengths:** - Findings are consistent with previous research that has revealed the resilience of children with CP and the significance of family and environmental factors in shaping psychosocial adaptation **Limitations:** - Small sample - Parent- or child-report only
Procedure: - Hyperbaric treatment involved 40 sessions over 2 months - Each session involved 1 hour in 100% oxygen at 1.75 atmospheres absolute - For the control group, treatment involved 40 sessions over the course of 2 months - Each session involved 1 hour of slightly pressurized air at 1.3 atmospheres absolute - Outcome measures were administered at baseline, after 20 sessions, 40 sessions, and 3 months following the end of treatment **Statistical Analyses:** - Analysis of covariance	**Strengths:** - Randomized - Control group - Double-blind **Limitations:** - Parent-report outcome measures - Parents were highly motivated and optimistic about treatment effects

(*Continued*)

Table 10.1 STUDIES EXAMINING AUTISM SPECTRUM DISORDER   (*Continued*)

Source of Research and Purpose of Study	Study Design: Recruitment of Participants, and Research Methodology

	Demographics:
	Age of children in treatment group:
	Mean: 7.2 SD: 2.6
	Age of children in control group:
	Mean: 7.2 SD: 2.6
	Gender of children in treatment group:
	Male: N = 30
	Female: N = 27
	Gender of children in control group:
	Male: N = 22
	Female: N = 32
	SES:
	Not reported
	Ethnicity:
	Not reported
	Research Methodology:
	- Randomized controlled trial
	Measures:
	- Primary outcome measure: Gross motor function (GMFM)
	- Secondary outcome measures included:
	  • Assessment of performance of activities of daily living
	  • Visual and auditory attention
	  • Visuospatial and verbal working memory
	  • Speech

Ketelaar, Gorter, Vermeer, Hart, & Helders, 2006 To evaluate the effectiveness of a functional therapy program on motor functioning of young children with CP	**Intervention group:** N = 28 children (2–7 years) with CP **Control group:** N = 27 children (2–7 years) with CP **Recruitment:** - Convenience sample - Recruited by physical therapists working in a primary health care setting in the Netherlands **Inclusion criteria:** - Diagnosis of CP - Between 2 and 7 years of age - Not enrolled in a special education program at school - Not receiving treatment at a rehabilitation center **Demographics of children in intervention group:** *Age:* Mean = 54 months; SD = 20 months; *Gender:* 16 male; 12 female *SES:* Not reported *Ethnicity:* Not reported **Demographics of children in control group:** *Age:* Mean = 56 months; SD = 20 months; *Gender:* 17 male; 10 female *SES:* Not reported

- Non-parametric tests used when appropriate

Results:
- Children in both groups improved significantly across all outcomes from pre- to post- intervention and these improvements persisted over time (maintained at 3-month follow-up)
- Children who received hyperbaric oxygen treatment experienced ear problems compared to children in the control group

Procedures:
- Children were assigned to either the intervention or control group
- Children in the intervention group received functional physical therapy (*see chapter for full description of therapy)
- Children in the control group continued in their previous course of therapy
- All children were pre-tested prior to intervention initiation, then again at 6 months, 12 months and 18 months
- Therapists received training in functional physical therapy prior to the initiation of therapy

Statistical Analyses:
- One-tailed repeated-measures analysis of variance

Results:
- No differences between groups were found over time on the GMFM
- However, the functioning skills in daily situations (PEDI) for children in the intervention group improved more than those of children in the control group
- Effect size of functional skills, as measured by the PEDI and calculated using pre-test and final assessment scores were 0.34 for self-care and 0.61 for mobility
- Parents in the intervention group reported statistically significantly higher/adaptive scores in terms of perceived parenting competency and perception of parenting

Strengths:
- Control group

Limitations:
- Follow-up ceased at 18 months; therefore, long-term effects are unknown
- Only children with mild forms of CP were included
- Pure random assignment was not achieved

(*Continued*)

Table 10.1 STUDIES EXAMINING AUTISM SPECTRUM DISORDER   *(Continued)*

Source of Research and Purpose of Study	Study Design: Recruitment of Participants, and Research Methodology
	Ethnicity: Not reported **Research Methodology:** - Quasi-experimental **Measures:** - Gross Motor Function Measure (GMFM-88) - Pediatric Evaluation of Disability Inventory (PEDI) - Questionnaire for therapists - Questionnaire for parents regarding their home program - Family functioning questionnaires for parents (Dutch)
Majnemer, Shevell, Rosenbaum, Law, & Poulin, 2007 To describe and identify the potential determinants of the quality of life of children with CP	N = 95 children with CP (6–12 years of age) **Recruitment:** - A neurologist's database was reviewed for all children with a diagnosis of CP (between July 1991 and June 2001) - Invited to participate by letter **Inclusion criteria:** - Children with CP - Between 6 and 12 years of age **Demographics of children with CP:** *Age:* Mean = 9.3 years; SD = 2.1 *Gender:* 63.2% male *SES:* Not reported *Ethnicity:* Not reported **Research Methodology:** - Historical cohort study **Measures:** - Child Health Questionnaire (CHQ) - Pediatric Quality of Life Inventory - Both completed by parent and child where possible
McCarton, Brooks-Gunn, Wallace, Bauer, Bennett, Berenbaum, Broyles, Casey, McCormick, Scott, Tyson, Tonascia, & Meinart, 1997 To assess the cognitive functioning, academic achievement, school performance, behavior, and health of low-birth weight (LBW) children at the age of 8 years who had participated in a randomized controlled trial of early intervention services from birth to age 3	Intervention group: N = 336 children Control group: N = 538 children **Recruitment:** - Reported elsewhere **Inclusion criteria:** - Birth weight of <2500 grams - Gestational age of <37 weeks - No severe medical condition or neurologic impairment **Demographics:** *Age:* Reported previously *Gender:* Reported previously *SES:* Reported previously *Ethnicity:* Reported previously **Research Methodology:** - Cohort study - Follow-up of a randomized controlled trial

Statistical Analyses:
- Descriptive statistics
- Univariate analyses were run: Pearson correlations and simple linear regressions
- Multiple linear regression models

Results:
- Children were less likely to report low psychosocial well-being
- More than half of the parents rated their child's psychosocial well-being as less than one SD lower than the norm
- Limitations on activities and higher restrictions on gross motor function was associated with poor physical well-being
- Very few variables were found to be associated with psychosocial well-being (including biomedical factors)
- In sum, results suggest that QOL among children with CP is variable and that many children may have a QOL similar to peers without a disability

Strengths:
- Inclusion of both child and parent reports

Limitations:
- Small sample size

Statistical Analyses:
- Multiple linear regression models were developed to assess outcome across the lighter and heavier birth weight groups

Results:
- Cognitive, school, and behavior outcomes were not statistically significantly different between the intervention and control groups
- However, the heavier LBW children in both groups scored significantly higher on cognitive and school outcomes
- While no differences in illness or hospitalization between groups were found, the intervention group was rated as having lower physical functioning than the control group (i.e., more limited in physical activities, etc.)

Strengths:
- Highlights an important distinction between LBW premature infants (in terms of birth weight)

(Continued)

Table 10.1 STUDIES EXAMINING AUTISM SPECTRUM DISORDER   (*Continued*)

Source of Research and Purpose of Study	Study Design: Recruitment of Participants, and Research Methodology
	Outcomes measured: - Cognitive functioning - Academic achievement - School performance - Behavior - Health
McCormick, McCarton, Tonascia, & Brooks-Gunn, 1993 To assess the effectiveness of an early educational intervention for low-birth weight infants following discharge from the hospital.	N = 280 infants VLBW Intervention group: N = 98 VLBW Control group: N = 182 ELBW Intervention group: N = 23 ELBW Control group: N = 57 **Recruitment:** Published elsewhere **Inclusion criteria:** - Birth weight of <2,500 grams - <37 weeks of gestation **Demographics:** (Presented according to very low birth weight [VLBW], extremely low birth weight [ELBW], intervention and control groups) **VLBW Intervention Group:** *Age of child:* Not reported *Gender of child:* 51% Male *SES:* Not reported *Ethnicity:* Black: 65.3% Hispanic: 11.2% Other (mostly white): 23.5% *Maternal age:* Median: 24 years; range: 14–41 years **VLBW Control Group:** *Age of child:* Not reported *Gender of child:* 49% Male *SES:* Not reported *Ethnicity:* Black: 57.7% Hispanic: 10.4% Other (mostly white): 31.9% *Maternal age:* Median: 25 years; range: 14–43 years **ELBW Intervention Group:** *Age of child:* Not reported *Gender of child:* 43.5% Male *SES:* Not reported

Procedure:
- The intervention group received home visits and group-based educational intervention until 36 months of age
- The control group was assessed but did not receive intervention
- Children were assessed every 4 months in the first year and every 6 months following the first year

Statistical Analyses:
- Multiple linear regression models were developed to assess outcome across the treatment and control groups

Results:
- At the 36-month assessment, 10% of the total sample were diagnosed with CP
- The VLBW intervention group improved significantly on measures of cognitive development compared to the VLBW control group
- When those children diagnosed with CP were removed from this analysis, improvement increased
- No significant differences between VLBW groups were found on measures of behavior or health (except for morbidity which was higher in the intervention group)
- Similar results were reported for the ELBW group but were not statistically significant

Strengths:
- Randomization
- Control group
- Low rates of attrition

Limitations:
- Maternal-report only
- Improved IQ scores could reflect improved test-taking abilities

(Continued)

Table 10.1 STUDIES EXAMINING AUTISM SPECTRUM DISORDER *(Continued)*

Source of Research and Purpose of Study	Study Design: Recruitment of Participants, and Research Methodology
	Ethnicity: Black: 65.2% Hispanic: 8.7% Other (mostly white): 26.1% *Maternal age:* Median: 26 years; range: 14–38 years **ELBW Control Group:** *Age of child:* Not reported *Gender of child:* 47.4% Male *SES:* Not reported *Ethnicity:* Black: 71.9% Hispanic: 10.5% Other (mostly white): 17.5% *Maternal age:* Median: 26 years; range: 14–43 years **Research Methodology:** - Randomized controlled trial **Outcomes measured:** - Cognitive development - Behavior - Health status - Functional status
Reddihough, King, Coleman, & Catanese, 1998 To compare the effectiveness of Conductive Education (CE) programs to traditional neurodevelopmental programs for children with CP	**CE Treatment Group** - N = 17 children with CP **Traditional program Group** - N = 17 children with CP - A total of 66 children took part in this study, but permission for randomization was not given for 32 of them, therefore, they were excluded from results **Recruitment:** - Not reported **Inclusion criteria:** - Children with CP **Demographics of children with CP:** *Age of children in both groups:* 12–36 months (Mean = 22 months 3 weeks) *Gender across both groups:* Male: N = 41 Female: N = 25 *SES:* Not reported *Ethnicity:* Not reported **Research Methodology:** - Randomized controlled trial **Measures:** - VABS (adaptive behavior) - Gross Motor Function Measure (GMFM) - Reynell Developmental Language Scale (RDLS) - QRS-F - Parenting Stress Index (PSI) - Satisfaction survey

Procedure:
- 6-month intervention period
- Children in the CE group received 75.6 hours of treatment (2.8 hours/week/child)
- Children in the traditional program received 79.8 hours of treatment (2.9 hours/week/child)
- Pre- and post-test administration of measures

Statistical Analyses:
- Analysis of variance

Results:
- Children with CP in both groups made significant developmental gains (regardless of program type)
- On the cognitive variable of the VABS, children in the traditional program demonstrated a lower score than children in the CE program
- On the expressive language variable of the VABS, both groups demonstrated statistically significant improvements from pre- to post
- Caregiver VABS reports indicate that both groups improved significantly from pre- to post-intervention in dressing, feeding, grooming, toileting, social interaction, expressive and receptive language, and organizational behavior
- Both groups demonstrated significant improvements on the developmental language scale
- Both groups of caregivers demonstrated significant improvement on the QRS-F over time, indicating improved coping and less stress

Strengths:
- Randomization
- Control group

Limitations:
- Variability in intervention "dosage"
- Children were not matched on all variables (such as SES)
- No follow-up

SUMMARY

Clearly, the care needed to raise a child with a NDD appears to be more challenging and stressful on parents psychologically, financially, and socially. Parents experience significant tension related to the multiple and competing demands, which include (a) finding and financing the various services and supports that their child requires, or from which the child would benefit; (b) fulfilling their multiple roles (parent to a special needs child; parent to other siblings; spouse to their partner; employee, etc.); (c) advocating for services that their special needs child requires; (d) negotiating various medical appointments; (e) managing interruptions in daily routines and plans; and (f) living with the general uncertainty about the child's future needs (Brown et al., 2008). Brown et al. (2008) also describe the undeniable impact, both positive and negative, of a child's disability on family dynamics, parent–child relationships, and the well-being of parents.

Ideally, in an intact family, a special needs child would have the benefit of two parents working cooperatively to meet the needs of their child. When parents separate and/or divorce, each parent must meet the challenges of parenting separately with varying degrees of cooperation by the other parent. Additionally, as the research indicates, the parents of children with a NDD are more likely to be compromised by physical and psychological health concerns than parents who do not have children with a NDD (Lach et al., 2009). Given that children with NDDs have greater emotional, behavioral, and social challenges that require different kinds of attention from their parents than do typically developing children, special consideration must be given to the development of parenting plans for these separated and/or divorcing families.

A number of common issues arise when a separated couple with a child who has a NDD begins to develop a co-parenting plan. It may be the case that one parent fully accepts the child's diagnosis, understands his or her needs, and actively advocates for the child, while the other parent does not. Years of clinical experience of forensic psychologists and family court judges suggest that it is very important for the parents to jointly attend an evaluation with the expert diagnosing the child, since a parent meeting separately with an expert may not provide a full and accurate developmental history to the expert or may provide inaccurate information to the other parent regarding the expert's findings (Saposnek, Perryman, Berkow, & Ellsworth, 2005). Early interventions may be very important to the special needs child reaching his or her full potential. With more severely impaired young autistic children under the age of 5 who have limited or no language, time is of the essence to get the child in intensive treatment, since it is generally believed that if language is not developed by age 5, it typically never develops adequately (Pickett, Olivia, O'Grady, & Gordon, 2009). However, these same researchers give some evidence of speech acquisition in autistic children between ages 5 and 13, but not older. Conservatively, it may be critical to get both parents to accept the ASD child's diagnosis and begin intensive treatment immediately.

Living as separated parents in two different household is more expensive than having the family share one household (Burton & Phipps, 2009; Czapanskiy, 2010; Lerman, 2002). Parish and Cloud (2006) report that in the United States at least 10% of families of children with disabilities have no form of health insurance coverage. In Canada, there is no harmonization of programs being offered for families of children with disabilities. Therefore, many families incur added expenses that need to be addressed when parents separate and/or divorce (Burton & Phipps, 2009). Coupled with the extra and regularly increasing costs of parenting a child with a NDD, the issues of how to share these extraordinary costs in the context of the increased costs of supporting two households can generate conflict between co-parents.

Separated parents may disagree on what educational settings and methods are best for their NDD child. One parent may want the child to be home-schooled to buffer the child from teasing or bullying by peers, to better individualize the unique learning needs of the child, and to have better control over the child's daily activities. The other parent may argue that the child needs to be socialized and mainstreamed with his or her peers in a regular school setting from the start. Whether the parents' convictions are based on their investigation of research or on unsubstantiated beliefs is notable. Separated parents may differ on the therapy needs of their NDD child. One parent may feel that their child with ASD needs five or six different therapies (e.g., occupational therapy, speech therapy, social thinking group therapy, individual psychotherapy, equine therapy) while the other does not believe in the validity of these therapies and believes that the best therapy is "just loving the child every day." Or, one parent may feel that a child with CP needs to have physical therapy and speech therapy several times a week, while the other parent feels that playing with the neighbor kids can accomplish just as much. Furthermore, the therapy-resistant parent may feel strongly about not wanting the child to feel stigmatized by having to go to special therapies. Parents may choose therapies that have little or no evidence-based validity, partly because they feel a need to do something—anything—therapeutic for their child, and partly because they may understand that the absence of validating evidence of efficacy does not necessarily mean there is no efficacy to a particular treatment approach.

In summary:

- Both parents together should meet with the child's medical care provider(s) to discuss the child's diagnosis and medical/psychological needs and to develop an integrated plan for managing the child's routines and care.
- Both parents should meet together at the same time with any relevant expert professional in order to get the same information and to reduce the chances that one parent will put a "spin" on the information for the other parent.
- The parents should meet together with an educational specialist who is knowledgeable about the child's particular NDD.
- Both the parents should read the research literature on the particular therapies suggested and discuss what they learned while meeting together with an expert on their child's particular NDD.

GUIDELINES: CONSIDERATIONS AND CAUTIONS

- The state of the research is still, in many ways, in its infancy with respect to the NDDs of ASD and CP. Caution should be taken in drawing conclusions from the published research about a particular child with any of these diagnoses.

- Research conclusions are usually drawn from the data about *groups* of children, not about an *individual child* with ASD or CP, and there is considerable heterogeneity of levels of functioning and impact of the child on the family within each group of children.
- Children with NDDs are not a homogenous group that is easily identified with a clearly prescribed treatment and management regimen. Therefore, forensic practitioners must carefully assess not just the relevant research for a child with NDD but also the individual child and the child's functional abilities in relation to both parents.
- In reviewing research, forensic practitioners must be aware of the limitations of the evidence base and must remember that science is not advanced enough to predict which intervention approach may or may not work for a specific child. Also, even though RCTs may demonstrate that a particular approach is not efficacious, that approach may still actually help a particular child, so it is important to take into consideration the experience of those who observe and interact with the child on a daily basis. This is particularly challenging when one parent is asking the court to allow the child to continue with a treatment that is costly and has little to no scientific evidence behind it.

ACKNOWLEDGMENTS

The authors express appreciation to Dr. Peter Rosenbaum, *CanChild* Centre for Childhood Disability Research, McMaster University, Hamilton, Ontario, Canada for reviewing an earlier draft of this chapter and providing his expertise as a pediatric researcher working with children who have neurodevelopmental disorders. See the *CanChild* Centre for Childhood Disability Research, McMaster University, Hamilton, Ontario, Canada for a comprehensive review of best practices and current state of the research literature about children with neurodevelopmental disorders and implications for parenting at: http://www.canchild.ca/en/ourresearch/focusonfunction.asp The authors, Birnbaum & Lach also wish to acknowledge the financial support of the Canadian Institute of Health Research (CIHR), Canada.

REFERENCES

Allik, H., Larsson, J.-O., & Smedje, H. (2006). Health-related quality of life in parents of school-age children with Asperger syndrome or high-functioning autism. *Health and Quality of Life Outcomes, 4*(1). doi: 10.1186/1477–7525-4–1

American Academy of Pediatrics, Committee on Children with Disabilities. (1998). Auditory integration training and facilitated communication for Autism. *Pediatrics, 102*(2), 431–433.

American Psychiatric Association. (2000). *Diagnostic and statistical manual of mental disorders* (4th ed., text rev.). Washington, DC: Author.

Andersen, G., Irgens, L., Haagas, I., Skranes, J., Meberg, A., & Torstein, V. (2008). Cerebral palsy in Norway: Prevalence, subtypes and severity. *European Journal of Pediatric Neurology, 12*, 4–13.

Arnaud, C., White-Koning, M., Michelsen, S. I., Parkes, J., Parkinson, K., Thyen, U., . . . Colver, A. (2008). Parent-reported quality of life of children with cerebral palsy in Europe. *Pediatrics, 121* (1), 54–64. doi: http://dx.doi.org/10.1542/peds.2007-0854

Bertrand, J., Mars, A., Boyle, C., Bove, F., Yeargin-Allsopp, M., & Decoufle, P. (2001). Prevalence of autism in a United States population: The Brick Township, New Jersey, investigation. *Pediatrics, 108,* 1155–1161.

Bishop, D. V. M. (2010). Which neurodevelopmental disorders get researched and why? Retrieved November 5, 2011, from http://www.plosone.org

Bishop, S. L., Richler, J., Cain, A. C., & Lord, C. (2007). Predictors of perceived negative impact in mothers of children with autism spectrum disorder. *American Journal on Mental Retardation, 112*(6), 450–461. doi: http://dx.doi.org/10.1352/0895-8017%282007%29112%5B450:POPNII%5D2.0.CO;2

Blair, E., & Stanley, F. J. (1997). Issues in the classification and epidemiology of cerebral palsy. *Mental Retardation and Developmental Disabilities Research Reviews, 3,* 184–193.

Brehaut, J. C., Kohen, D. E., Raina, P., Walter, R. P., Russell, D. J., Swinton, M., O'Donnell, M., & Rosenbaum, P. (2004). The health of primary caregivers of children with cerebral palsy: How does it compare with that of other Canadian caregivers? *Pediatrics, 114,* e182–e191.

Breslau, N., & Marshall, I. A. (1985). Psychological disturbance in children with physical disabilities: Continuity and change in a 5-year follow-up. *Journal of Abnormal Child Psychology, 13,* 199–215.

Brown, R. I., MacAdam-Crisp, J., Want, M., & Iarocci, G. (2006). Psychological functioning and coping among mothers of children with autism: A population-based study. *Journal of Policy and Practice in Intellectual Disabilities, 3*(4), 238–245.

Brown, R., Wiener, L., Kupst, M., Brennan, T., Behrman, R., Compas, B., . . . Zeltzer, L. (2008). Single parents of children with chronic illness: An understudied phenomenon. *Journal of Pediatric Psychology, 33*(4), 408–421.

Burton, P., & Phipps, S. (2009). Economic costs of caring for children with disabilities in Canada. *Canadian Public Policy, 35*(3), 269–290.

Butler, C. (1991). Augmentative mobility: Why do it? In K. M. Jaffe (Ed.), *Physical Medicine Rehabilitation Clinics of North America* 2, (4), 801–815.

Butler, C., & Campbell, S. (2000). Evidence of the effects of intrathecal baclofen for spastic and dystonic cerebral palsy: AACPDM treatment outcomes committee review panel. *Developmental Medical Child Neurology, 42,* 634–645.

Butler, C., & Darrah, J. (2001). Effects of neurodevelopmental treatment (NDT) for cerebral palsy: An AACPDM evidence report. *Developmental Medical Child Neurology, 43,* 778–790.

Cadman, D., Boyle, M., Szatmari, P., & Offord, D. R. (1987). Chronic illness, disability, and mental and social well-being: findings of the Ontario Child Health Study. *Pediatrics, 79*(5), 805–813.

Cascio, C. J. (2010). Somatosensory processing in neurodevelopmental disorders. *Journal of Neurodevelopmental Disorders, 2,* 62–69.

Centers for Disease Control. (2009). Prevalence of Autism Spectrum Disorders: Autism and Developmental Disabilities Monitoring Network, United States, 2006. *MMWR, 58*(SS10), 1–20. Retrieved from http://www.cdc.gov/mmwr/preview/mmwrhtml/ss5810a1.htm.

Charman, T., & Baird, G. (2002). Practitioner review: Assessment and diagnosis of autism spectrum disorders in the pre-school years. *Journal of Child Psychology and Psychiatry, 43*, 289–305.

Cheshire, A., Barlow, J. H., & Powell, L. A. (2010). The psychosocial well-being of parents of children with cerebral palsy: A comparison study. *Disability and Rehabilitation, 32*(20), 1673–1677. doi: 10.3109/09638281003649920

Cohen, E., Biran, G., Aran, A., & Gross-Tsur, V. (2008). Locus of control, perceived parenting style, and anxiety in children with cerebral palsy. *Journal of Developmental and Physical Disabilities, 20*, 415–423.

Collet, J. P., Vanasse, M., Marois, P., Amar, M., Goldberg, J., Lambert, J., & Majnemer, A. (2001). Hyperbaric oxygen for children with cerebral palsy: A randomised multicentre trial. HBO-CP Research Group. *Lancet, 357*(9256), 582–586.

Czapanskiy, K. S. (2010). Chalimony: Seeking equity between parents of children with disabilities and chronic illnesses. The Social Science Research Network Electronic Paper Collection. Retrieved from http://ssrn.com/abstract=1653927

Edgar, T. S. (2001). Clinical utility of botulinum toxin in the treatment of cerebral palsy: A comprehensive review. *Journal of Child Neurology, 16*, 37–46.

Eliasson, A. C., Krumlinde-Sundholm, L., Roshblad, B., Beckung, E., Arner, M., Ohrvall, A. M., & Rosenbaum, P. (2006). The Manual Ability Classification System (MACS) for children with cerebral palsy: Scale development and evidence of validity and reliability. *Developmental Medicine and Child Neurology, 48*, 549–554.

Farmer, J. E., & Deidrick, K. K. (2006). Introduction to childhood disability. In J. E. Farmer, J. Donders, & S. Warschausky (Eds.), *Treating neurodevelopmental disabilities: Clinical research and practice* (pp. 3–20). New York: Guilford Press.

Fayed, N., & Kerr, E. (2009). Identifying occupational issues among children with intractable epilepsy: Individualized versus norm referenced approaches. *Canadian Journal of Occupational Therapy, 76*(2), 90–97.

Fombonne, E. (2003). Epidemiological surveys of autism and other pervasive developmental disorders: An update. *Journal of Autism and Developmental Disorders, 33*, 365–382.

Fombonne, E., Zakarian, R., Bennett, A., Meng, L., & McLean-Heywood, D. (2006). Pervasive developmental disorders in Montreal, Quebec, Canada: Prevalence and links. *Pediatrics, 188*(1), e139–e150.

Freedman, B., Kalb, L., Zablotsky, B., & Stuart, E. (2010). *Relationship status among parents of children with Autism Spectrum Disorders: A population-based study.* Paper presented at the meeting of the International Society for Autism Research, Philadelphia. Retrieved from http://www.autism-insar.org/index.php?option=com_content&task=view&id=19&Itemid=82

Geytenbeek, J. (2011). Prevalence of speech and communication disorders. *Developmental Medicine and Child Neurology, 53*, 5–11.

Graham, H. K., Harvey, A., Rodda, J., Nattrass, G.R., & Pirpiris, M. (2004). The Functional Mobility Scale (FMS). *Journal of Pediatric Orthopedics, 24*, 514–520.

Hagopian, L. P., & Boelter, E. W. (2005). *Applied behaviour analysis and neurodevelopmental disorders: Overview and summary of scientific support.* Retrieved Feb. 17, 2011, from http://www.kennedykrieger.org/kki_misc.jsp?pid=4761&bl=1.

Hanna, S., & Law, M. (2006). *Prevalence of children with complex special needs in Ontario: Issues in measurement and forecasting. A report for the Ontario Ministry of Children and Youth Services*. Hamilton, ON: CanChild Centre for Childhood Disability Research.

Happe, F., Booth, R., Charlton, R., & Hughes, C. (2006). Executive function deficits in autism spectrum disorders and attention-deficit/hyperactivity disorder: Examining profiles across domains and ages. *Brain and Cognition, 61*, 25–39.

Hartley, S. L., Barker, E. T., Seltzer, M. M., Floyd, F. J., Greenberg, J. S., Orsmond, G. I., & Bolt, D. M. (2010). The relative risk and timing of divorce in families of children with an Autism Spectrum Disorder. *Journal of Family Psychology, 24*(4), 449–457.

Heller, K. W., Alberto, P. A., & Meagher, T. M. (1996). The impact of physical impairment on academic performance. *Journal of Developmental and Physical Disabilities, 8*, 233–245.

Hidecker, M. J. C., Paneth, N., Rosenbaum, P. L., Kent, R. D., Lillie, J., Eulenberg, J. B., & Taylor, K. (2011). Developing and validating the Communication Function Classification System (CFCS) for individuals with cerebral palsy. *Developmental Medicine and Child Neurology*. DOI: 10.1111/j.1469-8749.2011.03996.x

Hilton, J. C. (2005). *Communication skills of young children diagnosed with autism: Comparative effectiveness of applied behavior analysis and developmental, individual-difference, relationship-based interventions* (Doctoral dissertation). Harrisonburg: James Madison University.

Jesner, O. S., Aref-Adib, M., & Coren, E. (2007). Risperidone for Autism Spectrum Disorder. *Cochrane Database of Systematic Reviews, 1*(CD005040). doi: 10.1002/14651858. CD005040. pub2

Kazdin, A. E. (2008). Evidence-based treatment and practice—New opportunities to bridge clinical research and practice, enhance the knowledge base, and improve patient care. *American Psychologist, 63*(3), 146–159.

Kee, T. T. S. (2005). A cultural interpretation of locus of control, family and school experience, and school truancy: The case of Hong Kong. *International Journal of Adolescence and Youth, 124*, 325–349.

Ketelaar, M., Gorter, A., Vermeer, H., Hart, T., & Helders, P. J. M. (2006). The effects of a functional therapy program on children with cerebral palsy and on their parent. In H. D. Fong (Ed.), *Trends in cerebral palsy research* (pp. 69–108). New York: Nova Science Publishers, Inc.

Kim, J. A., Szatmari, P., Bryson, S. E., Streiner, D. L., & Wilson, F. J. (2000). The prevalence of anxiety and mood problems among children with Autism and Asperger's Syndrome. *Autism, 4*, 117–132.

Kogan, M. D., Strickland, B. B., Blumberg, S. J., Singh, G. K., Perrin, J. M., & van Dyck, P. C. (2008). A national profile of the health care experiences and family impact of autism spectrum disorder among children in the United States, 2005–2006. *Pediatrics, 122*(6), e1149–e1158. doi: http://dx.doi.org/10.1542/peds.2008-1057

Kuban, K. C. K., & Leviton, A. (1994). Cerebral palsy. *New England Journal of Medicine, 330*, 188–195.

Kuhn, J. C., & Carter, A. S. (2006). Maternal self-efficacy and associated parenting cognitions among mothers of children with autism. *American Journal of Orthopsychiatry, 76*, 564–575.

Lach, L. M., Kohen, D. E., Garner, R. E., Brehaut, J. C., Miller, A. R., Klassen, A. F., & Rosenbaum, P. L. (2009). The health and psychosocial functioning of caregivers of children with neurodevelopmental disorders. *Disability & Rehabilitation, 31*(9), 741–752. doi: 10.1080/08916930802354948

Lee, L.-C., Harrington, R. A., Louie, B. B., & Newschaffer, C. J. (2008). Children with autism: Quality of life and parental concerns. *Journal of Autism and Developmental Disorders, 38*(6), 1147–1160.

Lerman, R. I. (2002). *Marriage and the economic well-being of families with children: A review of the literature*. Washington, DC: Urban Institute and American University.

Levy, S. E., Mandell, D. S., & Schultz, R. T. (2009). Autism. *Lancet, 374,* 1627–1638.

Lord, C., Risi, S., Lambrecht, L., Cook, E. H., Jr., Leventhal, B. L., DiLavore, P. C., & Rutter, M. (2000). The autism diagnostic observation schedule-generic: A standard measure of social and communication deficits associated with the spectrum of autism. *Journal of Autism and Developmental Disorders, 30*(3), 205–223.

Lord, C., Rutter, M., & LeCouteur, A. (1994). Autism Diagnostic Interview-Revised: A revised version of a diagnostic interview for caregivers of individuals with possible pervasive developmental disorders. *Journal of Autism and Developmental Disorders, 24*(5), 659–685.

Majnemer, A., Shevell, M., Rosenbaum, P., Law, M., & Poulin, C. (2007). Determinants of life quality in school-age children with cerebral palsy. *Journal of Pediatrics, 151*(5), 470–475.

Mauger-Rothenberg, B., Samson, D. J., Aronson, N., Ziegler, K. M., Bonnell, C. J., & Gere, M. A. (2009). *Special report: Early intensive behavioral intervention based on applied behavior analysis among children with autism spectrum disorder* (Vol. 23, pp. 1–61). Blue Cross and Blue Shield Association, Technology Evaluation Center. Retrieved from *www.bcbs.com/blueresources/tec/vols/23/23_09.pdf*

McCarton, C. M., Brooks-Gunn, J., Wallace, I. F., Bauer, C. R., Bennett, F. C., Bernbaum, J. C., & Meinart, C. L. (1997). Results at age 8 years of early intervention for low-birth-weight premature infants. *Journal of American Medical Association, 277,* 126–132.

McCormick, M., McCarton, C., Tonascia, J., & Brooks-Gunn, J. (1993). Early educational intervention for very low birth weight infants: Results from the Infant Health and Development Program. *Journal of Pediatrics, 123,* 527–533.

McDermott, S., Coker, A. L., Mani, S., Krishnaswami, S., Nagle, R. J., Barnett-Queen, L. L., & Wuori, D. F. (1996). A population-based analysis of behavior problems in children with cerebral palsy. *Journal of Pediatric Psychology, 21*(3), 447–463.

McLaughlin, J., Bjornson, K., Temkin, N., Steinbok, P., Wright, V., & Reiner, A. (2002). Selective dorsal rhizotomy: Meta-analysis of three randomized control trials. *Developmental Medical Child Neurology, 44,* 17–25.

Mesibov, G. B., Shea, V., & Schopler, E. (2005). *The TEACCH approach to autism spectrum disorders*. New York: Kluwer Academic Plenum.

Miller, F. (2005). *Cerebral palsy*. New York: Springer Science + Business Media, Inc.

Millward, C., Ferriter, M., Calver, S. J., & Connell-Jones, G. G. (2008). Gluten- and casein-free diets for Autism Spectrum Disorder. *Cochrane Database of Systematic Reviews, 2*(CD003498). doi: 10.1002/14651858. CD003498. pub3

Montes, G., & Halterman, J. S. (2007). Psychological functioning and coping among mothers of children with autism: A population-based study. *Pediatrics, 119*(5), e1040–e1046. doi: http://dx.doi.org/10.1542/peds.2006-2819

Montes, G., & Halterman, J. S. (2008). Association of childhood autism spectrum disorders and loss of family income. *Pediatrics, 121*(4), e821–e826. doi: http://dx.doi.org/10.1542/peds.2007-1594

Mori, K., Ujiie, T., Smith, A., & Howlin, P. (2009). Parental stress associated with caring for children with Asperger's syndrome or autism. *Pediatrics International, 51*(3), 364–370. doi: http://dx.doi.org/10.1111/j.1442-200X.2008.02728.x

Myers, S. M., & Plauche-Johnson, C. (2007). Management of children with autism spectrum disorders. *Pediatrics, 120*(5), 1162–1182.

Nelson, K., & Ellenberg, J. (1986). Antecedents of cerebral palsy: Multivariate analysis of risk. *New England Journal of Medicine, 315*, 81–86.

Nelson, K. B. (2002). The epidemiology of cerebral palsy in term infants. *Mental Retardation and Developmental Disabilities, 8*, 146–150.

Nesseleroade, J. R., Musher-Eizenman, D. R., & Schmitz, B. (2002). Perceived control and academic performance: A comparison of high and low performing children on within person change patterns. *International Journal of Behavioural Development, 26*, 540–547.

Nielson, P. D., & McCaughey, J. (1982). Self-regulation of spasm and spasticity in cerebral palsy. *Journal of Neurology Neurosurgery Psychology, 45*, 320–330.

Ones, K., Yilmaz, E., & Cetinkaya, B. (2005). Assessment of the quality of life of Malaysian children with cerebral palsy: Predictors of child and parent-related stress. *Annals of Tropical Pediatrics, 18*, 334–340.

Orsmond, G. I., Krauss, M. W., & Seltzer, M. M. (2004). Peer relationships and social and recreational activities among adolescents and adults with autism. *Journal of Autism and Developmental Disorders, 34*(3), 245–256.

Ospina, M. B., Krebs Seida, J., Clark, B., Karkhaneh, M., Hartling, L., Tjosvold, L., & Smith, V. (2008). Behavioural and developmental interventions for autism spectrum disorder: A clinical systematic review. *PloS One, 3*(11), e3755. doi: 10.1371/journal. pone. 0003755

Ozonoff, S., & Cathcart, K. (1998). Effectiveness of a home program intervention for young children with autism. *Journal of Autism and Developmental Discord, 28*, 25–32.

Palisano, R. J., Rosenbaum, P., Bartlett, D., & Livingston, M. (2007). *GMFCS: E & R: Gross Motor Function Classification System Expanded and Revised.* Hamilton, Ontario: CanChild Centre for Childhood Disability Research, Institute for Applied Health Sciences, McMaster University.

Palisano, R. J., Rosenbaum, P., Walter, S., Russell, D., Wood, E., & Galuppi, B. (1997). Development and reliability of a system to classify gross motor function in children with cerebral palsy. *Developmental Medicine and Child Neurology, 39*, 214–223.

Palisano, R. J., Snider, L. M., & Orlin, M. N. (2004). Recent advances in physical and occupational therapy for children with cerebral palsy. *Seminars in Pediatric Neurology, 11*(1), 66–77.

Palmer, F. B. (1997). Evaluation of developmental therapies in cerebral palsy. *Mental Retardation and Developmental Disabilities Research Reviews, 3*, 145–152.

Panerai, S., Ferrante, L., & Zingale, M. (2002). Benefits of the treatment and education of autistic and communication handicapped children (TEACCH) programme as compared with a non-specific approach. *Journal of Intellectual Disability Research, 46*, 318–327.

Parish, S. L., & Cloud, J. M. (2006). Financial well-being of young children with disabilities. *Social Work, 51*, 223–232.

Parkes, J., & Hill, N. (2010). Number and needs of children and young people with cerebral palsy. *Paediatric Nursing, 22*(4), 14–19.

Peterson, M. C., & Palmer, F. B. (2001). Advances in prevention and treatment of cerebral palsy. *Mental Retardation and Developmental Disabilities Research, 1*(7), 30–37.

Pickett, E., Olivia, P., O'Grady, J., & Gordon, B. (2009). Speech acquisition in older nonverbal individuals with autism: A review of features, methods, and prognosis. *Cognitive and Behavioral Neurology, 22*(1), 1–21.

Pless, I. B., & Pinkerton, P. (1972). *Chronic childhood disorder: Promoting patterns of adjustment.* London: Henry Kimpton.

Rao, P. A., & Beidel, D. C. (2009). The impact of children with high-functioning autism on parental stress, sibling adjustment, and family functioning. *Behavior Modification, 33*(4), 437–451. doi: http://dx.doi.org/10.1177/0145445509336427

Reddihough, D. S., King, J., Coleman, C., & Catanese, T. (1998). Efficacy of programmes based on conductive education for young children with cerebral palsy. *Archives of Physical Medical Rehabilitation, 83,* 1157–1164.

Rosenbaum, P. (2003). Controversial treatment for spasticity: Exploring alternative therapies for motor function in children with cerebral palsy. *Journal of Child Neurology, 18,* 89–94.

Rosenbaum, P. (2006). Cerebral palsy: What parents and doctors want to know. *British Medical Journal, 326*(3), 970–974.

Rosenbaum, P. (2009). Cerebral palsy in the 21st century: Is there anything left to say? *Neuropediatrics, 40,* 56–60.

Rosenbaum, P. (2010). The randomized controlled trial: An excellent design, but can it address the big questions in neurodisability? *Developmental Medicine and Child Neurology, 52*(2), 111.

Rosenbaum, P., Paneth, N., Levitan, A., Goldstein, M., & Bax, M. (2007). Definition and classification of cerebral palsy. *Developmental Medicine and Child Neurology, 49*(s109), 1–44.

Sallows, G. O., & Graupner, T. D. (2005). Intensive behavioural treatment for children with autism: Four-year outcomes and predictors. *American Journal on Mental Retardation, 110*(6), 417–438.

Sameroff, A. J., & Mackenzie, M. J. (2003). Research strategies for capturing transactional models of development: The limits of the possible. *Development and Psychopathology, 15,* 613–640.

Saposnek, D. T., Perryman, H., Berkow, J., & Ellsworth, S. (2005). Special needs children in family court cases. *Family Court Review, 43*(4), 566–581.

Schaff, R., & Miller, L. J. (2005). Occupational therapy using sensory integrative approach for children with developmental disabilities. *Mental Retardation and Developmental Disabilities Research Reviews, 11,* 143–148.

Shevell, M. I., Majnemar, A., & Morin, I. (2003). Etiologic yield of cerebral palsy: A contemporary care series. *Pediatric Neurology, 28,* 352–359.

Siebes, R. C., Wijnroks, L., & Vermeer, A. (2002). Qualitative analysis of therapeutic motor intervention programmes for children with cerebral palsy: An update. *Developmental Medicine & Child Neurology, 49*(s109), 1–44.

Smith, T., Groen, A. D., & Wynn, J. W. (2000). Randomized trial of intensive early intervention for children with pervasive developmental disorder. *American Journal of Mental Retardation, 105*(4), 269–285.

Sobsey, D. (2004). Marital stability and marital satisfaction in families of children with disabilities: Chicken & egg? *Developmental Disabilities Bulletin, 32*(1), 62–83.

Stanley, F., Blair, E., & Alberman, E. (2000). *Cerebral palsies: Epidemiology and causal pathways*. Clinics in Developmental Medicine No. 151. London: MacKeith Press.

Stein, R. E., Bauman, L. J., Westbrook, L. E., Coupey, S. M., & Ireys, H. T. (1993). Framework for identifying children who have chronic conditions: The case for a new definition. *Journal of Pediatrics, 122*(3), 342–347.

Stein, R. E. K., & Jessop, D. J. (1982). A non-categorical approach to chronic childhood illness. *Public Health Reports, 97*, 354–362.

Stephenson, J., & Carter, M. (2009). The use of weighted vests with children with autism spectrum disorders and other disabilities. *Journal of Autism and Developmental Disorders, 39*, 105–114.

Su, Y. (2002). Investigation on mental health status of children with cerebral palsy and their parents. *Chinese Nursing Research, 16*, 257–258.

Vargas, S., & Camilli, G. (1999). A meta-analysis of research on sensory integration treatment. *American Journal of Occupational Therapy, 53*, 189–198.

Wakefield, A. J., Murch, S. H., Anthony, A., Linnell, J., Casson, D. M., Malik, M., & Walker-Smith, J. A. (1998). Ileal-lymphoid-nodular hyperplasia, non-specific colitis, and pervasive developmental disorder in children. *Lancet, 351*(9103), 637–641.

Wang, H. Y., & Jong, Y. J. (2004). Parental stress and related factors in parents of children with cerebral palsy. *Kaohsiung Journal of Medical Science, 20*, 334–340.

Welterlin, A. (2009). *The Home TEACCHing Program: A study of the efficacy of a parent training early intervention model* (Doctoral Dissertation). New Jersey: Rutgers University.

World Health Organization. (2007). *International Statistical Classification of Diseases and Related Health Problems* (ICD), 10th Revision. Retrieved from http://www.who.int/classifications/icf/en/

Yeargin-Allsopp, M., & Boyle, C. (2002). Overview: The epidemiology of neurodevelopmental disorders. *Mental Retardation and Developmental Disabilities, 8*, 113–116.

Yeargin-Allsopp, M., Rice, C., Karapurkan, T., Doernberg, N., Boyle, C., & Murphy, C. (2003). Prevalence of autism in a US metropolitan area. *Journal of the American Medical Association, 289*, 49–55.

Yude, C., & Goodman, R. (1999). Peer problems of 9-to 11-year old children with hemiplegia in mainstream school. Can these be predicted? *Developmental Medicine and Child Neurology, 41*, 4–8.

## 11

Co-parenting Children with Attention-Deficit/Hyperactivity Disorder and Disruptive Behavior Disorders

SUZANNE E.U. KERNS AND RONALD J. PRINZ ∎

Attention-deficit/hyperactivity disorder (ADHD) and disruptive behavior disorders, such as oppositional defiant disorder (ODD) and conduct disorder (CD), are the most commonly encountered childhood mental health concerns for families, practitioners, and the courts. Family court may be more likely to see families with children with ADHD or disruptive behavior disorders because families with children with these disorders are more likely to experience a range of adversities and marital problems.

ADHD and disruptive behavior disorders, especially when they occur together, can have a significant impact on families and the multiple systems in which the youth interfaces (especially school). There have been significant advances in the treatment of ADHD and disruptive behavior disorders, but challenges remain. One particular challenge is engaging parents and caregivers in appropriate, evidence-based treatments, despite research demonstrating that active caregiver involvement is essential in adequate treatment of these disorders. Considerations for family court are many, and the balance of this chapter first reviews the important characteristics of these disorders and then unpacks some of the more critical considerations related to effective treatment. In this chapter, a reference to "parents" refers to any individuals playing a parental role, not necessarily limited to biological or adoptive parents. This definition of parents includes any individuals with primary responsibility for caring for the youth, including individuals such as custodial grandparents, foster parents, kinship guardians, and other guardians.

NATURE OF ADHD AND DISRUPTIVE BEHAVIOR DISORDERS

ADHD

ADHD is typically diagnosed in childhood around the time of school entry (average age of first diagnosis is 7), although many parents report their children have challenging behaviors or symptoms earlier. ADHD is one of the most common childhood disorders, affecting approximately 1 in 11 to 20 children, and is approximately three to four times more common among boys (Barkley, Edwards, & Robin, 1999; Cantwell, 1996; Ramtekkar, Reiersen, Todorov, & Todd, 2010). While some youths experience decreased symptoms as they get older, ADHD symptoms typically persist through early adolescence and start to desist only as the youth approaches adulthood. Despite this, nearly 50% of youths diagnosed with ADHD will continue to experience impairment (especially problems related to inattention) into adulthood (Kessler et al., 2010). Symptoms of ADHD appear to be relatively consistent across cultures (Bauermeister, Canino, Polanczyk, & Rohde, 2010). However, a recent review article and meta-analysis of ethnic differences found that African American youths more often experience ADHD symptoms, yet they are less likely to receive a diagnosis (Miller, Nigg, & Miller, 2009).

As its name implies, difficulties in sustaining attention and/or engaging in behavior characterized as hyperactive or impulsive are prominent features of youths with ADHD (American Psychiatric Association [APA], 2000). For a diagnosis of ADHD to be made, the youth must experience symptoms in, and functional impairment across, two or more settings. The specific ADHD symptoms a particular youth expresses varies, with most youths having challenges "sustaining attention to tasks, persistence of effort, or vigilance" (Barkley, 1998, p. 57). There are three main subtypes of ADHD: ADHD, combined type; ADHD, predominantly inattentive type; and ADHD, predominantly hyperactive-impulsive type (APA, 2000). Because of these different subtypes, youths with a diagnosis of ADHD may present somewhat differently and thus experience a different set of functional challenges. For example, a youth with predominately inattentive type ADHD may have a teacher who expresses dismay about messy and careless schoolwork or parents who report their child often seems like "he has his head in the clouds" and that their child rarely finishes projects or tasks around the house. The child may experience difficulties in peer relationships because of challenges with focusing on basic rules for playing games or sustaining conversation.

A youth with primarily hyperactive-impulsive ADHD, however, may have a teacher who complains that the child cannot sit still in the classroom or often blurts out answers when it is not his turn. Parents may be concerned that their child is constantly climbing on things, running in the house, or talking when he should otherwise be quiet. This child's peers may become upset because the child takes things out of turn or is constantly "clowning around" and getting everyone in trouble. Furthermore, some environments might exacerbate or moderate symptoms to a certain degree, which can contribute to low cross-setting agreement on symptoms—for example, between parents and teachers (Barkley, 1998; Connolly & Vance, 2010).

Disruptive Behavior Disorders

Aside from ADHD, ODD and CD are the two most commonly diagnosed disruptive behavior disorders in childhood. Children with ODD typically start to develop symptoms prior to about age 8 (developing new symptoms of ODD in early adolescence is rare), while children diagnosed with CD can develop symptoms during childhood or during adolescence (APA, 2000). As with ADHD, the prevalence rates of ODD are fairly high, ranging from 2% to 16% of children. CD is somewhat less common, occurring in 1% to 10% of the population. While most youths with ODD do not go on to develop CD, a large proportion of youths with CD were previously diagnosed with ODD earlier in their development. There is significant overlap (comorbidity) for ADHD and ODD/CD, with several studies reporting comorbid rates at about 50%, primarily because disruptive behaviors associated with ADHD and aggressive behaviors associated with ODD and CD have similar topographies (Prinz, Connor, & Wilson, 1981). Youths diagnosed with combined ADHD and another disruptive behavior disorder during childhood are more likely to be verbally or physically aggressive as adolescents, compared with youths diagnosed with ADHD alone (Harty, Miller, Newcorn, & Halperin, 2009).

The primary behavioral features of ODD include general defiance, disobedience, and hostility, often directed towards adults (APA,2000). Parents of children with ODD often report that their children do not listen to them and do not seem to respect them, often arguing or blaming others for problems. Teachers report difficulties with maintaining children in the classroom, testing limits or inciting classroom problems.

CD, on the other hand, is generally expressed with more significant behavioral problems, often including aggression towards people, animals, or property, deceitfulness and theft, or breaking major rules, including the law. There are two subtypes of CD, each with implications for the course of the disorder. The first subtype is "childhood-onset type," which is characterized by problematic behaviors emerging prior to age 10. Research by Terry Moffitt et al. (1996) and others reveals that the earlier the youth engages in CD-related behaviors, generally the more significant problems emerge. Early-onset CD has been associated with increased involvement with the juvenile justice system and more significant problems with substance abuse. The second subtype is "adolescent-onset type," which is characterized by the absence of problematic behaviors prior to age 10. While these youths still experience functional impairment from the disorder, typically youths in this subtype "outgrow" CD by later adolescence and do not experience as many of the social and school-related difficulties as their childhood-onset counterparts.

Symptoms of CD can range from mild to severe. Mild symptoms generally have the most direct impact on the youths themselves, compared with others, and may include skipping school, avoiding curfew, etc. Severe symptoms generally incur significant pain or expense to others and may include behaviors such as forced sexual encounters, intentionally injuring or killing animals, or robbing others for money or goods.

Parents of a child with CD might express concern that their child "just doesn't seem to care" about others (low empathy) or that their child seems to get in more fights than other kids his age. Some parents and caregivers even report being intimidated or scared by their child. Parents might worry that their child is engaging in risky sexual behaviors, using drugs or alcohol, and generally engaging in risk-taking behaviors. Motor vehicle accidents for children with CD occur at a rate that is greater than the general population. School problems are almost always present, commonly marked by repeated suspensions, protracted periods of non-enrollment, or early dropout. It is often a struggle to get youths with CD re-enrolled in schools due to the disruptive nature of their behavior problems and the impact these behaviors have on others in the school environment.

OVERVIEW OF PRIMARY PARENTING CHALLENGES

As a field, research elucidating the impact of having a child with ADHD and/or disruptive behavior disorders on family life is only beginning to emerge (Johnston &Mash, 2001). While providing mixed findings with regard to the specific impact of having a child with these disorders, research to date points to a transactional relationship between family risk and protective factors that interact with the child with ADHD or a disruptive behavior disorder (Deault, 2010). In this way, merely having a child with ADHD does not necessarily equate to increased risk for problematic family functioning (Lindahl, 1998). When a child also exhibits symptoms of other disruptive behavior disorders, such as oppositional defiant behaviors or other conduct-related problems, the impact on family functioning can be greater, often reaching problematic levels (Johnston & Mash, 2001). However, research results are mixed and largely affected by methodological differences (see Johnson & Mash, 2001, for a comprehensive review).

Recent research highlights aspects of family life that are affected when one or more children have ADHD or a disruptive behavior disorder. A study of marital relationships when a child has ADHD found couples with a child with ADHD, compared to couples whose children did not have ADHD, experienced more significant challenges to the marital relationship and tended to divorce sooner (Wymbs et al., 2008). While identification of the particular family-interactional factors behind this finding require further research, it appears that one potential aggravating factor might be a bidirectional relationship between child behavior problems and interparental communication, whereby children who exhibit more difficult behaviors elicit more negative interactions between their parents (Wymbs& Pelham, 2010). Specifically, parents of children with ADHD are more likely to find fault in their partner's parenting, withdraw from parenting situations, or disagree about parenting tasks compared with parents of children without ADHD. Additionally, parents of children with comorbid ADHD and ODD or CD tend to exhibit more permissive (lax) and inconsistent parenting styles (Lindahl, 1998).

Caregiver strain is exacerbated when youths have ADHD plus comorbid ODD or conduct problems (Evans, Sibley, &Serpell, 2009). Mothers of children with ADHD tend to report greater symptoms of anxiety and depression compared to mothers of children without ADHD (Durukan et al., 2008). Parents of children with ADHD experience reduced interpersonal effectiveness, arrange and have their children participate in fewer play dates, and convey critical comments more often about their child's peer interactions (Mikami, Jack, Emeh, & Stephens, 2010). Furthermore, parental experiences with their child's school or educational placement may also be strained. A study examining parental participation in their child's learning at school, comparing parents of children with ADHD and not, found that parents of children with ADHD experienced lower self-efficacy when helping their child with schoolwork, felt less welcomed within the school environment, and were overall less involved with their child's learning (Rogers, Wiener, Marton, & Tannock, 2009).

Families of children with ADHD (especially combinedtype) tend to experience greater adversity compared to families of children without the disorder (Counts, Nigg, Stawicki, Rappley, & Von Eye, 2005). Examples of family adversity include low socioeconomic status, parental psychopathology, marital conflict, and other stressful events. Whether adversity precedes ADHD symptoms or ADHD symptoms interact with adversity requires further research; however, it is important to note that there are likely multiple risk factors in families with children with ADHD.

Families of children with ADHD experience several different types of stigma (dosReis, Barksdale, Sherman, Maloney, &Charach, 2010). Parents have general concerns about how others perceive their child being on medication. Other common parental concerns include worries about the labeling of their child or that they might be perceived as bad parents because their child has problems. Parents often report feeling socially isolated or rejected by other adults, including family, peers, and other community members. Parents also worry that their children experience similar social isolation, particularly in settings such as schools. Many also experience a feeling of being dismissed or rejected by other parents or even professionals with regard to their experiences.

Studies of family structure have indicated that non-intact families often experience greater degrees of challenging symptoms over time. In an interesting longitudinal look at the impact of family structure on ADHD symptoms over a 6-year period, findings revealed that youths from intact families tended to fare best. However, there was little difference overall between the trajectories of symptoms for youths from intact families and youths from families who got divorced during the time period. Children in stepfamilies appeared to experience the greatest challenges (Kerr & Michalski, 2007).

In summary:

- While not all families of children with ADHD or disruptive behavior disorders experience stress and adversity, many parents and caregivers report effects on their marital relationship, parenting strategies, general caregiver strain, and stigma.
- This is especially true for families with children who have both ADHD and comorbid disruptive behavior problems.

STATE OF TREATMENT SCIENCE

Treatment for ADHD, and more generally for disruptive behavior disorders, has received significant attention and advances over the past several decades. The following presents a brief summary of the most recent advances in treatments, including information about how parents play a direct role in the management of these disorders.

Treatment for ADHD

Effective treatment of ADHD generally falls within two major areas: pharmacologic treatments and psychosocial interventions. The past two decades have seen tremendous gains in both modalities. The general consensus is that treatment of ADHD is best managed by a combination of pharmacologic and psychosocial interventions—that one in the absence of the other has attenuated treatment effects (Pelham et al., 2005). The following reviews the most common treatment options available in each category.

PHARMACOLOGIC

Pharmacologic treatments of ADHD are highly effective, relative to pharmacologic treatments of other youth psychiatric disorders, and are reasonably safe and well-studied in children over the age of 6. Stimulant medications are the most effective medications for ADHD (Faraone&Buitelaar, 2010). There are more than 200 randomized controlled studies demonstrating the effectiveness of stimulants in school-age youths with ADHD. The most common stimulant medications include methylphenidate (e.g., Ritalin, Concerta), dextroamphetamine (e.g., Dexedrine, Dextrostat), and mixed-salts amphetamine (e.g., Adderall). There is relatively less evidence of treatment effectiveness for stimulants for youthsunder the age of 6. The Preschool ADHD Treatment Study (PATS), one of the more recent and better-designed studies of the treatment of preschool ADHD (Greenhill et al., 2006), found that although youths responded in a statistically significant and clinically meaning-ful manner to stimulants, the magnitude of response was not as great as for older children, and preschool youths were more likely to experience emotional outbursts (Wigal et al., 2006). The most common side effects of stimulants include insomnia and decreased appetite. Less common side effects are tics, repetitive behavior, and elevated blood pressure and pulse. Long-term use of stimulants is associated with decelerated growth and possibly shorter stature. Thus, height, weight, blood pressure, and pulse need to be regularly monitored when youths are prescribed stimulant medications for ADHD. There have been a few reports of sudden death associated with stimulants, which are believed to be related to preexisting cardiac conditions. If there is any family history or suspicion of youth cardiac problems, more cardiac testing is indicated. Finally, stimulants are associated with abuse potential, so medications should be administered only with a good safety and monitoring plan. As with any intervention, pharmacologic treatment should be regularly monitored by medical professionals for effectiveness and side effects, at least monthly.

Non-stimulant medications may be prescribed if the youth cannot tolerate stimulants, there is low responsiveness to stimulants, or there is significant risk that stimulants might be abused or diverted for use by others. While several non-stimulant medications have been found to be effective, the magnitude of their effectiveness is not as large as for stimulants (Faraone & Buitelaar, 2010), and they are not as well studied. Two of the better-studied and more effective non-stimulant medications are atomoxetine (e.g., Straterra) and guanfacine (e.g., Tenex, Intuniv).

It is important to note that most children receiving medication for ADHD do so through primary care settings. A recent study of 785 school-aged children demonstrated that while ADHD symptoms abate with appropriate medication management within primary care settings, the functional impairments associated with ADHD required additional coordination with mental health or educational services (Epstein et al., 2010).

PSYCHOSOCIAL INTERVENTIONS

Behavioral parent training (BPT) is the most effective psychosocial treatment for children with ADHD (Chronis, Chacko, Fabiano, Wymbs, & Pelham, 2004; Fabiano, Chacko, et al., 2009). Importantly, and as its name implies, BPT interventions focus on training the parents or caregivers on strategies to manage challenging child behavior. This distinction is important because some therapists purport to work directly with the child to address the problematic behavior (e.g., play therapy).

While teaching children coping skills and strategies for managing their symptoms can have some limited benefit, this type of therapy has not been shown to be effective in treating ADHD or any comorbid symptoms in the absence of targeted work directly with the parents.

Numerous BPTs have undergone rigorous scientific study and have proven effective for the treatment of ADHD (Fabiano, Pelham, et al., 2009). Examples include the parenting component of Pelham's Summer Treatment Program (Pelham & Hoza, 1996), Parent Child Interaction Therapy (Eyberg et al., 2001), and Triple P (Sanders, 1999), among others. While these programs represent a "gold standard" in research effectiveness, individual programs may or may not be available in certain communities or service sectors. A recent review by Kaminski et al. (2008) highlighted the common features across these interventions that have been associated with the most significant treatment effects. Specifically, they focus on promoting positive relationships between parents and their children through skillful parent–child interactions and effective communication, use of the time-out strategy, emphasizing consistency in use of parenting strategies, providing an opportunity for parents to practice skills they have learned with their own child, and receiving feedback from their therapist or coach (Kaminski et al., 2008).

BPT interventions are not without their challenges. Perhaps most importantly, the parents or caregivers themselves have historically been difficult to engage in treatment. No-show rates for treatment are generally high (McKay, McCadam, & Gonzales, 1996). Research has demonstrated that parental participation in treatment is an important mediator in treatment outcomes (Hinshaw, 2007). Even parents who participate may experience varying success in actually implementing treatment strategies. For example, a study of 101 mothers and their school-age children (ages 5–10) found that parenting self-efficacy was strongly related to use of the strategies and subsequent child benefit (Johnston, Mah, & Regambal, 2010).

A recent study of cultural differences in acceptability of different treatment modalities for youths with ADHD revealed that while most parents desire a combination of medication and behavioral interventions, ethnic minority parents are more likely to desire behavioral interventions to manage ADHD symptoms, compared with non-minority parents (Pham, Carlson, & Kosciulek, 2010). Another study on treatment response for various ethnic groups revealed that while there are baseline differences in parenting styles, there are no differences between ethnicities with regard to treatment effectiveness (Jones et al., 2010).

Treatment for Disruptive Behavior Disorders

Effective treatments for disruptive behavior disorders generally fall in one of three broad categories: individually based interventions, family-based interventions (mostly BPTs), and systemic or ecological interventions (Kerns & Prinz, 2002). Indeed, most of the interventions described in the above section on psychosocial ADHD treatments have also demonstrated effectiveness in treating the symptoms of disruptive behavior disorders.

For younger children (prior to adolescence), the clear treatments of choice are BPTs, for many of the same reasons outlined above. Examples of manualized BPTs that have the highest levels of evidence for their effectiveness include Parent Child

Interaction Therapy (Eyberg et al., 2001), Triple P Positive Parenting Program (Sanders, Markie-Dadds, Tully, & Bor, 2000), The Incredible Years (Webster-Stratton & Hammond, 1997), Helping the Noncompliant Child (McMahon & Forehand, 2005), and Parent Management Training (Reid, Patterson, & Snyder, 2002).

As youths enter adolescence, while parenting interventions continue to be helpful, there is increased effectiveness for more individual-based programs that teach coping and anger management. Also important during this developmental timeframe is for programs to exert an impact on adolescent substance use. Examples of individual-based programs that demonstrate effectiveness include Aggression Replacement Therapy (Goldstein, Glick, & Gibbs, 1998), Life Skills Training (Botvin, Griffin, & Nichols, 2006), Strengthening Families Program (Kumpfer & Tait, 2000), and Dialectical Behavior Therapy (Linehan et al., 1999). While not entirely individually focused, contingency management programs have also demonstrated effectiveness, especially when combined with other evidence-based treatment approaches (e.g., Stanger, Budney, Kamon, & Thostensen, 2009).

For adolescents whose behaviors have escalated to a degree that they are getting in trouble with the law (or at high risk for getting in trouble), exhibiting significant school problems, having difficulty in other community settings, engaging in extremely high-risk or reckless behaviors (including fighting, substance use, risky sexual behavior, and other dangerous behaviors such as carrying weapons), and/or experiencing significant challenges with their family, a class of interventions called "ecological" or "systemic" interventions may be required. These interventions are typically very intensive and involve working with the multiple systems that are affected by the youth's behaviors. Examples of such programs include Multisystemic Therapy (Henggeler, 1999), Functional Family Therapy (Alexander, Pugh, Parsons, & Sexton, 2000), and Multidimensional Treatment Foster Care (Chamberlain & Smith, 2003).

In general, psychopharmacologic treatments for disruptive behavior disorders (in the absence of other comorbid symptoms) should be considered only after psycho-social treatments have been attempted. For youths with both ADHD and disruptive behavior, a combination of anti-ADHD medications and behavioral treatment will provide greater reduction in disruptive behavior than behavioral treatment alone (Jensen et al., 2001).

For youths with primary disruptive behavior disorders, there is some evidence that medication classes, such as mood regulators (e.g., lithium, carbamazepine), α_2-agonists (e.g., clonidine, guanfacine), antidepressants (e.g., bupropion, desipramine, imipramine, nortriptyline), and atypical antipsychotics (e.g., risperidone) might provide some symptom relief (Turgay, 2009), although it is important to note that in many cases, studies were small in scope and short term, and future research is needed to promote confidence in these medications for treatment recommendations. Atypical antipsychotics are relatively better studied but are known to have problematic long-term side effects, including weight gain, dyslipidemias, glucose intolerance (which may lead to diabetes), and rare but serious side effects of irreversible movement disorders.

It is not uncommon for youths with disruptive behavior disorders to present on more than one medication (e.g., a stimulant and atypical antipsychotic). A great deal of caution should be applied around polypharmacy. It is highly recommended that families receive second opinions whenever youths are being managed on more than one psychotropic medication. Furthermore, there should be close scrutiny of any psychopharmacologic medications prescribed to youths under the age of 5.

In summary:

- Effective treatment of ADHD and disruptive behavior disorders requires active involvement on the part of parents or caregivers.
- Generally, parents or caregivers are the targets of treatment interventions, coaching parents to be more consistent, assertive, and proactive while enhancing their relationship with their child through positive parenting.
- There is little evidence, especially for children prior to adolescence, that individual work only with the child, and in absence of work with caregivers, results in any lasting change in his behavior or symptoms.
- Table 11.1 outlines programs that are considered "evidence-based parenting programs" and those that are either promising programs (one or two studies demonstrating initial effectiveness or feasibility) or programs for which there is little to no evidence but are still popular.

IMPACT OF PARENTING ON TREATMENT AND COURSE OF PROBLEMS

As mentioned above, effective treatment of ADHD and disruptive behavior disorders requires active involvement on the part of parents or caregivers. It is not always the case that parents or caregivers are in full agreement with regard to parenting strategies and demands, and this can have a significant impact on the course and effectiveness of treatment. There are several potential sources of such conflict. It has been well established that parents often differ on their ratings of their child's behavior problems, with mothers often providing higher ratings (noting more problematic behavior) than fathers (Langberg et al., 2010). Other sources of the conflict might be philosophical in nature. Parents often have strong feelings about particular intervention strategies, and it is not always the case that all caregivers feel the same way about particular approaches. Different parental beliefs concerning the importance or benefits/risks of taking medications is a classic example. Another source of conflict is poor communication across caregiver systems. Inadequate communication can lead to reduced effectiveness of intervention goals. For example, imagine that a youth steals $20 from his mother's wallet. When she finds out, she places the youth on restriction (no computer time) for one week. Mid-week, the youth visits with another caregiver who, because of poor communication, is unaware that he has lost the privilege. This caregiver allows the youth to have time on the computer, and also gives him $10 to spend after school. Thus, the impact of the consequence is almost completely diminished. Another source of conflict may be a function of the youth being in different settings at different times. Here, an example is that the youth may have a different curfew because of safety concerns in one setting versus another and, thus, presents more challenges to the curfew in the more restrictive setting.

Finally, when considering interventions to address ADHD or disruptive behavior disorders, parental preference for types of interventions may affect willingness to participate and "buyin" regarding the effectiveness of particular treatment approaches. A study by Cunningham et al. (2008) suggests that parents may be classified in different groups based on their preferences for treatment. In this study, parents were characterized in three groups: "Parents in Action," who preferred a solution-focused, active coaching-type intervention; "Information Segment," who preferred psychoeducational materials and programs that help to explain child behavior as opposed to strategies to solve behavioral challenges; and "Overwhelmed Segment," who preferred to solve problems on their own as opposed to getting help or assistance from others.

Because of these challenges, when there are multiple caregivers involved with a child with ADHD or a disruptive behavior disorder, there are several areas in which particular attention should be paid regarding parenting plans.

Consistency Between Caregivers

Parents and caregivers who are managing a youth with ADHD or a disruptive behavior disorder will need to consider strategies for being as consistent as possible with regard to expectations for behavior, rewards for positive behaviors, and consequences for misbehavior. Consistency in approaching behavioral difficulties has been shown to be essential in effective management of the disorders. While all parents and caregivers have their own approaches towards raising children, sometimes quite diverse in nature, it is important that youths with ADHD and disruptive behavior disorders receive consistent messages from as many caring adults in their lives as much as possible. While there is room for individual differences between households on some rules and expectations, it is important for children to have similar rules across settings regarding important areas such as homework expectations and curfew, and to have a similar schedule across settings.

Communication Plan

Related to the above principle of consistency, development of an effective communication plan between caregivers can be very helpful to reduce or eliminate areas of inconsistency and, especially for older children, opportunities for children to identify "loopholes" in parenting practices. For youths on psychotropic medications, communicating about last dose, response to treatment, and any issues or side effects is essential. Communication plans can also be useful in ensuring adequate communication between the school and multiple homes. Examples of important elements of communication plans may include youth's follow-through with rules and expectations, any consequences the youth has received as a result of not following rules, general areas of strength or concern, and any expectations for behaviors that would ideally be carried over into the other setting when possible.

Supervision and Monitoring

Especially for youths with disruptive behavior disorders, adequate supervision and monitoring is essential for effective management of the disorder. Because associations with deviant peers become increasingly predictive of engagement in high-risk,

Table 11.1 Evidence-Based and Other Common Parenting Interventions for Treatment of ADHD and Disruptive Behavior Disorders

Parenting Intervention	Source	Population of focus	Treatment modality
1-2-3 Magic	Developed by Thomas Phelan—no empirical or peer-reviewed articles	Parents of toddlers through adolescents. Magic 1-2-3 is not indicated for children with separation anxiety, physical violence, or self-punitive behavior.	1-2-3 Magic can be delivered in several different modalities, including self-directed, or under professional assistance (individual or group). There is also a professional development program for teachers. The group seminar is designed to last approximately 4–6 hours.
Black Parenting Strengths and Strategies	Coard, Foy-Watson, Zimmer, & Wallace (2007)	Parents of African American children between the ages of 3–7/8	Delivered in a group setting 1x/week, twelve 2-hour sessions
Defiant Children/ Defiant Teens (DC/DT)	Barkley, Edwards, & Robin (1999)	Children with oppositional/acting-out behaviors and/or ADHD between 2–12 years of age	This program can be delivered as a stand-alone parenting intervention or integrated within ongoing family therapy or other forms of therapy addressing other challenges in the family. DC/DT can be delivered in either individual or group format. There are "self-help" books available for parents.
Functional Family Therapy (FFT)	Alexander, Pugh, Parsons, & Sexton (2000); Waldron & Turner (2008).	Families of youths between 10/11 and 18 years of age, typically presenting with significant conduct problems and/or substance abuse	Generally, 3 months of intensive family-based intervention that can be delivered as either an outpatient therapy or a home-based model. Contexts in which FFT is delivered include schools, child welfare, probation, parole, mental health, and as alternatives to incarceration or other out-of-home placement.

Findings	Weaknesses	Strengths
There are no published studies of 1-2-3 Magic in the peer-reviewed literature. There has been one promising study, by Bradley etal. (), evaluating the effectiveness of brief parenting intervention that included the content and video segments of 1-2-3 Magic. Bradley and colleagues found significant results in improving parenting skills and decreasing problematic child behavior. For the most part, these results were maintained at the 1-year follow-up period.	There was significant attrition for the follow-up group. It is unclear how the way the research study delivered the intervention is similar to the way 1-2-3 Magic is typically delivered.	Popular program among parents. Easy to access (can readily purchase workbooks at most bookstores or online).
BPSS is still in the early stages of research. Studies thus far have demonstrated good effects (parental: increase in racial socialization strategies, positive parenting, and less harsh discipline; and child: reductions in conduct problems and increases in responsibility) and high rates of attendance and satisfaction with the intervention.	Not wide dissemination of the program	Program specifically designed to address unique cultural needs of African American families
While many of the strategies in this intervention are parts of other well-researched programs (such as PCIT and The Incredible Years), there has been very little research on the Defiant Child program. Additionally, the manual states that it is appropriate for youths up through age 12; however, none of the strategies suggested in the manual have any research for youths over age 10.	The evidence base for DC is not substantial, although it shares many similarities with several well-established programs.	Program manual and materials are widely available.
FFT is a highly regarded evidence-based program. It is one of the "Blueprint" programs and listed as a model program by the US Surgeon General. There has been extensive research demonstrating the effectiveness of FFT across a range of child behavior problems and with diverse families.	Program is intensive and expensive. Therefore, it is generally not widely available.	One of only a handful of evidence-based programs effective for adolescents with severe conduct problems

(Continued)

Parenting Intervention	Source	Population of focus	Treatment modality
Helping the Noncompliant Child (HNC)	McMahon & Forehand (2005)	Parents of children between the ages of 3 and 7/8 who are exhibiting mostly externalizing (acting-out) behaviors	Typically delivered in an office setting, with parents and child or children being seen together. The length of therapy varies, but typically lasts about 10 sessions (75–90 minutes), occurring 1 or 2 times per week. Length and progression in the program depends on demonstrated skill mastery in a clinical observation, so it can vary depending on the needs of a particular family.
The Incredible Years (IY)	Webster-Stratton (1997)	Parents of children age 0–12 (IY Babies; IY Toddlers; IY BASIC Preschool/Early Childhood Program; IY BASIC School Age Program). (*note, research is on children ages 2–8)	Typically delivered in a group format over 13–20 sessions. The BASIC parent training program is a 12- to 14-week program. The teacher training program includes a 6-day (or 42-hour) workshop for teachers, school counselors, and psychologists.
Love and Logic	Developed by Dr. Charles Fay. Information can be found at There are no peer-reviewed articles or research on this program.	Parents of children 8–9 months of age through adolescents	The Love and Logic training curriculum consists of 12–15 hours of curriculum materials (not specified), two instructional videos, CDs, and parent handbooks.
MATCH-ADTC	Chorpita, Daleiden, &Weisz (2005)	Children with internalizing (including anxiety, depression, and post-traumatic stress disorder) or externalizing behavior problems, between the ages of 7–13	Designed for youths with both singular or co-occurring internalizing problems and externalizing behavior problems. Outpatient, typically office- or home-based services. Typically designed to be delivered in 2–4 months, depending on which modules are delivered. Treatment could last up to a year or more if the youth has significant comorbid internalizing and externalizing behavior problems. The conduct modules can easily be delivered within 10 weeks.

Findings	Weaknesses	Strengths
There have been over 35 empirical outcome studies on various components of HNC, and it is generally regarded as an evidence-based practice.	Studies thus far have exclusively been conducted within a university setting. Not widely disseminated	High degree of empirical support. Families generally report high levels of satisfaction with the program.
The Incredible Years has been substantially researched and is a "Model" program (Center for Substance Abuse Prevention) and a Blueprint program (OJJDP). There have been 11 randomized control group evaluations (six by the developer, five independent replications). Furthermore, there has been substantial research outside of the United States.	Not all components are available across every setting. While one of the more widely disseminated evidence-based practices, may be difficult to find service providers in many locations.	Many studies of effectiveness with culturally diverse clients. Demonstrations of effectiveness within child welfare populations. Inclusion of school components.
No formal research studies	Love and Logic is a popular program in some regions of the US. While Love and Logic certainly offers some potentially useful tips and strategies for promoting a positive parent–child relationship and increasing child responsibility, there is little guidance about what to do if child behavior problems become overly concerning. Love and Logic appears to be designed for parents experiencing minimal difficulty with their child.	Widely disseminated and easy for parents to access
This program was developed through extracting the common, evidence-based strategies for treatment of the internalizing and externalizing behavior problems in youths. While each component has been well tested and evaluated, the process of putting the components together in a modular format is in early stages of being evaluated.	Research, while promising, is still early. Program is not widely available.	Flexible delivery modalities able to accommodate multiple simultaneous diagnoses

(Continued)

Parenting Intervention	Source	Population of focus	Treatment modality
Multidimensional Family Therapy (MDFT)	Liddle, Dakof, Parker, Diamond, Barrett, & Tejada (2001)	Adolescents (11–18) who abuse substances, and their parents	A full course of MDFT ranges between 16 and 25 sessions over 4 to 6 months. Clinicians work with the teen and parents. Sessions may occur multiple times during the week in a variety of contexts including in-home, in-clinic, or by phone.
Multisystemic Therapy (MST)	Henggeler, Cunningham, Pickrel, Schoenwald, & Brondino (1996)	Families of youths age 11–17 (typically involved, or at high risk for becoming involved, in the juvenile justice system)	Intensive ecological intervention that typically lasts 4 to 6 months. Treatment intervention targets may include the individual youth, the family, and interventions with community supports. Therapists carry very small caseloads and are available 24/7.
Parent–Child Interaction Therapy	Eyberg, Boggs, & Algina (1995)	Youth ages 2–6 with externalizing (acting-out) behavior problems	Weekly 1-hour sessions for an average of 12–16 sessions. Sessions include didactic instruction, modeling and role-plays, and in vivo skills training. Typically, the skills training is administered through use of "bug-in-the-ear" technology (therapist is behind a one-way mirror, providing coaching and feedback in realtime). Some recent research has investigated the success of PCIT as a home-based intervention.
Parenting Wisely	Gordon (2000)	Parents of youth ages 8–18	This program is delivered through a CD-ROM/DVD or online format. The intervention consists of 9 sessions and can be completed within 2–3 hours. The intervention can be administered in home or at a clinic.
Play Therapy	Bratton, Ray, & Rhine (2005)	Generally used with children ages 3 through 10 or 11	Generally conducted in an office setting. The "treatment" ranges in length, depending on the child's needs. It often lasts about 20 sessions or more.

Findings	Weaknesses	Strengths
There are at least four efficacy trials of MDFT demonstrating effectiveness in reducing adolescent substance use. MDFT is considered a "model program" by SAMHSA. MDFT has a high degree of research evidence.	Longitudinal investigations reveal that youths remain at high risk for relapse, although the magnitude of this risk does not differ from other evidence-based treatments.	Proven effective with ethnically and linguistically diverse clients. High treatment completion rates.
MST is a Blueprints program and considered a model program by SAMHSA. It has been extensively researched in multiple randomized controlled trials. MST was one of the first programs to demonstrate a clear relationship between program fidelity and outcomes (the better the fidelity, the better the outcomes).	The most significant findings have been with research conducted by the developer and his research team. Program is intensive and expensive. Therefore, it is generally not widely available.	One of only a handful of evidence-based programs effective for adolescents with severe conduct problems
PCIT has been extensively researched and evaluated (well over 30 studies). It is a SAMHSA model program. Research has demonstrated positive effects on parent–child relationships, parenting behaviors and skills, child compliance, reductions in child oppositional behavior, and parenting stress.	Not widely available	Provides intensive coaching via real-time "bug-in-the-ear" technology
Parenting Wisely is considered a model program by SAMHSA. The quality of the research is about average.	Most studies have been with Caucasian parents, with the exception of two unpublished studies on non-U.S. samples (ethnicity not specified).	The opportunity for wide dissemination is one feature that adds to the appeal of this program.
The research on play therapy is mixed, causing considerable controversy in the field. Positive findings of play therapy indicate it is successful in reducing symptoms such as trauma, anxiety, aggression, emotions related to parental divorce. In a recent meta-analysis, findings revealed an overall large effect size (ES=0.80) for play therapy, although filial therapy (in	Longer length of time to see effectiveness. Play therapy may not be the treatment of choice if there is imminent concern regarding a child's placement (e.g., if about to lose a foster care placement because of acting-out behavior) or school (e.g., child is about to be dismissed from his preschool).	Widely available in many community settings

(Continued)

Parenting Intervention	Source	Population of focus	Treatment modality
Strengthening Families	Kumpfer, Molgaard, & Spoth (1996)	Parents of children 3–16 years of age	Consists of 14 consecutive weekly 2-hour group skill-building sessions. Parents and children work separately in training sessions and then participate together in a session practicing the skills they learned earlier. There are Parenting Skills sessions, Children's Life Skills sessions, and Family Life Skills sessions. Participation in ongoing family support groups and booster sessions is encouraged to increase generalization and the use of skills learned.
Triple P Positive Parenting Program	Sanders (1999); Sanders, Markie-Dadds, Tully, & Bor (2000)	Parents of children birth–17 who are primarily exhibiting externalizing behavior problems or parents who demonstrate deficits in parenting effectiveness	There are several different levels of treatment intensity, ranging from one-session, brief intervention formats to more extensive parental support, up to 10 sessions. Additional support modules may be extended as well for parents having challenges with relationship problems or coping. Most frequently, Triple P is delivered in a consultation format or within group settings. Self-directed and media-based interventions are also available.

Findings	Weaknesses	Strengths
which parents actively participate in the play therapy) has a substantially larger effect size (ES=1.15).	With the exception of filial therapy, play therapy does not give parents the skills and knowledge to improve their parenting behavior.	
SFP was developed and found effective on a National Institute on Drug Abuse (NIDA) research grant in the early 1980s. More than 15 subsequent independent replications have found similar positive results with families in many different ethnic groups. SFP was found to significantly reduce problem behaviors, delinquency, and alcohol and drug abuse in children and to improve social competencies and school performance. Child maltreatment also decreases as parents strengthen bonds with their children and learn more effective parenting skills. Both culturally adapted versions and the core version of SFP have been found effective with African American, Hispanic, Asian, Pacific Islander, and First Nations families.	Most studies rely on parental reports of child behavior. At least one study found that community implementation of this program may result in iatrogenic effects for participating youth (Gottfredson et al.,).	Designed to be effective with addicted parents. Has been adapted to work with a variety of different cultural groups.
Triple P has received extensive empirical support, including over 35 randomized controlled studies of different program components and two meta-analyses. Recent studies of multiple diverse cultural contexts reveal robust findings and a high degree of acceptability.	Not widely available in many areas of the United States	Multiple levels of program "intensity" and delivery formats permit matching to parents' needs. High satisfaction ratings among participants.

antisocial activities, knowing a youth's whereabouts and with whom the youth is associating is a vital component of treatment (Henggeler, 1999). To the extent possible, it is important to ensure that youths engage in pro-social activities and have developmentally appropriate opportunities to participate with positive peers in well-supervised environments.

Managing School Issues

Youths with ADHD and disruptive behavioral disorders are at significantly greater risk to experience school-related academic and disciplinary problems (Loe & Feldman, 2007; Loeber, Green, Lahey, Frick, & McBurnett, 2000). Therefore, it is

Table 11.2 TABLE OF CITED STUDIES

Source	Focus of study	Participants or scope of review	Procedure
Comprehensive Review Articles			
Johnston & Mash (2001)	Review of parenting practices associated with child ADHD symptoms	Examined research findings from the past 20 years	Not stated
Deault (2010)	Review of parenting practices associated with child ADHD symptoms	22 articles meeting inclusion criteria, including published in peer-reviewed journals between 2000–2008	Systematic review

paramount to specifically address school issues. Evidence is mixed about the effectiveness of BPTs in generalizing to the school environment, and it should not be assumed that parental engagement in a BPT will necessarily improve the situation at school (McMahon & Wells, 1998). However, designing a treatment strategy that includes the school may provide at least incremental benefits. A study by Corkum, McKinnon, and Mullane (2005) found an enhanced generalization of a parenting intervention to the school environment when parents and teachers both received the intervention. Another study examined the effectiveness of a school intervention alone or in combination with a BPT. Researchers found the most robust impact on child externalizing behavior when the intervention was delivered both to the parents and within the school setting (Reid, Webster-Stratton, & Hammond, 2007).

Table 11.2 lists the research studies cited.

Analysis and Results	Weaknesses	Strengths
Provides a summary of research findings relevant to: • Conceptualizations of families and ADHD • Impact on family functioning • Observations of parent–child interactions • Impact on marital and family relationships • Family stress • Parental cognitions, including sense of competence, expectations and attributions • Parent psychological functioning Findings from the review highlight the need for further research in many areas of inquiry (due to inconsistencies in results across studies). Authors conclude that there is sufficient evidence across multiple studies to conclude that there is a bidirectional relationship between child ADHD and parent behavior and adjustment, and these findings are particularly strong for youths who also have other conduct-related problems.	Was not a systematic review; authors did not specify inclusion and exclusion criteria for articles included in the review. Most studies were limited by focusing on elementary-school-age boys (generally neglecting older youths and girls).	Provides a comprehensive and well-organized overview and synthesis of 20 years' worth of research on ADHD and the related impact on family functioning
Provided a critical summary of results from included articles. Findings revealed that family functional challenges are more likely to emerge for families of youths with disruptive behavior problems compared with families	Only examined PsycInfo and PubMed databases. While these are top-tier databases, the authors may have missed some relevant studies. Most included studies were correlational in design.	Good synthesis of recent literature pertinent to this topic area. Inclusion of high-quality studies. Ability to examine impact of design methodology on study outcomes across multiple studies.

(Continued)

Table 11.2 TABLE OF CITED STUDIES   (*Continued*)

Source	Focus of study	Participants or scope of review	Procedure

Research Articles

Source	Focus of study	Participants or scope of review	Procedure
Counts, Nigg, Stawicki, Rappley, & Von Eye (2005)	Examined family adversity of families with children who had two different ADHD subtypes and controls	337 mothers and fathers of 206 children ages 7–13. 134 children met DSM criteria for ADHD and an identified predominate subtype (inattentive=38, combined=96) and 72 children did not meet criteria and were included as controls.	Parents and teachers completed screening questionnaires over 2 years to assign ADHD/Control status. Child completed DISC-IV to determine ADHD subtype. Parents completed a series of questionnaires to measure SES, parental psychopathology, marital conflict, and stressful events. Parent-reported variables were combined into an adversity index.
Corkum, McKinnon, & Mullane (2005)	Examined the additive benefits of including a teacher intervention to a traditional behavioral parent training program	Parents and classroom teachers of 30 children between the ages of 5–12 who were clinically diagnosed with ADHD	Random assignment was used to assign families to either: 1) behavior parent training, or 2) behavior parent training plus teacher inclusion. Parents and teachers completed measures before and after the intervention. Measures examined child ADHD symptoms, parenting stress, knowledge of behavioral principles, ADHD knowledge, and treatment satisfaction. The parent intervention consisted of a 10-week group-based curriculum. The teacher inclusion condition consisted of psycho-educational materials about ADHD and communication about skills parents were learning in their parent group. They also received suggestions for how to implement strategies in their classroom.

Analysis and Results	Weaknesses	Strengths
of youths with ADHD. Variations in symptoms and family context warrant an individualized approach towards treatment, including possibly providing individual help for parents experiencing distress or mental health challenges.		
Families with children diagnosed with ADHD had higher levels of adversity, but this adversity was largely tied to cases with combined-subtype ADHD. When controlling for conduct problems, adversity remained associated with ADHD diagnosis. Regression analysis demonstrated that child symptomatology was differentially related to their perceptions of marital conflict and was related to maternal psychopathology.	Limited availability of data from biological fathers. Moderate levels of missing data. Family adversity was restricted to preclude extreme dysfunction.	Emphasis on the associations of both ADHD subtypes with family adversity and parental characteristics
ANOVAs were used to determine treatment effects. All families reported improvements regardless of condition. There were greater improvements for children whose teachers received information. Satisfaction across both conditions was high.	Very small sample size. Lack of a control group. Reliance on parent and teacher self-report. Did not report whether there were discrepancies in parent or teacher reports of ADHD symptoms.	Provides at least preliminary evidence that generalization of treatment to the school setting can be enhanced through a relatively low-cost, low-intensity intervention for the teachers, and that it is acceptable to teachers

(Continued)

Table 11.2 TABLE OF CITED STUDIES   *(Continued)*

Source	Focus of study	Participants or scope of review	Procedure
Cunningham et al. (2008)	Examined different parental preferences for information and treatment of child mental health problems	1,194 parents with a child between the ages of 6–18 who were receiving services from a community mental health center	Parents responded to either a web-based or paper survey, asking questions about treatment preferences, child mental health problems, child and family functioning, perception of the value of various information sources, and information barriers.
DosReis, Barksdale, Sherman, Maloney, & Charach (2010)	Qualitative study of parent experiences to examine stigmatizing situations related to child's ADHD diagnosis	48 parents or caregivers of children diagnosed with ADHD ages 6–18	Parents with children recently diagnosed with ADHD were recruited from health and behavioral/mental health outpatient clinics. Parents completed a phone or in-person interview within 1 month of diagnosis focused on events leading up to diagnosis.
Durukan et al. (2008)	Description of depression and anxiety in mothers who have children with or without DSM-diagnosed ADHD	30 mothers and children ages 7 to 12 years who received DSM diagnoses of ADHD and a control group of 30 mothers with the same age children who accessed a local pediatrics department	Mothers filled out the COPE (Coping Orientation to Problems Experienced), Beck Depression, and Beck Anxiety Scales.

Analysis and Results	Weaknesses	Strengths
Latent class analysis was used to determine groups of parents regarding treatment preferences. Results indicated that there were three distinct groups: Action, Information, and Overwhelmed groups. MANOVAs were used to examine differences between these three groups. Parents in the Action group preferred informational sources that provided evidence-based, active strategies, practice exercises, and regular meetings with their therapist. The Information group preferred written materials geared at psychoeducation (compared with problem-solving). This group preferred receiving information individually as opposed to in a group format. The Overwhelmed group generally did not want information or help with regard to their child's condition and preferred to seek out information on their own. The Overwhelmed group tended to have children with greater functional challenges compared with the Action and Information groups.	Respondents were all families already using mental health centers, thereby missing information about families who are not currently engaged in the MH system. Differential response rate for Internet-based surveys (65%) compared with paper-based surveys (32%).	Application of market research and health economy research methodology to apply to children's mental health. Large sample size. Study has clear clinical implications that may be useful in enhancing parental motivation to engage in treatment.
A grounded theory approach was used to code stigmatizing experiences into six categories (concerns with labeling, feelings of social isolation and rejection, perceptions of a dismissive society, influence of negative public views, exposure to negative media, and mistrust of medical assessments). Of the responding parents, 44% endorsed concerns with labeling, 40% social isolation, 21% negative media, 21% dismissive society, 17% mistrust of assessments, 6% influence of negative public views, and 23% did not report experiences with any of these themes.	Sample included only parents who were continuing to seek treatment for their child. Sample was not diverse in race or income level, so low generalizability to other populations. Low participation from biological fathers.	Recruitment from a variety of different clinics, both physical health and mental health, to account for a range of perspectives.
T-tests and chi-squares were used to assess relationships between the two different groups. Mothers of children with ADHD had significantly higher levels of depression and anxiety compared with mothers of children without ADHD. Mothers of children with ADHD had elevated maladaptive coping behavior on several subscales of the COPE	Small sample size limits ability to compare coping styles across ADHD subtypes. Exclusionary criteria (learning disabilities, CD, chronic illness) limits generalizability. Risk that results capitalized on Type I error for COPE subscales, warranting caution in interpretation of results.	Of note, youths with comorbid ADHD and ODD were included. Highlights clinical implications that family members of youth with ADHD may be experiencing challenges with depression and anxiety.

(Continued)

353

Table 11.2 TABLE OF CITED STUDIES   *(Continued)*

Source	Focus of study	Participants or scope of review	Procedure
Evans, Sibley, & Serpell (2009)	Examination of caregiver strain among caregivers of children with ADHD	52 caregivers of youth between the ages of 11–14 who have ADHD. Sample was of youths who were primarily Caucasian (94%) and mostly male (72.5%). Caregivers were predominately female (82%) and married (67.5%).	Caregivers completed questionnaires across two time periods, 1 year apart. Questionnaires measured caregiver strain, youth disruptive behavior disorders, and child grades (GPA) at school.
Johnston, Mah, & Regambal (2010)	Examined parenting beliefs and sense of efficacy on maternal experiences with behavioral parent training programs to address their child's ADHD symptoms	101 mothers of youths between the ages of 5–10 who have ADHD; most children were male (85%), Caucasian (81%). Mothers were mostly married (63%) or divorced (20%).	Mothers completed questionnaires on youth disruptive behavior symptoms, treatment history, parenting cognitions (self-efficacy, attributions of cause of ADHD), and treatment beliefs. After completing questionnaires, mothers then participated in a 1-hour behavioral parent training intervention. They returned 1 week later to report on their use of the strategies.
Kerr & Michalski (2007)	Analysis of a national longitudinal survey (NLSCY) to investigate relationship between family structure and hyperactivity trajectories	1,092 adult caregivers of children with data available in the NLSCY longitudinal survey at all four interview time points: 1994, 1996, 1998, & 2000	Caregivers of each selected child in the survey were interviewed using a brief scale measuring child hyperactivity. Family structure and other background data were also collected as part of the survey.

Analysis and Results	Weaknesses	Strengths
measure, including denial, emotion expression, suppression of competing activities, and total dysfunctional coping score.		
Multiple regression was used to examine the relationship between child symptoms and caregiver strain. Findings revealed that when youth also had symptoms of ODD and CD, caregivers were most likely to report caregiver strain. Change in perception of symptoms over time was also examined using multiple regression. The authors did not find any difference in caregiver strain given changes in symptoms between time 1 and time 2. Comorbid ADHD and ODD/CD symptoms predicted strain above and beyond severity of ADHD symptoms and school-related impairments.	Relatively small sample size, only two time points for analysis, largely homogeneous sample of families. Reliance on self-report measures.	Ability to investigate the relationships between constructs over the course of a year. Authors do a nice job relating findings to clinical implications (i.e., importance of behavioral parent training and teaching parents coping skills).
A number of analytic approaches were used, including exploratory and confirmatory factor analysis, and structural equation modeling. The main findings supported a relationship between attributions of child ADHD and beliefs about the acceptability of behavioral parent training. Use of the strategies, however, was most related to mother's sense of efficacy.	Only taught mothers two behavioral techniques in a 1-hr session. While the strategies were based on evidence-based behavioral management practices, the brevity of the treatment limits generalizability to actual treatment settings, which typically last 8–12 weeks.	Adequately dealt with missing data. Provided good evidence for the inter-relationship between parenting sense of efficacy and ability to use parenting strategies. This has important clinical implications.
Latent growth modeling was used to examine the relationship between constructs over time. Children in single-parent families had higher starting values but similar declines in hyperactivity symptoms over the course of the survey compared with children in dual parent families. Likewise, children whose parents separated during the study period showed no increased challenges at baseline and no difference in hyperactivity trajectories.	Authors suggest several potentially relevant factors that were not available in the dataset (structural factors, dynamic measures of family coping strategies, relationship characteristics).	Longitudinal survey with extremely high subject retention rates. Ability to examine trajectories over time enables causal inference.

(Continued)

Table 11.2 TABLE OF CITED STUDIES   (*Continued*)

Source	Focus of study	Participants or scope of review	Procedure

Lindahl (1998)	Examination of marital and family factors associated with ADHD, ODD, and comorbid ADHD and ODD	110 two-parent families with at least one male child between the ages of 7–11.
		  7% African American
		  36% Caucasian
		  57% Hispanic/Latino (10% responding to questionnaires translated into Spanish)
			Families completed questionnaires about child behavior and marital and family functioning. Parents participated in a marital problem discussion task; parents and the child participated in a discussion of a recent family argument.

Mikami, Jack, Emeh, & Stephens (2010)	Compared children with ADHD and controls on their peer relationships and effects of parent social competence and parent behavior around child's peers	124 parents of children ages 6 to 10 with or without ADHD who were recruited from schools, clinics, and primary health offices	Parents and teachers completed the Child Symptom Inventory used to determine which children met criteria for ADHD.
			  Parents completed additional measures about child's behavior, and self-reported social competence.
			  Children were assigned to playgroups of children they had never met, and the parent and child played in the playgroup for an hour. Parents were instructed to help their child make friends. After the play session, parents debriefed their child about their behavior in the group and finally, all children completed a measure of how much they liked peers in the playgroup.

Rogers, Wiener, Marton, & Tannock (2009)	Compared factors that influenced parental involvement and differences in level of parent school-related involvement	Parents of 101 children ages 8 to 12 with and without diagnosed ADHD	Child completed screener and structured interview for ADHD determination and study screening. Parents completed the Parent Involvement Project-Parent Questionnaire (PIP-PQ)

Analysis and Results	Weaknesses	Strengths
Examined differences in parent ratings among the four groups (ADHD alone, ODD alone, co-morbid ADHD and ODD, and a control group) using MANOVA, with income as the covariate, and discriminant analysis to further determine the nature of differences between groups. Findings revealed that families with boys with ADHD only tended to have more coercive interactions, but there was more limited impact on the marital relationship. Parents with boys with ODD or comorbid ADHD/ODD reported the most significant impact on family life (less cohesive), conflict over childrearing, and greater problems with their marital relationship.	Only looked at male children. Relatively small sample size. Cross-sectional study, thereby providing information at only one data point. Evolution of impacts on family life over time was not able to be assessed given the research design.	Ethnically diverse sample. Multiple strategies for obtaining information (questionnaires and direct observation).
Differences between parents of children with and without ADHD were examined using ANCOVAs with ADHD status as the independent variable and CD/ODD symptoms as a covariate. Hierarchical linear modeling (HLM) was used because children were nested within playgroups. Parents of children with ADHD reported lower interpersonal competence themselves, hosting fewer playdates, and were more critical of their children during playdates. Parents who engaged in more socializing with other parents had children who were rated higher on peer acceptancemeasures by their teachers. Increased parent socializing was also linked with higher positive social ratings by the child's peers.	Few fathers participated in the study. Relatively small sample size. Playtime observation involved a much higher ratio of ADHD to non-ADHD children than would be expected in usual interactions.	Examined differences between inattentive and combined types of ADHD. Comparison group was recruited from the same local school as the ADHD sample. Broad inclusionary criteria. Multi-informant method of assessing ADHD symptoms and peer acceptance.
Used 2 (ADHD status) × 2 (child grade level) ANCOVAs to examine differences in parental involvement between the two groups of children. Covariates included parent education level. Parents of children with ADHD had lower parental efficacy and time	Limited participation from fathers in the sample. ADHD and non-ADHD samples were drawn using different procedures (clinicreferrals and general community sample). Relatively small sample size.	Investigated both theorized contributing factors and self-reported parent involvement in child learning. This study has clear clinical and practical implications.

(Continued)

Table 11.2 Table of Cited Studies   (*Continued*)

Source	Focus of study	Participants or scope of review	Procedure
			measuring factors that influence parent involvement and then completed the Family School Questionnaire (FSQ) to measure self-reported involvement in child's home-based learning.
Wymbs et al. (2008)	Examination of rates of divorce, comparing parents of youths with and without ADHD	Participants included 282 youths with ADHD and 206 youths without ADHD and their parents. Participants were mostly male (88%) and Caucasian (87%), with an average age of 17 at the time of the study. All participants were part of a larger study (PALS; see Molina et al., 2007).	Longitudinal study using interview and survey methodology. Childhood data (severity of ADHD and ODD/CD symptoms; parental relationship information) were collected approximately 8 years prior. Divorce history and current ADHD and ODD/CD symptoms were collected at follow-up.
Wymbs & Pelham (2010)	Examined the impact of child effects on the marital relationships, particularly considering interactions with a child with or without ADHD on parental conflict	90 couples with children between the ages of 9–12 with ADHD (N=51) and without ADHD (N=39). Most children were male (84%) and predominately Caucasian (96%). Most couples were married (94%).	Experimental study. Parents were randomly assigned to have to interact with a confederate child who was either acting "disruptive" or "typical." After interacting with the child, couples then were asked to discuss issues related to co-parenting (how they could work together better as parents).

Analysis and Results	Weaknesses	Strengths
and energy to devote to involvement. These parents also reported fewer general school invitations but more specific teacher invitations than parents of children who did not have an ADHD diagnosis. No differences were found in self-reported mother's involvement in child learning (active participation, academic pressure, or encouragement). Fathers of children with ADHD self-reported lower levels of active participation and higher academic pressure compared to controls.		
Used Kaplan-Meier survival analyses to examine the time until divorce, comparing youths with ADHD and controls. Cox regression analyses were used to simultaneously examine the impact of other child and parent risk factors on time to divorce. Findings revealed that families of youths with ADHD divorced more often and were married for shorter lengths of time compared with families of the control youths. Other factors related to time to divorce included lower education levels of mothers, fathers who had more education and more antisocial behavior, and for youths who were younger, ethnically diverse, and also had ODD/CD problems.	Of note, only 147 of the 282 youths with ADHD were able to be included in the primary analyses due to availability of data. Significant missing data between data points (although the researchers examined the impact of the missing variables on outcomes and found no difference). Families were relatively homogeneous, thereby limiting generalizabiltiy of findings.	Ability to examine outcomes over time, both prospectively and retrospectively. Examination of both parent and youth variables. Highlights the importance of examining the impact of divorce on families with children with ADHD since the base rate may be much higher.
2 (ADHD/no ADHD) × 2 (parent gender) × 2 (confederate disruptive or normal) MANCOVA analyses were used to assess parent ratings of partner communication. Other covariates included parent educational level and length of relationship with children. ANCOVAs and chi-square analyses were used to assess the observer-rated communication. Findings revealed that parents interacting with "disruptive" confederate children engaged in less positive and more negative communi-cation patterns, especially when the parents had their own child with ADHD and/or comorbid ADHD and ODD/CD.	Potential limitations with regard to external validity (given the highly controlled environment). Relatively small sample size, largely homogeneous population of families, and reports from parents that communication may not have been realistic compared to how they typically communicate at home.	Experimental study provides good corroboration with other prospective studies examining the impact of child characteristics on the marital relationship. Researchers adequately examined the validity of the experimental manipulation.

In summary:

- Treatment of ADHD and disruptive behavior disorders can be compromised if parents disagree on intervention targets and strategies.
- Lack of consistency between caregivers can attenuate the effectiveness of treatment.
- Communication plans may be a helpful strategy to increase consistency and strategies for decision-making.
- Adequate supervision and monitoring of youths, especially youths with ODD or CD, is an essential component of any parenting plan.
- School issues can be significant and will likely require additional intervention targets and goals.

SUMMARY

ADHD and disruptive behavior disorders are among the most common behavioral health disorders in childhood. The functional impairments associated with these disorders can greatly affect youths across a range of domains, including home, school, and the community. There is mounting evidence that youths with these disorders and their families experience increased challenges. Therefore, appropriate and timely treatment is paramount to prevent more significant levels of impairment. There have been significant advances in treatment options. The most effective treatments for ADHD include a combination of behavioral interventions and medications, with the best evidence with stimulant medication. The most effective treatments for disruptive behavior disorders are behavioral parent training programs for younger children and behavioral parent training programs or systemic/ecological treatments for adolescents. Parents play a critical role in supporting such treatments, including monitoring and supervising medications and participating in behavioral training programs when indicated. Identifying strategies to promote consistency between caregivers, developing clear communication plans, supporting realistic and effective supervision and monitoring, and adequately managing school issues are all important considerations within the family court context.

Guidelines: Considerations and Cautions

- Children and adolescents with ADHD and disruptive behavior problems experience a range of functional impairments that span individual, family, academic, and community settings.
- Families with children with ADHD and/or disruptive behavior problems often experience increased challenges across a number of domains, including marital relationships, parent–teacher relationships, and general coping and parental well-being.
- Research demonstrates that effective treatment of ADHD and disruptive behavior problems relies on parental involvement as a key component to intervention success.

- Parental involvement in treatment has been historically challenging, and while research is beginning to identify strategies to increase parental motivation and/or match interventions to parental preferences, as a field there is not a strong research base in this area.
- There is a proliferation of non-researched, ineffective, and even iatrogenic strategies for managing ADHD and disruptive behavior disorders. Examples include many cases of polypharmacy, psychopharmacologic interventions for very young children, and purported psychosocial interventions that have strong marketing campaigns yet very little research regarding their effectiveness. Caution should be undertaken with regard to these approaches.

REFERENCES

Alexander, J. F., Pugh, C., Parsons, B. V., & Sexton, T. L. (2000). Functional family therapy. In D. S. Eliott (Ed.), *Blueprints for violence prevention* (2nd ed., Book 3). Boulder, CO: Center for the Study and Prevention of Violence, Institute of Behavioral Science, University of Colorado.

American Psychiatric Association. (2000). *Diagnostic and statistical manual of mental disorders* (4th ed., text rev.).Washington, DC: APA. doi: 10.1176/appi.books.9780890423349

Barkley, R. A. (1998). Attention-deficit/hyperactivity disorder. In E. J. Mash & R. A. Barkley (Eds.), *Treatment of childhood disorders* (2nd ed., pp. 55–110). New York: Guilford Press.

Barkley, R. A., Edwards, G. H., & Robin, A. L. (1999). *Defiant teens: A clinician's manual for assessment and family intervention.* New York: Guilford Press.

Bauermeister, J. J., Canino, G., Polanczyk, G., & Rohde, L. A. (2010). ADHD across cultures: Is there evidence of a bidimensional organization of symptoms? *Journal of Clinical Child and Adolescent Psychology, 39*(3), 362–372. doi:10.1080/15374411003691743

Botvin, G. J., Griffin, K. W., & Nichols, T. R. (2006). Preventing youth violence and delinquency through a universal school-based prevention approach. *Prevention Science, 7*, 403–408. doi:10.1007/s11121–006-0057-y

Bradley, S.J., Jadaa, D.-A., Brody, J., Landy, S., Tallett, S.E., Watson, W., . . . Stephens, D. (2003). Brief psychoeducational parenting program: An evaluation and 1-year follow up. *Journal of the American Academy of Child and Adolescent Psychiatry, 42*,1171–1178. doi: 10.1097/01.chi.0000081823.25107.75

Bratton, S., Ray, D., & Rhine, T. (2005).The efficacy of play therapy with children: A meta-analytic review of treatment outcomes. *Journal of Professional Psychology Research and Practice, 36*(4), 376–390. doi: 10.1037/0735–7028.36.4.376

Cantwell, D. (1996). Attention deficit disorder: A review of the past 10 years. *Journal of the American Academy of Child and Adolescent Psychiatry, 35*,978–987. doi:10.1097/00004583–199608000-00008

Chamberlain, P., & Smith, D. K. (2003). The Oregon multidimensional treatment foster care model. In A. E. Kazdin & J. R.Weisz (Eds.), *Evidence-based psychotherapies for children and adolescents* (pp. 282–300).New York: Guilford Press.

Chorpita, B. F., Daleiden, E. L., & Weisz, J. R. (2005). Modularity in the design and application of therapeutic interventions. *Applied and Preventive Psychology, 11*(3), 141–156. doi: 10.1016/j.appsy.2005.05.002

Chronis, A. M., Chacko, A., Fabiano, G. A., Wymbs, B. T., & Pelham, W. E. (2004). Enhancements to the behavioral parent training paradigm for families of children with ADHD: Review and future directions. *Clinical Child and Family Psychology Review, 7*(1), 1–27. doi:10.1023/B:CCFP.0000020190.60808.a4

Coard, S. I., Foy-Watson, S., Zimmer, C., & Wallace, A. (2007). Considering culturally relevant parenting practices in intervention development and adaptation: A randomized controlled trial of the black parenting strengths and strategies (BPSS) program. *Counseling Psychologist, 35*(6), 797–820. doi: 10.1177/0011000007304592

Connolly, A., & Vance, A. (2010). Psychosocial factors associated with parent and teacher reports of aggression in children and adolescents with attention deficit hyperactivity disorder. *Australian and New Zealand Journal of Psychiatry, 44*(7), 667–675. doi:10.3109/00048671003664697

Corkum, P., McKinnon, M., & Mullane, J. (2005). The effect of involving classroom teachers in a parent training program for families of children with ADHD. *Child and Family Behavior Therapy, 27*(4), 29–49. doi:10.1300/J019v27n04_02

Counts, C. A., Nigg, J. T., Stawicki, J. A., Rappley, M. D., & Von Eye, A. (2005). Family adversity in DSM-IV ADHD combined and inattentive subtypes and associated disruptive behavior problems. *Journal of the American Academy of Child and Adolescent Psychiatry, 44*(7), 690–698. doi:10.1097/01.chi.0000162582.87710.66

Cunningham, C. E., Deal, K., Rimas, H., Buchanan, D. H., Gold, M., Sdao-Jarvie, K., & Boyle, M. (2008).Modeling the information preferences of parents of children with mental health problems: A discrete choice conjoint experiment. *Journal of Abnormal Child Psychology, 36*(7), 1123–1138. doi:10.1007/s10802–008-9238–4

Deault, L. C. (2010). A systematic review of parenting in relation to the development of comorbidities and functional impairments in children with Attention-Deficit/Hyperactivity Disorder.*Child Psychiatry and Human Development, 41*(2), 168–192. doi:10.1007/s10578–009-0159–4

dosReis, S., Barksdale, C. L., Sherman, A., Maloney, K., & Charach, A. (2010). Stigmatizing experience of parents of children with a new diagnosis of ADHD. *Psychiatric Services, 61*(8), 811–816. doi:10.1176/appi.ps.61.8.811

Durukan, I., Erdem, M., Tufan, A. E., Congoluglu, A., Yorbik, O., & Turkbay, T. (2008). Depression and anxiety levels and coping strategies used by mothers of children with ADHD: A preliminary study. *Anatolian Journal of Psychiatry, 9*(4), 217–223. Retrieved fromhttp://sites.google.com/site/anatolianpsychiatry/

Epstein, J. N., Langberg, J. M., Lichtenstein, P. K., Altaye, M., Brinkman, W. B., House, K., & Stark, L.J. (2010).Attention-deficit/hyperactivity disorder outcomes for children treated in community-based pediatric settings. *Archives of Pediatrics and Adolescent Medicine, 164*(2), 160–165. doi:10.1001/archpediatrics.2009.263

Evans, S. W., Sibley, M., & Serpell, Z. N. (2009). Changes in caregiver strain over time in young adolescents with ADHD: The role of oppositional and delinquent behavior. *Journal of Attention Disorders, 12*(6), 516–524. doi:10.1177/1087054708322987

Eyberg, S. M., Boggs, S. R., & Algina, J. (1995). Parent-child interaction therapy: A psychosocial model for the treatment of young children with conduct problem behavior and their families. *Psychopharmacology Bulletin, 31*, 83–91.

Eyberg, S. M., Funderburk, B. W., Hembree-Kigin, T. L., McNeil, C. B., Querido, J. G., & Hood, K. K. (2001). Parent-child interaction therapy with behavior problem children: One and two year maintenance of treatment effects in the family. *Child and Family Behavior Therapy, 23*(4), 1–20. doi:10.1300/J019v23n04_01

Fabiano, G. A., Chacko, A., Pelham, W. E., Robb, J., Walker, K. S., Arnold, F., . . . Pirvics, L. (2009). A comparison of behavioral parent training programs for fathers of children with attention-deficit/hyperactivity disorder. *Behavior Therapy, 40*(2), 190–204. doi:10.1016/j.beth.2008.05.002

Fabiano, G. A., Pelham, W. E., Coles, E. K., Gnagy, E. M., Chronis, A. M., & O'Connor, B. C. (2009). A meta-analysis of behavioral treatments for Attention-Deficit/ Hyperactivity Disorder. *Clinical Psychology Review, 29*(2), 129–140. doi:10.1016/j. cpr.2008.11.001

Faraone, S. V., & Buitelaar, J. (2010). Comparing the efficacy of stimulants for ADHD in children and adolescents using meta-analysis. *European Child and Adolescent Psychiatry, 19*(4), 353–364. doi: 10.1007/s00787–009-0054–3

Gordon, D.A. (2000). Parent training via CD-ROM: Using technology to disseminate effective prevention practices. *Journal of Primary Prevention, 21*(2), 227–251. doi: 10.1023/A:1007035320118

Gottfredson, D., Kumpfer, K., Polizzi-Fox, D., Wilson, D., Puryear, V., Beatty, P. & Vilmenay, M. (2006). The Strengthening Families Washington DC Project: A randomized effectiveness trial of family-based prevention. *Prevention Science, 7*(1), 57–74.

Goldstein, A. P., Glick, B., & Gibbs, J. C. (1998). *Aggression Replacement Training: A comprehensive intervention for aggressive youth.* Champaign, IL: Research Press.

Greenhill, L., Kollins, S., Abikoff, H., McCracken, J., Riddle, M., Swanson, J., . . . Cooper, T. (2006). Efficacy and safety of immediate-release methylphenidate treatment for preschoolers with ADHD. *Journal of the American Academy of Child and Adolescent Psychiatry, 45*(11), 1284–1293. doi: 10.1097/01.chi.0000235077.32661.61

Harty, S. C., Miller, C. J., Newcorn, J. H., & Halperin, J. M. (2009). Adolescents with childhood ADHD and comorbid disruptive behavior disorders: Aggression, anger, and hostility. *Child Psychiatry and Human Development, 40*(1), 85–97. doi:10.1007/s10578–008-0110–0

Henggeler, S. W. (1999). Multisystemic Therapy: An overview of clinical procedures, outcomes, and policy implications. *Childand Adolescent Mental Health, 4*(1), 2–10. doi:10.1111/1475–3588.00243

Henggeler, S. W., Cunningham, P. B., Pickrel, S. G., Schoenwald, S. K., & Brondino, M. J. (1996). Multisystemic therapy: An effective violence prevention approach for serious juvenile offenders. *Journal of Adolescence, 19*(1), 47–61. Retrieved fromhttp://www.elsevier.com/wps/find/journaldescription.cws_home/622849/descriptiondescription

Hinshaw, S. P. (2007). Moderators and mediators of treatment outcome for youth with ADHD: Understanding for whom and how interventions work. *Journal of Pediatric Psychology, 32*(6), 664–675. doi:10.1093/jpepsy/jsl055

Jensen, P. S., Hinshaw, S. P., Kraemer, H. C., Lenora, N., Newcorn, J. H., Abikoff, H. B., . . .Vitiello, B. (2001). ADHD comorbidity findings from the MTA study: Comparing comorbid subgroups. *Journal of the American Academy of Child and Adolescent Psychiatry, 40*(2), 147–158. doi:10.1097/00004583–200102000-00009

Johnston, C., Mah, J. W. T., & Regambal, M. (2010). Parenting cognitions and treatment beliefs as predictors of experience using behavioral parenting strategies in families of children with Attention-Deficit/Hyperactivity Disorder. *Behavior Therapy, 41*(4), 491–504. doi:10.1016/j.beth.2010.02.001

Johnston, C., & Mash, E. J. (2001). Families of children with Attention Deficit/ Hyperactivity Disorder: Review and recommendations for future research. *Clinical Child and Family Psychology Review, 4,* 183–207. doi:10.1023/ A:1017592030434

Jones, H. A., Epstein, J. N., Hinshaw, S. P., Owens, E. B., Chi, T. C., Arnold, L. E., . . .Wells, K.C. (2010). Ethnicity as a moderator of treatment effects on parent-child interaction for children with ADHD. *Journal of Attention Disorders, 13*(6), 592–600. doi:10.1177/1087054709332158

Kaminski, J. W., Valle, L. A., Filene, J. H., & Boyle, C. L. (2008). A meta-analytic review of components associated with parent training program effectiveness. *Journal of Abnormal Child Psychology, 36,* 567–589. doi:10.1007/s10802–007–9201–9

Kerns, S. E. U., & Prinz, R. J. (2002). Critical issues in the prevention of violence-related behavior in youth.*Clinical Child and Family Psychology Review, 5*(2), 133–160. doi:10.1023/A:1015411320113

Kerr, D., & Michalski, J. H. (2007). Family structure and children's hyperactivity problems: A longitudinal analysis. *Canadian Journal of Sociology, 32*(1), 85–112. doi:10.2307/20460617

Kessler, R. C., Green, J. G., Adler, L. A., Barkley, R. A., Chatterji, S., Faraone, S. V., . . . Van Brunt, D.L. (2010). Structure and diagnosis of adult Attention-Deficit/ Hyperactivity Disorder. *Archives of General Psychiatry, 67,* 1168–1178. doi:10.1001/ archgenpsychiatry.2010.146

Kumpfer, K. L., Molgaard, V., & Spoth, R. (1996). The Strengthening Families program for prevention of delinquency and drug use in special populations. In R. Dev Peters & R. J. McMahon (Eds.), *Childhood disorders, substance abuse, and delinquency: Prevention and early intervention approaches* (pp. 241–267). Newbury Park, CA: Sage Publications.

Kumpfer, K. L., & Tait, C. M. (2000). *Family skills training for parents and children.*Washington, DC: Office of Juvenile Justice and Delinquency Prevention. Retrieved from http://www.ojjdp.gov/

Langberg, J. M., Epstein, J. N., Simon, J. O., Loren, R. E. A., Arnold, L. E., Hechtman, L., . . . Wigal, T. (2010). Parent agreement on ratings of children's Attention Deficit/ Hyperactivity Disorder and broadband externalizing behaviors.*Journal of Emotional and Behavioral Disorders, 18*(1), 41–50. doi:10.1177/1063426608330792

Liddle, H. A., Dakof, G. A., Parker, K., Diamond, G. S., Barrett, K., & Tejada, M. (2001). Multidimensional Family Therapy for adolescent substance abuse: Results of a randomized clinical trial. *American Journal of Drug and Alcohol Abuse, 27*(4), 651–687. doi: 10.1081/ada-100107661

Lindahl, K. M. (1998). Family process variables and children's disruptive behavior problems. *Journal of Family Psychology, 12,* 420–436. doi:10.1037/0893–3200. 12.3.420

Linehan, M. M., Schmidt, H., Dimeff, L. A., Craft, J. C., Kanter, J., & Comtois, K. A. (1999). Dialectical Behavior Therapy for patients with borderline personality disorder and drug dependence. *American Journal on Addictions, 8,* 279–292. doi:10.1080/105504999305686

Loe, I. M., & Feldman, H. M. (2007). Academic and educational outcomes of children with ADHD. *Journal of Pediatric Psychology, 32*(6), 643–654. doi:10.1093/jpepsy/jsl054

Loeber, R., Green, S. M., Lahey, B. B., Frick, P. J., & McBurnett, K. (2000). Findings on disruptive behavior disorders from the first decade of the Developmental Trends Studies. *Clinical Child and Family Psychology Review, 3*,37–60. doi:10.1023/A:1009567419190

McKay, M. M., McCadam, K., & Gonzales, J. J. (1996). Addressing the barriers to mental health services for inner city children and their caretakers. *Community Mental Health Journal, 32*, 353–361. doi:10.1007/BF02249453

McMahon, R. J., & Forehand, R. L. (2005). *Helping the noncompliant child.* New York: The Guilford Press.

McMahon, R. J., & Wells, K. C. (1998). Conduct problems. In E. J. Mash & R. A. Barkley(Eds.), *Treatment of childhood disorders* (2nd ed., pp.111–207). New York: Guilford Press.

Mikami, A. Y., Jack, A., Emeh, C. C., & Stephens, H. F. (2010). Parental influence on children with Attention-Deficit/Hyperactivity Disorder: I. Relationships between parent behaviors and child peer status. *Journal of Abnormal Child Psychology, 38*(6), 721–736. doi:10.1007/s10802-010-9393-2

Miller, T. W., Nigg, J. T., & Miller, R. L. (2009). Attention-Deficit/Hyperactivity Disorder in African American children: What can be concluded from the past 10 years? *Clinical Psychology Review, 29*(1), 77–86. doi:10.1016/j.cpr.2008.10.001

Moffitt, T. E., Caspi, A., Dickson, N., Silva, P. A., & Stanton, W. (1996). Childhood-onset versus adolescent-onset antisocial conduct in males: Natural history from age 3 to 18. *Development and Psychopathology, 8*, 399–424. doi:10.1017/S0954579400007161

Molina, B. S. G., Flory, K., Hinshaw, S.P., Greiner, A. R., Arnold, L. E., Swanson, J., . . . & Wigal, T. (2007). Delinquent behavior and emerging substance use in the MTA at 36-months: Prevalence, course, and treatment effects. *Journal of the American Academy of Child and Adolescent Psychiatry, 46*, 1028–1040. doi:10.1097/chi.0b013e3180686d96

Pelham, W. E., Burrows-MacLean, L., Gnagy, E. M., Fabiano, G. A., Coles, E. K., Tresco, K. E., . . . Hoffman, M.T. (2005). Transdermal methylphenidate, behavioral, and combined treatment for children with ADHD. *Experimental and Clinical Psychopharmacology, 13*(2), 111–126. doi:10.1037/1064-1297.13.2.111

Pelham, W. E., & Hoza, B. (1996). Intensive treatment: A summer treatment program for children with ADHD. In E. Hibbs & P. Jensen(Eds.), *Psychosocial treatments for child and adolescent disorders: Empirically based strategies for clinical practice* (pp. 311–340). New York: APA Press. doi:10.1037/10196-013

Pham, A.V., Carlson, J.S., & Kosciulek, J.F. (2010). Ethnic differences in parental beliefs of Attention-Deficit/Hyperactivity Disorder and treatment. *Journal of Attention Disorders, 13*(6), 584–591. doi: 10.1177/1087054709332391

Prinz, R. J., Connor, P. A., & Wilson, C. C. (1981). Hyperactive and aggressive behaviors in childhood: Intertwined dimensions. *Journal of Abnormal Child Psychology, 9*, 191–202. Retrieved fromhttp://www.springerlink.com/content/104756/

Ramtekkar, U. P., Reiersen, A. M., Todorov, A. A., & Todd, R. D. (2010). Sex and age differences in Attention-Deficit/Hyperactivity Disorder symptoms and diagnoses: Implications for DSM-V and ICD-11. *Journal of the American*

Academy of Child and Adolescent Psychiatry, 49(3), 217–228. doi:10.1016/j.jaac. 2009.11.011

Reid, J. B., Patterson, G. R., & Snyder, J. (2002). *Antisocial behavior in children and adolescents: A developmental analysis and model for intervention.* Washington, DC: American Psychological Association. doi:10.1037/10468–000

Reid, M. J., Webster-Stratton, C., & Hammond, M. (2007). Enhancing a classroom social competence and problem-solving curriculum by offering parent training to families of moderate-to-high-risk elementary school children. *Journal of Clinical Child and Adolescent Psychology, 36*(5), 605–620. doi:10.1080/15374410701662741

Rogers, M. A., Wiener, J., Marton, I., & Tannock, R. (2009). Parental involvement in children's learning: Comparing parents of children with and without attention-deficit/hyperactivity disorder. *Journal of School Psychology, 47*(3), 167–185. doi:10.1016/j.jsp.2009.02.001

Sanders, M. R. (1999). Triple P-Positive Parenting Program: Towards an empirically validated multilevel parenting and family support strategy for the prevention of behavior and emotional problems in children. *Clinical Child and Family Psychology Review, 2*(2), 71–90. doi:10.1023/A:1021843613840

Sanders, M. R., Markie-Dadds, C., Tully, L., & Bor, B. (2000). The Triple P-Positive Parenting Program: A comparison of enhanced, standard and self-directed behavioural family intervention for parents of children with early onset conduct problems. *Journal of Consulting and Clinical Psychology, 68*, 624–640. doi:10.1037/0022–006X.68.4.624

Stanger, C., Budney, A. J., Kamon, J. L., & Thostensen, J. (2009). A randomized trial of contingency management for adolescent marijuana abuse and dependence. *Drug and Alcohol Dependence, 105*(3), 240–247. doi: 10.1016/j.drugalcdep. 2009.07.009

Turgay, A. (2009). Psychopharmalogical treatment of oppositional defiant disorder. *CNS Drugs, 23*(1), 1–17. doi:10.2165/0023210–200923010-00001

Waldron, H.B., & Turner, C.W. (2008). Evidence-based psychosocial treatments for adolescent abusers: A review and meta-analysis. *Journal of Clinical Child and Adolescent Psychology, 37*,1–24. doi: 10.1080/15374410701820133

Webster-Stratton, C., & Hammond, M. (1997). Treating children with early-onset conduct problems: A comparison of child and parent training interventions. *Journal of Consulting and Clinical Psychology, 65*(1), 93–109. doi:10.1037/0022–006X.65.1.93

Wigal, T., Greenhill, L., Chuang, S., McGough, J., Vitiello, B., Skrobala, A., . . . Stehli-Nguyen, A. (2006). Safety and tolerability of methylphenidate in preschool children with ADHD. *Journal of the American Academy of Child and Adolescent Psychiatry, 45*(11), 1294–1302. doi: 10.1097/01.chi.0000235082.63156.27

Wymbs, B. T., & Pelham, W. E. (2010). Child effects on communication between parents of youth with and without Attention-Deficit/Hyperactivity Disorder. *Journal of Abnormal Psychology, 119*(2), 366–375. doi:10.1037/a0019034

Wymbs, B. T., Pelham, W. E., Molina, B. S. G., Gnagy, E. M., Wilson, T. K., & Greenhouse, J. B. (2008). Rate and predictors of divorce among parents of youths with ADHD. *Journalof Consulting and Clinical Psychology, 76*(5), 735–744. doi:10.1037/a0012719

Parent Behaviors Affecting Co-parenting and the Stability of the Parent–Child Relationships

## 12

Gatekeeping after Separation and Divorce

LAWRENCE GANONG, MARILYN COLEMAN,
AND GRAHAM McCAULLEY ∎

When parents separate and divorce they often struggle with continuing to relate to each other as co-parents of their children while ending the couple relationship (Ahrons, 2007). Being able to develop a positive co-parental relationship is important because there is ample research evidence that children's adjustment following divorce is dependent on the quality of post-divorce family relationships. For instance, the quality of the co-parental relationship is connected to children's well-being—children are harmed when parents argue frequently, try to undermine each other, and put children in the middle of their disputes (Buchanan, Maccoby, & Dornbusch, 1996; Sandler, Miles, Cookston, & Braver, 2008). Co-parenting quality is associated with another important post-divorce relationship: children's bonds with non-residential parents (Sobolewski & King, 2005). Maintaining close emotional relationships with non-residential parents has been found in several studies to be predictive of children's successful adjustment to divorce (Amato & Gilbreth, 1999; Carlson, 2006; King & Sobolewski, 2006).

Researchers have shown that co-parental relationships and parent–child relationships after divorce are positively related (Amato & Sobolewski, 2004). When parents cooperate in childrearing, then children's relationships with both parents are closer and more satisfying, and children benefit. Consequently, helping individuals make transitions from spouses or cohabiting partners to physically separated but functional co-parents that allow children to maintain positive ties with both of their parents is the focus of many parent education programs (e.g., Pollett & Lombreglia, 2008) and interventions (e.g., Cowan, Cowan, Pruett, & Pruett, 2007; Pruett, Arthur, & Ebling, 2007) designed for divorcing and separating parents.

The research evidence on the effects of positive family relationships on children after divorce has been so compelling that over the past two decades researchers have studied various factors that facilitate or hinder divorced parents' connections with their children and each other. One phenomenon that has received attention is gatekeeping (Pruett et al., 2007). Although previous reviewers have concluded that empirical support for gatekeeping "is not robust" (Pleck & Masciadrelli, 2004, p. 249), the potential effects of gatekeeping are so significant that research on this construct persists.

In this chapter the authors review and critique empirical research and theorizing about gatekeeping after separation and divorce.

CONCEPTUALIZING GATEKEEPING

Researchers initially thought of gatekeeping primarily as mothers' efforts to restrict fathers' involvement with their children. For example, maternal gatekeeping was defined in a widely cited study as "a collection of beliefs and behaviors that ultimately inhibit a collaborative effort between men and women in family work by limiting men's opportunities for learning and growing through caring for home and children" (Allen & Hawkins, 1999, p. 200). Another frequent conceptualization was blunter: Gatekeeping was defined as "mothers' preferences and attempts to restrict and exclude fathers from child care and involvement with children" (Fagan & Barnett, 2003, p. 1021). Maternal gatekeeping was conceptualized by researchers as a common aspect of motherhood that was independent of parents' marital status. This view of gatekeeping as consisting of beliefs and behaviors of one parent that endeavored to limit the other parent's involvement with children has been labeled *restrictive gatekeeping* (Austin, 2008) or *negative control* (Berger, Brown, Joung, Melli, & Wimer, 2008).

Although researchers have recognized that fathers as well as mothers may gate-keep (Allen & Hawkins, 1999; Pruett, Williams, Insabella, & Little, 2003; Trinder, 2008), research on gatekeeping has been almost exclusively focused on mothers as gatekeepers (Adamsons, 2010). Mothers are more likely to have physical custody of children after divorce, particularly when children are young (Berger et al., 2008), so they have more opportunities than fathers to gatekeep. It should be noted, however, that even the research on married parents has focused on mothers as gatekeepers, primarily because motherhood is seen as consisting of "clearly specified roles, rights, and responsibilities" (Adamsons, 2010, p. 137), whereas fatherhood is a more socially constructed and ambiguous status.

In general, most researchers have proposed that restrictive gatekeeping has nega-tive effects on children and nonresidential parents, but other scholars have pointed out that there often is a rational motivation for gatekeeping that may have beneficial results for children, such as in families where there has been intimate partner vio-lence, child abuse, or parental substance abuse (Austin, 2008). The term *protective gatekeeping* was applied to these situations by Leslie Drozd (cited in Austin, 2008). A primary difference between restrictive and protective gatekeeping is contextual—if being with the other parent is a potentially dangerous situation for children, the main intention of protective gatekeeping is to control or monitor the other parent's access in order to shield the child from harm, whereas multiple intentions have been proposed as motivations for restrictive gatekeeping (Pruett et al., 2007).

In recent years scholars have called attention to the fact that parents not only engage in restrictive gatekeeping but also facilitate each other's interactions with children (Pruett et al., 2003; Sano, Richards, & Zvonkovic, 2008; Schoppe-Sullivan, Brown, Cannon, Mangelsdorf, & Sokolowski, 2008; Trinder, 2008). Pruett and col-leagues (2003) broadened the definition of gatekeeping as "facilitative and inhibitory functions exercised by one or both parents that determine who will have access to their children, and the nature of that access" (p. 171). Trinder (2008) suggested that gatekeeping be defined as a nondirectional concept, with *gate closing* being used as a term to describe actions that restrict parental engagement with children and *gate opening* to describe behaviors that enhance the other parent's involvement.

Austin (2005) has proposed that inhibitory and facilitative gatekeeping behaviors are two ends of a single continuum, with such actions as withholding information about the child, refusing to let the other parent see or speak to the child, and denigrating the other parent to the child at the inhibitory end of the continuum. Freely sharing information, flexibly allowing involvement of the other parent with the child, and cooperatively co-parenting would be at the facilitative end. Toward the middle of this gatekeeping continuum, according to Austin (2005), parents experience ambivalence about the role of the other parent and may vacillate between facilitating and prohibiting involvement of the other parent with the children.

Trinder's (2008) qualitative British study indicates that maternal gatekeeping is a more complex process than most researchers have envisioned, involving the thoughts and actions of both parents, and with parents exerting continual and bidirectional influences on each other. She argued that gatekeeping cannot be understood by examining only one parent's actions or one parent's beliefs because gatekeeping is a dynamic process in which both parents have input. Unfortunately, most studies of gatekeeping have done just what Trinder advised against: Gathering data from one parent about her beliefs and, less often, her behaviors, without collecting data from fathers or children. Although scholars have not reached consensus about how to conceptualize gatekeeping, there is general agreement that facilitative, restrictive, and protective gatekeeping involves multidimensional processes that are motivated by multiple factors.

In summary:

- Gatekeeping may be done by either parent, but researchers have centered their attention on maternal gatekeeping.
- Maternal gatekeeping has been conceptualized as a process that is independent of a mother's marital status.
- Gatekeeping may be restrictive, protective, or facilitative. These categories of gatekeeping indicate diverse and multiple motivations.
- Most researchers have focused on restrictive gatekeeping, which is intended to reduce the other parent's involvement in order to punish, control, and minimize the value of the other parent.
- Protective gatekeeping is aimed at limiting or eliminating contact with the other parent, with the goal of ensuring the child's safety and well-being.
- Facilitative gatekeeping involves encouraging interactions between the children and their other parent. It has been called "gate opening."
- A parent may engage in all three categories of gatekeeping.

DIMENSIONS OF GATEKEEPING

Gatekeeping generally has been conceptualized as a constellation of both parental beliefs and behaviors (Allen & Hawkins, 1999; DeLuccie, 1995; Fagan & Barnett,

2003: McBride et al., 2005; Trinder, 2008). Researchers have hypothesized that mothers' beliefs influence their gatekeeping behaviors and interactions with fathers and children (e.g., Allen & Hawkins, 1999; Hoffman & Moon, 1999; Pruett et al., 2007). These hypothesized maternal beliefs range from cultural gender ideologies about the differentiated parental roles of men and women to mothers' personal

Table 12.1 EXAMPLES OF RELEVANT GATEKEEPING STUDIES

Source	Participants	Procedures
Fagan & Barnett (2003)	102 residential mothers with a child ages 3–16. Children had 30 nonresidential and 72 residential fathers/father figures.	Mothers filled out instruments relating to family background, beliefs on importance of fathers (Role of the Father Questionnaire), perceptions of father's abilities (Inventory of Father Involvement), extent to which mothers gatekeep, and amount of father involvement.
Herzog, Umana-Taylor, Madden-Derdich, & Leonard (2007)	121 mothers (M age = 18, M age of child = 13 mos.) receiving public assistance in a Southwestern city, recruited via an educational program. Most had not finished high school, were non-white (63% Latino). About half were in relationships with their children's fathers (M age = 20.66 years).	During small-group sessions mothers completed survey packets with assistance from research assistants. Survey packets contained measures on fathers' support during pregnancy, financial support, and involvement with target child. Grandparents' support of teen fathers' involvement was also assessed, as were mothers' feelings towards fathers, romantic relationships with fathers, gatekeeping beliefs, and co-parental interaction.

evaluations about the fathers of their children and about themselves as mothers (i.e., maternal identities). Researchers also have speculated about a variety of other maternal cognitions (i.e., idealization of parents, self-esteem, thoughts about the past relationship with the father, and desire for control and power). The research evidence about these diverse beliefs is examined separately (Table 12.1).

Analysis and Results	Weaknesses	Strengths
Analyses included factor analyses for data reduction, bivariate correlations, path analyses to examine the model, and multiple regression to test for mediation. Maternal gatekeeping was negatively related to father involvement, while father nonresidential status was associated with maternal gatekeeping. Father competence was related to maternal gatekeeping and father involvement. Gatekeeping mediated effects of maternal beliefs on father competence and involvement. Only 18% of the variance in father involvement was explained by maternal gatekeeping.	Data were from mother self-report only, limited generalizability due to convenience sampling. Causal inferences should be tempered with correlational data.	About half of the mothers were married and half remarried, never married, divorced, or separated; racially diverse sample. Examined gatekeeping beliefs and behaviors.
Mothers who were in a romantic relationship with fathers reported more frequent father–child contact and more involvement in co-parental interaction than mothers who were not romantically involved with fathers. Objective 2 of the study used regression analysis to examine a mediational model concerning father involvement in couples who were no longer romantically involved. Mothers' satisfaction with and desire for fathers' involvement mediated the relationship between fathers' support during pregnancy, presence at birth, financial support, maternal grandparent support, and frequency of father–child contact and co-parental interaction. Objective 3 examined mothers in romantic relationships with their children's fathers and found correlations between mothers' satisfaction with and desire for fathers' involvement. Frequency of father–child contact and co-parental interaction were not significant so testing the mediation model was not possible. Romantically involved mothers were more satisfied and desired more paternal involvement, more father–child contact, and co-parental interaction than non-romantically involved mothers.	Study was conducted in English and not designed specifically for Latinos so they may have not assessed culturally relevant variables. Sample size did not permit comparisons for racial/ethnic groups. Gathering data from mothers only on father and grandparent behaviors may introduce reporter bias and shared method variance bias. The lack of information on fathers (e.g., mental health, substance use) limits contextual factors that may affect father involvement.	Sample was low-income and diverse (roughly 90% non-white). Study examined developmental-contextual framework to understand teenage fathers' involvement, and the assessment of co-parental interaction furthered the study of father involvement beyond just father–child contact.

(Continued)

Table 12.1 EXAMPLES OF RELEVANT GATEKEEPING STUDIES   *(Continued)*

Source	Participants	Procedures
King & Heard (1999)	1,565 mothers in households with children younger than 18 years old who had a father living elsewhere (includes both divorced and never-married families). The final analyses examining child well-being is limited to children at least 5 years old, resulting in a sample of 1,172.	Data drawn from the first wave of the National Survey of Families and Households (NSFH; collected from 1987 to 1988). Data are based on mother reports on whether conflict exists between the parents over the father's visitation, if the mother is satisfied or dissatisfied with the father's level of contact with the focal child, the frequency of father visitation with a focal child, and the focal child's well-being (i.e., adjustment, global well-being, behavior problems).
Kulik & Tsoref (2010)	88 married Israeli women (M age = 34, most had postsecondary education and all worked) with young children aged 2–6 (52% had 2 children, 24% had 3 children)	Mothers were recruited through community and school settings as well as through snowball sampling. Mothers completed a survey packet in Hebrew in their homes. Maternal gatekeeping was measured via Fagan and Barnett's (2003) scale assessing mothers' attitudes toward fathers' involvement in child care and child-related activities. Data were gathered on mothers' gender role ideology; desire for control; satisfaction with husband's involvement in child care; perceived support from extended family; and family background variables.

Analysis and Results	Weaknesses	Strengths
Bivariate relationships showed that mothers were more satisfied when there was less conflict and when fathers visited more often. More mothers were satisfied when fathers had no contact than when fathers had low levels of contact. Conflict over visitation increased as father contact increased, although conflict declined for families reporting the highest levels of contact. Most mothers (77%) did not report conflict over visitation and most (70%) were satisfied with visitation. Families were grouped by conflict, satisfaction, and visitation and analyses were performed to see how family type affected child well-being. Conflict over visitation does not appear to make a difference. Frequent contact does not benefit children more than infrequent contact, even when mothers are satisfied. Children are least well off in families in which mothers are dissatisfied and there are high levels of father contact. Using OLS regression an interaction effect between father contact and mother dissatisfaction was found. Mother's dissatisfaction predicted poor child well-being only when the fathers' contacts were high. Logistic regression analyses found that with high contact, mothers were more likely to be dissatisfied if they had been married to the father, the father had little influence, and they rarely discussed the child.	Data on child well-being are mothers' reports; richer data would add context to how maternal satisfaction is related to father contact and conflict. Some information is lost by dichotomizing these variables when considering family types and child well-being. Conclusions about the role of conflict over fathers' visitation should be interpreted cautiously, as the sample displayed modest levels of conflict and there was no information on the context in which conflict occurred.	Study aided in providing a fuller picture of the relationship between non-resident father contact and mother, and examines a previously neglected facet of non-resident parenting: the role of the mother's satisfaction with the father's contact. Person-centered approach to data analysis (people, not variables, are the main focus) by grouping families via combinations of key measures. Large, national dataset used.
Relationships between research variables and maternal gatekeeping were examined through Pearson's correlations and hierarchical regression analyses were performed to examine the overall contribution of research variables in explaining maternal gatekeeping. No correlation was found between mothers' desire for control and gatekeeping. When mothers were more educated, wealthier, held more liberal gender role ideologies, and perceived more support from extended family, they were significantly less likely to gatekeep. Mothers who were more satisfied with fathers' involvement were also more confident in fathers' abilities to care for children and less likely to gatekeep.	Israeli sample may limit generalizability to other cultural groups, and particular sample may not represent all dual-earner families with young children in Israeli society, as it focused mainly on upper-class, married, heterosexual couples. Correlational cross-sectional design prohibits determining causal relationships.	Study examined gatekeeping in an understudied context and provided a basis for conducting research among additional socioeconomic and cultural groups. Information on factors affecting gatekeeping was advanced by examining maternal, family, and background characteristics, which may help identify mothers who gatekeep.

(Continued)

Table 12.1 Examples of Relevant Gatekeeping Studies   (*Continued*)

Source	Participants	Procedures
Madden-Derdich & Leonard (2000)	62 nonresidential fathers (mean age of 38 with average of two children) who had divorced in the past 3 months were recruited from a Southwestern city. Fathers were predominantly white, middle-class, and well educated. Fathers had been divorced a mean of 11 months and 13% had remarried.	Fathers completed survey packets at home and returned them by mail. Measures assessed fathers' satisfaction with their own parenting performance, satisfaction with the parent–child relationship, involvement in co-parental interaction, co-parental support from former spouse, and co-parental conflict.
Pruett, Arthur, & Ebling (2007)	142 families in the process of divorce/separation in Connecticut (24% never married, the rest married average of 8 years). Sample was primarily white yet economically diverse. Target children in the sample were the youngest in families (if applicable, mean age 3.3 years). The youngest child from each family served as the target child for the study.	Divorcing or separating parents were recruited by mail or in person, were randomly assigned as either recipients of an intervention emphasizing both parents' involvement with children or as control group families. Data collection began when parents began legal proceedings, 6 months later, and again 15–18 months later. Data on gatekeeping attitudes, family demographics, parent and children's adjustment, legal outcomes, custody, non-residential parental involvement, and co-parental and parent–child relationship quality were collected. In addition, collateral information was obtained from attorneys, teachers, and court records.

Analysis and Results	Weaknesses	Strengths
Gatekeeping behaviors were not related to child characteristics (i.e., large family size, young children). Overall, mothers' gender role ideologies and evaluations of fathers' involvement in child care appear to be the more dominant factors affecting maternal gatekeeping.		
Authors used multiple regression to determine how well parenting role variables predicted co-parental interaction. Custody arrangement, co-parental conflict, and satisfaction with the parent–child relationship were not significant predictors of co-parental interaction. Fathers' perceptions of amount of parenting support received from former spouses and their satisfaction with their own parenting performance were significant predictors of co-parental involvement, with co-parental involvement having the strongest relationship to co-parental interaction. Regressions were conducted to determine main and interaction effects for the four independent variables and custody arrangement on co-parental interaction. When fathers had joint legal custody, their satisfaction with parenting performance was positively associated with involvement in co-parental interaction, yet when fathers did not share legal custody their satisfaction with parenting performance was negatively related to involvement in co-parental interaction.	Data from both parents would have contributed to a fuller picture of the co-parenting relationship, and the overall response rate of 34% suggests considerations may be warranted regarding differences between responders and non-responders. Generalizability is also limited by the sample containing divorced (versus never-married), predominantly white fathers with some post-secondary education.	Study involved non-resident fathers in the year after divorce and contributed to the literature on factors affecting post-divorce fathering by gathering data from fathers rather than relying on mother reports. Data captured fathers' perceptions of their parenting and considered the role of legal custody context on fathers' co-parenting.
Parents' answers to open-ended questions were transcribed and coded. Mothers were twice as likely to report facilitating ex-partners' access to children as they were to report hindering contact. Fathers viewed mothers as facilitators and as restrictors in equal numbers. Both parents reported being flexible with father visitation as the most common facilitative behavior of mothers. Most fathers saw maternal behaviors as affecting their parental involvement; most reported more negative effects. Correlational analyses found that both parents' reports of maternal gatekeeping attitudes were negatively related to co-parenting quality and father involvement.	Some generalizability limited by predominately white sample with young children, although sample was economically diverse and included both married and never-married parents.	Study design was longitudinal and collected data from both parents as well as others via several methods. Interviews and questionnaires allowed researchers to gather good qualitative data on gatekeeping and parenting in the transition to divorce.

(Continued)

Table 12.1 EXAMPLES OF RELEVANT GATEKEEPING STUDIES   (*Continued*)

Source	Participants	Procedures
Pruett, Williams, Insabella, & Little (2003)	102 nonresidential fathers and 110 mothers with primary physical custody of children age 6 or younger (59% boys, 41% girls) who started the legal divorce process. Sample was mainly white (85%); 80% were married (average length = 8 years); sample was educated but economically diverse.	Parents were recruited as part of a larger longitudinal study, and data were derived from their initial survey responses. Mothers and fathers completed questionnaires regarding family demographics, parents' and children's adjustment, legal outcomes, custody arrangements, non-residential parents' involvement, and quality of the co-parenting and parent–child relationships. Data on children's adaptation were assessed through phone interviews with mothers conducted by a trained clinician.
Roy & Dyson (2005)	Sample of 40 incarcerated non-resident fathers (78% had children with one woman, 20% with two women, 2% with three women) in a work-release program in a Midwestern urban area	Researchers used participant observation and 11 weeks of field work to look at individual, group, and neighborhood processes related to non-residential father involvement. A subsample of fathers was recruited for more in-depth, life-history interviews related to father roles and involvement.

Analysis and Results	Weaknesses	Strengths
Regression analyses found that mothers' gatekeeping attitudes mediated the relationships between their perceptions of the past couple relationship and their current cooperation with fathers and perceptions of father involvement. Mothers and fathers in the intervention group, which received information and assistance to identify maternal gatekeeping and encouragement to involve both parents, were more likely to endorse facilitative gatekeeping than parents in the control group. Intervention group mothers were more aware of ways they may hinder fathers' access to children.		
Structural equation modeling was used to examine relations among family dynamics, attorney involvement, and child adjustment at the time of parents' separation. Authors employed a two-group (mothers vs. fathers) path analysis and examined differences. Fathers felt they were more involved with children than mothers perceived them to be, reported more maternal gatekeeping than did mothers, and more negative changes in parent–child relationships. Gatekeeping was conceptualized as the degree to which parents valued the importance of and fostered the other parent's involvement, positive feelings about the other parent from the marriage and the effects of affection for a child, and parents' perception of support received from other parent during marriage and its impact on past and present parenting. Mothers with greater psychological symptomatology were more likely to view fathers' support as an influence on their parenting. Conflict was associated with less positive views of the other parent. No gatekeeping factors were correlated with child outcomes or father involvement.	Generalizability limited by sample being mainly white and primarily having young children, and only non-residential fathers were involved in the study. Although the operationalizing of gatekeeping was novel, model received mixed support.	Captured parents at the beginning of the legal divorce process. Considered how the marital context may contribute to gatekeeping. Gatekeeping factors were not limited to maternal gatekeeping; both positive and negative factors were examined. Fairly large sample obtained and dyadic data were collected.
Data were coded for fatherhood themes with the basic elements of grounded theory and analytic induction. Mothers both discouraged men's involvement as parents (48% of fathers described such experiences) and encouraged their involvement (74% of fathers reported encouragement). 26% of fathers	Small sample limits generalizability. Study may have more reports of maternal encouragement due to the context of incarceration—the work-release program was supportive of relationships among fathers, mothers, and children.	Study is one of the few to examine non-resident, low-income fathers; had a diverse sample in age and race. One of the few studies to look at father reports or collect data over time.

(Continued)

Table 12.1 Examples of Relevant Gatekeeping Studies   (*Continued*)

Source	Participants	Procedures
Sano, Richards, & Zvonkovic (2008)	83 low-income, rural residential mothers (mean age 30.8 years) from 13 states (children's mean age = 7.3 yrs.).	As part of a larger longitudinal study, mothers were interviewed on a variety of topics including family well-being, parenting, financial issues, and family relationships.
Trinder (2008)	43 mothers and 33 non-resident fathers (22 with former partners interviewed separately and 32 interviewed without partners)	Semi-structured interview was designed to elicit a history of contacts, and thoughts, feelings, and judgments about arrangements. Parents were questioned on what they thought helped or hindered parent–child contact.

Maternal Beliefs that Affect Gatekeeping

Gender Ideology and Gatekeeping

One of the underlying motivations proposed to explain restrictive maternal gate-keeping is the extent to which mothers adhere to belief systems about the differentiated roles of mothers and fathers (Adamsons, 2010; Allen & Hawkins, 1999; DeLuccie, 1995; Fagan & Barnett, 2003; Gaunt, 2008). Women who strongly adhere to gendered ideology are hypothesized to be reluctant to relinquish childrearing responsibility to fathers because traditional gender ideologies view mothers as the primary and most effective caregivers for children. According to Braverman (1989), a powerful cultural ideology that she called the *myth of motherhood* mandates that motherhood is natural and instinctive for all women and is the highest "calling" a woman

Analysis and Results	Weaknesses	Strengths
identified discouragement and encouragement from the same mother. Maternal gatekeeping is more than mothers' values or beliefs about paternal involvement, but is instead an active process of negotiating overlapping role expectations that require an active response from fathers.		
Mothers' responses to open-ended questions were inductively coded for major themes regarding relationships with non-resident fathers. Four themes regarding mothers' concerns about fathers: child support issues, frustration about father–child contact, distrust in fathers' skills, and concerns for children's safety. Most mothers did not receive child support but did not limit fathers' involvement. Primary concerns were father–child relationship quality.	Although theoretical saturation was reached and sample size was appropriate for qualitative work, generalizability may be limited to rural, low-income mothers and fathers. Data reflect only mothers' perspectives.	Study examined the complexities involved in maternal gatekeeping, considered gatekeeping in mothers' own words.
Data were analyzed using grounded theory methods and found five approaches to maternal gate work: proactive and contingent gate opening, passive gatekeeping, and justifiable and proactive gate closing. Although it was variable, individuals did not change approaches. Gate work was seen as transactional processes where parents exert continual bidirectional influences on each other via co-parental relationship, maternal perceptions of paternal competence and commitment, child safety concerns, and role issues.	Small sample size reduced ability to identify pathways between maternal gate work and contextual factors. Unclear whether gate work is a gender- or status-based practice. Almost exclusively white parents.	Interviews with both partners from former couples allowed verification of accounts and how men perceive maternal gate work. Method designed to develop theory.

may pursue. Beliefs that mothers and fathers have differentiated roles are related to beliefs about what children need from each of their parents and what parents should offer their children (Sano et al., 2008; Trinder, 2008). From this perspective, mothers are seen as providing unique resources for children—resources that fathers and other adults, even grandparents, cannot provide. The perceived importance of fatherhood and fathers' roles in children's lives is hypothesized to be a component of gender ideologies as well (DeLuccie, 1995; Fagan & Barnett, 2003; Gaunt, 2008; Pruett et al., 2007). In gendered ideologies fathers are thought to be necessary complements to mothers, but only as secondary parents.

Adherence to gender ideologies is hypothesized to affect not only the role behaviors of mothers in gatekeeping but maternal identities are thought to be influenced as well (Allen & Hawkins, 1999; DeLuccie, 1995; Gaunt, 2008; Markham, Ganong, &

Coleman, 2007). How women see themselves as mothers and the extent to which they evaluate themselves doing well as mothers, thus validating their maternal identities, are hypothesized to affect the degree to which they restrict fathers' involvement with children (Allen & Hawkins, 1999; Pruett et al., 2007). Conversely, egalitarian beliefs have been proposed as influencing mothers' facilitative gatekeeping and sharing of childrearing responsibilities with fathers (Bulanda, 2004; Hoffman & Moon, 1999). Mothers who believe that men and women are equally adept at caring for children, it has been proposed, will readily share co-parenting responsibilities with the children's fathers.

Research evidence for the influence of gender ideologies on maternal gatekeeping generally has been consistent in that most studies have supported hypotheses about gendered motivations, but effect sizes have been small. For example, maternal beliefs about the importance of fathers' involvement for children's development were directly related to the frequency of father involvement, as reported by mothers, in two studies (DeLuccie, 1995; Fagan & Barnett, 2003). Married mothers' beliefs about a limited role for fathers in children's lives were related to reductions in fathers' accessibility to their children even when the men expressed high commitment to parenting (McBride et al., 2005). The perceived importance of fathers also was found to be indirectly related to paternal involvement, mediated through married mothers' satisfaction with fathers' involvement (DeLuccie, 1995), and mediated through divorced parents' perceptions of their marriage and current co-parenting (Pruett et al., 2007).

Allen and Hawkins (1999) found that the extent to which traditional maternal roles were part of a woman's identity as a mother was related to mothers' restrictive gatekeeping. This also was supported in another study testing this hypothesis: Maternal identity salience was predictive of maternal gatekeeping and paternal involvement with children (Gaunt, 2008). Similarly, nontraditional beliefs held by married women about fathers' roles have been found to be associated with greater father involvement (Cannon, Schoppe-Sullivan, Mangelsdorf, Brown, & Sokolowski, 2008; Schoppe-Sullivan et al., 2008) and more support by mothers for paternal engagement with children (Hoffman & Moon, 1999). These findings suggest that facilitative gatekeeping or gate opening may be linked to egalitarian gender attitudes. Not all investigations, however, have found nontraditional gender role ideologies to be related to paternal involvement (Bulanda, 2004).

In two qualitative studies of rural, mostly low-income women who were separated from the fathers of their children, mothers reported that they encouraged fathers to be involved with their children partly because the mothers believed that fathers play an important function in children's development (Laakso, 2004; Sano et al., 2008). Other considerations, including children's safety when they were with potentially violent or substance-abusing men, somewhat offset these facilitative behaviors that were stimulated by gendered beliefs, leading mothers to protectively gatekeep at times. Other researchers have reported that maternal beliefs about the importance of fathers for children's development led mothers to agree to joint physical and legal custody with men who had physically and emotionally abused them during the marriage (Hardesty & Ganong, 2006). These formerly abused women also actively engaged in gate-opening behaviors to facilitate the men's involvement, but they did so watchfully, and carefully, attuned to possible problems in how the men interacted with them and their children.

Some of this facilitative behavior may be rooted in gendered ideologies that go beyond beliefs about fathers' roles—one aspect of traditional motherhood is *kinkeeping*, or managing relationships in families and encouraging everyone to get along. Seery and Crowley (2000) found that most of the women in their study, regardless of marital status (e.g., married, remarried, and divorced), engaged in a variety of kinkeeping, or relationship management work, for their children and the children's fathers. These mothers offered suggestions for joint father–child activities, praised fathers for being involved, passed along positive comments from child to father and back, and did what they could to promote a positive image of fathers to their children. In many ways these mothers acted as mediators whose jobs were to promote and maintain positive father–child bonds. This mediating or kinkeeping role has been found in several studies of divorced mothers (Hardesty & Ganong, 2006; Madden-Derdich & Leonard, 2000; Trinder, 2008). A related construct, *kinscripting*, also has been found to be related to maternal recruiting efforts directed towards never-married, low-income fathers to be involved with their children (Roy & Burton, 2007). Kinscripting, originally applied to low-income African American families, is a framework for examining how mothers engage extended maternal and paternal kin, including unrelated or fictive kin, in doing family work. Kinscripting, like kinkeeping, is seen as an aspect of maternal identities that affect co-parental interactions.

Mothers' beliefs also have been found to be related to fathers' beliefs and engagement in childrearing behaviors in some, but not all, aspects of fathering (Cannon et al., 2008; McBride et al., 2005). This finding led McBride and colleagues to speculate that the function of gendered beliefs on maternal gatekeeping, at least among married co-parents, may be more complex than researchers initially thought.

Although researchers have found associations between mothers' gendered beliefs, gatekeeping, and father involvement, the designs of most of the studies generally have not allowed researchers to carefully examine the underlying processes that link maternal beliefs and gatekeeping behaviors (Pleck & Masciadrelli, 2004; see Cannon et al., 2008; Gaunt, 2008; McBride et al., 2005; and Pruett et al., 2007, for exceptions). Fathers' beliefs and behaviors are also relevant (Adamsons, 2010; Madden-Derdich & Leonard, 2000), although rarely have researchers examined fathers' contributions to maternal gatekeeping.

MATERNAL BELIEFS ABOUT PATERNAL COMPETENCE

A common motivation for restricting fathers' access to children is the perception that fathers are incompetent at childrearing. Both mothers and fathers reported that divorced mothers were more accommodating to changes in visitation when they were more satisfied with their former spouses' childrearing skills (Madden-Derdich & Leonard, 2002).

Some scholars have suggested that mothers' views regarding paternal incompetence are due to their need to be seen as good mothers by others, so they set impossibly high standards for child care that fathers cannot meet (Allen & Hawkins, 1999). There is some empirical support for higher standards predicting lower engagement in family work by fathers and higher engagement by mothers (Allen & Hawkins, 1999; Gaunt, 2008). Perceived incompetence by fathers has been found to be related to maternal beliefs about the differential roles of mothers and fathers (DeLuccie, 1995; Pruett et al., 2007) but not to beliefs about the importance of fathers (Fagan & Barnett, 2003).

Most studies indicate that mothers are expressing concerns about fathers' abilities to safely and effectively provide care for children that are based on more than gendered beliefs about men's abilities to care for children (Herzog, Umana-Taylor, Madden-Derdich, & Leonard, 2007). For instance, divorced mothers' concerns about their former spouses' parenting abilities both shortly after filing for divorce and 3 years later were related to perceived visitation problems such as the father spoiling the child, being a bad role model, not providing a religious upbringing, and children's depression after visiting the father (Wolchik, Fenaughty, & Braver, 1996). Presumably some divorced mothers base their judgments about fathers' childrearing capabilities on observations made during marriage, when some fathers may not have been as engaged in childrearing as they are after separating from the mothers (Amato & Sobolewski, 2004).

Divorced mothers who wanted to facilitate the connection among their children and the fathers of those children have expressed qualms about encouraging contacts with fathers who are not perceived by them to be good at parenting (Sano et al., 2008; Trinder, 2008). Such qualms led them to what Trinder (2008) called *contingent gate opening*—allowing contact with fathers only under certain conditions. These conditions were set by mothers to ensure that children would be safe when they were with fathers who had substance abuse problems (Laakso, 2004; Trinder, 2008), who had been physically abusive to mothers (but not to the children) in the past (Hardesty & Ganong, 2006; Laakso, 2004), or who were perceived by mothers to be irresponsible in fulfilling what the mothers saw as paternal roles (Sano et al., 2008). These contingent gate-opening mothers would be in the middle of Austin's (2005) gatekeeping continuum because they want to facilitate father–child contacts but are concerned and hesitant about doing so because of worries about children's safety and well-being when they are with their fathers.

Although there have been only a few studies of gatekeeping that have examined perceptions of paternal incompetence, the findings are consistent in showing that mothers actively restrict fathers' involvement with children when they believe that fathers are incapable at parenting. What is less clear from these studies is the degree to which these maternal perceptions are a function of fathers' actual inability to take care of children because of inexperience or lack of childrearing knowledge and skills, or if they are due to past relationship problems between co-parents that may have little to do with childrearing skills (Pruett et al., 2007). Current relationship issues also may be involved: When men make greater financial contributions, mothers perceive them to be more competent (Fagan & Barnett, 2003).

MATERNAL PERCEPTIONS OF FATHERS' INTEREST IN CHILDREARING

Maternal assessment of fathers' competence in caring for children may be due, in part, to their perceptions of how willing fathers are to be involved in raising children (Laakso, 2004). For divorced mothers these perceptions may be based on fathers' actions during the marriage or since separation, or they may be due to unresolved couple issues. These assessments may be due also to mothers' gendered beliefs about fathers. Unfortunately, few researchers have observed fathers' interactions with children (Cannon et al., 2008) or examined fathers' self-reported interest (McBride et al., 2005), and those that have were investigating married couples with infants. Among divorced couples, mothers sometimes conclude that fathers who do not contact or pick up children when they say they will or who break other promises to children do so because of disinterest in parenting (Laakso, 2004; Sano et al., 2008). This judgment by mothers causes them to be more selective about when children see their fathers and contributes to restrictive gatekeeping.

"Payback" for the Past and Maternal Gatekeeping

Post-divorce co-parenting is affected by marital and parental dynamics before the separation (Pruett et al., 2007). In marriage, the man's husband and father roles mutually influence and are influenced by the woman's wife and mother roles; over the course of a marriage these couple and co-parental dynamics develop, are maintained, and eventually change, resulting in partner differences in satisfaction with each of these roles (Van Egeren, 2004). After divorce, marital roles end but co-parental roles and behaviors continue. Co-parenting changes after divorce because parents live in separate households, children typically spend more time in the household of one parent than the other, and the nature of the couple union has changed significantly.

When marriages end, the quality of those marriages and the ways in which those unions were dissolved have been hypothesized to affect post-divorce co-parenting and, specifically, maternal gatekeeping. Pruett and her colleagues (2007) tested what they called a theory of maternal gatekeeping in which one of the major predictors of gatekeeping was mothers' thoughts and feelings about how she and her children "were treated during the marriage and its termination" (p. 25). In this theory, perceived mistreatment during marriage should lead to restrictive maternal gatekeeping and less paternal involvement and less cooperative co-parenting after divorce. Positive perceptions about the marriage should lead to facilitative gatekeeping and more paternal involvement and shared co-parenting. Support for these hypotheses was found in correlational data from parents enrolled in a post-divorce intervention study (Pruett et al., 2007). Mothers used gatekeeping as a way to pay fathers back for their marital and post-marital actions.

Other studies support the view that anger and hurt feelings about the marriage ending contribute to strife between co-parents, and mothers respond by controlling fathers' contacts with their children (Laakso, 2004; Wolchik et al., 1996). Moreover, a woman who resented her husband for not meeting her expectations as a co-parent during the marriage may retaliate by limiting his contacts with children after the marriage ends (Van Egeren, 2004).

These findings suggest that educational and interventional programs designed to reduce anger and hostility between divorcing co-parents are addressing important family dynamics. Marital conflicts that continue through the dissolution of the union and into post-divorce family life make it hard for divorced parents to cooperate in raising their children. Parenting plans need to reflect the realities of the continuation of couple and co-parental dynamics (Kelly, 2007).

Satisfaction with Co-parenting

Several studies have examined separated and divorced mothers' satisfaction with various aspects of co-parenting and custody. In general, satisfied mothers appear to be more accommodating to father involvement with children, have less conflict with fathers, and are less prone to restrictive gatekeeping. For example, mothers' satisfaction with fathers' involvement with children was significantly related to less restrictive maternal gatekeeping (Herzog et al., 2007; Kulik & Tsoref, 2010). Mothers' satisfaction with custody arrangements and fathers' parenting skills have been found to be related to lower conflict between parents, which may facilitate gate-opening behaviors (Blackwell & Dawe, 2003; Madden-Derdich & Leonard, 2002). Mothers' satisfaction with the fathers' contacts with children was highest when there was no co-parental conflict and contacts were frequent. Satisfaction was lowest when there was low contact frequency but conflict. Moreover, children's adjustment was better when mothers were satisfied, regardless of the amount of father contact (King & Heard, 1999).

Beliefs About Pleasing the Court

Although the authors could find no studies of this phenomenon, some legal scholars and behavioral scientists (Austin, 2008; Dore, 2004; Pruett et al., 2007) have raised the issue of parents acting as if they were open and facilitative gatekeepers in order to convince judges to award physical custody to them under what has been called the "friendly parent doctrine" (Dore, 2004, p. 41). This principle is included in some statutes as a guideline for judges to award custody to the parent whom they perceive is most likely to allow children to have contact with the other parent. The concern is that parents who have filed for divorce may engage in friendly, facilitative actions only to influence legal decisions. After a judgment has been rendered, the fear is that the custodial parent will engage in restrictive gatekeeping. Parental beliefs about how to sway legal authorities may be something that social science researchers should examine.

Critique of Research on Gatekeeping Beliefs

Virtually every study reviewed in this section was based, either explicitly or implicitly, on the theoretical perspective that gatekeeping beliefs influence behaviors. One major problem in sorting out the relationship among gatekeeping beliefs and behaviors is the cross-sectional designs used in most of these studies (Adamsons, 2010). Gathering data at one point in time, which is what is done in cross-sectional designs, makes it difficult to infer the direction of causality. Researchers may have theoretical models about cause and effect, but unless they have experimental designs (impossible to do in gatekeeping research) or well-controlled longitudinal designs that follow families over time, causal inferences are difficult to make with confidence. Quantitative studies where data are gathered at one point in time can really only indicate whether variables are related significantly or not (i.e., beyond chance). Similarly, qualitative studies of gatekeeping can only indicate what participants *perceive* to be causal effects. This is valuable information into the thought processes of gatekeeping mothers; however, qualitative designs do not allow easy causal inferences.

Another characteristic of much of the gatekeeping beliefs research is the reliance on self-report methods. Of course, it is impossible to assess beliefs without obtaining self-report data: Researchers have to ask mothers what they think about fathers, co-parenting, and other constructs in order to understand maternal beliefs. What is problematic to consumers of this research, however, is that behaviors are also based on someone's self-report rather than on observations. Father involvement with children and children's reactions to them, and mother's own actions are often based solely on perceptions of behaviors, rather than observations, and typically these perceptions are gathered from only one family member. Usually, mothers' self-reports are used in these studies. Mothers' perceptions are filtered through their own experiences, and in the case of post-divorce contexts, mothers may have profound biases about fathers and their involvement that color their reports. It is difficult to obtain observational research when mothers and fathers live apart from each other, which is why the only observational gatekeeping research reviewed in this chapter is of married parents of very young children or infants (e.g., Cannon et al., 2008). In general, collecting information from study participants by using more than one method of data collection is preferred; research designs that use multiple methods enhance the validity of findings and reduce concerns about biases and errors in the conclusions drawn from only one data-gathering method. Not only is the body of research on gatekeeping beliefs after divorce *about* mothers only, it is a body of research almost exclusively *from* mothers and their self-reports (for exceptions that include fathers, see Pruett et al., 2007; Wolchik et al., 1996).

A final critique worth noting is that what the authors have done in this review is what other scholars have done before (e.g., Pleck & Masciadrelli, 2004), which is to combine studies on maternal gatekeeping beliefs about married mothers with those about divorced mothers. Although it makes sense to argue that a mother's gatekeeping beliefs in marriage influence her beliefs after divorce, what the authors criticize here is drawing conclusions from married mothers of young children and generalizing them, and the theories based on them, to divorced mothers of children of various ages. The degree to which maternal beliefs are similar between these two broad groups of mothers is an empirical question, but it is a question that has not yet been addressed by researchers. The potential problem is when researchers, reviewers of research, or practitioner-consumers of research do not take caution when drawing conclusions and making generalizations from this collective body of scholarship.

In summary:

- Researchers hypothesize that maternal gatekeeping is based on a variety of maternal beliefs. These beliefs affect restrictive, protective, and facilitative gatekeeping and paternal involvement.
- Gender ideology (i.e., a strong maternal identity, beliefs about differentiated roles of men and women, beliefs about the importance of fathers in children's lives, and beliefs about mothers' kinkeeping roles) has often been studied. There is overall empirical support for gendered beliefs affecting maternal gatekeeping, but findings are mixed.
- Other maternal gatekeeping beliefs that have been proposed to be relevant to gatekeeping include beliefs about paternal competence, beliefs about the father's interest in childrearing, perceptions of paternal treatment during the marriage and how that should be repaid, satisfaction with paternal involvement and co-parenting, and beliefs about parental behaviors that would be positively viewed by the court.
- Mothers will restrictively gatekeep or will at least gatekeep conditionally when they perceive fathers to be incompetent at parenting.
- Gatekeeping is more likely when mothers think fathers are not interested in childrearing.
- Maternal perceptions about how children and mothers were treated by fathers during the marriage affect gatekeeping and father involvement.

- Satisfaction with co-parenting and fathers' involvement with children are related to lower levels of co-parental conflict and less restrictive gatekeeping.
- Most studies of maternal gatekeeping beliefs have not included both mothers and fathers.
- Research on maternal gatekeeping beliefs have gathered data at one time point, making conclusions about cause-and-effect relationships difficult, if not impossible, to draw.
- Most investigations of maternal gatekeeping have relied on mothers' self-report data.
- Caution should be taken when generalizing findings from research on married mothers to mothers in divorced families.

Behavioral Factors in Gatekeeping

Beliefs are only part of the complex phenomenon of gatekeeping; behaviors also must be considered. Perhaps surprisingly, studies of gatekeeping have focused less on behaviors and more on beliefs. This may be why, after reviewing the gatekeeping research literature, Pleck and Masciadrelli (2004) concluded that *maternal beliefs and attitudes* were critical in predicting fathers' involvement with children.

Domestic Violence and Substance Abuse

Some restrictive gatekeeping behaviors are connected clearly to maternal beliefs about fathers' behaviors. For instance, mothers' perceptions of the fathers as threats to children's safety because of past violence against mothers or abuse of the children or because of father's substance abuse are related to a variety of severe gatekeeping behaviors by mothers, including totally refusing to allow fathers to have any contact with children (Roy & Dyson, 2005; Sano et al., 2008) and refusing to communicate about the children with the father (Roy & Dyson, 2005). Evidence from qualitative studies suggest that even when mothers want to encourage a relationship between their children and the children's fathers, they monitor father–child interactions much more closely when fathers have a history of violence or substance abuse (Hardesty & Ganong, 2006; Laakso, 2004; Sano et al., 2008; Trinder, 2008). Concerns about safety take precedence over the desire to help children maintain ties with the fathers.

Remarriage or Repartnering

When a divorced parent remarries, the dynamics of co-parenting children from prior unions often change (Ganong & Coleman, 2004). Most researchers have found that nonresidential fathers reduce their involvement with children when either the mother (Blackwell & Dawe, 2003; Hetherington & Kelly, 2002) or the father remarries (Hetherington & Kelly, 2002; Stephens, 1996).

Manning and Smock (1999) found that reductions in father involvement were due to the number of new children acquired in later unions. Remarriage for fathers often results in complex parenting arrangements for them because they may have non-residential children from prior relationships, and they may take responsibility for the new partner's children who usually are living in their households as well (Manning, Stewart, & Smock, 2003). The birth of children to remarried couples also potentially affects maternal gatekeeping or fathers' reactions to maternal gatekeeping (Blackwell

& Dawe, 2003). Fathers with children born to the remarital union tend to turn their attention to raising the children residing in their households, both their biological children and stepchildren (Manning & Smock, 1999; Manning et al., 2003). This makes it less necessary for mothers to restrictively gatekeep, and in fact encourages them to direct energies toward helping their children maintain ties with their fathers (Ganong & Coleman, 2004). Some custodial remarried mothers reproduce in an effort to bring household members together (Ganong & Coleman, 1988); whether this enhances or reduces gatekeeping actions is not clear. It also is not known if gatekeeping following remarriage is similar to gatekeeping after parents acquire new cohabiting partners.

Reduced paternal involvement after remarriage is an important issue to consider because remarriage and stepfamilies are common. The effects of subsequent unions on paternal involvement are known, but it is less well known how gatekeeping affects involvement.

Mothers may prefer to have new stepfathers assume paternal functions because it simplifies the lives of the adults in stepfamilies to have the stepfamily operate as if it was a first marriage nuclear family (Ganong & Coleman, 2004). By regarding the stepfather as the replacement father, stepfamilies avoid being marginalized, and stepfathers and stepchildren avoid being stigmatized by passing as a nuclear family (Ganong & Coleman, 2004). Moreover, stepfathers are often willing to assume paternal roles with stepchildren (Ganong, Coleman, & Jamison, 2011; Manning & Smock, 1999; Marsiglio, 2005), and many stepchildren accept stepfathers as additional parents (Ganong at al., 2011; King, 2006; White & Gilbreth, 2001).

Recreating the remarriage as if it were a first marriage nuclear family involves severing ties with the non-residential parent, usually the father. For this adaptation to be successful and for stepfathers to successfully replace fathers, children as well as non-residential fathers have to allow this to happen, either by not fighting it or by withdrawing (if they have not withdrawn already). If children do not want to lose their connection to their fathers, this often leads to conflicts between children and their stepfathers and mothers. If non-residential fathers do not agree to being replaced, then this also leads to co-parental conflicts as fathers fight these maximally restrictive gatekeeping efforts to cut them off (Roy & Dyson, 2005). In general, stepfathers replacing fathers is more likely to be successful when children are young, fathers are not involved, and everyone agrees to the arrangement (Ganong & Coleman, 2004).

Not every remarried mother goes to such gatekeeping extremes, however. Rather than cutting off the father's ties with children totally, some mothers, with the support and cooperation of their new partners, become more restrictive in gatekeeping without attempting to end the father's involvement completely. Clinicians assert that they do this by making it harder for fathers to talk to children, planning activities for their new family that disrupt the father's plans for being with children, and subtly encouraging children to think of their stepfather as the primary paternal figure in their lives (Visher & Visher, 1996). Stepfathers may participate in gatekeeping against non-residential fathers by supporting mothers, engaging in gatekeeping behaviors themselves, and encouraging children to bond with them in place of their fathers (Marsiglio, 2005).

When children in stepfamilies are not allowed to maintain ties with non-residential parents, or are discouraged from doing so, and are encouraged instead to bond with stepparents, they often experience loyalty conflicts or loyalty binds, feeling torn between the stepfather and father and/or their mother and father (Afifi, 2003). Such binds are stressful for children who feel caught in a no-win situation because regardless of what they do or say, they perceive themselves to be upsetting someone they care about (Afifi, 2003). Although the negative effects of feeling caught between parents often fade over time for children of divorced parents (Amato & Afifi, 2006), this is still a divisive and distressful experience for adolescents and younger children.

There is some research evidence to suggest that non-custodial fathers who remarry also engage in gatekeeping when they have the children in their households, attempting to keep the children with them longer than was planned or longer than the parenting plan allows. Clinicians have pointed out that remarried fathers, encouraged at times by their new wives who want to demonstrate that they are better moms than the biological mothers, sometimes feel emboldened to seek changes in custody arrangements for children from prior unions, particularly when former spouses remain single (Visher & Visher, 1996). Other nonresidential stepmothers inadvertently help mothers with gatekeeping by competing with visiting stepchildren for the father's attention and time, actions that gradually drive stepchildren away from fathers and make them reluctant to visit fathers' households (Ganong et al., in press).

GATEKEEPING AS NEGOTIATING TACTICS

Although a few studies have reported that mothers engage in facilitative gatekeeping behaviors regardless of whether or not fathers have paid child support to them (Sano et al., 2008; Trinder, 2008), other researchers have found that restrictive gatekeeping behaviors may be part of the negotiating strategies of mothers who are trying to elicit child support payments from fathers or who want to punish fathers for not paying (Fagan & Barnett, 2003; Roy & Dyson, 2005). Low-income mothers are less likely than middle-class mothers to do this because they understand the social and employment constraints that the fathers face (Sano et al., 2008). Nonetheless, low-income mothers will negotiate with fathers of their children, offering to trade contact with the children for either payments of child support or other resources (e.g., diapers, formula, food; Ispa, Thornburg, & Fine, 2006).

CRITIQUE OF RESEARCH ON GATEKEEPING BEHAVIORS

In general, research on maternal gatekeeping behaviors is more limited in focus and breadth than research on maternal gatekeeping beliefs. Researchers often do not assess behaviors that constitute gatekeeping—in some studies statistical associations among maternal beliefs and paternal involvement are examined without measuring gatekeeping behaviors at all (e.g., Allen & Hawkins, 1999; Bulanda, 2004; DeLuccie, 1995; Gaunt, 2008). In these studies, changes in paternal involvement were assumed to be evidence that maternal gatekeeping has occurred. Because researchers often have not measured behaviors, it is not clear how often mothers try to prevent, reduce, or facilitate fathers' contacts with children (King & Heard, 1999).

The research on gatekeeping after remarriage sometimes does not fit well with the literature on gatekeeping beliefs because this research on beliefs primarily focuses on gatekeeping within mother–father dyads. Gatekeeping after remarriage may involve three or even four adults. Although maternal gatekeeping beliefs about fathers (e.g., gendered views about the importance of fathers, concerns about father's competence, beliefs about differentiated roles of mothers and fathers) may operate in post-remarriage gatekeeping, other beliefs also may serve as motivations in post-remarriage gatekeeping. For instance, Ganong and Coleman (2004) have argued that adherence to a nuclear family ideology motivates adults in stepfamilies to try to refashion themselves into nuclear families, which involves often extreme gatekeeping actions against non-residential parents.

In summary:

- Maternal perceptions about threats to children's safety are related to a variety of gatekeeping behaviors, including severing paternal contact with children and refusing to communicate with the father.
- Non-residential fathers reduce their involvement with children when either parent remarries.
- Reductions in father involvement after remarriage are due primarily to the number of new children acquired in later unions by fathers.
- Gatekeeping in remarriage may involve stepparents as well as parents.
- Gatekeeping in remarriage may result in children feeling stressful loyalty binds.
- Restrictive gatekeeping may be part of mothers' negotiating strategies when trying to elicit more child support from fathers.
- Research on gatekeeping behaviors is limited in terms of the issues examined and in the methods used.
- Gatekeeping behaviors are seldom measured in gatekeeping studies; instead, beliefs are assessed.

Measuring Gatekeeping

The lack of measures of gatekeeping behaviors is of concern, and until better conceptualizations and operational definitions of gatekeeping behaviors are delineated, progress in gatekeeping research will be restricted. A few researchers have developed observational assessments of maternal gatekeeping, but these have been designed for interactions between married parents of infants or young children (e.g., Cannon et al., 2008), so they have limited utility for divorced parents and families with older children.

Gatekeeping beliefs have been operationalized in studies of divorced parents with researcher-developed instruments that often were created to test a particular set of hypotheses about gatekeeping. For instance, Pruett and colleagues (2003) created a questionnaire with three subscales that assesses beliefs about (a) Enhancing Spouse's Parenting, (b) Positive Views of Spouse, and (c) Spouse's Influence on Parenting. This instrument did not fit well for the model they tested in one study (Pruett et al., 2003), but it did fit with a later model of gatekeeping, co-parental relationships, and father involvement (Pruett, et al., 2007). In the latter study, a brief measure of paternal perceptions of maternal gatekeeping was also developed. Of course, more work with these instruments is needed before researchers and practitioners can have confidence in their validity and reliability estimates. Further endeavors such as these that specifically assess gatekeeping after divorce, and are bolstered by a theoretical framework, are badly needed. Until such measures are developed and thoroughly tested with different samples, progress in understanding gatekeeping will be hampered.

Parent's Mental Health and Gatekeeping

Few researchers have directly looked at how the psychological characteristics of parents affect gatekeeping. Pruett et al. (2003) assessed divorcing parents' symptomatology and found that mothers who reported greater symptomatology were more likely to view the fathers' support as influential on their own parenting both during marriage and after. In married couples with young children, Gaunt (2008) found that married mothers with low self-esteem were more likely to gatekeep. In another study of married parents, there was an interaction effect between parents—when one parent more rapidly expressed negative emotions such as anger and fear and the other parent held traditional beliefs about fathers' roles, then maternal gatekeeping behavior was more likely (Cannon et al., 2008). These authors also found that although parents' communion (i.e., extent to which one is interpersonally oriented and feels integrated with others), a trait that has been linked to better psychological well-being, was predictive of father involvement, it was not related to maternal gatekeeping (Cannon et al., 2008). The mental health of fathers also appears to affect maternal gatekeeping, inasmuch as alcohol or substance abuse, physical violence, and criminal activity may reflect poorer mental health in fathers.

Gatekeeping and Parental Alienation

Does gatekeeping contribute to parental alienation? A child is alienated from a parent when the child rejects and expresses intense negative feelings toward the targeted parent (Baker & Darnall, 2006). This rejection is theoretically the result of "a parent's alienating behavior towards the child for the purpose of harming the relationship with the other parent" (Baker & Darnall, 2006, p. 98). This is similar to definitions of restrictive gatekeeping, with the addition of an intention of damaging the non-residential parent–child relationship.

The authors could find no studies that link maternal gatekeeping with children's alienation. The alienating behaviors and strategies described by samples of alienated adult children of divorced parents and targeted alienated parents in Baker and Darnall's (2006) descriptive study were similar to the restrictive gatekeeping actions reported in qualitative data from studies, such as not answering the phone, refusing overnights and other visits, not reminding fathers of the schedule, and arguing in front of children as a way to convince them to side with her (Laakso, 2004; Pruett et al., 2007; Sano et al., 2008). The strategies and behaviors of alienating parents also contained a variety of extreme actions (e.g., hiding the child, having the child keep secrets from the targeted parent, beating the targeted parent in front of the child) that have not been reported in restrictive gatekeeping studies. In the absence of research it is hard to know precisely if restrictive gatekeeping is related to parents' intentions to have the children denigrate and dislike the other parent. Of course, gatekeeping parents do not only engage in restricting parental involvement; there is research showing that parents facilitate and protect as well as restrict, so it may be that parental alienation is a concern only when parents limit gatekeeping to extreme forms of restricting non-residential parents' access and do so chronically. This speculation remains to be tested. This is clearly an area of needed research.

SUMMARY

Gatekeeping after separation and divorce may be done by either parent and may involve multiple motivations, but researchers have focused on restrictive maternal gatekeeping, which is intended to reduce fathers' involvement in order to punish, control, and minimize their value as parents. Protective gatekeeping is designed to limit or eliminate contact with the other parent in order to protect the child's safety and well-being. Facilitative gatekeeping involves encouraging interactions between the children and their other parent.

Maternal gatekeeping is based on a variety of beliefs. Gender ideology (i.e., strong maternal identity, beliefs that men and women should have different familial roles, beliefs about the value of fathers, and beliefs about mothers' kinkeeping roles) has often been studied and has received some, albeit mixed, research support. Maternal beliefs related to greater restrictive gatekeeping include judgments about paternal competence and about the father's interest in childrearing, perceptions of paternal treatment during the marriage and how that should be repaid, satisfaction with paternal involvement and co-parenting, and perceptions about behaviors that would be positively viewed by the courts. Less restrictive gatekeeping occurs when mothers are satisfied with co-parenting and fathers' involvement with children and when there are lower levels of co-parental conflict. Maternal perceptions about threats to children's safety are related to a variety of gatekeeping behaviors, including severing paternal contact with children and refusing to communicate with the father. Non-residential fathers reduce their involvement with children when either parent remarries. Reductions in father involvement after remarriage are due primarily to the number of new children acquired in later unions by fathers. Stepparents also gatekeep. Children often feel loyalty binds due to gatekeeping after remarriage.

Research on gatekeeping behaviors is limited in the issues examined and in the methods used. Gatekeeping behaviors are seldom measured in gatekeeping studies. Most studies of maternal gatekeeping have relied on mother's reports only, have not examined fathers' behaviors, and have gathered data at only one point in time, making conclusions about cause-and-effect relationships difficult to draw. Findings from married mothers should not be generalized to mothers in divorced families.

GUIDELINES: CONSIDERATIONS AND CAUTIONS

- Both parents may gatekeep, but researchers have focused on mothers.
- Gatekeeping may be restrictive, protective, or facilitative. A parent may engage in all three categories of gatekeeping.
- Protective gatekeeping is aimed at limiting or eliminating contact with the other parent, with the goal of ensuring the child's safety and well-being.

- Facilitative gatekeeping involves encouraging interactions between the children and their other parent. It has been called "gate opening."
- Gatekeeping may be better thought of as a characteristic of "gate work," which is a dynamic, multidirectional process in which both mothers and fathers influence both gate opening and gate closing.
- Gatekeeping is driven by many diverse beliefs and motivations. There is mixed research support for the effects of gender ideologies (e.g., beliefs about the familial roles of men and women, a strong maternal identity, and beliefs about the importance of fathers) on maternal gatekeeping.
- A strong maternal motive to restrict children's contact with fathers is perceived paternal incompetence at childrearing.
- Maternal perceptions about how fathers treated mothers and children during marriage affect gatekeeping and paternal involvement after divorce.
- In some post-divorce families, the behavior of mothers may be considered as gatekeeping by fathers yet may not reflect negative beliefs about father involvement. Instead, these behaviors arise from concerns about children's welfare or attempts to negotiate more acceptable father behavior.
- Maternal satisfaction with co-parenting and with fathers' involvement with children is related to less conflict between parents and less restrictive gatekeeping.
- Remarriage or repartnering, particularly when new children are involved, changes co-parenting and father involvement after divorce. Non-residential fathers reduce their involvement with children after either parent remarries.
- Gatekeeping in remarriage may involve stepparents as well as parents.
- Research on gatekeeping is limited in terms of the issues that are studied and the methods used. Much more research is needed.
- Most studies are based on maternal self-reports rather than on gatekeeping behaviors.
- Fathers are seldom studied in post-divorce gatekeeping.
- The effects of gatekeeping over time have rarely been examined.
- The association between gatekeeping and parental alienation is unknown.

REFERENCES

Adamsons, K. (2010). Using identity theory to develop a mid-range model of parental gatekeeping and parenting behavior. *Journal of Family Theory & Review, 2*, 137–148. doi: 10.1111/j.1756-2589.2010.00047.x

Afifi, T. D. (2003). "Feeling caught" in stepfamilies: Managing boundary turbulence through appropriate privacy coordination rules. *Journal of Social and Personal Relationships, 20*, 729–756. doi:10.1177/0265407503206002

Ahrons, C. (2007). Family ties after divorce: Long-term implications for children. *Family Process, 46*, 53–65. doi:10.1111/j.1545-5300.2006.00191.x

Allen, S. M., & Hawkins, A. J. (1999). Maternal gatekeeping: Mothers' beliefs and behaviors that inhibit greater father involvement in family work. *Journal of Marriage and Family, 61*, 199–212. doi:10.2307/353894

Amato, P., & Afifi, T. D. (2006). Feeling caught between parents: Adult children's relations with parents and subjective well-being. *Journal of Marriage and Family*, *68*, 222–236. doi:10.1111/j.1741–3737.2006.00243.x

Amato, P. R., & Gilbreth, J. G. (1999). Nonresident fathers and children's well-being: A meta-analysis. *Journal of Marriage and Family*, *61*, 557–573. doi:10.2307/353560

Amato, P. R., & Sobolewski, J. M. (2004). The effects of divorce on fathers and children: Nonresidential fathers and stepfathers. In M. E. Lamb (Ed.), *The role of the father in child development* (4th ed., pp. 341–367). Hoboken, NJ: John Wiley & Sons.

Austin, W. G. (2005). Considering the process of support for the other parent and gatekeeping in parenting evaluations. *Colorado IDC News: The Newsletter of the State of Colorado Interdisciplinary Committee*, *7*(1), 10–13.

Austin, W. G. (2008). Relocation, research and forensic evaluation part II: Research support for the relocation risk assessment model. *Family Court Review*, *46*, 347–365. doi:10.1111/j.1744–1617.2008.00205.x

Baker, A. J. L., & Darnall, D. (2006) Behaviors and strategies of parental alienation: A survey of parental experiences. *Journal of Divorce and Remarriage*, *45*, 97–124. doi:10.1300/J087v45n01_06

Berger, L. M., Brown, P. R., Joung, E., Melli, M. S., & Wimer, L. (2008). The stability of child physical placements following divorce: Descriptive evidence from Wisconsin. *Journal of Marriage and Family*, *70*, 273–283. doi: 10.1111/j.1741–3737.2008.00480.x

Blackwell, A., & Dawe, F. (2003). *Non-residential parental contact final report. Social and Vital Statistics Division*. London, England: ONS.

Braverman, L. (1989). Beyond the myth of motherhood. In M. McGoldrick, C. M. Anderson, & F. Walsh (Eds.), *Women in families* (pp. 227–243). New York: Norton.

Buchanan, C. M., Maccoby, E. E., & Dornbusch, S. M. (1996). *Adolescents after divorce*. Cambridge, MA: Harvard University.

Bulanda, R. E. (2004). Paternal involvement with children: The influence of gender ideologies. *Journal of Marriage and Family*, *66*, 40–45. doi:10.1111/j.0022–2455.2004.00003.x

Carlson, M. (2006). Family structure, father involvement, and adolescent behavioral outcomes. *Journal of Marriage and Family*, *68*, 137–154. doi:10.1111/j.1741–3737.2006.00239.x

Cannon, E. A., Schoppe-Sullivan, S. J., Mangelsdorf, S. C., Brown, G. L., & Sokolowski, M. S. (2008). Parent characteristics as antecedents of maternal gatekeeping and fathering behavior. *Family Process*, *47*, 501–519. doi:10.1111/j.1545–5300.2008.00268.x

Cowan, C. P., Cowan, P. A., Pruett, M. K., & Pruett, K. (2007). An approach to preventing coparenting conflict and divorce in low-income families: Strengthening couple relationships and fostering fathers' involvement. *Family Process*, *46*, 109–121. doi:10.1111/j.1545–5300.2006.00195.x

DeLuccie, M. F. (1995). Mothers as gatekeepers: A model of maternal mediators of father involvement. *Journal of Genetic Psychology*, *156*, 115–131. doi:10.1080/00221325.1995.9914811

Dore, M. K. (2004). The "friendly parent" concept: A flawed factor for child custody. *Loyola Journal of Public Interest Law*, *6*, 41–56.

Fagan, J., & Barnett, M. (2003). The relationship between maternal gatekeeping, paternal competence, mothers' attitudes about the father role, and father involvement. *Journal of Family Issues, 24,* 1020–1043. doi:10.1177/0192513X03256397

Ganong, L., & Coleman, M. (1988). Do mutual children cement bonds in stepfamilies? *Journal of Marriage and the Family, 50,* 687–698.

Ganong, L. & Coleman, M. (2004). *Stepfamily relationships.* New York: Kluwer/Plenum.

Ganong, L., Coleman, M., & Jamison, T. B. (2011). Patterns of stepchild-stepparent relationship development. *Journal of Marriage and Family, 73,* 396–413.

Gaunt, R. (2008). Maternal gatekeeping: Antecedents and consequences. *Journal of Family Issues, 29,* 373–395. doi:10.1177/0192513X07307851

Hardesty, J., & Ganong, L. (2006). How women make custody decisions and manage coparenting with abusive former husbands. *Journal of Social and Personal Relationships, 23,* 543–563. doi:10.1177/0265407506065983

Herzog, M. J., Umana-Taylor, A. J., Madden- Derdich, D. A., & Leonard, S. A. (2007). Adolescent mothers' perceptions of fathers' parental involvement: Satisfaction and desire for involvement. *Family Relations, 56,* 244–257. doi:10.1111/j.1741-3729.2007.00456.x

Hetherington, E. M., & Kelly, J. (2002). *For better or for worse.* New York: W.W. Norton.

Hoffman, C. D., & Moon, M. (1999). Women's characteristics and gender role attitudes: Support for father involvement with children. *Journal of Genetic Psychology, 160,* 411–418. doi:10.1080/00221329909595554

Ispa, J. M., Thornburg, K. R., & Fine, M. A. (2006). *Keepin' on.* Baltimore, MD: Brookes.

Kelly, J. B. (2007). Children's living arrangements following separation and divorce: Insights from empirical and clinical research. *Family Process, 46,* 35–52. doi:10.1111/j.1545-5300.2006.00190.x

King, V. (2006). The antecedents and consequences of adolescents' relationships with stepfathers and nonresident fathers. *Journal of Marriage and Family, 68,* 910–928. doi:10.1111/j.1741-3737.2006.00304.x

King, V., & Heard, H. E. (1999). Nonresident father visitation, parental conflict, and mother's satisfaction: What's best for child well-being? *Journal of Marriage and Family, 61,* 385–396.

King, V., & Sobolewski, J. M. (2006). Nonresident fathers' contributions to adolescent well-being. *Journal of Marriage and Family, 68,* 537–557. doi:10.2307/353756

Kulik, L., & Tsoref, H. (2010). The entrance to the maternal garden: Environmental and personal variables that explain maternal gatekeeping. *Journal of Gender Studies, 19*(3), 263–277. doi: 10.1080/09589236.2010.494342

Laakso, J. (2004). Key determinants of mothers' decisions to allow visits with noncustodial fathers. *Fathering, 2,* 131–145. doi:10.3149/fth.0202.131

Madden-Derdich, D. A., & Leonard, S. A. (2000). Parental role identity and fathers' involvement after divorce: Fathers' perspectives. *Family Relations, 49,* 311–318. doi:10.1111/j.1741-3729.2000.00311.x

Madden-Derdich, D. A., & Leonard, S. A. (2002). Shared experiences, unique realities: Formerly married mothers' and fathers' perceptions of parenting and custody after divorce. *Family Relations, 51,* 37–45. doi:10.1111/j.1741-3729.2002.00037.x

Manning, W. D., & Smock, P. J. (1999). New families and nonresident father-child visitation. *Social Forces, 78*, 87–116. doi:10.2307/3005791

Manning, W. D., Stewart, S., & Smock, P. J. (2003). The complexity of fathers parenting responsibilities and involvement with nonresident children. *Journal of Family Issues, 24*, 627–644. doi:10.1177/0192513X03024005004

Markham, M., Ganong, L., & Coleman, M. (2007). Coparental identity and mothers' cooperation in coparental relationships. *Family Relations, 56*, 369–377. doi:10.1111/j.1741-3729.2007.00466.x

Marsiglio, W. (2005). Contextual scenarios for stepfathers' identity construction, boundary work, and "fatherly" involvement. In W. Marsiglio, K. Roy, & G. L. Fox (Eds.), *Situated fathering: A focus on physical and social spaces* (pp. 73–97). Lanham, MD: Rowman & Littlefield.

McBride, B. A., Brown, G. L., Bost, K. K., Shin, N., Vaughn, B., & Korth, B. (2005). Paternal identity, maternal gatekeeping, and father involvement. *Family Relations, 54*, 360–372. doi:10.1111/j.1741-3729.2005.00323.x

Pleck, J. H., & Masciadrelli, B. (2004). Paternal involvement in U.S. residential fathers: Levels, sources, and consequences. In M. E. Lamb (Ed.), *The role of the father in child development* (4th ed., pp. 222–271). New York: Wiley.

Pollet, S. L., & Lombregalia, M. (2008). A nationwide survey of mandatory parent education. *Family Court Review, 46*, 375–408. doi:10.1111/j.1744-1617.2008.00207.x

Pruett, M. K., Arthur, L. A., & Ebling, R. (2007). The hand that rocks the cradle: Maternal gatekeeping after divorce. *Pace Law Review, 27*, 709–739. Retrieved from http://digitalcommons.pace.edu/plr/vol27/iss4/8

Pruett, M. K., Williams, T. Y., Insabella, G., & Little, T. D. (2003). Family and legal indicators of child adjustment to divorce among families with young children. *Journal of Family Psychology, 17*, 169–180. doi:10.1037/0893-3200.17.2.169

Roy, K., & Burton, L. (2007). Mothering through recruitment: Kinscription of nonresidential fathers and father figures in low-income families. *Family Relations, 56*, 24–39. doi:10.1111/j.1741-3729.2007.00437.x

Roy, K. M., & Dyson, O. L. (2005). Gatekeeping in context: Babymama drama and the involvement of incarcerated fathers. *Fathering, 3*, 289–310. doi:10.3149/fth.0303.289

Sandler, I., Miles, J., Cookston, J. T., & Braver, S. L. (2008). Effects of father and mother parenting on children's mental health in high- and low-conflict divorces. *Family Court Review, 46*, 282–296. doi:10.1111/j.1744-1617.2008.00201.x

Sano, Y., Richards, L. N., & Zvonkovic, A. M. (2008). Are mothers really "gatekeepers" of children? Rural mothers' perceptions of nonresident fathers' involvement in low-income families. *Journal of Family Issues, 29*, 1701–1723. doi:10.1177/0192513X08321543

Schoppe-Sullivan, S. J., Brown, G. L., Cannon, E. A., Mangelsdorf, S. C., & Sokolowski, S. C. (2008). Maternal gatekeeping, coparenting quality, and fathering behavior in families with infants. *Journal of Family Psychology, 22*, 389–398. doi:10.1037/0893-3200.22.3.389

Seery, B., & Crowley, M.S. (2000). Women's emotion work in the family: Relationship management and the process of building father-child relationships. *Journal of Family Issues, 21*, 100–127. doi:10.1177/019251300021001005

Sobolewski, J. M., & King, V. (2005). The importance of the coparental relationship for nonresident fathers' ties to children. *Journal of Marriage and Family, 67,* 1196–1212. doi:10.1111/j.1741-3737.2005.00210.x

Stephens, L. S. (1996). Will Johnny see daddy this week? An empirical test of three theoretical perspectives of postdivorce contact. *Journal of Family Issues, 17,* 466–494. doi:10.1177/019251396017004003

Trinder, L. (2008). Maternal gate closing and gate opening in postdivorce families. *Journal of Family Issues, 29,* 1298–1324. doi:10.1177/0192513X08315362

Van Egeren, L. A. (2004). The development of the coparenting relationship over the transition to parenthood. *Infant Mental Health Journal, 25,* 453–477. doi:10.1002/imhj.20019

Visher, E. B., & Visher, J. S. (1996). *Therapy with stepfamilies.* New York: Brunner/Mazel.

White, L., & Gilbreth, J. G. (2001). When children have two fathers: Effects of relationships with stepfathers and noncustodial fathers on adolescent outcomes. *Journal of Marriage and Family, 63,* 155–167. doi:10.1111/j.1741-3737.2001.00155.x

Wolchik, S. A., Fenaughty, A. M., & Braver, S. L. (1996). Residential and nonresidential parents' perspectives on visitation problems. *Family Relations, 45,* 230–237. doi:10.2307/585295

## 13

Empirical Studies of Alienation

MICHAEL SAINI, JANET R. JOHNSTON,
BARBARA JO FIDLER, AND NICHOLAS BALA ■

INTRODUCTION

The dilemma posed by a child's strident rejection of one parent, generally accompanied by strong resistance or refusal to contact that parent after divorce, has increasingly troubled family courts, professionals, and parents alike. Definitions of the problem vary in the literature. "Parental alienation" (PA) is a generic term used broadly to refer to a child who has been influenced to reject one parent, in extreme cases "brainwashed" or indoctrinated by an embittered/malicious other parent. PA can also refer to those behaviors by a parent that negatively influence or poison the child's relationship with the other parent (Darnall, 1998). More specifically, Gardner (1998) proposed the concept of parental alienation syndrome (PAS) and defined it as a child's unjustified campaign of denigration against a parent that results from the combination of two contributing factors: programming or brainwashing by one parent, and the child's own contributions to the vilification of the target parent. Kelly and Johnston (2001) define an alienated child as one who expresses, freely and persistently, unreasonable negative feelings and beliefs (such as anger, hatred, rejection, or fear) towards a parent that are disproportionate to the child's actual experience with that parent. By contrast, children who have reasonable cause to have such attitudes and beliefs (e.g., due to parental neglect or abuse) are termed "estranged" and are categorically excluded in all of the above conceptualizations. Others, avoiding all reference to cause, define the problem in behavioral terms as a child who resists or refuses visitation (Friedlander & Walters, 2010; Johnston, 1993).

While there is a rapidly growing body of literature on "alienation" within parent–child relationships, there remains great debate whether the current body of evidence is sufficiently robust to accurately make assertions about the etiology, prevalence, and consequences of alienation for children and families. The majority of academic literature documenting the presence and sources of alienation remains based on clinical illustrations and expert opinions. There are also books by parents reporting on their own experiences (Adams, 2009; Baldwin & Tab, 2008; Jeffries & Davies, 2009; Richardson, 2006). Turkat (2002) opines that if clinical observations "receive attention in the literature from others, that is usually a sign that the idea has some degree of merit" (p. 155). Clinical observations and first-person accounts are important building blocks for an emerging field in inquiry, but alone they do not constitute "empirical evidence." In contrast, evidence from empirically tested methods provides the confidence to make assertions from the findings across multiple samples and helps to build a solid knowledge base that is transparent, highlights the strengths and limitations of the evidence, and helps to accurately depict the generalizability of findings across populations. In this chapter we undertake a review of the incipient collection of empirically based studies, searched and retrieved in the fall of 2010 to help to shape the knowledge base about parent alienation with these goals in mind.

In assessing the credibility and precision of the current scientific evidence, it is important to recognize that not all research designs are equal in minimizing biases and controlling for risk of error in the results. Some research methods provide better evidence than other methods when seeking answers to specific questions. Qualitative interviews are preferred for an in-depth exploration of participants' experiences and are valued for their hypothesis-generating capacity, but they are not well suited for making inferences beyond the study sample. Qualitative studies often include small sample sizes and in-depth interviewing techniques and consider the local contextual factors of the sample, making it difficult and perhaps misleading to make generalizations beyond the sample participants. To make more sound inferences beyond the sample, it is best to use quantitative surveys using random sampling techniques from a known population. For example, if a random sample of custody evaluations is drawn from a national registry of litigated cases, then the results of the sample could theoretically be generalized back to the "population" of litigated cases, and inferences about the sample could be made. Moreover, when randomized control comparison groups are used within quantitative surveys, studies are better able to isolate any associational relationships found in the target sample that are different from the comparison group.

In rating the quality of evidence across study designs, it is important to consider the unique methodological considerations for each of the methods used, as there is no "one-size-fits-all" approach for assessing quality. The quality assessment tool used in this chapter, therefore, has been adapted from conventional quality appraisal tools to provide sufficient flexibility in rating studies across designs. We acknowledge, however, that this quality assessment tool favors quantitative designs because of its ability to produce the empirical generalizations needed for making sound evidence-based policies and programs in response to the impact of alienation on children and families.

This chapter provides a cautious review of the findings for making sensible, responsible generalizations from the multiple findings. The overall lack of empirical quality of individual studies necessitates restraint in making inferences based on a limited number of known studies. Rather, it is important to consider the consensus or concordance across studies in making generalized knowledge claims by paying particular attention to the methodological weight, the strengths and limitations, and the overall contribution of each study for generating generalized statements across studies.

In summary:

• There remains no consensus for a single definition for alienation (parental alienation, child alienation, parental alienation syndrome, etc.).

- The evidence that supports alienation is largely based on clinical opinions and expert opinions.
- Further research is needed to distinguish alienation from other types of strained parent–child relationships.
- A standard rating system is needed to assess the strengths and limitations of current empirical research specific to alienation.

CRITERIA FOR INCLUSION OF EMPIRICAL RESEARCH STUDIES

A systematic protocol for information retrieval was developed by the authors to search, screen, and independently assess the methodological quality of included studies. Published and unpublished materials (e.g., dissertations) relevant to the topic were retrieved using an iterative electronic search strategy of applying and modifying key terms, as this allows for those with null findings as well as those with significant findings.

The inclusion criteria included empirical studies of alienation. The topic of the study pertained to children who have negative, rejecting attitudes and beliefs about one parent that appear to be, wholly or in part, unjustified. This phenomenon has been variously described in the literature as "alienation", "parental alienation," "parental alienation syndrome," "child reluctance or refusal to visit," "child alienation," the "Medea syndrome," and "malicious mother syndrome." It also included studies of the psychological tactics used by one parent to instill negative attitudes and beliefs about the other parent in the child (referred to as alienating, indoctrinating, or brainwashing behaviors, relationship distancing) that are often associated with high-conflict divorcing parents, perpetrators of intimate partner violence, parental abduction, and hostage taking of the child.

The purpose or goals of the study could broadly encompass any one or more of the tasks listed in Box 13.1 with respect to the topic of the research.

The study should have a qualitative or quantitative research design that reports on the sample size, how cases were selected for study, what data-gathering procedures and measures were systematically used, and how the data were analyzed, along with the findings. This means that numerous clinical and opinion articles on the subject of PA that may offer valuable insight into the causes, consequences, treatment, or management of the problem are not included as they do not provide this important information about research design that enables one to evaluate their findings.

ASSESSMENT OF RESEARCH QUALITY

The quality of the research report was assessed independently by two of the co-authors on the basis of the eight criteria described in Box 13.2. One point was assigned for each item when a criterion was met, and 0 was assigned when it was not met. Partial credit (0.5) was assigned when a criterion was partly met. Very high agreement between raters (90%) was achieved after definitional differences on a few items were resolved. The scores were then summed and divided by 2 to calculate

Box 13.1

VARIED PURPOSES OF THE RESEARCH STUDIES

Prevalence
- Estimate its incidence or prevalence within intact, separated and divorced, or custody-litigating families based on survey data or review of court cases

Diagnosis/Assessment

Identification
- Identify the defining and associated features of the phenomena (cluster of symptoms) and the distinctive features that differentiate it from other conditions (i.e., differential diagnosis)

Description
- Describe psychological traits or profiles of both parents and children and parent–child relationships typically involved in cases of alienation

Measurement
- Test the reliability, validity, and/or sensitivity of a measure or tool to assess the presence of the phenomena

Etiology
- Test hypothesis about the predictors and possible causal and moderating factors (escalating or buffering variables) of the phenomena

Prognosis and Long-Term Effects
- Retrospective or longitudinal data on the long-term prognosis, outcomes, or consequences of the phenomena

Evaluation of Intervention/Treatment
- Evaluate the process and outcomes of different intervention strategies, programs, and policies in response to the dilemmas posed by the phenomena

Professional Views
- Survey the views of mental health and legal professionals and/or family court and legal responses to the problem

an overall methodological rating, consistent with the Grading of Recommendations Assessment, Development and Evaluation (GRADE) system for grading evidence when submitting a clinical guidelines article by the GRADE Working Group (Atkins et al., 2004). The benefit of using a systematic rating system across studies is that it can minimize bias in grading the strength and limitations of each study, and it provides the field with a standard approach for making clinical and policy decisions

Box 13.2

Criteria for Rating the Quality of Research Reports

1. Did the study use a comparison or control group that helps to verify the hypothesized preconditions or presence of the effect (or conduct systematic intragroup comparisons)?
2. Did the study use standard measures (those consistently applied within the study) or standardized measures with reported psychometric properties (those consistently applied across studies) for the dependent and independent variables?
3. Are data gathered from multiple sources of informants (versus a single source) so that different perspectives of relevant observers are considered (e.g., mothers, fathers, child, clinician)?
4. Did the study systematically control for extraneous variables that may have influenced the magnitude of the effect (e.g., influence of siblings, age, gender, severity of alienation) and/or alternative explanatory factors for the effect (e.g., interparental conflict that might explain long-term outcomes or problematic/abusive parenting that might explain child's attitudes to the rejected parent)?
5. Did the study design establish a temporal order between the dependent and independent variables in order to test for direction of effects or causality?
6. Were the selection and exclusion criteria, response rates, and subject attrition explicitly defined and explained so the kind of sample the findings pertain to is clear?
7. Did the study use a random selection from the population parameters that would allow one to generalize the results of the study widely to other similar populations?
8. Is there sufficient sample power (as determined by sample size and magnitude of expected effects for independent and control variables) in order to be able to detect robust, statistically significant, and clinically important findings?

based on the quality of the evidence to guide these decisions. GRADE is based on the four levels of quality for decision making:

1. *Very low quality* (scores 2 or less). Any estimate of effect is very uncertain.
2. *Low quality* (scores 3–4). Further research is very likely to have an important impact on confidence in the estimate of effect and is likely to change the estimate.
3. *Moderate quality* (scores 5–6). Further research is likely to have an important impact on confidence in the estimate of effect and may change the estimate.
4. *High quality* (scores 7–8). Further research is very unlikely to change confidence in the estimate of effect.

OVERALL FINDINGS

A total of 29 published papers and 10 doctoral dissertations met these criteria. Table 13.1 provides a summary of the purpose, research design and methodology, principal findings, limitations, and ratings of each empirical study in alphabetical order.

With respect to quality, all of the studies were scored in the range of 1 to 3 (mean = 1.79, SD = 0.73). Of the 39 empirical studies, no studies (0%) were scored as

Table 13.1 EMPIRICAL EVIDENCE OF ALIENATION STUDIES

#	Source of Research and Purpose of Study	Study Design: Recruitment of Participants, and Research Methodology
1.	**Baker (2005a, 2005b, 2005c, 2006)** *Diagnosis/assessment* of alienating parents' personality traits, patterns of alienation, and parental behavioral strategies that turn child against other parent. *Prognosis and long-term effects* on child victims as adults.	N = 40 adults Recruited by word of mouth and from postings on internet message boards, including PAS. Criteria for inclusion were an adult who self-defined as having been turned against other parent as a child. An additional 2 subjects dropped out and 2 tapes inaudible. Age: 19–67 (M = 40.5, SD = 11.5) Gender: 15 male, 25 females Ethnicity: Not stated SES: Not stated Mothers more often were alienating parents. Qualitative semi-structured interviews, transcribed. All retrospective accounts. Compared subjects' accounts to general findings about behavior of followers of cult leaders.
2.	**Baker (2007)** *Professional views* of PAS: its importance to assess in custody evaluations, its admissibility as evidence in court, and its prevalence as an allegation in custody cases	N = 104 custody evaluators Recruited from a total professional membership of 140 (PACE) Age: M = 56, SD = 6.9 Gender: 77 males, 27 females Ethnicity: Not stated SES: Not stated Experience ranged from 1 to 49 years.

high quality, 7 (18%) were scored as moderate quality, 17 (43%) were scored as low quality, and 15 (39%) were scored as very low quality according to GRADE four levels of quality for decision making. The problem is that the majority of the empirically based studies of alienation lack the critical design elements described in Box 13.2 that warrant generalizability of their findings. Rather, they are plagued by small, non-random samples, data analyzed retrospectively, the use of descriptive statistics rather than mathematically calculated comparisons, a lack of consensus on the definitions of alienation, and the use of varying non-standardized measures

Principal Findings	Study Strengths, Limitations, and Explanation of Ratings	Rating[3]
In Baker (2005a) subjects described alienating parent as narcissistic, requiring excessive devotion, loyalty. Used emotional manipulation to maintain their dependency. Researcher conceptualized phenomena as similar to cult involvement. In Baker (2005b) subjects attributed their negative feelings and behavior to long-term effects of parent alienation. Seven major themes: 1) Low-self-esteem; 2) Depression; 3) Drug/alcohol use; 4) Lack of trust; 5) Alienation from own children; 6) Divorce; 7) Other, including not having a sense of belonging and low achievement. Baker (2005c) reported the strategies the alienating parent used to effectively turn the subjects against the other parent: 1) General bad-mouthing; 2) Limiting contact; 3) Withdrawal of love; 4) Saying other does not love child; 5) Forcing to choose; 6) Saying other is dangerous; 7) Confiding in child; 8) Limiting mention of other; 9) Forcing to reject other; 10) Limiting contact; 11) Exposure to belittling other; and 12) Inducing conflict between child and other parent. Findings of Baker (2006) pertain to the process of alienation from the target/rejected parent. Three patterns of alienation: 1) Narcissistic alienating mothers in divorce families; 2) Narcissistic alienating mothers in intact families; and 3) Abusive/rejecting mothers and fathers.	1. Used no comparison or control group 2. Standard(ized) measures not used 3. Target parent was single source informant 4. No systematic controls for extraneous and alternative explanatory factors for subjects' views, beliefs, and feelings 5. Retrospective design is unable to ensure temporal ordering of dependent and independent variable nor test for direction of effects. 6. Non-random sample; ability to generalize results low 7. Selection criteria clear but exclusion criteria vague 8. Sample power insufficient	1
Almost all subjects were "mostly" or "somewhat" familiar with PAS as a concept and endorsed the importance of assessing for alienation in custody evaluations; 3/4 believe it is possible for a parent to turn children against the other parent. No consensus on whether PAS should be included in DSM-V and whether PAS meets Daubert standard. Estimates of proportion of alienation cases ranged from 1% to 55% with an average of 11%.	1. Used no comparison or control group 2. Used standard measure 3. Single source informant 4. Some control for extraneous variables 5. Cross-sectional survey cannot determine causal direction 6. Non-random sample; ability to generalize results limited 7. Selection criteria clear 8. Sufficient sample power	2

(Continued)

Table 13.1 Empirical Evidence of Alienation Studies (*Continued*)

#	Source of Research and Purpose of Study	Study Design: Recruitment of Participants, and Research Methodology
3.	**Baker and Darnall (2006)** *Diagnosis/assessment* of behavioral strategies that turn the child against the other parent	N = 97 parents self-identified as targets of alienating behaviors by the other parent—80% response rate. Age: 22–63 years (M = 42.4, SD =7.8) Gender: 60 males, 37 females Ethnicity: Not stated SES: Not stated
4.	**Baker and Darnall (2007)** *Diagnosis/assessment* Test validity of Gardner's 8 symptoms as a measure that can identify PAS	N = 68 parents self-identified as targets of alienating behaviors by the other parent where the child was 18 years of age or younger Age: M = 44, SD = 7 Gender: 38 males, 30 females Ethnicity: Not stated SES: Not stated Only subjects reporting severe cases of PAS were eligible.
5.	**Bala, Hunt, and McCarney (2010)** *Prevalence* To examine court-based rates of substantiated and unsubstantiated allegations of alienation, including gender differences, and disposition of alienation cases in legal proceedings	N = 175 court cases in Canada where the term *alienation* was used. Searches were made of all cases in two major commercial Canadian databases of judicial decisions (Westlaw and Quicklaw) that had records between 1989 and 2008 in order to identify those that were eligible. Age: Not stated Gender: 175 males, 175 females Ethnicity: Not stated SES: Not stated These court decisions were content-analyzed and coded, from which descriptive statistics were developed.
6.	**Bow, Gould, and Flens(2009)** *Professional views* of PAS and its relevance to assessment, and admissibility as evidence in child custody litigation	N = 448 mental health and legal professionals. U.S. National Internet search was conducted to locate e-mail addresses of professionals involved in custody cases. Age: M = 53, SD = 8.04 Gender: 43% males, 57% females Ethnicity: 93% Caucasian, 2% African American, 2% Hispanic, 4% other SES: Not stated Completed a cross-sectional Internet survey (from a total of 1,172 invited to participate).

Principal Findings	Study Strengths, Limitations, and Explanation of Ratings	Rating
Categories of alienating strategies commonly identified were bad-mouthing, limiting visitation, limiting phone contact, limiting symbolic interaction, interfering with information, emotional manipulation, unhealthy alliance, and other. Mild, moderate, and severe levels were identified. Found no significant differences in strategies used based on gender of parent and/or child.	1. Used no comparison or control group 2. Used standard measure 3. All data derived from one source, the target parent 4. Controlled for some extraneous variables but not for alternative explanatory factors for child's attitudes 5. Cross-sectional design cannot test for directionality of effects 6. Non-random selection of sample; unable to generalize results 7. Selection criteria clear 8. Sufficient sample power	2
Subjects reported child behaviors consistent with Gardner's eight symptoms of a child with severe PAS (70–90% noted 6 symptoms and 40–50% 2 symptoms). Subjects reported that their severely alienated children "always" or "mostly" exhibited these behaviors but also showed some positive inclination toward the targeted parent at times.	1. Used no comparison or control group 2. Used standard measures 3. Single source informant was target parent 4. No systematic controls for extraneous or alternative explanatory factors of child's attitudes (e.g., abusive parent) 5. Unable to test for direction of effects 6. Non-random sample; ability to generalize results is low 7. Selection criteria mostly clear except for that of severe cases 8. Sufficient sample power	2
Alienation was found by the court in 106 cases, with more frequent incidence in recent years (doubled in a decade). Mother was alienating parent for 68%, father was alienating parent for 31% (related to who had primary care of child). Court-ordered counseling in 27% cases; custody changed to the alienated parent in 49% of cases. Alienation was rejected by the court is 69 cases for the following reasons: "justified estrangement" (29); " focused on the parenting of the rejected parent" (24); "child's independent decision not to see other parent" (14); "insufficient evidence to establish alienation" (26).	1. Used no comparison or/control group 2. Used standard coding (extraction of data from decisions) 3. Documents coded by single source but contents reflected multiple views 4. Controls for multiple extraneous factors 5. Unable to test for direction of effects 6. Used total population of records but only Canadian officially recorded legal proceedings using PA terminology were data source 7. Selection criteria clear 8. Sufficient sample power	2
As a group, subjects considered themselves as being moderately to extremely knowledgeable about alienation. Overall, respondents perceived a lack of research to support the concept, although they acknowledged the existence of alienation dynamics within the child custody field. Almost all viewed it as a multidimensional construct. The majority did not endorse PAS as a syndrome as meeting either the Frye or Daubert standards. Different professions varied in the importance they placed on assessment of multiple factors that are hypothesized to contribute to alienation.	1. Used no comparison or control group but examined intergroup differences between professionals 2. Used standard measures 3. All data from one source 4. Some control for extraneous variables in *post-hoc* analysis 5. Cross-sectional survey cannot determine causal direction 6. Non-random sample; ability to generalize results limited (likely to change over time) 7. Selection criteria clear 8. Sufficient sample power	2

(Continued)

Table 13.1 Empirical Evidence of Alienation Studies *(Continued)*

#	Source of Research and Purpose of Study	Study Design: Recruitment of Participants, and Research Methodology
7.	**Braver, Coatsworth, and Peralta (n.d.)** *Diagnosis/assessment:* Relative extent of mothers' and fathers' alienating behaviors in intact and divorced families. *Prognosis and long-term effects* on emotional well-being and adjustment of young adults.	N = 86 students and their families, including 142 mothers, 100 fathers. Subjects were recruited from 6 psychology classes and then invited their parents to participate. Age: Not stated Gender: Not stated Ethnicity: Not stated SES: Not stated Written survey design. Retrospective reports of independent variable. Students from non-divorced families were used as a comparison group.
8.	**Burril-O'Donnell (2001)** (dissertation) *Diagnosis/assessment*	N = 30 custody evaluation cases, including 50 children Recruitment by author completing a search of court cases involving PAS Age: 2–17 years (M = 9.6, SD = 3) Gender: 33 females, 26 males Ethnicity: 49 Caucasian, 6 African American, 4 Asian SES: Not stated Content analysis.
9.	**Carey (2003)** (dissertation) *Prognosis and long-term effects* of PAS	N = 10 young adults Participants recruited from website in the volunteer section and one was recruited from Parental Alienation Research Foundation. Further screening for at least 3/8 of Gardner's symptoms confirmed in 8/10 of the sample. Age: 19–31 (M = 27) Gender: 6 females, 4 males Ethnicity: 9 Caucasian; 1 Asian American SES: Not stated Qualitative interviews were transcribed and interpreted by author and research assistant. Some descriptive quantitative data.
10.	**Cox (2010)** (dissertation) *Professional views* of PAS and its relevance to assessment, and admissibility as evidence in child custody litigation, all as a function of professional orientation and years of experience	N = 119 professionals Recruited based on professional residence in the U.S. and membership in AFCC. Total N = 350 Age: Not stated Gender: 40% male, 60% female Ethnicity: Not stated SES: Not stated 9 judges; 28 attorneys, 64 psychologists, 1 psychiatrist, 6 social workers, 7 mental health counselors, 4 marriage and family therapists Survey design with closed-ended questions.

Principal Findings	Study Strengths, Limitations, and Explanation of Ratings	Rating
Found co-occurrence of mothers' and fathers' alienating behaviors but with each parent reporting that the other parent alienated significantly more often. Their offspring, however, did not report a significant difference between mothers' and fathers' alienating behavior. Alienating behaviors was almost 3 times higher in divorced families than in intact families according to their offspring's report. Only two low significant correlations with adult student's current adjustment and well-being, both with the father's reports of mother's alienation.	1. Used a comparison group 2. Used standard measures 3. Multiple sources of informants 4. Some controls for extraneous and alternative explanatory factors 5. Retrospective design unable to test for direction of effects 6. Not a random sample, unable to generalize results 7. Selection criteria clear 8. Sufficient sample power for some of the findings	2
Based on Gardner's definition of PAS, author found corroborating evidence of PAS in court cases. Children's and parents' behaviors were related to the severity of PAS.	1. Used no comparison or control groups 2. Used no standard measures 3. Data derived primarily from one parent and court files 4. Controlled for few extraneous or alternative explanatory variables 5. Cross-sectional studies cannot ensure independent variable precedes dependent variable 6. Non-random sample pre-selected for PAS, unable to generalize results 7. Selection criteria clear 8. Insufficient sample power	1
Subjects believed that alienation dynamics affected their development, especially the development of romantic relationships. 7/10 recovered relationship with target parent as an older youth or young adult, mostly as a result of maturation. Although none of the sample experienced a reversal of custody as children, those who were severely alienated as children lived away from the alienating parent as teens.	1. Used no comparison or control group 2. Standardized measures not used 3. Subjects were single source informant 4. No systematic controls for alternative explanatory factors of subjects' views, beliefs, and feelings 5. Retrospective design is unable to test for direction of effects 6. Non-random sample; unable to generalize results 7. Selection criteria somewhat unclear 8. Insufficient sample power	1
95% were "somewhat" and "very much" familiar with the concept of PA. 72% were of view that determination of whether PA has occurred is of utmost importance. Most were of the view that the current knowledge on PA does not meet the Frye standards. 63 of 119 were of the view that in cases of severe PA, custody reversal is somewhat warranted. 16 viewed reversal as not warranted even in cases of severe PA. No relationships between type and experience of professional and his or her views.	1. Used no comparison or control group 2. Used standard measure 3. Multiple professionals were informants 4. Some control for extraneous and other explanatory variables 5. Cross-sectional survey cannot determine direction of effects 6. Non-random sample; ability to generalize results limited 7. Selection criteria clear 8. Sufficient sample power	2

(Continued)

Table 13.1 Empirical Evidence of Alienation Studies (*Continued*)

#	Source of Research and Purpose of Study	Study Design: Recruitment of Participants, and Research Methodology
11.	**Darnall and Steinberg (2008)** *Etiology:* Exploration of factors that produce an alienated or estranged child	N = 27 children who were alienated and/or estranged who made spontaneous requests for reunification with their previously rejected parent. Requests for success stories via the Internet from both of the authors' professional websites, parents bringing to the authors' attention successful reunification, and from follow-up inquiries to family members in cases previously served. Age: 4–17 years Gender: 13 boys, 12 girls Ethnicity: Not stated SES: Not stated Archival records, interviews with children or adults who met the criteria of having been alienated from the rejected parent, and rejected parents.
12.	**Dunne and Hedrick (1994)** *Diagnosis/Assessment* To apply Gardner's criteria for PAS in child and corresponding alienating behaviors by aligned parent	N = 16 cases, including 26 children Referred to one or both of the authors for forensic evaluation or treatment. Cases were selected on the basis of at least one child in the family having intensely rejected one of the parents for trivial or unsubstantiated accusations. Age: 2–16 years Gender: 14 girls, 12 boys Ethnicity: Not stated SES: Not stated Case study analysis.
13.	**Gardner (2001)** *Evaluation of treatment/intervention:* Outcomes of change of custody for severe cases of PAS	N = 99 PAS children from 52 families Recruitment based on whether author had been personally directly involved in the case; custodial transfer or restriction of time with the alienating parent was warranted because of the tenacity of the alienating behaviors and/or the severity of the PAS; follow-up information was available Age: Not stated Gender: Not stated Ethnicity: Not stated SES: Not stated Case study analysis.
14.	**Gordon, Stoffey, and Bottinelli (2008)** *Diagnosis/Assessment* Examine the relationship between parenting behaviors of alienating and rejected parents and selected personality variables	N = 158 from court-ordered custody evaluations from seven forensic psychology practices. Subjects were identified as alienating parent, target parent, and control parent. 76 were PAS cases and 82 were custody cases without PAS (controls). Age: Not stated Gender: Father–mother pairs Ethnicity: Not stated SES: Not stated Two different MMPI-2 indexes were used to measure primitive defenses: $L + K - F$ and $(L + Pa + Sc) - (Hy + Pt)$.

Principal Findings	Study Strengths, Limitations, and Explanation of Ratings	Rating
Four types of motivational models identified: 1) Hurting Stalemate 2) Recent Catastrophe 3) Impending Catastrophe/Deteriorating Position 4) Enticing Opportunity. Of the 27 spontaneous reunifications reviewed, 9 were considered successful because the child felt a bond and was accepted by both parents. The 18 remaining were not considered as successful because contact between the child and both parents was not bilateral, and in some cases contact with the rejected parent was severely limited or had completely stopped.	1. Used no comparison or control group 2. Standard(ized) measures not used 3. Multiple informants but coded by single source 4. No systematic controls for alternative extraneous or alternative explanatory factors for subjects' views, beliefs, and feelings 5. Retrospective design is unable to test for direction of effects 6. Not a random sample; ability to generalize results low 7. Selection criteria clear 8. Insufficient sample power	1
All of the alienating parents experienced intense dysphoric feelings, which they blamed on their former spouses. Function of the pathology of the alienating parent and that parent's relationship with the children. Concluded that Gardner's PAS 8 symptoms were a valid portrayal of the problem.	1. Used no comparison or control group 2. Standard(ized) measures were not used 3. Data gathered from multiple informants but single source clinical opinion reported 4. No systematic controls for extraneous or alternative explanatory factors of subjects' views, beliefs, and feelings 5. Cross-sectional design is unable to test for direction of effects 6. Non-random sample; ability to generalize results low 7. Selection criteria clear 8. Insufficient sample power	1
The court chose either to restrict the children's access to the alienator or to change custody in 22 of the children with significant reduction or even elimination of PAS in all 22 of these cases. The court chose not to transfer custody or reduce access to the alienator in 77 cases. In these cases there was an increase in PAS in 70 (90.9%).	1. Used no comparison or control group 2. Standard(ized) measures were not used 3. Single source informant was target parent 4. No systematic controls for extraneous or alternative explanatory factors of child's attitudes (e.g., abusive parent) or for why court chose custody reversal 5. Case study analysis is unable to test for direction of effects 6. Non-random sample; ability to generalize results is low 7. Selection criteria clear 8. Sufficient sample power	1
Alienating parents (mothers and fathers) had clinical-range scores, while the control parents (mothers and fathers who were in custody litigation, but without PAS) had normal range scores in both measures of favoring primitive defenses, $L + K - F$, and the Goldberg Index $(L + Pa + Sc) - (Hy + Pt)$.	1. Used a comparison group 2. Used standardized measures 3. Multiple sources of informants 4. No systematic controls for extraneous or alternative explanatory factors 5. Unable to ensure temporal ordering of dependent and independent variable to test for direction of effects 6. Non-random sample; unable to generalize results 7. Selection criteria clear 8. Sufficient sample power	3

(Continued)

Table 13.1 Empirical Evidence of Alienation Studies   (*Continued*)

#	Source of Research and Purpose of Study	Study Design: Recruitment of Participants, and Research Methodology

15.	**Johnston (1993)**
	Prevalence of visitation resistance and strong alliances
	Direction of effects:
	To identify factors contributing to child's reluctance or refusal to visit one parent and strong alliances with the other
		Study 1: N = 80 families, 100 children
		Study 2: N = 60 families, 75 children
		    All referred from local family courts after failing to settle custody and child-related disputes in litigation, mediation, or evaluation.
		Study 1
		Age: 1–12 years
		Gender: Not stated
		    Ethnicity: 64% Caucasian, 13% Hispanic, 8% African American, 8% Asian, 8% other
		SES: average low–middle incomes
		Study 2
		Age: 3–12 years
		Gender: Not stated
		    Ethnicity: 80% Caucasian, 8% Hispanic, 3% African American, 3% Asian, 5% other
		SES: average low–middle incomes
		    Exploratory descriptive study of clinical observations supported by correlational data analysis.

16.	**Johnston (2003)**
	Prevalence: the frequency and extent of parent–child alliances of one parent against the other in community and court samples
	Etiology: tested a model of multiple factors hypothesized to contribute to children's negative attitudes and behavior towards a parent
		N = 215 children, 91 from the community and 124 in custody litigation.
		    Recruited to research study in exchange for counseling/mediation on sliding-scale fee.
		Age: 5–14 years at follow-up
		Gender: 108 girls, 107 boys Ethnicity: 81% Caucasian
		SES: diverse incomes
		    Re-analysis of archives of clinical research data collected 2–3 years after divorce (1981–91). Measures developed from ratings by clinician who saw family and factor-analyzed to produce scales. Parent report using some standardized measures.
		    Cross-sectional design with follow-up.
		Multivariate data analysis including path models.

17.	**Johnston and Goldman (2010);**
	Johnston, Roseby, and Kuehlne (2009)
	Prognosis and long-term effects of young adults who were children of high-conflict custody-disputing families, with special focus on those who had been alienated or estranged from one parent as children. Examine current relationships with both parents, and occupational, emotional, and relational functioning of young adult.
		N = 37 young adults from 22 families.
		    This longitudinal study gathered data 15–20 years later from a representative one third of 90 custody-disputing families, initially referred by family courts between 1989–1993.
		Age: 20–30 years
		Gender: Not stated
		Ethnicity: Majority was Caucasian (83%)
		SES: varied income
		    All had been provided with 20–30 hours of family-focused counseling at the time of the custody dispute when they were ages 4–14 years.

Principal Findings	Study Strengths, Limitations, and Explanation of Ratings	Rating
In Study 1 and 2 respectively, visitation resistance manifest in 63% and 71%; strong alliances with one parent against the other in 7% and 27% of children. 6 explanatory themes: 1) Normal separation anxiety in very young child; 2) Child's social cognitive capacity to consider parents' opposing perspectives; 3) Intensity and longevity of parental disputes; 4) Child exposure to traumatic abuse and violence; 5) Child's enmeshment with emotionally disturbed parent; 6) Counter-rejection by other parent.	1. Used no comparison or control groups 2. Used standard measures 3. Data derived from multiple family members but rated by one source 4. No systematic controls extraneous or alternative explanatory variables 5. Cross-sectional design cannot test for directionality of effects 6. Non-random sample; limited ability to generalize results 7. Selection criteria clear 8. Sufficient sample power	2

15% of community and 21% of court sample aligned with one parent against the other. Mother–child alignments were twice as frequent in custody litigating group compared to those in the community comparison group.
 	
    Rejection of father was linked to his own socioemotional problems and multi-determined by: 1) Aligned mothers' use of child for their own emotional support and sabotage of the rejected parents' relationship with child; 2) Lack of warm involved parenting by rejected father; and 3) Vulnerabilities of children themselves, specifically those who were older, emotionally more disturbed, or socially less competent or had problematic self-esteem; 4) Chronic custody litigation in family court.
    Rejection of mother was linked to her own socioemotional problems and to 2, 3, and 4 above.
	1. Used comparison or control groups and made intragroup comparisons
	2. Used standard measures
	3. Data derived from multiple family members but rated by one source
	4. Controlled for multiple explanatory variables
	5. Cross-sectional design cannot test for directionality of effects
	6. Non-random sample; limited ability to generalize results
	7. Selection criteria clear
	8. Sufficient sample power
		3

Ratings by one fifth of subjects who recalled predominantly negative feelings towards one parent (mostly fathers) as children were generally consistent with counselors' ratings at the time of the custody dispute. The proportion of youths with predominantly negative feelings in this sample tripled during their mid-teens. As young adults, however, most had reverted to having relatively positive feelings towards both parents. Virtually all of the children and youths who had actively resisted or refused visitation subsequently, on their own accord, initiated reconciliation with the rejected parent some time during their late teens and early twenties.	1. Used no comparison or control groups but made intragroup comparisons 2. Used standard(ized) measures 3. Data derived from multiple family members but ratings only by subjects 4. Controlled for few extraneous or alternative explanatory variables 5. Longitudinal study ensured independent variable preceded dependent variable in time in order to determine direction of effects 6. Random sample but small N; limited ability to generalize results	2

(Continued)

Table 13.1 EMPIRICAL EVIDENCE OF ALIENATION STUDIES   (*Continued*)

#	Source of Research and Purpose of Study	Study Design: Recruitment of Participants, and Research Methodology
		Both parents and the grown children of the disputes, when able to be located, were interviewed by the same counselor (the first author) who had seen them originally (yielding a 70% response rate) and completed questionnaires and standardized measures of emotional adjustment and attachment security in intimate relationships.
18.	**Johnston, Walters, and Olesen (2005a)** *Diagnosis/assessment* Are alienated children emotionally disturbed and at risk for psychological problems or relationship difficulties later in life?	N = 74 children Referred by family courts for counseling or evaluation. Included only cases that had completed family reports and child psychological test data on at least one of the two criterion measures. Archival clinical and research records of families disputing custody. Age: 5–12 years Gender: 36 boys, 38 girls Ethnicity: 82% Caucasian SES: diverse incomes Cross-sectional design with interviews and rating scales completed by clinician and standardized psychological measures completed by parents (Child Behavior Checklist) and child (Rorschach).
19.	**Johnston, Walters, and Olesen (2005b)** *Etiology*: Tested four alternative theories as to why children reject a parent: (1) *PAS Perspective*: Primarily a brainwashing parent who indoctrinates the child in a campaign of denigration of a good, loving parent; (2) *Abuse Perspective*: Child abuse and family violence perpetrated by the rejected parent; (3) *Family Structure Perspective*: Role reversal, parent–child boundary diffusion and enmeshment; or (4) *Multi-factor Perspective*: Combination of all of above	N = 125 children from custody-litigating families referred by courts for counseling or custody evaluations. Drawn from archival database of documentary records describing parent–child relationships in separating divorced families. Age: 13 and under Gender: 65 girls, 60 boys Ethnicity: Caucasian (85%) and the remainder (15%) included African American, Hispanic, and Asian-Pacific Islander SES: upper-income parents Data were rated on multiple items by 2 clinicians (one original counselor), factor-analyzed to produce scales measuring each concept, and subjected to multivariate analysis.

Principal Findings	Study Strengths, Limitations, and Explanation of Ratings	Rating
A residual 19% during their young adult years expressed strong negative feelings towards one parent (all fathers) and continued to refuse all contact. These subjects were judged as estranged from an abusive parent rather than alienated. The occupational, emotional, and relational functioning of this sub-group ranged broadly and was no different from those who had relatively positive feelings towards both parents as young adults.	7. Selection criteria clear 8. Insufficient sample power	
Child alienation was defined as persistent, strong negative attitudes and rejecting behaviors toward one parent and absence of affection, lack of pleasure and enjoyment in contact with that parent, with a corresponding emotional enmeshment or boundary diffusion with the other parent, demonstrated by separation anxieties and parent–child role reversal. According to their aligned parent (whether mother or father), alienated children had more behavioral problems of clinically serious proportions (including depression, withdrawal, somatic complaints, and aggression) than children who were able to maintain relationships with both parents. Pattern of Rorschach personality variables suggested alienated children and non-alienated children used different coping styles in response to ongoing parental disputes, both potentially problematic.	1. Used no comparison or control groups but made intragroup comparisons between alienated and non-alienated groups 2. Used standard(ized) measures 3. Data derived from multiple sources 4. Controlled for multiple extraneous and explanatory variables 5. Cross-sectional study cannot determine directionality of effects 6. Non-random sample; limited ability to generalize results 7. Selection criteria clear 8. Sufficient sample power	3
Extreme rejection of parent: 11% fathers and 7.2% mothers. Co-occurrence of mother's and father's alienating behaviors was common. The multi-factor model was best predictor. Child's rejection of father was predicted by six independent variables: alienating by mother, separation anxieties with mother, mother's warm/involved parenting, lack of father's warm/involved parenting, older age of child, and father's abuse of child. Rejection of mother was predicted by three independent variables: alienating by father, separation anxieties with father, and child abuse by mother. Role reversal and alienating behaviors by parents were highly correlated. Male domestic violence perpetrators attempted to alienate their child from the victim mother rather than vice versa.	1. Used no comparison or control groups but systematically examined variations within the group 2. Used standard(ized) measures 3. Data derived from multiple family members but ratings mostly made by one source 4. Controlled for multiple explanatory variables 5. Cross-sectional study cannot test for directionality of effects 6. Non-random sample; limited ability to generalize results 7. Selection criteria clear 8. Sufficient sample power	3

(Continued)

Table 13.1 Empirical Evidence of Alienation Studies *(Continued)*

#	Source of Research and Purpose of Study	Study Design: Recruitment of Participants, and Research Methodology
20.	**Johnston, Walters, and Olesen (2005c)** *Diagnosis/Assessment* Examine the relationship between parenting behaviors of alienating and rejected parents and selected personality variables from the Rorschach	N = 98 parents from 49 families undergoing custody evaluations (from a total sample of 87 families, since only those with children under 13 years were selected) Drawn from an archival database of custody evaluation records describing parent–child relationships in separating and divorced families. Age: 13 and under Gender: Not stated Ethnicity: Majority was Caucasian (90%) SES: Relatively high socioeconomic status for fathers and moderate status for mothers. Extensive interviews with each family member and full battery of psychological tests were administered to all parents, and with children when indicated.
21.	**Kumar, (2003)** (dissertation) *Evaluation of treatment/intervention* of a supervised (facilitated) visitation program: To examine what factors interfere with resolution of visitation refusal within that setting	N = 105 families who attended the Smart Parenting Office were invited to participate if their case was closed with the Smart Parenting program and the reason for attendance was due to the child's refusal to have contact with a parent. Cases were excluded if allegations of abuse, currently in treatment, being monitored or in evaluation. Age: M = 7, SD = 3.8 Gender: Not stated Ethnicity: Not stated SES: Parents mostly well educated Mother custody 77%, father custody 23%. All family members completed questionnaires. Passive-observational design using archival data.
22.	**Lampel (1996a)** *Prevalence* of alienation in custody-litigating cases	Study I, N = 24 sets of parents and children. Inclusion criteria were that the child's entire family had been referred for a child custody evaluation by the family court during 1989 and 1990. Age: 7–14 years (M = 10 years, SD = 26.5 months) Gender: 10 boys, 14 girls Ethnicity: 23 Caucasian, 1 Latino SES: Not stated Cross-sectional descriptive study. Administered the Revised Slosson Intelligence Test and the Family Relations Test to each child as part of the standard evaluation procedure for the court-ordered psychological evaluation.
23.	**Lampel (1996b)** *Diagnosis assessment* Compared personality traits and psychological functioning of aligned and non-aligned parents and children in custody-litigating families	Study 2: N = 20 sets of parents and their children Age: 7–14 years (M = 10 years, SD = 25 months) Gender: 12 boys, 8 girls Ethnicity: 14 Caucasian, 8 other SES: Not stated Half the children were aligned and similar in age and gender with non-aligned children. Each child completed the Revised Slosson Intelligence Test, the Family Relations Test, and

Principal Findings	Study Strengths, Limitations, and Explanation of Ratings	Rating
Alienating co-parenting behavior by fathers was directly correlated with their narcissism, self-preoccupation, cognitive slippage, and rigid authoritarian style. Alienating co-parenting behavior by mothers was inversely correlated with their need for interpersonal closeness, and was directly correlated with cognitive slippage and a passive stance in fantasy. To the extent that rejected parents (mothers and fathers) were prone to be abusive and/or lack warm involvement with their children, they were likely to be depressed and anxious and have coping deficits and difficulty modulating emotions.	1. Used no comparison or control groups but made systematic intragroup comparisons 2. Used standard(ized) measures 3. Data derived from multiple family members 4. Controlled for some alternative explanatory variables 5. Cross-sectional study design cannot test for directionality of effects 6. Non-random sample; limited ability to generalize results 7. Selection criteria clear 8. Sufficient sample power	3
60% of children reconciled with a parent after using the Smart Parenting program. Older children (>13) were less likely to reconcile than younger children. Length of time since visits and level of parental conflict had little impact on reconciliation. The more willing parents were to communicate and ameliorate their relationship with the other parent, the more likely the child reconciled with the other parent.	1. Used no comparison or control groups but made intragroup comparisons 2. Used standard measures 3. Data derived from multiple family members and clinicians 4. Controlled for few extraneous or alternative explanatory variables 5. Cross-sectional study cannot test for directionality of effects 6. Non-random sample of less severe cases; unable to generalize results 7. Selection criteria clear 8. Sufficient sample power	2
Study 1: Alignments were defined as having more positive than negative responses towards one parent on the FRT. 46% were non-aligned, with positive scores for both parents; 42% were aligned and had positive scores for mother and negative scores for father. None had positive scores for father and negative scores for mother. All children were of average intelligence.	1. Used no comparison or control groups 2. Used standard(ized) measures 3. Data derived from multiple family members 4. No controls for extraneous or alternative explanatory variables 5. Cross-sectional design cannot test for directionality of effects 6. Non-random sample; limited ability to generalize results 7. Selection criteria clear 8. Insufficient sample power	2
Both parents of aligned children were more rigid, naively defended, and less emotive than were parents of non-aligned children. Aligned children preferred the more emotive, problem-solving, and outgoing of the two parents. Aligned children were less adept at conceptualizing complex problems than were non-aligned children, but they were more self-confident. No differences in intelligence between groups.	1. Used comparison or control groups 2. Used standard(ized) measures 3. Data derived from multiple family members 4. No systematic controls for extraneous or other explanatory variables 5. Cross-sectional study cannot test for directionality of effects 6. Non-random sample, unable to generalize results	2

(Continued)

Table 13.1 EMPIRICAL EVIDENCE OF ALIENATION STUDIES   *(Continued)*

#	Source of Research and Purpose of Study	Study Design: Recruitment of Participants, and Research Methodology
		Roberts Apperception Test for Children and each parent the Minnesota MultiphasicPersonality Inventory-2, Mother-Child Relationship Evaluation, and Parent Stress Index as part of the standard evaluation procedure for the court-ordered psychological evaluation.
24.	**Laughrea (2002)** *Measurement*: To develop a self-report measure of family alienation from young adult's viewpoint	N = 493 undergraduate students, 417 were from intact families (IF) and 76 were from divorced/separated families (DF). Recruited throughout all of the faculties at the University of Moncton. Age: 17–22 years (M = 19 years, SD = 1.8) Gender: 363 women, 117 men Ethnicity: Not stated SES: diverse incomes of parents
25.	**Moné (2007)** (dissertation) *Diagnostic/assessment* To understand and interpret internal dynamics and family relationships of divorced parents who engage in ongoing interparental conflict and parental alienation	N = 3 families Sent over 400 letters and flyers and attended workshops to recruit parents into the study. Qualitative interviews. Age: 37–44 years Gender: 1 father, 2 mothers Ethnicity: Not stated SES: Not stated
26.	**Moné and Biringen (2006)** *Prevalence* of alienation in intact and divorced families. *Measurement*: To develop an instrument to measure relationship distancing (alienating) parental behavior. *Prognosis and long-term effects*: To examine the connection between "feeling parent–child alienation" during the growing-up years and subjects' report of adulthood relationships with both parents	N = 227 undergraduates, 25% from separated or divorced families. Recruited from several applied human science courses at a large public university in the western U.S. Questionnaires were distributed to 382 students; 60% returned completed forms one week later. Age: Not stated Gender: predominantly females Ethnicity: predominantly Caucasian SES: Not stated Cross-sectional written survey included the Relationship Distancing Questionnaire (RDQ) and numerous other relationship questionnaires.

Principal Findings	Study Strengths, Limitations, and Explanation of Ratings	Rating
	7. Selection criteria clear 8. Insufficient sample power	

The "Alienated Family Relationship Scale" (AFRS) comprised three sections:
  1) Interparental Conflict, 2) Alienating Attitude of the father toward the mother and of the mother toward the father, and 3) Alienated Attitude of the young adult toward both parents.
  Results suggested good reliability, and convergent and construct validity. The AFRS also discriminated between IF and DF groups.
	1. Used comparison or control group
	2. Used standardized measures
	3. Young adult was single source informant
	4. Some systematic controls for extraneous or alternative explanatory factors for subjects' attitudes (e.g., abusive parent)
	5. Retrospective design is unable to test for direction of effects
	6. Non-random sample; ability to generalize results is low
	7. Selection criteria clear; classes invited to participate
	8. Sufficient sample power
		3

Parental alienation involves a family relational dynamic. Three meta-themes identified: 1) parents and children are engaged in dichotomous construction of meaning and views of one another; 2) the need for control seems to be the underlying motivation for family members' response to the conflict and alienation; 3) multiple family members contribute to the alienation.	1. Used no comparison or control groups 2. Used no standard(ized) measures 3. Data derived from only 3 families and interpreted by one source 4. No systematic control for extraneous or alternative explanatory variables 5. Cross-sectional design cannot test for direction of effects 6. Non-random sample; limited ability to generalize results 7. Selection criteria unclear 8. Insufficient sample power	1
Psychometric properties of the Relationship Distancing Questionnaire (RDQ): Alpha = 7.6 and 0.79 for the factors that make up the mother and father section respectively. Test–retest was 0.94 and 0.88. Convergent validity showed RDQ connected to assessment of feelings of parent–child alienation. More negative adulthood relationships with both parents were reported by subjects who felt parent–child alienation during childhood, especially with the alienating parent (a backfiring effect). Parental conflict was a better predictor than parents' marital status of whether alienation occurred.	1. Used no comparison or control groups but used multiple intragroup comparisons 2. Used standard measures 3. Data derived from single source 4. Some systematic control for extraneous or alternative explanatory variables 5. Cross-sectional design cannot establish direction of effects 6. Non-random sample; limited ability to generalize results 7. Selection criteria clear 8. Sufficient sample power	2

(Continued)

419

Table 13.1 Empirical Evidence of Alienation Studies *(Continued)*

#	Source of Research and Purpose of Study	Study Design: Recruitment of Participants, and Research Methodology
27.	**Morrison (2006)** (dissertation) *Measurement–Diagnosis Assessment–Professional Views:* To examine interrater reliability of Gardner's 8 symptoms of PAS and professionals' recognition of the range of child and parent behaviors associated with PAS	Part I: N = 20 mental health professionals who returned test–retest written surveys from a total of 300 solicitations for participation from American Psychological Association, American Psychiatric Association, and organizations affiliated with PAS. Subjects were given 5 case vignettes and asked to identify the presence of Gardner's 8 PAS symptoms. Age: 25–65 Gender: 30% female, 65% male Ethnicity: 90% Caucasian SES: Not stated Part 2: N = 36 guardian *ad litems* who returned surveys from a total of 259 solicitations from family courts and Internet. Subjects estimated frequency of 8 PAS child behaviors and alienating parent behaviors in their caseloads of custody disputing families. Age: Not stated Gender: 31% male, 69% female Ethnicity: 77% Caucasian, 11% Hispanic, 11% African American SES: Not stated
28.	**Racusin, Copans, and Mills(1994)** *Prevalence* of refusal to visit in divorced families *Diagnosis/assessment* To examine the characteristics of children, the psychopathology of parents, and custodial arrangements of families where a child refused to visit	N = 100 children and adolescents Examined 100 consecutive clinical records in a psychiatric outpatient clinic of child and adolescent cases involving parental divorce that were seen by one of the authors. Compared the 12 children who refused post-divorce visits with non-custodial parents with 88 non-refusers. Age: 2–17 years (M = 10, SD = 4.2) Gender: 70 boys, 30 girls Ethnicity: All Caucasian SES: Not stated Archival data analysis, clinical ratings.
29.	**Rand, Rand, and Kopetski (2005)** *Evaluation of treatment/intervention:* To evaluate the efficacy of structural and therapeutic interventions for interrupting PAS in more severe cases	N = 45 PAS children from 25 families whom one author had evaluated over a period of 20 years, starting in 1976. Archival data analysis on litigated custody cases referred by family court with longitudinal follow-up on 45 of a total of 84 PAS cases seen 20 years previously. Age: 3–16 years Gender: Not stated Ethnicity: Not stated SES: Not stated

Principal Findings	Study Strengths, Limitations, and Explanation of Ratings	Rating
Part I: In 4 of 5 vignettes professionals were able to identify PAS in child. Alphas ranged from 0.78–0.95; minimum ICC = 0.77, replicating Rueda's (2003) interrater reliability study. Part 2. The behavioral survey also provides support for identifying PAS child behaviors but found that relationship-destructive (alienating) behaviors by parents were observed more frequently with a high level of false allegations of abuse in custody-litigated cases. Findings provide support for Gardner's eight PAS behaviors but revealed unresolved debates about whether PAS is a syndrome.	1. Used no comparison or control group 2. Used standard measure 3. Multiple professionals were informants 4. Lacks systematic control for extraneous variables 5. Cross-sectional survey cannot determine directionality of effects 6. Non-random sample; ability to generalize results limited 7. Selection criteria unclear 8. Insufficient sample power	1
12% prevalence of visitation refusal. Children who refused post-divorce visits with their non-custodial parents were significantly more likely to be female, the oldest child at home, and in special education, and to have at least one parent with evidence of psychopathology. Substance abuse and violence toward spouse were more frequent in the non-custodial parent; suicidal behavior, psychosis, and violence towards spouse were more frequent in custodial parents in refusers than non-refusers.	1. Used no comparison or control groups but made intragroup comparisons 2. Used no standard measures 3. Data derived from multiple family members but rated by one source 4. Controlled for some explanatory variables 5. Cross-sectional study design cannot test for directionality of effects 6. Non-random sample; limited ability to generalize results 7. Selection criteria clear 8. Insufficient sample power for refuser group	1
Mother was alienating parent (AP) in 18 cases and father was AP in 7 cases. At follow-up, 20 children from 12 families had the PAS process "interrupted"; 11 in 5 families had "mixed outcomes"; and 14 from 8 families had alienation "completed." The court's decisions with respect to custody and visitation were viewed as essential for interrupting or preventing alienation. If therapy was the primary intervention, it was ineffective for interrupting alienation and sometimes made things worse.	1. Used no comparison or control groups 2. Used no standard(ized) measures 3. Data derived from multiple family members but rated by one source 4. Controlled for some explanatory variables 5. Longitudinal design ensured independent variable preceded dependent variable in time to establish directionality of effects 6. Non-random sample; limited ability to generalize results 7. Selection criteria clear 8. Insufficient sample power	1

(Continued)

Table 13.1 EMPIRICAL EVIDENCE OF ALIENATION STUDIES   (*Continued*)

#	Source of Research and Purpose of Study	Study Design: Recruitment of Participants, and Research Methodology
30.	**Reay (2007)** (dissertation) *Prognosis and long-term effects* : To explore the long-term (adult) consequences of parent alienation as a child	N = 150 adults from separated and divorced families of origin. The majority were recruited through advertisements in newspapers. Other by snowball sampling of local professionals for participants who may have experienced PAS in childhood and/or adolescence. Age: 18–35 years (M = 27.01, SD = 5.8) Gender: Not stated Ethnicity: 85% Caucasian, 2% Asian-Canadian, 5% Métis, 4% First Nations/Inuit, 1% Black-Canadian, 3% biracial SES: Not stated Causal-comparative research design: Subjects completed several measures of mother and father alienating behaviors they remembered experiencing as a child and a symptom checklist of their current level of emotional distress.
31.	**Rueda (2003, 2004)** (dissertation and publication) *Measurement–Professional views* To examine the degree of acceptance and validity of the concept and the syndrome of PAS among professionals	N = 14 Ph.D.-level professional practitioners familiar with child custody evaluations. Selected from professionals in the field in U.S., Canada, and Europe. Out of 58 approached, only 14 surveys were usable. Age: Not stated Gender: Not stated Ethnicity: Not stated SES: Not stated An interrater reliability study: The respondents analyzed five cases using Gardner's differential diagnosis chart (8 criteria) built into a questionnaire for the potential alienating parent and child.
32.	**Sarrazin (2009)** (dissertation) *Etiology*: To examine factors that might predict which children become alienated in custody-litigating families	N = 93 case files from an agency undertaking a psycholegal analysis because of parental disputes concerning child custody. Among these files, 36 had previously been identified with a high likelihood of being in a PA dynamic. Both groups were matched regarding socioeconomic variables and the child's age. Age: 2–15 years (M = 8, SD, 3) Gender: 44 girls, 49 boys Ethnicity: Not stated SES: Not stated Archival data analysis.

Principal Findings	Study Strengths, Limitations, and Explanation of Ratings	Rating
Findings demonstrated that adult children of divorce who perceived experiencing greater levels of PAS also perceived experiencing greater levels of psychological distress.	1. Used no comparison or control group 2. Used standard(ized) measures 3. Subjects were single source informant 4. No controls for extraneous or alternative explanatory factors for subjects' views, beliefs, and feelings 5. Retrospective design is unable to test for direction of effects 6. Non-random sample; ability to generalize results low 7. Selection criteria clear 8. Sufficient sample power	2
A significant level of concordance was found among raters in 4/5 cases; in 1/5 cases there was a lower consensus on the presence of PAS or meeting Gardner's criteria due to the complexity of the case presentation. Overall, agreement about the symptoms of PAS prevailed over the agreement regarding the concept of syndrome.	1. Used no comparison or control group 2. Used standard measure 3. Different professionals were single source informants 4. Lacks systematic control for extraneous variables 5. Cross-sectional survey cannot determine causal direction 6. Non-random sample; ability to generalize results limited 7. Selection criteria unclear 8. Insufficient sample power	1
Two variables that predicted a child's risk of being a victim of parental alienation were: 1) the child's lack of communication with his or her surroundings and 2) the absence of exteriorized disorders in the child.	1. Used a comparison group 2. Used standard measures 3. Multiple family informants but ratings made by clinician 4. Controlled for some extraneous variables 5. Cross-sectional survey cannot determine causal direction 6. Non-random sample; ability to generalize results limited 7. Selection criteria clear 8. Sufficient sample power	2

(Continued)

Table 13.1 EMPIRICAL EVIDENCE OF ALIENATION STUDIES *(Continued)*

#	Source of Research and Purpose of Study	Study Design: Recruitment of Participants, and Research Methodology
33.	**Siegel and Langford (1998)** *Diagnosis/Assessment* To compare pertinent personality variables of mothers who engaged in parental alienating behaviors with those mothers who did not in custody-litigating families	N = 34 females who completed the MMPI-2 in the course of child custody evaluations. All but 4 were from the authors' practice. These test results were separated from the rest of the records of the evaluations, which were reviewed and subjects classified into a PA group (n = 16) and a non-PA group (n = 18). Age: 2–15 years (M = 8, SD, 3) Gender: all females Ethnicity: Not stated SES: Not stated MMPI-2 validity scales of the two groups were compared.
34.	**Spruijt, Eikelenboom, Harmeling, Stokkers, and Kormos (2005)** *Professional views* as to the extent of PAS and the validity of Gardner's 8 symptoms in detecting it	N = 138 professionals and 69 divorced non-resident parents. Respondents replied to an invitation sent to 150 members of the Dutch Association of Family Lawyers and divorce mediators, and divorced non-resident parents. Age: 27–45 years Gender: all females Ethnicity: Not stated SES: Not stated Structured questionnaires. The questions were derived from Gardner's eight symptoms.
35.	**Stoner-Moskowitz (1998)** (dissertation) *Etiology:* To compare the self-concept of children in different family structures with the hypothesis that alienated children would have the lowest level	N = 141 children (5 from intact families, 30 from divorced, 23 from high-conflict parents, and 30 alienated). Children in the first 2 groups were recruited through several public schools and the last 2 groups from family courts, where family court services determined eligibility into the study. Age: 7 to 13 years Gender: 73 males, 68 females Ethnicity: Equal distribution of Caucasian, Hispanic, African American, Asian SES: Not stated Administration of standard tests of child's self-concept.
36.	**Sullivan, Ward, and Deutsch (2010)** *Evaluation of treatment/intervention:* of a 5-day intensive educational and therapeutic group camp intervention for both parents and their alienated children	N = 21 parents from 10 families involved in program that was conducted twice (5 families per group). Families were recruited by word of mouth through authors' professional networks and selected for pragmatic reasons (e.g., timing, cost, and availability). Age: 7–14 years Gender: Not stated

Principal Findings	Study Strengths, Limitations, and Explanation of Ratings	Rating
Mothers exhibiting PA behaviors had significantly higher scores on the K scale and significantly lower scores on the F scale than both the standard MMPI-2 normative sample and the sample of divorcing mothers who did not engage in PA. This was interpreted to mean PA mothers were more likely to deny and project. No significant difference in L scale scores between the alienating and non-alienating groups, although both were higher than the published normative sample.	1. Used a comparison group 2. Used standardized measures 3. Multiple sources of informants 4. Lacking controls for extraneous or alternative explanatory factors 5. Cross-sectional design is unable to test for direction of effects 6. Non-random sample; limited ability to generalize results 7. Selection criteria clear 8. Insufficient sample power	2
PAS occurred in a mild form in 33% of cases and in a moderate form in 9% of cases. There were very few serious cases of PAS. 58% of professionals thought PAS either does not occur or rarely occurs in the Netherlands, and 42% thought it does occur, and at mild (33%) or moderate (9%) levels. Gardner's classification of eight symptoms of parental alienation was not evident in the findings. However, distinguished four factors or symptoms, two concerning alienation by the resident parent and two concerning alienation by the child.	1. Used no comparison or control group 2. Used standard measure 3. Multiple professionals were informants 4. Lacks control for extraneous variables 5. Cross-sectional survey cannot determine causal direction 6. Non-random sample; ability to generalize results limited 7. Selection criteria mostly clear 8. Sufficient sample power	2
The children from intact families had significantly higher self-concept than those from the other family structures. However, no significant differences in children's self-concept were found between divorced, high-conflict, and PAS groups.	1. Used a comparison group 2. Used standardized measures 3. Multiple sources of informants 4. Used controls for extraneous or alternative explanatory factors 5. Cross-sectional design is unable to ensure temporal ordering of dependent variable and independent variable or test for direction of effects 6. Non-random sample; limited ability to generalize results 7. Selection criteria somewhat unclear 8. Sufficient sample power	3
The adult ratings of the camp experience in general were positive (all 4–5 on a 5-point scale). Children provided advice to parents and other peers in their situation. A range of preliminary outcomes have been observed to date with respect to resolution of the parent–child relationship difficulties and normalization of visiting arrangements.	1. Used no comparison or control groups 2. Used only standard satisfaction survey 3. Data derived from multiple family members and clinicians 4. Controlled for no extraneous or alternative explanatory variables	1

(Continued)

Table 13.1 Empirical Evidence of Alienation Studies (*Continued*)

#	Source of Research and Purpose of Study	Study Design: Recruitment of Participants, and Research Methodology
		Ethnicity: Not stated SES: Not stated All participants were approached to complete satisfaction survey at the completion of the camp, 1 month and 6 months later, and group leaders made ratings.

37.	**Vassiliou (2005)**
	(dissertation)
	Diagnosis/assessment
	    Part 1: To describe the experience and understanding of PAS from the "lost" parents' perspective.
	    Part 2. To compare the characteristics of litigated custody cases of false allegations of abuse (FA) with those of PAS.
		Part 1. N = 9 parents meeting Gardner's 8 symptoms.
		    Participants recruited via flyers, Internet postings, and e-mails. Of the 200 packages sent out, 12 met the criteria (Gardner's 8 symptoms), but 3 were dropped because difficult to contact.
		Age: Not stated
		Gender: 5 fathers, 1 mother
		Ethnicity: Not stated
		SES: Not stated
		Part 2. N = 39 court cases
		20 FA; 19 PAS
		    Searches on court-based databases for judgments made about FA and PAS
		Age: Not stated
		Gender: 22 females, 7 males
		Ethnicity: Not stated
		SES: Not stated
		Mixed-method design of qualitative interviews and court-based analysis (Part 2).

38.	**Vassiliou and Cartwright(2001)**
	Diagnosis/assessment
	    To describe the experience and understanding of PAS from the "lost" parents' perspective
		N = 6 target parents' perception of parental alienation syndrome (PAS).
		    Participants recruited via flyers, Internet postings, and e-mails.
		Age: 36 to 54 years
		Gender: 1 mother, 8 fathers
		Ethnicity: Not stated
		SES: Not stated
		    Semi-structured, open-ended interview questionnaires.

39.	**Warshak (2010)** *Evaluation of treatment/intervention:* of an experiential educational intervention for children and their rejected parents in families suffering from severe parental alienation	N = 23 children in 12 families All cases referred by court orders mandating child's participation with the "hated" parent. Cases were selected based on author's involvement with them during the intervention; 10 of the 12 rejected parents provided updates and documents such as report cards, award certificates, and photographs in a follow-up period ranging from months to several years.

Principal Findings	Study Strengths, Limitations, and Explanation of Ratings	Rating
	5. Post-treatment measures only cannot establish direction of effects 6. Non-random sample, unable to generalize results 7. Selection criteria somewhat unclear 8. Insufficient sample power	

Part 1. Findings focused on the difficulties of parents decoupling after separation and its influence on the presence of PAS.
    Part 2. Mothers more likely to make FA and to be alienating parents; PAS children were more likely to be older than those with FA. No difference between the 2 groups in length of litigation or number of siblings. FA seems to be a precursor for the presence of PAS.
    Subjects believed that courts do not use their powers to sanction and so PAS seems to continue unabated.
	1. Used no comparison or control groups
	2. Used no standard(ized) measures
	3. Data derived primarily from one parent and court files; single source rating
	4. Controlled for few extraneous or alternative explanatory variables
	5. Cross-sectional studies cannot ensure independent variable precedes dependent variable
	6. Non-random samples, limited ability to generalize results
	7. Selection criteria clear
	8. Insufficient sample power
		1

PAS children were "enlisted" by the alienating parent as secondary alienators to them (i.e., to the primary alienator) to contribute to the alienation. Lost parents reported feeling powerless as a result of the alienating situation.	1. Used no comparison or control groups 2. Used no standard(ized) measures 3. Data derived only from rejected parent 4. Controlled for no extraneous or alternative explanatory variables 5. Cross-sectional study cannot ensure independent variable preceded dependent variable in time for causal inference 6. Non-random sample of cases, unable to generalize results 7. Selection criteria unclear 8. Insufficient sample power	1
The brief, intensive workshop is based on social psychological principles (e.g., common errors in perception, suggestibility, response to authority, negative stereotype formation) and teaches critical thinking, communication, problem-solving, and parenting skills. By the conclusion of the workshop, 22 of the 23 children, all of whom were severely alienated at the outset and had prior failed experiences	1. Used no comparison or control groups 2. Used no standard(ized) measures 3. Data derived primarily from rejected parent and author-clinician 4. No systematic control for extraneous or alternative explanatory variables 5. Pre-experimental design cannot establish direction of effects	1

(Continued)

Table 13.1 Empirical Evidence of Alienation Studies   (*Continued*)

#	Source of Research and Purpose of Study	Study Design: Recruitment of Participants, and Research Methodology
		Age: age range <3 years to >17 years Gender: Not stated Ethnicity: Not stated SES: Not stated

[3] Rating of studies is based on a systematic and transparent process for grading the strengths and limitations of included studies. Two of the co-authors independently rated the quality of studies according to a predetermined rating scale based on eight criteria for the quality of studies (see Box 13.2). The rating scale was adapted from the Grading of Recommendations Assessment, Development and Evaluation (GRADE) for the purpose of assessing the strengths and limitations of studies to make sound and empirically based inferences regarding alienation. Total scores ranged from 0 to 8 and were divided by 2 to come up with a rating ranging from 1 to 4. A rating of 1 indicates very low quality and any estimate of effect is very uncertain. A rating of 2 indicates low quality and further research is very likely to have an important impact on confidence in the estimate of effect and is likely to change the estimate. A rating of 3 indicates moderate quality and further research is likely to have an important impact on confidence in the estimate of effect and may change the estimate. A rating of 4 indicates a high-quality study and further research is very unlikely to change confidence in the estimate of effect. The ability to make inferences of what is known about alienation is considered stronger for high-quality studies compared to low-quality studies.

and procedures. The review of empirical evidence clearly suggests that research in this area is still in its infancy. It also reflects the fact that it is very challenging (and expensive) to do research in this area in a methodologically sound fashion.

SUMMARY OF COMPOSITE FINDINGS

Prevalence

In the absence of randomly drawn samples, and lacking common definitions of alienation, to date there are no defensible estimates of the prevalence or incidence of the problem. Among the seven studies that aimed to estimate the extent of alienation, widely varying rates among separated parents were reported (#5, 15, 16, 22, 26, 28, 34).[1] There is general agreement that PA may occur regardless of gender of parent or child (i.e., sons and daughters can become alienated from either their fathers or mothers) and that the phenomenon can occur within intact, separated and divorced or custody-litigating families. However, parental alienation occurs more frequently in disrupted families and litigating cases (#5, 7, 16, 26), suggesting that parental conflict is a formative factor. In litigated custody cases, fathers are more likely to be the rejected parent, but this may be in part because mothers are more often the primary custodian or have the major share of residential care of the children (#5, 16, 29).

Principal Findings	Study Strengths, Limitations, and Explanation of Ratings	Rating
with counseling, had restored a positive relationship with the rejected parent, as evidenced by the children's own statements and by the observations of the rejected parent, workshop leaders, and aftercare specialist (primarily the author).

    Among the 22 children, four regressed after the court renewed their contact with the favored parent. | 6. Non-random small sample of cases, limited ability to generalize results
7. Selection criteria clear
8. Insufficient sample power | |

Furthermore, the problem of PA is being raised increasingly more often in custody litigation matters during the past decade (possibly because of growing professional and public awareness and widespread use of this terminology to describe the problem) (#5).

Diagnosis and Assessment

The most frequently stated purpose of the research has been to assess for or identify the presence of PA or PAS in the child, and parental alienating behaviors (PABs) in the parents. In general, these efforts have been very promising, showing that it appears possible to develop valid and reliable measures of these phenomena. However, to date, there has been little systematic development of these instruments with reports of adequate psychometric properties.

    More specifically, eight studies have examined Gardner's eight-symptom checklist[2] of a PAS child and all but one (#34) supported preliminary face and content validity (#4, 8, 12, 27, 31, 34, 37, 38). However, these studies seldom assessed for more complex methods of validity testing, including concurrent, convergent, predictive, and discriminant. In terms of consistency of the criteria, only two of these studies (#27, 31) assessed inter-rater reliability between professional custody evaluators using the Gardner measure. Two alternative checklists to measure the child's rejection of a parent have been developed by others (#17, 18, 24, 32) with good scale consistency, interrater reliability, and preliminary evidence of concurrent and predictive validity.

Although this subset of consistent findings is encouraging, a number of limitations should be noted. First, to date, there has been little systematic empirical control for extraneous variables that might influence the degree or seriousness of alienation. Among others, these include age of child, presence of siblings and birth order, child temperament, role of significant others (like therapists and relatives who support the child's negative beliefs), child's exposure to the interparental conflict, and the like. Second, the above measures are primarily based upon a third-party professional's viewpoint, and in some cases the non-preferred parent's viewpoint. Children and their preferred parent's perspectives have not been assessed using these measures. Third, there have been no systematic attempts to differentiate a diagnosis of PA or PAS from other conditions that might share similar features, for example from realistic estrangement or pathological bonding due to parental neglect, abuse, and exposure to intimate partner violence; from psychological enmeshment and boundary diffusion due to family structural aberrations; or from psychotic states like *folie à deux*. Most importantly, although the majority of the researchers purport to exclude from their studies cases where abuse of the child had occurred, few have reported working definitions of child abuse and systematic methods for identifying and excluding them from their samples. Despite considerable controversy in the field over the extent to which child abuse and intimate partner violence cases are wrongfully judged in family courts to be alienation cases or vice versa, whether estrangement as a consequence of abuse co-occurs with alienation, and the likelihood that allegations of abuse are false when they are associated with or precede alienation, few empirical studies have tried to sort these issues out, and to date no clear concurrence of findings have emerged (#18, 27, 37).

On the other hand, the identification of PABs has been the focus of research in at least eight studies and has produced a set of remarkably concordant findings, derived from researchers with diverse perspectives and variability in the quality of the studies (#1, 3, 7, 16, 18, 19, 24, 26). Mothers, fathers, children, young adults, and counselors alike have been able to describe the explicit behaviors that may be perpetrated by one parent and have the capacity to distance, damage, or destroy a child's relationship with the other parent. The psychometric properties of a set of PABs are being verified in some of these studies (interrater reliabilities, alpha scale consistencies, concurrent and predictive validities; #16, 18, 19, 20, 24, 26), but much further scale development is needed to demonstrate adequate psychometric properties of PAB measures. A further problem is that there is no commonly accepted measure of PABs; each of the researchers has developed parallel and separate instruments to measure the phenomena.

A promising, fruitful domain of research was pursued by five studies that tested hypotheses about the psychological profiles of both preferred and non-preferred parents and alienated children using psychological testing results (e.g., MMPI(2) or Rorschach) and custody evaluation records (#14, 17, 19, 23, 33). These research designs were usually stronger because they employed a comparison group of non-alienation cases in custody evaluations, used standardized measures and procedures for collecting data, and had access to data collected from multiple family members and collaterals. In three of four studies, the findings supported the hypothesis that alienating parents tended to use more narcissistic and primitive defenses and had poor reality testing (#14, 19, 33). The findings with respect to the rejected parent were mixed: some did (#14) and others did not (#23) differentiate them from the alienating parent; some found them similar to parents in non-alienation cases (#14); others found them to have different problems, such as having coping deficits and difficulty modulating emotions (#19). Interestingly, although alienated children are often thought to be emotionally disturbed compared to their non-alienated counterparts in custody-disputing families, empirical support for this hypothesis is also mixed, with findings of clinical levels of emotional problems according to some ratings (#23) and null findings on others (#17, 23, 35). The problem is that these studies are too few, lacked sample power, or examined only a limited number of the many relevant personality variables to draw definitive conclusions.

Etiology

To the extent that some researchers have adopted Gardner's conceptualization of PA or PAS as a syndrome primarily instigated in a child by an alienating parent, the search for alternative explanations of the child's negative attitudes and behavior is not assumed to be important. Other researchers, however, have challenged this assumption. At least eight studies (#11, 15, 16, 18, 25, 28, 32, 35) have explored child and family dynamics that are associated with PA, and several have tested causal models or used multivariate analysis to examine multiple predictive, buffering, or moderating factors that are hypothesized to produce the kind of family dynamics conducive to a child's alienation from one parent. The findings generally support these more complex models of effects. It is apparent that both parents in conflicted families may engage in reciprocal PABs (possibly in response to one another) (#7, 16, 18, 24), and that their children are differentially affected, depending upon their age, birth order, social-cognitive capacity, and socioemotional problems (#16, 28, 32). Three studies, all by the same research group (#15, 16, 18), implicate both parents as contributing to the problem. The preferred parent is more likely to engage in PABs along with providing conditional warm involvement with the child, while the non-preferred parent lacks warm involvement and is more prone to actual abuse of the child.

Data used to test these multivariate models have all been derived from cross-sectional studies that are unable to assess the directionality of effects. It is therefore difficult to assess the temporal order between a child's rejection of a parent and associational factors, such as a parent's alienating behaviors, poor parenting capacities, or critical incidents of child abuse. Although all of these factors have been found to be associated with the child's rejection of a parent, only longitudinal studies can ensure that the independent variables precede the dependent variables in time in order to assert causal direction. It could be argued that rejected parents have been rendered powerless to parent by the alliance against them. Alternatively, it could be argued that concerned parents, in *response* to their child's angry troubled relationship with their ex-partner, empathically support their child's negative views and become alienators. In the absence of longitudinal data that could help sort out whether the "chicken or the egg" came first and whether this temporal order was constant, good theoretical models predicting the child's rejection of a parent—those that are built upon fundamental knowledge about child development, parent–child attachment, the impact of intrusive parenting processes, and family structural aberrations—need to be tested using large, representative samples drawn from relevant populations. The extant body of empirical research about PA, by and large, has not drawn from basic social science knowledge about children and families that could shed light on the problem.

Prognosis and Long-Term Effects

Eight of the studies examined long-term outcomes and residual effects of PA/PAS and PAB (#1, 7, 9, 11, 20, 24, 26, 30). The findings are inconclusive as to the degree and type of negative consequences. Spontaneous reunifications (ones initiated by the teenagers or young adults) were reported with varying frequency, for different reasons, and with a range of outcomes both positive and negative (#9, 11, 20). One study (#26) found compromised relationships with both parents and a "boomerang effect" of later rejection of the alienating parent. Three studies (#1, 9, 30) documented profoundly negative effects on the adult's mental health and capacity to form trusting intimate relationships; however, these studies had no control group and used small samples (ranging from 10 to 38), and all three employed retrospective designs wherein subjects were recruited precisely because they self-identified as victims of PAB as a child. It is possible that subjects were over-attributing all of their negative feelings and experiences to PAB. Another three studies (#7, 24, 26) that gathered data from college students and used a comparison group of intact families found weak to moderate negative effects on long-term emotional well-being or capacity for secure intimate relationships. Because this subset of studies all employed retrospective designs that cannot determine directionality of effects and ruled out few if any alternative explanatory factors (e.g., parental divorce, conflict, parental psychopathology), there is no way of definitively attributing these negative outcomes to PA/PAS. The only longitudinal study (#20) that potentially could examine directionality of effects produced null findings: that is, although alienated offspring as young adults scored high using standardized measures of emotional distress and attachment insecurity in intimate relations, they were not more disturbed than their non-alienated counterparts in custody-disputed cases. Unfortunately, this was a small sample (n = 22 families) that employed no control group, so the findings are deemed unreliable.

Evaluation of Treatment and Interventions

Five studies evaluated the outcome effectiveness of diverse interventions for PA/PAS families, all claiming varying levels of success (#13, 21, 29, 36, 39). Two evaluated custody change from the preferred to the rejected parent by court order for severely alienated cases as the intervention of choice, comparing outcomes of cases where the court had followed the recommendations of the evaluator with those cases where the recommendation of custody reversal was not followed by the court (#13, 29). A third study evaluated a therapeutic supervised visitation program for visitation-resistant children (#21). A fourth study followed up a court-mandated 4-day educational program for alienated children and the rejected parent (#39). A fifth study included a post-treatment client survey following a one-week psychotherapeutic group workshop for all members of multiple PA families (#36).

Outcomes in response to treatment in these studies—defined differently and sometimes from a limited perspective of one family member—could range from complete restoration of a relationship with both parents, to a partial softening of the negativity and resistance towards the rejected parent, to a reversal of parent preference, to no change or even a consolidation of the youngster's negativity. Successful outcomes were associated with a number of factors, including early intervention; the capacity of parents to communicate about their offspring; younger age of child; absence of reactive or retaliative abuse, neglect, or abandonment by either parent; court orders that protect the child's right of access to the non-preferred parent; and the opportunity for the alienated child to live away from his or her alienating parent(s) (#13, 20, 21, 28, 39). While these findings might suggest that in severe cases court-ordered reversal of custody can be an effective response, often requiring a suspension of contact with the alienating parent, there are a number of reasons for viewing this research as preliminary and requiring confirmation with further studies. Almost all of these studies employed the weakest research design (i.e., a post-treatment evaluation of different interventions designed by the researcher-clinician). None used a comparison or control group, nor were standardized measures of outcome used. In four of five cases, the sample size of independent subjects was small, and the cases were mostly derived from the researcher-clinician's own caseload. Further, there were no systematic controls for many other variables that might have affected outcome.

Professional Views

Finally, a set of six studies surveyed mental health and/or legal professionals to ascertain their opinion about a range of issues including their knowledge of PA/PAS, its prevalence in their caseloads, the importance of assessing for it in custody evaluations, and their opinions as to its admissibility in court during expert testimony (#2, 6, 10, 27, 31, 34). The findings were remarkably concordant across studies and in general agreement with the overall conclusions reached in our literature review as to the status of the empirical research on the subject of alienation. As a group, professionals in the family justice field considered themselves moderately to extremely knowledgeable about alienation and endorsed the importance of assessing for it in custody cases. Estimated prevalence ranged broadly depending upon the composition of their practice caseloads. Overall, respondents recognized the lack of sound research to support the concept, although they acknowledged the existence of alienation dynamics within the child custody field and the cases that they are involved with. Almost all viewed it as a multidimensional construct. In some studies there was no consensus, and in other studies the majority did not endorse PAS as a syndrome meeting either the Frye or Daubert standards for admission as a diagnosis by an expert witness. Where the question was asked, there were divided views about having PA included in the DSM-V. However, it would appear that most professionals believe that expert testimony about children's resistance to contact with a parent can assist family courts in making decisions.

Summary

- All of the studies were scored in the range of 1 to 3, clearly suggesting that research in this area is still in its infancy.
- The lack of consensus on the definitions of alienation and the use of varying non-standardized measures and procedures limit the ability of researchers to perform methodologically sound research in this area.
- Studies of alienation generally use small, non-random samples with no comparison group, suggesting that more large-scale empirical studies are needed to inform the field.
- Many of the studies employ cross-sectional or retrospective research designs to test simple hypotheses, suggesting the need for prospective longitudinal studies to disentangle complex interactive effects and compare outcomes over time.

SUMMARY AND GUIDELINES FOR USE

An overview of the status of empirical research findings on parental alienation can be found in Box 13.3.

In summary, at this stage of the empirical research, it is apparent that PABs are characteristics often associated with high-conflict separations and post-divorce parental disputes. PA/PAS is not a diagnostic syndrome at this time but rather a cluster of commonly recognized symptoms; there is little empirically validated evidence about cause, prognosis, and treatment. The present research findings suggest that multiple other factors also contribute to the problem, including higher levels of interparental conflict, age of children, personality predispositions of family members, parenting and parent–child relationship patterns, living arrangements, and ongoing custody litigation. For this reason, alienation should be viewed as a family relational problem rather than an individual pathology of one parent or child. This does not mean that both parents are always equally accountable: there are cases where one parent may have primary responsibility for "alienating" a child from the other parent. The complexity of these situations places the onus on custody evaluators to conduct an ecologically oriented and comprehensive assessment of the various factors that may impede or facilitate parent–child contact problems, rather than prematurely determining that the accountability rests specifically with one parent's individual pathology or misconduct.

PA allegations may be reified in the adversarial legal system. A finding of PA or PAS by a court may appear to offer simple, clear-cut answers as to which parent is "right" and which parent is "wrong" in cases where the reality may be more complex. Parental blaming, mistrust, and polarization may be increased, and capacity for (co) parenting is undermined in this context such that a diagnosis of PA can have the potential of doing more harm than good. Rather than make a simple diagnosis of PA or PAS—with its potential for simplification of issues or misuse in custody litigation—clinicians should consider using a more specific description of the parents' and child's behavior in the context of the family, together with a thorough assessment of all factors potentially contributing to the child's negative beliefs and behaviors vis-à-vis the other parent. When a child is reluctant or refuses to contact, PAB is

Box 13.3

CONSIDERATIONS AND CAUTIONS FOR RESEARCH ON
PARENTAL ALIENATION

- *State of the Evidence:* The extant body of empirical research on parental alienation comprising 39 studies was reviewed and assessed by conventional standards of quality in order to draw empirically supported general conclusions. As a group the empirical studies were found to be methodologically weak, with very limited ability to generalize the results of any one study. The clinician should be wary of the numerous knowledge claims in this field and realize that the empirically supported findings are relatively few. However, these conclusions are likely to change as new and better-quality research becomes available.
- *Prevalence:* To date, there are no defensible estimates of the prevalence of PA or PAB, but the problem can occur regardless of age and gender of parent and child in all family structures. However, adolescents are likely to be more entrenched in their stance and fathers are more likely than mothers for a variety of reasons to suffer the rejection of their children in custody-litigating families.
- *Diagnosis/Assessment:* There is remarkable agreement about the kind of behavioral strategies that parents can use that have the potential to manipulate their children's feelings, attitudes, and beliefs in ways that may interfere with their relationship with the other parent (PAB). The cluster of symptoms or behaviors that indicate the presence of alienation in the child can also be reliably identified.
- *Measurement:* There has been little systematic development of assessment tools for PA or PAB that have adequate psychometric properties.
- *Differentiation:* There is a virtual absence of empirical studies on the differential diagnosis of alienation in children from other conditions that share similar features with PA, especially child estrangement in response to parental abuse and witness to intimate partner violence.
- *Description:* Whereas a consistent psychological profile of a parent who engages in PAB is beginning to emerge, there are mixed or inconsistent findings about the psychological functioning of alienated children and the non-preferred or rejected parent.
- *Etiology:* Multiple factors (including PAB) are associated with children's alienated stance. Clearly PAB by a parent may be a contributing factor; however, it is not uncommon for both parents in high-conflict cases to engage in PAB, and both may have problematic parenting practices that appear to contribute to the problem—with intrusive or protective parenting practices by the preferred parent and lack of warm involvement or punitive (re)actions by the non-preferred parent. Children are differentially affected, depending upon their age, birth order, social-cognitive capacity, and socioemotional functioning.
- The problem with assessing the etiology of alienation is that the data used to test these multivariate models have all been derived from cross-sectional studies that are unable to assess the directionality of effects. Only longitudinal

studies can ensure that independent variables precede dependent variables in time in order to assert causal direction.

- **Prognosis:** Although a range of profoundly negative long-term consequences of PA and PAB have been asserted, empirical findings about the nature and extent of those effects have been mixed and inconclusive.
- The problem with all but one of the studies of long-term effects is that they have used retrospective reports that are unable to ensure that the independent variables precede the dependent variables in time. None of the studies have systematically controlled for extraneous variables or ruled out alternative explanatory factors for any observed long-term effects.
- **Treatment/Intervention:** The development and evaluation of interventions (both legal and psychological) are in their formative stages, and outcomes are inconclusive or unreliable at this time due mainly to very weak evaluation methodology.
- **Professional Views:** Surveys of mental health and legal professionals indicate that as a group they consider themselves knowledgeable about PA/PAS and its clinical manifestations, consider it important to assess in custody matters, and are aware of its limited empirical research basis. The majority does not consider that it meets the Frye or Daubert standards for admission of expert testimony as a "syndrome."
- **Implications for Custody Evaluations:** PA/PAS is not a diagnostic syndrome at this time, but rather a cluster of commonly recognized symptoms; there is insufficient empirically validated evidence about etiology, prognosis, and treatment. For this reason and because of the complexity of these situations, the onus is on custody evaluators to conduct a comprehensive assessment of the various factors that may impede or facilitate parent–child contact problems.
- **Implications for Intervention:** Court orders for change of custody and access arrangements, and mandates for psychological treatment should: 1) be based upon the needs of the individual child within his or her particular family situation; 2) address the factors that appear to be maintaining the child's reluctance or refusal to contact; and 3) ensure a timely follow-up to review progress and determine the direction and need for further intervention.

---

an important factor to consider, but it should not be the sole focal point of attention and censure. Moreover, interventions need to address the child's overall adjustment considering the dynamics of the particular child and the family situation.

If there are specific indications that the young person is suffering emotional or social problems, or is at risk for negative long-term outcomes, irrespective of the source of the problem, court-ordered therapy may be warranted. Importantly, the therapy will vary depending on the assessment of the multiple factors and the nature and severity of the parent–child contact problem. However, there is a lack of clear empirical evidence that children who resist or refuse contact with one of their parents are universally emotionally disturbed or necessarily at risk for long-term negative outcomes. A range of different educational, therapeutic, and structural interventions are being proposed and piloted—like early preventive education or counseling, parent–child reunification, family therapy—but to date there is insufficient research evidence as to what works best with whom. In the absence of these data, individually crafted interventions need to be based on a thorough assessment of what appears to be causing or maintaining the problem, and timely follow-ups on progress should guide the continuation and direction of the treatment.

A not uncommon judicial response to severe alienation is to remove children from the care of the "alienating" parent and place him or her in the custody of the rejected parent. While some studies conclude that in severe cases a court-ordered reversal of custody can be an effective response, often requiring a temporary suspension of contact with the alienating parent, there are a number of reasons for viewing this research as preliminary and requiring confirmation with further research, as these studies employed very weak research designs. Equally, there is a lack of empirical support for leaving children with the favored parent in cases of parental alienation. Clearly more and better empirical research is warranted to unravel these complex family situations.

NOTES

1 The numbers in parentheses refer to the numbers assigned to the research studies listed alphabetically in Table 13.1.
2 These eight symptom behaviors are the child (1) engaged in a campaign of denigration against one parent; (2) gave a frivolous, weak, or absurd rationale for the alienation; (3) lacked ambivalence towards the alienated parent; (4) lacked guilt or remorse; (5) claimed to be an independent thinker; (6) reflexively took the side of the alienating parent in the disputes; (7) cited borrowed scenarios in support of his or her position; and (8) spread alienation to the extended family.

REFERENCES

Adams, K. (2009). *The parentectomy—A memoir: A perspective on rising above parental alienation*. Bloomington, IN: Xlibris Corporation.
Atkins, D., Eccles, M., Flottorp, S., Guyatt, G. H., Henry, D., Hill, S., . . . Williams, J. W., Jr. (2004). Systems for grading the quality of evidence and the strength of recommendations I: Critical appraisal of existing approaches. The GRADE Working Group. *BMC Health Services Research, 4*(1), 38–45. doi:10.1186/1472-6963-4-38
Baker, A. J. L. (2005a). The cult of parenthood: A qualitative study of parental alienation. *Cultic Studies Review, 4*(1), 1–29.
Baker, A.J.L. (2005b). The long-term effects of parental alienation on adult children: A qualitative research study. *American Journal of Family Therapy, 33*(4), 289–302. doi:10.1080/01926180590962129
Baker, A. J. L. (2005c). Parent alienation strategies: A qualitative study of adults who experienced parental alienation as a child. *American Journal of Forensic Psychology, 23*(4), 41–63.

Baker, A. J. L. (2006). Patterns of parental alienation syndrome: A qualitative study of adults who were alienated from a parent as a child. *American Journal of Family Therapy, 34*(1), 63–78.

Baker, A. J. L. (2007). Knowledge and attitudes about the parental alienation syndrome: A survey of custody evaluators. *American Journal of Family Therapy, 35*(1), 1–19. doi:10.1080/01926180600698368

Baker, A. J. L., & Darnall, D. (2006). Behaviors and strategies employed in parental alienation: A survey of parental experiences. *Journal of Divorce and Remarriage, 45*(1–2), 97–124. doi:10.1300/J087v45n01_06

Baker, A. J. L., & Darnall, D. (2007). A construct study of the eight symptoms of severe parental alienation syndrome: A survey of parental experiences. *Journal of Divorce and Remarriage, 47*(1–2), 55–75. doi:10.1300/J087v47n01_04

Bala, N., Hunt, S., & McCarney, C. (2010). Parental alienation Canadian court cases 1989–2008. *Family Court Review, 48*(1), 164–179. doi:10.1111/j.1744–1617.2009.01296.x

Baldwin, A., & Tab, M. (2008). *A promise to ourselves: A journey through fatherhood and divorce.* Atlanta, GA: St. Martin's Press.

Bow, J. N., Gould, J. W., & Flens, J. R. (2009). Examining parental alienation in child custody cases: A survey of mental health and legal professionals. *American Journal of Family Therapy, 37*(2), 127–145. doi:10.1080/01926180801960658

Braver, S. J., Coatsworth, D., & Peralta, K. (n.d.). Alienating behavior within divorced and intact families: Matched parents' and now-young adult children's reports. Retrieved online on Dec. 17, 2010, at http://www.uea.ac.uk/swp/iccd2006/Presentations/tues_pm/ps12%20High%20conflict%20&%20Enforcement/Braver%20summary.pdf

Burril-O'Donnell, J. (2001). *Parental alienation syndrome in court referred custody cases* (Doctoral dissertation). Northcentral University. Retrieved online on Dec. 14, 2010, at http://www.bookpump.com/dps/pdf-b/1121490b.pdf

Carey, K. M. (2003). *Exploring long-term outcomes of the parental alienation syndrome* (Psy.D. dissertation). Alliant International University, San Francisco, California. Dissertations and Theses: Full Text. (Publication No. AAT 3088909).

Cox, M. (2010). *Bridging the gap on parental alienation: A survey for legal and mental health professionals in family law* (Psy.D. dissertation). Alliant International University, Los Angeles, California. Dissertations and Theses: Full Text. (Publication No. AAT 3421110).

Darnall, D. (1998). *Divorce casualties: Protecting your children from parental alienation.* Lanham, MD: Taylor Publishing Co.

Darnall, D., & Steinberg, B.F. (2008). Motivational models for spontaneous renunciation with the alienated child: Part II. *American Journal of Family Therapy, 36*(3), 253–261. doi:10.1080/01926180701643230

Dunne, J., & Hedrick, M. (1994). The parental alienation syndrome: An analysis of sixteen selected cases. *Journal of Divorce and Remarriage, 21*, 21–38. doi:10.1300/J087v21n03_02

Fidler, B. J., & Bala, N. (2010). Children resisting postseparation contact with a parent: Concepts, controversies, and conundrums. *Family Court Review, 48*(1), 10–47 doi:10.1111/j.1744–1617.2009.01287.x

Friedlander, S., & Walters, M. G. (2010). When a child rejects a parent: Tailoring the intervention to fit the problem. *Family Court Review, 48*, 97–110. doi:10.1111/j.1744–1617.2009.01291.x

Gardner, R. A. (1998). *The parental alienation syndrome* (2nd ed.). Cresskill, NJ: Creative Therapeutics Inc.

Gardner, R. (2001). Should courts order PAS children to visit/reside with the alienated parent? A follow-up study. *American Journal of Forensic Psychology, 19*(3), 61–106.

Gordon, R. M., Stoffey, R., & Bottinelli, J. (2008). MMPI-2 findings of primitive defenses in alienating parents. *American Journal of Family Therapy, 36*(3), 211–228. doi:10.1080/01926180701643313

Jeffries, M., & Davies, J. (2009) *A family's heartbreak: A parent's introduction to parental alienation.* Stamford, CT: A Family's Heartbreak, LLC.

Johnston, J. R. (1993). Children of divorce who refuse visitation. In J. H. Bray & C. Depner (Eds.), *Nonresidential parenting: New vistas in family living* (pp. 109–135). Newbury Park, CA: Sage Publishing Co.

Johnston, J. R. (2003). Parental alignments and rejection: An empirical study of alienation in children of divorce. *Journal of American Academy of Psychiatry and the Law, 31*, 158–170. PMid:12875493

Johnston, J. R., & Goldman, J. R. (2010). Outcomes of family counseling interventions with children who resist visitation: An addendum to Friedlander and Walters. *Family Court Review, 48*(1), 112–115. doi:10.1111/j.1744–1617.2009. 01292.x

Johnston, J., Roseby, V., & Kuehnle, K. (2009). *In the name of the child: A developmental approach to understanding and helping children of conflicted and violent divorce.* New York: Springer Publishing Company.

Johnston, J. R., Walters, M. G., & Olesen, N. W. (2005a). The psychological functioning of alienated children in custody disputing families: An exploratory study. *American Journal of Forensic Psychology, 23*(3), 39–64.

Johnston, J. R., Walters, M. G., & Olesen, N. W. (2005b). Is it alienating parenting, role reversal or child abuse? A study of children's rejection of a parent in child custody disputes. *Journal of Emotional Abuse, 5*(4), 191–218. doi:10.1300/ J135v05n04_02

Johnston, J. R., Waters, M. G. & Olesen, N. W. (2005c). Clinical ratings of parenting capacity and Rorschach protocols of custody-disputing parents: An exploratory study. *Journal of Child Custody, 2*, 159–178. doi:10.1300/J190v02n01_09

Kelly, J. B., & Johnston, J. R. (2001). The alienated child: A reformulation of parental alienation syndrome. *Family Court Review. Special Issue: Alienated Children in Divorce, 39*(3), 249–266.

Kumar, S. (2003). *Factors affecting reconciliation in visitation refusal cases* (Doctoral dissertation). Adelphi University, The Institute of Advanced Psychological Studies. Garden City, NY. Dissertations and Theses: Full Text. (Publication No. AAT 3069406).

Lampel, A. K. (1996a). Children's alignments with parents in highly conflicted custody cases: Study 1. *Family Conciliation Court Review, 34*, 229–239. doi:10. 1111/j.174–1617.1996.tb00416.x

Lampel, A. K. (1996b). Children's alignments with parents in highly conflicted custody cases: Study 2. *Family Conciliation Court Review, 34*, 229–239. doi:10. 1111/j.174–1617.1996.tb00416.x

Laughrea, K. (2002). Alienated family relationship scale: Validation with young adults. *Journal of College Student Psychotherapy, 17*(1), 37–48. doi:10.1300/J035v17n01_05

Moné, J. (2007). *Family members' narratives on divorce and interparental conflict* (Doctoral dissertation). Colorado State University, Colorado. Dissertations and Theses: Full Text. (Publication No. AAT 3299791).

Moné, J. G., & Biringen, Z. (2006). Perceived parent-child alienation: Empirical assessment of parent-child relationships within divorced and intact families. *Journal of Divorce and Remarriage, 45*(3–4), 131–156.

Morrison, S. (2006). *Parental alienation syndrome: An inter-rater reliability study. Alienating behaviors—related justice system issues* (Ph.D. dissertation). University of Southern Mississippi, Mississippi. Dissertations and Theses: Full Text. (Publication No. AAT 3268461).

Racusin, R., Copans, S. A., & Mills, P. (1994). Characteristics of families of children who refuse post-divorce visits. *Journal of Clinical Psychology, 50*, 792–801. doi:10.1002/1097–4679(199409)50:5<792::AID-JCLP2270500518>3.0.CO;2-K

Rand, D. C., Rand, R. & Kopetski, L. (2005). The spectrum of parental alienation syndrome, Part III: The Kopetski follow-up study. *American Journal of Forensic Psychology, 23*, 15–43.

Reay, K. (2007). *Psychological distress among adult children of divorce who perceive experiencing parental alienation syndrome in earlier years* (Ph.D. dissertation). Capella University, Minnesota. Dissertations and Theses: Full Text. (Publication No. AAT 3266272).

Richardson, P. (2006). A kidnapped mind: A mother's heartbreaking story of parental alienation syndrome: Toronto, ON: University of Toronto Press

Rueda, C. A. (2003). *Parental alienation syndrome: An inter-rater reliability study* (Ph.D. dissertation). Walden University, Minnesota. Dissertations and Theses: Full Text. (Publication No. AAT 3117194).

Rueda, C. A. (2004). An inter-rater reliability study of parental alienation syndrome. *American Journal of Family Therapy, 32*(5), 391–403. doi:10.1080/01926180490499864

Sarrazin, J. (2009). *Les conflits parentaux et le phenomene de l'alienation parentale: Conditions aggravantes pour l'enfant de parents separes* (Ph.D. dissertation). Universite de Montreal, Canada. Dissertations and Theses: Full Text. (Publication No. AAT NR52908).

Siegel, J. C., & Langford, J. S. (1998). MMPI-2 validity scales and suspected parental alienation syndrome. *American Journal of Forensic Psychology, 16*(4), 5–14.

Spruijt, E., Eikelenboom, B., Harmeling, J., Stokkers, R., & Kormos, H. (2005). Parental alienation syndrome (PAS) in the Netherlands. *American Journal of Family Therapy, 33*(4), 303–317. doi:10.1080/01926180590962110

Stoner-Moskowitz, J. (1998). *The effect of parental alienation syndrome and interparental conflict on the self-concept of children of divorce* (Psy.D. dissertation). Miami Institute of Psychology of the Caribbean Center for Advanced Studies, Florida. Dissertations and Theses: Full Text. (Publication No. AAT 9829488).

Sullivan, M., Ward, P., & Deutsch, R.M. (2010). Overcoming barriers family camp: A program for high-conflict divorced families where a child is resisting contact with a parent. *Family Court Review, 48*(1), 116–135. doi:10.1111/j.1744–1617.2009.01293.x

Turkat, I. (2002). Parental alienation syndrome: A review of critical issues. *Journal of the American Academy of Matrimonial Lawyers, 18*, 131.

Vassiliou, D. (2005). *The impact of the legal system on parental alienation syndrome* (Ph.D. dissertation). McGill University, Canada. Dissertations and Theses: Full Text. (Publication No. AAT NR21706).

Vassiliou, D., & Cartwright, G.F. (2001). The lost parents' perspective on parental alienation syndrome. *American Journal of Family Therapy, 29*(3), 181–191. doi:10.1080/019261801750424307

Warshak, R. A. (2010). Family Bridges: Using insights from social science to reconnect parents and alienated children. *Family Court Review, 48*(1), 48–80. doi:10.1111/j.1744–1617.2009.01288.x

## 14

Domestic Violence and Child Custody

JENNIFER L. HARDESTY, MEGAN L. HASELSCHWERDT,
AND MICHAEL P. JOHNSON ■

Approximately half of U.S. marriages end in divorce, with half of divorcing couples having dependent children (U.S. Census, 2002). In addition, two fifths of U.S. births are to unmarried women (Ventura, 2009), many of whom also experience relationship dissolution. Of divorcing parents, about 20% are unable to develop parenting plans (i.e., custody agreements) on their own; estimates for unmarried parents are unknown. When parents are unable to reach agreements on their own, judicial intervention is required. Legal and mental health professionals face the complex task of evaluating these families to determine what parenting plans best meet the children's needs. In general, professionals are guided by the "best interest of the child" standard, which encourages child-centered parenting plans that favor ongoing contact between children and both parents. This standard is based on a substantial body of literature pointing to the benefits to children of co-parental cooperation and low co-parental conflict (Amato, 2010). When there is adult domestic violence (DV), however, the complexity of making child-centered decisions is compounded, as professionals must weigh the benefits of cooperative co-parenting alongside potential threats to the safety and long-term adjustment of both mother and children.

Broadly defined, DV refers to physical, sexual, or psychological harm caused by a current or former partner (Centers for Disease Control [CDC], 2010). Allegations of DV are very common among separating parents who require judicial intervention (Jaffe, Crooks, & Poisson, 2003; Johnston, Lee, Oleson, & Walters, 2005). Despite mandates requiring courts to factor DV into parenting plans, other factors, such as preference for joint custody and cooperative co-parenting, are often favored over efforts to ensure safety (Dragiewicz, 2010). A number of factors contribute to this pattern. First, as professionals weigh the benefits of cooperative co-parenting versus the risks posed by DV, they have access to a far more substantial body of literature on the former (e.g., Adamsons & Pasley, 2006; Amato, 2000, 2010). Empirical research on post-separation parenting when there is a history of DV is in its infancy, and validated tools for assessing risk or the potential for effective co-parenting in this context are lacking. A second contributing factor is inadequate DV training for custody evaluators. Studies indicate that many U.S. custody evaluators espouse common misconceptions about DV that minimize its seriousness (Jaffe, Lemon, & Poisson, 2003). In one quasi-experimental vignette study of 603 custody evaluators across the United States, recommendations were influenced by characteristics of the mother but not by characteristics of the DV. Specifically, when mothers were described as hostile (vs. pleasant), custody evaluators favored fathers for custody regardless of the type, severity, and frequency of fathers' violence (Hardesty, Hans, Haselschwerdt, Khaw, & Crossman, 2010). Open-ended data revealed a belief that "real" DV victims should have a passive demeanor (Hardesty et al., 2010; Haselschwerdt, Hardesty, & Hans, 2011). Misconceptions such as this can lead to misperceptions of the potential danger of DV for families experiencing separation.

Finally, DV allegations in the context of custody disputes can be challenging to substantiate (Johnston et al., 2005). Empirical data on the extent to which DV allegations in custody disputes are substantiated are limited. In one study of 120 high-conflict custody disputes, the rate of substantiation of allegations of adult abuse (which combined DV and substance abuse) was 55% substantiation of accusations against mothers and 67% against fathers (Johnston et al., 2005). Substantiations were defined as any corroborating evidence of abuse that had not been dismissed as unfounded (e.g., self-admissions, eyewitness reports, medical records, police reports). Even when corroborating evidence is available, DV still may be ignored or minimized. For example, a comparison of custody dispute cases with substantiated DV ($n = 44$) and with no DV ($n = 36$) found little difference in the evaluation process or custody outcomes (Logan, Walker, Jordan, & Horvath, 2002). This study also found that information on the history of DV (e.g., protection from abuse orders) that was available in case files was often excluded from evaluation reports. Hardesty and colleagues' (2010) vignette study suggests that even when such information is available there is a tendency to minimize or ignore DV. In this study, evaluators initially rated the believability of a mother's DV allegations as presented in a vignette, and then the vignette continued by indicating whether any documentation was available to substantiate the DV allegations. Evaluators' believability ratings did not increase among those who heard that there was a protection from abuse order; however, believability ratings declined among those who heard that there was *not* a protection from abuse order. Open-ended data revealed conflicting beliefs: on one hand, if the violence really happened, then the victim would have obtained a protection from abuse order; on the other hand, a protection from abuse order is easy to obtain and thus proves nothing.

The purpose of this chapter is to review empirical research that will inform the process of evaluating separating parents in the context of DV. The authors begin by introducing distinctions among types of DV, distinctions that are important for understanding the relevant research and for evaluating the implications of DV for custody decisions. To help establish the relevance of DV to child custody, a summary of the effects of DV exposure on children is provided. Then the research on parenting in the context of DV is reviewed. This growing body of research provides insight into post-separation relationship dynamics and parenting characteristics of victims and abusers. The chapter concludes with the options available for parenting plans that prioritize both safety and the long-term adjustment of parents and children affected by DV.

TYPES OF DOMESTIC VIOLENCE

In 2007, the Association of Family and Conciliation Courts (AFCC) and the National Council of Juvenile and Family Court Judges (NCJFCJ) convened a group of leading DV scholars and practitioners to develop consensus points for improving service to families (Ellis, 2008; Frederick, 2008; Jaffe, Johnston, Crooks, & Bala, 2008; Kelly & Johnson, 2008; Salem & Dunford-Jackson, 2008; VerSteegh & Dalton, 2008; Warrier, 2008). The group concluded that appropriate decisions regarding child custody must take into account the major differences among types of DV.

Kelly and Johnson (2008) identify three major types of DV (coercive controlling violence, violent resistance, situational couple violence) and one subtype of situational couple violence (separation-instigated violence) that is often encountered in the family court setting (Johnston & Campbell, 1993a). Differences among the three major types are well established by research conducted by different researchers, using different measures, with different sampling frames, in different countries (Ansara & Hindin, 2010; Frye, Manganello, Campbell, Walton-Moss, & Wilt, 2006; Graham-Kevan & Archer, 2003; Hardesty, Khaw, Chung, & Martin, 2008; Johnson, 2008).

Coercive controlling violence, which Johnson (2008) has termed *intimate terrorism*, involves physical violence as just one among many coercive tactics (e.g., threats, intimidation, monitoring time and activities) that abusers use to dominate their partners while creating a climate of oppression, fear, and isolation. In heterosexual relationships, this violence is perpetrated more often by men against women and on average is more severe, frequent, and injurious (Ansara & Hindin, 2010; Frye et al., 2006; Graham-Kevan & Archer, 2003; Johnson, 2006; Johnson & Leone, 2005; Johnson, Leone, & Xu, 2008; Laroche, 2005; Leone, Johnson, & Cohan, 2007). Coercive controlling violence is what is traditionally thought of as battering, and in many contexts the term "domestic violence" is used to refer specifically to this type of intimate partner violence.

Violent resistance is violence enacted in resistance to coercive controlling violence. It is most often either an attempt to stop the partner's violence or to exact retribution. Because in heterosexual relationships coercive controlling violence is mostly male-perpetrated, violent resistance is seen primarily among women (Ansara & Hindin, 2010; Graham-Kevan & Archer, 2003; Johnson, 2006; Johnson et al., 2008; Laroche, 2005).

Situational couple violence and its subtype, separation-instigated violence, involve violence that occurs when couple conflict escalates. In the case of separation-instigated violence, the conflict is over the separation itself, and it occurs for the first time in that context (Johnston & Campbell, 1993a, 1993b). For many other couples, however, situational couple violence has been a part of their relationship before the separation was initiated. Situational couple violence arises in the context of conflict and is extremely variable in its patterns and causes (Johnson, 2008). For many couples, the violence is mild and rare, often involving only one incident. For others, however, the violence is chronic and/or severe, even life-threatening. Potential causes of such chronic violence include chronic conflict, poor communication, substance abuse, or poor anger management skills, among others. Compared to coercive controlling violence, situational couple violence is more likely to be perpetrated by both men and women and may be mutual (Ansara & Hindin, 2010; Graham-Kevan & Archer, 2003; Johnson, 2006; Johnson et al., 2008; Laroche, 2005).

Understanding these distinctions is important for several reasons. First, differentiating among types of DV explains seemingly contradictory findings regarding the prevalence and nature of DV (e.g., whether DV is perpetrated more often by men or women; Johnson, 2006). Divergent findings result from using different samples that involve different types of DV. Specifically, studies using samples from agencies such as DV shelters, hospitals, and police departments typically involve reports of coercive controlling violence, whereas general community samples typically involve reports of situational couple violence (Ansara & Hindin, 2010; Graham-Kevan & Archer, 2003; Johnson, 2006; Johnson et al., 2008). Thus, although findings from these different types of samples may appear to be contradictory, they actually address different types of DV.

Second, families experiencing different types of DV probably require different parenting plans and interventions (Hardesty & Chung, 2006; Jaffe et al., 2008). Parents who experience situational couple violence may benefit from traditional interventions, such as parent education and anger management classes. Because the violence is conflict-instigated, parents may be responsive to learning more constructive ways to resolve arguments before they escalate. Indeed, evidence suggests that interventions aimed at reducing violence may be successful with situational couple violence because the issue is about conflict management (Eckhardt, Holtzworth-Munroe, Norlander, Sibley, & Cahill, 2008; Lawrence, Ro, Barry, & Bunde, 2006). Traditional interventions may not be appropriate with coercive controlling violence and violent resistance, however, because they ignore the inherent power imbalance between parents. Instead, parenting plans and interventions aimed at preventing post-separation violence and coercive control as well as promoting safety and recovery from DV trauma are more appropriate (Hardesty & Chung, 2006; Jaffe et al., 2003).

Although there is no research that distinguishes among types of DV in a sample of all separating couples requiring judicial intervention, there are a few studies that provide some relevant evidence. In a 4-year longitudinal study of 56 couples, Lawrence and Bradbury (2001) found that those who reported physical violence by either partner had a significantly greater risk of divorce than couples with no violence, and that among couples with DV, the risk was greater with severe versus moderate levels of violence. A more recent study using two waves of data from 2,610 mothers found that mothers' reports of fathers' controlling behaviors were associated with more relationship dissolution (Adkins & Kamp Dush, 2010). Although Johnston and Campbell's (1993b) study of a sample of high-conflict divorces found situational couple violence to be the most common type of DV, there were a significant number of cases of coercive controlling violence. In Crossman and colleagues' (Crossman, Khaw, Hardesty, & Raffaelli, 2010) sample of 50 divorcing mothers who experienced DV, coercive controlling violence was more commonly reported than situational couple violence. These studies suggest that professionals working with separating parents may encounter more coercive controlling violence than one would find in the general population.

To summarize the types of DV:

• Decisions regarding child custody must take into account the major differences among types of DV.

- Coercive controlling violence involves physical violence as one of many tactics used to dominate one's partner. It is perpetrated more often by men against women and on average is more frequent, severe, and injurious. Violent resistance is seen primarily among women and is used to resist coercive controlling violence by male perpetrators. Situational couple violence arises in the context of conflict and is extremely variable in its patterns and causes. It is more likely than coercive controlling violence to be perpetrated by both men and women, and it may be mutual. Separation-instigated violence is a subtype of situational couple violence in which the conflict is over the separation itself and violence occurs for the first time during separation.
- Differentiating among types of DV explains seemingly contradictory research findings regarding the prevalence and nature of DV.
- Families experiencing different types of DV probably require different parenting plans and interventions.

In the discussion to follow, the authors point to any conclusions that differentiate among types of DV when possible. For the most part, however, research relevant to DV and child custody has an implicit focus on coercive controlling violence. Before discussing post-separation issues in more depth, a review on the effects of DV exposure on children is presented. This research provides an important context for understanding the relevance of DV to child custody.

EFFECTS OF DOMESTIC VIOLENCE EXPOSURE ON CHILDREN

Based on data from four large-scale surveys of adults recalling their exposure to violence as children as well as data from teens across school districts in five cities, Carlson (2000) conservatively estimates that from 10% to 20% of U.S. children (including adolescents) are exposed to adult DV each year. Based on recent U.S. Census data, this would indicate that approximately 7 to 14 million U.S. children are exposed to adult DV annually (Edleson et al., 2007). Children's exposure to DV can take many forms; they experience prenatal exposure, are eyewitnesses or overhear the violence, intervene, and experience the aftermath of violence (Holden, 2003). Children are likely to experience more than one type of exposure, and the form and frequency of exposure can vary for different children in the same family and from family to family as well as over time (Wolfe, Crooks, Lee, McIntyre-Smith, & Jaffe, 2003).

To date, there are no child exposure studies that make distinctions among types of DV. Because research has shown that coercive controlling violence is more likely in agency samples and situational couple violence is more likely in general community samples, it is possible to draw tentative conclusions about types of DV and child exposure based on which samples are used in the research study (Johnson, 2008). Of the child exposure studies reviewed in this chapter, half used mixed samples from DV shelters and the general community (Becker & McCloskey, 2002; Graham-Bermann, Howell, Miller, Kwek, & Lilly, 2010; Herrera & McCloskey, 2001; Huth-Bocks, Levendosky, & Semel, 2001; Levendosky, Huth-Bocks, & Semel, 2002; Lichter & McCloskey, 2004; McCloskey & Lichter, 2003; McCloskey & Stuewig,

2001), about one third relied on general community samples (Ireland & Smith, 2009; Levendosky, Huth-Bocks, Semel, & Shapiro, 2002; Moylan et al., 2010; Rigterink, Katz, & Hessler, 2010; Zinzow et al., 2009), and about one fifth relied solely on agency samples, including a DV shelter (Blackburn, 2008), a correctional facility for aggressive and delinquent youths (Moretti, Obsuth, Odgers, & Reebye, 2006), and participants referred for mental health issues pertaining to DV (Smith Stover, Van Horn, Turner, Cooper, & Lieberman, 2003). Only one study using a mixed sample from a DV shelter and the general community measured and reported different outcomes based on sampling (McCloskey & Stuewig, 2001).

Over the past decade, there have been multiple meta-analyses and literature reviews describing the relationship between child exposure to DV and various developmental outcomes (Evans, Davies, & DiLillo, 2008; Holt, Buckley, & Whelan, 2008; Kitzmann, Gaylord, Holt, & Kenny, 2003; Wolfe et al., 2003). Although meta-analyses have consistently shown that DV exposure puts children at high levels of risk for emotional and behavioral problems (Holt et al., 2008), there are also differences in those effects as a function of age and gender of the child. For example, some studies suggest that younger or preschool-aged children are more negatively affected by DV exposure (Levendosky, Huth-Bocks, & Semel, 2002), while two meta-analyses did not find significant differences across developmental stages (Evans et al., 2008; Wolfe et al., 2003). Similarly, younger children may be more vulnerable to violence or threats towards their mother, given their dependency (Gerwitz & Edleson, 2007), whereas older children may be able to escape the violence in their home because they have more resources available to them. The authors' review of the research on DV exposure is organized according to the following domains: emotional and behavioral, cognitive, and social and relational development. Given the unique tasks and competencies that children develop as they progress through life, differences in findings for children at different developmental stages are discussed.

Emotional and Behavioral Development

Research has shown that children who have been exposed to DV display elevated levels of emotional and behavioral problems compared to their non-exposed peers. Preschool-aged children from a general community sample who were exposed to DV had elevated posttraumatic stress disorder (PTSD) symptoms (Levendosky, Huth-Bocks, Semel, & Shapiro, 2002). In another general community sample, young children exposed to DV were less able to regulate their emotions than their non-exposed peers (Rigterink et al., 2010).

Research on older youths exposed to DV has found similar trends. A recent study of a general community sample of adolescents found that those exposed to DV had higher levels of internalizing and externalizing behaviors than non-exposed adolescents (Moylan et al., 2010). Another general community sample study found that exposed adolescents were more likely to report PTSD symptoms and major depressive disorder than non-exposed youths (Zinzow et al., 2009). Levendosky, Huth-Bocks, and Semel (2002) relied on a general community sample and found that exposed adolescents were more likely than non-exposed adolescents to have avoidant attachment. Becker and McCloskey (2002) compared a mixed sample (general community and agency sample) with a non-exposed sample and found that exposed adolescents are more likely to meet the clinical cutoff for attention-deficit/ hyperactive disorder. Another study using the same samples found that exposed adolescents report higher levels of delinquency (Herrera & McCloskey, 2001). Although both general community and shelter samples were included, the authors did not report differences based on the two sampling methods. Finally, a study with general community samples found that adolescents exposed to DV partook in more antisocial behavior and participation in general and violent crime than adolescents not exposed to DV (Ireland & Smith, 2009).

Negative effects on children have been more pronounced when their exposure includes more frequent and severe DV. For example, Jouriles, Norwood, McDonald, and Peters (2001) summarized the literature through 2001, stating that, in general, more severe and frequent DV increases the likelihood of child difficulties. Specifically, in general community and agency samples, exposure to more frequent and severe violence (e.g., punching, choking, and kicking) increased the risk of PTSD symptoms in young children (Levendosky, Huth-Bocks, Semel, & Shapiro, 2002) and aggressive and antisocial behaviors in young children and adolescents (Ireland & Smith, 2009; Smith Stover et al., 2003) when compared to peers exposed to less frequent and severe violence or no violence. The greater likelihood of participation in antisocial and criminal behavior continued into early adulthood for adolescents exposed to more frequent and severe violence, but not for adolescents exposed to less frequent and severe violence (Ireland & Smith, 2009).

Cognitive Development

Based on general community and agency samples, exposed preschool children have significantly poorer verbal ability than non-exposed children (Graham-Bermann et al., 2010; Huth-Bocks, Levendosky, & Semel, 2001). The impact of DV exposure on cognitive outcomes also extends to school-aged children and adolescents. Blackburn (2008) compared an agency sample with a control sample and found that DV exposure had a negative impact on school-aged children's reading phonological awareness, especially children exposed to both physical violence and more severe psychological aggression (i.e., coercive controlling violence). Significantly more children in the physical violence and more severe psychological aggression group (i.e., coercive controlling violence) had more reading difficulties than children in the physical violence and minor to no psychological aggression group (i.e., situational couple violence) and the non-DV group (Blackburn, 2008).

Social and Relational Development

A recent review concluded that DV exposure is associated with lower levels of social competence as well as less positive and less effective interactions with other children (Berman, Hardesty, Lewis-O'Connor, & Humphreys, 2011). Indeed, elevated levels of externalizing or internalizing problems can negatively affect peer relations. For example, children who have elevated levels of externalizing problems may act more aggressively towards their peers, which may lead to rejection (Berman et al., 2011).

School-aged children from a mixed general community and agency sample (e.g., DV shelter) who were exposed to DV were lonelier, reported more conflict with their best friends, and reported more peer problems and conflict than children who did not witness DV (McCloskey & Stuewig, 2001). Children residing in the DV shelter, who were likely exposed to coercive controlling violence, reported more social and friendship problems than children from the general community (McCloskey & Stuewig, 2001).

Studies using agency (Moretti et al., 2006) and general community samples (Ireland & Smith, 2009) have also found an association between exposure to DV and aggression in dating relationships, towards parents, and with peers. Youths exposed to severe and frequent DV during adolescence (which is more likely to be coercive controlling violence) were at an increased risk for severe violent partner interactions during early adulthood when compared to youths exposed to less severe and frequent DV (Ireland & Smith, 2009). They were also more accepting of violence against women than youths from nonviolent homes (Lichter & McCloskey, 2004).

Increased Risk of Direct Child Abuse

The limited number of empirical studies on the dual experience of DV exposure and direct child abuse find more negative outcomes for children who experience both compared to children exposed to only DV, only child abuse, or no violence (Bourassa, 2007; Sousa et al., 2011; Spilsbury et al., 2007; Wolfe et al., 2003). Furthermore, children living in homes with adult DV are at an increased risk for direct physical abuse and other forms of child maltreatment, such as neglect (Appel & Holden, 1998; Edleson, 1999). However, different sampling methods (i.e., general community vs. agency samples) and definitions of child abuse make it difficult to establish concrete rates of the co-occurrence of child abuse and DV exposure (Appel & Holden, 1998; Edleson, 1999; Jouriles, McDonald, Smith Slep, Heyman, & Garrido, 2008). Almost by definition, studies that define child abuse broadly (e.g., pushing, spanking) will yield higher rates of overlap than studies that define child abuse more narrowly (Jouriles et al., 2008).

When child abuse is defined more narrowly, meta-analyses have found the co-occurrence rate of child abuse and DV to range from 18% to 67% (Edleson, 1999; Jouriles et al., 2008). Studies that used DV shelters and other agency samples report a significantly higher co-occurrence rate than studies using general community and general population samples (Jouriles et al., 2008). A meta-analysis conducted by Jouriles et al. associates (2008) revealed that the frequency of DV was significantly related to more frequent physical child abuse, which was more likely to be found in agency-based samples. Thus, these findings suggest that children are at greater risk of child abuse in cases of coercive controlling violence than they are in cases of situational couple violence (Johnson, 2005).

It is important to acknowledge that children are capable of positive outcomes and adaptations even when exposed to the risk factor of DV (Grych, Jouriles, Swank, McDonald, & Norwood, 2000; Hughes & Luke, 1998) Indeed, studies have shown that 26% to 37% of children exposed to DV are asymptomatic, at least in the short term (Grych et al., 2000; Hughes & Luke, 1998; Kitzman et al., 2003). In a sample of children residing in DV shelters, those who were functioning within or above average on measures of adjustment were exposed to lower levels of self-reported DV than their peers who scored below average (Grych et al., 2000). These children also had less fear that their father would do something harmful to their mother or to them and reported greater family problem-solving ability (Grych et al., 2000). Similarly, a study relying on a community sample of 2- to 4-year-olds exposed to DV found that constant exposure to DV predicted the development of internalizing or externalizing problems, but exposure to one-time or intermittent exposure did not (Martinez-Torteya, Bogat, von Eye, & Levendosky, 2009). Based on these findings, it is possible that children who show more positive outcomes and adaptation are those who experienced situational couple violence as opposed to coercive controlling violence.

To summarize the effects of DV exposure on children:

- Exposure to DV has the potential to negatively affect children emotionally, behaviorally, cognitively, and socially.
- Exposure to more severe and frequent DV, and to coercive controlling violence, increases risks of poor adaptation in comparison to situational couple violence or DV that occurs one time or intermittently.

Table 14.1 EMPIRICAL STUDIES ON POST-SEPARATION RELATIONSHIPS

Source	Participants	Procedure
Beeble, Bybee, & Sullivan (2009)	160 mothers from three DV-related agencies with at least one child ages 5–12. Reported experiencing physical abuse in past 4 months.	Mothers were interviewed 6 times over 2 years about their involvement with the abuser, physical and psychological abuse, depression, quality of life, and social support.
Campbell et al. (2003)	220 DV femicide victims identified in 11 cities from police or medical examiner records (cases). Proxy informants were identified for each case and consisted of relatives or friends that were knowledgeable about the victim–perpetrator relationship. 343 abused women (controls) who had been physically assaulted or threatened with a weapon by a current or former partner in past 2 years were randomly sampled in the same cities as the cases.	Proxies and controls were interviewed about risk factors for homicide; demographic and relationship characteristics; type, frequency, and severity of violence; psychological abuse and harassment; substance use; and weapon availability.

- Children living in homes with DV, especially those experiencing coercive controlling violence, are at an elevated risk for direct physical abuse or other forms of neglect.

The studies reviewed above provide ample justification for concerns about DV in child custody, not because of the effects of prior DV alone, but because of the potential risk of ongoing DV exposure and child abuse after separation. Further justification is provided in the sections that follow, which discuss what is known about the effects of DV on post-separation relationship dynamics.

EFFECTS OF DOMESTIC VIOLENCE ON POST-SEPARATION RELATIONSHIPS

Research on post-separation relationships when there is a history of DV is minimal compared to the extensive research on child exposure to DV. The research related to post-separation relationships falls into two categories: effects of DV on former-partner relationship dynamics (including co-parenting and ongoing abuse) and the effects of DV on parenting practices and parent–child relationships. Table 14.1 summarizes the relevant research discussed in this section.

Analysis & Results	Weaknesses	Strengths
Used longitudinal, multilevel modeling to examine impact of physical and psychological abuse on depression over time with social support as a moderator. Mean levels of physical and psychological abuse and average depression scores decreased over time. Social support and average quality of life scores increased over time. Social support mediated, moderated, and had a main effect on well-being. Effects were strongest for mothers who experienced lower levels of abuse.	Overall mean levels of violence were relatively low and may not be generalizable to populations with higher levels of violence. Unclear whether controlled for relevant variables, such as income, employment, and community violence. Does not make distinctions among types of violence.	Used repeated measures over time. Distinguished between high and low levels of violence.
Factor analysis of risk items was used to construct scales measuring partner's controlling and stalking behaviors. Logistic regression was used to estimate the association between hypothesized risk factors and risk of femicide. Risk factors for femicide included: abuser's lack of employment (strongest risk factor), abuser's access to a firearm, use of illicit drugs (not alcohol), highly controlling behaviors and separation after living together, having a child who is not the abuser's living in the home, and previous threats to harm or kill with a weapon.	Reliance on proxies who may not know all of the details surrounding the victim–perpetrator relationship.	Used a case–control design to match femicide victims with abused women. Included contextual factors such as controlling, harassing, and stalking behaviors that reflect the dynamics of coercive control.

(Continued)

Table 14.1 Empirical Studies on Post-separation Relationships (*Continued*)

Source	Participants	Procedure
Campbell & Soeken (1999)	General community sample of 98 women who had experienced at least one act of severe violence, two acts of minor physical aggression, or had been forced into sex by an intimate partner in the past year.	Women were interviewed three times over 3.5 years about the severity of physical and sexual abuse and emotional abuse, risk factors for homicide, and health and stress outcomes.
Fleury, Sullivan, & Bybee (2000)	135 women recruited from a DV shelter program in a medium-sized industrial city. Women were included if they were involved with their partner when they entered the shelter but were no longer involved with the partner 10 weeks after shelter exit.	Women were interviewed six times, including at shelter exit, 10 weeks later, and then every 6 months for the next 2 years. Abuser's behavior was measured, including physical violence, threats, sexual suspicion, alcohol and drug use, previous DV arrests, and proximity to the survivor. Women's behavior was measured, including number of times she contacted the police, number of previous separations, involvement with a new intimate partner, and help-seeking efforts.
Ford-Gilboe, Wuest, & Merritt-Gray (2005)	40 single-parent mothers who had left abusive partners and 11 of their children (children over age 12 were included if mothers consented)	In-depth, open-ended interviews were conducted. Interviews focused on the effects of abuse on family health promotion processes.

Analysis & Results	Weaknesses	Strengths

Used longitudinal predictive correlational analysis.
 	
    Women were in one of three groups: abuse at Time 1 only; abuse at Times 1 and 2; abuse at Times 1, 2, and 3 Used a 3 (pattern) × 3 (time) mixed repeated measures ANOVA to measure change or growth in health and stress outcomes across time.
 	
    Women who reported abuse at all three time points had significantly poorer health outcomes at Time 3 than women who reported abuse at Times 1 or Times 1 and 2. Women who reported abuse at all three time points scored significantly higher on risk factors for homicide.
	Longitudinal methods highlight various processes rather than treating abuse as a one-time event.
	
	    Assessed abuse and health outcomes at three time points, which allowed analyses to focus on the change that occurs when abuse stops, but also highlights the deleterious effects of abuse, especially long-term continuous abuse.
	
	    Contributes to literature by describing different depression trajectories based on abuse experiences and ethnicity.
		Limitations in the use of ANOVA created two problems in their sampling. First, they cannot account for missing data at any of the three time points, so they had to exclude participants who did not participate at all three time points.
		
		    Second, the participants had to have equal spacing between time points in order to include their data.

Event history analysis was used to examine factors such as re-involvement with the abusive partner.
 	
    A logistic regression model was used to create separate cases for each time that a specific woman was known to be at risk for violence by the ex-partner.
 	
    One in three women (36%) was assaulted by an ex-partner prior to either reuniting or the end of the study, and the majority (72%) of assaults was severe. The majority of initial assaults occurred soon after the end of the relationship. Factors including the length of relationship prior to shelter stay, frequency of threats against women since the prior interview, and sexual suspicion were related to an increased risk of violence at the subsequent time point.
 	
    The majority of women who were assaulted sought both informal and formal help.
	Results may not be generalizable beyond shelter samples.	Uses longitudinal data to identify specific factors that put women at risk for assault after they leave a shelter and separate from their abusive partner.

Used grounded theory methods, starting with line-by-line coding and constant comparative analysis and then moving to creating categories and descriptive theoretical coding. Member checking occurred by discussing the categories and theoretical findings with participants.
 	
    Most women (60%) reported multiple forms of abuse (e.g., physical and emotional). The majority of children (85%) witnessed violence; there were six cases of direct physical or sexual child abuse. The majority of women (58%) reported current harassment from their abusive former partners.
 	
    "Strengthening the capacity to limit intrusion" emerged as the core process of family health promotion after leaving an abusive partner.
	Does not differentiate among types of DV or consider differences based on frequency or severity of DV.	Rigorous and detailed description of grounded theory methods used.
		
		    Used a strength-based approach to analyze the experiences of mothers and their children.

Table 14.1 EMPIRICAL STUDIES ON POST-SEPARATION RELATIONSHIPS   (*Continued*)

Source	Participants	Procedure
Hardesty & Ganong (2006)	19 mothers who left abusive husbands were recruited from a court-mandated education program for all divorcing parents. Mothers were eligible for inclusion if they reported that their former husband had physically hurt them, or threatened or attempted to physically hurt them, more than once before or after separation. All women in the sample reported abuse that had the potential to cause injury.	In-depth semi-structured interviews were conducted using broad questions about violence, custody, and co-parenting as well as factors related to their divorce and family structure.
Hardesty, Khaw, Chung, & Martin (2008)	25 divorced mothers who experienced at least 2 incidents of violence by their former husband during marriage	In-depth, semi-structured interviewers were conducted with questions focused on IPV, fathers' contact and involvement with children, women's relationships with former partners, and parent–child relationships
Hilton (1992)	20 mothers who had separated from an abusive partner. Participants were from agency samples (e.g., DV shelters and nonresidential services for women).	Semi-structured interviews that focused on violent incidents with their former partner and the conflicts preceding the violence. Questions pertaining to their children were also asked, including whether the child witnessed the

Analysis & Results	Weaknesses	Strengths
Grounded theory methods of analysis were used, including open coding and constant comparative analysis, axial coding, and selective coding. Analysis moved from descriptive to theoretical coding. Mothers reported one of three patterns of marital abuse: chronic physical abuse with coercive control ($n = 12$), episodic physical abuse with coercive control ($n = 3$), and episodic physical abuse without coercive control ($n = 4$). Mothers' custody decisions were influenced by a complex combination of fears (e.g., child-related, legal system), pragmatic concerns, and family ideology. All mothers who experienced coercive controlling violence in marriage were actively co-parenting with their former husbands and reported ongoing issues with abuse and coercive control.	Reliance on self-report, retrospective accounts. Reliance on mothers' reports of co-parenting relationships.	Differentiates between coercive controlling and situational couple violence. Addresses factors that make it more difficult for mothers to co-parent with their abusive former husbands despite the desire for their children to maintain contact with their fathers.
Grounded theory methods of analysis were used, including open coding and constant comparative analysis, axial coding, and selective coding. Analysis moved from descriptive to theoretical coding. "Differentiation of parental/spousal and parental roles" emerged as the core variable. Three distinct patterns emerged: poorly differentiated, well differentiated, and absent former husbands. Poorly differentiated former husbands had a history of coercive controlling violence and continued to exert control over their partners after separation. The majority of well-differentiated former husbands had a history of situational couple violence and was able to work out effective co-parenting relationships with mothers. Absent former husbands were not distinguished by type of DV.	Reliance on self-report retrospective accounts. Reliance on mothers' reports of co-parenting relationships.	Differentiates between coercive controlling and situational couple violence.
For 45% of mothers, children were often the focus of the conflict preceding violence. 70% of mothers reported that their children witnessed the violence or its after-effects, and 55% reported that their children were direct witnesses.	Reliance on only maternal retrospective reports of children's exposure. Reliance on shelter population limits generalizability. No discussion of what constituted physical or	Contributes to the literature by describing the context of child-focused conflicts that precipitated violent acts. Indicates the many ways in which children are either part of violent incidents or

(Continued)

Table 14.1 Empirical Studies on Post-separation Relationships   (*Continued*)

Source	Participants	Procedure
		violence, what the child said or did at that time or later, and whether the former partner was violent towards the children. Mothers were also asked about their beliefs regarding intergenerational transmission of violence and the role that her children played in her decision to leave and since leaving.
Holden & Ritchie (1991)	37 battered mothers recruited from a DV shelter and 37 comparison mothers recruited from community advertisements as well as their children aged 2–8 years old	Four methods were used over the course of two sessions: an interview, three questionnaires, a mother–child observation, and computer-presented social situations, which used contextualized vignettes. Instruments included Conflict Tactics Scales, Child Behavior Checklist, and the Temperament Assessment Battery for Children. The observation entailed a structured block play task in which visual and verbal observations were made based on the mother's teaching behaviors and quality of interaction. The computer- presented social situations vignettes were simulated as a day in the life of the family with commonly occurring family situations or childrearing problems.
Levendosky& Graham-Bermann (1998)	121 mothers and their children aged 7–12 ($n = 60$ shelter residents; $n = 61$ non-shelter residents). Sample was primarily low income.	Mothers completed questionnaires assessing children's adjustment (Child Behavior Checklist), parenting stress (Parenting Stress Index), physical violence (Conflict Tactics Scales), and psychological abuse (Violence Against Women Scales)

Analysis & Results	Weaknesses	Strengths
Children played an important role in mothers' decision to stay or leave. One third stayed in the relationship for the children; 55% left out of concern for their children. 45% of mothers were concerned about intergenerational transmission of violence, and many were taking active steps to prevent it.	emotional abuse for inclusion in the study. Type, severity, and frequency of violence and exposure were not reported.	are catalysts for women's eventual exit from the relationship.
Significant differences between the fathers of the two groups. Specifically, abusive fathers were more irritable and less involved. Levels of stress and inconsistency in parenting were the only two significant differences between the groups of mothers. Children from violent homes had poorer outcomes than comparison children. Maternal stress and paternal irritability were significant predictors of behavioral problems in the battered women group.	Different locations for completing the study (for the battered mothers vs. comparison mothers) could contribute to different results. Does not differentiate among types of DV.	Used a variety of methods to test hypotheses. Although there are some methodological problems, the use of a comparison group helps to determine parenting differences between abused and non-abused mothers.
Hierarchical multiple regressions were performed separately to predict parent domain stress and child domain stress. These regressions were also used to predict child behavioral symptoms, with income, psychological and physical abuse, and parenting stress as independent variables. Psychological and physical DV were associated with higher levels of parenting stress, but parenting stress did not differ significantly between the two groups. Parenting stress had a negative effect on children's adjustment, independent of DV. Parenting stress served as a unique vulnerability factor for internalizing and externalizing behaviors. Psychological abuse was a stronger predictor of children's adjustment than physical abuse.	Reliance on mother reports only. Sample was primarily low income. Results may not be generalizable to other income groups.	Contributes to a more thorough understanding of how DV affects children by measuring direct and indirect pathways

(Continued)

Table 14.1 Empirical Studies on Post-separation Relationships *(Continued)*

Source	Participants	Procedure
Levendosky & Graham-Bermann (2000)	95 mother–child dyads from predominately low-income communities were recruited from local communities as well as DV shelters and community support groups. Children were 7–12 years old.	Participants completed questionnaires and participated in a 10-minute videotaped interaction task. Questionnaires included measures of income, negative life events (Life Stress Scale), social support (Social Support Quality of Life scale), physical abuse (Conflict Tactics Scales), psychological abuse (Violence Against Women Scales), depression (Beck Depression Inventory), PTSD (Post-Traumatic Stress Scale for Family Violence), and children's emotional and behavioral problems (Child Behavior Checklist). Observations followed the family interaction coding manual in which the dyad was asked to choose one issue about which they most disagree and to spend 10 minutes trying to resolve the disagreement.
Levendosky & Graham-Bermann (2001)	121 mother–child dyads recruited from the general community and from DV shelters. Children were 7–12 years old. Sample was predominately low income and included a wide range of abuse experiences. Mothers from DV shelters reported significantly more psychological and physical abuse than the non-sheltered mothers.	Family violence, including domestic violence, child abuse perpetrated by the mother, and maternal history of child abuse were assessed. Also, they assessed negative maternal psychological functioning, marital satisfaction, negative life events, quantity and quality of social support, social isolation, parenting style, and children's adjustment.
Levendosky, Leahy, Bogat, Davidson, & von Eye (2006)	203 pregnant women were recruited from community fliers and from various community agencies, including women's health clinics and social service programs. All women experienced either threats of physical violence, physical violence, sexual violence, or a combination of the three.	Women were interviewed at two time points. At Time 1 and 2, the Severity of Violence Against Women Scale was administered. At Time 2, mother–infant dyads were observed for maternal parenting during a 10- minute free-play. The Norbeck Social Support Scale, Infant Toddler Social and Emotional Assessment, Posttraumatic Stress Scale for Family Violence, Brief Symptom Inventory, Beck Depression Inventory, and the Rosenberg Self-Esteem Scale were administered at Time 2.

Analysis & Results	Weaknesses	Strengths
Hierarchical multiple regression analyses were used to examine the effects of ecological factors on maternal parenting styles and children's observed behaviors. DV significantly predicted parenting warmth but not parenting authority-control over other systemic and individual factors. Psychological abuse of mothers predicted children's antisocial behavior. Psychological and physical abuse were both highly related to observed maternal warmth. In general, psychological abuse had a more significant negative influence on parenting. Physical abuse of mothers was not related to children's observed behaviors.	Developmental interpretations are not possible due to the cross-sectional nature of the study. Findings may not be generalizable to broader populations given that the sample is from high-risk (violent and low-income) communities.	Measured various types of DV in order to make distinctions and more accurate assessments regarding child-related outcomes. Highlights the negative indirect effect of DV on children through its effect on maternal parenting.
Structural equation modeling was used. Effect of DV on parenting was mediated by the negative effects of DV on mothers' psychological functioning and marital satisfaction. Lack of social support, negative life events, and maternal history of child abuse were related to mothers' psychological functioning. In turn, psychological functioning was related to poorer parenting.	Reliance on mother reports only. The parenting style scale may not adequately assess the experiences of mothers exposed to trauma. No analysis of fathering and its influence on children's adjustment. No analysis of variations in outcomes according to the continuum of DV referenced in the methods, which is problematic given the wide range of DV experiences.	Addresses a variety of ecological factors that contribute to maternal and child adjustment.
Descriptive statistics and models of mediation were used to analyze the latent variables and indicators. Experiencing DV at Time 1 only was not related to maternal parenting, but experiencing DV at Time 2 (current DV) was negatively related to parenting. Past (Time 1) and current (Time 2) DV were related to maternal mental health. At both time points, experiencing more DV was negatively associated with mental health. Social support was directly and positively related to mental health. DV reported at Time 1 was directly related to infants' externalizing behaviors.	Reliance on mother reports only. Validation of the model was not possible given the small sample tested. No differentiation among types of violence, severity, or frequency of violence. No analysis distinguishing between experiencing threats versus actual violence.	Tested experiences of DV before and after childbirth. Used multiple assessments of maternal parenting. Analyzed both direct and indirect effects on infant behavior.

(Continued)

Table 14.1 Empirical Studies on Post-separation Relationships   *(Continued)*

Source	Participants	Procedure
Levendosky, Lynch, & Graham-Bermann (2000)	95 mothers recruited from community locations (*n* = 61) and DV shelters (*n* = 34). Mothers reported high levels of frequent and severe DV. Sample was predominately low income.	The Conflict Tactics Scales and the Violence Against Women Scales were used to assess physical and psychological violence. Mothers were also asked about threats of violence and verbal abuse. Open-ended questions were asked about how DV had affected their parenting, if there were times when it is was more difficult to parent and why, and what kind of parent they would be if they did not have a violent partner.
Margolin, Gordis, Medina, & Oliver, (2003)	Two different samples were recruited from the community (e.g., church bulletins, newspapers, parenting magazines). The first sample (two-parent sample) consisted of 181 families, including both biological parents. The second sample (mother-only sample) consisted of 65 mother–child dyads.	The mother-only sample took part in a 2-hour meeting in a research lab, and the two-parent sample took part in a 4-hour research lab session and 6 weeks of daily data collection. Family-of-origin aggression was asked of both samples, but the questions slightly differed. For the two-parent sample, both parents were asked if they were physically abused as a child and how often physical abuse occurred between their parents. The mother-only sample was asked how often they were hit or slapped during their childhood and how often their parents hit or slapped each other. All parents completed questionnaires assessing husband-to-wife aggression, parent's potential for child abuse, parental relationships, and interactions with the child. Children completed a parent–child relationship questionnaire in the two-parent study and a perception of parenting scale in the mother-only sample.

Analysis & Results	Weaknesses	Strengths
Narratives were coded by four trained coders. Similar responses were grouped into categories for each question. The majority of mothers believed that DV affected their parenting and that they would be different parents if they did not have a violent partner. Mothers reported both negative and positive influences of DV on their parenting (e.g., positive in that they sought resources to respond to DV on behalf of their children). Mothers' narratives reflected awareness and concern over how children were affected by DV.	Interviews were short in duration and lacked depth. Lacks a thorough description of the methods of analysis. No differentiation based on severity and frequency of DV. Cross-sectional design limits ability to compare mothers currently in a relationship to those who have left.	Sample was recruited from diverse locations. Open-ended questions provided a more in-depth look at mothers' perceptions of parenting and how they believe DV influences their parenting and affects their children.
Physical aggression was measured as both continuous and categorical variables. Logistic regressions were used when treating physical aggression as a categorical variable in order to predict the likelihood of various forms of family violence when physical aggression was present or absent. Correlations were used when physical aggression was treated as a continuous variable. ANOVAs were conducted to compare parenting in mothers and fathers when they experienced various amounts of family aggression risk variables. Mother and father reports suggest that husband-to-wife aggression and child abuse are potentially positively correlated with higher levels of controlling, coercive forms of discipline and negatively correlated with various aspects of positive parenting. Fathers who experienced family-of-origin aggression were more likely to be aggressive towards their wives than fathers who did not. Husband-to-wife aggression was positively associated with child abuse potential in both mothers and fathers.	The two samples were asked different questions regarding violence in their family of origin. No distinctions among types of violence or severity and frequency of violence. Generalizability is limited to similar community samples in which mostly minor acts of violence are reported.	Examined multiple types of family aggression and histories of family aggression in the parents' family of origin. Highlights the importance of studying husband-to-wife aggression in the context of other forms of family aggression, such as child abuse.

(Continued)

Table 14.1 Empirical Studies on Post-separation Relationships   (*Continued*)

Source	Participants	Procedure
Wuest, Ford-Gilboe, Merritt-Gray, & Berman (2003)	40 single-parent families with a history of woman abuse. Recruited using community advertisements. Mothers and children over the age of 12 were interviewed.	In-depth, open-ended interviews were conducted.

Former-Partner Relationship Dynamics

Studies indicate that parents involved in high-conflict custody disputes are unlikely to be able to develop cooperative parenting agreements without intensive interventions. High levels of conflict have been found to persist among these parents for 2 to 3 years, after which parents evolve into disengaged or parallel parenting relationships (Johnston, 1995). More frequent contact with one another after separation due to joint custody or visitation (vs. less contact with sole custody options) is associated with more physical violence, especially at visitation exchanges (Johnston, 1995). However, this research includes violent and nonviolent high-conflict parents. Thus, it is not clear how those with violence might be unique, and of course this research does not distinguish among types of DV.

In two more recent qualitative studies, Hardesty and Ganong (2006) and Hardesty and associates (2008) focused on mothers with a history of DV and made distinctions among types. They found that mothers who experienced coercive controlling violence in marriage reported violence and coercive control after separation that interfered with their ability to develop safe and cooperative co-parenting relationships. In contrast, mothers who experienced situational couple violence reported that either their former husbands did not remain involved with the children or that they were eventually able to develop cooperative relationships. The primary problem appeared to be one of role differentiation. Abusers who were controlling were less able to separate their spousal/partner and parental roles in order to continue

Analysis & Results	Weaknesses	Strengths
Used grounded theory methods, starting with line-by-line coding and constant comparative analysis and then moving to creating categories and descriptive theoretical coding. Member checking occurred by discussing the categories and theoretical findings with participants. "Intrusion" was identified as central to families' experiences after separation. Intrusion included continued harassment and violence (e.g., disrupting family routines, purposely violating family expectations, withholding child support). When intrusion was high, mothers had to focus on day-to-day struggles to avoid intrusion instead of planning for families' overall well-being. Mothers' ability to manage and limit intrusion was essential for long-term health and security of mothers and children.	No distinctions among types of violence or severity or frequency of violence.	Provides practical implications for policymakers and service providers working to assist single-parent families after leaving an abusive husband/father. Provides detailed description of qualitative methods. Documents how controlling behaviors may shift from violence in the relationship to intrusion after separation in the form of harassment.

relationships with their children that were kept separate from their motive to control their former partners. These studies highlight the significance of coercive control in shaping post-separation co-parenting dynamics. As with high-conflict divorces, Hardesty and colleagues (2008) found that former partners who had experienced coercive controlling violence (i.e., physical violence in the context of other coercive controlling tactics, such as monitoring activities and isolating one's partner) when they were together evolved over time into disengaged or parallel relationships in which they each maintained individual relationships with their children but had minimal to no contact or communication with each other.

Although conflict and violence both may dissipate over time after separation, the period immediately following separation appears to be particularly risky for abused women. Research clearly indicates that violence continues for some women even after they leave and that separation itself is a risk factor for physical and sexual violence (DeKeseredy, Rogness, & Schwartz, 2004; Fleury, Sullivan, & Bybee, 2000), including homicide (Campbell et al., 2003). For the purposes of this discussion, the most important issue is risk of further violence among those who experienced violence while they were together. In a follow-up interview of 24 women 4 to 6 months after their stay in a shelter, Giles-Sims (1983) found that 44% of those women who had not returned to their abuser had experienced violence at least once subsequent to leaving the shelter. Based on a shelter sample of 135 women who had left their batterer, Fleury et al. (2000) reported that 36% had been assaulted by their ex-partner during a 2-year period. The 1999 Canadian General

Social Survey (GSS) data show that, among women with a former marital or common-law partner who had been violent during the relationship, 39% reported experiencing violence by their ex-partner after separation (Hotton, 2001). Although all of these studies involve samples in which most of the violence would have been coercive controlling violence (see Ansara & Hindin, 2010; Graham-Kevan & Archer, 2003; Johnson, 2006; Johnson et al., 2008), none of them make distinctions among types of violence.

Hardesty and colleagues (2006, 2008) made distinctions between coercive controlling violence and situational couple violence and have shown that the likelihood of post-separation violence and control is greater for cases of coercive controlling violence than situational couple violence. In a sample of 19 divorced mothers who completed a parent education class required of all divorcing parents, 13 of the 15 mothers who reported coercive controlling violence during marriage reported some type of abuse after separation (Hardesty & Ganong, 2006). Abuse was defined broadly to include threats to physically harm, threats to kill, attempted sexual assault, physical violence, and stalking. Four mothers who reported situational couple violence did not report any type of abuse after separation. Likewise, in a sample of 25 divorced mothers recruited primarily through community fliers, 11 of the 17 mothers who experienced coercive controlling violence during marriage reported controlling intrusion after separation, which included threats, physical violence, and use of children and the courts to reassert control (Hardesty et al., 2008).

In the initial period following separation, mothers may believe that the violence will end. In Hardesty and Ganong (2006), mothers reported hopes of being able to co-parent safely once their relationships ended. They wanted their children to maintain relationships with their fathers. Their idealized notions shifted over time if the violence and harassment continued, which was more likely in cases of coercive controlling violence than situational couple violence. Mothers who experienced coercive controlling violence found themselves less focused on facilitating father–child contact over time and more focused on preventing violence and protecting their children from exposure (Hardesty & Ganong, 2006; Hardesty et al., 2008). To do so, they set increasingly rigid boundaries between themselves and their former partners, which for some meant obtaining protection from abuse orders or seeking changes to custody agreements. Mothers who experienced situational couple violence were better able to informally negotiate safe co-parenting relationships with their former husbands.

Parenting Practices and Parent–Child Relationships

Research on the effects of DV on parenting practices has focused primarily on how being abused affects mothers' parenting and little on the parenting practices of abusive fathers. In a review of the literature, Edleson, Mbilinyi, and Shetty (2003) found that abused mothers reported greater levels of stress than non-abused mothers. However, heightened stress does not necessarily translate to parenting deficits (Holden, Stein, Ritchie, Harris, & Jouriles, 1998; Levendosky & Graham-Bermann, 1998). Indeed, Van Horn and Lieberman's (2002) review determined that battered and non-battered mothers do not differ in beliefs about parenting, self-reported parenting behaviors, or observed parent–child interactions.

Battered and non-battered mothers were also similar in the extent to which they provided structure, warmth, emotional support, and positive reinforcement. Research has indicated that abused mothers alter their parenting behaviors when in the presence of their abusers, perhaps to avoid angering the abuser (Holden et al., 1998). Other studies indicate that abused mothers are more likely than non-abused mothers to use aggression against their children, but less likely to do so once they are safe (Edleson et al., 2003). Thus, when assessing abused mothers' parenting, it is important to consider ways in which the abusers' presence may interfere with mothers' parenting practices (Levendosky, Lynch, & Graham-Bermann, 2000).

Furthermore, when under extreme levels of stress, abused mothers have some-times been found to compensate by being more nurturing and protective of their children (Levendosky et al., 2000). The protective strategies that abused mothers use when managing DV are not always recognized when evaluating custody decisions (Edleson et al., 2003). Yet, research indicates that abused mothers make decisions to stay or leave violent relationships based on their perceptions of their children's needs. For example, mothers may stay to protect the economic security of their children or to prevent the escalation of violence than can follow separation. They make decisions to leave when violence spreads to the children or when they see the effects of expo-sure on their children (Hardesty & Ganong, 2006; Hilton, 1992).

Nonetheless, mothers may experience depression or PTSD symptoms as a result of DV, and mental health problems have been shown to negatively influence mothers' parenting practices. For example, depressed mothers may be less available or involved with their children (Levendosky & Graham-Bermann, 2000, 2001; Margolin, Gordis, Medina, & Oliver, 2003). Levendosky and Graham-Bermann (2001) found that DV negatively affected mothers' psychological functioning (e.g., changes in affect or mood) and that lower psychological functioning had both direct and indirect (through its effect on parenting) influences on child adjustment. Levendosky, Leahy, Bogat, Davidson, and von Eye (2006) found that changes in DV produced changes in both mothers' mental health and parenting, which then influenced child functioning.

Furthermore, Levendosky and colleagues (2006) found that while current DV negatively affected parenting, past DV did not. They posit that current parent–child interactions may offer new opportunities for positive parenting that are not nega-tively affected by past DV. This suggests that the negative effects of DV may dissipate once mothers are safe. Thus, when evaluating mothers' mental health, professionals should be aware of what may be reasonable responses in the context of DV (e.g., fear, paranoia, depression) that have the potential for improvement when mother and child are safe. Indeed, longitudinal research indicates that mental health improves after women leave, but only for those for whom the violence ends (Campbell & Soeken, 1999). Thus, protecting mothers from ongoing violence is critical. Also, because social and practical support has been shown to moderate the effects of DV (Beeble, Bybee, & Sullivan, 2009; Levendosky & Graham-Bermann, 2001; Levendosky et al., 2006), services targeted at providing support after separation may be helpful for mitigating lasting effects of DV on parenting. Increasing social support may be particularly important in cases of coercive controlling violence, where abusers often isolate their partners (Levendosky & Graham-Bermann, 2001); however, Beeble and colleagues (2009) found that the buffering effect of social support was most effective at lower levels of violence. Thus, when violence is severe, as is more often the case with coercive controlling violence, comprehensive services, in addition to social support, are likely needed.

Studies by Ford-Gilboe and colleagues have addressed health promotion for single mothers and their children after leaving violent and controlling partners and found that, although violence and its consequences for women's health may intensify after separation, both the violence and women's health do improve over time (Ford-Gilboe, Varcoe, Wuest, & Merritt-Gray, 2011). Based on qualitative interviews with abused mothers who had separated, they identified "intrusion" as central to women's post-separation experiences (Ford-Gilboe, Wuest, & Merritt-Gray, 2005; Wuest, Ford-Gilboe, Merritt-Gray, & Berman, 2003). High levels of unwanted interference from continued harassment and violence, cumulative physical and mental health consequences of the violence, and the costs of getting help interfered with mothers' efforts to recover from the trauma of violence, restructure their families, and promote their own and their children's health. Instead of focusing their energy on their family's future well-being, mothers were forced to manage the day-to-day stress of ongoing intrusion. Thus, limiting intrusion and increasing mothers' capacity to manage intrusion are essential for the long-term health and security of mothers and their children in the aftermath of DV (Ford-Gilboe et al., 2005; Wuest et al., 2003).

Importantly, none of this research considers how abusive fathers' parenting behaviors contribute to children's outcomes; the focus has been on mothers only. In fact, there is little empirical work on abusers as fathers and how their parenting affects children. What little is known is based on clinical evidence and abused mothers' reports. This evidence indicates that abusers parent differently than non-abusers. Controlling abusers in particular demonstrate a lack of warmth, coercive tactics, and rejection of their children as well as inconsistent parenting (e.g., switching from permissive to rigid approaches; Jaffe et al., 2008). Based on clinical work, Bancroft and Silverman (2002) report that abusive fathers are more controlling and authoritarian, less consistent, and more manipulative with their children than non-abusive fathers. Abused mothers, compared to non-abused mothers, report that fathers are less involved, use less positive parenting practices, and are more likely to be angry with their children (Holden & Ritchie, 1991; Holden et al., 1998). Emotional abuse of children (e.g., name calling) is also common among controlling abusers (Jaffe et al., 2008). Finally, abusers are poor role models. Children learn from observing DV that violence is acceptable. Whether they observe DV that is used to control one's partner or to resolve specific conflicts, children may learn to expect this behavior as a normal part of intimate and family relationships (Jaffe et al., 2008).

To summarize the effects of DV on post-separation relationships:

- Qualitative research indicates that coercive controlling violence in marriage is related to violence and coercive control after separation, which interferes with the development of safe and cooperative co-parenting relationships. The period immediately following separation is particularly risky for abused women, especially those who have experienced coercive controlling violence.

- DV can create high levels of stress for mothers, but this stress does not necessarily result in diminished parenting. Although abused mothers may experience depression and PTSD, which can have a negative impact on parenting, women's health and children's health do improve once protected from DV.
- Clinical evidence and mothers' reports indicate that abusers, especially those who use coercive controlling violence, exhibit poor parenting practices compared to non-abusers.

DIFFERENT TYPES OF DOMESTIC VIOLENCE, DIFFERENT PARENTING PLANS

For parenting plans to promote secure and healthy adjustment, they must address the different needs of families who experience different types of DV. Jaffe and his colleagues (2008) propose an empirically based approach to guide professionals toward the appropriate next steps for developing parenting plans that match a family's individual needs. Specifically, their approach involves screening for risk based on potency, pattern, and primary perpetrator of the DV. *Potency* refers to the degree of severity, danger, and potential risk of serious injury or death. *Pattern* refers to whether there is a history of coercive control or domination over time in addition to the violence, or if the violence was an isolated incident. *Primary perpetrator* refers to whether there is a primary aggressor or whether both parents initiate violence absent a context of control. Jaffe and colleagues (2008) provide measures of all three of these factors, which could be used to determine which type of DV the couple has been experiencing.

The specific pattern or type of DV provides insight into the degree of stress or trauma experienced by the abuse victim and children, suggests the potential for ongoing violence and control after separation, and has implications for post-relationship custody arrangements. In cases of coercive controlling violence, for example, custody agreements should probably facilitate disengaged or parallel parenting with minimal contact and shared decision-making rather than cooperative co-parenting arrangements (Jaffe et al., 2008). Parenting plans probably also should include comprehensive support services for the victim (e.g., parenting support to improve skills and abilities to support children's recovery), interventions for the abuser (e.g., batterer's treatment, substance abuse treatment), specific conditions to be met for the abuser to have contact with children (e.g., supervision of contact, completion of treatment, desistence of violence), and consequences for violating agreements (e.g., rules for returning to court). Safety should be the primary concern in these cases. Continued monitoring of the abuser's contact with children and the abuser's willingness to be held accountable are central to ensuring safety (Edleson et al., 2003).

In cases of situational couple violence, parenting plans might include interventions to help both parents learn more effective ways to resolve conflict. These parenting plans can assist in equalizing power between parents, setting enforceable boundaries, and minimizing the potential for conflict to escalate to violence. In cases of separation-instigated violence, attention to safety in the immediate aftermath of separation is necessary but will become less important as strong emotions subside.

CONCLUSION

For most separating families, the best interests of children can be met by establishing cooperative co-parenting arrangements. For families with DV, however, this goal may not be realistic. Rather than apply a one-size-fits-all approach to families with DV, this chapter reviews research that demonstrates the importance of applying a differentiated approach to assessing individual families with DV and creating tailored parenting plans that match their needs.

GUIDELINES: CONSIDERATIONS AND CAUTIONS

- There are three major types of DV. *Coercive controlling violence* involves physical violence as only one of many coercive tactics that abusers use to dominate their partners. *Violent resistance* is violence enacted in resistance to coercive controlling violence. *Situational couple violence* arises in the context of conflict and is extremely variable in its patterns and causes. *Separation-instigated violence* is a subtype of situational couple violence that arises in response to the separation itself and occurs for the first time in that context. Differentiating among types of DV explains seemingly contradictory findings in the literature regarding the prevalence and nature of DV.
- Exposure to DV has a myriad of negative effects on children, including emotional, behavioral, cognitive, social, and relationship effects as well as increased risk of direct child abuse.
- DV is relevant to child custody not only because of effects of prior DV, but also because of the risk of ongoing exposure to violence and the impact on parenting practices after separation.
- To promote safety and healthy adjustment after separation, differential parenting plans are needed to address the different needs of families who experience different types of DV.

REFERENCES

Adamsons, K., & Pasley, K. (2006). Coparenting following divorce and relationship dissolution. In M. A. Fine & J. H. Harvey (Eds.), *Handbook of divorce and relationship dissolution* (pp. 241–261). Mahway, NJ: Erlbaum.

Adkins, K. S., & Kamp Dush, C. M. (2010). The mental health of mothers in and after violence and controlling unions. *Social Science Research, 39*(6), 925–937. doi:10.1016/j.ssresearch.2010.06.013

Amato, P. (2000). The consequences of divorce for adults and children. *Journal of Marriage and the Family, 62,* 1269–1288. doi: 10.1111/j.1741-3737.2000.01269.x

Amato, P. R. (2010). Research on divorce: Continuing trends and new developments. *Journal of Marriage and Family, 72*(3), 650–666. doi:10.1111/j.1741-3737.2010.00723.x

Ansara, D. L., & Hindin, M. J. (2010). Exploring gender differences in the patterns of intimate partner violence in Canada: A latent class approach. *Journal of Epidemiology and Community Health, 64,* 849–854.

Appel, A. E., & Holden, G. W. (1998). The co-occurrence of spouse and physical child abuse: A review and appraisal. *Journal of Family Psychology, 12,* 578–599. doi:10.1037/0893–3200.12.4.578

Bancroft, L., & Silverman, J. G. (2002). *The batterer as parent: Addressing the impact of domestic violence on family dynamics.* Thousand Oaks, CA: Sage.

Becker, K., & McCloskey, L. (2002) Attention and conduct problems in children exposed to family violence. *American Journal of Orthopsychiatry, 72,* 83–91. doi:10.1037/0002–9432.72.1.83

Beeble, M. L., Bybee, D., & Sullivan, C. M. (2009). Main, mediating and moderating effects of social support on the well-being of survivors of intimate partner violence across two years. *Journal of Consulting and Clinical Psychology, 77*(4), 718–729. doi:10.1037/a0016140

Berman, H., Hardesty, J. L., Lewis-O'Connor, A., & Humphreys, J. (2011). Childhood exposure to intimate partner violence. In J. Humphreys & J. C. Campbell (Eds.), *Family violence and nursing practice* (2nd ed., pp. 279–317). New York: Springer.

Blackburn, J. F. (2008). Reading and phonological awareness skills in children exposed to domestic violence. *Journal of Aggression, Maltreatment, & Trauma, 17*(4), 415–438. doi:10.1080/10926770802463396

Bourassa, C. (2007). Co-occurrence of interparental violence and child physical abuse and its effect on the adolescents' behavior. *Journal of Family Violence, 22,* 691–701. doi:10.1007/s10896–007–9117–8

Campbell, J. C., & Soeken, K. L. (1999). Women's responses to battering over time: An analysis of change. *Journal of Interpersonal Violence, 14,* 21–40. doi:10.1177/088626099014001002

Campbell, J. C., Webster, D., Koziol-McLain, J., Block, C., Campbell, D., Curry, M. A., . . . & Laughon, K. (2003) Risk factors for femicide in abusive relationships: Results from a multisite case control study. *American Journal of Public Health, 93*(7), 1089–1097. doi:10.2105/AJPH.93.7.1089

Carlson, B. E. (2000). Children exposed to intimate partner violence: Research findings and implications for intervention. *Trauma, Violence, & Abuse, 1*(4), 321–342–587. doi: 1 0.1177/1524838000001004002

Centers for Disease Control and Prevention (CDC). (2010). *Intimate partner violence: Definitions.* Retrieved from http://www.cdc.gov/ViolencePrevention/intimatepartnerviolence/definitions.html

Crossman, K., Khaw, L., Hardesty, J. L., & Raffaelli, M. (2010, November). *Coparenting quality after separation: The role of intimate terrorism and boundary ambiguity.* Paper presented at the annual conference of the National Council on Family Relations, Minneapolis, MN.

DeKeseredy, W. S., Rogness, M., & Schwartz, M. D. (2004). Separation/divorce sexual assault: The current state of social scientific knowledge. *Aggression and Violent Behavior, 9,* 675–691. doi:10.1016/j.avb.2003.08.004

Dragiewicz, M. (2010). Gender bias in the courts: Implications for battered mothers and their children. In M. T. Hannah & B. Goldstein (Eds.), *Domestic violence, abuse, and child custody: Legal strategies and policy issues* (pp. 1–19). Kingston, NJ: Civic Research Institute.

Eckhardt, C. I., Holtzworth-Munroe, A., Norlander, B., Sibley, A., & Cahill, M. (2008). Readiness to change, partner violence subtypes, and treatment outcomes among men in treatment for partner assault. *Violence and Victims, 23*(4), 446–477. doi:10.1891/0886–6708.23.4.446

Edleson, J. L. (1999). Children's witnessing of adult domestic violence. *Journal of Interpersonal Violence, 14*(8), 839–870. doi:10.1177/088626099014008004

Edleson, J. L., Ellerton, A. L., Seagren, S. L., Kirchberg, S. O., Schmidt, S. O., & Ambrose, A. T. (2007). Assessing child exposure to domestic violence. *Children and Youth Services Review, 29*(7), 961–971. doi:10.1016/j.childyouth.2006.12.009

Edleson, J. L., Mbilinyi, L. F., &Shetty, S. (2003). *Parenting in the context of domestic violence.* San Francisco, CA: Judicial Council of California, Administrative Office of the Courts, Center for Families, Children & the Courts.

Ellis, D. (2008). Divorce and the family court: What can be done about domestic violence? *Family Court Review, 46*(3), 531–536. DOI: 10.1111/j.1744–1617.2008.00218.x

Evans, S. E., Davies, C., &DiLillo, D. (2008). Exposure to domestic violence: A meta-analysis of child and adolescent outcomes. *Aggression and Violent Behavior, 13*(2), 1–15. doi:10.1016/j.avb.2008.02.005

Fleury, R. E., Sullivan, C. M., & Bybee, D. I. (2000). When ending the relationship does not end the violence: Women's experiences of violence by former partners. *Violence Against Women, 6*, 1363–1383. doi:10.1177/10778010022183695

Ford-Gilboe, M., Varcoe, C., Wuest, J., & Merritt-Gray, M. (2011). Intimate partner violence and nursing practice. In J. Humphreys & J. C. Campbell (Eds.), *Family violence and nursing practice* (2nd ed., pp. 115–153). New York: Springer.

Ford-Gilboe, M., Wuest, J., & Merritt-Gray, M. (2005). Strengthening capacity to limit intrusion: Theorizing family health promotion in the aftermath of woman abuse. *Qualitative Health Research, 15*(4), 477–501. doi:10.1177/1049732305274590

Frederick, L. (2008). Questions about family court and domestic violence screening and assessment. *Family Court Review, 46*(3), 523–530. DOI: 10.1111/j.1744–1617.2008.00217.x

Frye, V., Manganello, J., Campbell, J. C., Walton-Moss, B., & Wilt, S. (2006). The distribution of and factors associated with intimate terrorism and situational couple violence among a population-based sample of urban women in the United States. *Journal of Interpersonal Violence, 21*(10), 1286–1313. doi:10.1177/0886260506291658

Gerwitz, A., & Edleson, J. (2007). Young children's exposure to intimate partner violence: Towards a developmental risk and resilience framework for research and intervention. *Journal of Family Violence, 22*(3), 151–163. doi:10.1007/s10896–007–9065–3.

Giles-Sims, J. (1983). *Wife battering: A systems theory approach.* New York: The Guilford Press.

Graham-Bermann, S. A., Howell, K. H., Miller, L. E., Kwek, J., & Lilly, M. M. (2010). Traumatic events and maternal education as predictors of verbal ability for preschool children exposed to intimate partner violence (IPV). *Journal of Family Violence, 25*(4), 383–392. doi:10.1007/s10896–009–9299–3

Graham-Kevan, N., & Archer, J. (2003). Intimate terrorism and common couple violence: A test of Johnson's predictions in four British samples. *Journal of Interpersonal Violence, 18*(11), 1247–1270. doi:10.1177/0886260503256656

Grych, J. H., Jouriles, E. N., Swank, P. R., McDonald, R., & Norwood, W. D. (2000). Patterns of adjustment among children of battered women. *Journal of Consulting and Clinical Psychology, 68*(1), 84–94. doi:10.1037//0022–006X.68.I.84

Hardesty, J. L., & Chung, G. H. (2006). Intimate partner violence, parental divorce, and child custody: Directions for intervention and future research. *Family Relations, 55*(2), 200–210. doi:10.1111/j.1741–3729.2006.00370.x.

Hardesty, J. L., & Ganong, L. H. (2006). How women make custody decisions and manage co-parenting with abusive former husbands. *Journal of Social and Personal Relationships, 23*(4), 543–563. doi:10.1177/0265407506065983

Hardesty, J. L., Hans, J. D., Haselschwerdt, M. L., Khaw, L., & Crossman, K. (2010, November). *The effect of domestic violence allegations on custody evaluators' recommendations.* Paper presented at the annual conference of the National Council on Family Relations, Minneapolis, MN.

Hardesty, J. L, Khaw, L., Chung, G. H., & Martin, J. M. (2008). Coparenting relationships after divorce: Variations by type of marital violence and fathers' role differentiation. *Family Relations, 57*(4), 479–491. doi:10.1111/j.1741–3729.2008.00516.x.

Haselschwerdt, M. L., Hardesty, J. L., & Hans, J. D. (2011). Custody evaluators' beliefs about domestic violence allegations during divorce: Feminist and family violence perspectives. *Journal of Interpersonal Violence, 26*(8). doi:10.1177/0886260510370599

Herrera, V. M., & McCloskey, L. A. (2001). Gender differences in the risk for delinquency among youth exposed to family violence. *Child Abuse and Neglect, 25,* 1037–1051. doi:10.1016/S0145–2134(01)00255–1

Hilton, N. Z. (1992). Battered women's concerns about their children witnessing wife assault. *Journal of Interpersonal Violence, 7,* 77–86. doi:10.1177/088626092007001007

Holden, G. W. (2003). Children exposed to domestic violence and child abuse: Terminology and taxonomy. *Clinical Child and Family Psychology Review, 6*(3), 151–160. doi:10.1023/A:1024906315255

Holden, G. W., & Ritchie, K. L. (1991). Linking extreme marital discord, child rearing, and child behavior problems: Evidence from battered women. *Child Development, 62,* 311–327. doi:10.2307/1131005

Holden, G. W., Stein, J. D., Ritchie, K. L., Harris, S. D., & Jouriles, E. N. (1998). Parenting behaviors and beliefs of battered women. In G. W. Holden, R. Geffner & E. N. Jouriles, (Eds.), *Children exposed to marital violence: Theory, research, and applied issues* (pp. 185–222). Washington, DC: American Psychological Association.

Holt, S., Buckley, H., & Whelan, S. (2008). The impact of exposure to domestic violence on children and young people: A review of the literature. *Child Abuse & Neglect, 32,* 797–810. doi:10.1016/j.chiabu.2008.02.004

Hotton, T. (2001). Spousal violence after marital separation. *Juristat, 21,* 1–19.

Hughes, H. M., & Luke, D. A. (1998). Heterogeneity in adjustment among children of battered women. In G. W. Holden, R. Geffner, & E. N. Jouriles (Eds.), *Children exposed to marital violence: Theory, research, and applied issues* (pp. 185–221). Washington, DC: American Psychological Association.

Huth-Bocks, A. C., Levendosky, A. A., & Semel, M. A. (2001). The direct and indirect effects of domestic violence on young children's intellectual functioning. *Journal of Family Violence, 16,* 269–290. doi:10.1023/A:1011138332712

Ireland, T. O., & Smith, C. A. (2009). Living in partner-violent families: Developmental links to antisocial behavior and relationship violence. *Journal of Youth and Adolescence, 38,* 323–339. doi:10.1007/s10964-008-9347-y

Jaffe, P. G., Crooks, C.V., & Poisson, S. E. (2003). Common misconceptions in addressing domestic violence in custody disputes. *Juvenile and Family Court Journal, 54,* 57–67. doi:10.1111/j.1755–6988.2003.tb00086.x

Jaffe, P. G., Johnston, J. R., Crooks, C. V., & Bala, N. (2008). Custody disputes involving allegations of domestic violence: Toward a differentiated approach to parenting plans. *Family Court Review, 46*(3), 500–522. doi:10.1111/j.1744–1617.2008.00216.x

Jaffe, P. G., Lemon, N., & Poisson, S. (2003). *Child custody and domestic violence: A call for safety and accountability.* Thousand Oaks, CA: Sage.

Johnson, M. P. (2005). Apples and oranges in child custody disputes: Intimate terrorism vs. situational couple violence. *Journal of Child Custody, 2*(4), 43–52. doi:10.1300/J190v02n04_03

Johnson, M. P. (2006). Conflict and control: Gender symmetry and asymmetry in domestic violence. *Violence Against Women, 12*(11), 1003–1018. doi:10.1177/1077801206293328

Johnson, M. P. (2008). *A typology of domestic violence: Intimate terrorism, violent resistance, and situational couple violence.* Boston, MA: Northeastern University.

Johnson, M. P., & Leone, J. M. (2005). The differential effects of intimate terrorism and situational couple violence: Findings from the National Violence Against Women Survey. *Journal of Family Issues, 26*(3), 322–349.doi: 10.1177/0192513X04270345

Johnson, M. P., Leone, J. M., & Xu, Y. (2008, November). *Gender, intimate terrorism, and situational couple violence in general survey data: The gender debate revisited—again.* Paper presented at the annual meeting of the National Council on Family Relations, Little Rock, AR.

Johnston, J. R. (1995). Research update: Children's adjustment in sole custody compared to joint custody families and principles for custody decision making. *Family and Conciliation Courts Review, 33*(4), 415–425. doi:10.1111/j.174–1617.1995.tb00386.x

Johnston, J. R., & Campbell, L. E. (1993a). A clinical typology of interparental violence in disputed custody divorces. *American Journal of Orthopsychiatry, 63*(2), 190–199. doi:10.1037/h0079425

Johnston, J. R., & Campbell, L. E. (1993b). Parent-child relationships in domestic violence families disputing custody. *Family & Conciliation Courts Review, 31*(3), 282–298.

Johnston, J. R., Lee, S., Oleson, N. W., & Walters, M. G. (2005). Allegations and substantiations of abuse in custody-disputing families. *Family Court Review, 43*(2), 283–294. doi: 10.1111/j.1744–1617.2005.00029.x

Jouriles, E. N., McDonald, R., Smith Slep, A. M., Heyman, R. E., & Garrido, E. (2008). Child abuse in the context of domestic violence: Prevalence, explanations, and practice implications. *Violence and Victims, 23*(2), 221–235. doi:10.1891/0886–6708.23.2.221

Jouriles, E. N., Norwood, W. D., McDonald, R., & Peters, B. (2001). Domestic violence and child adjustment. In J. H. Grych & F. D. Fincham (Eds.), *Interparental conflict and child development: Theory, research, and applications* (pp. 315–336). New York: Cambridge University Press.

Kelly, J. B., & Johnson, M. P. (2008). Differentiation among types of intimate partner violence: Research update and implications for interventions. *Family Court Review, 46*(3), 476–499. doi:10.1111/j.1744–1617.2008.00215.x

Kitzman, K. M., Gaylord, N. K., Holt, A. R., & Kenny, E. D. (2003). Child witness to domestic violence: A meta-analytic review. *Journal of Consulting and Clinical Psychology, 71*(2), 339–352. doi:10.1037/0022–006X.71.2.339

Laroche, D. (2005). *Aspects of the context and consequences of domestic violence: Situational couple violence and intimate terrorism in Canada in 1999.* Government of Quebec: Institut de la statistique du Québec, Quebec. Retrieved from http://www.stat.gouv.qc.ca/publications/conditions/pdf/AspectViolen_an.pdf

Lawrence, E., & Bradbury, T. N. (2001). Physical aggression and marital dysfunction: A longitudinal analysis. *Journal of Family Psychology, 15,* 135–154. doi:10.1037//0893–3200.15.1.135

Lawrence, E., Ro, E., Barry, R., & Bunde, M. (2006). Mechanisms of distress and dissolution in physically aggressive romantic relationships. In M. A. Fine & J. H. Harvey (Eds.), *Handbook of divorce and relationship dissolution* (pp. 263–286). Mahway, NJ: Erlbaum.

Leone, J. M., Johnson, M. J., & Cohan, C. L. (2007). Victim help-seeking: Differences between intimate terrorism and situational couple violence. *Family Relations, 56,* 427–439. doi: 10.1111/j.1741–3729.2007.00471.x

Levendosky, A. A., & Graham-Bermann, S. A. (1998). The moderating effects of parenting stress on children's adjustment in woman-abusing families. *Journal of Interpersonal Violence, 12*(3), 383–397. doi:10.1177/088626098013003005

Levendosky, A. A., & Graham-Bermann, S. A. (2000). Behavioral observations of parenting in battered women. *Journal of Family Psychology, 14,* 1–15. doi: 10.1037//0893–3200.14.I.80

Levendosky, A. A., & Graham-Bermann, S. A. (2001). Parenting in battered women: The effects of domestic violence on women and their children. *Journal of Family Violence, 16*(2), 171–192. doi:10.1023/A:1011111003373

Levendosky, A. A., Huth-Bocks, A., & Semel, M. A. (2002). Adolescent peer relationships and mental health functioning in families with domestic violence. *Journal of Clinical Child Psychology, 31*(2), 206–218. doi:10.1207/153744202753604485

Levendosky, A. A., Huth-Bocks, A. C., Semel, M. A., & Shapiro, D. L. (2002). Trauma symptoms in preschool age children exposed to domestic violence. *Journal of Interpersonal Violence, 17*(3), 150–164. doi:10.1177/0886260502017002003

Levendosky, A. A., Leahy, K. L., Bogat, G. A., Davidson, W. S., & von Eye, A. (2006). Domestic violence, maternal parenting, maternal mental health, and infant externalizing behavior. *Journal of Family Psychology, 20*(4), 544–552. doi:10.1037/0893–3200.20.4.544

Levendosky, A. A., Lynch, S. M., & Graham-Bermann, S. A. (2000). Mothers' perceptions of the impact of woman abuse on their parenting. *Violence Against Women, 6*(3), 247–271. doi:10.1177/10778010022181831

Lichter, E. L., & McCloskey, L. A. (2004). The effects of childhood exposure to marital violence on adolescent gender-role beliefs and dating violence. *Psychology of Women Quarterly, 28,* 344–357. doi:10.1111/j.1471–6402.2004.00151.x.

Logan, T. K., Walker, R., Jordan, C. E., & Horvath, L. S. (2002). Child custody evaluations and domestic violence. *Violence and Victims, 17*(6), 719–742.

Margolin, G., Gordis, E. B., Medina, A. M., & Oliver, P. H. (2003). The co-occurrence of husband-to-wife aggression, family-of-origin aggression, and child abuse potential in a community sample: Implications for parenting. *Journal of Interpersonal Violence, 18,* 413–440. doi:10.1177/0886260502250835

Martinez-Torteya, C. G, Bogat, A., von Eye, A, & Levendosky, A. A. (2009). Resilience among children exposed to domestic violence: The role of risk and protective factors. *Child Development, 80*(2), 562–577. doi: 10.1111/j.1467–8624.2009. 01279.x

McCloskey, L. A., & Lichter, E. L. (2003). The contribution of marital violence to adolescent aggression across different relationships. *Journal of Interpersonal Violence, 4,* 390–412. doi:10.1177/0886260503251179

McCloskey, L. A, & Stuewig, J. (2001). The quality of peer relationships among children exposed to family violence. *Development and Psychopathology 13,* 83–96. doi:10.1017/S0954579401001067

Moretti, M. M., Obsuth, I., Odgers, C. L., & Reebye, P. (2006). Exposure to maternal vs. paternal partner violence, PTSD, and aggression in adolescent girls and boys. *Aggressive Behavior, 32*(4), 385–395. doi:10.1002/ab.20137.

Moylan, C. A., Herrenkohl, T. I., Sousa, C., Tajima, E. A., Herrenkohl, R. C., & Russo, M. J. (2010). The effects of child abuse and exposure to domestic violence on adolescent internalizing and externalizing behavior problems. *Journal of Family Violence, 25,* 53–63. doi:10.1007/s10896–009–9269–9

Rigterink, T., Katz, L. F., & Hessler, D. M. (2010). Domestic violence and longitudinal associations with children's physiological regulation abilities. *Journal of Interpersonal Violence, 25*(9), 1669–1683. doi:10.1177/0886260509354589

Salem, P., & Dunford-Jackson, B. L. (2008). Beyond politics and positions: A call for collaboration between family court and domestic violence professionals. *Family Court Review, 46*(3), 437–453. DOI: 10.1111/j.1744–1617.2008.00213.x

Smith Stover, C., Van Horn, P., Turner, R., Cooper, B., & Lieberman, A. F. (2003). The effects of father visitation on pre-school aged witnesses of domestic violence. *Journal of Interpersonal Violence, 18*(10), 1149–1166. doi:10.1177/0886260503255553

Sousa, C., Herenkhol, T. I., Moylan, C. A., Tajima, E. A., Klika, J. B., Herenkohl, R. C., & Russo, M. J (2011). Longitudinal study on the effects of child abuse and children's exposure to domestic violence, parent-child attachments, and antisocial behavior in adolescence. *Journal of Interpersonal Violence, 26*(1), 111–136. doi:10.1177/0886260510362883

Spilsbury, J. C., Belliston, L., Drotar, D., Drinkard, A., Kretschmar, J., Creeden, R.,. . . & Friedman, S. (2007). Clinically significant trauma symptoms and behavioral problems in a community-based sample of children exposed to domestic violence. *Journal of Family Violence, 22,* 487–399. doi:10.1007/s10896–007–9113-z

U.S. Census. (2002). *Number, timing, and duration of marriages and divorces: 1996.* Washington, DC: Author.

Van Horn, P., & Lieberman, A. (2002). *Domestic violence and parenting: A review of the literature.* San Francisco, CA: Judicial Council of California, Administrative Office of the Courts, Center for Families, Children & the Courts.

Ventura, S. J. (2009). *Changing patterns of nonmarital childbearing in the United States* (NCHS Data Brief, No. 18). Hyattsville, MD: National Center for Health Statistics.

VerSteegh, N., & Dalton, C. (2008). Report from the Wingspread Conference on Domestic Violence and Family Courts. *Family Court Review, 46*(3), 454–475. doi:10.1111/j.1744–1617.2008.00214.x

Warrier, S. (2008). "It's in their culture": Fairness and cultural considerations in domestic violence. *Family Court Review, 46*(3), 537–542. DOI: 10.1111/j.1744-1617.2008.00219.x

Wolfe, D. A, Crooks, C. V., Lee, V., McIntyre-Smith, A., & Jaffe, P. G. (2003). The effects of children's exposure to domestic violence: A meta-analysis and critique. *Clinical Child and Family Psychology Review, 6*(3), 171–186. doi:10.1023/A:1024910416164

Wuest, J., Ford-Gilboe, M., Merritt-Gray, M., & Berman, H. (2003). Intrusion: The central problem for family health promotion among children and single mothers after leaving an abusive partner. *Qualitative Health Research, 13*(5), 597–622. doi:10.1177/1049732303013005002

Zinzow, H. M., Ruggiero, K. J., Resnick, H., Hanson, R., Smith, D., Saunders, B., & Kilpatrick, D. (2009). Prevalence and mental health correlates of witnessed parental and community violence in a national sample of adolescents. *Journal of Child Psychology and Psychiatry, 50*(4), 441–450. doi:10.1111/j.1469-7610.2008.02004.x

Present and Future Cultural and Political Issues

## 15

Never-Married Parents in Family Court

LIZA COHEN HITA AND SANFORD L. BRAVER ■

INTRODUCTION

One of the newest types of family populations to confront family courts and associated professionals consists of unmarried parents. While only 12% of children were born outside of marriage in the United States in 1970, today nearly one third of all children are born to an unwed mother (Parke, 2004; Sigle-Rushton & McLanahan, 2002; U.S. Bureau of the Census, 2003; Ventura & Bachrach, 2000). The rate is especially high in some subpopulations. For example, 40% of Latino and 70% of African American children are born to unwed mothers (Parke, 2004). Giving birth without being married is also more common among lower income and less educated parents (Ellwood & Jencks, 2004; Hao, 1996; Manning & Brown, 2003; McLanahan & Sandefur, 1994; Sigle-Rushton & McLanahan, 2002; U.S. Bureau of the Census, 2009)

The term usually given to unmarried couples who have children together is "never-married parents" (NMPs). Because NMPs have no formal legal status, unlike divorcing parents, they are not required to use the court in formalizing the details of their arrangements when separating. Indeed, many NMPs have no arrangements between them except informal ones, and the court is uninvolved in their lives; in fact, the court may never be aware of their existence. Nonetheless, both the greatly increased rate of children born to NMPs and the outreach of the court and other government agencies to this population have prompted many more NMPs than previously to bring their issues before a court to assist in their legal resolutions, including their parenting arrangements. As a result, court administrators report that caseloads in current court dockets consist of about one third NMPs and two thirds parents pursuing a legal divorce ("legally divorcing parents" [LDPs]). Moreover, the indications are that the proportion of court cases involving NMPs is going to continue to grow even further, consistent with the increasing population trends (Kennedy & Bumpass, 2008; Lichter, Turner, & Sassier, 2010).

The largest subgroup of NMPs (about half) and the one about which the most is known is couples who at one time were living together, or *cohabiting* (McLanahan & Garfinkel, 2002). There are other subtypes of NMPs who have never cohabited (*non-cohabiters*). These include parents who never lived together but who did have a committed relationship; those who had dating or other more casual relationships that did not involve monogamous commitment; those who were never in a relationship at all and who had either infrequent sexual encounters or a "one-night stand"; and parents who would primarily consider themselves "friends" at the time of the child's conception. For many writers (e.g., Heiland & Liu, 2005), the best way of distinguishing among the non-cohabiting parents is to identify whether they continue to have a romantic (or what they term *visiting*) relationship after the child's birth (about two thirds of the non-cohabiters do). While the above descriptors apply to the parents' relationship, an additional distinction is whether each parent had a relationship with the child, especially prior to coming to court.

Virtually no empirical data specific to parenting plans for NMPs exist. Nonetheless, there is a substantial empirical literature on the characteristics and dynamics of cohabiting families, and a smaller literature on non-cohabiting NMPs. Since many NMPs never come to the attention of the court—it is only those who do that concern the present chapter—what is known about court-bound NMPs will be discussed. A key goal of this chapter is to delineate for the professional reader the distinctions between various subtypes of court-bound NMPs. Both the similarities and the differences from LDPs will be presented; where they are similar, helping professionals can extrapolate principles on which to base parenting plans for NMPs from those for LDPs. Where they are different, the professional must be keenly aware of how that may affect parenting plans.

LITERATURE ABOUT NMPs

Until fairly recently, relatively little was known about NMPs. Researchers were restricted to using large-scale data sets such as census records that contained little specific questioning of NMPs. This changed in the current decade with the advent of the Fragile Families and Child Wellbeing Study (FF; Reichman, Teitler, Garfinkel, & McLanahan, 2001). The FF researchers approached mothers at the time of the children's birth in 75 hospitals in 16 large cities (with populations of 200,000 or more) across the United States between 1998 and 2000. If the father was identified and present in the hospital, the researchers attempted to interview him as well. Biological parents in approximately 4,700 births were interviewed soon after childbirth and subsequently every 2 years; about 3,600 of the births were to unmarried parents, while the rest were to married couples. In the FF data set, a large number of family socioeconomic, demographic, relationship quality, and child development outcome variables are assessed. FF is the basis for many of the findings presented in the next sections. Nonetheless, findings are just beginning to emerge as the data set becomes ready for analyses.

In the following, distinctions between cohabiting, visiting, and non-visiting families are presented, since the dynamics of each have been shown to be different.

Cohabiting Families

Cohabitation enables couples to have and jointly parent children without dealing with common barriers to marriage, such as economic instability and uncertain relationship status (Edin & Reed, 2005; Smock, Manning, & Porter, 2005). About half of cohabiting couples eventually marry (Parke, 2004; Smock, 2000). Nonetheless, data show that cohabiting parents are at greater risk of separating than their married counterparts: 40% will not be together by the child's fifth birthday (McLanahan & Beck, 2010). In fact, cohabitation seems to increase the rates of dissolution even if the couple later marries. Among children born to cohabiting parents who later marry, 15% will have their parents separate by the time they are one year old, half will not be living with both parents by age 5, and two thirds will not live with both parents by age 10 (Manning, Smock, & Majumdar, 2004).

Visiting Families vs. Non-Visiting Families

Visiting relationship parents (those with a romantic relationship, but non-cohabiting) are in most respects in between cohabiting and non-visiting (where the parents have no ongoing romantic relationship) parents. While, as reported above, about 60% of cohabiters are still together 5 years after the child's birth, only about one fifth of visiting couples are then still romantically involved, and, by definition, no non-visiting relationship parents are together (McLanahan & Beck, 2010). While virtually all cohabiting fathers provided financial support or other types of assistance during the pregnancy, came to the hospital to see the mother and baby, and said they wanted to help raise the child, all of these factors were true for at least three quarters of visiting fathers as well. But all three of these factors were only found with one quarter to one third of non-visiting fathers. Virtually all visiting fathers said that they wanted to be involved in raising their child, according to the mothers, who in turn wanted the fathers so involved. Three fourths of non-visiting couples reported a desire for involvement (McLanahan & Beck, 2010).

The interaction between the mothers and fathers in NMPs was surprisingly good at the time of the child's birth, with parents indicating a high level of commitment to co-parent their child. Co-parenting quality was measured by questions that asked mothers whether the father "acts like the father you want for your child"; "can be trusted to take good care of the child"; "respects your schedules and rules"; "supports you in the way you want to raise the child"; "talks with you about problems that come up with raising the child"; and "can be counted on to help when you need someone to look after the child for a few hours." On a scale from 1 (*rarely true*) to 3 (*always true*), cohabiting mothers gave an average score of 2.77; non-cohabiting mothers gave a lower, but still rather high, score of 2.12 (Carlson, McLanahan, & England, 2004).

NMPs AND THE LEGAL SYSTEM

While the literature deriving from FF is a rich source of information for court professionals, it is important to recognize that it contains virtually no information concerning when NMPs come to family court. In fact, such data are virtually nonexistent. Court records are generally of little help in this regard. In many jurisdictions, in fact, there is no official demarcation labeling the file that even indicates whether parents are LDPs or NMPs. Perhaps this is because, for purposes of handling parenting issues, there is generally little legal distinction once the man's biological and social paternity are established. However, courts' handling of strictly financial issues, such as alimony and property division, allows—indeed requires—clear differentiation between the two. Unlike spouses, even cohabiting partners generally have no financial claims against one another arising from their non-marital relationship (as opposed to their common parentage), although they may have rights arising from a contract, explicit or, more commonly implicit, if they had one. This means that claims to share in property accumulated during their relationship, or for alimony as opposed to child support, are generally unavailable to non-marital partners who do not have a contract establishing them (Ellman et al., 2010).

Nonetheless, the court is enjoined by statute and precedent to handle the parenting issues of NMPs identically to that of LDPs, although they are permitted to base dispositions on factors that co-vary with marital status, such as length of parental relationship or the parent–child relationship (Thornton, Axinn, & Xie, 2007). In fact, there are multiple legal precedents that have been enacted to protect and afford privileges to long-term relationships that are often considered to be *common-law marriages* or *marriage-like* (Blumberg, 2001).

LDPs and NMPs Seeking Legal Assistance

Virtually all LDPs initially come to the attention of the court at the time they begin the process of seeking a legal divorce. They normatively expect some sort of court involvement because they are seeking dissolution of a legal marriage, corresponding property settlements, child support orders, and as part of their decree, a formalized parenting plan. In contrast, there is no set time or circumstance that compels NMPs into legal action, and as a result, the timing of their commerce with the court and with professionals assisting them with parenting plan development is considerably more variable. Although many cohabiting NMPs originally come to court at or near the time of the separation (or in the case of visiting NMPs, of the relationship breakup), many do not. Instead, formerly cohabiting NMPs may wait until disagreements arise such as about child support, a change of employment or income, access to child(ren), a perceived change in parental fitness, or simply disputes about what they see as the best interest of the child (e.g., a new partner; Raisner, 2004; Skaine, 2003). It is often the aggregate of smaller disputes that catalyzes litigation.

Another key difference is that, generally with LDPs, the family is coming into the court system because at least one of the parents has initiated litigation. Yet with NMPs, it is much more common that neither parent initiated litigation, but rather both are involuntary litigants. Forced litigants are brought into the family court system by an administrative order of the superior court by state government where public assistance (Temporary Assistance for Needy Families) is being or has been received. Since these "IV-D" parents do not file their own petitions, they can be uninformed about the process and discontent with the prospects of having external management of important aspects of their life, such as paying child support for a child they may or may not have visitation with, sharing parenting time with a parent they may or may not have a relationship with, and/or repaying the state to recoup the cost of public assistance to the other parent. In most courts, there is not even any official indicator in the file to indicate whether the family consists of LDPs or NMPs.

As a result, courts lack official figures and have only unofficial guesstimates of the proportion of NMPs in its overall parenting-issues caseload (Salem, personal communication, Sept. 14, 2010).

In summary:

- Research is sparse on NMPs, though they are a burgeoning population. Their increases have been sizeable, with current figures estimating approximately one third of all children being born to NMPs.
- NMPs have various living arrangements, including cohabiting, visiting, and non-visiting, with each having different relationship and familial dynamics.
- In comparison to LDPs, NMPs have a somewhat different entry path into the court system with unique circumstances at times; however, they have a similar legal process without obvious distinction from their divorcing counterparts.

DEMOGRAPHIC DISTINCTIONS BETWEEN HIGH-CONFLICT NMPS VS. LDPS: THE FAMILY TRANSITIONS STUDY

Despite this lack of definitive data, there is widespread recognition throughout the family court system that NMPs are a distinct though overlapping population from LDPs, and they have disparate needs (Raisner, 2004). But exactly how they are distinct and exactly how they are overlapping remains to be further elucidated. To help fill that gap, Braver, Sandler, and Hita initiated the Family Transitions Study (FTS)[1] in 2005 to examine the differences and the commonalities among LDPs and NMPs in the court subpopulation deemed *high conflict.* This project, conducted in collaboration with the Maricopa Court, collected data on over 600 LDPs and NMPs ordered by the judge in their case to a program for high-conflict litigating couples. High conflict was not well defined; the judges were told to use any criteria they chose. The program to which judges ordered participation was one of two, chosen randomly (these programs are the subject of later publications by the authors). The sample represents the most comprehensive, empirically grounded comparative study so far existing of high-conflict court-bound NMPs versus LDPs. Below (in the first presentation of the results of this survey), the demographic characteristics results are presented.

First, NMPs represent 40% of the sample, LDPs 60%. Thus, the actual proportion of NMPs in this high-conflict sample is a bit higher than what is anecdotally assumed to be the family court's caseload: one third. Second, about 33% of the LDPs and 47% of NMPs are ethnic minority. Thus, as is the case for single parents more generally, high-conflict court-bound NMPs also consist disproportionately of ethnic minorities. An appreciation of the cultural issues is vital for forensic professionals dealing with minority litigants. Saini and Ma (Chapter 17 in this volume) provide excellent guidance in regard to the cultural competence required for mediators, parent educators, forensic custody evaluators, and courts.

Figure 15.1 shows the educational attainment data; as can be seen, the primary differences are that NMPs are less likely to have graduated college and correspondingly are more likely to have had no college than LDPs. Thus, as is true in general for NMPs, those NMPs who appear in family court and are considered high conflict

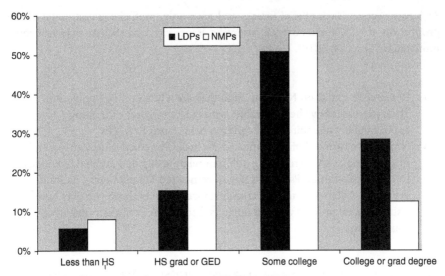

Figure 15.1 Education Levels of LDPs and NMPs in FTS

are less likely than parents who have married and are now divorcing to have college degrees.

Finally, Table 15.1 shows the age and relationship statistics. Court-going NMPs are younger, have younger children, and have been together only half as long as LDPs. Thus, reflecting the general tendency for NMPs to be younger, have younger children, and have shorter-term relationships with the other parent than LDPs, those NMPs who are court-going and deemed high conflict also have these characteristics.

In addition to these demographic differences, the literature cited below points to the respects in which the NMPs' risk factors of a psychosocial nature may be different from those of LDPs.

Psychosocial Risk Factors

The voluminous general literature on divorced families certainly gives reason to think that NMPs who use family court services face considerable stresses and that their children are at elevated risk. The neighboring literature reviewed in this volume (e.g., Kelly; Lamb) suggest that most children whose parents separate and go to court

Table 15.1 STATISTICAL DIFFERENCES BETWEEN LEGALLY DIVORCING PARENTS (LDPs) AND NEVER-MARRIED PARENTS (NMPs) IN FAMILY TRANSITIONS STUDY DATA SET

	Mean LDP	Mean NMP	Difference
Parent's age	37.0	31.2	5.7
Child's age	9.5	5.4	4.1
Length of relationship (months)	109.3	51.8	57.5
Time apart (months)	49.4	45.5	3.9

are more likely to experience tribulations, including higher rates of mental health problems (Bream & Buchanon, 2003; Carlson & McLanahan, 2010; Clarke-Stewart & Brentano, 2006; Johnston & Campbell, 1988; Pedro-Carroll, Nakhnikian, & Montes, 2001; Zill, Morrison, & Coiro, 1993). Nonetheless, experts caution that "outcomes for children and adolescents following divorce were complexly determined, varied considerably, and could be best understood within a framework of familial and external factors increasing risk and fostering resilience" (Kelly, Chapter 3 in this volume). Lamb points out that "approximately 20% to 25% of children in post-separation and divorced families give evidence of adjustment problems, compared to 12% in married families. Thus, the majority of children from separated families evince no psychopathology or behavioral symptoms" (Lamb, Chapter 8 in this volume).

While research specifically on NMPs is far more sparse, the studies that do exist suggest that their children appear to have generally poorer outcomes than the children of LDPs across a myriad of indicators, including academic performance, emotional and behavioral problems, depression, and delinquency (Acs & Nelson, 2002, 2004; Brown, 2004, 2006; DeLeire & Kalil, 2002; Hofferth, 2006; Manning, 2004; Manning & Brown, 2003; Manning & Lichter, 1996; Osborne & McLanahan, 2007). While acknowledging this elevated risk, it should be noted that, as with children of LDPs, the average child of NMPs will emerge without permanent impairment, and the variability of their reactions is related to a number of risk factors.

It is here proposed that this elevated risk confronting cohabiting NMPs using family court is generally a difference in degree rather than in kind; that is, cohabiting NMPs are likely to face substantially the same types of issues or challenges as LDPs do, but they commonly experience higher levels of certain adversities (described below). As a result, they themselves are more distressed or compromised, and their children are accordingly faced with environments—both parental and otherwise— that are more debilitating. The empirical literature has identified a constellation of factors or variables along which NMPs may differ from LDPs, all of which increase the psychological risks their children face. Within this chapter, these factors are collectively termed *chaotic environment* (cf. Evans, Gonnella, Marcynyszyn, Gentile, & Salpekar, 2005). In particular, the environments of cohabiting NMPs appear more chaotic and toxic than LDPs in four respects. First, they are more likely to experience economic decline and to recede to dangerously low economic levels than LDPs (Bramlett & Mosher, 2002; Teachman & Paasch, 1994). Second, cohabiting NMPs are more likely to have inadequate support networks and to fail to receive appropriate assistance from friends and family (Wang & Amato, 2000). Third, cohabiting NMPs are more prone to relocating and other changes in their physical environment (i.e., forcing the child to attend a new school) (McLanahan & Sandefur, 1994). Finally, cohabiting NMPs appear to differ in the rapidity of changes and fluidity in family restructuring, including new romantic relationships that either parent may have (Carlson & Corcoran, 2001). These factors are summarized in Table 15.2.

Economic Strain

According to most research, the majority of NMPs exist at stressful economic levels, with their poverty rate at about 35%, compared to the more general rate

Table 15.2 PSYCHOSOCIAL FACTORS ALONG WHICH NMPs FACE MORE ADVERSE LEVELS THAN LDPs, AND WHICH ARE LIKELY TO HARM THE CHILDREN

Chaotic Environment
• Economic strain
• Lack of social support
• Relocation
• Family restructuring

of around 20% (U.S. Bureau of the Census, 2009). If they were non-cohabiters, this level of hardship has tended to be chronic. Among former cohabiters, on average their level of economic well-being was always somewhat lower than their married counterparts, although higher than non-cohabiters; it drops to very low levels upon separation (Bramlett & Mosher, 2002; Braver, Gonzalez, Wolchik, & Sandler, 1989; Klebanov, Brooks-Gunn, & Duncan, 1994; Teachman & Paasch, 1994; Wang & Amato, 2000). Both chronic economic hardship and decreases in economic level (experienced by formerly cohabiting NMPs at separation) are each associated with problems for the parents as well as for the children (Barnett, 2008; Bradley & Corwyn, 2002; Mistry, Vandewater, Huston, & McLoyd, 2002).

Of course, not all NMPs are from the economic underclass; there is a full continuum of NMPs of varying economic background. Some NMPs with higher socioeconomic status make a deliberate choice not to marry for a myriad of reasons, such as personal beliefs and diverse worldviews, including rejecting both gendered ideas of marriage and pressures to conform to social constructions (DePaulo & Morris, 2005). For other well-off NMPs, the choice not to marry is a temporary one; they appear to be waiting until they are certain the relationship "will last" before marrying (Smock et al., 2005). While the FTS sample contained few NMPs who were affluent (less than 15% had received a BA or BS or higher), upper-income parents are undoubtedly disproportionately represented among the NMPs who retain the services of private forensic custody evaluators. Unfortunately, there is a severe paucity of empirical literature on these affluent NMPs, who not infrequently come to the attention of forensic professionals for parenting plan guidance.

However, even relatively wealthy NMPs are likely to have experienced substantial economic declines upon separation, even though they remain far from destitute (Braver et al., 1989). Even at high levels of earnings, making the transition from a dual-income to a single-income household can create a sense of strain when lifestyle change is inevitable and generally undesirable.

In terms of its effects on NMP children's well-being, declines in parental economic well-being (no matter to what eventual level) appear to have both direct effects and indirect effects through the parenting they experience. Children are directly affected by declines when their parents spend less on them. The indirect effects arise from the parent's psychological distress in dealing with the economic challenges (Cutrona, Russell, Hessling, Brown, & Murry, 2000; Jones, Forehand, Brody, & Armistead, 2003). In turn, this distress results in impaired parenting: more harsh and inconsistent discipline as well as expressing less parental warmth (Klebanov et al., 1994). When mothers are in a position of economic strain due to stress over income or employment changes, mother–child interaction can suffer (Duncan & Brooks-Gunn, 2000). New or unsatisfying employment patterns can also create strains as NMP mothers attempt to balance family life and work with limited resources (Osborne & Knab, 2007).

Although they receive somewhat less attention, NMP fathers, both custodial and non-custodial, also experience financial strain and its attendant distress upon separation. NMP fathers with low incomes have less supportive co-parenting relationships, particularly if the mother was also economically disadvantaged (Bronte-Tinkew & Horowitz, 2010). There are a subset of never-married fathers who have difficulty maintaining formal employment, given the changing economic climate, and may have increased dependence on the underground economy or "hustling," which does not provide dependable income (and is sometimes illegal) (Woldoff & Cina, 2007). On the other hand, affluent non-custodial NMPs appear somewhat immune from this particular source of distress.

Lack of Social Support

Social support has been shown to protect children from many community-related adverse events such as exposure to negative peer groups, as well as internal family strain, which would otherwise pose difficulties (Murry, Bynum, Brody, Willert, & Stephens, 2000). Social support thus provides a buffering effect in stressful situations (Cohen & Wills, 1985). In addition, social support appears to also link directly to positive psychological outcomes (Pierce, Sarason, & Sarason, 1996). Informal social support from family and friends is particularly salient for certain ethno-racial communities that often rely on extended family networks for support in childrearing and parenting duties (Forehand & Kotchick, 1996). For parents, higher levels of social support may serve to enhance positive parenting, mainly by decreasing parental psychological distress (MacPhee, Fritz, & Miller-Heyl, 1996), leading to increased child well-being outcomes.

When parents are parenting alone, the social support benefits of the other parent, such as caregiving and providing financial and emotional resources, are lost (Sigle-Rushton & McLanahan 2002). In addition, NMPs may be less adept at harnessing broader social support networks than LDPs. Thus, NMPs are less likely to have adequate social support networks than LDPs (Cairney, Boyle, Offord, & Racine, 2003) and are more likely to feel isolated and alone. These feelings of isolation often affect the children, who feel equally isolated and who feel a sense of loss regarding the different relationship dynamics and lack of social support (Kelly & Emery, 2003).

Relocation

NMPs are particularly likely to have unstable physical environments, either as a result of separation (for formerly cohabiting NMPs) or because of their lower financial levels. Moving or relocation can be a stressful experience for children, posing its own set of risk factors (Austin, 2008). Moving often involves attending a new school, which causes children stress due to changes in their peer networks and community ties (Astone & McLanahan, 1994; McLanahan & Sandefur, 1994), especially during key developmental periods of their life. Children have natural social pathways that mark developmental transitions, such as entering middle school (Elder, 1998). The aggregate of multiple stressors that disrupt these social pathways can lead to problem behaviors with school-aged children, such as disruptive behaviors with teachers (Cavanagh & Huston, 2006). The more times a child changes schools, with the exception of normal transition times (kindergarten, middle school, and high school), the lower his or her academic success rate (Pribesh & Downey, 1999). Children who moved more frequently were also more likely to have failing grades and/or to have repeated a grade than children who had never moved or who moved infrequently (Wood, Halfon, Scarlata, Newacheck, & Nessim, 1993).

Family Restructuring

Family restructuring refers to the amount of change children experience in their family structure, which includes revisions in parenting time and creation, termination, or changes in parental repartnering. The partner referred to is not necessarily restricted to new parental romantic partners but includes any person who has a significant role in the parent's life that also involves contact with the child. For example, new babysitters, new platonic friends, or even significantly changed time with extended family members may qualify (Raley & Wildsmith 2004; Teachman 2003). These events involve familial transitions for children and accordingly constitute major stressors in children's lives (Amato, 2001). Children from homes with more transitions and/or more restructuring exhibit more externalizing behaviors, classroom disruptions, and negative interactions with peers than did children from more stable homes (Cavanagh & Huston, 2006; Osborne & McLanahan, 2007).

NMPs commonly experience more family restructuring than divorcing parents, and their children thus experience more transitions in their family structure than do children of traditional marriages (Osborne & McLanahan, 2007). The quantitative research data show that family transitions can also be linked to dramatic changes in income and residential moves (Amato, 2000; Astone & McLanahan, 1994; McLanahan & Sandefur, 1994), which can affect children's well-being (Teachman, 2003). Families who experience one major family transition are more likely to experience additional transitions, thus compounding the stresses that accompany these life changes (Martinson & Wu, 1992).

In summary:

- The FTS study provided data regarding how NMPs (whose family formation has been researched in other large data sets, e.g., FF) fare in their separation process, an area of considerable void in the literature.
- NMPs are at elevated risk for poor child behavior outcomes on a myriad of indicators, somewhat more so than LDPs.
- Salient risk factors include, but are not limited to, chaotic environment variables, including economic strain, lack of social support, family restructuring, and relocation.
- Not all NMPs experience these risk factors in the same way. There is a full spectrum of socioeconomic diversity within this population that affects the intensity and duration of these variables.

SUMMARY

As this chapter has discussed, there is very large and growing population of NMPs who are turning to the court for assistance in parenting plan development. Currently, among litigants who have been determined to be high conflict, one study found that approximately 40% are NMPs, and if current trends continue, the figure might well reach half in the next decade or so. The scientific literature has patently lagged behind this trend, but with the advent of the FF study, there is reason to expect more will soon be known (Table 15.3). However, the FF is not specific to NMPs in the court, and so far, only the FTS, described for the first time in these pages, contains information pertinent to these litigants.

Obviously, this situation should be remedied as quickly as possible by high-quality research. The divorce rate began to explode in the late 1960s (Braver & Lamb, in press). Within a decade, a matching explosion of research followed to help professionals and scholars understand the issues such families are grappling with. Thus, since 1975, over 8,500 papers have been published with *divorce* listed as a key topic (ISIWeb of Science bibliographic database); nearly 2,000 have been published in the past decade alone (Amato, 2010). Research on NMPs must now begin to replicate that trend, with investigations accumulating to match the scope of the current problem.

While investigations using FF will no doubt begin to fill that gap soon, nonetheless, to be maximally useful to court professionals, the explorations must give special attention to those NMPs who come to court for the resolution of their problems. It is unclear whether the FF data set contains information to illuminate these matters. A simple device the courts can implement should have great effect in facilitating non-FF research: making sure there is an indicator in the official court file that specifies whether the couple has been legally married or not. Without such a marker, neither researchers wishing to use court records alone, nor those who wish to identify and then survey NMPs, can proceed.

Another understudied subpopulation of NMPs of substantial interest is middle- to upper-class NMPs who present for forensic custody evaluations in family court. While at present they are a statistical minority among court-bound NMPs, their numbers are growing, and they disproportionately contract the services of private forensic professionals. Perhaps the most promising avenue for increasing information about this group is the case files of forensic professionals who have seen a substantial number of such families: in other words, qualitative and ethnographic investigations rather than quantitative ones.

When considering NMPs, two main categories should be distinguished: cohabiters and non-cohabiters. Cohabiters are different primarily in degree, rather than qualitatively, from the divorcing parents more traditionally treated by forensic professionals. They are likely to be younger, to have younger children, to have been together for a shorter period, and to be less educated, and they are more likely of ethnic minority status than LDPs. They are also likely to be more stressed and distressed than LDPs along the four chaotic environment dimensions.

Non-cohabiters (about half of NMPs) represent a greater departure from LDPs for forensic professionals to consider than cohabiters. They are extremely variable in terms of the extent of their relationship to the other parent and to the child and in their co-parenting experience.

Table 15.3 RELEVANT RESEARCH STUDIES

Data Set	Research Agenda	Participants
Fragile Families and Child Wellbeing Study	The core FF Study was designed primarily to address four questions of great interest to researchers and policy makers: (1) What are the conditions and capabilities of unmarried parents, especially fathers? (2) What is the nature of the relationships between unmarried parents? (3) How do children born into these families fare? and (4) How do policies and environmental conditions affect families and children? Information collected focused on relationships, parenting behavior, demographic characteristics, health (psychological and physical), economic and employment status, neighborhood characteristics, and program participation.	The parent(s) of approximately 4,700 (3,600 non-marital and 1,100 marital) children born in large U.S. cities between 1998 and 2000. Parent(s) were interviewed in four waves as core data: at the time of child's birth and at age 1, 3, and 5 years old. A 9-year follow-up initiated in 2007 and concluded in 2010.
National Longitudinal Survey of Youth	Surveys included questions on labor market experiences, training investments, schooling, community background, family income, health conditions, geographic residence and environmental characteristics, household composition, and marital and fertility histories.	NLSY79: The NLSY79 is a nationally representative sample of 12,686 young men and women who were 14 to 22 years of age when first surveyed in 1979 and again annually until 1994. Thereafter, participants were interviewed biennially. Interviewing for round 21 of the NLSY79 began in January 2004 and ended in the winter of 2005. NLSY97 cohort, 8,984 respondents originated from 6,819 unique households
National Survey of Families and Households	Designed explicitly for the research community and under advisement of many consultants, the survey gathered life history information, including the respondent's family living arrangements in childhood; departures and returns to the parental home; current living arrangements; and histories of marriage, cohabitation, education, fertility, and employment; as well as the analysis of the consequences of earlier patterns on current states, marital and parenting relationships, kin contact, and economic and psychological well-being.	The national sample of 13,007 included a main cross-section of 9,637 households with one randomly selected participant, plus an oversampling of Blacks, Puerto Ricans, Mexican Americans, single-parent families, families with stepchildren, cohabiting couples, and recently married persons. Interviews were conducted in 1987–88, 1992–94, and 2001–2003.

Relevant Papers*	Shortfalls of the Research in Regards to NMPs in Transition
Bronte-Tinkew, J., & Horowitz, A. (2010) Heiland, F., & Liu, S. (2005) Carlson, M., McLanahan, S., & England, P. (2004) Beck, A.N., Cooper, C.E., & McLanahan, S. (2010)	Studies focus on families with young children. No discussion on dynamic of separation experience for parents or children.
Carlson, M. J., & Corcoran, M. E. (2001) Kowaleski-Jones, L., & Duniforn, R. (2006) Falci, C. (2006) Day, R., & Acock, A. (2004)	No discussion on dynamic of separation experience for parents or children
Wolfinger, N. H. (2001) Pascoe, J. M., Stolfi, A., & Ormond, M. B. (2006) Marcussen, K. (2005) Goldscheider, F., & Kaufman, G. (2006)	No discussion on litigation experiences with NMPs and their children.

(Continued)

Table 15.3 RELEVANT RESEARCH STUDIES   *(Continued)*

Data Set	Research Agenda	Participants
Current Population Survey	Conducted by the Bureau of the Census for the Bureau of Labor Statistics. Information gathered includes employment, unemployment, earnings, hours of work, and other indicators. They are available by a variety of demographic characteristics including age, sex, race, marital status, and educational attainment, including information on occupation, industry, and class of worker. The data gathered are used by government policymakers and legislators as important indicators of the nation's economic situation and for planning and evaluating many government programs, as well as by the press, students, academics, and the general public.	Repeated monthly cross-section of over 50,000 households
National Longitudinal Study of Adolescent Health	Research focuses on key potential influences that shape trajectories of resilience and vulnerability from adolescence to young adulthood. Objectives focus on potential factors that influence the likelihood of these trajectories among youths from disadvantaged and advantaged origins, such as personal resources, family dynamics, influences beyond the family, mastery experiences in school and work, and role transitions, as well as the generalizability of these causal processes.	National sample consisted of approximately 20,000 youths in Grades 7–12 in 1994: Wave I (1994–1995), the in-school survey and in-home interviews with the adolescent and caregiver; Wave II (1996), interview with the adolescent; and Wave III (2001–2002).

*This is only a small selection of numerous relevant papers.

This chapter contends that cohabiting NMPs differ only in degree, not in kind, from LDPs. The same cannot be said with respect to NMPs who have never lived together, or who have never lived simultaneously with the child. It is likely that the dynamics of the latter non-cohabiting families vary tremendously. This chapter also draws attention to the necessity for researchers to concentrate especially on this burgeoning subgroup. The authors hope that when the next edition of this volume is published, much more about this group can be documented in the literature.

In summary:

- New research and a more nuanced research agenda are needed on NMPs to better serve this population, including more focus on economic diversity, particularly upper-income earners who disproportionately present for forensic custody evaluations, as well as non-cohabiting NMPs.
- NMPs can be seen as a two-pronged population, with cohabiting NMPs sharing considerable similarities with LDPs in regards to familial dynamics and child well-being outcomes, while non-cohabiters are especially diverse.

Relevant Papers*	Shortfalls of the Research in Regards to NMPs in Transition
McKeever, M., & Wolfinger, N. H. (2011) Huang, C. (2006) Lichter, D. T., & Crowley, M. L. (2004) Yoo, J., & Younghee, L. (2009)	Main focus on economic indicators. No research on litigation process with NMPs.
Blum, R. W., Beuhring, T., Shew, M. L., Bearinger, L. H., Seiving, R. E., & Resnick, M. D. (2000) Manning, W. D., & Lamb, K. A. (2004) Demuth, S., & Brown, S. L. (2004) Marsigilio, W., Amato, P., Day, R., & Lamb, M. (2004)	Focus primarily on adolescents. No discussion on the affects of litigation with NMPs.

GUIDELINES: CONSIDERATIONS AND CAUTIONS

- Never-married parents (NMPs) are a burgeoning court population, with over a third of all modern births being to unwed parents and a higher proportion being court-bound; NMPs represent an even higher proportion of the high-conflict population (based on the FTS sample).
- Ethnoracial minorities are more highly represented among NMPs than in legally divorcing parents (LDPs), with disproportionately high representation in court-identified high-conflict families. They also tend to be younger, to have younger children, and to have less educational attainment than LDPs. NMPs tend to have shorter relationships than LDPs prior to separation.
- NMPs are a heterogeneous group that comprise multiple sub-populations. This chapter has divided NMPs into cohabiters and non-cohabiters. Living status is important to consider because it reflects the interparental dynamic

before separation as well as the child–parent relationship and level/quality of contact.

- Entry into the court system varies by relationship status. LDPs enter into their initial litigation to dissolve a legal marriage, so the court intervenes at an early and voluntary stage of the separation process. NMPs are often entering into the court system to manage longstanding problems, crises they could not resolve independently, or involuntarily through state-ordered proceedings. However, relitigation does not appear to differ between groups.
- There are not legal distinctions within the court system, outside the public record of a divorce decree or explicit reference within the narrative of an evaluative report, to delineate between NMPs and LDPs in the court's records.
- Socioeconomic and cultural variables are salient factors in assisting NMPs.
- Key considerations with NMPs are what the authors call chaotic environment. These include economic strain, lack of social support, relocation, and family restructuring. In the literature on cohabiting and single parents, these are identified as key determinants for child well-being. As a constellation of factors, they indicate increased risk for child behavior problems.

NOTE

1 The project is funded by both the William T. Grant Foundation and the National Institute of Mental Health.

REFERENCES

Acs, G., & Nelson, S. (2002). The kids are alright? Children's well-being and the rise in cohabitation. Washington, DC: The Urban Institute. *Assessing the New Federalism* Policy Brief B-48.

Acs, G., & Nelson, S. (2004). Changes in living arrangements during the late 1990s: Do welfare policies matter? *Journal of Policy Analysis and Management, 23*(2), 273–290.

Amato, P.R. (2000). The consequences of divorce for adults and children. *Journal of Marriage and the Family, 62,* 1269–1287.

Amato, P.R. (2001). Children of divorce in the 1990s: An update of the Amato and Keith (1991) meta-analysis. *Journal of Family Psychology, 15*(3), 355–370.

Amato, P. R. (2010). Research on divorce: Continuing trends and new developments. *Journal of Marriage and Family, 72,* 650–666.

Astone, M., & McLanahan, S. S. (1994). Family structure, residential mobility, and school dropout: A research note. *Demography, 31,* 575–584.

Austin, W. G. (2008). Relocation, research, and forensic evaluation: Part II. Research support for the relocation risk assessment model. *Family Court Review, 46*(2), 347–365.

Barnett, M. A. (2008). Economic disadvantage in complex family systems: Expansion of family stress models. *Clinical Child and Family Psychology Review, 11*(3), 145–160.

Beck, A. N., Cooper, C. E., & McLanahan, S. (2010). Partner transitions and maternal parenting. *Journal of Marriage and Family, 72,* 219–233.

Blum, R. W., Beuhring, T., Shew, M. L., Bearinger, L. H., Seiving, R. E., & Resnick, M. D. (2000). The effects of race/ethnicity, income, and family structure on adolescent risk behaviors. *American Journal of Public Health, 90*(12), 1879–1884.

Blumberg, G. (2001). The regularization of nonmarital cohabitation: Rights and responsibilities in the American welfare state. *Notre Dame Law Review, 76*(5), 1265–1310.

Bradley, R. H., & Corwyn, R. F. (2002). Socioeconomic status and child development. *Annual Review of Psychology, 53,* 371–399.

Bramlett, M. D., & Mosher, W. D. (2002). Cohabitation, marriage, divorce, and remarriage in the United States. *Vital and Health Statistics, 23*(22), 1–34.

Braver, S. L., Gonzalez, N., Wolchik, S. A., & Sandler, I. N. (1989). Economic hardship and psychological distress in custodial mothers. *Journal of Divorce, 12*(4), 19–34.

Braver, S. L., & Lamb, M. E. (in press). Marital dissolution. In G. W. Peterson & K. R. Bush (Eds.), *Handbook of marriage and the family* (2nd ed.). New York: Springer Publishing Company.

Bream, V., & Buchanan, A. (2003). Distress among children whose separated or divorced parents cannot agree on arrangements for them. *British Journal of Social Work, 33,* 227–238.

Bronte-Tinkew, J., & Horowitz, A. (2010). Factors associated with unmarried, nonresident fathers' perceptions of their coparenting. *Journal of Family Issues, 3*(1), 31–65.

Brown, S. L. (2004). Family structure and child wellbeing: The significance of parental cohabitation. *Journal of Marriage and Family. 66*(2), 351–367.

Brown, S. L. (2006). Family structure transitions and adolescent wellbeing. *Demography, 43*(3), 447–461.

Cairney, J., Boyle, M., Offord, D. R., & Racine, Y. (2003). Stress, social support, and depression in single and married mothers. *Social Psychiatry and Psychiatric Epidemiology, 38*(8), 442–449.

Carlson, M. J., & Corcoran, M. E. (2001). Family structure and children's behavioral and cognitive outcomes. *Journal of Marriage and Family, 63,* 779–792.

Carlson, M. J., & McLanahan, S. S. (2010). Fathers in fragile families. In M. E. Lamb (Ed.), *The role of the father in child development* (5th ed., pp. 241–269). Hoboken, NJ: Wiley.

Carlson, M. J., McLanahan, S. J., & England, P. (2004). Union formation in fragile families. *Demography, 41*(2), 237–261.

Cavanagh, S. E., & Huston, A.C. (2006). Family instability and children's early problem behavior. *Social Forces, 85*(1),551–581.

Clarke-Stewart, A., & Brentano, C. (2006). *Divorce: Causes and consequences.* New Haven, CT: Yale University Press.

Cohen, S., & Wills, T. A. (1985). Stress, social support, and the buffering hypothesis. *Psychological Bulletin, 98,* 310–357.

Cutrona, C., Russell, D., Hessling, R., Brown, P., & Murry, V. (2000). Direct and moderating effects of community context on the psychological well-being of African American women. *Journal of Personality and Social Psychology, 79,* 1099–1101.

Day, R., & Acock, A. (2004). Youth ratings of family processes and the father role performance of resident and nonresident fathers. In R. D. Day & M. Lamb (Eds.), *Conceptualizing and measuring father involvement* (pp. 273–292). London: Lawrence Erlbaum Associates Publisher.

DeLeire, T., & Kalil, A. (2002). Good things come in threes: Single-parent multi-generational family structure and adolescent adjustment. *Demography, 39*(2), 393–412.

Demuth, S., & Brown, S. L. (2004). Family structure, family processes, and adolescent delinquency: The significance of parental absence versus parental gender. *Journal of Research in Crime and Delinquency, 41*, 58–81.

DePaulo, B. M., & Morris, W. L. (2005). Singles in society and in science. *Psychological Inquiry, 16*, 57–83

Duncan, G., & Brooks-Gunn, J. (2000). Family poverty, welfare reform, and child development. *Child Development, 71*, 188–196.

Edin, K., & Reed, J. M. (2005). Why don't they just get married? Barriers to marriage among the disadvantaged. *The Future of Children, 15*(2), 117–137.

Elder, G. H. (1998). The life course and human behavior. In W. Damon (Ed.), *Handbook of child psychology* (Vol. 1, pp. 939–991). New York: John Wiley and Sons.

Ellman, I. M., Kurtz, P., Weithorn, L. A, Bix, B. H., Czapanskiy, K., & Eichner, M. (2010). *Family law: Cases, text, problems* (5th ed.). Newark, NJ: LexisNexis.

Ellwood, D., & Jencks, C. (2004). The spread of single-parent families in the United States since 1960. In D. P. Moynihan, T. Smeeding, & L. Rainwater (Eds.), *The future of the family* (pp. 25–65). New York: Russell Sage Foundation.

Evans, G. W., Gonnella, C., Marcynyszyn, L. A., Gentile, L., & Salpekar, N. (2005). The role of chaos in poverty and children's socioemotional adjustment. *Psychological Science, 16*(7), 560–565.

Falci, C. (2006). Family structure, closeness to residential and nonresidential parents, and psychological distress in early and middle adolescence. *Sociological Quarterly, 47*(1), 123–146.

Forehand, R. L., & Kotchick, B. A. (1996). Cultural diversity: A wake-up call for parent training. *Behavior Therapy, 27*, 187–206.

Goldscheider, F., & Kaufman, G. (2006). Single parenthood and the double standard. *Fathering, 4*(2), 191–208.

Hao, L. (1996). Family structure, private transfers, and the economic well-being of families with children. *Social Forces, 75*(1), 269–292.

Heiland, F., & Liu, S. (2005). *Family structure and wellbeing of out-of-wedlock children: The significance of the biological parents relationship.* Retrieved from http://www.demographic-research.org/volumes/vol15/4/

Hofferth, S. L. (2006). Residential father family type and child wellbeing: Investment versus selection. *Demography, 43*(1), 53–77.

Huang, C. (2006). Child support enforcement and father involvement for children in never-married mother families. *Fathering, 4*(1), 97–111.

Johnston, J. R., & Campbell, L. E. G. (1988). *Impasses of divorce: The dynamics and resolution of family conflict.* New York: Free Press.

Jones, D. J., Forehand, R., Brody, G., & Armistead, L. (2003). Parental monitoring in African American single mother-headed families: An ecological approach to the identification of predictors. *Behavior Modification, 27*, 435–457.

Kelly, J. (2012). Risk and protective factors associated with child and adolescent adjustment following separation and divorce: Social science applications.

In K. Kuehnle & L. Drozd (Eds.), *Parenting plan evaluations: Applied research for the family court*. New York: Oxford University Press.

Kelly, J. B., & Emery, R. (2003). Children's adjustment following divorce: Risk and resilience perspectives. *Family Relations, 52*, 352–362.

Kennedy, S., & Bumpass, L. (2008). Cohabitation and children's living arrangements: New estimates from the United States. *Demography Research, 19*, 1663–1692.

Klebanov, P., Brooks-Gunn, J., & Duncan, G. (1994). Does neighborhood and family poverty affect mothers' parenting, mental health, and social support? *Journal of Marriage and the Family, 56*, 412–455.

Kowaleski-Jones, L. & Duniform, R. (2006). Family structure and community context: Evaluating influences on adolescent outcomes. *Youth and Society, 38*(1), 110–130.

Lamb, M. (2012). Critical analysis of research on parenting plans and children's well-being. In K. Kuehnle & L. Drozd (Eds.), *Parenting plan evaluations: Applied research for the family court*. New York: Oxford University Press.

Lichter, D. T., & Crowley, M. L. (2004). Welfare reform and child poverty: Effects of maternal employment, marriage, and cohabitation. *Social Science Research, 33*, 385–408.

Lichter, D. T., Turner, R. N., & Sassler, S. (2010). National estimates of the rise in serial cohabitation. *Marriage and family in the new millennium: Papers in honor of Steven L. Knock, 39*(5), 754–765.

MacPhee, D., Fritz, J., & Miller-Heyl, J. (1996). Ethnic variations in personal social networks and parenting. *Child Development, 67*, 3278–3295.

Manning, W. D. (2004). Children and the stability of cohabiting couples. *Journal of Marriage and Family, 66*, 674–689.

Manning, W. D., & Brown, S. (2003). *Children's economic well-being in cohabiting parent families: An update and extension*. Paper presented at the annual meeting of the Population Association of America, Minneapolis, MN.

Manning, W. D., & Lamb, K. A. (2004). Adolescent well-being in cohabiting, married, and single-parent families. *Journal of Marriage and Family, 65*(4), 876–893.

Manning, W. D., & Lichter, D. T. (1996). Parental cohabitation and children's economic well-being. *Journal of Marriage and the Family, 58*, 998–1010.

Manning, W. D., Smock, P. J., & Majumdar, D. (2004). The relative stability of marital and cohabiting unions for children. *Population Research and Policy Review, 23*, 135–159.

Marcussen, K. (2005). Explaining differences in mental health between married and cohabiting individuals. *Social Psychology Quarterly, 68*(3), 239–257.

Martinson, B., & Wu, L. (1992). Parent histories: Patterns of change in early life. *Journal of Family Issues, 13*, 351–377.

Marsigilio, W., Amato, P., Day, R., Lamb, M. (2004). Scholarship on fatherhood in the 1990s and beyond. *Journal of Marriage and Family, 62*(4), 1173–1191.

McKeever, M., & Wolfinger, N.H. (2011). Thanks for nothing: Income and labor force participation for never-married mothers since 1982. *Social Science, 40*(1), 63–76.

McLanahan, S., & Beck, A. (2010).Parental relationships in fragile families. *The Future of Children, 20*(2), 17–37.

McLanahan, S., & Garfinkel, I. (2002).*Unwed parents: Myths, realities, and policy-making* (Working Paper 2002-15-FF). Princeton, NJ: Center for Research on Child Wellbeing.

McLanahan, S., & Sandefur, G. (1994).*Growing up with a single parent: What hurts, what helps?* Cambridge, MA: Harvard University Press.

Mistry, R. S., Vandewater, E. A., Huston, A. C., & McLoyd, V. C. (2002). Economic well-being and children's social adjustment: The role of family process in an ethnically diverse low-income sample. *Child Development, 73*, 667–681.

Murry, V. M., Bynum, M. S., Brody, G. H., Willert, A., & Stephens, D. (2000). African American single mothers and children in context: A review of studies on risk and resilience. *Clinical Child and Family Psychology Review, 4*, 133–155.

Osborne, C., & Knab, J. (2007). Work, welfare, and young children's health and behavior in the Fragile Families and Child Wellbeing study. *Children and Youth Services Review, 29*, 762–781.

Osborne, C., & McLanahan, S. (2007). Partnership instability and child wellbeing. *Journal of Marriage and Family, 69*, 1065–1083.

Parke, M. (2004). *What are "fragile families" and what do we know about them?* Couples and Marriage Series, Brief No.4. Washington, DC: Center for Law and Social Policy. Available on-line at www.clasp.org.

Pascoe, J. M., Stolfi, A., & Ormond, M. B. (2006). Correlates of mothers' persistent depressive symptoms: A national study. *Journal of Pediatric Health Care, 20*(4), 261–269.

Pedro-Carroll, J., Nakhnikian, E., & Montes, G. (2001). Assisting children through transition: Helping parents protect their children from the toxic effects of ongoing conflict in the aftermath of divorce. *Family Court Review, 39*(4), 377–392.

Pierce, G. R., Sarason, I. G., & Sarason, B. R. (1996). Coping and social support. In M. Zeidner & N. S. Endler (Eds.), *Handbook of coping: Theory, research, applications* (pp. 434–451). New York: John Wiley & Sons.

Pribesh, S., & Downey, D. (1999). Why are residential school moves associated with poorer school performance? *Demography, 36*(4), 521–534.

Raisner, J. K. (2004). Mediation with never-married parents. In J. Folberg, A. L. Milne, & P. Salem (Eds.), *Divorce and family mediation: Models, techniques, and applications* (pp. 283–303). New York: The Guilford Press.

Raley, R. K., & Wildsmith, E. (2004). Cohabitation and children's family instability. *Journal of Marriage and Family, 66*, 210–219.

Reichman, N., Teitler, J., Garfinkel, I., & McLanahan, S. (2001). Fragile Families: Sample and design. *Children and Youth Services Review, 23*(4), 303–326.

Saini, M., & Ma, J. (2012). Cultural dynamics of divorce and parenting after divorce. In K. Kuehnle & L. Drozd (Eds.), *Parenting plan evaluations: Applied research for the family court.* New York: Oxford University Press.

Sigle-Rushton, W., & McLanahan, S. S. (2002). The living arrangements of new unmarried mothers. *Demography, 39*, 415–433.

Skaine, R. (2003). *Paternity and American law.* Jefferson, NC: McFarland & Company, Inc. Publishers.

Smock, P. J. (2000). Cohabitation in the United States: An appraisal of research themes, findings, and implications. *Annual Review of Sociology, 26*, 1–20.

Smock, P. J., Manning, W. D., & Porter, M. (2005). "Everything's there except money": How money shapes decisions to marry among cohabiters. *Journal of Marriage and Family, 67*(3),680–696.

Teachman, J. (2003). Childhood living arrangements and the formation of coresidential unions, *Journal of Marriage and Family, 65*, 507–524

Teachman, J., & Paasch, K. M. (1994). Financial impact of divorce on children and their families. *The Future of Children, 4*(1), 63–82.

Thornton, A., Axinn, W. G., & Xie, Y. (2007). *Marriage and cohabitation.* Chicago, IL: The University of Chicago Press.

U.S. Bureau of the Census.(2003, February). *Married-couple and unmarried partner households: 2000.* Census 2000 Special Reports. Washington, DC: Author.

U.S. Bureau of the Census. (2009, November). *Custodial mothers and fathers and their child support: 2007.* Census 2007 Special Reports, Washington, DC: Author.

Ventura, S., & Bachrach, C. (2000). *Nonmarital childbearing in the United States, 1940–1999.* National Vital Statistics Reports, 48(16). Hyattsville, MD: National Center for Health Statistics.

Wang, H., & Amato, P. R. (2000). Predictors of divorce adjustment: Stressors, resources, and definitions. *Journal of Marriage and Family, 62,* 655–668.

Woldoff, R. A., & Cina, M. G. (2007). Regular work, underground jobs, and hustling: An examination of paternal work and father involvement. *Fathering: A Journal of Theory, Research, and Practice about Men as Fathers, 5*(3), 153–173.

Wolfinger, N. H. (2001). The effects of family structure of origin on offspring cohabitation duration. *Social Inquiry, 71*(3), 293–313.

Wood, D., Halfon, N., Scarlata, D., Newacheck, P., & Nessim, S. (1993). Impact of family relocation on children's growth, development, school function, and behavior. *Journal of the American Medical Association, 270*(11), 1334–1138.

Yoo, J., & Younghee, L. (2009). The trend in income status of children in female-headed families: A replication and update. *Children and Youth Services Review, 31*(4), 482–488.

Zill, N., Morrison, R. D., & Coiro, M. J. (1993). Long-term effects of parental divorce on parent-child relationships, adjustment, and achievement in young adulthood: Families in transition. *Journal of Family Psychology, 7*(1), 91–103.

## 16

Gay and Lesbian Parents and Their Children

Research Relevant to Custody Cases

SUZANNE M. JOHNSON AND ELIZABETH O'CONNOR ■

Gay and lesbian parents and their children live in every county in the United States (Smith & Gates, 2001). Over 600,000 gay or lesbian families were reported in the 2000 Census, and this is almost certainly an underestimation of the true number of families with same-sex parents. Gay and lesbian parents are a diverse group of families. Many, possibly a majority, had their children within the context of a previous heterosexual relationship or marriage. There is evidence that suggests that this may be changing, with younger gay parents more likely to have created their families within the context of a gay relationship (Tornello & Patterson, 2010). There are a number of pathways to parenthood that gays or lesbians may take. Some lesbians pursue biological parenthood through the use of sperm donors, either anonymous or known. The known donor may act as anything from a third parental figure to a fairly uninvolved family friend. Gay couples may choose surrogacy as a route to biological parenthood, with the role of the surrogate in the child's life varying along similar dimensions. In some couples, both parents choose to become biological parents. Other gay or lesbian couples opt for adoption; some data (Farr & Patterson, 2009a) suggest that gay and lesbian parents are more likely than heterosexuals to adopt transracially. Individual families may include children who arrived through a combination of these pathways.

As these families vary in their composition, so too do they vary in the legal ties they have available to them. Currently, same-sex adoptions are recognized in 11 states (New Jersey, New York, Indiana, Maine, California, Connecticut, Illinois, Massachusetts, Oregon, Vermont, and Florida) as well as in the District of Columbia. In states that do not legally recognize two parents of the same sex, such families are without protection under the law. Should these families seek relief in the court system for any reason, they will do so from a very vulnerable position.

Gay and lesbian parents may become involved in the legal system for a variety of reasons. This could occur when the dissolution of a heterosexual marriage involves the adoption of a gay or lesbian identity by one of the parents, and a custody battle ensues. A previously agreed-upon custody decision between heterosexual parents may be challenged when one parent enters into a same-sex relationship. Legal challenges to surrogacy, or sperm or egg donor arrangements, may also arise. A gay or lesbian relationship may dissolve, leading to a custody case.

In each of these cases, issues regarding the suitability of gays and lesbians serving as parents may be raised in custody decisions. Research that addresses this question—whether gays and lesbians are capable of raising well-functioning children—will be the focus of this chapter.

RESEARCH ON GAY AND LESBIAN PARENTS AND THEIR CHILDREN

Some points regarding the literature need to be made. First, the term *research on gay and lesbian parents* is a bit misleading; there is actually much more research on lesbian mothers than on gay fathers. While this disparity has begun to be addressed in recent years, there still remains much more empirical data on lesbian mothers and their children. More work needs to be undertaken in the future to expand the current knowledge of gay fathers and their children.

Gay and lesbian parents, as noted, are geographically diverse and are a difficult group for researchers to reach. Historically, and particularly in the early years, this has resulted in researchers relying on fairly small convenience samples. These samples generally overrepresented White, middle-class gays and lesbians. It is encouraging that more recent data (for example, Wainwright & Patterson, 2008) have been drawn from random national surveys. However, there is still a need for more research focusing on ethnic and racial minorities, multiracial families, lower-class families, adoptive families, and those living in rural areas.

Methodological advances in the field have been made, but the progress needs to continue. Many studies rely on self-reports of parents and children, and while these provide valuable information, other types of data collection, such as teacher and peer reports and direct observation, need to become more commonly used.

It also is important to bear in mind that given changes in societal acceptance of gays and lesbians as parents, it is likely that each successive cohort will have different experiences. Continued research is needed to ascertain how changes in laws regarding same-sex marriage and adoption—and societal acceptance of gays and lesbians in general—will affect these families in the future.

Given the focus on the current chapter, it is unfortunate that there is virtually no research on gay and lesbian parents who dissolve their relationship. Similarly, there is a lack of research on child outcomes of gay or lesbian family dissolution. As gays and lesbians create their own families in increasing numbers, it is inevitable that some of their relationships will dissolve. Research focusing on this sub-group of gay and lesbian parents, and the effects of their relationship dissolution, custody arrangements, and long-term outcomes for both children and adults, is an area crying out for study.

Table 16.1 shows empirical research on lesbian mothers, gay fathers, and their children. Each study's methodology and findings are described as well as evaluated as to the methodological strengths and weaknesses. The following characteristics of each study will be assessed: whether a comparison group was used; whether standardized measures were used; the source of reporting (parent or child self-reports, reports of teachers or peers, etc.); if the study sample was random; if selection criteria

Table 16.1 Empirical Research on Lesbian Mothers, Gay Fathers, and Their Children

Source of Research	Study Design
Bailey, J. M., Bobrow, D., Wolfe, M., & Mikach, S. (1995)	82 adult sons of gay fathers
Bos, H. M., Van Balen, F., & Van den Boom, D. C. (2007) Bos, H. M., Van Balen, F., & Van den Boom, D. C. (2004)	100 planned lesbian-parent families, 100 heterosexual-parent families
Bos, H., & Sandfort, T. (2010)	63 8- to 12-year-old children with lesbian parents, 68 8- to 12-year-old children with heterosexual parents
Chan, R. W., Brooks, R. S., Raboy, B., & Patterson, C. J. (1998) Chan, R. W., Raboy, B., & Patterson, C. J. (1998)	30 lesbian couples, 16 heterosexual couples; all had conceived using an anonymous sperm donor (a) 55 lesbian-headed families, 25 heterosexual-headed families; all had conceived using an anonymous sperm donor (b)
Farr, R., & Patterson, C. (2009a)	26 lesbian-headed, 29 gay-headed, and 50 heterosexual adoptive families
Flaks, D. K., Ficher, I., Masterpasqua, F., & Joseph, G. (1995)	15 lesbian couples and their children
US National Longitudinal Lesbian Family Study. Gartrell, N., Banks, A., Hamilton, J., Reed, N., Bishop, H., & Rodas, J. (1999) Gartrell, N., Banks, A., Reed, N., Hamilton, J., Rodas, C., & Deck, A. (2000) Gartrell, N., Deck, A., Rodas, C., Peyser, H., & Banks, A. (2005) Gartrell, N., & Bos, H. M. (2010)	A cohort of planned lesbian families has been studied since the late 1980s, beginning during pregnancy or attempts to become pregnant via donor insemination. 84 families initially, 70 of whom had 2 mothers; 93% retention rate.

Analysis & Results	Rating (Number of 6 possible criteria met)	Study Limitations
Over 90% of sons rate themselves as heterosexual.	3	1) Comparison group used 2) Non-standardized measures used 3) Self-reports used 4) Non-random sample 5) Selection criteria clear 6) Adequate sample size
No differences in child adjustment by family type (2007); No differences in parental competence by family type; lesbian mothers less concerned with conformity as a childrearing goal (2004)	5	1) Comparison or control group used 2) Standardized measures used 3) Self-reports used 4) Random sample 5) Selection criteria clear 6) Adequate sample size
Children with lesbian parents reported less pressure to conform to gender stereotypes; less certainty regarding future heterosexual involvement	4	1) Comparison group used 2) Standardized measures used 3) Self-reports used 4) Non-random sample 5) Selection criteria clear 6) Adequate sample size
No differences in child adjustment by family type as reported by parents or teachers	6	1) Comparison group used 2) Standardized measures used 3) Parent and teacher reports used 4) Random sample 5) Selection criteria clear 6) Adequate sample size
Same-sex couples more likely to complete transracial adoption; children in all groups well adjusted	6	1) Comparison group used 2) Standardized measures used 3) Parent and teacher reports used 4) Random sample 5) Selection criteria clear 6) Adequate sample size
Teacher and mother reports indicate children in normal range on behavioral adjustment and social competence	3	1) No comparison group used 2) Standardized measures used 3) Teacher and mother reports used 4) Non-random sample 5) Selection criteria clear 6) Small sample
Gartrell et al. (1999): Subjects described egalitarian parenting 　　Gartrell et al. (2000): Subjects reported their 5-year-olds as well adjusted 　　Gartrell et al. (2005): Subjects rated their children in the normal range on Child Behavior Checklist 　　Gartrell & Bos (2010): Subjects rated their adolescents as more socially competent, and with fewer behavior problems, than reported norms	3	1) No comparison or control group used 2) Standardized measures used (2005, 2010) 3) Self-reports used 4) Non-random sample 5) Selection criteria clear 6) Adequate sample size

(Continued)

Table 16.1 Empirical Research on Lesbian Mothers, Gay Fathers, and Their Children (*Continued*)

Source of Research	Study Design
Tasker, F. L., & Golombok, S. (1997) Golombok, S., & Tasker, F. (1996)	25 adolescents and young adults with lesbian mothers; 21 with heterosexual mothers
Golombok, S., Tasker, F., & Murray, C. (1997)	30 lesbian mother families; 42 single and 41 two-parent heterosexual families
Johnson, S., & O'Connor, E. (2002)	79 gay fathers; 336 lesbian mothers
Kurdek, L. A. (2001)	150 gay couples; 102 lesbian couples; 90 heterosexual couples with children; 108 non-parent heterosexual couples
MacCallum, F., & Golombok, S. (2004)	25 lesbian mother families, 3 families with a single heterosexual mother, and 38 two-parent heterosexual families
Patterson, C. J. (1994)	37 lesbian mothers and their children
Siegenthaler, A., & Bigner, J. J. (2000)	25 lesbian mothers, 26 heterosexual mothers

Analysis & Results	Rating (Number of 6 possible criteria met)	Study Limitations
No differences in self-reported family or peer relationships, sexual orientation, or psychological adjustment by family type (1997); those with lesbian mothers more likely to have considered the possibility of same-sex attraction (1996)	3; 2	1) Comparison group used 2) Standardized measures used (1997); non-standardized interviews (1996) 3) Self-reports used 4) Non-random sample 5) Selection criteria clear 6) Small sample
No differences in child behavior or maternal psychological functioning by family type as reported by parents	4	1) Comparison group used 2) Standardized measures used 3) Self-reports used 4) Non-random sample 5) Selection criteria clear 6) Adequate sample size
Self-reports indicate couples in normal range on relationship satisfaction	3	1) No comparison group used 2) Standardized measures used 3) Self-reports used 4) Non-random sample 5) Selection criteria clear 6) Adequate sample size
Gay and lesbian couples report less support from their families	5	1) Comparison group used 2) Standardized measures used 3) Self-reports used 4) Random sample 5) Selection criteria clear 6) Adequate sample size
No differences between father-absent and father-present families in children's psychological adjustment, peer relationships, behavior problems, or self-esteem. Boys in father-absent homes showed more feminine characteristics, but no fewer masculine characteristics, than other boys.	5	1) Comparison group used 2) Standardized measures used 3) Child, parent, and teacher reports used 4) Random sample 5) Selection criteria clear 6) Small sample
Mother reports indicate children in normal range on gender role behavior, social competence, behavioral adjustment, and self-concept	2	1) No comparison group used 2) Standardized measures used 3) Mother reports used 4) Non-random sample 5) Selection criteria clear 6) Small sample
No differences on 5 of 6 subscales on reason for having children (including personal satisfaction, achieving a sense of family, accomplishment, ability to influence, and adult status); heterosexual mothers more likely to endorse to strengthen marital bond and achieve higher purpose	4	1) Comparison group used 2) Standardized measures used 3) Self-reports used 4) Random sample 5) Selection criteria clear 6) Small sample

(Continued)

Table 16.1 Empirical Research on Lesbian Mothers, Gay Fathers, and
Their Children   *(Continued)*

Source of Research	Study Design
Vanfraussen, K., Ponjaert-Kristoffersen, I., & Brewaeys, A. (2002)	24 children with lesbian parents, 24 children with heterosexual parents

Wainright, J. L., & Patterson, C. J. (2008)
  Wainright, J. L., & Patterson, C. J. (2006)
  Wainright, J. L., Russell, S. T., &
Patterson, C. J. (2004)
	44 adolescents with same-sex parents; 44 with heterosexual parents. Subjects drawn from a national sample, matched on demographics.

were clearly stated; and whether the sample was of adequate size. The focus of the chapter will now shift to a brief review of empirical studies that have focused on children raised by gays and lesbians.

Social Relationships

Research focusing on the social functioning of children and adolescents with gay or lesbian parents has been undertaken. The issue that has been addressed is whether these children and adolescents suffer teasing, bullying, or ostracism from their peers as a result of their different families. If children of gays and lesbian did, in fact, experience high rates of teasing and bullying from their peers, they would be at risk for impaired social relationships. Fortunately, research has consistently found that these concerns are not borne out.

Vanfraussen, Ponjaert-Kristofferson, and Brewaeys (2002) found similar rates of teasing experienced by children of lesbian parents and children of heterosexual parents. Both groups of children reported being teased because of their physical appearance, intelligence, or clothing choices. What did differ between the groups was their experience of being teased about their families. Children of lesbians reported being teased more frequently about their families than did children of heterosexual parents. The children of heterosexuals were teased as frequently, just over different issues.

Flaks, Ficher, Masterpasqua, and Joseph (1995) found that children of lesbian mothers were rated within the average range on social competence by both their

Analysis & Results	Rating (Number of 6 possible criteria met)	Study Limitations
No differences in child adjustment by family type as reported by parents; more attentional problems in children of lesbians reported by teachers; more teasing over family reported by children of lesbians	5	1) Comparison group used 2) Standardized measures used 3) Child, parent, and teacher reports used 4) Random sample 5) Selection criteria clear 6) Small sample
No differences in adolescent peer relationships as a function of family type (2008); no differences in substance use, delinquent behavior, or quality of family relationships (2006); no differences in psychosocial adjustment, school outcome, or romantic attraction and behavior (2004)	4.5	1) Comparison or control group used 2) Standardized measures used 3) Self- and mother reports used (2008; 2004); self-reports used (2006) 4) Random sample 5) Selection criteria somewhat vague; parents not asked directly about sexual identity 6) Adequate sample size

mothers and their teachers. MacCallum and Golombok (2004) found no differences in the quality of peer relationships between children who had heterosexual parents and children with lesbian mothers.

Tasker and Golombok (1997) compared the self-reported peer relationships of adolescents and young adults with lesbian mothers to self-reports of adolescents with heterosexual mothers. No differences in the quality of peer relationships were found. Wainwright and Patterson (2008) drew from a national sample to examine the quality of adolescent peer relationships in adolescents with same-sex parents in comparison to those with heterosexual parents. In this sample, too, no differences as a function of family type emerged.

In summary, the research on social relationships of children raised by gay or lesbian parents indicates that:

- Children and adolescents raised by same-sex parents do not experience greater levels of bullying and teasing from their peers than do children with heterosexual parents.
- What may be different is what children are teased about. Children and adolescents with lesbian mothers may be more likely to be teased about their family and about their own sexuality than their peers with heterosexual parents.
- When compared to children of heterosexual mothers, children of lesbian mothers exhibit peer relationships that are just as positive.
- Adolescents with lesbian mothers do not differ in the quality of their peer relationships, in comparison to adolescents with heterosexual parents.

Gender Behavior

Questions regarding the development of gender role behavior in children of gays and lesbians have also been addressed in a number of studies. The concern is that children who do not have a parent of one gender in their home may not acquire appropriate socialization in terms of their gender identity or sex role behavior. Essentially, the issue is whether a boy needs a father to teach him how to be a boy or man, or whether a girl needs a mother in order to develop into a woman. Researchers have focused on preferences for activities, toys, and friends in young children, and on attitudes toward gender-typical behavior in older children and adolescents. Concern that children of non-heterosexual parents develop atypical gender role behavior has been examined in numerous studies, and again fears appear to be unfounded.

For example, Golombok et al. (2003) assessed activity preferences in children of lesbian, single heterosexual, and heterosexual married mothers. They found no significant differences based on the type of family in which the children were being raised. Similarly, Patterson (1994) found that children of lesbian mothers report preference for toys, activities, friends, and characters to be typical for children of their age.

Another study (Sutfin, Fulcher, Bowles, & Patterson, 2008) indicates that children with lesbian mothers have less stereotyped environments and less traditional attitudes toward gender. Lesbian mothers in this sample seem less invested in promoting gendered stereotyped behavior in their children. Bos and Sandfort (2010) found that children of lesbians report less pressure to conform to gender stereotypes, being more comfortable with androgyny than children of heterosexuals.

In summary, research indicates that:

- In terms of toy and activity preferences and understanding of gender stereotypes, children with lesbian mothers do not differ from children of heterosexual parents.
- Children of lesbian mothers do show more acceptance of androgynous behavior and attitudes.

Psychological Functioning, Behavior Disorders, and Delinquency

Child and adolescent psychological functioning among offspring of gays or lesbians has also been a focus of research. The question is whether children of gays and lesbians are at heightened risk for maladjustment, problem behavior, or delinquency. Might children of gays and lesbians be more likely to develop anxiety or depression, or acting-out behaviors, as a result of the supposed stress of growing up in a stigmatized family? The answer appears to be "no"; empirical research finds no such elevated risk.

In comparing two-parent lesbian-headed families to two-parent heterosexual-headed families, Chan, Raboy, and Patterson (1998) found that children's adjustment and behavior problems were not related to structural variables such as the number of parents or the sexual orientation of the parents. Factors that were associated with children's adjustment, in both lesbian and heterosexual families, were levels of parenting stress, parental interpersonal conflict, and levels of love expressed between the parents (Chan, Brooks, Raboy, & Patterson, 1998). This finding was supported by a more recent study that used a larger sample and found similar results (Bos, Van Balen, & Van den Boom, 2007).

The psychological adjustment of adolescents of gay and lesbian parents has also been examined, yielding no significant differences between adolescents with heterosexual parents and adolescents with gay or lesbian parents on measures of anxiety, depression, self-esteem, school connectedness, or delinquent behavior (Farr & Patterson, 2009b; Wainwright & Patterson, 2006; Wainwright, Russell, & Patterson, 2004).

Research on behavior disorders demonstrates that:

- Children with lesbian mothers are no more likely to exhibit emotional or behavior disorders than are children with heterosexual parents.
- Adolescents with same-sex parents are no more likely to engage in delinquent behavior or substance use than adolescents with both a male and a female parent.

Sexual Orientation

Will children raised by gays or lesbians be less likely to grow up to become heterosexual? This issue is, in some ways, an extension of the debate over gender identity. The concern is that same-sex parents, perhaps through modeling or implicit or explicit encouragement, will increase the odds that their children will grow up to identify as non-heterosexual. Research on reported sexual orientation of adolescent and adult children of gays and lesbians will be reviewed.

Young adult women who grew up with lesbian mothers have not been found to identify themselves any differently regarding their sexual orientation than do young women raised by heterosexual parents (Golombok & Tasker, 1996: Tasker & Golombok, 1997). What is interesting is that these researchers found that the young adult daughters of lesbians were more likely to have considered the possibility that they might one day experience an attraction to someone of the same sex or have a same-sex relationship than daughters raised by heterosexual mothers. Bos and Sandfort (2010) also found that among prepubescent children, those with lesbian mothers expressed less certainty regarding future heterosexual attractions and involvement.

Bailey, Bobrow, Wolfe, and Mikach (1995) focused on adult sons of gay fathers. They found that the overwhelming majority of these young men identified themselves as heterosexual.

Regarding the adult sexual orientation of children with gay or lesbian parents, the following conclusions may be drawn:

- The overwhelming majority of children with gay or lesbian parents identify as heterosexual in adulthood. Rates of identification as anything other than heterosexual do not appear to be significantly higher.

- Young adults with lesbian mothers do appear more likely to have considered the possibility of a same-sex attraction or relationship than young adults with heterosexual parents.

Gay and Lesbian Parents

Research on gay and lesbian parents will be reviewed, with a focus on the parents' goals and concerns for their children. The intent of this section will be to inform professionals who deal with this population as to the mindset of these parents.

Gartrell et al. (Gartrell et al., 1996, 1999, 2000; Gartrell & Bos, 2010; Gartrell, Deck, Rodas, Peyser, & Banks, 2005) are conducting the longest-running longitudinal study of planned lesbian families. The study began when the mothers were pregnant or attempting to become pregnant; the oldest children are now in their teens. Prospective mothers identified concerns about stigmatization of their children; most co-mothers reported egalitarian parenting and being actively involved in the lesbian community. Of interest in terms of the focus of this chapter is what this study found concerning custody arrangements in couples who had split up while their children were young. Among those couples who had been able to procure legal parental rights for both parents (i.e., obtain second-parent adoption), the majority were sharing custody after the separation. This was not the most common pattern in those couples where second-parent adoption was not obtained.

Family functioning within gay and lesbian families has also been studied. Siegenthaler and Bigner (2000) queried mothers about their reasons for having children; they found few differences in a comparison of lesbians and heterosexual mothers. In their study the heterosexual mothers were more likely to cite strengthening their marital bond and having children in order to serve a higher purpose than were lesbian mothers. Golombok, Tasker, and Murray (1997) found no differences in maternal psychological health between lesbian and heterosexual mothers. Vanfraussen et al. (2002) found that children with heterosexual parents talked only to their mothers about emotional issues while children of lesbians talked to both parents equally. Likewise, non-biological lesbian mothers were more involved in child care than their heterosexual father counterparts. When examining broader family functioning variables such as measures of family relationship quality, parental attitudes, and dyadic adjustment, McNeil, Reinzi and Kposowa (1998) and Johnson and O'Connor (2002) found that lesbian couples who were co-parenting perform as well or better on these measures than their heterosexual couple co-parenting counterparts. Bos, Van Balen, and Van den Boom (2004) found lesbian mothers were less concerned with instilling conformity in their children than were heterosexual parents.

Schacher, Auerbach, and Silverstein (2005) found that gay fathers perceive prejudice on the basis of heterosexist gender roles as well as on the basis of non-heterosexual parenting. This suggests the possibility of additional parental stress on the part of gay fathers. McPherson (1993) compared two-parent families: families where there were gay co-parents and families where there were heterosexual co-parents. Gay couples reported a more even division of household responsibilities and child care than did heterosexual couples. Research on gay fathers indicates that families headed by gay fathers are functioning as well or better than heterosexual couples on measures of relationship satisfaction and parenting alliance (Kurdek, 2001, 2004).

CONCLUSION

Gay and lesbian family relationships that present in the legal system can bring with them complicated legal and psychological situations. A solid literature exists on the functioning of children and adolescents who were raised by gays or lesbians. What the research clearly demonstrates is that concerns regarding dysfunction in these children and adolescents are unfounded. In terms of psychological adjustment, peer relationships, experience of teasing, gender role development, and ultimate sexual orientation, there are very few differences between children who are raised by gays or lesbians and those raised by heterosexual parents. Family functioning, both in terms of the quality of the adult relationships and the parent–child relationships, is also not determined by the sexual orientation of the parents. While there continue to be gaps in the research that need to be addressed, all current evidence points to the ability of gays and lesbians to raise happy, well-functioning children.

Guidelines: Considerations and Cautions

- Gays and lesbians with children are a diverse group of families, including planned gay and lesbian families; gay and lesbian stepfamilies, which include a heterosexual parent from a prior relationship; families with three or more identified parents; and families where parental figures have no legal ties to the children.
- Research demonstrates that children raised by gays and lesbians suffer no adverse effects in terms of social relationships, gender role development, and behavior, and there is no heightened risk for behavioral disorders.
- There is not a strong base of research on this population in terms of the effects of parental separation, divorce, or custody issues. There is no reason to believe, however, that factors that facilitate positive adjustment to parental divorce in typical families (continued parental involvement by all parents, positive communication, and low levels of conflict) are different in this population.
- Professionals who encounter these families should educate themselves about the unique characteristics and legal challenges they face.

REFERENCES

Bailey, J. M., Bobrow, D., Wolfe, M., & Mikach, S. (1995). Sexual orientation of adult sons of gay fathers. *Developmental Psychology, 31*(1), 124–129.

Bos, H., & Sandfort, T. (2010). Children's gender identity in lesbian and heterosexual two-parent families. *Sex Roles, 62*(1–2), 114–126.

Bos, H. M., Van Balen, F., & Van den Boom, D. C. (2004). Experience of parenthood, couple relationship, social support, and child-rearing goals in planned lesbian mother families. *Journal of Child Psychology and Psychiatry, 45*(4), 755–764.

Bos, H. M., Van Balen, F., & Van den Boom, D. C. (2007). Child adjustment and parenting in planned lesbian-parent families. *American Journal of Orthopsychiatry, 77*(1), 38–48.

Chan, R. W., Brooks, R. S., Raboy, B., & Patterson, C. J. (1998). Division of labor among lesbian and heterosexual parents: Associations with children's adjustment. *Journal of Family Psychology, 12*(3), 402–419.

Chan, R. W., Raboy, B., & Patterson, C. J. (1998). Psychosocial adjustment among children conceived via donor insemination by lesbian and heterosexual mothers. *Child Development, 69*(2), 443–457.

Farr, R., & Patterson, C. (2009a). Transracial adoption by lesbian, gay, and heterosexual couples: Who completes transracial adoptions and with what results? *Adoption Quarterly, 12*(3–4), 187–204.

Farr, R., & Patterson, C. (2009b). *Adoptive families led by gay fathers: Family processes and outcomes.* Paper presented at the meeting of the Society for Research in Child Development, Denver, CO.

Flaks, D. K., Ficher, I., Masterpasqua, F., & Joseph, G. (1995). Lesbians choosing motherhood: A comparative study of lesbian and heterosexual parents and their children. *Developmental Psychology, 33*(1), 105–114.

Gartrell, N., Banks, A., Hamilton, J., Reed, N., Bishop, H., & Rodas, J. (1999). The National Lesbian Family Study: 2. Interviews with mothers of toddlers. *American Journal of Orthopsychiatry, 69*(3), 362–369.

Gartrell, N., Banks, A., Reed, N., Hamilton, J., Rodas, C., & Deck, A. (2000). The National Lesbian Family Study: 3. Interviews with mothers of 5-year-olds. *American Journal of Orthopsychiatry, 70*(4), 542–648.

Gartrell, N., & Bos, H. M. (2010). US National Longitudinal Lesbian Family Study: Psychological adjustment of 17-year-old adolescents. *Pediatrics, 126*(1), 1–9.

Gartrell N., Deck, A., Rodas, C., Peyser, H., & Banks, A. (2005). The National Lesbian Family Study: 4. Interviews with the 10-year-old children. *American Journal of Orthopsychiatry, 75*(4), 518–524.

Gartrell, N., Hamilton, J., Banks, A., Mosbacher, D., Reed, N., Sparks, C. H., & Bishop, H. (1996). The National Lesbian Family Study: 1. Interviews with prospective mothers. *American Journal of Orthopsychiatry, 66*(2), 272–281.

Golombok, S., Perry, B., Burston, A., Murray, C., Mooney-Somers, J., Stevens, M. & Golding, J. (2003) Children with lesbian parents: A community study. *Developmental Psychology, 39*(1), 20–33.

Golombok, S., & Tasker, F. (1996). Do parents influence the sexual orientation of their children? Findings from a longitudinal study of lesbian families. *Developmental Psychology, 32*(1), 3–11.

Golombok, S., Tasker, F., & Murray, C. (1997). Children raised in fatherless families from infancy: Family relationships and the socioemotional development of children of lesbian and single heterosexual mothers. *Journal of Child Psychology and Psychiatry, 38*(7), 783–791.

Johnson, S., & O'Connor, E. (2002). *The gay baby boom: The psychology of gay parenthood.* New York: New York University Press.

Kurdek, L. (2004). Are gay and lesbian cohabitating couples really different from heterosexual married couples? *Journal of Marriage and the Family, 66,* 880–900.

Kurdek, L. A. (2001). Differences between heterosexual-nonparent couples and gay, lesbian, and heterosexual-parent couples. *Journal of Family Issues, 22*(6), 727–754.

MacCallum, F., & Golombok, S. (2004) Children raised in fatherless families from infancy: A follow-up of children of lesbian and single heterosexual mothers at early adolescence. *Journal of Child Psychology and Psychiatry, 45*(7), 1407–1419.

McNeil, K. F., Reinzi, B. M., & Kposowa, A. (1998). Families and parenting: a comparison of lesbian and heterosexual mothers. *Psychological Reports, 82*(1), 59–62.

McPherson, D. (1993). *Gay parenting couples: Parenting arrangements, arrangement satisfaction, and relationship satisfaction* (Unpublished doctoral dissertation). Pacific Graduate School of Psychology, Palo Alto, CA.

Patterson, C. J. (1994). Children of the lesbian baby boom: Behavioral adjustment, self-concepts, and sex role identity. In B. Green & G. Herek (Eds.), *Lesbian and gay psychology & theory, research, and clinical applications* (pp. 156–175). Thousand Oaks, CA: Sage.

Schacher, S. J., Auerbach, C. F., & Silverstein, L. B. (2005). Gay fathers expanding the possibilities for us all. *Journal of GLBT Family Studies, 1*(3), 31–52.

Siegenthaler, A., & Bigner, J. J. (2000). The value of children to lesbian and non-lesbian mothers. *Journal of Homosexuality, 39*, 73–92.

Smith, D. M., & Gates, G. J. (2001). *Gay and lesbian families in the United States: Same-sex unmarried households. A Preliminary Analysis of 2000 United States Census Data: A Human Rights Campaign Report*. Retrieved from http://www.urban.org/uploadedpdf/1000491_gl_partner_households.pdf.

Sutfin, E. L., Fulcher, M., Bowles, R. P., & Patterson, C. J. (2008). How lesbian and heterosexual parents convey attitudes about gender to their children: The role of gendered environments. *Sex Roles, 58*, 501–513.

Tasker, F. L., & Golombok, S. (1997). *Growing up in a lesbian family: Effect on child development*. New York: Guilford Press.

Tornello, S. L., & Patterson, C. (2010, May). *Gay fathers' pathways to parenthood: Is there a generational shift?* Paper presented at the meeting of the Association for Psychological Science, Boston, MA.

Vanfraussen, K., Ponjaert-Kristoffersen, I., & Brewaeys, A. (2002). What does it mean for a youngster to grow up in a lesbian family created by means of donor insemination? *Journal of Reproductive and Infant Psychology, 20*(4), 237–252.

Wainright, J. L., & Patterson, C. J. (2006). Delinquency, victimization, and substance use among adolescents with female same-sex parents. *Journal of Family Psychology, 20*(3), 526–530.

Wainright, J. L., & Patterson, C. J. (2008). Peer relations among adolescents with female same-sex parents. *Developmental Psychology, 44*(1), 117–126.

Wainright, J. L., Russell, S. T., & Patterson, C. J. (2004). Psychological adjustment, school outcomes, and romantic relationships of adolescents with same-sex parents. *Child Development, 75*(6), 1886–1898.

## 17

Cultural Dynamics of Divorce and Parenting

MICHAEL SAINI AND JENNIFER MA ∎

Increased ethnic and racial diversity is one of the most compelling sociodemographic changes affecting North American families today (Vanier Institute of the Family, 2010). High levels of immigration from diverse countries (Sabo, 2000; Statistics Canada, 2008) and significant changes in the composition of families are transforming notions of multiculturalism, multilinguistic services, and multi-religious observances. In the United States, for example, the number of first- and second-generation immigrant children increased by 28% between 2000 and 2009 to 174 million, accounting for nearly one in four children in the United States (Child Trends, 2010). In Canada, Statistics Canada (2007) reported that in 2006, approximately 6.2 million individuals were born outside of Canada, representing one in five (19.8%) of the overall population. This is the highest ratio reported in 75 years. Moreover, 223,200 newcomers were children under the age of 15 in 2006, representing one in five (21%) of the foreign-born population. Nearly 1.1 million recent immigrants came to Canada between 2001 and 2006, increasing Canada's foreign-born population by 13.6%, which was four times higher than the increase (3.3%) in the Canadian-born population.

Increased immigration in both the United States and Canada adds to the complexity of working with children and families from diverse cultural backgrounds, given that children in immigrant families generally experience additional adversities stemming from families' migration and acculturation experiences (Dettlaff, Vidal de Haymes, Velazquez, Midell, & Bruce, 2009; Pine & Drachman, 2005; Roer-Strier, 2001). These challenges include stress and pressure related to differences in culture, language, and traditions (Dettlaff, 2010); feelings of isolation and discrimination; and adjustment to new and foreign systems (Alaggia & Maiter, 2006). Immigrant families are also at increased risk of poverty due to a greater likelihood of unemployment and underemployment following settlement (Beiser, Hou, Kaspar, & Noh, 2000). Given the complexity of issues experienced by diverse families, their distinct needs must be reflected in the family courts to facilitate the provision of effective services and in turn to promote positive outcomes.

The increased diversity of families involved in family courts challenges court-based services to re-evaluate how families are understood and how therapeutic and legal services can best function to collectively support the unique needs of diverse families. Cultural sensitivity is relevant to all mental health practitioners and legal professionals working in family courts, as it provides an overview of the various ways that cultural differences can influence complex decision-making processes when working with families from diverse backgrounds and heritages.

Due to the high rates and potential negative consequences of separation and divorce for children and families, considerable attention has been placed on investigating the risk and protective factors that either facilitate or impede families' adjustment to family breakdown (Das, 2010). With the ever-increasing levels of immigration and a substantial increase in the number of intercultural marriages in both the United States and Canada (Crippen & Brew, 2007; Vanier Institute of the Family, 2010), it is likely that mental health practitioners and legal professionals involved with family courts will work with families from racial and ethnic cultures different from their own. The rich cultural, linguistic, and ethnic diversity of separating and divorcing families makes it imperative that court-based services explore the systematic relationships among culture, family dynamics, childrearing patterns, and perceptions about separation and divorce to foster culturally competent practices based on the unique needs of children and families.

Interparental conflict, co-parenting relationships, and psychosocial health of separating and divorcing families may vary across different cultures (Cummings & Davies, 2010). Moreover, parenting after separation and divorce may be influenced by parent–child relationships, attachment, parenting styles, parenting attitudes and beliefs, and parent involvement, which also may vary across cultures. Because of the cultural variability of children and parents' experiences involved in custody disputes, cultural differences can dramatically increase the complexity of a child custody dispute. Two decades ago, Myricks and Ferullo (1986) noted that when culturally based disputes were brought to the courts, issues of race, ethnicity, and culture were either completely ignored or were made to be the deciding factor in determining child custody decisions, irrespective of other important factors affecting the child's best interest. For example, in *Ward v. Ward* (1950), one of the first known custody cases to address race in the United States, the court offered a one-dimensional view of race while de-emphasizing the children's complex connections with their parents:

> He is colored; she is white . . . both children are colored. We do not question the mother's love for her children. But we have always stated, in divorce cases, that our primary concern is the welfare of the children. We owe that duty to all children brought into a divorce court, regardless of race, color or creed. These unfortunate girls are the victims of a mixed marriage and a broken home. They will have a much better opportunity to their rightful place in society if they are brought up among their own people (qtd. in Myricks & Ferullo, 1986, p. 326)

Although cultural sensitivity has been steadily emerging as a prominent framework for the past 20 years across various disciplines (Buenker & Ratner, 1992; Irving & Benjamin, 1995), including family therapy, counseling, child psychology, and social work (Devore & Schlesinger, 1999; Falicov, 1995; McGoldrick, Pearce, & Giordano, 1982; Sue, Ivey, & Pederson, 1996), less attention has focused on the complexity of working with culturally diverse families in the context of family courts. McKinley (1980) lamented three decades ago that most legal professionals had not received adequate training to work collaboratively with families of diverse cultures. Based on the review of the current evidence, it appears little has changed since then.

Requirements for diversity training are now included in model standards for practice for child custody evaluations (Association of Family and Conciliation Courts, 2006; American Psychological Association, 1994), but there remains little guidance for the types of training services that would be most effective in fostering cultural sensitivity and self-awareness when working with diverse court-based clients. Professionals must be aware of their personal values, practices, and biases based on their own cultural experiences. Without a clear culturally sensitive framework, professionals may rely too heavily on universalistic standards for child custody evaluations (Gunning, 1995; Irving & Benjamin, 1995). A lack of culturally competent insight can result in court-based services not adeptly responding to cultural differences, pathologizing these differences as deficiencies in the child and/or family, and can bias data collection and assessment, thus interfering with the development of scientifically based opinions and recommendations (American Psychological Association, 1994).

Developing a culturally sensitive framework for understanding multicultural, multiethnic, and multilingual families within the context of separation and divorce is complicated and requires thoughtful considerations in how best to deal with cultural differences. The current literature focuses on descriptive profiles of ethnic and racial differences found within divorcing families (Barrett, 2003; Bulanda, & Brown, 2006; Coleman, Ganong, & Rothrauff, 2006; Irving & Benjamin, 1995; Irving & Benjamin, San-Pedro, 1999; Kalmijn, 2010; Lau, 2004; Lopez, Melendez, & Rice, 2000; McKenry & Fine, 1993; McKenry & McKelvey, 2003; Myricks & Ferullo, 1986; Shek, 2008; Sullivan, 2005). Although these differences provide an exploratory point of reference for understanding how culture is experienced among cultural groups, it is equally important to avoid stereotyping families based on perceived differences. The chapter emphasizes, therefore, a multicultural framework of both similarities and differences among and between cultures to enhance cultural sensitivity when working with diverse families within the context of family law.

THE MEANING OF CULTURE FOR FAMILIES

Culture is a complex concept with many different definitions. Ting-Toomey (1999) describes culture consisting of "patterns of traditions, beliefs, values, norms, symbols, and meanings" (p. 10). Culture is a shared experience, influencing values, beliefs, attitudes, and interactions with social structures (McGoldrick, 1989). These experiences can influence the choices of food, language, clothing, faith, customs, living arrangements, perspective on education, socioeconomic status, country of birth, and family structures, to name a few. These shared experiences among the cultural group are passed on from generation to generation and provide members with an ability to identify with the group and differentiate from other cultural groups. Triandis (2000) suggests that culture functions to improve the "adaptation of members of the culture to a particular ecology, and it includes the knowledge that people need to have in order to function effectively in their social environment" (p. 146).

This knowledge is created in sets of rules and social standards that govern behaviors considered both acceptable and adaptable for the longevity of the group.

Each of these descriptions provides an understanding of the collective glue that maintains individuals' connection to their cultural milieu. When working with children and families across cultural groups, it is important to consider both the importance of these shared experiences and the significant functions they contribute in shaping norms and expectations within a shared heritage. Internalized cultural beliefs and values influence both family relationships and interactional patterns based on these shared experiences and expectations of conformity to the group norms (Kagitcibasi, 1996; Triandis, 1995).

Phillips (1995) formulated six concepts to describe the intergenerational transmission of culture. First, culture is learned rather than biologically transmitted. Children learn cultural rules and expectations through daily interactions within the cultural groups. Second, culture is characterized and socially located within group formation. Individual personality traits within the cultural groups are distinguished from cultural traits along a continuum of individuality and conformity. Third, culture is a set of rules for behaviors. As Phillips explains, "the essence of culture is in the rules that produce the behaviors, not the behaviors themselves" (p. 5). Behaviors alone are not culture, but the expectation of behaviors according to the group norms is considered culturally based. Fourth, individuals are not fixed within culture and may experience different degrees of inclusion within various cultural groups. Families place different emphasis on cultural traditions and vary in their connections to the values, beliefs, and expectations set by cultural norms. Fifth, culture is not static. Rules and expectations can change over time and can be influenced by other cultures. Lastly, members of a cultural group may be unable to describe the sets of rules, expectations, and values, even though they may be proficient in the cultural behaviors of the group. Nevertheless, culture plays a vital role in the lives of children and families, regardless of their level of consciousness about the reasons for their behaviors.

In summary:

- Increased diversity among divorcing families challenges universalistic approaches to family law services.
- Culture is a complex, dynamic, and fluid phenomenon, and the definitions of culture vary across diverse groups.
- Culture is generally considered a shared experience among group members to provide knowledge across generations and to guide expectations within the group and/or affiliation.
- It is important to consider the shared experiences of children and families, as cultural beliefs and values influence family relationships.

THE IMPORTANCE OF CULTURE

Differences in the socialization patterns across cultural groups are often compared along a continuum from individualism and collectivism dimensions (Hofstede, 1991; Markus & Kitayama, 1991; Triandis, 1995). Individualist cultures emphasize autonomy, independence, and a right to privacy (Hofstede, 1991; Hui & Triandis, 1986). Collectivism, in contrast, "stands for a society in which people from birth onwards are integrated into strong cohesive in-groups, which throughout people's lifetime continue to protect them in exchange for unquestioning loyalty" (Hofstede, 1991, p. 51). In collectivist cultures, socialization practices emphasize interdependence and conformity because these values are believed to be necessary in preserving group harmony (Chao, 2001; Triandis, 1995). This perception of relationships reinforces the adherence to conventions and obedience, which are strongly encouraged. In return for the group loyalty, the adherents enjoy the group's protection and security when faced by challenges from outside the group. Among collectivist cultures, individual or personal goals are subordinate to communal goals, and thus independence and autonomy are discouraged.

Although the continuum of individualism and collectivism dimensions provides an important framework to understand differences in parenting, childrearing, and behaviors, it seems premature to assume that families from individualistic cultures are individualist and families from collectivistic cultures organize their families according to a collectivist framework. Dutta-Bergman and Wells (2002), for example, provide evidence of within-culture variations in terms of individualism and collectivism and consequent differences exhibited in behavioral indicators. Developments in cross-cultural psychology have also suggested that the traditional conceptualization of individualism versus collectivism is a simplified dichotomy that can limit understanding family formations, expectations, and experiences.

The influence of culture on parenting and divorce is perhaps best understood within an ecological theory (Bronfenbrenner, 1979), to highlight the interactions among individual differences, family characteristics, and environmental factors such as cultural expectations. An ecological perspective is relevant for understanding children's development because it provides a framework for assessing the influences of each level in the child's system (individual, parents, family, extended families, social networks, cultural affiliations, etc.) without obscuring the power of each of these influences in tandem. Within the ecological theory, children and parents are both directly and indirectly influenced by the family's cultural identifications, including race, ethnicity, religion, socioeconomic status, geographical location, and so on. The continuum of individualist and collectivist dimensions of culture can influence the family structure, but these differences are experienced in connection with other individual, family, and environmental factors.

Family systems theory (McGoldrick, 1989) also places importance on cultural considerations affecting families as connections to cultural expectations can influence the families' beliefs, practices, and values. There is an assumption within family systems theory, though, that the degree to which culture is important to a given family varies. For example, families who live close to others of the same ethnic, racial, and cultural background may maintain similar norms to the group, while those who move away from their cultural milieu may become more influenced by cultures experienced in their new social surroundings. Likewise, a teenager attending public school may gravitate more towards the school's dominant culture and be more acculturated to these social norms shared by peers compared to the teenager's parents, who may not have similar outlets for cultural integration.

Segal and Mayadas (2005) posit that the experience of acculturation is another critical factor in understanding diverse families. Newcomers, for example, are confronted with language, social structures, norms, expectations, and values that may differ considerably from those that have been fundamental in their lives. Adjusting to a new culture and lifestyle can be extremely stressful, with detrimental consequences. Cunradi, Caetano, and Shafer (2002), for example, found that high levels of acculturative stress are associated with an increased risk for family conflict and violence. Similarly, Choi, He, and Harachi (2008) found that parent–child conflict among Vietnamese and Cambodian immigrant families was associated with intergenerational cultural discrepancies due to differences in levels of acculturation between children and their parents. Ying and Hun (2008) explored the effect of parental acculturation, parental involvement, and intergenerational relationship on adolescent well-being among Southeast Asian American refugee families and found significant paths from parental English proficiency to parental involvement, from parental involvement to intergenerational relationships, and from intergenerational relationships to positive child outcomes. In other words, parents' increased language skills in English were associated with a significant increase in discussions about the child's education, engagement with the school, and extrafamilial social world. Educational involvement and social support significantly decreased familial conflict, and parental participation in the school increased family cohesion. Family conflict was found to increase the child's depressive symptoms and decrease the child's self-esteem, whereas family cohesion had an inverse effect, decreasing depressive symptoms and increasing self-esteem. Likewise, Ying and Han (2008) investigated the effect of parental acculturation, parental involvement, and intergenerational relationships on adolescent well-being among Filipino American immigrant families and found parental acculturation to mediate parents' involvement with their children's school, education at home, and social settings.

In summary:

- Socialization across cultural groups is often compared along a continuum of individualism and collectivism.
- Examining families solely on the traditional definitions of individualism and collectivism limits understanding of family formations, expectations, and experiences.
- An ecological framework identifies interactions among individual characteristics, family characteristics, and environmental factors and can be used to examine the influence of culture on parenting and divorce.
- Family systems theory identifies the impact of culture on familial beliefs, values, and practices, which varies across families.
- Acculturation among newcomers may be extremely stressful and can increase the risk of family conflict and violence, which may negatively affect child functioning.

INTRACULTURAL, INTERCULTURAL, AND TRANSCULTURAL FAMILIES

Since culture is a multidimensional construct, it is important to consider the differences in culture across intracultural, intercultural, transcultural, and multicultural families (Barnett & Lee, 2002). Intracultural refers to cultural elements shared within the same cultural group and reflects a particular group of people who may share a common language, customs, values, and beliefs (Samovar & Porter, 2001). Intracultural relationships, for example, are referred to as homogenous relationships among people who share similar race, ethnicity, and religion. Intracultural families often live in similar neighborhoods, frequent the same community services, and share close ties to their cultural surroundings.

Intercultural relationships, such as mixed marriages, are an integration of two different cultural backgrounds into one relationship (Crippen & Brew, 2007). Intercultural relationships are heterogeneous relationships among people with dissimilar cultures and may include interracial, interethnic, and/or interfaith pairings. Horowitz (1999) suggests that intercultural couples often face the challenge of negotiating and realigning individual cultural backgrounds, cultural values, and cultural realities to form a new cultural reality conjointly experienced by the couple. Research has documented increased conflict between intercultural couples following the birth of the first child and at each developmental stage, as these may trigger sources of stress as the couple negotiates contradictory goals, universal versus culturally specific processes of parenting, divergent values and beliefs, educational and disciplinary styles, and expectations of parent–child relationships (Bhugra & De Silva, 2000; Ho, 1990; Mackey & O'Brien, 1998; Mann & Waldron, 1977; Romano, 2001).

Transcultural family systems, a creation of a new, shared family identity, occurs when disparate cultural backgrounds are negotiated to form an integrated set of values and beliefs shared by all members of the family (Crippen & Brew, 2007). Moving from intercultural to transcultural requires reconstruction of each parent's identity and construction of a new family identity formed through marriage and then consolidated during the childrearing years (Bennett, Wolin, & McAvity, 1988; Crippen & Brew, 2007). There is a dearth of empirical evidence on the process of moving towards transcultural families. Vivero and Jenkins (1999) found that some of the benefits of transcultural families include more equitable division of household labor between parents, increased feelings of family support, and the family's ability to both recognize and resolve cultural impasses. But even if couples are able to achieve a transcultural union, they will most likely need to renegotiate their cultural values and beliefs at the point of the birth of their first child (Ho & Johnson, 1990; Romano, 2001). For example, Ho and Johnson (1990) found that the birth of a child within transcultural couples reactivated each parent's own childhood experiences, which connected them back to their individual cultural standpoints about preferred childrearing practices and goals.

Understanding the differences of culture across dimensions of intracultural, intercultural, and transcultural families can provide court-based professionals with yet another framework for understanding the evolving influences of culture experienced by children and families. Culture is not static, nor should it be considered unidimensional.

In summary:

- Intracultural families comprise individuals with common elements shared within a cultural group.
- Intercultural families comprise a combination of two different cultural groups.

- Transcultural families comprise a new, shared cultural identity created from an integration of values and beliefs shared by all members.
- Culture is not static and is experienced differently among children and families.

CULTURE AND DIVORCING FAMILIES

Any attempt to explain the reasons couples separate and divorce must take into account both the nature of marriage as an institution within a given social and cultural context and its particular meaning for the individuals involved (Wolcott & Hughes, 1999). The dramatic rise in divorce in Western societies during the past century is generally attributed to structural changes in society, including the movements towards industrialization, urbanization, individualization, and the subsequent changes in attitudes and laws governing divorce (Fu, 2006). In comparing divorce rates across cultures, societies with more emphasis on cultural individualism, such as the United States and Canada, have consistently demonstrated higher divorce rates compared to collectivist societies, which tend to place greater emphasis on adherence to social conventions (Toth & Kemmelmeier, 2009). A comprehensive search for this literature has uncovered a limited number of studies (Table 17.1) that have specifically considered factors that influence parents' decisions to separate and the adjustment process for children and parents after separation and divorce across cultural groups.

Although there is a tendency to focus on racial differences in union formation and separation trends, research highlights the importance of considering a combination of factors that contribute to family breakdown and divorce adjustment. Research that focuses on cultural differences suggests that there is a constellation of factors that can contribute to marital unhappiness, conflict, and divorce adjustment, including the nature and timing of mental health effects on marital dissolution (Barrett, 2003; McKenry & McKelvey, 2003); the presence of substance abuse (Barrett, 2003); the availability of social supports (Bulanda & Brown, 2006; McKenry & McKelvey, 2003); and religious affiliations (Bulanda & Brown, 2006). Cohen and Savaya (2003) found that positive adjustment to divorce among Muslim Arab citizens of Israel, for both men and women, was related to levels of education, employment status, levels of satisfaction with the court hearings, and their living conditions. McKenry and McKelvey (2003) found, after controlling for education and the time elapsed since a divorce, that African American mothers demonstrated lower levels of psychosocial well-being in personal mastery, informal support, and perceived economic well-being compared to Caucasian mothers. They also found that remarriage as a mechanism for adjusting to divorce is less likely for African American mothers due to systemic and structural factors, including focusing on counseling and job training to become more self-supportive and less dependent on marriage.

Although consequences of divorce vary between racial and ethnic groups (Fine, 1986; Gharaibeh & Oweis, 2009; Kung, Hung, & Chan, 2004; Rao, & Sekhar, 2002; Schovanec, & Lee, 2001; Van Praagh, 1997), the level of perceived social support provided to parents and children is positively associated with divorce adjustment regardless of cultural affiliations (Bulanda & Brown, 2006; Gohm, Oishi, Darlington, & Diener, 1998). For example, Gohm et al. (1998) found that children's experience

Table 17.1 Studies of Culture and Divorcing Families

Source	Relevant Divorce Factor	Participants	Procedure
Gohm, Oishi, Darlington& Diener (1998)	Marital conflict	6,820 college students from 39 countries, ages 18–35; 60% female, 40% male	Data collected in college classes. Participants completed assessment tools measuring life satisfaction, emotional experience, parents' marital status, and marital quality.
Bulanda & Brown (2006)	Marital quality	6,231 adults; 316 Mexican American, 743 black, and 5,172 white participants. Divorce subgroup: 5,282 adults, including 225 Mexican American, 585 black, and 4,472 white participants.	Data obtained from the National Survey of Families and Households. During the second wave, the analysis was limited to participants who were divorced.
Barrett (2003)	Psychosocial well-being	1,941 adults; 616 black and 1,325 white participants; 54% female, 46% male	Data obtained from the Piedmont Health Survey. Participants completed interviews regarding their mental health.
Cohen & Savaya (2003)	Psychosocial well-being	312 Muslim Arab divorced adults; 47% female, 53% male	Data obtained from the Shari'a courts. Names of couples who had divorced in 1993 and 1994 were provided. Snowball sampling also used through Arab interviewers who were able to locate divorced individuals.
McKenry & McKelvey (2003)	Psychosocial well-being	739 divorced or separated and not remarried mothers; 181 black and 558 white participants	Data obtained from two waves of the National Survey of Families and Households. One adult per household was randomly selected.
Molina & Abel (2010)	Psychosocial well-being	24 Latina women (23 immigrants and one American-born)	Data obtained from domestic violence groups offered at the SafetyNet Program

Findings	Weaknesses	Strengths
Parents' marital conflict was associated with low levels of life satisfaction of adult offspring across individualist and collectivist cultures.	Retrospective bias. Did not examine the potential moderating effect of marital conflict. No cross-cultural validation of measures.	A large sample size across various nations
Mexican Americans and whites report similar levels of marital quality, while blacks report poorer marital quality. Blacks are at increased risk for marital disruption due to lower marital quality. Economic factors do not play a significant role in racial-ethnic differences in marital quality.	The analysis was limited to three categories of culture, and interracial couples were not included. Measure of marital quality may not be valid across all cultures. Measure consisted of one item for each factor. Data were collected in the late 80s to early 90s.	A large sample size across the nation; longitudinal, repeated measures design
Gender was found to interact with race and influenced the impact of separation and divorce on mental health. The nature and timing of mental health effects vary by race. Separation is stressful for white participants and divorce is associated with diminished mental health among black participants.	The analysis was limited to two categories of culture. Data were cross-sectional and were collected in the 80s.	A large sample size including participants across the nation was used for the study. The researchers employed random sampling.
Being educated, male, employed, satisfied with the court hearing, having fewer stressful events around divorce, and improved living conditions were associated with positive post-divorce adjustment. Perception of stigma was a major factor in adjustment.	Did not distinguish between custodial and non-custodial parents, which may have affected predictive power. The results may not be generalizable to American population. Tools did not measure adjustment to divorce as defined by the population of interest.	Study of limited-researched area (Muslim Arab men and women living in Israel)
After controlling for education and time since divorce/ separation, white mothers demonstrated higher levels of psychosocial well-being in personal mastery, informal support, and perceived economic well-being.	The analysis was limited to two categories of culture and the groups were not proportioned. Furthermore, the researchers did not employ standardized measures.	A large sample size including participants across the nation was used for the study. The researchers employed a longitudinal, repeated measures design.
Participants (all but two) indicated that Latino culture does not help them with their post-divorce adjustment. Remaining married because family unity is valued, and stigma of divorce is detrimental.	Analysis was limited to a small sample size and was specific to Latina women who experienced domestic violence.	Qualitative interviews provide detailed information about psychosocial well-being after divorce.

of social support by other family members (e.g., siblings, grandparents) or community members (e.g., religious leaders) following divorce had positive influences on reported life satisfaction regardless of cultural affiliations. Also connected to perceived social support, the presence of stigma is important to consider across cultures. Cohen and Savaya (2003), for example, found that adjustment following divorce was related to perceptions of stigma among Muslim Arab citizens of Israel due to negative images of the divorced man and woman within Arab cultural values and traditions. Likewise, Molina and Abel (2010) found that Latina women who had experienced domestic violence felt unsupported by their Latino communities and reported feeling pressured to stay married despite the presence of violence. Divorce was considered detrimental to the community, as family unity is valued above all else within the Latino culture.

Based on this evidence, it is important to consider levels of social support offered and available for children and families within their cultural context. Significant relationships with siblings, grandparents, and other important contact with family members can be overlooked or not given adequate weight. Levels of shame, stigma, and blame experienced by children and families can differ based on cultural affiliations and social connections to group norms. Although these cultural profiles provide a source for investigating the importance of these transactions, cultural differences are best served as a proxy measure for assessing levels of social support and stigma within various cultural groups to help assess for risk and protective factors that either interfere or buffer against negative consequences of divorce for children and families.

In summary:

- The impact of culture on divorcing families is associated with conflict and adjustment after divorce, substance abuse issues, social support, and religion.

Table 17.2 STUDIES OF CULTURE AND PARENTING AFTER DIVORCE

Source	Relevant Divorce Factor	Participants	Procedure
Coleman, Ganong, & Rothrauff, (2006)	Parent–child relations	3,316 adults; 492 African American, 121 Asian American, 362 Latino, and 2,122 white European American participants	Data obtained from national multistage probability sampling using random-digit dialing of phone numbers. Participants were interviewed and responded to case vignettes.
Kalmijn (2010)	Parent–child relations	7,470 adults with married and divorced parents; 6,753 white and 717 Caribbean participants	Data obtained from a larger study with a representative national sample. Participants completed assessment tools measuring the effects of parental divorce on children.
Shek (2008)	Parent–child relations	2,374 Chinese adolescents, 2,140 from intact families and 234 from non-intact families	Data obtained from three waves of a larger longitudinal study of parental control processes among secondary school students in Hong Kong

- Psychosocial well-being, level of support, and perceived economic well-being after divorce vary across cultures.
- Higher level of perceived social support is positively associated with divorce adjustment for children and parents across cultures.
- Stigma related to divorce is negatively related to adjustment following a divorce.

PARENTING AFTER DIVORCE

Separation results in the restructuring of relationships, including changes in parenting dynamics, parent–child relationships, sibling relationships, and co-parent relationships with former partners (Madden-Derdich, Leonard & Arditti, 1999). Separation also affects parents and the ways in which they fulfill their parental functions and duties across cultures. Research suggests that a period of less effective parenting often occurs following separation for both emotional and practical reasons (Amato, 2000). Positive parenting after separation can help moderate the impact of separation on the children and protect children from the negative consequences of separation and divorce (Amato, 2000; Hetherington & Kelly, 2002; Kelly, 2007; Saini, 2008). Despite the importance of parenting after separation and divorce, research in this area is only beginning to emerge (Saini, 2007). Table 17.2 includes empirical studies that specifically address parenting across cultures within the context of separation and divorce.

Parenting across cultural groups is influenced by group norms, values, and previous experiences that influence parenting competencies considered adaptive for childrearing within different environmental contexts (Forehand & Kotchick, 1996;

Findings	Weaknesses	Strengths
Asian Americans and African Americans expressed the belief that younger adults should assist older kin after divorce and remarriage more often than European Americans and Latinos.	Limited to responses to case vignettes. Measurement tool not valid across cultural backgrounds. The analysis was also limited to four cultural categories.	A large sample size including random sampling of participants across the nation was used for the study. Mixed method design. Qualitative interviews provide detailed information.
No effects of parental divorce on own divorce, choice of cohabitation, age at leaving home, and contact frequency with father among Caribbean adults in comparison to white participants	The analysis was limited to two categories of culture. The Caribbean sample was disproportionate to the white sample.	A large sample size was used for the study. Study of limited-researched area of the effect of parental divorce and single parenthood on children living in a non-American society.
Perceived parental behavioral control and parent–child relational qualities were poorer in non-intact families in comparison to intact families over a period of 3 years.	Limited to child perceptions and did not examine parent perceptions. Limited to adolescents from Hong Kong. Although it was a longitudinal study, the results are indicative of short-term effects.	A large sample size was used for the study. Researchers employed a longitudinal design. Study of limited-researched area of Asian families, especially in the area of divorce.

(Continued)

Table 17.2 STUDIES OF CULTURE AND PARENTING AFTER DIVORCE   *(Continued)*

Source	Relevant Divorce Factor	Participants	Procedure
Lopez, Melendez, & Rice (2000)	Adult attachment	487 undergraduate students, 338 from intact families and 149 from non-intact families; 329 white, 89 Hispanic, and 69 black participants; 67% female and 33% male	Data obtained from two independent surveys previously conducted. Participants completed assessment tools measuring parental bonding and adult attachment.
McKenry & Fine (1993)	Parenting attitudes and beliefs	573 single mothers, 444 white and 129 black	Data obtained from the National Survey of Families and Households. One adult per household was randomly selected.
Lau (2004)	Parent involvement	69 post-divorce families with at least one child living in Hong Kong	Data from purposive sampling. Resident parents, non-resident parents, and children completed assessment tools measuring mutual support between parents, conflict resolution strategies, quality of parent–child relation, and role flexibility.

Harkness & Super, 1995; Ogbu, 1981). Within a specific cultural milieu, parenting behaviors are significantly influenced by the customary practices of the group believed to successfully foster culturally valued child behaviors. Most empirical support for the relevance of cultural values and beliefs in parenting practices across cultures has emerged from the work of anthropologists and ethnographers who have observed childrearing practices in non-Western societies (Barry, Child, & Bacon, 1967; Harkness & Super, 1991; Meade, 1968). Far less progress has been made in observing cultural differences in childrearing in the context of separation and divorce.

Cultural variations in parenting behaviors, attitudes, and beliefs have been found to vary across cultural groups within Western societies, including differences in attitudes about parental protection, parental warmth, parent–child attachment, parenting styles, parent's expectations of children, and the use of corporal punishment and discipline (Crippen & Brew 2007; Jambunathan, Burts, & Pierce, 2000; Julian, McKenry, & McKelvey, 1994; Kalmijn, 2010; Kagitcibasi, 1996; McKenry & Fine, 1993). Julian et al. (1994) underscore that many of these perceived parenting

Findings	Weaknesses	Strengths
Participants from Hispanic and black non-intact families reported early relationships with both parents as significantly less warm and caring. Participants from black non-intact families viewed mothers as significantly less controlling and more encouraging of autonomy.	Limited to three categories of culture. Did not control for the potential influence of acculturation and cultural mistrust on adult attachment orientations of minorities. Moreover, the researchers did not assess attachment orientations with ethnically similar and dissimilar peers.	A large sample size was used for the study. Researchers employed standardized measures.
No racial/ethnic differences were found among parenting behaviors, parenting involvement, or parental satisfaction. There were racial/ethnic differences among parenting expectations. Black single mothers had higher expectations than white single mothers.	The analysis was limited to two categories of culture. The black sample was disproportionate to the white sample. Measures employed in this study may not be valid across cultures. Measurement tools were completed by only one parent.	A large sample size including participants across the nation was used for the study. Socioeconomic status and length of time since divorce controlled as these factors are highly related to divorce adjustment.
Mutual non-resident parent–child relationship, mutual support between parents, and flexible parental role had mutually facilitative relationships with non-resident parents' involvement in child care.	Limited to adolescents from Hong Kong. Measures employed in this study may not be valid across cultures. The families included in this study reported low conflict levels; thus, high-conflict families were not examined.	Study of limited-researched area of Asian families, especially in the area of divorce

behaviors are more similar than different when systemic and environmental factors, such as socioeconomic status, are controlled. Forehand and Kotchick (1996) emphasize that the environmental context of parenting can influence parents' values and perceptions of childrearing. For example, in poor urban communities, children's emotional independence and self-sufficiency are considered important competencies to acquire to increase their chances to adapt in often dangerous and violent neighborhoods (dense traffic, high crime rates, unsafe playground equipment). Strict and authoritarian parenting in African American communities, for example, has been linked to positive outcomes for children living in dangerous environments (Deater-Deckard, Dodge, Bates, & Pettit, 1996; Gonzales, Pitts, Hill, & Roosa, 2000; Mandara & Murray, 2000; Mason, Cauce, Gonzales, & Hiraga, 1996; Whaley, 2000). Similar positive outcomes of authoritarian parenting and parental behavior controls have been reported in Asian families which is considered to be responsible parenting and valued with Asian communities (Bernstein, Harris, Long, Iida, & Hans, 2005; Chao, 1994; Shek, 2008).

Attachment patterns also vary across family status and racial and ethnic groups for divorcing families (Lopez et al., 2000). Attachment patterns across cultures are one of the most researched aspects of parent–child relationships (Saini, 2007). The Strange Situation (Ainsworth, Blehar, Waters, & Wall, 1978) has been used to assess parent–child attachment patterns in Germany (Grossmann & Grossmann 1991), Africa (Keromoian & Leiderman, 1986; True, 2001), Japan (Bornstein et al., 1992; Durrett, Otaki, & Richards, 1984; Takahashi, 1986), China (Hu & Meng, 1996), Israel (Sagi et al., 1985), Canada (Fernyhough, Audet, & Le Mare, 2002), and the United States (Waters, Weinfield, & Hamilton, 2000). Although the expressions of parent–child relationships vary across cultures, attachment patterns have been found to be both universal and comparable across cultures. Grossmann and Grossmann (1991) found, for example, a higher proportion of avoidant styles in Western European countries, whereas anxious/ambivalent styles have been found to be more prominent in Israel (Sagi et al., 1985) and Japan (Miyake, Chen, & Campos, 1985). Differences in attachment styles are related to both environmental and cultural differences in parenting across cultures (Saini, 2007). Children in the Japanese culture, for example, often remain in closer proximity to their caregivers compared to North American children, and therefore may perceive separation from their caregiver as more threatening (Kondo-Ikemura, 1993). Understanding the environmental context of these differences is therefore critical in considering parenting, parenting expectations, and systemic differences in the meanings of attachment behaviors across cultures (Akaragian & Dewa, 1992; De Wolff & van IJzendoorn, 1997; George & Solomon, 1999; Harwood, Miller, & Isizarry, 1995; Hayes, 1995; Nugent, Lester, & Brazelton, 1991; Stevenson-Hinde, 1990). Van IJzendoorn (1990) states that cross-cultural study of attachment must move beyond "the search for a so-called culture-free test . . . to [a] search for differences in outcome in different cultures" (p. 7). As Grossmann and Grossmann (1991) suggest, "it may well be that the behavior strategies are universal, but that the relevance for them may be culture-specific" (p. 37).

In summary:

- Divorce affects familial relationships and parenting practices across cultures.
- Parenting is influenced by cultural norms, values, and prior experiences.
- The environmental context of parenting can influence parenting values and perceptions of caregiving.
- Attachment patterns and meaning among divorcing families may vary across cultural groups.

CULTURALLY SENSITIVE INTERVENTIONS FOR FAMILIES

Cultural considerations in family mediation services have received the most attention in the divorce literature (Barsky, 2007; Irving & Benjamin, 1995; Irving, 2002; Kruk, 1997; Meierding, 1992; Pankaj, 2000; Saposnek, 1991). Pankaj (2000) noted that mediation services were underused by minority groups when such services did not adequately address issues of cultural sensitivity and respect for diverse beliefs and cultural values. Increasing cultural sensitivity within mediation services involves exploring cultural-specific strategies for confidentiality, communication styles, language services, and the inclusion of informal supports within the mediation process. Once engaged in mediation services, cultural issues can severely affect the mediation process, especially when conflict is between parties from different cultural backgrounds (Barksy, 2007). Unaddressed or unresolved cultural impasses can both exacerbate the conflict and prevent the parties from resolving underlying differences of values, beliefs, and cultural expectations of parenting and parenting plans. Based on focus groups and interviews with members of different minority ethnic groups, Pankaj (2000) suggests that the recruitment of mediators and outside community members from minority ethnic cultures is essential to help users identify with family mediation services, to identify cultural issues within mediation, and to facilitate translating cultural nuances and language needs of families from various cultures.

The review of the literature of parenting training did not reveal studies comparing the effectiveness of parenting training services across cultural groups; in fact, cultural, linguistic, and ethnic diversities of divorcing families are rarely mentioned (Geasler & Blaisure, 1999; McIntosh & Deacon-Wood, 2003; Whitworth, Capshew, & Abell, 2002). Without such discussion, it is difficult to modify current parenting training programs for particular cultural groups. In the absence of modified programs, universal programs geared for all divorcing parents fail to meet the unique cultural differences among and between groups.

There is a significant gap in evidence regarding the influence of culture in the context of conducting custody evaluations. Without adequate attention to the child's cultural interests, recommendations made by child custody evaluators can severely affect the child's sense of cultural self-identity. Additionally, focusing exclusively on universal standards for optimal parenting arrangements, without considering the unique cultural frameworks of each member in the family, introduces methodological biases in child custody investigations and limits the validity and applicability of recommendations. Similarly, drawing inferences about parenting and parent–child relationships based on cultural stereotypes and generalization desensitizes evaluators to individual differences found within members of a common cultural community (Bernstein et al., 2005). Moreover, the degree of acculturation of immigrant and racial minorities into the dominant North American culture further limits the generalizability based on perceived cultural differences.

In summary:

- There is a dearth of literature examining the effectiveness of court-based services for children and families across cultural groups.
- Court-based services for families that are not culturally sensitive or tailored to diverse cultures may not be effective in working with culturally diverse families.
- Recruitment and retention of families from culturally diverse families into court-based services can be compromised if services are not culturally sensitive to the unique needs of diverse families.

GAPS IN EVIDENCE

Separating and divorcing families from different cultures may exhibit both similar and unique family interactions and dynamics (Cummings & Davies, 2010; Parke,

2000), but there remains a significant gap in knowledge regarding the intersections of parenting, parent–child relationships, and children's adjustment across cultural groups within the context of separation and divorce. Based on a comprehensive search of the literature regarding culture and divorce, the literature is predominantly written from a North American context that attempts to profile bounded cultural communities, typically comparing differences among Caucasians, African Americans, Mexican Americans, Asians, and to a lesser extent Native Americans living within the United States or Canada. Although studies of race and ethnicity provide initial starting points for the study of culture, categorizing differences based on the imprecise categories is predicated on the assumption that cultural values and beliefs are static, fixed, and uniquely bounded within these categories of race and ethnicity. Cummings and Davies (2010) note, "The wide variability in the adoption of specific cultural beliefs within any given racial or ethnic group should serve as a reminder that race and ethnicity are not synonymous with culture and resulting beliefs" (p. 151).

It remains premature to make conclusions about any direct paths towards the influence of culture for separating and divorcing families. By focusing exclusively on the differences among racial groups, the current research does not fully capture the broader discourse of culture and fails to consider the heterogeneity within and across racial and ethnic groups. This narrow view of culture attempts to isolate racial differences (McLoyd, Harper, & Copeland, 2001), resulting in a diminished capacity to explore co-occurring ecological factors, including the family's socioeconomic status, differences in parenting, family structures, use of social supports, and stigma and social discrimination experienced by families.

In summary:

- There is a lack of empirical knowledge on the intersection of parenting, parent–child relationships, and children's adjustment in separating and divorcing families across cultural groups.
- There is a need for research to consider the complexity of culture rather than considering cultural values and beliefs that are bound to categories of race and ethnicity.
- Ecological factors such as family socioeconomic status, divergent parenting, family structures, social support, and stigma must be examined.

CONCLUSION

It is evident that culturally sensitive practices must vary when working with children and families across cultural groups. A review of the current evidence provides a framework for working with diverse groups. Due to the confounding factors of socioeconomic status, housing, parents' employment status, access to resources, and the presence of informal and formal supports, cross-cultural studies of parenting should be considered with caution, and generalizations should be avoided. The purpose of cross-cultural awareness should not be to extrapolate steadfast rules of the differences in parenting across groups, but rather to explore the perceived cultural frameworks and cultural constructions by parents and children across groups to guide culturally sensitive and individualized approaches when working with diverse families. In doing so, it is important to remember that optimal parenting practices, parent–child relationships, and child development can follow many different paths. What may appear deficient in one cultural context may be considered adaptable in another. Nevertheless, parenting practices from different cultures may be considered unacceptable, if illegal, in the country where the family currently resides.

Culturally based impasses between professionals and families can occur when professionals lack basic understanding about the multidimensional and culturally specific realities of family breakdown, are not able to engage with families because of differences in worldviews and cultural values, take on a universal approach rather than being curious about the cultural nuances within family interactions, and pay inadequate attention to the idiosyncrasies related to the family's identified cultures (Webb, 2001).

GUIDELINES: CONSIDERATIONS AND CAUTIONS

- Children are best understood and supported within an ecological approach that considers their individual differences, their complex relationships with their parents, external supports, and their interactions with their cultural environments.
- Cultures differ in the degree that children and families are connected to cultural group norms and social expectations (e.g., collectivist or individualist cultural frameworks). It is important to assess the degree of connection to cultural group norms and its impact on perceived support, stigma, and blame for the breakdown of the family unit.
- It is important to recognize and respect that family childrearing values, parenting strategies, and parent–child relationships may be rooted in culture and may be considered adaptive within the family cultural heritage. The research points to the fact that insecure attachment styles, for example, may be considered adaptive to the cultural environment rather than indicating deficiencies in the parent–child relationship.
- Children across different cultures may experience family dynamics differently (e.g., parenting styles), but there remain significant gaps in the research to adequately understand and address these differences based solely on racial and ethnic profiles of difference.
- While avoiding cultural stereotypes, comprehensive assessments should include cultural protective factors that serve to buffer children during stressful adjustment problems, such as active involvement of extended family members; extensive kinship networks; church or religious affiliations; strong racial identities; close attachment to the ethnic community; and supportive social and cultural environments.
- Race and ethnicity can be considered a rough proxy for various cultural differences, but it is premature to conclude that families will necessarily have stronger connections to cultural values, beliefs, and traditions simply because of their race and ethnicity. Research has not readily supported the role of race and ethnicity as significant moderators in post-divorce adjustment.

- Assessing for cross-cultural difference should include the investigation of co-occurring variables that may be mediating differences, such as socioeconomic status, family structure, use of informal and formal supports, connections to community, and the experience of discrimination.
- The dignity of each family and its culture, language, customs, and beliefs should be both respected and accommodated on a case-by-case basis. Since the meanings and experiences of one's cultural traditions may be different for children and families within the same cultural context, it is important to be curious about the importance that families place on cultures while avoiding overgeneralizations based solely on expected cultural differences.

REFERENCES

Ainsworth, M. S., Blehar, M. C., Waters, E., & Wall, (1978). *Patterns of attachment: A psychological study of the Strange Situation.* Hillsdale, NJ: Erlbaum.

Akaragian, S., & Dewa C. (1992). Standardization of the Denver Development Screening Test for American Children. *Journal of Pediatric Nursing, 7*(2), 106–109. PMid:1373771

Alaggia, R., & Maiter, S. (2006). Domestic violence and child abuse: Issues for immigrant and refugee families. In R. Alaggia & C. Vine (Eds.), *Cruel but not unusual: Violence in Canadian families* (pp. 99–126). Ontario, Canada: Wilfrid Laurier University Press.

Amato, P. R. (2000). The consequences of divorce for adults and children. *Journal of Marriage and the Family, 62*(4), 1269–1288. doi:10.1111/j.1741-3737.2000.01269.x

American Psychological Association. (1994). Guidelines for child custody evaluations in divorce proceedings. *American Psychologist, 4,* 677–680.

Association of Family and Conciliation Courts. (2006). *Models standards of practice for child custody evaluations.* Retrieved Dec. 2, 2011, from http://www.afccnet.org/pdfs/Model%20Stds%20Child%20Custody%20Eval%20Sept%202006.pdf.

Barnett, G. A., & Lee, M. (2002). Issues in intercultural communication. In W.B. Gudykunst & B. Mody (Eds.), *Handbook of international and intercultural communication* (pp. 275–290). Thousand Oaks, CA: Sage.

Barrett, A. E. (2003). Race differences in the mental health effects of divorce: A reexamination incorporating temporal dimensions of the dissolution practice. *Journal of Family Issues, 4*(8), 995–1019. doi:10.1177/0192513X03256396

Barry, H., III, Child, I. L., & Bacon, M. K. (1967). Relation of child training to subsistence economy. In C. S. Ford (Ed.), *Cross-cultural approaches: Readings in comparative research* (pp. 246–258). New Haven, CT: HRAF Press.

Barsky, A. E. (2007). *Conflict resolution for the helping professions* (2nd ed.). Belmont, CA: Brooks/Cole.

Beiser, M., Hou, F., Kaspar, V., & Noh, S. (2000). *Changes in poverty status and developmental behaviours: A comparison of immigrant and non-immigrant children in Canada.* Hull, QC: Applied Research Branch. Retrieved Jan. 11, 2011, from http://www.hrsdc.gc.ca/eng/cs/sp/sdc/pkrf/publications/research/2000-001332/page06.shtml

Bennett, L. A., Wolin, S. J., & McAvity, K. J. (1988). Family identity, ritual and myth: A cultural perspective on life cycle transition. In C. J. Falicov (Ed.), *Family transitions* (pp. 211–234). New York: Guilford.

Bernstein, V. J., Harris, E., Long, C., Iida, E., & Hans, S. (2005). Issues in the multicultural assessment of parent-child interaction: An exploratory study from the starting early starting smart collaboration. *Journal of Applied Developmental Psychology, 26,* 241–275.

Bhugra, D., & De Silva, P. (2000). Couple therapy across cultures. *Sexual and Relationship Therapy, 15,* 183–192.

Bornstein, M. H., Tamis-LeMonda, C. S., Tal, J., Ludemann, P., Toda, S., Rahn, C. W., . . . Vardi, D. (1992). Maternal responsiveness to infants in three societies: The United States, France, and Japan. *Child Development, 63,* 808–821. doi:10.2307/1131235

Bronfenbrenner, U. (1979). *The ecology of human development: Experiments by nature and design.* Cambridge, MA: Harvard University Press.

Buenker, J. D., & Ratner, L. A. (1992). *Multiculturalism in the United States: A comparative guide to acculturation and ethnicity.* New York: Greenwood Press.

Bulanda, J. R., & Brown, S. L. (2006). Race-ethnic differences in marital quality and divorce. *Social Science Research, 36,* 945–967. doi:10.1016/j.ssresearch.2006.04.001

Chao, R. (1994). Beyond parental control and authoritarian parenting style: Understanding Chinese parenting through the cultural notion of training. *Child Development, 65,* 1111–1119. doi:10.2307/1131308

Chao, R. (2001). Extending research on the consequences of parenting style for Chinese Americans and European Americans. *Child Development, 72,* 1832–1843. doi:10.1111/1467-8624.00381

Child Trends. (2010). *Immigrant children.* Retrieved online on Feb. 27, 2011, from www.childtrendsdatabank.org/?q=node/333.

Choi, Y., He, M., & Harachi, T. W. (2008). Intergenerational cultural dissonance, parent-child conflict and bonding, and youth problem behaviors among Vietnamese and Cambodian immigrant families. *Journal of Youth and Adolescence, 37,* 85–96.

Cohen, O., & Savaya, R. (2003). Adjustment to divorce: A preliminary study among Muslim Arab citizens of Israel. *Family Process, 42*(2), 269–290. doi:10.1111/j.1545-5300.2003.42206.x

Coleman, M., Ganong, L. H., & Rothrauff, T. C. (2006). Racial and ethnic similarities and differences in beliefs about intergenerational assistance to other adults after divorce and remarriage. *Family Relations, 55,* 576–587. doi:10.1111/j.1741-3729.2006.00427.x

Crippen, C., & Brew, L. (2007). Intercultural parenting and the transcultural family: A literature review. *The Family Journal: Counseling and Therapy for Couples and Families, 15*(2), 107–115. doi:10.1177/1066480706297783

Cummings, E. M., & Davies, P.T. (2010). *Marital conflict and children: An emotional security perspective.* New York: Guildford Press.

Cunradi, C., Caetano, R., & Shafer, J. (2002). Socioeconomic predictors of intimate partner violence among white, black, and Hispanic couples in the United States. *Journal of Family Violence, 17,* 377–389.

Das, S. (2010). Resilience, risk and protective factors for British-Indian children and divorce. *Journal of Social Science 25*(1-2-3), 97–108.

De Wolff, M., & van IJzendoorn, M. H. (1997). Sensitivity and attachment: A meta-analysis on parental antecedents of infant attachment. *Child Development, 68*(4), 571–591. doi:10.2307/1132107

McIntosh, J., & Deacon-Wood, H. (2003). Group interventions for separated parents in entrenched conflict: An exploration of evidence-based frameworks. *Journal of Family Studies*, 9(2), 187–199.

Deater-Deckard, K., Dodge, K., Bates, J., & Pettit, G. (1996). Physical discipline among African American and European American mothers: Links to children's externalizing behavior. *Developmental Psychology, 32*, 1065–1072. doi:10.1037/0012-1649.32.6.1065

Dettlaff, A. J. (2010). Child welfare practice with immigrant children and families: Challenges and responses. *Journal of Public Child Welfare, 4*, 241–244.

Dettlaff, A. J., Vidal de Haymes, M., Velazquez, S., Midell, R., & Bruce, L. (2009). Emerging issues at the intersection of immigration and child welfare: Results from a transnational research and policy forum. *Child Maltreatment, 88*(2), 47–67.

Devore, W., & Schlesinger, E. G. (1999). *Ethnic-sensitive social work practice* (5th ed.). Boston, MA: Allyn & Bacon.

Durrett, M. E., Otaki, M., & Richards, P. (1984). Attachment and the mother's perception of support from the father. *International Journal of Behavioral Development, 7*, 167–176.

Dutta-Bergman, M., & Wells, W. D. (2002). The values and lifestyles of idiocentrics and allocentrics in an individualist culture. *Journal of Consumer Psychology, 12*, 42–54.

Falicov, C. J. (1995). Cross-cultural marriages. In N. S. Jacobson & A. S. Gurman (Eds.), *Clinical handbook of couple therapy* (pp. 231–246). New York: Guilford.

Fernyhough, L., Audet, K., & Le Mare, L. (2002). A longitudinal study of service use in families of children adopted from Romania. *International Journal of Behavioral Development, 31*, 242–251.

Fine, S. (1986). Divorce: Cultural factors and kinship factors in the adjustment of children. *Child Psychiatry and Human Development, 17*(2), 121–128. doi:10.1007/BF00706651

Forehand, R., & Kotchick, B. A. (1996). Cultural diversity: A wake-up call for parent training. *Behavior Therapy, 27*, 187–206. doi:10.1016/S0005-7894(96)80014-1

Fu, X. (2006). Impact of socioeconomic status on inter-racial mate selection and divorce. *Social Science Journal, 43*, 239–258. doi:10.1016/j.soscij.2006.02.004

Geasler, M. J., & Blaisure, K. R. (1999). 1998 nationwide survey of court-connected divorce education programs. *Family and Conciliation Courts Review, 37*, 36–63. doi:10.1111/j.174-1617.1999.tb00527.x

George, C., & Solomon, J. (1999). Attachment and caregiving: The caregiving behavioral system. In J. Cassidy & P. R. Shaver (Eds.), *Handbook of attachment: Theory, research, and clinical applications* (pp. 649–670). New York: Guilford Press.

Gharaibeh, M., & Oweis, A. (2009). Why do Jordanian women stay in an abusive relationship: Implications for health and social well-being. *Journal of Nursing Scholarship, 41*(4), 376–384. doi:10.1111/j.1547-5069.2009.01305.x

Gohm, C. L., Oishi, S., Darlington, J., & Diener, E. (1998). Culture, parental conflict, parental marital status, and the subjective well-being of young adults. *Journal of Marriage and the Family, 60*, 319–334. doi:10.2307/353851

Gonzales, N. A., Pitts, S. C., Hill, N. E., & Roosa, M. W. (2000). A mediational model of the impact of interparental conflict on child adjustment in a multiethnic, low-income sample. *Journal of Family Psychology, 14*, 365–379. doi:10.1037/0893-3200.14.3.365

Grossmann, K. E., & Grossmann, K. (1991). Attachment quality as an organizer of emotional and behavioral responses in a longitudinal perspective. In C. M. Parkes, J. Stevenson-Hinde, & P. Marris (Eds.), *Attachment across the life cycle* (pp. 93–114). London, England: Routledge.

Gunning, I. R. (1995). Diversity issues in mediation: Controlling negative cultural myths. *Journal of Dispute Resolution, 1,* 55–93.

Harkness, S., & Super, C. M. (1991). East Africa. In H. R. Hiner & J. M. Hawes (Eds.), *Children in comparative and historical perspective: An international handbook and research guide* (pp. 217–240). Westport, CT: Greenwood Press.

Harkness, S., & Super, C. M. (1995). Culture and parenting. In M. H. Bornstein (Ed.), *Handbook of parenting: Biology and ecology of parenting* (Vol. 2, pp. 211–234). Mahwah, NJ: Lawrence Erlbaum.

Harwood, R. L., Miller, J. G., & Isizarry, N. L. (1995). *Culture and attachment: Perceptions of the child in context.* New York: The Guildford Press.

Hayes, P. A. (1995). Multicultural applications of cognitive-behavior therapy. *Professional Psychology: Research and Practice, 26,* 309–315. doi:10.1037/0735-7028.26.3.309

Hetherington, E. M., & Kelly, H. (2002) *For better or for worse: Divorce reconsidered.* New York: W. W. Norton.

Ho, C. K. (1990). An analysis of domestic violence in Asian-American communities: A multicultural approach to counseling. *Women & Therapy, 9*(1–2), 129–150.

Ho, F. C., & Johnson, R. C. (1990). Intra-ethnic and inter-ethnic marriage and divorce in Hawaii. *Social Biology, 37*(1–2), 44–51. PMid:2270506

Hofstede, G. (1991). *Cultures and organizations: Software of the mind.* London, England: McGraw-Hill.

Horowitz, J. A. (1999). Negotiating couplehood: The process of resolving the December dilemma among interfaith couples. *Family Process, 38*(3), 303–323. doi:10.1111/j.1545-5300.1999.00303.x

Hu, P., & Meng, Z. (1996, August). *An examination of infant-mother attachment in China.* Poster presented at the meeting of the International Society for the Study of Behavioral Development, Quebec City, Quebec, Canada.

Hui, C. H., & Triandis, H. C. (1986). *Individualism-collectivism: A study of cross-cultural perspectives.* Lincoln, NE: Nebraska University Press.

Irving, H. (2002). *Family mediation: Theory and practice with Chinese families.* Hong Kong: University Press.

Irving, H., & Benjamin, M. (1995). *Family mediation contemporary issues.* London, England: Sage Publications.

Irving, H. H., Benjamin, M., & San-Pedro, J. (1999). Family mediation and cultural diversity: Mediating with Latino families. *Mediation Quarterly, 16*(4), 325–339. doi:10.1002/crq.3900160403

Jambunathan, S., Burts, D., & Pierce, S. (2000). Comparisons of parenting attitudes among five ethnic groups in the United States. *Journal of Comparative Family Studies, 31*(4), 395–408.

Julian, T. W., McKenry, P. C., & McKelvey, M. W. (1994). Cultural variations in parenting: Perceptions of Caucasian, African-American, Hispanic, and Asian-American parents. *Family Relations, 43*(1), 30–37. doi:10.2307/585139

Kagitcibasi, C. (1996). *Family and human development across cultures.* Mahwah, NJ: Lawrence Erlbaum.

Kalmijn, M. (2010). Racial differences in the effects of parental divorce and separation on children: Generalizing the evidence to a European case. *Social Science Research, 39,* 845–856. doi:10.1016/j.ssresearch.2010.05.002

Kelly, J. (2007, May-June). *Domestic violence: Research on differentiation of types of intimate partner violence.* Paper presented at the 44nd Annual Conference of the Association of Family and Conciliation Courts. Washington, DC.

Keromoian, R., & Leiderman, P. H. (1986). Infant attachment to mother and child caretaker in an East African community. *International Journal of Behavioral Development, 9,* 455–469.

Kondo-Ikemura, K. (1993). Current issues in attachment research: The use of Q-sort methodology. *Japanese Journal of Developmental Psychology, 4*(2), 108–116.

Kruk, E. (1997). *Mediation and conflict resolution in social work and the human services.* Chicago, IL: Nelson-Hall.

Kung, W. W., Hung, S., & Chan, C. L. (2004). How the socio-cultural context shapes women's divorce experience in Hong Kong. *Journal of Comparative Family Studies, 33*(24), 33–50.

Lau, Y. K. (2004). Nonresident parents' participation in nonresidential parenting in a Chinese context. *Journal of Divorce & Remarriage, 40*(3/4), 149–159. doi:10.1300/J087v40n03_10

Lopez, F. G., Melendez, M. C., & Rice, K. G. (2000). Parental divorce, parent-child bonds, and adult attachment orientations among college students: A comparison of three racial/ethnic groups. *Journal of Counselling Psychology, 47*(2), 177–186. doi:10.1037/0022-0167.47.2.177

Mackey, R., & O'Brien, B. A. (1998). Marital conflict management: Gender and ethnic differences. *Social Work: Journal of the National Association of Social Workers, 43,* 128–141.

Madden-Derdich, D. A., Leonard, S. S. & Christopher, F. S. (1999). Boundary ambiguity and coparental conflict after divorce: An empirical test of a family systems model of the divorce process. *Family Relations: Interdisciplinary Journal of Applied Family Studies, 48,* 37–45.

Mann, E., & Waldron, J. A. (1977). Intercultural marriage and child rearing. In W.-S. Tseng, J. F. McDermott, Jr., & T. W. Maretzki (Eds.), *Adjustment in intercultural marriage* (pp. 62–80). Honolulu, HI: University of Hawaii.

Mandara, J., & Murray, C. B. (2000). Effects of parental marital status, income and family functioning on African American adolescent self-esteem. *Journal of Family Psychology, 14,* 475–490. doi:10.1037/0893-3200.14.3.475

Markus, H., & Kitayama, S. (1991). Culture and self: Implications for cognition, emotion and motivation. *Psychological Review, 98,* 224–253. doi:10.1037/0033-295X.98.2.224

Mason, C. A., Cauce, A. M., Gonzales, N,. & Hiraga, Y. (1996). Neither too sweet nor too sour: Problem peers, maternal control, and problem behavior in African American adolescents. *Child Development, 67,* 2115–2130.

McGoldrick, M. (1989). Ethnicity and the family life cycle. In B. Carter & M. McGoldrick (Eds.), *The changing family life cycle* (69- 86) (2nd ed.). Needham Heights, MA: Allyn & Bacon.

McGoldrick, M., Pearce, J. K., & Giordano, J. (1982). *Ethnicity and family therapy.* New York: Guilford Press.

McKenry, P. C., & Fine, M. A. (1993). Parenting following divorce: A comparison of black and white single mothers. *Journal of Comparative Family Studies, 24*(1), 99–111.

McKenry, P. C., & McKelvey, M. W. (2003). The psychosocial well-being of black and white mothers following marital dissolution: A brief report of a follow-up study. *Psychology of Women Quarterly, 27,* 31–36. doi:10.1111/1471–6402.t01-2-00004

McKinley, C. (1980). Custody disputes following the dissolution of interracial marriages: Best interest or judicial racism? *Journal of Family Law 19*(1), 97–136.

McLoyd, V. C., Harper, C. I., & Copeland, N. L. (2001). Ethnic minority status, interparental conflict, and child adjustment. In J. H. Grych & F. D. Fincham (Eds.), *Interparental conflict and child development: Theory, research and applications* (pp. 98–125). New York: Cambridge University Press. doi:10.1017/CBO9780511527838.006

Mead, M. (1968). *Coming of age in Samoa: A psychological study of primitive youth for Western civilization.* New York: Dell. (Original work published in 1928)

Meierding, N. R. (1992). The impact of cultural and religious diversity in the divorce mediation process. *Mediation Quarterly, 9,* 297–305.

Miyake, K., Chen, S., & Campos, J. (1985). Infant temperament, mother's mode of interaction and attachment in Japan: An interim report. In I. Bretberton & E. Waters (Eds.), Growing points of attachment. *Monographs of the Society for Research in Child Development, 50* (1–2, Serial No. 209), 276–298.

Molina, O., & Abel, E. M. (2010). Abused Latina women's perceptions of their postdivorce adjustment. *Journal of Divorce and Remarriage, 51,* 124–140. doi:10.1080/10502550903455190

Myricks, N., & Ferullo, D. (1986). Race and child custody disputes. *Family Relations, 35*(2), 325–328. doi:10.2307/583642

Nugent, J. K., Lester, B. M., & Brazelton, T. B. (1991). *Cultural context of infancy: Volume 2: Multicultural and interdisciplinary approaches to parent–infant relations.* Santa Barbara, CA: Greenwood Publishing Group.

Ogbu, J. U. (1981). Origins of human competence: A cultural-ecological perspective. *Child Development, 52,* 413–429. doi:10.2307/1129158

Pankaj, V. (2000). *Family mediation services for minority ethnic families in Scotland.* Glasgow, Scotland: The Scottish Executive Central Research.

Parke, R. D. (2000). Beyond White and middle class: Cultural variations in families—Assessments, processes, and policies. *Journal of Family Psychology, 14,* 331–333.

Phillips, C. B. (1995). Culture: A process that empowers. In P. L. Mangione (Ed.), *Infant/toddler caregiving: A guide to culturally sensitive care* (pp. 2–9). Sacramento, CA: California Department of Education.

Pine, B. A., & Drachman, D. (2005). Effective child welfare practice with immigrant and refugee children and their families. *Child Welfare, 84*(5), 537–562.

Rao, A. B. S. V. R., & Sekhar, K. (2002). Divorce: Process and correlates a cross-cultural study. *Journal of Comparative Family Studies, 33*(4), 541–563.

Roer-Strier, D. (2001). Reducing risk for children in changing cultural contexts: Recommendations for intervention and training. *Child Abuse and Neglect, 25,* 231–248.

Romano, D. (2001). *Intercultural marriage: Promises and pitfalls* (2nd ed.). Yarmouth, ME: Intercultural Press.

Sabo, S. R. (2000). Diversity at work. *Techniques, 75*(2), 26–28.

Sagi, A., Lamb, M. E., Lewkowicz, K. S., Shoham, R., Dvir, R., & Estes, D. (1985). Security of infant-mother, -father, and -metapelet attachments among kibbutz-reared Israeli children. *Monographs of the Society for Research in Child Development, 50*(1–2), 257–275 *doi:10.* 2307/3333837

Saini, M. (2007). *Parenting after divorce: Contributions from adult attachment and interparental conflict* (Doctoral dissertation). University of Toronto, Toronto, Ontario, Canada.

Saini, M. (2008). Evidence base of custody and access evaluations. *Journal of Brief Treatment and Crisis Intervention. 8*(1), 111–129. doi:10.1093/brief-treatment/mhm023

Samovar, L. A., & Porter, R. E. (2001). *Communication between cultures* (4th ed.). Belmont, CA: Wadsworth/Thomson.

Saposnek, D. T. (1991). The value of children in mediation: A cross-cultural perspective. *Conflict Resolution Quarterly, 8*, 325–342. doi:10.1002/crq.3890080408

Schovanec, B., & Lee, C. (2001). Culture & divorce: The relationship of values and attitudes in a Protestant sample. *Journal of Divorce & Remarriage, 36*(1/2), 159–177. doi:10.1300/J087v36n01_09

Segal, U. A., & Mayadas, N. S. (2005). Assessment of issues facing immigrant and refugee families. *Child Welfare, 84*(5), 563–583.

Shek, D. T. L. (2008). Perceived parental control processes, parent-child relational qualities, and adolescent psychological well-being in intact and nonintact families: Longitudinal findings in Chinese culture. *Journal of Divorce and Remarriage, 49*(1), 171–189. doi:10.1080/10502550801973187

Statistics Canada. (2007). Immigration in Canada: A portrait of the foreign-born population, 2006 census. Catalogue no. 97–557-XIE. Ottawa: Social and Aboriginal Statistics Division, Statistics Canada. Retrieved Jan. 11, 2011, from http://www12.statcan.ca/census-recensement/2006/as-sa/97-557/index-eng.cfm.

Statistics Canada (2008). *Canada's ethnocultural mosaic, 2006 Census.* Catalogue no. 97–562-X. http://www12.statcan.ca/english/census06/analysis/ethnicorigin/pdf/97-562-XIE2006001.pdf

Stevenson-Hinde, J. (1990). Attachment within family systems: An overview. *Infant Mental Health Journal, 11*, 218–227. doi:10.1002/1097-0355(199023)11:3<218::AID-IMHJ2280110304>3.0.CO;2-1

Sue, D. W., Ivey, A. E., & Pedersen, P. B. (1996). *Multicultural counseling theory.* Belmont, CA: Brooks/Cole.

Sullivan, P. L. (2005). Culture, divorce, and family mediation in Hong Kong. *Family Court Review, 43*(1), 109–123. doi:10.1111/j.1744-1617.2005.00011.x

Takahashi, K. (1986). Examining the Strange-Situation procedure with Japanese mothers and 12-month-old infants. *Developmental Psychology, 22*, 265–270. doi:10.1037/0012-1649.22.2.265

Ting-Toomey, S. (1999). *Communicating across cultures.* New York: Guilford.

Toth, K., & Kemmelmeier, M. (2009). Divorce attitudes around the world: Distinguishing the impact of culture on evaluations and attitude structure. *Cross-Cultural Research, 43*(3), 280–297. doi:10.1177/1069397109336648

Triandis, H. C. (1995). *Individualism and collectivism.* Boulder, CO: Westview Press.

Triandis, H. C. (2000). Culture and conflict. *International Journal of Psychology, 35*(2), 145–152. doi:10.1080/002075900399448

True, M. M. (2001). Mother-infant attachment and communication among the Dogon of Mali. *Child Development, 72*(5), 1451–1466. doi:10.1111/1467-8624.00359

van IJzendoorn, M. H. (1990). Developments in cross-cultural research on attachment: Some methodological notes. *Human Development, 33*, 3–9. doi:10.1159/000276498

Van Praagh, S. (1997). Religion, custody and a child's identities. *Osgoode Hall Law Journal 35*(2), 309–378.

Vanier Institute of the Family. (2010). Family diversity. *Transitions, 4*(2), retrieved online Dec. 14, 2010, from http://www.cccabc.bc.ca/res/pubs/pdf/Family_Diversity.pdf

Vivero, V. N., & Jenkins, S. R. (1999). Existential hazards of the multicultural individual: Defining and understanding "cultural homelessness." *Cultural Diversity and Ethnic Minority Psychology, 5,* 6–26.

Ward v. Ward, 36 Wash. 2d 143, 216 P. 2d 755 (1950).

Waters, E., Weinfield, N. S., & Hamilton, C. E. (2000). The stability of attachment security from infancy to adolescence and early adulthood: General discussion. *Child Development, 71,* 703–706. doi:10.1111/1467-8624.00179

Webb, N. B. (2001). *Helping culturally diverse children and their families.* New York: Columbia University Press.

Whaley, A. (2000). Sociocultural differences in the developmental consequences of the use of physical discipline during childhood for African Americans. *Cultural Diversity and Ethnic Minority Psychology, 6,* 5–12. doi:10.1037/1099-9809.6.1.5

Whitworth, J., Capshew, T., & Abell, N. (2002). Children caught in the conflict: An overview of court-endorsed divorced parenting classes. *Journal of Divorce and Remarriage, 37*(3/4), 1–18. doi:10.1300/J087v37n03_01

Wolcott, I., & Hughes, J. (1999), *Towards understanding the reasons for divorce.* Working Paper No. 20, Australian Institute of Family Study, Melbourne.

Ying, Y., & Han, M. (2008). Parental contributions to Southeast Asian American adolescents' well-being. *Youth and Society, 40*(2), 289–306.

Ying, Y., & Hun, M. (2008). Parental acculturation, parental involvement, intergenerational relationship and adolescent outcomes in immigrant Filipino American families. *Journal of Immigrant and Refugee Studies, 6*(1), 112–131.

## 18

Relocation, Research, and Child Custody Disputes

WILLIAM G. AUSTIN ■

Relocation disputes are one of the most complex types of cases that family courts encounter. These cases involve one parent requesting to remove the child a substantial geographic distance away from the home community of the child and other parent, either at the time of divorce or subsequent to it. Relocation creates both a psychological and physical separation between the child and non-moving parent. Since the United States has always been a highly mobile society, it is to be expected that following separation and divorce parents frequently will want to relocate for a variety of reasons. Divorcing and divorced parents are about the most mobile of all identifiable types of family groups (U.S. Census Bureau, 2009). Litigation is common in relocation cases; such disputes are almost impossible to mediate and settle because there usually is no middle ground to find a compromise on the core issue of moving. Frequent moves of a non-residential parent typically do not trigger litigation on the relocation issue but will require modification to determine how to implement a long-distance parenting time arrangement.

In the 1990s, relocation of divorced or divorcing parents began to receive increased attention from state appellate courts. States began to develop and clarify relocation law via state Supreme Court case law and with the passage of statutes. Researchers and child custody scholars have been called upon to help courts forge law on this difficult topic by presenting amici briefs in hotly contested, high-profile relocation cases that analyzed the relocation dilemma against the background of the scientific research on children and divorce (Shear et al., 2004; Warshak et al., 2004; see also Wallerstein et al., 2004). This chapter will address U.S. relocation law and research findings on the psychological and behavioral effects of relocation on children of divorce. Social policy issues involved in relocation disputes are discussed in light of the extensive research literature on the contribution of non-residential parents to the healthy adjustment of children of divorce and the impact of relocation on these relationships. Theory and research on parental gatekeeping is discussed as particularly important in relocation and long-distance parenting arrangements. The organizing concept of social capital is presented as an explanation for why some children of divorce who relocate will likely fare better while others will be at risk for adjustment problems.

RELOCATION LAW IN THE UNITED STATES

Relocation law in the United States follows the different standards and procedures adopted by the 50 states and the District of Columbia. Atkinson (2010) provides a comprehensive description of the various approaches to relocation found in state law. Relocation law has shown a clear pattern of evolution over the past several decades and reflects changing family roles and responsibilities, where fathers are now much more involved in child rearing (Lamb, 2004). Relocation law is governed both by statute (37 states) and case law. There are variations across states in both the legal standards and civil procedures that govern child custody litigation for relocation cases.

In the 1970s there generally was a presumption that the custodial parent (usually the mother) could relocate with the child, and in the vast majority of custody decisions the mother was granted primary or sole custody. One prominent case was influential, and it proposed a list of factors for courts to consider (*D'Onofrio v. D'Onofrio*, 1976). Because of social change towards gender equality in many areas of society and the law, as reflected in greater frequency of joint custody, father custody, and the requirement for gender-neutral custody laws, the legal standard for relocation was reexamined with considerable frequency in most states.

Several prominent cases in the 1990s addressed relocation, especially in California (*In re* Marriage of Burgess, 1996) and New York (*Tropea v. Tropea*, 1996), and they garnered the attention of other states. The trend in state high court decisions in the past decade (see Atkinson, 2010) has been to avoid the use of legal presumptions on relocation, either for or against, in favor of a "best interests of the child" standard and for the court to consider a list of "relocation factors" in each case. The opinions in the more recent state high court decisions were based on a review of the evolution of relocation law and a search for trends and consensus (*Dupré v. Dupré*, 2004; *Goldfarb v. Goldfarb*, 2004; *In re Marriage of LaMusga*, 2004). These cases embody the contemporary approach, which is one of a best interest of the child plus consideration of specific legal factors to consider as the legal standard. The clear trend also emphasizes the importance of basing the judicial determination on the facts (Atkinson, 2010), or *individualized determination*, even when there may be a legal presumption as the legal standard (*In re* Marriage of Burgess, 1996; *In re Marriage of Francis*, 1996).

Courts and custody evaluators generally need to assess both the statutory best-interest factors (if the state has a list of factors) and any relocation factors that are identified in the statute and controlling case law. For example, Colorado requires the court to explicitly address all of the 11 best-interest factors and 9 relocation factors (*In re Marriage of Ciesluk*, 2005). Relocation factors that are typically found in state law include the stated reasons for relocation by the moving parent; reasons for opposing relocation by the non-moving parent; how the move will enhance the quality of life for the moving parent and child; the impact of the move on the relationship between the non-moving parent and child; and any past history of domestic violence.

Relocation statutes and case law generally address the situation of a post-divorce modification of an existing parenting plan where one parent wishes to relocate with the child so that parenting plan would need to be changed. The moving parent generally will be the residential or majority-time parent, though there will be post-decree cases where there is shared custody. When the relocation issue coincides with the parental dissolution of marriage, for example, a pre-decree case, then a different legal standard may apply, and the relocation statute and case law may not be controlling. Typically the case would not be distinguishable legally from other custody disputes at the time of divorce except for the issue of geographic location of the parents' intended residences. Case law in one state explicitly requires the court to assume each parent will be living in the geographic location where he or she intends to live and decide on a residential parent accordingly (*Spahmer v. Gullette*, 2005).

Atkinson's review of relocation law concerning legal standards and procedural requirements shows the following:

- Four states have a presumption in favor of relocation by a residential parent and one state a presumption against relocation.
- A presumption for relocation may be dependent on the parent's status as a primary residential parent; there may be no presumption if there has been equal parenting time.
- The burden of proof is assigned to the moving party in 10 states and to the opposing party in four states.
- The burden of proof is split in eight states, where it initially is assigned to the moving party but shifts to the opposing party if a *prima facie* case is sufficiently established by the moving party.[1]

RELOCATION AND SOCIAL POLICY

Many states in the United States have social policy embedded in their statutes on the importance and inherent value of both parents having the opportunity for continuing involvement with their children following separation and divorce. It is represented in legislative declarations, such as the following passage from Colorado legislation:

> The general assembly finds and declares that it is in the best interests of all parties to encourage frequent and continuing contact between each parent and the minor children of the marriage after the parents have separated or dissolved their marriage. In order to effectuate this goal, the general assembly urges parents to share the rights and responsibilities of child-rearing and to encourage the love, affection, and contact between the children and the parents. (Colorado Revised Statutes, 2010, 14-10-124(1))

Research strongly supports this type of goal and declaration. Children of divorce show the best long-term adjustment when they enjoy quality relationships with both parents, especially if the level of parent conflict is low (Amato & Sobolewski, 2001). The legal context and practical realities in a relocation dispute make it more difficult to achieve continuing contact and to sustain a high-quality and meaningful relationship between a child and the non-moving parent. In addition, there are the competing constitutional rights of the litigating parents on the right to travel and the right to exercise care and control over one's child, as noted in the introduction. The mother holds a constitutional right to travel (*Shapiro v. Thompson*, 1969), and the father asserts a constitutional right to have care and control over his child—for example, reasonable access (*Prince v. Massachusetts*, 1944; *Santosky v. Kramer*, 1982; *Troxel v. Granville*, 2000). These rights translate into competing social policies (e.g., not impeding a parent's wish to pursue opportunities and encouraging strong parent–child relationships). The court in a New Jersey decision that helped shape relocation law in many states reflected on the judicial dilemma in relocation cases: "The court is keenly aware that of all adjudicatory proceedings none require greater judicial thoughtfulness" (*D'Onofrio v. D'Onofrio*, 1976, p. 28).

In summary:

- Relocation disputes occur in a psycho-legal context of social policy considerations for courts and custody evaluators.
- Relocation law recognizes the countervailing parental constitutional rights to travel versus to have access to and control over one's child.
- State laws promulgate the social policy to encourage the continuing involvement of both parents with children following divorce.
- The challenge for courts and evaluators is to craft suitable long-distance parenting plans when relocation is allowed so both parents can enjoy meaningful relationships with the child.

THE MAIN RELOCATION ISSUE

Non-residential Parent–Child Relationship Harm

When a parent wants to relocate with a child following separation and divorce, the main issues in the legal dispute concern potential harm to the non-moving parent–child relationship and how to keep the parent meaningfully involved with the child. It is assumed that this "relationship harm" will translate to developmental harm to the child because of the non-residential parent's diminished involvement in the life of the child. This view is equivalent to a social capital perspective; for example, with a very long-distance move and a very young child, the psychological resources from the distant parent will largely be unavailable to the child.[2] Courts recognize that there is a certain degree of expectable distress for the child associated with relocation (*In re Marriage of Littlefield*, 1997). Courts have pointed out that if the sole criterion to deny relocation was to show some degree of relationship harm, then no relocation petition would ever succeed (*Goldfarb v. Goldfarb*, 2004; *In re Marriage of LaMusga*, 2004). Austin (2000) argued that there is a hypothetical threshold of harm in relocation cases to be determined by the court where the degree of predicted harm is sufficient to deny the relocation (*In re Marriage of LaMusga*, 2004).

Crafting Long-Distance Parenting Plans to Mitigate Harm

A common relocation factor in state statutes is whether a suitable alternative parenting time schedule can be established. The court's legal calculus in any given relocation dispute addresses the question of how to keep the non-moving parent involved through a new parenting plan and time-sharing schedule. The proposed new plan is the chief vehicle to manage the risk of relationship and developmental harm. The focus of the plan is to facilitate parent involvement by the non-moving parent.

Relocation usually results in less time with the non-residential parent, typically the father. When these cases reach state appellate courts, gender politics may surface since it still is the statistical reality that usually it is a custodial parent/mother who is requesting to relocate with the child (Bruch & Bowermaster, 1996; see also Wallerstein & Tanke, 1996 for the feminist position on relocation). Most children want ready access to both of their parents after divorce. Fabricius and Hall (2000) found the majority of college students whose parents had divorced wished they could have spent more time with their father or even equal time.

In summary:

- Relocation creates a risk of harm to the nonresidential parent–child relationship.
- The courts expect a certain degree of distress and adjustment issues for the child who relocates.
- It is useful for evaluators and the courts to conduct a social capital or resource availability analysis in anticipating a child's adjustment to relocation.
- Parenting plans and access schedules try to manage the risk of relocation-associated harm for the child.
- Relocation as an issue has yielded a gender-based social policy discourse.

MOBILITY STATISTICS

Scholars have long observed how mobile the United States has been as a society (Triandis, 1995; Turner, 1921), and analyses of census data demonstrate the impressive frequency with which Americans move (U.S. Census Bureau, 2009). Exploration and the pioneering spirit has been a vital part of American history, and mobility has been associated with seeking new opportunities since early in the development of the United States (Toqueville, 1835/2003). Many other Western, industrialized countries show high mobility rates, such as Canada (Statistics Canada, 2006) and England (Office for National Statistics, 2009).

Frequency of Residential Mobility

During a one-year period (2002–2003) in the United States, 14% of the U.S. population moved. The most mobile groups were people in the age ranges of 20 to 24, 25 to 29, and 30 to 34, with respective moving rates of 30.1%, 28.1%, and 19.8% (Schacter, 2004). The group that moves most frequently is adults in the 20- to 34-year-old range, and this is the group most likely to have young children (Schacter, 2004). Demographic data from 2002–2003 showed high moving rates for children: 21.4% for ages 1 to 4; 15.9% for ages 5 to 9; and 13.2% for ages 10 to 14. In examining the distance of moves, the data for these years showed "the median distance was 160 miles for an inter-county move, while the mean (average) move was a much longer 400 miles"

(Schacter, 2004, p. 10). U.S. Census data (Schacter, 2001) show that moves in 1999 were made for housing reasons (21.5 million), family-related matters (11 million), and work-related reasons (6.7 million). Eleven percent of divorced/separated parents moved. These data indicate that a high percentage of parents who move will be divorced, will have young children, and will move a substantial distance.

Post-Divorce Mobility

The destabilizing effect of divorce accentuates residential mobility. Marital separation usually means one parent is going to move to a new physical residence—and often both parents. These moves often are temporary and may be followed by subsequent moves, including out-of-county and interstate moves. The statistics on residential mobility for the population of families following divorce are quite staggering. In Arizona, 30% of custodial parents in one community moved out of the area within the first 2 years after separation (Braver, Ellman, & Fabricius, 2003). Results from a 40-year longitudinal study of a large Virginia sample, 10 years after divorce, found that the average distance between the parents' residences was 400 miles (Hetherington & Kelly, 2002).

In summary:

- The United States historically has been a highly mobile society.
- The most mobile family group consists of younger, divorced parents with young children.
- Longitudinal research shows long-distance parent–child relationships are very common 10 years after divorce.

RELOCATION AND PSYCHOLOGICAL ADJUSTMENT

Table 18.1 summarizes research on the effects of residential mobility on children of divorce.

Relocation and Risk to Children of Divorce

The relocation paradox is that residential mobility is a general risk factor for children of divorce both during their growing-up years (McLanahan & Sandefur, 1994; Tucker, Marx, & Long, 1998) and into adulthood (Dong, Anda, Felitti, Williamson et al., 2005), but it is something that occurs with great frequency. One state high court remarked that something that occurs with such regularity (in light of U.S. Census data) cannot be assumed to be too harmful (*In re Marriage of Ciesluk*, 2005). This general statement is incorrect based on the scientific research (McLanahan & Sandefur, 1994; South, Haynie, & Bose, 2005; Wood, Halfon, Scarlata, Newacheck, & Nessim, 1993), but most children who relocate will probably show a reasonable level of adjustment, just as with the case of children who experience divorce (Emery, 1998).

Austin (2008a) reviewed the extensive research literature in sociology and demography on residential mobility and children's adjustment following divorce compared

Table 18.1 REVIEW OF RESEARCH ON EFFECTS OF RESIDENTIAL MOBILITY ON CHILDREN OF DIVORCE

Source	Participants	Procedures
Tucker, Marx, & Long (1998)	17,000 parents interviewed on children, aged 7–12. Family types grouped as both biological parents; biological mother only; stepfamilies; other family types—father only or other relatives	1988 National Health Survey. Effects of age, race, socioeconomic status, family type, and frequency of residential mobility on school achievement & behavior problems.
Braver, Ellman, & Fabricius (2003)	602 university students in introductory psychology class whose parents divorced	Questionnaire, retrospective reports. Measures of general health, hostility, depression, distress, life satisfaction, parent contribution to tuition, & perceived parent support.
South, Haynie, & Bose (2005)	5,000 adolescents	Longitudinal survey measuring residential mobility & onset of adolescent sexual intercourse
Artis (2007)	10,511 kindergarten children	National, representative survey with stratified cluster sampling by U.S. Census Bureau. Parent reports on child functioning. Measures on family stability including residential mobility and effect on child well-being. Number of moves measured.
Wood et al. (1993)	9,915 children who were 6–18 years old	National, representative survey with stratified cluster sampling by U.S. Census Bureau. Face-to-face interviews with parents. Predictor variables: number of residential moves, poverty status, family structure, employment, education. Achenbach Behavior Check List to measure child behavior problems. Risk categories created.
Simpson & Fowler (1994)	10,362 school-age children; grades 1–12	National, representative survey with stratified cluster sampling by U.S. Census Bureau on child health; measures of frequency of residential mobility.

Findings	Strengths	Weaknesses
Academic-behavioral problems: 16.7% in families with both biological parents; 29.5% mother only custody; 27% stepfamilies; 28% other family types. Median no. moves: 1.14 in families with two biological parents; 2.6 mother only; 3.36 stepfamilies.	Large, national, representative survey. Number of moves measured. Children in a particular age range studied. The age range is the one where children are more likely to adjust well with relocation. It is a less mobile age range group. Family structure examined. SES & race controlled. Results explained by greater social capital in intact family structure.	Parent interview data only; no observational data; teachers not interviewed; school records not reviewed
Relocation effect associated with either parent moving; effect on parent contribution to college; perceived parent support; parents as good role models; parent conflict; non-significant or marginal differences on health, satisfaction, and adjustment	Adult-child self-report data; data on moving by either parent	College sample expected to be higher functioning, higher IQ, so more resilient. Significant effects not found on measures of mental health and social functioning.
Recent moving adolescents one-third more likely to experience first premarital intercourse; higher delinquency; poor academic performance	Large representative sample; study of adolescence and effect of relocation; explanation using social networks & fitting in with positive peer group influence; social capital	
Type of family structure creates different level of stability in life of young children and significantly related to cognitive and psychological outcomes. Children with cohabiting parents score lower on cognitive tests compared to children from two biological, married parent families. Stability due to number of parent relationship changes and number of residences.	Studied cohabiting parents. Study of young age group population. Large sample. Conceptual analysis of relocation as part of family stability.	Limits from survey approach
In families with more frequent moves children showed more behavior problems and failing a grade in school.	Large sample with control for confounding variables such as poverty. Discussion of reasons due to disruption in relationships, schools, etc. associated with moves, even for short distance. Social capital explanation.	Authors did not report different relocation effects for divorced vs. intact families.
24% never moved; 35% 1 or 2 times; 39% 3 or more in lifetime. Children who moved 3 or more times: 2 times more likely behavioral/emotional problems, receive mental health treatment, repeated a grade & suspended or expelled from school.	Control for demographic variables; wide range of child outcome measures; frequency of residential mobility data	Inherent limitations with survey approach and lack of corroborative data. Results not differentiated by type of family structure or age group.

(Continued)

Table 18.1 Review of Research on Effects of Residential Mobility on Children of Divorce   (*Continued*)

Source	Participants	Procedures
Pruett et al. (2003)	102 primary caretaker mothers; 102 non-residential fathers; children ages 0–6 years; parents involved in child custody litigation	Longitudinal study; gatekeeping scale developed; multiple measures of parent characteristics & child outcome; measure of parent conflict

to children in intact families who experience residential mobility. He found that relocation and economic changes associated with divorce are the two most potent predictors of the children's adjustment. Relocation and economic changes together explain about two thirds of the difference between children in intact family versus children in other family structures on a variety of outcome measures, including academic achievement, school dropout, child psychological well-being, and teenage pregnancy (McLanahan & Sandefur, 1994). Multiple moves create more risk (Wood et al., 1993), but only one move produces the relocation effect, or the statistical differences between the averages for outcomes for children from intact versus other family structures (Tucker et al., 1998). Austin (2008a) concluded that it was possible to estimate a base rate of harm associated with relocation for children of divorce by using this research data. For example, in the Tucker et al. study, the difference in school behavior problems was 13% greater for children in other family structures compared to children from intact families, controlling for number of moves. Relocation, then, is a general risk factor for children of divorce.

Children's Developmental Stage

Theory and research suggest that very young children (Kelly & Lamb, 2003) and adolescents (Simpson & Fowler, 1994; South et al., 2005) are at higher risk for adjustment problems due to relocation. There may be a "developmental window" where children of divorce in the age range of 8 to 12 are at lower risk for adjustment problems following relocation (Austin, 2008a). However, research has not been conducted to substantiate this hypothesis.

Mobility During Childhood

There is a large empirically based literature showing the long-term effects of frequent childhood mobility on adult well-being (Bures, 2003; Oishi, 2010; Oishi & Schimmack, 2010). Because this research did not control for the type of family structure in which these highly mobile children lived, the extrapolation of these findings to the context

Findings	Strengths	Weaknesses
Children showed better adjustment with higher father involvement even with restrictive maternal gatekeeping attitudes and parent conflict. Poorer adjustment with more mother symptomatology. Poor quality in parent–child relationships predicted child outcomes. Mothers' symptoms associated with gatekeeping attitudes.	Gatekeeping & child outcomes measured in families involved in custody litigation; development of gatekeeping scale; relevance to custody relocation cases. Data on very young children. Multiple measures used.	Data on young children only. Only gatekeeping attitudes were measured, not actual behaviors.

of divorce and relocation is problematic. In contrast, the research on children of divorce shows when type of family structure is controlled, then the negative "relocation effect" on child outcomes is consistently stronger for children of divorce compared to children living in intact families with two biological parents (McLanahan & Sandefur, 1994; Tucker et al., 1998).

Another limitation of the residential mobility research is that the type and distance of the move has seldom been studied or controlled for in the research designs. In a divorce context, an interstate move, for example, would be expected to have a much greater impact on the child and the relationship between the child and the non-moving parent compared to a move of an hour away. One would produce a qualitative change in the relationship, whereas the other would be an inconvenience to everyone.[3] Custody evaluators and courts face the task in every case of predicting long-term child outcomes partly as a function of a recommended parenting plan and time-sharing arrangement. This predictive task is more complex in relocation cases.

In summary:

- Research shows that relocation/residential mobility is a general risk factor for children of divorce.
- There is a base rate of harm associated with relocation that can be established for children of divorce.
- Children living in intact families with two biological parents show significantly better adjustment than children from all other family structures.
- Theory and research strongly suggest that very young children and adolescents from divorced parents are at greater risk when they relocate.
- Research on the effects of relocation has generally not controlled well for the number and qualitative type of residential moves.

RELOCATION, SOCIAL CAPITAL, AND GATEKEEPING

Austin (2008b) hypothesized that the key to the child having a good adjustment with relocation (that is, a successful relocation) lies in the attitudes and actions of the moving, residential parent. Important factors for the parent and child adjustment to relocation include how well the moving parent adjusts to the move, copes with the stress involved with relocation (i.e., new housing, job, finding a school), and opens up new sources of social capital for herself and the child. How supportive the moving parent is of the non-moving parent's relationship with the child can have a protective function as the child tries to adjust to the extended separation from the other parent. The hypothesis is that how well the social capital from the distant parent makes its way to the child depends not just on the efforts of the non-moving parent to stay involved despite the geographic barrier, but also on the efforts of the residential parent to facilitate the other parent's involvement. Future research needs to be designed to investigate these hypotheses.

Role of Non-residential Parents and Fathers on Children's Adjustment

Research findings indicate that a main protective factor for children of divorce is to have at least one consistent relationship with a stable, competent caregiver if the caregiver provides warmth and an effective parenting style (Kelly & Emery, 2003). Custodial mothers tend to be this main protective factor following divorce (Hetherington, Bridges, & Insabella, 1998; Kelly & Emery, 2003). The importance and unique contributions of fathers have also been empirically established (Amato & Sobolewski, 2004; Flouri, 2005; Lamb, 2004). However, research is robust in showing that the best outcomes for children of divorce are associated with competent involvement and quality relationships with both parents (Ahrons, 1994; Hetherington & Kelly, 2002). In a prominent California case (*In re Marriage of LaMusga*, 2004), numerous amici briefs were submitted to the Supreme Court by prominent divorce researchers and child custody scholars on the issue of the contributions of both parents for children of divorce. The court accepted the view of the researchers that quality relationships with both parents were important in the relocation context. The fact pattern in the *LaMusga* case involved allegations of restrictive gatekeeping, or possible attempts by the mother to alienate the children from the father.

Parental Gatekeeping

Support for the other parent–child relationship (or SOPCR) is a common statutory best-interest factor. It is also the second part of the legislative declaration described above. It often becomes the focus of a relocation dispute. For example, in Michigan the statutory factor is worded as "The willingness and ability of each of the parties to facilitate and encourage a close and continuing parent-child relationship between the child and the other parent or the child and the parents" (M.C.L.A., Child Custody Act of 1970, §722.23(j)).

The concept of parental gatekeeping encompasses the SOPCR statutory factor. Gatekeeping emerged from the literature on co-parenting (Pleck, 1985) and father involvement (Lamb, 1981), and family studies research followed in the investigation of *maternal gatekeeping* (Allen & Hawkins, 1999; De Luccie, 2001; Fagan & Barnett, 2003; McBride, Brown, Bost, Shin et al., 2005). One definition of gatekeeping was "mother's preferences and attempts to restrict and exclude fathers from child care and involvement with children" (Fagan & Barnett, 2003, p. 1021). Research was almost exclusively on maternal gatekeeping in intact families. Allen and Hawkins (1999) proposed that gatekeeping could vary on a continuum, or there were different types of gatekeeping: restrictive, intermediate, and cooperative co-parenting. They found that 21% of mothers were restrictive in intact families.

Co-parenting theorists and gatekeeping researchers have focused on the outcome measure of father involvement because of the belief that the mother's support for the father's involvement was a key determinant of how involved fathers became in parenting. Further, it was assumed that the father's involvement was important for the children's adjustment and healthy development (Pruett, 2000). Researchers have documented how the mother's support for the father's involvement and the father's perception of the mother's support is associated with the father's actual involvement in parenting (Beitel & Parke, 1998; McBride et al., 2005; Schoppe-Sullivan, Brown, Cannon, & Mangelsdorf, 2008).

Theorists have recently proposed that gatekeeping can apply to mothers and fathers and that gatekeeping conflict may occur in the context of divorce and custody disputes (Adamson, 2010; Pruett, Arthur, & Ebling, 2007; Trinder, 2008). One could argue that a custody dispute is by definition focused on gatekeeping, or the amount and pattern of access to the child. Disputes concern foremost issues surrounding parental involvement. Research has found that restrictive or inhibitory gatekeeping indeed is more common among divorced parents (Fagan & Barnett, 2003; Pruett, Williams, Insabella, & Little, 2003; Trinder, 2008).

The gatekeeping continuum among divorced parents has been described as ranging from facilitative to restrictive or inhibitory (Austin, Eidman, Gould, & Kirkpatrick, 2006; Austin, Flens, & Kirkpatrick, 2010; Trinder, 2008). The facilitative gatekeeper is proactive, cooperative, and inclusive of the other parent's involvement. The very restrictive gatekeeper may make access difficult, derogates the other parent to the child, and attempts to undermine the child's relationship with the other parent. Extreme examples of restrictive gatekeeping would be severe alienation and child abduction. Most divorced parents who are engaging in the co-parenting process will fall somewhere along the continuum, with most in the middle, meaning they are mostly cooperative but in an emotionally disengaged way (Maccoby & Mnookin, 1992).

The limited research on gatekeeping with divorced or divorcing parents has described the *gate opening* and *gate closing* behaviors of custodial parents (Trinder, 2008). A study involving children ages 0 to 6 found that children showed better adjustment when fathers were involved, even if the mother described negative gate-keeping attitudes (Pruett et al., 2003). The qualitative data in this same study found that mothers and fathers both reported a high level of supportive behaviors by the mother towards the father, but fathers naturally reported a lower level of gate-opening behaviors and a higher level of gate-closing behaviors compared to mothers' perceptions.

In relocation disputes, gatekeeping takes on even more significance, as it usually will be a point of emphasis by both parents. If the court believes the moving parent will be a restrictive gatekeeper, then it greatly increases the likelihood the relocation will not be allowed because the court will anticipate that any long-distance parenting plan will not accomplish the goal of facilitating sufficient involvement by the non-moving parent. The divorce context points to the need to examine gatekeeping by both parents (Adamsons, 2010; Austin et al., 2010), but researchers have not yet studied fathers' gatekeeping behaviors either in intact or divorced family systems.

In summary:

- Research shows that a mother's support for a father and her view of his competency influences his actual involvement in parenting in intact families.
- Gatekeeping captures mothers' attitudes and behaviors about fathers' involvement in parenting.
- Gatekeeping varies on a continuum from proactive/facilitative to restrictive/inhibitory.
- Research shows that gatekeeping is more likely to be restrictive following divorce.
- Both parents engage in gate-closing and gate-opening behaviors following divorce.
- Following divorce, children show better adjustment when they have high-quality relationships with both parents.
- Gatekeeping is the prominent issue in child custody disputes and may be accentuated in relocation cases.
- Facilitative gatekeeping is the key to a successful relocation by the child.

SUMMARY

Child custody relocation disputes pose unique dilemmas for family law courts and custody evaluators. There are competing constitutional rights and social policy considerations that are unique to such cases. It is an area of family law where research clearly has direct application for the interpretation of evidence and data and can help guide the court in making judicial predictions about children's outcomes associated with relocation.

The United States and other Western, industrialized countries are highly mobile societies. Families that experience divorce have a high rate of residential mobility. Research has established that relocation, or residential mobility, is a general risk factor for children of divorce in terms of their psychological adjustment and well-being, but children in all types of family structures move substantial distances with considerable frequency. With the proper social supports or social capital in place, most children who relocate with a parent will likely show an adequate long-term adjustment. The same conclusion might be drawn concerning children when a parent moves a substantial distance, the children remain in the home community with the non-moving parent, and there is a long-distance parenting arrangement in place. Relocation cases are highly individualized and dependent on the facts in the case, but research hypotheses can be helpful to the decision-maker and child custody evaluator. However, further research is needed to investigate these hypotheses.[4]

Relocation law in the United States varies considerably among the 50 states, but there has been a clear trend in state case law and statutes towards a legal standard of the best interests of the child and requirement that courts consider a list of relocation factors. Such factors include the child's anticipated adjustment to relocation; impact of the move on the relationship between the child and the non-moving parent;

presence of extended family members in the two communities; and a history of domestic violence. Relocation law emphasizes the fact-driven nature of relocation disputes. States vary in the procedural aspects surrounding relocation, including requirements to give notice to the other parent about the proposed relocation, listing the reasons for the move, and which parent has the burden to prove (or disprove) that the move will be in the child's best interests.

The concept and research surrounding parental gatekeeping is highly relevant to relocation disputes. How well the moving parent will support the relationship between the child and the non-moving parent may be the key to a child having a successful adjustment to the move. A past pattern of restrictive or inhibitory gate-keeping by the moving parent makes it more likely that the other parent will have difficulty sustaining a quality relationship with the child in a long-distance parenting arrangement.

GUIDELINES: CONSIDERATIONS AND CAUTIONS

- *Social Policy and Judicial Dilemmas*: When courts and custody evaluators apply research to relocation disputes, they do so in the legal context that encourages the continuing involvement of both parents while recognizing the important social policy of not interfering with a parent's right to relocate with a child. The legal and psychological analysis requires a comparative analysis on the relative advantages and disadvantages to the child associated with living primarily with each parent in different communities and experiencing life in a long-distance parenting arrangement.
- *Relocation Law*: There is considerable variation to relocation disputes among the 50 states in the United States. The trend is avoidance of legal presumptions for or against relocation of a child with the moving parent; emphasis on the facts and family context of the case; and a legal standard of the best interests of the child, with a list of specific relocation factors to consider.
- *Research on Residential Mobility and Effects on Children of Divorce*: A very large research literature shows that relocation is a general risk factor for children of divorce compared to those in intact families with two legal parents, as measured on a variety of measures of long-term child outcomes. Research shows a large number of post-divorce moves creates a higher risk for adjustment and developmental problems.
- *Research on Contributions of Non-residential Parents/Fathers*: A substantial research literature has found that children of divorce show the best short- and long-term adjustment when they enjoy high-quality relationships with both parents, especially under conditions of low parent conflict. While research shows that the main protective factor for children's adjustment lies in having a consistent relationship with a custodial mother who shows warmth and uses an authoritative parenting style, research also convincingly demonstrates the important contributions of fathers to

children's development, both in intact and divorced families. Even when there is substantial parent conflict, children show better adjustment when fathers remain highly involved, especially if they are competent in their parenting skills and show warmth to the child. The implications of these research literatures for children's adjustment following relocation are straightforward.

- **Rates of Residential Mobility:** Younger parents with young children have some of the highest rates of mobility, according to U.S. Census data and regional samples gathered by divorce researchers. A significant proportion of the moves by divorced parents and children will be inter-county and interstate. Research on the median and average distance for moves is impressive, and the figures correspond to longitudinal research on the geographic separation between parents 10 years after divorce. There are social policy implications of these mobility data in light of the research on the risk of harm to children of divorce associated with residential mobility. The clear conclusion is that courts and custody evaluators must develop risk-management and harm-mitigation strategies in each contested relocation case. The most effective risk-management intervention will be to create a long-distance parenting plan that facilitates continuing involvement by the non-moving parent with the child despite the logistical obstacles created by the geographic distance.

- **Explanations for Effects of Relocation:** Divorce researchers and forensic child custody scholars have proposed the concept of social capital as an efficient explanation for why children in intact families show better overall adjustment compared to children of divorce. Researchers have also explained better adjustment for some children of divorce in terms of the greater degree of social capital available in the child's post-divorce environment. Exposure to ongoing parent conflict, perhaps exacerbated by a parent moving away with the child, may also explain a particular child's poor adjustment. Parent conflict would be an example of "negative social capital," or aversive environmental influences on the child.

- **Parental Gatekeeping and Relocation:** This concept refers to attitudes and behaviors by parents that are intended to limit the involvement with the other parent and the influence of the other parent over the child. Theorists propose that facilitative/proactive gatekeeping will increase the child's social capital and lower the risk to the child associated with relocation. It will be a key factor for courts and evaluators to consider in the individual assessment in a relocation dispute. Research provides support for this hypothesis, though it is preliminary in nature.

- **Cautions on Using Research Hypotheses in a Forensic Setting:** Research on relocation provides a basis for hypotheses on children's adjustment associated with relocation and the role of specific risk and protective factors. These hypotheses will be based on aggregate data or group averages. Courts and evaluators need to treat research hypotheses and forensic frameworks developed on the basis of research as just a first step in considering factors and data for individual cases. State case law also often reminds courts to keep the facts foremost in mind in resolving relocation disputes.

- *Need for Research on Effects of Relocation:* Research on residential mobility shows correlations between children of divorce moving and their post-divorce adjustment. When courts and evaluators make predictions about children's outcomes associated with proposed relocation by a parent and child, it requires extrapolation from research on divorce to how children (and parents) will cope with residential mobility following litigation. Research is needed that will consist of substantial sample sizes and quantitative as well as qualitative measures, especially child outcome data.

NOTES

1 A *prima facie* case is made for relocation when the court determines the moving parent has presented sufficient evidence based on the pleadings or at a temporary hearing until this initial offer of proof is sufficiently disproven by later evidence from the other parent.

2 Social capital is defined as the psychological, emotional, and social contributions that are provided to the child by parents, siblings, extended family, peers, etc., and also by organizations and groups (Coleman, 1990). Researchers have applied social capital to explanations for children's adjustment to divorce (Amato & Sobolewski, 2004; Hetherington, 1999). The application of a social capital analysis to child custody disputes allows for a comparative analysis of the expected types and degrees of social capital or human resources that will be available to the child in the two alternative residential living arrangements and with competing parenting time arrangements.

3 While research shows that a move of an hour away by either parent (Braver et al., 2003) or a geographical separation of 75 miles or more (Hetherington & Kelly, 2002) can have long-term negative effects on children of divorce and father involvement, there are qualitatively different types of residential moves with predictable effects on the child's access to social capital.

4 Preliminary qualitative, longitudinal research on how families experience the resolution of legal relocation disputes and the resultant long-distance parenting arrangements is being conducted in Australia, England, and New Zealand (see Parkinson, Cashmore, & Single, 2010; Taylor & Freeman, 2010).

REFERENCES

Adamsons, K. (2010). Using identity theory to develop a midrange model of parental gatekeeping and parenting behavior. *Journal of Family Theory and Review, 2*(2), 137–148.

Ahrons, C. (1994). *The good divorce: Keeping your family together when your marriage comes apart.* New York: HarperPerennial.

Allen, S. M., & Hawkins, A. J. (1999). Maternal gatekeeping: Mother's beliefs and behavior that inhibit greater father involvement in family work. *Journal of Marriage and Family, 61,* 199–212. doi: 10.2307/353894

Amato, P. R., & Sobolewski, J. M. (2001). The effects of divorce and marital discord on adult children's psychological well-being. *American Sociological Review, 66,* 900–921. doi: 10.2307/3088878

Amato, P. R., & Sobolewski, J. M. (2004). The effects of divorce on fathers and children. In M. E. Lamb (Ed.), *The role of the father in child development* (pp. 341–367). New York: Wiley.

Artis, J. E. (2007). Maternal cohabitation and child well-being among kindergarten children. *Journal of Marriage and Family, 69,* 222–236.

Atkinson, J. (2010). The law of relocation of children. *Behavioral Sciences and the Law, 28,* 563–579. PMid: 20607727

Austin, W. G. (2000). Relocation law and the threshold of harm: Integrating legal and behavioral perspectives. *Family Law Quarterly, 34,* 63–82.

Austin, W. G. (2008a). Relocation, research, and forensic evaluation: Part I: Effects of residential mobility on children of divorce. *Family Court Review, 46*(1), 136–149.

Austin, W. G. (2008b). Relocation, research, and forensic evaluation: Part II: Research support for the relocation risk assessment model. *Family Court Review, 46*(2), 347–365. doi: 10.1111/j. 1744–1617.2008.00205. x

Austin, W. G., Eidman, M., Gould, J. W., & Kirkpatrick, H. D. (2006, Oct. 20). *Application of gatekeeping to child custody evaluation.* Workshop presented at the meeting of Association of Family and Conciliation Courts, Seventh International Symposium on Child Custody Evaluations, Atlanta, GA.

Austin, W. G., Flens, J. R., Kirkpatrick, H. D. (2010, June 3). *Gatekeeping and child custody evaluation: Theory, measurement & applications.* Association of Family and Conciliation Courts, 47th Annual Conference, Denver, CO.

Beitel, A. H., & Parke, R. D. (1998). Paternal involvement in infancy: The role of maternal and paternal attitudes. *Journal of Family Psychology, 12*(2), 268–288. doi: 10.1037/0893–3200.12.2.268

Braver, S. L., Ellman, I. M., & Fabricius, W. V. (2003). Relocation of children after divorce and children's best interests: New evidence and legal considerations. *Journal of Family Psychology, 17,* 206–219. doi: 10.1037/0893–3200.17.2.206PMid: 12828017

Bruch, C. S., & Bowermaster, J. M. (1996). The relocation of children and custodial parents: Public policy, past and present. *Family Law Quarterly, 30,* 245–265.

Bures, R. M. (2003). Childhood residential stability and health at midlife. *American Journal of Public Health, 93*(7), 1144–1148. doi: 10.2105/AJPH. 93.7.1144PMid: 12835200 PMCid: 1447924

Burgess, *In re* the Marriage of, 913 P. 2d 473 (Cal. 1996).

Ciesluk, *In re* Marriage of, 113 P. 3d 135 (Colo. 2005).

Coleman, J. S. (1990). *Foundations of social theory.* Cambridge, MA: Harvard University Press.

Colorado Revised Statutes. (2010). *Domestic matters. Dissolution of marriage– parental responsibilities.* §14–10–124(1).

DeLuccie, M. F. (2001). Mothers as gatekeepers: A model of maternal mediators of father involvement. *Journal of Genetic Psychology, 156,* 115–131. doi: 10.1080/ 00221325.1995.9914811

Dong, M., Anda, R. F., Felitti, V. J., Williamson, D. F., et al. (2005). Childhood residential mobility and multiple health risks during adolescence and adulthood. *Archives of Pediatric and Adolescent Medicine, 159,* 1104–1110. doi: 10.1001/ archpedi. 159.12.1104 PMid: 16330731

D'Onofrio v. D'Onofrio, 365 A. 2d 27 (N.J. 1976).

Dupré v. Dupré, 857 A. 2d 242 (R.I. 2004).

Emery, R. E. (1998). *Marriage, divorce, and children's adjustment* (2nd ed.). Thousand Oaks, CA: Sage.

Fabricius, W. J., & Hall, J. A. (2000). Young adults' perspectives on divorce: Living arrangements. *Family and Conciliation Courts Review, 38,* 446–461. doi: 10.1111/j. 174–1617.2000. tb00584. x

Fagan, J., & Barnett, M. (2003). The relationship between maternal gatekeeping, paternal competence, mothers' attitudes about the father role, and father involvement. *Journal of Family Issues, 24,* 1020–1043. doi: 10.1177/0192513X03256397

Flouri, E. (2005). *Fathering & child outcomes*. West Sussex, England: John Wiley.

Francis, *In re* the Marriage of, 919 P. 2d 776 (Colo. 1996).

Goldfarb v. Goldfarb, Superior Ct., 861 A. 2d 340 (Pa. Super 2004).

Hetherington, E. M. (1999). Social capital and the development of youth from non-divorced, divorced, and remarried families. In W. A. Collins & B. Laursen (Eds.), *Relationships as developmental contexts: The Minnesota symposium on child psychology* (Vol. 30, pp. 177–210). Mahwah, NJ: Erlbaum.

Hetherington, E. M., Bridges, M., & Insabella, G. M. (1998). What matters? What does not? Five perspectives on the association between marital transitions and children's adjustment. *American Psychologist, 53,* 167–184. doi: 10.1037/0003-066X. 53.2.167PMid: 9491746

Hetherington, E. M., & Kelly, J. (2002). *Divorce reconsidered: For better or for worse*. New York: Norton.

Kelly, J. B., & Emery, R. (2003). Children's adjustment following divorce: Risk and resilience perspectives. *Family Relations, 52,* 352–362. doi: 10.1111/j. 1741-3729.2003.00352. x

Kelly, J. B., & Lamb, M. E. (2003). Developmental issues in relocation cases involving young children: When, whether, and how? *Journal of Family Psychology, 17,* 193–205. doi: 10.1037/0893-3200.17.2.193PMid: 12828016

Lamb, M. E. (Ed.). (1981). *The role of the father in child development* (2nd ed.). Hoboken, NJ: Wiley.

Lamb, M. E. (Ed.). (2004). *The role of the father in child development* (4th ed.). Hoboken, NJ: Wiley.

LaMusga, *In re* the Marriage of, 88 P. 3d 81 (Cal. 2004).

Littlefield, *In re the Marriage of*, 940 P. 2d 1362 (Wash. 1997).

Maccoby, E. E., & Mnookin, R. H. (1992). *Dividing the child: Social & legal dilemmas of custody*. Cambridge, MA: Harvard University Press.

McBride, B. A., Brown, G. L., Bost, K. K., Shin, N., Vaughn, B., & Korth, B. (2005). Paternal identity, maternal gatekeeping, and father involvements. *Family Relations, 54,* 360–372. doi: 10.1111/j. 1741-3729.2005.00323. x

McLanahan, S., &Sandefur, G. (1994). *Growing up with a single parent: What hurts, what helps*. Cambridge, MA: Harvard University Press.

Michigan Code of Laws Annotated, Child Custody Act of 1970, §722.23(j).

Office for National Statistics. (2009). *Migration statistics national report*. [Statistical Bull]. Retrieved from www.statistics.gov.uk/cci/nugget.asp?id=260.

Oishi, S. (2010). The psychology of residential mobility: Implications for the self, social relationships, and well-being. *Perspectives on Psychological Science, 5*(1), 5–21. doi: 101177/1745691609356781

Oishi, S., & Schimmack, U. (2010). Residential mobility, well-being, and mortality. *Journal of Personality and Social Psychology, 98*(6), 980–994. doi: 10.1037/a0019389 PMid: 20515253

Parkinson, P., Cashmore, J., & Single, J. (2010). The need for reality testing in relocation cases. *Family Law Quarterly, 44*(1), 1–34.

Pleck, J. H. (1985). *Working wives/working husbands.* Beverly Hills, CA: Sage.

Prince v. Massachusetts, 321 U.S. 158 (1944).

Pruett, K. D. (2000). *Fatherneed: Why father care is essential as mother care for your child.* New York: Free Press.

Pruett, M. K., Arthur, L. A., &Ebling, R. (2007). The hand that rocks the cradle: Maternal gatekeeping after divorce. *Pace Law Review, 27*(4), 709–739. doi: 10.1177/1531244504421004

Pruett, M. K., Williams, T. Y., Insabella, G., & Little, T. D. (2003). Family and legal indicators of child adjustment to divorce among families with young children. *Journal of Family Psychology, 17,* 169–180. doi: 10.1037/0893-3200.17.2.169PMid: 12828014

Santosky v. Kramer, 455 U.S. 745 (1982).

Schacter, J. (2001). *Why people move: Exploring the March 2000 current population survey.* (Current Population Reports, U.S. Census Bureau). Washington, DC: U.S. Department of Commerce.

Schacter, J. P. (2004). *Geographic mobility: 2003–2003.* (U.S. Census Bureau, No. P20–549). Washington, DC: U.S. Department of Commerce.

Schoppe-Sullivan, S. J., Brown, G. L., Cannon, E. A., & Mangelsdorf, S. C. (2008). Maternal gatekeeping, coparenting quality, and fathering behavior in families with infants. *Journal of Family Psychology, 22*(3), 389–398. doi: 10.1037/0893-3200.22.3.389PMid: 18540767

Shapiro v. Thompson, 394 U.S. 618, 629–631 (1969).

Shear, L. E., Fuller, M. G., Olesen, N. M., Stettman, P. P., Lamb, M. E., Gray, D., & McNeil, M. (2004). Amici Curiae brief, *In re* the Marriage of LaMusga, Supreme Court of California.

Simpson, G. A., & Fowler, M. G. (1994). Geographic mobility and children's emotional/behavioral adjustment and school functioning. *Pediatrics, 93*(2), 303–309.

South, S. J., Haynie, D. L., & Bose, S. (2005). Residential mobility and the onset of adolescent sexual activity. *Journal of Marriage and Family, 67,* 499–514. doi: 10.111/j. 0022-2445.2005.00131. x

Spahmer v. Gullette, 113 P. 3d 158 (Colo. 2005).

Statistics Canada. (2006). *A portrait of the mobility of Canadians between 2001 and 2006.* Retrieved from www.statcan.gc.ca/pub/91-209-x/2004000/part2/p1-eng.htm

Taylor, N., & Freeman, M. (2010). International research evidence on relocation: Past, present, and future. *Family Law Quarterly, 44*(3), 317–340.

Toqueville, A. (2003). *Democracy in America.* New York: Penguin Books. (Original work published in 1835)

Triandis, H. C. (1995). *Individualism and collectivism.* Boulder, CO: Westview Press.

Trinder, L. (2008). Maternal gate closing and gate opening in postdivorce families. *Journal of Family Issues, 29*(10), 1298–1324. doi: 10.1177/0192513X08315362

Tropea v. Tropea, 665 N.E. 2d 145 (1996).

Troxel v. Granville, 530 U.S. 57 (2000).

Tucker, C. J., Marx, J., & Long, L. (1998). "Moving on": Residential mobility and children's school lives. *Sociology of Education, 71*, 111–129. doi: 10.2307/2673244

Turner, F. J. (1921). *The frontier in American history*. New York: Henry Holt.

U.S. Census Bureau, Housing and Households Economics Statistics Division. *Geographical Mobility Detailed Tables 2008 to 2009*. Retrieved from: www.census.gov/population/www/socdemo/migrate/cps2009.html

Wallerstein, J. S., Kernberg, P. F., Silberg, J. L., Lewis, J. M., Sikorski, J. B., & Dallam, S. J. (2004). Amici Curiae brief, *In re* the Marriage of LaMusga, Supreme Court of California.

Wallerstein, J. S., &Tanke, T. J. (1996). To move or not to move: Psychological and legal considerations in the relocation of children following divorce. *Family Law Quarterly, 30*, 305–332.

Warshak, R. A., Braver, S. L., Kelly, J. B., Bray, J. H., Austin, W. G., & Rick, G. R. (2004). Amici Curiae brief, *In re* the Marriage of LaMusga, Supreme Court of California.

Wood, D., Halfon, N., Scarlata, D., Newacheck, P., & Nessim, S. (1993). Impact of family relocation on children's growth, development, school function, and behavior. *Journal of the American Medical Association, 270*, 1334–1338. PMid: 7689659

Science and the Law

## 19

Judicial Impact

The Best Interests of the Child and the Daubert and Frye Evidentiary Frameworks

DANIEL W. SHUMAN† AND ALEXANDER S. BERK ∎

INTRODUCTION

The legal process of divorce is a common experience for many children today: An estimated 40% of all children will be faced with the divorce of their parents, and 6% to 20% will have their custodial placement determined for them through litigation, a contentious way to have one's future planned indeed (Krauss & Sales, 2000). Given the profound effect that custodial placement decisions have on children, it is not unreasonable to think that a straightforward and unambiguous judicial framework would be in place. However, the practical effect of the standard for legal determinations of custodial placement, the best interest of the child, has been confusion and uncertainty, with the judicial system turning to the widespread use of mental health professionals as experts for answers. Complicating the issue, the standard for admissibility of expert testimony requires judges to scrutinize the relevance and reliability of these experts' testimony. Amazingly, even with these inoperable standards, there is relatively no case law on the issue of admissibility of mental health expert testimony in the child custody context. This is true even in the face of scholarly criticism arguing that mental health expert testimony, much of which is the product of psychological tests that are based on theoretical constructs well outside the scope of custody litigation, fails to meet the relevance and reliability threshold. Whereas other areas of the law have seen judicial scrutiny of expert testimony, this has certainly not been the case in custody determinations, which instead receive a laissez-faire attitude from courts regarding the evidentiary threshold and admissibility of expert testimony (Shuman, 2002).

THE "BEST INTERESTS OF THE CHILD" STANDARD

Legal determinations of custodial placement are based on the psychological "best interest of the child standard" (BICS). An indeterminate standard incapable of being

† Deceased

operationalized, criticism has surrounded the BICS since its inception (Emery, Otto, & O'Donohue, 2005). Its inherent ambiguity is a focal point for much of the criticism, with legal scholars arguing it leads to detrimental outcomes for all parties involved in custody litigation (Krauss & Sales, 2000). Much of the ambiguity is caused by the variation between jurisdictions as to the makeup of child custody statutes setting forth factors to be considered when determining the BICS. More specifically, while most custody statutes incorporate many of the factors originally set out in the Uniform Marriage and Divorce Act of 1970 (UMDA) (e.g., the wishes of the child's parent or parents with respect to custody, the wishes of the child as to his or her custody), and as amended, this is certainly not true for all jurisdictions. The inconsistency between jurisdictions is exacerbated by the fact that many elect to include additional factors outside of the UMDA in their statutes (Krauss & Sales, 1999). This piecemeal framework is complicated by the lack of guidance as to how these statutory factors should be weighed or applied by the judiciary (Krauss & Sales, 1999). The result is widespread judicial discretion in application of the BICS, opening the door for judicial bias to influence custodial determinations. Often this entails judges imputing their own beliefs as the basis for their decisions (Krauss & Sales, 2000).

The influx of mental health professionals as experts in custody determinations has been attributed to the indeterminate BICS and the difficulty judges have in adjudicating these cases. Scholars have attributed what appears to be a dependency on mental health professionals on the hope these experts will provide an answer to the psychological, rather than legal, question of what is in the best interest of the child (Krauss & Sales, 2000). Exacerbating this dependency was the influential work of Goldstein, Freud, and Solnit (1979), who helped originate and give life to the legal movement that precipitated the BICS. Their psychological parent theory, requiring psychological evaluations in child custody disputes to determine the level of psychological attachment between parent and child, necessitated a call for active participation by mental health professionals, namely psychologists and psychiatrists, in custody disputes. Though the psychological parent theory was never adopted, the underlying notion of Goldstein, Freud, and Solnit's work advocating for an increased role of mental health professionals has taken hold, given their overwhelming presence today in child custody determinations (Shuman, 2002).

In summary:

- The inherent ambiguity of the BICS has led to judicial subjectivity regarding its application, creating a risk for adjudication that is based on personal bias and beliefs rather than clear statutory guidelines.
- The indeterminate BICS and the resulting judicial difficulty in applying the standard have led to the frequent use of mental health professionals in custody determinations, the hope being that these experts would provide an answer to the psychological best interest of the child.

RELEVANCE AND RELIABILITY: THE EVIDENTIARY THRESHOLD

At the same time as BICS was taking root as the standard for judicial determination of custodial placement, the U.S. Supreme Court, over a 76-year period (1923–1999), was reinventing the standard for judicial determination of the admissibility of expert testimony (Shuman, 2002). Initially the admissibility standard of expert testimony only required on expert qualification, to have an expert's testimony admitted the proponent of the testimony merely had to show the expert was qualified to make the claim. This is about as lenient of a standard as one can find. Through a series of cases, beginning in 1923 with *Frye v. United States* and culminating with *Daubert v. Merrell Dow Pharmaceuticals, Inc.* (1993), the Court reworked the admissibility standard from one of qualification only to one scrutinizing experts' methods and procedures by requiring proof of testimonial relevance and reliability (Shuman, 1997).

Prior to *Daubert*, *Frye* required that the basis of expert testimony be "generally accepted" within the relevant scientific community before the testimony could be admitted as valid (*Frye*, 1923). Although there was no question of the expert's qualifications in *Frye*, the Court could not justify admitting testimony based on a test that amounted to a precursor of the polygraph, unknown to other scientific professionals at the time (*Frye*, 1923). Although stricter than a mere qualifications standard, the "general acceptance" test was still remarkably lenient, with legal scholars emphasizing that an expert could always be located who would swear that his or her theory was generally accepted (Grove & Barden, 1999). Other flaws were prevalent as well. Though *Frye* attempted to limit the admissibility of novel scientific evidence, it failed to define either "science" or "novel science," thereby leaving little direction for application of its rule or to determine what science would fall under its purview. The decision whether to admit expert testimony was left not to trial judges, but rather to the relevant scientific community's acceptance of the basis for the testimony. Further, the notion was that *Frye* equated validity with popularity (Shuman, 1997). Though imperfect, the importance of *Frye* was the core of its holding, namely the focus on relevance and reliability of expert testimony as the means by which to gauge admissibility.

The 1993 *Daubert* decision was an attempt to remedy the flaws inherent in *Frye* by delineating a heightened scrutiny of experts in the face of the liberal thrust of the Federal Rules of Evidence (FRE). Specifically, the Court determined that FRE 702, not *Frye*, controlled the determination of admissibility of expert testimony. Per FRE 702, expert testimony is admissible "if scientific, technical, or other specialized knowledge will assist the trier of fact to understand the evidence or to determine a fact in issue." Interpreting FRE 702, the Court held that admissibility of expert testimony in federal court hinges on the reliability of an expert's knowledge and its relevance to an issue in a case:

> The trial judge must determine…whether the expert is proposing to testify to scientific knowledge that will assist the trier of fact to understand or determine a fact in issue. This entails a preliminary assessment of whether the reasoning or methodology underlying the testimony is scientifically valid and of whether that reasoning or methodology properly can be applied to the facts in issue. (*Daubert*, 1993, pp. 592–593)

To aid in this gatekeeping function, the Court laid out a non-exhaustive list of five pragmatic factors for trial judges to consider: whether

1. the proffered expert testimony can be, and has been, tested;
2. the technique or theory has been subject to peer review or publication;

3. it has a known or potential error rate;

4. it is generally accepted within the appropriate scientific community; and

5. there are any other factors that should be included that might speak to the evidentiary reliability of the testimony (Daubert, 1993, p. 593).

As an interpretation of the FRE, *Daubert* is binding only in federal court. Therefore, as the typical forum for child custody disputes is state court, *Daubert* has no application unless a state adopts it by statute or common law. Though many states have elected to do this, some have chosen to follow *Frye* or some variation of the *Daubert-Frye* analysis instead. The effect is a typical requirement in most, if not all states, requiring some level of analysis regarding the relevance and reliability of expert testimony (Shuman, 2002).

More recently, the Court *in Khumo Tire Co., Ltd.,* et al. *v. Carmichael* et al. (1999) expanded the *Daubert* relevance and reliability framework to include relatively all expert testimony, thereby implicating the testimony of mental health professionals (Grove & Barden, 1999). The Court opined that in performing their gatekeeping function, trial judges were obliged to analyze all expert testimony based on FRE 702. Specifically, the Court found that judges would be unable to distinguish between "scientific," "technical," and "specialized knowledge," and that even if they could, there was no need to make the distinction due to the practice of allowing nonscientific experts to testify regardless if they showed "the same level of intellectual rigor that characterizes the practice of an expert in the relevant field" (*Khumo*, 1999, pp. 7–9). With the *Khumo* holding, the admissibility of expert testimony proffered by mental health professionals triggers a *Daubert* analysis, "thus present[ing] a basis for challenging the long-standing practice of receiving psychological testimony in best interests hearings in state courts that apply these evidentiary standards" (Wah, 2002, p. 154).

In summary:

- In 1923, *Frye* held that the basis of expert testimony must be "generally accepted" within the relevant scientific community before the testimony could be admitted as valid.
- In 1993, *Daubert* interpreted FRE 702 to require that expert methods and procedures be relevant and reliable.
- As an interpretation of the Federal Rules, *Daubert* is mandatory only in federal court. As child custody determinations are adjudicated in state court, for *Daubert* to apply it must be statutorily enacted or adopted through common law.
- Jurisdictions vary in their evidentiary standards. While many states have adopted the *Daubert* framework, others remain tied to *Frye* or a variation of both.
- *Khumo* applied the *Daubert* evidentiary threshold to all experts, thereby implicating mental health expert testimony within its framework.

JUDICIAL LAISSEZ-FAIRE ATTITUDE TOWARD THE EVIDENTIARY THRESHOLD

Surprisingly, even with the indeterminate BICS standard for judicial determination of custodial placement, coupled with the reliability and relevance standard for judicial determination of admissibility of expert testimony, there is relatively no case law on the admissibility of mental health expert testimony in child custody proceedings. While a few courts have been able to avoid the question altogether by finding procedural error, such as an objection to admissibility being insufficiently clear (*In re C.J.B.*, 137 S.W.3d 814 (Tex.App.–Waco 2004)) and counsel failing to lay the proper predicate identifying and qualifying a witness as an expert (*Morris v. Morris*, 783 So.2d 681 (Miss. 2001)), what case law there is on point shows a disturbing trend of trial judges either overlooking, ignoring, or making bare mention of either relevance or reliability in their determinations (*Robb v. Robb*, 687 N.W.2d 195 (Neb. 2004)).

> Notwithstanding the federal and state high court decisions instructing trial judges about their threshold responsibility to address the reliability and relevance of expert testimony and the expression of concern that this had not occurred in the case of expert testimony addressing the interests of children, little has changed in the admissibility of expert testimony in the trial of custodial issues post-*Daubert* and its progeny. (Shuman, 2002, p. 139)

Multiple reasons have been suggested for this trend. While Frye suggests a liberal policy of admissibility, *Daubert* expounds a stringent relevance and reliability framework, leaving trial judges unsure as to the level of rigidity to apply in their admissibility determinations. It is also unclear from *Daubert* whether trial judges are required to determine the reliability of expert testimony using the five pragmatic factors given, and if so, what weight is to applied to each. Another likely explanation is the effect of *General Electric v. Joiner* (1997), in which the Supreme Court held the obligation for determining admissibility of expert testimony under *Daubert* to be exclusively on trial judges rather than appellate courts. Specifically, *Joiner* held that a trial judge's determination of whether to admit scientific expert testimony should be reviewed only for abuse of discretion. This is a difficult feat: To prove a trial judge abused his or her discretion, an appealing party must show that the trial judge's determination was manifestly erroneous. As a practical matter, the difficulty in meeting this standard likely prevents many parties from attempting review, and those who do likely face the refusal of appellate courts to second-guess trial courts' determinations of admissibility. As the great majority of published opinions come from appellate courts, the lack of published opinions concerning mental health expert testimony in custodial determinations is not surprising. Importantly, the lack of appellate review necessarily means that trial courts will have little to no guidance in the proper application of *Daubert* (Krauss & Sales, 1999).

The fact remains that trial judges are continuing to admit expert mental health testimony regardless of the relevance/reliability evidentiary threshold. Psychological tests commonly employed in custody evaluations therefore pass muster without much, if any, judicial scrutiny. Given the pervasive questions and debate that have surrounded these tests in terms of their relevance to custody determinations and scientific reliability, legal scholars and critics are questioning the role, if any, that mental health experts should play in this context.

In summary:

- Regardless of the ambiguous BICS coupled with the rigid *Daubert* evidentiary framework, there is a paucity of case law on the issue of

admissibility of mental health expert testimony in child custody
determinations.

- Even with intense debates regarding the relevance and reliability of this
expert testimony, including that based on psychological testing, the
judiciary has continued to take an apathetic approach to the evidentiary
standard, regularly admitting this expert testimony without due scrutiny.

THE QUALIFICATION ISSUE

One of the commonalities shared between the *Daubert* and *Frye* holdings is the
importance of separating an expert's qualifications from an analysis into the reliability of the science employed by that expert (Zervopoulos, 2008). Making clear there is
no per se reliability in an expert's methods and procedures merely through qualifications, the Supreme Court opined in *Joiner* (1997) that "nothing in either *Daubert* or
the Federal Rules of Evidence requires a district court to admit opinion evidence that
is connected to existing data only by the *ipse dixit* of the expert." Recent case law
reflects this rule that an expert's opinion will not be admitted merely because of the
writing on his or her diploma, as testimony from experts has been both admitted and
excluded regardless of degree or licensure. Courts have admitted expert testimony
from not only psychologists (*Surman v. Surman*, 745 N.W.2d 802 (Mich.App. 2007)
and *In re K.C.F.*, 928 A.2d 1046 (Pa.Super. 2007)) but also from social workers (*Minter
v. Minter*, 29 So.3d 840 (Miss.App. 2009), *Smith v. Tierney*, 906 So.2d 586 (La.App. 1
Cir. 2005), and *Giannaris v. Giannaris*, 960 So.2d 462 (Miss. 2007)) and counselors
(*LaMoria v. LaMoria*, 762 A.2d 1233 (Vt. 2000) and *In re K.L.R.*, 162 S.W.3d 291
(Tex.App.-Tyler 2005)). At the same time, it is not uncommon to see judicial determinations hanging their admissibility hat on an analysis of qualifications:

> I think education is the key word. This lady has as much education or more than
> many people who have been well qualified and have testified before this court
> primarily on the basis of long experience. Certainly the twenty years alone that
> she has been experienced in these matters, that is particularly family counsel-
> ing, child/adolescent counseling, and abuse/neglect proceedings or counseling,
> she's well qualified in all three matters, and the Court accepts those qualifica-
> tions and her expertise in those matters. (*Surman v. Surman*, 745 N.W.2d 802
> (Mich.App. 2007))

Given the inconsistent case law, the question remains whether proper application
of *Daubert* and *Frye*, in the context of admissibility of opinions offered by mental
health professionals, is being undertaken by trial judges or whether subjective
judicial determinations are being made on an ad hoc basis.

In summary:

- A commonality between *Daubert* and *Frye* is separation of qualification
from reliability of testimony.
- While recent case law reflects this proposition, as courts have admitted
expert testimony from psychologists, social workers, and counselors, there
are cases reflecting admissibility based on education.

- Whether advocating for admissibility of expert testimony or challenging the admissibility, it is important for litigants to remember proper procedural rules in this regard.

JUDICIAL AND COUNSEL GUIDELINES FOR IDENTIFYING RELIABLE EXPERT TESTIMONY

Whether testimony, including that which is scientifically based, is admissible depends on an assessment of both an expert's qualifications and the expert's methods and procedures (Zervopoulos, 2008). In essence, the question confronting a presiding judge, and that which counsel must be cognizant of and prepare for, is: "How do you [the expert] know what you claim to know?" (Zervopoulos, 2008, page 28). The following five-part model, incorporating factors set out by John A. Zervopoulos (2008) to assist mental health professionals in the role of witness, is provided as judicial and counsel guidelines for identifying reliable expert testimony.

First, the witness must be qualified as an expert (Zervopoulos, 2008). Those qualified may include trained professionals, such as psychologists, social workers, and counselors, as seen above, or individuals lacking scientific training as long as the proper foundation for their testimony is laid (Zervopoulos, 2008). Second, as the 5th Circuit stated in *Watkins v. Talsmith, Inc.* (1997), "The [district] court should ensure that the [expert] opinion comports with applicable professional standards outside the courtroom, and that it will have a reliable basis in the knowledge and experience of the discipline" (Zervopoulos, 2008, p. 30). Ethical codes, professional guidelines, and the means by which the expert gathered their information on which scientific testimony is based, therefore, should be assessed (Zervopoulos, 2008). Third, as mandated by the Supreme Court in *Joiner*, a judge must assess the existence of "empirical and logical connections between the data arising from the expert's methods and the expert's conclusions" (Zervopoulos, 2008, p. 33) and ensure the "analytical gap" between the two is not "too great" (*Joiner*, 1997). Fourth, a judge must assess whether the expert's conclusions, inferences, opinions, and resulting recommendations appropriately speak to the prevailing legal standard (i.e., best interest of the child) at issue (Zervopoulos, 2008). Of the many questions that arise in this analysis, one of the most significant concerns an assessment of the expert's objectivity (Shuman & Zervopoulos, 2010, p. 592). More specifically, an inquiry into whether bias, if any, impeded an expert's ability to provide objective testimony is likely necessary. This should include an examination into inappropriate use of therapeutic empathy or empathy-bias, the latter defined as "forensic examiner's personal views and mindset towards the examination's purpose" (Shuman & Zervopoulos, 2010, p. 592,). Factors to consider in determining impartiality may include an inquiry into whether:

1. The examiner's *competence* permits him or her to provide an opinion on the legal issue
2. The "facts or data" underlying the expert opinion are *relevant* to the legal issue (Fed. R. Evid. 705)
3. The *perspectives* of each party to the litigation have been taken into consideration

4. There existed a *balance* between the attention paid to the differing perspectives
5. The expert's testimony was done with *candor* and was not selectively based (Shuman & Greenberg, 2003)

In addition, to help ensure that objective reliable testimony is admitted, judges and counsel within family court should familiarize themselves with these concepts.

Fifth, the judge must assess his or her own objectivity and determine whether empathy, if any, toward a litigant(s) may impede an appropriate judicial determination (Shuman & Zervopoulos, 2010). Judges are no less susceptible to the effects emotion may play on objectivity, and in the child custody context, emotions typically run high. Therefore, it is imperative that presiding judges regularly remind themselves of their objective adjudicative duty.

In summary, the five-part judicial guidelines model for identifying reliable expert testimony consist of:

- Determine whether the witness is qualified as an expert
- Determine whether the expert opinion comports with applicable professional standards outside the courtroom and that it has a reliable basis in the knowledge and experience of the expert's discipline
- Determine whether the analytical gap between the expert's data and conclusions is not "too great"
- Determine whether the expert's testimony speaks to the legal standard at issue, including an assessment for the existence of expert bias
- Judicial self-assessment for objectivity

SUMMARY

Psychology and law, two areas that have historically remained at arm's length from each other, are practically inseparable in the family court setting. Arguing that psychologists and psychiatrists were the sole parties capable of determining the correct custodial placement for children, Goldstein, Freud, and Solnit (1979) spurred a legal movement effectuating in the inundation of mental health professionals as experts in determinations of the best interests of the child (Shuman, 2002). Though the frequent use of these experts in BICS determinations has drawn the criticism of scholars regarding the relevance and reliability of the methods and procedures they employ, such as the different psychological tests used in custody evaluations, the admissibility of their testimony is rarely challenged (Shuman, 2002). Whereas judicial evidentiary scrutiny is routinely applied in other areas of the law, the demanding *Daubert* framework appears to have bypassed child custody determinations; this is an area ripe with evidentiary relevance and reliability concerns begging for evaluation specifically allowed for under *Khumo*.

The BICS ambiguity and the lack of adherence to the evidentiary framework has led to subjective admissibility decisions based on judicial biases and preferences, resulting in inconsistent and variable custodial determinations. This unpredictable nature has led litigants to undertake various strategic actions contrary to honest and ethical negotiation, such as forum-shopping and extending litigation in the hopes of either settlement or one party dropping the claim (Krauss & Sales, 2000). This latter move often incorporates a battle of private experts, a common, expected practice that Justice Learned Hand feared would eventuate if the use of experts was not scrutinized: "[My] serious objections [to the use of experts] are, first, that the expert becomes a hired champion on one side; second, that he is the subject of examination and cross-examination and a contradiction of other experts" (Wah, 2002, p. 154). Regarding court-appointed experts, litigants may reasonably expect a judge to blindly follow the recommendation of a court-appointed mental health expert, illustrating the impact and power these appointed experts have in custody determinations (Shuman, 2002). Clearly, legal scholars have cause for concern regarding who is actually adjudicating these cases, the elected or appointed judiciary or the mental health expert.

The everyday use of mental health professionals is likewise illustrative of an about-face from evidentiary concerns regarding the ability of the expert to, as the FRE requires, "assist the trier of fact." Illustrative of this concern, Justice Hand opined, "The expert is necessary and logical only to supply to the jury certain propositions of general applicability, or laws of nature, which are not the heritage of the ordinary man [and to provide] specialized experience such as the ordinary man does not possess" (Wah, 2002, p. 154). As a significant amount of mental health expert testimony is drawn from interviews with parties to the litigation, it is likely many experts are acting merely as reporters of information the trier of fact could receive directly otherwise (Wah, 2002). Moreover, testimony introduced merely to gain a strategic advantage, such as to increase costs in an attempt to spur settlement, or testimony based on "evidence" that an expert believes *should* be admitted, clearly does not assist the fact-finder in either understanding the evidence or determining a fact in issue. As such, this type of testimony should be excluded (Shuman, 2002).

Given the debate that has plagued the issue of admissibility of mental health expert testimony in child custody determinations since the inception of the BICS and the handing down of the *Daubert* framework, the judiciary needs to determine whether it is capable of undertaking the required evidentiary scrutiny in order to appropriately adjudicate these cases. If not, alternative approaches should be considered. As the only consistency in adjudicating custody determinations is judicial inconsistency, it is clear that more cogent research and judicial activism is needed in this area, given those at risk if the situation remains at the current status quo: our children.

GUIDELINES: CONSIDERATIONS AND CAUTIONS

- The combination of the indeterminate BICS with the relevant and reliability frameworks of both *Daubert* and *Frye* has not resulted in the case law that scholars have expected regarding the admissibility of mental health expert testimony in child custody determinations.
- Case law research has resulted in sparse findings. Over the past decade, the number of published opinions speaking on this issue can almost be counted on two hands. Judicial scrutiny of expert testimony is needed to give guidance and consistency to custody determinations. Rather than

leaving this responsibility solely in the hands of trial judges, appellate courts should scrutinize this expert testimony as well in order to delineate guidance through controlling precedence.

- With the lack of judicial guidance, custody litigation has become an inconsistent endeavor not only between jurisdictions, but within jurisdictions as well. Because of this inconsistency, many litigants choose to engage in behavior typically adverse to proper and ethical adjudication, such as forum-shopping and extending litigation in the hopes the adverse party will either quit or choose to settle. A battle of privately hired experts typically ensues, leaving judicial determination based on equally compelling evidence.
- The recommendations of court-appointed psychologists are typically followed without question, leaving concern regarding the proper role of these experts. Further discussion is needed regarding the role these experts should undertake as compared with that of the judiciary.
- Complicating the issue is the indefinable BICS. For a test to be valid it must have a definable target. Therefore, inquiry is needed into the veracity of the BICS. Alternative standards need to be developed and tested.

REFERENCES

Daubert v. Merrell Dow Pharmaceuticals, Inc., 509 U.S. 579 (1993).

Emery, R. E., Otto, R. K., & O'Donohue, W. T. (2005). A critical assessment of child custody evaluations: Limited science and a flawed system. *Psychological Science in the Public Interest, 6*, 1–29.

Fed. R. Evid. 702.

Fed. R. Evid. 705.

Frye v. United States, 293 U.S. 1013 (D.C. Cir. 1923)

General Electric Co. v. Joiner, 522 U.S. 136 (1997)

Giannaris v. Giannaris, 960 So.2d 462 (Miss. 2007) (court held chancellor abused its discretion in admitting testimony by social worker that was not based on any data or facts nor the product of reliable principles or methods)

Goldstein, J., Freud, A., & Solnit, A. J. (1979). *Before the best interests of the child.* New York: The Free Press.

Grove, W. M., & Barden, R. C. (1999). Protecting the integrity of the legal system the admissibility of testimony from mental health experts under Daubert/Khumo analyses. *Psychology, Public Policy, and Law, 5*, 224–242.

In re C.J.B., 137 S.W.3d 814 (Tex.App.–Waco 2004)

In re K.C.F., 928 A.2d 1046 (Pa.Supper. 2007) (trial court did not abuse discretion in finding clinical psychologist qualified)

In re K.L.R., 162 S.W.3d 291 (Tex.App.–Tyler 2005) (court held trial court erred in admitting testimony of licensed professional counselor with a Ph.D. because she did not state counseling was a legitimate field and did not state her testimony was within the scope of her field, nor could it be implied from her testimony, and she did not state her testimony properly relied upon and/or used principles involved in her field)

Krauss, D. A., & Sales, B. D. (1999). The problem of "helpfulness" in applying Daubert to expert testimony child custody determinations in family law as an exemplar. *Psychology, Public Policy, and Law, 5*, 78–99.

Krauss, D. A., & Sales, B. D. (2000). Legal standards, expertise, and experts in the resolution of contested child custody cases. *Psychology, Public Policy, and Law, 6*, 843–879.

Khumo Tire Co. v. Carmichael, 526 U.S. 137 (1999).

LaMoria v. LaMoria, 762 A.2d 1233 (Vt. 2000) (counselor with a Ph.D. held qualified as an expert to give clinical opinion only)

Minter v. Minter, 29 So.3d 840 (Miss.App. 2009) (chancellor did not abuse discretion in finding social worker with a Ph.D. in sociology qualified)

Morris v. Morris, 783 So.2d 681 (Miss. 2001)

Robb v. Robb, 687 N.W.2d 195 (Neb. 2004) (trial judge admitted expert psychological testimony on parenting abilities when that expert failed to conduct a full custody evaluation)

Shuman, D. W. (1997). What should we permit mental health professionals to say about "the best interests of the child"? An essay on common sense, Daubert, and the Rules of Evidence. *Family Law Quarterly, 31*, 551–569.

Shuman, D. W. (2002). The role of mental health experts in custody decisions: Science, psychological tests, and clinical judgment. *Family Law Quarterly, 36*, 135–162.

Shuman, D. W., & Greenberg, S. A. (2003). The expert witness, the adversary system, and the voice of reason: reconciling impartiality and advocacy. *Professional Psychology: Research and Practice, 34*(3), 219–224.

Shuman, D. W., & Zervopoulos, J. A. (2010). Empathy or objectivity: the forensic examiner's dilemma? *Behavioral Sciences and the Law, 28*, 585–602.

Smith v. Tierney, 906 So.2d 586 (La.App. 1 Cir. 2005) (court did not abuse discretion in finding social worker qualified)

Surman v. Surman, 745 N.W.2d 802 (Mich.App. 2007) (trial court did not abuse discretion in finding psychologist with a limited license and LPC qualified to testify)

Uniform Marriage & Divorce Act of 1970, amended 1971 and 1973

Wah, C. R. (2002). The changing nature of psychological expert testimony in child custody cases. *Judicature, 86*, 152–161.

Watkins v. Telsmith, Inc., 121 F.3d 984, 991 (5th Cir. 1997)

Zervopoulos, J. A. (2008). A legal perspective. In J. A. Zervopoulos, *Confronting mental health evidence: A practical guide to reliability and experts in family law*. Chicago: American Bar Association, Section of Family Law.

Conclusion

## 20

Evidence-Based Practice

KATHRYN F. KUEHNLE AND LESLIE M. DROZD ■

Social science research must be the foundation of mental health experts' conclusions and opinions about parents and children in litigated time-sharing cases. When research does not guide the mental health expert in forensic activities, expert opinions may be emotionally or capriciously derived and families and children may be harmed. The scientific process used in forensic mental health assessment places a high value on intellectual honesty. When conducting a forensic assessment, there is an explicit acknowledgement that subjective beliefs could be wrong and that scientific procedures are designed to protect the evaluator from relying on unfounded assumptions (Lilienfeld, 2010). Scientific procedures are intended to reduce human error.

Lilienfeld (2010) wrote that "science is a set of systematic safeguards against confirmation bias, that is, the tendency to seek out evidence consistent with our hypotheses and to deny, dismiss, or distort evidence that runs counter to them." B.F. Skinner (1953) concluded that science requires a "willingness to accept facts even when they are opposed to wishes" (p. 12). Among the errors the evidence-based child custody evaluator's procedures intend to minimize are confirmatory bias, confirmatory distortion, primacy and recency effects, and other types of bias (Martindale, 2005). A fundamental distinction is made between scientists and pseudoscientists. A scientist relies on the scientific method and empirical investigation, while the pseudoscientist relies on subjective clinical judgments and intuition.

Social scientists, including many of the chapter authors in this volume, employ and evaluate quantitative research designs to investigate social phenomena through quantifiable evidence. The results drawn from well-designed empirical studies have given professionals a better understanding of children's developmental needs and the familial and external factors that may affect long term risk or resilience in children of divorce (Kelly, Chapter 3 in this volume). The identification of adequate from inadequate social science research (see Kelly & Ramsey, 2007; Ramsey & Kelly, 2004 & 2007) is profoundly important when mental health professionals claim expertise in domains where their testimony can ruin lives and where knowledge of reliable data derived from good science can enhance lives. The courts must be assisted in distinguishing science from pseudoscience in order to give the appropriate weight to an expert's testimony.

Scientists design studies to test rival alternative hypotheses and/or to seek confirmation of existing hypotheses. They are conservative in generalizing findings from a group of subjects to a specific individual or another group, who may or may not have the same characteristics as the subjects studied. In contrast to the scientific process, pseudoscientists tend to seek confirmation of their assumptions through selective attention to data, minimize the opportunity for constructive feedback by failing to examine rival, alternative hypotheses, and ignore data that refutes their hypotheses. Much of pseudoscience is based on interpretation of negative or anomalous findings as corroborations of assumptions, sometimes interpreting worse than chance performance as positive findings (Lilienfeld, Lynn, & Lohr, 2003). As a result, assumptions that are false or unconfirmed may be presented to the court as supported by the social science literature and with that families and children could be hurt.

Mnookin and Gross (2003) note that the biggest draw back to expert testimony is the unwarranted confidence with which some colleagues express their opinions. If an expert is acting as a scientist, the process of scientific inquiry serves to subject "our most cherished hypotheses to the risk of falsification" (Lilienfeld, 2010, p. 2). Science is a prescription for humility (McFall, 1996) and a method of "arrogance control" (Tavris & Aronson, 2007). The confidence and perhaps arrogance of the testifying expert is not always equal to his or her level of competence.

Scientific inquiry requires evaluators to override more automatic, effortless, and intuitive modes of thinking with more controlled, effortful, and reflective modes of thinking (Stanovich, 2009).

> All non-scientific systems of thought accept intuition, or personal insight, as a valid source of ultimate knowledge . . . . Science, on the other hand, is the rejection of this belief, and its replacement with the idea that knowledge of the external world can come only from objective investigation." (Cromer, 1993, p. 21)

Shuman and Berk (Chapter 19 in this volume) report that the use of mental health experts in litigated family law cases has drawn the criticism of scholars regarding the relevance and reliability of the methods and procedures they employ. Scholars also argue that judicial evidentiary scrutiny that is routinely applied in other areas of the law appear to have a lower threshold in time-sharing determinations. The authors agree with these scholars' criticisms and opine the threshold for screening out testimony based on poor research and pseudoscience is not high enough in some jurisdictions and with some individual judges. When the bar has been too low, mental health practitioners have been allowed to testify about their conclusions based on assessment techniques that lack a rigorous scientific foundation and are based on pseudoscience claims (e.g., identifying components of children's drawings or play behaviors as associated with sexually abused children. Murrie, Martindale, & Epstein, 2009; Weiner & Kuehnle, 1998). Zervopoulos (2008) opines that simply citing research studies does not support reliable expert testimony, and lawyers and the courts should look critically at the research that mental health practitioners invoke in their testimony. Tavris (2003) writes, "Pseudoscience is particularly attractive because pseudoscience by definition promises certainty, whereas science gives us probability and doubt. Pseudoscience is popular because it confirms what we believe; science is unpopular because it makes us question what we believe" (pp. xv-xvi).

Judges, attorneys and parents can be seduced by the expert who offers certainty in a context of uncertainty. Experts have the responsibility to inform the court of the multiple interacting variables that confound a linear decision (e.g., children under age 3 should have overnights solely with the primary parent; children under age 3 should have overnights with both parents) when addressing parenting plans regarding aspects of children's developmental needs and parenting skills that will optimize children's psychological development. Courts must be kept informed of new findings as empirical studies improve in sample size and diversity, methodology, and advanced statistical analyses. Improved research over the past several decades has shown that outcomes for children and adolescents following divorce are complexly determined and vary considerably. Experts who do not keep abreast of this evolving research may misinform the court by citing early studies that lacked methodological sophistication and that produced results that cannot be generalized beyond the specific group of subjects used in the study. The evolving research is robust in demonstrating that there are no simple solutions to the complex problem of time-sharing determinations.

As noted by Lamb (Chapter 8 in this volume), some of the relevant research has elucidated normative developmental processes by investigating both the typical experiences of young children and the multiple factors associated with variations in the outcomes for children of divorced and intact families. However, numerous issues related to children's development and to parenting plans have not been empirically studied, and the academic literature addressing these issues remains based on clinical illustrations, expert subjective opinions, or weak research designs.

Experts must identify for the courts those issues that can be addressed with reliable conclusions based on empirical investigations and those that cannot. Although clinical observations and preliminary research are important building blocks for an emerging field of interest, independently they do not constitute "empirical evidence" from which reliable conclusions can be drawn for individuals outside the subject sample studied. Several areas of research identified in this volume remain in the stage of preliminary investigation with continuing research in these areas promising to offer new insights for parenting plans that will enhance the psychological development for children of divorce. These areas of ongoing investigation include parent insightfulness (Oppenheim & Koren-Karie, Chapter 2 in this volume), parenting time, quality versus quantity (Fabricius, Sokol, Diaz, & Braver, Chapter 7 in this volume), and parent gatekeeping (Ganong, Coleman, & McCaulley, Chapter 12 in this volume). Overnight time-sharing for infants, toddlers, and preschoolers is also an emerging area of research where general conclusions based on research cannot yet be offered and where there remains important debate (see Lamb, Chapter 9 in this volume; McIntosh & Smyth, Chapter 6 in this volume). Regarding research on overnights for young children, McIntosh and her colleague echo the voices of other child development experts and researchers when they write that "the empirical base is embryonic, and further research is needed" p. xx).

In contrast to preliminary research, evidence from empirically investigated methods based on findings from a number of subject samples provides the confidence to offer opinions. Furthermore, empirical studies help to build a solid knowledge base that is transparent, highlights the strengths and limitations of the evidence, and helps to accurately identify whether the findings can be generalized to the population of interest (Saini, Johnston, Fidler, & Bala., Chapter 13, in this volume). Forensic experts unfamiliar with the range of empirical data on the complex factors that optimize children's psychological development and with the quantity and quality of the parent-child relationship in divorced families may do harm by leaving the court uninformed or misinformed. In this volume, Saini and his colleagues (Chapter 13) provide some guidance to judges, lawyers, and mental health professionals who are unfamiliar with disentangling the strengths and weaknesses of empirical studies.

Forensic experts perceived as most credible by judges and juries are those experts who present themselves as the most confident in their testimony. However, experts' confidence in the information they impart to the court may or may not be associated with the accuracy of the information they provide. Zervopoulos (2008) opines that attorneys and courts face one of their greatest challenges when they attempt to gauge the analytical gaps among the quality of the mental health experts' data, the conclusions, and the opinions. He advocates that attorneys attempt to extricate information from the mental health practitioners to answer the question "How do you know what you say you know?" (p. 39). He identifies the analytical gaps as hidden by: (a) overly abstract psychological concepts, (b) "common sense" notions unsupported by empirical or logical reasoning, (c) *ipse dixit* assertions whereby experts offer opinions devoid of support, (d) reliance on general acceptance factors absent in other support, (e) misapplication or misrepresentation of research, and (f) confirmatory bias (p. 6).

The chapters in this volume reflect empirical findings based upon studies that rely upon the use of the scientific method. Chapter authors present their empirical studies and also analyze the findings from other major research studies that form the foundation of concepts addressed in their chapters. The chapters in this book present a unique opportunity to review the strengths and weaknesses of research that is the current foundation of timesharing and parenting plan concepts. As illustrated by the research reviews, prior to offering information to the court as empirically sound, not only must experts review multiple studies, but they must also analyze the quality of the studies and the robustness of the findings. As experts engage in referencing empirically sound studies and as they engage in evidence-based practices, the statement, "Your Honor, I know because I know" or the vague statement "The research (or the literature) shows," will in time fade away and no longer be part of the lexicon of family court.

ACKNOWLEDGMENTS

We would like to express our appreciation to Jonathan Gould, Ph.D., who is one of the first to write about the need for the use of scientific methodology in child custody, for his input on this chapter.

REFERENCES

Cromer, A. (1993). Uncommon sense: The heretical nature of science. *Science, 265*, 688.

Fabricius, W. V., Sokol, K. R., Diaz, P., & Braver, S. L. (2012). Parenting time, parent conflict, parent-child relationships, and children's physical health. In K. F. Kuehnle & L. M. Drozd (Eds.), *Parenting plan evaluations: Applied research for the family court*. New York: Oxford University Press.

Ganong, L., Coleman, M., & McCaulley, G. (2012). Gatekeeping after separation and divorce. In K. F. Kuehnle & L. M. Drozd (Eds.), *Parenting plan evaluations: Applied research for the family court.* New York: Oxford University Press.

Kelly, J. B. (2012). Risk and protective factors associated with child and adolescent adjustment following separation and divorce: Social science application. In K. F. Kuehnle & L. M. Drozd (Eds.), *Parenting plan evaluations: Applied research for the family court.* New York: Oxford University Press.

Kelly, R.F. & Ramsey, S.H. (2007). Perspectives on family law & social science research: Assessing and communicating social science information in family and child judicial settings: Standards for judges and allied professionals. *Family Court Review, 45,* (2), 22–41. doi:10.1111/j.1744-1617.2007.00126.x

Lamb, M. E. (2012). Critical analysis of research on parenting plans and children's well-being. In K. F. Kuehnle & L. M. Drozd (Eds.), *Parenting plan evaluations: Applied research for the family court.* New York: Oxford University Press.

Lilienfeld, S. O., Lynn, S. J., & Lohr, J. M. (2003). Science and pseudoscience in clinical psychology: Initial thoughts, reflections and considerations. In S. O. Lilienfeld, S. J. Lynn, & J. M. Lohr (Eds.), *Science and pseudoscience in clinical psychology* (pp.1–14). New York: Guilford.

Lilienfeld, S. O. (2010). Can psychology become a science? *Personality and Individual Differences. 49,* 281–288. doi:10.1016/j.paid.2010.01.024

Martindale, D. A. (2005). Confirmatory bias and confirmatory distortion. *Journal of Child Custody, 2*(1/2), 31–48. Haworth Press, New York. doi:10.1300/J190v02n01_03

McFall, R. M. (1996). Making psychology incorruptible. *Applied and Preventive Psychology, 5,* 9–16. doi:10.1016/S0962-1849(96)80021-7

McIntosh, J., & Smyth, B. (2012). Shared-time parenting: An evidence-based matrix for understanding risk. In K. F. Kuehnle & L. M. Drozd (Eds.), *Parenting plan evaluations: Applied research for the family court.* New York: Oxford University Press.

Mnookin, J. L. and Gross, S. R. (2003). Expert information and expert testimony: A preliminary taxonomy. *Seton Hall Law Review, 34,* 139–185.

Murrie, D., Martindale, D., & Epstein, M. (2009). Unsupported assessment techniques in child sexual abuse evaluations. In K. Kuehnle & M. Connell (Eds.), *The evaluation of child sexual abuse allegations: A comprehensive guide to assessment and testimony,* pp. 397–420). Hoboken, NJ: Wiley & Sons, Inc.

Oppenheim, D., & Koren-Karie, N. (2012). Parents' insightfulness: The importance of keeping the inner world of the child in mind for parenting plan evaluations. In K. F. Kuehnle & L. M. Drozd (Eds.), *Parenting plan evaluations: Applied research for the family court.* New York: Oxford University Press.

Ramsey, S. H., & Kelly, R. F. (2004). Social science knowledge in family law cases: Judicial gate-keeping in the Daubert era, *59. University of Miami Law Review, 1*(59), 46–47.

Ramsey, S. H. & Kelly, R. F. (2007). Law-making through the adversarial process: The need for standards for social science briefs in family law cases. In Lynn D. Wardle and Camille Williams (Eds.), *Family Law: Balancing Interests and Pursuing Priorities.* Wm. S. Hein & Co., 2007. (SSRN: http://ssrn.com/abstract=987362)

Saini, M., Johnston, J. R., Fidler, B. J., & Bala, N. (2012). Empirical studies of alienation. In K. F. Kuehnle & L. M. Drozd (Eds.), *Parenting plan evaluations: Applied research for the family court.* New York: Oxford University Press.

Shuman, D., & Berk, A. (2012). Judicial impact: The best interests of the child and the *Daubert* and *Frye* evidentiary frameworks. In K. F. Kuehnle & L. M. Drozd (Eds.), *Parenting plan evaluations: Applied research for the family court.* New York: Oxford University Press.

Skinner, B. F. (1953). *Science and human behavior.* New York: MacMillan.

Stanovich, K. E. (2009). *What intelligence tests miss: The psychology of rational thought.* New Haven, CT: Yale University Press.

Tavris, C. (2003). The widening scientist–practitioner gap. In S. O. Lilienfeld, S. J. Lynn, & J. M. Lohr (Eds.), *Science and pseudoscience in clinical psychology,* pp. ix-xviii). New York: Guilford.

Tavris, C., & Aronson, E. (2007). *Mistakes were made (not by me): Why we justify foolish beliefs, bad directions, and hurtful actions.* Boston, MA: Houghton-Mifflin.

Weiner, I., & Kuehnle, K. (1998). Projective assessment of children and adolescents. In M.Hersen & A. Bellack (Eds.), *Comprehensive clinical psychology,* 3, (431–458). Tarrytown, NY: Elsevier Science, Inc.

Zervopoulos, J. A. (2008). *Confronting mental health evidence: A practical guide to reliability and experts in family law.* Chicago, IL: American Bar Association Publishing.

Page numbers followed by " *f* ", " *t* ", or " *n* " denote figures, tables, or notes, respectively.

children experiencing transitions
  structure, 71
children from intact, 425*t*
children influenced by restructuring,
  488
children's chronic medical conditions
  influenced by, 254–55
children's health relationships, 203–4
children with chronic medical
  conditions stressors, 252
cultural considerations, 531–32
cultural diversity, 516–17
culturally sensitive interventions for,
  528–29
culture divorcing, 521–25
divorced family adjustment children
  compared, 50–51
divorce or separation's culturally
  unique interactions, 529–30
economic resources as risk factor,
  71–72, 75
ethnic groups, 528
family systems theory influencing, 518
father's role, 146
intracultural, 519–20
law, 578
LDPs, NMPs restructuring, 488
NMPs children's risks compared,
  51–52
non-intact, 525*t*, 527*t*
parental alienation dynamics
  associated with, 431–32
parents insightfulness, 43
risky, 203–4
shared-time parenting risk, 172-173
stress response system with, 204–5
transcultural, 520
U.S. diversity, 514–15
visiting compared non-visiting, 481
families, post-divorce, 385
  children, 50–51
  children refusing visits, 421*t*
  conflict, 227
  co-parenting relationships, 127–28
  intrusion, 463*t*, 466
  marital conflicts, 385
  psychologically adequate parents, 62
family courts
  child custody evaluations, 489, 541

child custody litigation, 25
cultural diversity, 515–16
domestic violence, 174–75
forensic custody evaluations, 489
issues facing, 127–28
LDPs and NMPs representation,
  493–94
marital conflict consideration, 205–7
material bias, 200–201
mental health experts, 580
NMPs data nonexistent, 481–82
NMPs uninvolved, 479
parental alienation court-ordered
  custody reversals, 433
parental alienation findings, 434–37
prima facie case, 555n1
processing LDPs, 482–83
relocation issue, 543
visitation guidelines from, 67–68
Ward v. Ward, 515
Family of origin aggression, 460*t*
Family Quality Life Survey (FQLS), 286*t*
Family Relationship Centres (FRCs), 228
family systems theory, 518
Family Transition Study, 483–88, 484*t*
Farr, R., 502*t*
father-child relationships
  Cashmore's findings on, 107
  child behavior problems, 111–12
  child's distress after divorce, 66–67, 74
  child's emotional security from,
    189, 196
  contact time spent, 109
  father-child contact associations
    with, 197*t*
  father's characteristics influencing,
    108–9
  frequency contact, 190
  intervention programs influence
    on, 113
  maternal gatekeeping risk factor,
    129–30
  mother-child relationship mirrored
    by, 194
  overnights, 141
  parentg time influencing, 202–3, 206
  protecting against relationship loss,
    67–69, 74
  quality of time, 189–90

Mulls, L. L., 251
Multidimensional Family Therapy, 344*t*
Multidimensional Treatment Foster
  Care, 337
multiple regression, 93*t*, 355*t*
Multisystemic Therapy, 337, 344*t*
Murray, C., 504*t*, 510
Murrie, D., 578
Musher-Eizenman, D. R., 280
mutual support, 527*t*
Myricks, N., 515

National Council Juvenile Family Court
  Judges (NCJFCJ), 444
National Institute on Drug Abuse
  (NIDA), 347*t*
National Longitudinal Study Adolescent
  Health, 191, 492*t*
National Longitudinal Study Youth, 220
National Longitudinal Survey, 354*t*
National Longitudinal Survey Youth, 490*t*
National Survey Families Households
  (NSFH), 374*t*, 490*t*, 522*t*
NCJFCJ. *See* National Council Juvenile
  Family Court Judges
NDDs. *See* neurodevelopmental disorders
negative control, 370
Nelson, K. B., 279
Nesseleroade, J. R., 280
neurodevelopmental disorders (NDDs),
  270–73. *See also* children, with
  NDDs
neurological development, 270–71
never-married parents (NMPs), 479
  children's outcomes, 485
  children's well-being influenced by,
    486–87
  cohabitation, 480–81, 489
  cohabiting-family children risks
    compared, 51–52
  co-parenting qualities, 481
  economic strains experienced by,
    485–87
  education levels, 484*f*
  family court data nonexistent for,
    481–82
  family court representation, 493–94
  family courts uninvolved, 479
  family restructuring, 488

Family Transition Study statistical
    differences, 484*t*
  fathers as, 487
  high-conflict families and study,
    483–88, 493
  legal assistance sought by, 482–83
  literature about, 480–81
  psychosocial risk factors, 484–85
  relocation, 487–88
  social support lacking for, 487
  studies on, 490–93
New Beginnings program, 104
New Jersey, 543
Newschaffer, C. J., 290*t*
NIDA. *See* National Institute on Drug
  Abuse
Nigg, J. T., 350*t*
NMPs. *See* never-married parents
non-tact families, 525*t*, 527*t*
non-residential parents
  children's relationship with, 225
  fathers actively parenting as, 220
  fathers as, 146
  stepfamilies, 389–90
non-visiting families, 481
Norwood, W. D., 448
NSFH. *See* National Survey Families
  and Households

O'Connor, E., 500, 504*t*, 510
O'Connor, T. G., 220
ODD. *See* oppositional defiant disorder
O'Donnell, M., 306*t*
Oishi, S., 522*t*
Olesen, N. W., 414*t*, 416*t*
Oliver, P. H., 460*t*
1-2-3 Magic, 340*t*–341*t*
one-sided parents, 32–33, 33*t*, 36
Oppenheim, D., 25, 38*t*, 40*t*
  children with secure attachments
    findings, 36–37
  insightfulness association with child
    secure attachment from, 40–42
  insightfulness operationalized by, 35
oppositional defiant disorder (ODD),
  330–32
Orsmond, G. I., 294*t*
Osterberg, L., 260*t*
Otsuki, M., 253, 260*t*